# Agatha Christie's

## COMPLETE SECRET NOTEBOOKS

Mousetrap II ?

A reunion dinner - The Survivors
of (Revolution?) (that?)

(Aircrew & Passengers Lost in desert)

1 Man - Gale crashes - A lawyer?
Elderly? Marryward? Felix Ceylin?
Type? I or a Richardson

A murder - Here - One of you
is a murderer - One of you is
a victim -
Don't know v.t -----

End of Scene - Is the prospective
victim, and ?

(Really murderer -)

Possibility of house in street Soho hired for party - waiters
hired for jobs!

One man is waiter - brings
drinks to guests - Later enters
as guest - with moustache.

P.T.O

*From Notebook 4 a tantalising glimpse of a project,
never realised, from the 1960s.*

# Agatha Christie's

## COMPLETE SECRET NOTEBOOKS

### Stories and Secrets of
### Murder in the Making

JOHN CURRAN

HarperCollins*Publishers*

HarperCollins*Publishers*
1 London Bridge Street
London SE1 9GF
www.harpercollins.co.uk

HarperCollins*Publishers*
Macken House, 39/40 Mayor Street Upper
Dublin 1
D01 C9W8 Ireland

Paperback edition 2020

3

Fully revised and expanded edition published 2016
First published in Great Britain in two volumes by HarperCollins*Publishers*
as *Agatha Christie's Secret Notebooks* and *Murder in the Making* 2009, 2011

ISBN 978-0-00-812963-7

Printed and bound in the UK using
100% renewable electricity at CPI Group (UK) Ltd

MIX
Paper | Supporting
responsible forestry
FSC™ C007454

This book contains FSC™ certified paper and other controlled
sources to ensure responsible forest management.

For more information visit: www.harpercollins.co.uk/green

For
Joseph, Conor,
Francis, Oisin and Lorcan

And for
Mathew, Lucy and Mahler,
without whom . . .

# Contents

## Part IV: The Fourth Decade

# Foreword

When John Curran's book *Agatha Christie's Secret Notebooks* was published in 2009, the reading public was given something very rare: perhaps the most complete document for any author of the notes and sketches of their novels. Reading the book was like studying the preliminary sketches of any great artist, and in doing so we automatically found ourselves searching for clues. It gave us an insight into the workings of Agatha Christie's mind – plus the gift of two new unpublished Poirot stories!

John Curran not only gives us the facts of what is written in Mrs Christie's notebooks, but he uses conjecture firmly based upon these facts to show us how her remarkable novels came to be written. He even manages to get into her mind and into her psychology. He studies her life and her relationships (both personal and professional), and places these facts together with what is in her 'secret' notebooks to inform us how she wrote and how her writings were influenced by her daily life and the current affairs of the time.

Poirot is often heard to exclaim to Hastings, '*The facts, Hastings ... the facts!*' These for Poirot are the most important matters to 'arrange'. And now John Curran in his book becomes himself the veritable Hercule – well ... almost!

DAVID SUCHET

Cont. _Autobiography_                    Jan. 1965.

Recap —

   Parents' Marriage —
   Ho— - 3ʳᵈ birthday — my
mother - Sam - Stories - Reading

   Goes to the Curran Ref.

I.    The nursery
    Servants — Jane & (in woods
(Insert anecdote on "Such Cads" in my early
married days")

Insert from bit about Servants?
   Census -
   Dog. Tony.

Nurse's Sister
Early - Games with Granny

*Notes dated 1965 in Notebook 27 summarising the early chapters of*
An Autobiography, *eventually published in 1977.*

# Introduction

Quite a few years ago, my first wife, Angela, and I made a trip to Calgary in western Canada to see a world premiere of a very early Agatha Christie play called *Chimneys*. At the first reception we met a quiet, bespectacled Irishman called John Curran. He took with his customary good humour my opening gambit that he must be mad to travel from Dublin to Calgary to see an Agatha Christie play and we have been friends ever since.

After my parents died at Greenway in Devon, which has recently been taken over by the National Trust (and has just been reopened), John was a frequent visitor. Most people who visit Greenway are transfixed by the gardens and the walks by the river. Not John. He spent all his time in the 'fax room', a room on the first floor about ten feet by four in which the Agatha Christie archive was kept. He had to be prised out for meals, sometimes spending 12 hours a day immersed in the history of Agatha Christie's work.

It was here that John's love affair with Agatha Christie's Notebooks blossomed, and neither he nor I could believe our (and your) good fortune when HarperCollins agreed to publish John's book about them. I think you will find that his fascination and enthusiasm for them emerge very clearly.

I never cease to be astounded that over 30 years since she died, interest in every aspect of Agatha Christie's life and work is still at fever pitch. To John's credit, he has always concentrated on her work, leaving to others more morbid fascination about the person behind the books, and here is a book which deals with the very kernel, the raw material of all this great work. It is highly personal and certainly a piece of literary history. John has produced a treat for us all – I hope you enjoy it.

MATHEW PRICHARD

# Shadows in Sunlight – Interlude at Greenway, Summer 1954

As she watches the river below, a pleasure steamer chugs towards Dartmouth, sun glinting on the water in its wake. The laughter of the holidaymakers on board reaches her vantage point in the Battery, and the dog at her feet raises his head peering inquisitively towards the river. A drowsy bee is the only other sound that disturbs her peace. Elsewhere in this haven the gardener, Frank, is busy preparing for the flower show and Mathew is following the treasure hunt she set for him, but here in this semicircular battlement at the edge of the garden overlooking the river she has peace. And a temporary solitude to think about her next project after a wonderful period of leisure – eating the glorious produce of the garden and swimming in the sea and picnicking on the nearby moors and lazing on the lawn and enjoying the company of her family and friends.

She knows that if she lets her mind wander inspiration will come; after all, for over 35 years her imagination has never let her down and there is no reason to suppose that in this tranquil setting it will fail her. She gazes vaguely around. Just visible to her left is the roof of the Boathouse, and behind and to the right the garden continues its upward climb towards the imposing Georgian house. She can now hear occasional rustles in the undergrowth as Mathew follows her trail of clues.

*If he has followed them properly he should, by now, be heading in the direction of the tennis court . . . Wonder if he'll spot the tennis ball . . . it has the next clue. Very like a detective story really . . . but more fun and less planning . . . and no editing or proofreading . . . and nobody writes to you afterwards and points out mistakes . . . But if there were a few participants it would be even better – more fun and more of a contest. Perhaps next time I could arrange for some of Max's nephews to join him and that would make it more exciting. Or the next time I have a garden party for the local school . . . maybe I could work in the Battery and the Boathouse . . . although the Boathouse could seem slightly sinister . . . especially if you were there on your own . . .*

She is now gazing unseeingly over the river and imagining her surroundings in a more ominous light . . .

*If the lawn was a scene of light-hearted enjoyment . . . a family event . . . no, it would need more people than that . . . a garden party . . . a fund-raiser? For the Scouts or the Guides – they were always in need of funds . . . yes, possibilities there . . . There could be stalls on the lawn and teas in a tent, perhaps by the magnolia . . . people in and out of the house . . . a fortune-teller and a bottle stall . . . and confusion about where everyone was . . . And else-where in the grounds a darker force at work . . . unrecognised . . . unsuspected . . . What about here in the Battery? No – too open and . . . too . . . too . . . unmenacing, and you couldn't really hide a body here; but the Boathouse . . . now, that has possibilities – far enough away to be lonely, down those rickety steps, and yet perfectly accessible to anyone. And you can lock the door . . . and it can be reached from the river . . .*

*What about Mrs Oliver? . . . perfect for planning a treasure hunt . . . and it could go wrong for some reason and somebody dies. Let's see . . . how about a murder hunt instead of a treasure hunt . . . like Cluedo except around a real house and grounds instead of a board. Now, Poirot or Marple . . . Marple or Poirot . . . can't see Miss M walking around Greenway, bad enough for Poirot but not really credible that she would . . . and she doesn't know Mrs Oliver anyway, and I have to use her . . . So . . . Mrs O would have to bring in Poirot for some reason . . . perhaps she could call him down to the house on some pretext . . . she needs his help with some of the clues? . . . or could he know the Chief Constable . . . but I've used that a few times already . . . how about handing out the prize for the winner of the hunt . . .*

She reaches into her bag and extracts a large red note-book . . .

*Not really suitable for carrying around but to use the Scouts' own motto – be prepared. Now, I'm sure there's a pen here somewhere . . . Best to get this down while it is still fresh – it can be changed later but I think the basic idea has distinct possibilities.*

She opens the notebook, finds an empty page and starts to write.

Basic ideas usable
Mrs Oliver summons Poirot
She is at Greenway – professional job – arranging a Treasure
Hunt or a Murder Hunt for the Conservative Fete, which is
to be held there –

She is totally absorbed, covering the pages with character-istically large, sprawling handwriting, getting ideas down on paper even if they are to be discarded at a later stage. The real Greenway has disappeared as she peoples it with the children of her imagination: foreign students, girl guides, boy scouts, murder hunt solvers, policemen – and Hercule Poirot.

Some ideas
Hiker (girl?) from hostel Next door – really Lady Bannerman

*Yes, the youth hostel next door could be put to some good use . . .
foreign students . . . possibilities of disguising one of them as . . .
who? They're always coming and going and nobody knows who they
are – they could be anyone, really. A girl is easier to disguise than
a man . . . perhaps she could double as the lady of the house.
Mmmmm, that would mean nobody really knowing her well . . .
perhaps she could be ill . . . an invalid . . . always in her room . . .
or stupid and nobody pays attention to her . . . or recently married
and new to everyone. But then someone from her past arrives . . .
her real husband, maybe . . . or a lover . . . or a relative . . . and
she has to get rid of them . . .*

Young wife recognised by someone who knows she is
married already – blackmail?

*I can adapt one of the treasure hunts I've done for Mathew and
work in the Boathouse somehow . . . and invent Mrs Oliver's hunt
. . . I could use the Cluedo idea of weapons and suspects . . . but
with a real body instead of a pretend one . . .*

Mrs Oliver's plan
The Weapons
Revolver – Knife – Clothes Line

*Who will I murder? The foreign student . . . no, she has to be part
of the plan . . . someone very unexpected then . . . how about the
lord of the manor? . . . no, too clichéd . . . needs to have impact . . .
what about a stranger? . . . but who . . . and that brings a lot of
problems . . . I'll leave that for next year maybe . . . How about a
child? . . . needs to be handled carefully but I could make it a not-
very-nice child . . . perhaps the pretend body, could be one of the
scouts, turns out to be really dead . . . or, better again, a girl guide
. . . she could be nosy and have seen something she shouldn't . . .
Don't think I've had a child victim before . . .*

Points to be decided – Who first chosen for victim?
(?a) 'Body' to be Boy Scout in boat house – key of which
has to be found by 'clues'

She gazes abstractedly into the distance, blind to the pano-
ramic view of the river and the wooded hillside opposite. She
is Poirot, taking afternoon tea in the drawing room, carefully exiting through the French windows and wandering
down through the garden. She is Hattie, intent on preserving
her position and money at all costs. She is Mrs Oliver, dis-
tractedly plotting, discarding, amending, changing . . .

Next bits – P at house – wandering up to Folly – Finds?

Hattie goes in as herself – she changes her clothes and
emerges (from boathouse? Folly? fortune teller's tent?)
as student from Hostel

*Now, I have to provide a few family members . . . how about an
elderly mother . . . she could live in the Gate Lodge. If I make her
mysterious, readers will think she is 'it' . . . little old ladies are
always good as suspects. Could she know something from years
earlier? . . . perhaps she knew Hattie from somewhere . . . or thinks
she does . . . or make Poirot think she does, which is almost as
good . . . Let's see . . .*

Mrs Folliat? suspicious character – really covering up for
something she saw. Or an old crime – a wife who 'ran away'

She stops writing and listens as a voice approaches the Battery
calling 'Nima, Nima.'

'Here, Mathew,' she calls and a tousled 11-year-old runs
down the steps.

'I found the treasure, I found the treasure,' he chants
excitedly, clutching a half-crown.

'Well done. I hope it wasn't too difficult?'

'Not really. The clue in the tennis court took me a while but then I spotted the ball at the base of the net.'

'I thought that one would puzzle you,' she smiles.

She closes the notebook and puts it away in her bag. Hercule Poirot's questioning of Mrs Folliat and the identity of a possible second victim will have to wait.

'Come on,' she says. 'Let's see if there is anything nice to eat in the house.'

Agatha Christie, Queen of Crime, is finished for the day and Agatha Christie, grandmother, climbs the steps from the Battery in search of ice-cream for her grandson.

And the Christie for Christmas 1956 was *Dead Man's Folly*.

# 1

## *The Beginning of a Career*

That was the beginning of the whole thing. I suddenly saw my way clear. And I determined to commit not one murder, but murder on a grand scale.

*And Then There Were None*, Epilogue

---◄○►---

**SOLUTIONS REVEALED**

*Death on the Nile • Evil under the Sun • The Hollow • Lord Edgware Dies • The Murder at the Vicarage • The Mysterious Affair at Styles • Ordeal by Innocence • Witness for the Prosecution*

---◄○►---

The Golden Age of British detective fiction is generally regarded as the period between the end of the First World War and that of the Second, i.e. 1920 to 1945. This was the era of the country house weekend enlivened by the presence of a murderer, the evidence of the adenoidal under-housemaid, the snow-covered lawn with no footprints and the baffled policeman seeking the assistance of the gifted amateur. Ingenuity reached new heights with the fatal air embolism via the empty hypodermic, the poison-smeared postage stamp, and the icicle dagger that evaporates after use.

During these years all of the names we now associate with

the classic whodunit began their writing careers. The period ushered in the fiendish brilliance of John Dickson Carr, who devised more ways to enter and leave a locked room than anyone before or since; it saluted the ingenuity of Freeman Wills Crofts, master of the unbreakable alibi, and Anthony Berkeley, pioneer of multiple solutions. It saw the birth of Lord Peter Wimsey, created by Dorothy L. Sayers, whose fiction and criticism did much to improve the literary level and acceptance of the genre; the emergence of Margery Allingham, who proved, with her creation Albert Campion, that a good detective story could also be a good novel; and the appearance of Ngaio Marsh, whose hero, Roderick Alleyn, managed to combine the professions of policeman and gentleman. Across the Atlantic it welcomed Ellery Queen and his penultimate chapter 'Challenge to the Reader', defying the armchair detective to solve the puzzle; S.S. Van Dine and his pompous creation Philo Vance breaking publishing records; and Rex Stout's overweight creation Nero Wolfe, solving crimes while tending his orchid collection.

Cabinet ministers and archbishops extolled the virtues of a good detective story; poets (Nicholas Blake, otherwise Cecil Day Lewis), university dons (Michael Innes, otherwise Professor J.I.M. Stewart), priests (Rev. Ronald Knox), composers (Edmund Crispin, otherwise Bruce Montgomery) and judges (Cyril Hare, otherwise Judge Gordon Clark) contributed to and expanded the form. R. Austin Freeman and his scientific Dr John Thorndyke sowed the seeds of the modern forensic crime novel; Gladys Mitchell introduced a psychologist detective in her outrageous creation Mrs Bradley; and Henry Wade prepared the ground for the police procedural with his Inspector Poole. Books were presented in the form of correspondence in Sayers' *The Documents in the Case*, as verbatim question-and-answer evidence in Philip Macdonald's *The Maze* and, ultimately, as actual police dossiers complete with physical clues of telegrams and train tickets in Dennis Wheatley's *Murder off Miami*. Floor plans, clue-finders, timetables and footnotes proliferated; readers became intimately acquainted with the properties of arsenic, the interpretation of train timetables and the intricacies of the 1926 Legitimacy Act. Collins Crime Club and the Detection Club were founded; Ronald Knox issued a Detective Story Decalogue and S.S. Van Dine wrote his Rules.

And Agatha Christie published *The Mysterious Affair at Styles*.

### Poirot Investigates . . .

In *An Autobiography* Christie gives a detailed account of the genesis of *The Mysterious Affair at Styles*. By now the main facts are well known: the immortal challenge – 'I bet you can't write a good detective story' – from her sister Madge, the arrival in Torquay of First World War Belgian refugees who inspired Poirot's nationality, Christie's knowledge of poisons from her work in the local dispensary, her intermittent work on the book and its eventual completion during a two-week seclusion in the Moorland Hotel, at the encouragement of her mother. This was not her first literary effort, nor was she the first member of her family with literary aspirations. Both her mother and sister Madge wrote, and Madge actually had a play, *The Claimant*, produced in the West End before Agatha did. Agatha had already written a long dreary novel (her own words) and a few stories and sketches. She had even had a poem published in the local newspaper. While the story of the bet is plausible, it is clear that this alone would not be spur enough to plot, sketch and write a successful book. There was obviously an inherent gift and a facility with the written word.

Although she began writing the novel in 1916 (*The Mysterious Affair at Styles* is actually set in 1917), it was not published for another four years. And its publication was to demand consistent determination on its author's part as more than one publisher declined the manuscript. Until, in 1919, John

Lane, The Bodley Head asked to meet her with a view to publication. But, even then, the struggle was far from over.

The contract, dated 1 January 1920, that John Lane offered Christie took advantage of her publishing naivety. (Remarkably, the actual contract is for *The Mysterious Affair* of *Styles*.) She was to get 10 per cent only after 2,000 copies were sold in the UK and she was contracted to produce five more. This clause led to much correspondence over the following years. Possibly because she was so delighted to be published or because she had no intention then of pursuing a writing career, it is entirely possible that she did not read the small print carefully.

When she realised what she had signed, she insisted that if she *offered* a book she was fulfilling her part of the contract whether or not John Lane accepted it. When John Lane expressed doubt as to whether *Poirot Investigates*, as a volume of short stories rather than a novel, should be considered part of the six-book contract, the by now confident writer pointed out that she had offered them a novel, the non-crime *Vision*, as her third title. The fact that the publishers refused it was, as far as she was concerned, their choice. It is quite possible that if John Lane had not tried to take advantage of his literary discovery she might have stayed longer with the company. But the prickly surviving correspondence shows that those early years of her career were a sharp learning curve in the ways of publishers – and that Agatha Christie was a star pupil. Within a relatively short space of time she is transformed from an awed and inexperienced neophyte perched nervously on the edge of a chair in John Lane's office into a confident and businesslike professional with a resolute interest in every aspect of her books – jacket design, marketing, royalties, serialisation, translation and cinema rights, even spelling.

Despite favourable readers' reports a year earlier, in October 1920 Christie wrote to Mr Willett of John Lane wondering if her book was 'ever coming out' and pointing out that she had almost finished a second novel. This resulted in her receiving the projected cover design, which she approved. Ultimately, after a serialisation in 1920 in *The Weekly Times*, *The Mysterious Affair at Styles* was published later that year in the USA. And, almost five years after she began it, Agatha Christie's first book went on sale in the UK on 21 January 1921. Even after its appearance there was much correspondence about statements and incorrect calculations of royalties as well as cover designs. In fairness to John Lane, it should be said that cover design and blurbs were also a recurring feature of her correspondence with Collins throughout her career.

### *Verdict . . .*

The readers' reports on the Styles manuscript were, despite some misgivings, promising. One gets right to the commercial considerations: 'Despite its manifest shortcomings, Lane could very likely sell the novel . . . There is a certain freshness about it.' A second report is more enthusiastic: 'It is altogether rather well told and well written.' And another speculates on her potential future 'if she goes on writing detective stories and she evidently has quite a talent for them'. They were much taken with the character of Poirot, noting 'the exuberant personality of M. Poirot who is a very welcome variation on the "detective" of romance' and 'a jolly little man in the person of has-been famous Belgian detective'. Although Poirot might take issue with the description 'has-been', it is clear that his presence was a factor in the book's acceptance. In a report dated 7 October 1919 one very perceptive reader remarked, 'but the account of the trial of John Cavendish makes me suspect the hand of a woman'. And because her name on the manuscript had appeared as A.M. Christie, another reader refers to Mr Christie.

All the reports agreed that Poirot's contribution to the Cavendish trial did not convince and needed revision. They were referring to the denouement of the original manuscript, where Poirot's explanation of the crime comes in the form of his evidence given in the witness box during the trial of John Cavendish. This simply did not work, as Christie herself accepted, and Lane demanded a rewrite. She obliged and, although the explanation of the crime itself remains the same, instead of giving it as witness box evidence Poirot holds forth in the drawing room of Styles, in the type of scene that was to be replicated in many later books.

Sutherland Scott, in his 1953 history of the detective story, *Blood in their Ink*, perceptively calls *The Mysterious Affair at Styles* 'one of the finest firsts ever written'. It contained some of the features that were to distinguish many of her later titles.

## Poirot and the Big Four

### Hercule Poirot

There is an irony in the fact that although Agatha Christie is seen as a quintessentially British writer, her most famous creation is 'foreign', a Belgian. The existence of detective figures with which she would have been familiar may have been a contributing factor. Poe's Chevalier Dupin, Robert Barr's Eugène Valmont, Maurice Leblanc's Arsène Lupin and A.E.W. Mason's Inspector Hanaud of the Sûreté were already, in 1920, established figures in the world of crime fiction. And a title Christie specifically mentions in *An Autobiography* is Gaston Leroux's 1908 novel *The Mystery of the Yellow Room*, with its detective, Monsieur Rouletabille. Although largely forgotten nowadays, Leroux was also the creator of *The Phantom of the Opera*.

At the time it was also considered necessary for the detective figure to have a distinguishing idiosyncrasy, or, even better, a collection of them. Holmes had his violin, his cocaine and his pipe; Father Brown had his umbrella and his deceptive air of absent-mindedness; Lord Peter Wimsey had his monocle, his valet and his antiquarian book collection. Lesser figures had other no less distinctive traits: Baroness Orczy's Old Man in the Corner sat in an ABC Teashop and tied knots, Ernest Bramah's Max Carrados was blind and Jacques Futrelle's Professor Augustus S.F.X. Van Dusen was known as The Thinking Machine. So Poirot was created Belgian with impressive moustaches, little grey cells, overweening vanity, both intellectual and sartorial, and a mania for order. Christie's only mistake was in making him, in 1920, a *retired* member of the Belgian police force; this, in turn, meant that by 1975 and *Curtain: Poirot's: Last Case*, he was in his thirteenth decade. Of course, in 1916 Agatha Christie had no idea that the fictional little Belgian would outlive herself.

### Readability

As early as this first novel one of Christie's great gifts, her readability, was in evidence. At its most basic, this is the ability to make readers continue from the top to the bottom of the page and then turn that page; and then make them do that 200 times in the course of any, and in her case, every, book. This facility deserted her only in the very closing chapter of her writing career, *Postern of Fate* being the most challenging example. This gift was, with Christie, innate; and it is doubtful whether it can be learned anyway. Thirty years after *The Mysterious Affair at Styles* the reader at Collins, reporting on *They Came to Baghdad*, wrote in an otherwise damning report: 'It is eminently readable and passes the acid test of holding the interest throughout.'

Christie's prose, while by no means distinguished, flows easily, the characters are believable and differentiated, and much of each book is told in dialogue. There are no long-winded scenes of question-and-answer, no detailed scientific explanations, no wordy descriptions of people or places. But there is sufficient of each to fix the scene and its protagonists clearly in the mind. Every chapter, indeed almost every scene, pushes the story on towards a carefully prepared solution and climax. And Poirot does not alienate the reader with either the irritating facetiousness of Sayers' Lord Peter Wimsey, the pedantic arrogance of Van Dine's Philo Vance or the emotional entanglements of Bentley's Philip Trent.

A comparison with almost any other contemporaneous crime title shows what a chasm existed between Christie and other writers, most of them now long out of print. As illustration, the appearance of two other detective-story writers also coincided with the publication of *The Mysterious Affair at Styles*. Freeman Wills Crofts, a Dubliner, published *The Cask* in 1920 and H.C. Bailey published *Call Mr Fortune* the previous year. Crofts' detective, Inspector French, showed painstaking attention in following every lead, and specialised in the unbreakable alibi. However, this very meticulousness militated against an exciting reading experience. H.C. Bailey began his career as a writer of historical fiction but turned to crime fiction, much of it featuring his detective, Reginald Fortune. The two writers, although skilled plot technicians in both novel and short story form, lacked the vital ingredient of readability.

### Plotting

Christie's plotting, coupled with this almost uncanny readability, was to prove a peerless combination. An examination of her Notebooks shows that although this gift for plotting was innate and in profusion, she worked at her ideas, distilling and sharpening and perfecting them, and that even the most inspired titles (e.g. *Crooked House, Endless Night, The ABC Murders*) were the result of meticulous planning. The secret of her ingenuity with plot lies in the fact that this dexterity is not daunting. Her solutions turn on everyday information: some names can be male or female, a mirror reflects but it also reverses, a sprawled body is not necessarily a dead body, a forest is the best hiding place for a tree. She knows she can depend on the reader's erroneous interpretation of an eternal triangle, an overheard argument or an illicit liaison. She counts on our received prejudice that retired Army men are harmless buffoons, that quiet, mousy wives are objects of pity, that all policemen are honest and all children innocent. She does not mystify us with the mechanical or technical; or insult us with the clichéd or the obvious; or alienate us with the terrifying or the gruesome.

In almost every Christie title the mise-en-scène features a closed circle of suspects: a strictly limited number of potential murderers from which to choose. A country house, a ship, a train, a plane, an island – all of these provided her with a setting that limits the number of possible killers and ensures that a complete unknown is not unmasked in the last chapter. In effect, Christie says, 'Here is the flock of suspects from which I will choose my villain. See if you can spot the black sheep.' It can be as few as four (*Cards on the Table*) or five (*Five Little Pigs*) or as many as the coach full of travellers on the Orient Express. *The Mysterious Affair at Styles* is typical of the country-house murders beloved of Golden Age writers and readers: a group of assorted characters sharing an isolated setting long enough for murder to be committed, investigated and solved.

Although an element of the solution in *The Mysterious Affair at Styles* turns on a scientific fact, it is not unfair as the reader is told from the outset of the investigation what the poison is. Admittedly, anyone with knowledge of toxicology has a distinct advantage, but the information is readily available. Other than this mildly controversial item, all the information necessary to arrive at the solution is scrupulously given: the coffee cup, the scrap of material, a fire lit during a July heatwave, the medicine bottle. And, of course, it is Poirot's passion for neatness that gives him the final proof; and in a way that was to be reused, a decade later, in the play *Black Coffee*. But how many readers will notice that Poirot has to tidy the mantelpiece twice (Chapters 4 and 5), thereby discovering a vital link in the chain of guilt?

*Fairness*

Throughout her career Christie was quite happy to provide her readers with clues, confident in the knowledge that, in the words of her great contemporary R. Austin Freeman, 'the reader would mislead himself'. How many readers will properly interpret the clue of the calendar in *Hercule Poirot's Christmas*, or the velvet stole in *Death on the Nile*, or the love letters in *Peril at End House*? Or who will correctly appreciate the significance of the wax flowers in *After the Funeral*, or Major Palgrave's glass eye in *A Caribbean Mystery*, or the telephone call in *Lord Edgware Dies*, or the beer bottle in *Five Little Pigs*?

While not in the same class of 'surprise solution' as *Murder on the Orient Express*, *The Murder of Roger Ackroyd* or *Crooked House*, the solution to *The Mysterious Affair at Styles* still manages to surprise. This is due to the use of one of Christie's most effective ploys: the double-bluff. It is the first example in her work of this powerful weapon in the detective-story writer's armoury. Here the most obvious solution, despite an initial appearance of impossibility, transpires to be the correct one after all. In *An Autobiography* she explains that 'The whole point of a *good* detective story was that it must be somebody obvious but at the same time for some reason, you would then find that it was not obvious, that he could not possibly have done it. Though really, of course, he *had* done it.' She returned throughout her career to this type of solution; and particularly when the explanation revolves around a murderous alliance: *The Murder at the Vicarage*, *Evil under the Sun*, *Death on the Nile*. Lethal partnerships aside, *Lord Edgware Dies* and *The Hollow* also feature this device. And she can take the bluff one step further, in *Ordeal by Innocence* and, devastatingly, in *Witness for the Prosecution*.

In *The Mysterious Affair at Styles* we are satisfied that Alfred Inglethorp is both too obvious and too dislikeable to be the murderer; and, on a more mundane level, he was absent from the house on the night of his wife's death. So we discount him. As a further strengthening of the double-bluff, part of his plan depends on being suspected, arrested, tried and acquitted, thus ensuring his perpetual freedom. Unless carefully handled this solution runs the risk of producing an anticlimax. Here it is skilfully avoided by uncovering the presence of an unexpected conspirator in the person of hearty Evelyn Howard, who, throughout the novel, has denounced her employer's husband (her unsuspected lover) as a fortune hunter – as indeed he is.

## *Productivity*

Although no one, least of all Christie herself, knew it at the time, *The Mysterious Affair at Styles* was to be the first in a substantial corpus of books that were to issue from her typewriter over the next half century. She was equally successful in the novel and the short story form and alone among her contemporaries she also conquered the theatre. She created two famous detectives, a feat not duplicated by other crime writers. During the height of her powers publication could hardly keep pace with creation – 1934 saw the publication of no fewer than four crime titles and a Mary Westmacott, the name under which she wrote six non-crime novels published between 1930 and 1956. And this remarkable output is also a factor in her continuing success. It is possible to read a different Christie title every month for almost seven years; at which stage one can start all over again. And it is possible to watch a different Agatha Christie dramatisation every month for two years. Very few writers, in any field, have equalled this record.

And so Christie's work continues to transcend every barrier of geography, culture, race, religion, age and sex; she is read as avidly in Bermuda as in Balham, she is read by grandparents and grandchildren, she is read on e-book and in graphic novel format in this twenty-first century as eagerly as in the green Penguins and *The Strand* magazine of the last.

Why? Because no other crime writer did it so well, so often or for so long; no one else has ever matched her combination of readability, plotting, fairness and productivity.

And no one ever will.

# The Evidence of the Notebooks

Like a conjuror, he whipped from a drawer in the desk two shabby exercise books.

*The Clocks*, Chapter 28

---

**SOLUTIONS REVEALED**

*The Murder of Roger Ackroyd* • *Sad Cypress*

---

Although mentioned by both of her biographers, Janet Morgan and Laura Thompson, Agatha Christie's Notebooks remain a closely protected, and largely unknown, treasure. After the death of her mother, Rosalind Hicks ensured their safety in Greenway House and, with the exception of Torquay Museum, they have never been publicly displayed. But Christie does briefly mention them in *An Autobiography*:

*Of course, all the practical details are still to be worked out, and the people have to creep slowly into my consciousness, but I jot down my splendid idea in an exercise book. So far so good – but what I invariably do is lose the exercise book. I usually have about half a dozen on hand, and I used to make notes in them of ideas that had struck me, or about some poison or drug, or a clever little bit of swindling that I had read about in the paper. Of course, if I had kept all these things neatly sorted and filed and labelled, it would save me a lot of trouble. However, it is a pleasure sometimes, when looking vaguely through a pile of old note-books to find something scribbled down, as:* Possible plot – do it yourself – girl and not really sister – August *– with a kind of sketch of a plot. What it's all about I can't remember now; but it often stimulates me, if not to write that identical plot, at least to write something else.*

A closer examination of some of these remarks will give a clearer idea of what she meant. Using Christie's own words as a guide, we can begin to see the part these Notebooks played in her creative process.

### . . . *idea in an exercise book* . . .

Considered as the notes, drafts and outlines for the greatest body of detective fiction ever written (and in many cases, unwritten) these Notebooks are unique and priceless literary artefacts. Viewed as physical objects they are somewhat less impressive. They are before mc as I write these words and, at a passing glance, look like the piles of exercise books gathered by teachers at the end of class in schools the world over. Because most of them are just that – exercise books. Red and blue and green and grey exercise books, coverless copybooks ruled with wide-spaced blue lines, small black pocket-sized notebooks: The Minerva, The Marvel, The Kingsway, The Victoria, The Lion Brand, The Challenge, The Mayfair exercise books, ranging in price from The Kingsway (Notebook 72) for 2d to The Marvel (Notebook 28) for a shilling (5p); Notebook 5 represented particularly good value at 4 for 7½d (3p). Inside covers often have 'useful' information: a map of the UK, capitals of the world, decimal conversion rates (obviously bought just before or after the introduction of decimal coinage in February 1971). There are covers illustrated by the New York skyline (Notebook 23) or a Mexican volcano (Notebook 18).

Some of them are more worthy recipients of their contents: hard-backed multi-paged notebooks with marbled covers or spiral binding with embossed covers; some are even grandly inscribed on the cover 'Manuscript'. Notebook 7 is described inside the back cover as 'spongeable PVC cover from WHS', and Notebook 71 is a 'Cahier' with 'Agatha Miller 31 Mai 1907' written on the cover and containing French homework from her time in Paris as a young woman. Notebook 31 is an impressive wine-coloured hardback from Langley and Sons Ltd., Tottenham Court Rd. and costing 1s 3d (6p).

In a few cases their unpretentiousness is now a liability as some of them have suffered on their journey down the years – they have lost their covers (and perhaps some pages – who knows?), staples have become rusted, pencil has faded and in some cases the quality of the paper, combined with the use of a leaky biro, has meant that notes written on one page have seeped on to the reverse also. And, of course, as many of them date from the war years, paper quality was often poor.

It would seem that some Notebooks originally belonged to, or were temporarily commandeered by, Christie's (then young) daughter Rosalind, as her name and address in her own neat handwriting appears on the inside cover (Notebook 41). And Notebook 73, otherwise blank, has her first husband Archie Christie's name in flowing script inside the front cover. The name and address lines on the front cover of Notebook 19 have been filled in: 'Mallowan, 17 Lawn Road Flats'.

The number of pages Christie used in each Notebook varies greatly – Notebook 35 has 220 pages of notes while Notebook 72 has a mere five; Notebook 63 has notes on over 150 pages but Notebook 42 uses only 20. The average lies somewhere between 100 and 120.

Although they are collectively referred to as 'The Notebooks of Agatha Christie', not all of them are concerned with her literary output. Notebooks 11, 40 and 55 consist solely of chemical formulae and seem to date from her days as a student dispenser; Notebook 71 contains French homework and Notebook 73 is completely blank. Moreover, she often used them for making random notes, sometimes on the inside covers – there is a list of 'furniture for 48' [Sheffield Terrace] in Notebook 59; Notebook 67 has reminders to ring up Collins and to make a hair appointment; Notebook 68 has a list of train times from Stockport to Torquay. And her husband Max Mallowan has written accurately in his small, neat hand, '*The Pale Horse*' on the front of Notebook 54.

### . . . *what I invariably do is lose the exercise book* . . .

In a career spanning over half a century and two world wars, some loss is inevitable but reassuringly this seems to have happened hardly at all. Of course, we cannot be sure how many Notebooks there should be, but the 73 we still have are an impressive legacy.

Nevertheless, no notes or outlines exists for *The Murder on the Links* (1923), *The Murder of Roger Ackroyd* (1926), *The Big Four* (1927) or *The Seven Dials Mystery* (1929). From the 1920s we have notes only for *The Mysterious Affair at Styles* (1920), *The Man in the Brown Suit* (1924), *The Secret of Chimneys* (1925) and *The Mystery of the Blue Train* (1928). When we remember that *The Murder of Roger Ackroyd* was published just before Christie's traumatic disappearance and subsequent divorce it is perhaps not surprising that these notes are no longer extant. The same applies to *The Big Four*, despite the fact that this episodic novel had appeared earlier as individual short stories. And there is nothing showing the genesis of the first adventure of Tommy and Tuppence in *The Secret Adversary* (1922); for the 1929 collection *Partners in Crime*, there are only sketchy notes. This is a particular disappointment as it might have given us an insight into the thoughts of Agatha Christie on her fellow crime writers, who are affectionately pastiched in this collection.

From the 1930s onwards, however, the only missing book titles are *Murder on the Orient Express* (1934), *Cards on the Table* (1936) and *Murder is Easy* (1939). This would seem to suggest that very few notebooks were, in fact, lost. Why notes for *Murder is Easy* are missing – apart from a passing reference in Notebook 66 – is a minor mystery when the notes for the novels on either side survive.

In some cases the notes are sketchy and consist of little more than a list of characters (*Death on the Nile* – Notebook 30). And some titles have copious notes: *They Came to Baghdad* (100 pages), *Five Little Pigs* (75 pages), *One, Two, Buckle my Shoe* (75 pages). Other titles outline the course of the finished book so closely that I am tempted to assume that there were earlier, rougher notes that have not survived. A case in point is *Ten Little Niggers*[1] (aka *And Then There Were None*). In *An Autobiography* Dame Agatha remembers: 'I had written the book *Ten Little Niggers* because it was so difficult to do that the idea fascinated me. Ten people had to die without it becoming ridiculous or the murderer becoming obvious. I wrote the book after a tremendous amount of planning.' Unfortunately, none of this planning survives; what there is in Notebook 65 follows almost exactly the progress of the novel. It is difficult to believe that this would have been written straight on to the page with so few deletions or so little discussion of possible alternatives. Nor are there, unfortunately, any notes for her dramatisation of this famous story. For the rest of her career we are fortunate to have notes on all of the novels. In the case of most of the later titles the notes are extensive and detailed – and legible.

Fewer than 50 of almost 150 short stories are discussed in the pages of the Notebooks. This may mean that, for many of them, Christie typed directly on to the page without making

---

1 Although this title is now officially *And Then There Were None*, the use of the original, and now unacceptable, title at some points in this book is unavoidable.

*Two examples of Agatha Christie, the housekeeper. The heading 'Wallingford' on the lower one confirms that they are both lists of items to bring to or from her various homes.*

any preliminary notes. Or that she worked on loose pages that she subsequently discarded. When she wrote the early short stories she did not consider herself a writer in the professional sense of the word. It was only after her divorce, and the consequent need to earn her living, that she realised that writing was now her 'job'. So the earliest adventures of Poirot as published in 1923 in *The Sketch* magazine do not appear in the Notebooks at all, although there are, thankfully, detailed notes for her greatest Poirot collection, *The Labours of Hercules*. And many ideas that she sketched for short stories did not make it any further than the pages of the Notebooks (see 'Unused Ideas').

There are notes on most of her stage work, including unknown, unperformed and uncompleted plays. There are only two pages each of notes for her most famous and her greatest play, *Three Blind Mice* (as it still was at the time of writing the notes) and *Witness for the Prosecution* respectively. But these are disappointingly uninformative, as they contain no detail of the adaptation, merely a draft of scenes without any of the usual speculation.

And there are many pages devoted to *An Autobiography*, her poetry and her Westmacott novels. Most of the poetry is of a personal nature as she often wrote a poem as a birthday present for family members. There are only 40 pages in total devoted to the Westmacott titles, mainly of quotations that might provide titles, and those for *An Autobiography* are, for the most part, diffuse and disconnected, consisting of what are little more than reminders to herself.

### . . . *I usually have about half a dozen on hand* . . .

It could reasonably be supposed that each Agatha Christie title has its own Notebook. This is emphatically not the case. In only five instances is a Notebook devoted to a single title. Notebooks 26 and 42 are entirely dedicated to *Third Girl*; Notebook 68 concerns only *Peril at End House*; Notebook 2 is

*A Caribbean Mystery*; Notebook 46 contains nothing but extensive historical background and a rough outline for *Death Comes as the End*. Otherwise, every Notebook is a fascinating record of a productive brain and an industrious professional. Some examples should make this clear.

Notebook 53 contains:
> Fifty pages of detailed notes for *After the Funeral* and
> > *A Pocket Full of Rye* alternating with each other every
> > few pages
>
> Rough notes for *Destination Unknown*
> A short outline of an unwritten novel
> Three separate and different attempts at the radio play
> > *Personal Call*
>
> Notes for a new Mary Westmacott
> Preliminary notes for *Witness for the Prosecution* and
> > *The Unexpected Guest*
>
> An outline for an unpublished and unperformed play,
> > *Miss Perry*
>
> Some poetry

Notebook 13 contains:
> 38 pages for *Death Comes as the End*
> 20 pages for *Taken at the Flood*
> 20 pages for *Sparkling Cyanide*
> 6 pages for Mary Westmacott
> 30 pages of a foreign Travel Diary
> 4 pages each for *The Hollow, Curtain, N or M?*

Notebook 35 contains:
> 75 pages for *Five Little Pigs*
> 75 pages for *One, Two, Buckle my Shoe*
> 8 pages for *N or M?*
> 4 pages for *The Body in the Library*
> 25 pages of ideas

### . . . *if I had kept all these things neatly sorted* . . .

One of the most frustrating aspects of the Notebooks is the lack of order, especially the uncertainty of the chronology. Although there are 73 Notebooks, we have only 77 examples of dates most of them incomplete. A page can be headed 'October 20th' or 'September 28th' or just '1948'. There are only six examples of complete (day/month/year) dates all from the 1960s and 70s. In the case of incomplete dates it is sometimes possible to deduce the year from the publication date of the title in question, but in the case of notes for an unpublished or undeveloped idea, this is almost impossible. This uncertainty is compounded for a variety of reasons.

First, use of the Notebooks was utterly random. Christie opened a Notebook (or, as she says herself, any of half a dozen contemporaneous ones), found the next blank page and began to write. It was simply a case of finding an empty page, even one between two already filled pages. And, as if that wasn't complicated enough, in almost all cases she turned the Notebook over and, with admirable economy, wrote from the back also. In one extreme case, during the plotting of 'Manx Gold' she even wrote sideways on the page! It should be remembered that many of these pages were filled during the days of paper rationing in the Second World War. In compiling this book I had to devise a system to enable me to identify whether or not the page was an 'upside-down' one.

Second, because many pages are filled with notes for stories that were never completed, there are no publication dates as a guideline. Deductions can sometimes be made from the notes immediately preceding and following, but this method is not entirely flawless. A closer look at the contents of Notebook 13 (listed above) illustrates an aspect of this random chronology. Leaving aside *Curtain*, the earliest novel listed here is *N or M?* published in 1941 and the latest

Jan. 1935.

A.

Rose without Thorn _ _

B. Ventriloquist _ on board _

C. A & B _ _ A _ _
_ murder B _ _ _ _
murder C

D. Man in E. Africa. 3 women Lady
Pat _ Barbara Kevins _ the & girls
of ship _

*This page, in Notebook 66, is from Christie's most prolific and ingenious period and list ideas that became* Sad Cypress, 'Problem at Sea' and They Do It With Mirrors. *It was one of very few pages in the Notebooks to bear a date, and the stories were published between 1936 and 1952.*

nov 2nd 1973

Book of Stories

The White Horse stories.
First one

The White Horse Party
(Rather Similar to Jane Marple's Tuesday Night
Club )

Each story might be based on a
particular White Horse in England —
The White Horse in question plays a part in
Some Particular Incident — a Problem, or
Some Criminal happening — a Likeness
to Mr Quin — A White Horse always
partakes — a ghostly Side to it

*Another rare page with a date, demonstrating a marked change in
handwriting, these are among the last notes that Christie wrote and appear
in Notebook 7. Although she continued making notes, no new material
appeared later than* Postern of Fate, *published in October 1973.*

is *Taken at the Flood* published in 1948. But many of the intervening titles are missing from this Notebook – *Five Little Pigs* is in Notebook 35, *Evil under the Sun* in Notebook 39 and *Towards Zero* in Notebook 32.

Third, in many cases jottings for a book may have preceded publication by many years. The earliest notes for *The Unexpected Guest* are headed '1951' in Notebook 31, i.e. seven years before the first performance; the germ of *Endless Night* first appears, six years before publication, on a page of Notebook 4 dated 1961.

The pages following a clearly dated page cannot be assumed to have been written at the same time. For example:

page 1 of Notebook 3 reads 'General Projects 1955'
page 9 reads 'Nov. 5th 1965' (and there were ten books in the intervening period)
page 12 reads '1963'
page 21 reads 'Nov. 6 1965 Cont.'
page 28 is headed 'Notes on Passenger to Frankfort [sic] 1970'
page 36 reads 'Oct. 1972'
page 72 reads 'Book Nov. 1972'

In the space of 70 pages we have moved through seventeen years and as many novels and, between pages 9 and 21, skipped back and forth between 1963 and 1965.

Notebook 31 is dated, on different pages, 1944, 1948 and 1951, but also contains notes for *The Body in the Library* (1942), written in the early days of the Second World War. Notebook 35 has pages dated 1947, sketching *Mrs McGinty's Dead*, and 1962, an early germ of *Endless Night*.

### *. . . and filed . . .*

Although the Notebooks are numbered from 1 through to 73, this numbering is completely arbitrary. Some years before she died, Christie's daughter Rosalind arranged, as a first step towards analysing their contents, that the Notebooks should be numbered and that the titles discussed within be listed. The analysis never went any further than that, but in the process every Notebook was allocated a number. This numbering is completely random and a lower number does not indicate an earlier year or a more important Notebook. Notebook 2, for instance, contains notes for *A Caribbean Mystery* (1964) and Notebook 3 for *Passenger to Frankfurt* (1970), while Notebook 37 contains a long, deleted extract from *The Mysterious Affair at Styles* (1920). So the numbers are nothing more than an identification mark.

### . . . *and labelled* . . .

Some of the Notebooks show attempts on the part of the elderly Agatha Christie to impose a little order on this chaos. Notebook 31 has a loose-page listing inside the front cover in her own handwriting; others have typewritten page-markers indicating where each title is discussed. These brave attempts are rudimentary and the compiler (probably not Christie herself) soon wearied of the daunting task. Most Notebooks contain notes for several books and as three novels can often jostle for space among twenty pages, the page markers soon become hopelessly cumbersome and, eventually, useless.

To give some idea of the amount of information contained, randomly, within their covers, for the purposes of this book I created a table to index the entire contents. When printed, it ran to seventeen pages.

### . . . *something scribbled down* . . .

Before discussing the handwriting in the Notebooks, it is only fair to emphasise that these were working notes and jottings; there was no reason to make an effort to maintain a certain standard of calligraphy as no one but Christie herself was ever intended to read them. These were, essentially, personal journals and not written for any purpose other than to clarify her thoughts.

Our handwriting changes as we age and scrambled notes of college or university days soon overtake the copperplate efforts of our early school years. Accidents, medical conditions and age all take their toll on our writing. In most cases it is safe to assert that as we get older our handwriting deteriorates. In the case of Agatha Christie the opposite is the case. At her creative peak (roughly 1930 to 1950) her handwriting is almost indecipherable. It looks, in many cases, like shorthand and it is debatable if even she could read some sections of it. I have no doubt that the reason for this was that, during these hugely prolific years, her fertile brain teemed with ideas and it was a case of getting them on to paper as fast as possible. Clarity of presentation was a secondary consideration.

The conversion of the Notebooks into an easily readable format, for the purposes of this book, took over six months. A detailed knowledge of all of Dame Agatha's output was not just an enormous help but a vital necessity. It helped to know, for instance, that a reference to 'apomorphine' is not a misprint, a mistake or a mis-spelling but a vital part of the plot of *Sad Cypress*. But it did not help in the case of notes for an unpublished title or for discarded ideas. As the weeks progressed I was surprised how used to the handwriting I became, so that converting the last batch of Notebooks was considerably quicker than the first. I also discovered that if I left a seemingly indecipherable page and returned to it a few days later, I could often make sense of it. But some words or sentences still defied me and in a number of cases I had to resort to an educated guess.

From the late 1940s onwards the handwriting steadily 'improved' so that by the early 1950s and, for example, *After the Funeral* in Notebook 53, the notes are quite legible. Agatha

Christie was ruefully aware of this herself. In November 1957, in a letter about *Ordeal by Innocence*, she writes, 'I am asking Mrs. Kirwan [her secretary Stella Kirwan] to type this to you knowing what my handwriting is like', and again in August 1970 she describes her own handwriting as 'overlarge and frankly rather illegible'. And she writes this *after* the improvement!

For some years, there has been a theory in the popular press that Agatha Christie suffered from dyslexia. I have no idea where this originated but even a cursory glance at the Notebooks gives the lie to this story. The only example that could be produced in evidence is her struggle with 'Caribbean' and 'Carribean' throughout the notes for *A Caribbean Mystery*: but I think in that she would not be alone!

### . . . *a kind of sketch of a plot* . . .

Dotted irregularly throughout the Notebooks are brief jottings dashed down and often not developed any further at the time. This is what Christie means by 'a sketch of a plot'; these jottings were all she needed to stimulate her considerable imagination. The ideas below are reproduced exactly as they appear on the page of the Notebooks, and some of them occur in more than one Notebook (examples of similar jottings are given later in this book). All of them were to appear, to a greater or lesser degree, in her titles. The first two are major plot devices and the remaining two are minor plot features:

Poirot asked to go down to country – finds a house and various fantastic details [see *The Hollow*]

Saves her life several times [see *Endless Night*]

Dangerous drugs stolen from car [see *Hickory Dickory Dock*]

Inquire enquire – both in same letter [see *A Murder is Announced*]

### *. . . it often stimulates me, if not to write that identical plot at least to write something else . . .*

Throughout her career one of Christie's greatest gifts was her ability to weave almost endless variations on seemingly basic ideas. Murderous alliances, the eternal triangle, victim-as-murderer, disguise – down the years she used and reused all these ploys to confound reader expectation. So when she writes about being stimulated to write 'something else' we know that she could do this effortlessly. Something as seemingly unimportant or uninspiring as the word 'teeth' could inspire her and, in fact, she used that very idea in at least two novels: *One, Two, Buckle my Shoe* and, as a minor plot element, in *The Body in the Library*.

Identical twins (one killed in railway smash) survivor – claims to be the rich one (teeth?)

Poor little rich girl – house on hill – luxury gadgets etc. – original owner

Stamp idea – man realises fortune – puts it on old letter – a Trinidad stamp on a Fiji letter

Old lady in train variant – a girl is in with her – later is offered a job at the village – takes it

As we shall see, the 'Stamp idea' features in a short story and a play over 15 years apart; the 'Old lady in train' ploy appears in two novels almost 20 years apart; and the 'Poor little rich girl' inspired a short story and, 25 years later, a novel.

Finally, it is a major disappointment that there remains nothing from the creation of two of Christie's most famous titles: *The Murder of Roger Ackroyd* and *Murder on the Orient Express*. About the latter we know absolutely nothing, as it is not mentioned even in passing. Notebook 67 does have an incomplete list of characters from *The Murder of Roger Ackroyd* but nothing more. There is, however, some background to its creation contained in an intriguing correspondence with Lord Mountbatten of Burma.

In a letter dated 28 March 1924 Mountbatten wrote to 'Mrs Christie, Author of The Man who was No. 4, c/o The Sketch' (this was a reference to the recently finished serial publication of *The Big Four* in that magazine). Writing in the third person, he expressed his admiration for Poirot and Christie and begged to offer an idea for a detective story. He explained that, although he had had a few stories published under a pseudonym, his career at sea did not leave a lot of time for writing.

Briefly, his idea was that Hastings, before he leaves for South America, should introduce a friend, Genny, to Poirot. When a murder occurs Poirot writes to inform Hastings and explains that Genny will write subsequent letters keeping him abreast of developments. The plot involves the drugging of the victim to appear dead; when the body is 'discovered', the murderer stabs him. Genny's alibi appears impeccable as he is with Poirot until the discovery. Only in the final chapter is Genny unmasked as the killer. As can be seen, Christie retained the underlying suggestion, the narrator/murderer idea. All the surrounding detail, however, was her embroidery on his basic pattern.

On 26 November 1969 Mountbatten wrote again to congratulate Christie on *The Mousetrap*'s seventeenth birthday. She replied within the week and apologised in case she had not acknowledged his suggestion of 45 years earlier (he subsequently assured her that she had), thanked him for his kind words and enclosed her latest book, *Hallowe'en Party* ('not as good as Roger Ackroyd but not too bad'). She also mentioned that her brother-in-law, James, had suggested a similar narrator/murderer plot to her around the same time, although she had thought then that it would be very difficult to carry off.

# Agatha Christie at Work

'I mean, what *can* you say about how you write your books?
What I mean is, first you've got to think of something, and
then when you've thought of it you've got to force yourself
to sit down and write it. That's all.'

*Dead Man's Folly*, Chapter 17

———————◄○►———————

**SOLUTIONS REVEALED**

*Crooked House* • *Endless Night* • *Mrs McGinty's Dead* •
*A Murder is Announced* • *Murder in Mesopotamia* •
*One, Two, Buckle my Shoe*

———————◄○►———————

How did Agatha Christie produce so many books of such a
high standard over so many years? A close examination of
her Notebooks will reveal some of her working methods,
although, as will be seen, 'method' was not her strong suit.
But that, I contend, *was* her secret – even though she was
unaware of this paradox herself.

### Dumb Witnesses

In February 1955, on the BBC radio programme *Close-Up*,
Agatha Christie admitted, when asked about her process of

working, that 'the disappointing truth is that I haven't much method'. She typed her own drafts 'on an ancient faithful typewriter that I've had for years' but she found a Dictaphone useful for short stories. 'The real work is done in thinking out the development of your story and worrying about it until it comes right. That may take quite a while.' And this is where her Notebooks, which are not mentioned in the interview, came in. A glance at them shows that this is where she did her 'thinking and worrying'.

Up to the early-1930s her Notebooks are succinct outlines of the novels with relatively little evidence of rough notes or speculation, deletions or crossing-out. And, unlike later years, when each Notebook contains notes for a few titles, at that early stage the bulk of the notes for any title is contained within one Notebook. These outlines follow closely the finished novel and would seem to indicate that the 'thinking and worrying' was done elsewhere and subsequently destroyed or lost. Notes for *The Mysterious Affair at Styles* (Notebook 37), *The Man in the Brown Suit* (Notebook 34), *The Mystery of the Blue Train* (Notebook 54), *The Murder at the Vicarage* (Notebook 33), *The Sittaford Mystery* (Notebook 59), *Peril at End House* (Notebook 68) and *Lord Edgware Dies* (Notebook 41) are accurate reflections of the novels. But from the mid-1930s and *Death in the Clouds* on, the Notebooks include all her thoughts and ideas, accepted or rejected.

She did all her speculating on the page of the Notebook until she was happy with the plot, although it is not always obvious from the Notebook alone which plan she has adopted. She worked out variations and possibilities; she selected and discarded; she explored and experimented. She 'brainstormed' on the page, and then sorted the potentially useful from the probably useless. Notes for different books overlap and intersect; a single title skips throughout a Notebook or, in extreme cases, through a dozen Notebooks.

When asked by Lord Snowdon in a 1974 interview how she would like to be remembered, Agatha Christie replied,

'I would like to be remembered as a rather good writer of detective stories.' This modest remark, coming after a lifetime as a bestseller in bookshop and theatre, is unconscious confirmation of another aspect of Christie evident from the Notebooks, her lack of self-importance. She saw these unpretentious jotters as no more precious a tool in her working life than the pen or pencil or biro she held to fill them. She employed her Notebooks as diaries, as scribblers, as telephone-message pads, as travel logs, as household accounts ledgers; she used them to draft letters, to list Christmas and birthday presents, to scribble to-do reminders, to record books read and books to read, to scrawl travel directions. She sketched maps of Warmsley Heath (*Taken at the Flood*) and St Mary Mead in them; she doodled the jacket design for *Sad Cypress* and the stage setting for *Afternoon at the Seaside* in them; she drew diagrams of the plane compartment from *Death in the Clouds* and the island from *Evil under the Sun* in them. Sir Max used them to do calculations, Rosalind used them to practise her handwriting and everyone used them as bridge-score keepers.

### Pigeon among the Cats

As with reading a Christie novel, the unexpected, within the Notebooks, is to be expected. The plotting of the latest Poirot novel can be interrupted by a poem written for Rosalind's birthday; a page headed, optimistically, 'Things to do' is sandwiched between the latest Marple and an unfinished stage play. A phone number and message interrupts the creation of a radio play; a list of new books disrupts the intricacies of a murderer's timetable; a letter to *The Times* disturbs the new Westmacott novel.

A random flick through the Notebooks illustrates some of these points: the original ending to *Death Comes as the End* or a crossword clue ('– *I* – *T* – –'); the draft of an unfinished Poirot story or a list of tulips ('Grenadier – Really scarlet,

Don Pedro – good bronze purple'); a letter to *The Times* ('I have read with great interest the article written by Dr. A. L. Rowse on his discovery of the identity of Shakespeare's Dark Lady of the Sonnets') or a sketch for *Mousetrap* II. A page of jottings – a short list of books (all published in 1970), arrangements for Christmas shopping and a quotation that caught her attention – interrupts the notes for *Nemesis*:

> At some place in (Ireland?) (Scotland?) (Cornwall?) a family lives – writes her to stay for a day or two or weekend – rejoin tour later – (Has she been taken slightly ill? fever? Sickness – some drug administered)

> Notes on books
> Deliverance – James Dickey
> The Driver's Seat – Muriel Spark
> A Start in Life – Alan Sillitoe

> Let's go to Syon Lodge Ltd. (Crowthers) – 20 mins. by car from Hyde Park Corner – on way to airport – Xmas shopping? Collingwood in Conduit St

> Remark made by McCauley 'To be ruled by a busybody is more than human nature can bear'

> What is this focal point of (an accused person imprisoned) – R's son – a failure – R. always knew when he was lying

The plotting of *One, Two, Buckle my Shoe* and a listing of possible short story ideas is interrupted by a social message from her great friend Nan Gardner:

> H.P. not satisfied – asks about bodies – at last – one is found

> All away weekend – can we go Thursday Nan

> Ideas (1940)
> A. 2 friends – arty spinsters – <u>one</u> a crook – (other camouflage) they give evidence – possible for Miss Marple

A list of ideas, some of which became *Death in the Clouds, The ABC Murders* and 'Problem at Sea', is put on hold for three pages of Christmas presents:

C. Stabbed by an arrow – Stabbed by dart (poison) from blow pipe

Jack [her brother in law] – Dog?
Mrs E – Menu holders
Aunt Min – blotter and notepaper stand
Barbara – bag and scarf
Joan – Belt?

D. Ventriloquist

E. Series of murders – P gets letter from apparent maniac – First – an old woman in Yorkshire

*Three Act Tragedy* is preceded by an address and phone number:

Toby, 1 Granville Place, Portman Street Mayfair 1087

P suggests Egg should tackle Mrs Dacres

Travel details appear in the middle of 'The Capture of Cerberus' ('Robin' was possibly Robin McCartney, who drew the jacket designs for *Death on the Nile, Murder in Mesopotamia* and *Appointment with Death*):

Young widow – husband missing believed killed – P sees him in 'Hell'

Any Thursday by afternoon train Robin

Combine with idea of man who has gone under – Dead?
A waiter in Hell?

As can be seen, Christie's creativity was not exclusive – she was able to plot a murder while making a social appointment,

Aunt Grace (Cannan)
Murder Abroad (Punshon)
D Stop Press (Innes)
Flight from a Lady (MacDonell)
Twenty-Four Short Stories (Graham Greene, Jan Lane)
By the Waters of Babylon – (R. Neumann)
D Deliver (Taste American)
D Some Day I'll Kill You (an Nove)
The Death Guard (William Bawley)
The Ghost of a Rose.
In the Teeth of the Evidence (D. Sayers)
The Trial of Harry Court.
Nation Road (Kiki Barry)
x Murder at Charters
John Arrison (Edward Thompson)
Murder in Stained Glass
The People of the Experience
Escape with me Osbert Sitwell
x The Footprints on the Ceiling (Mahine)
x Before Lunch (Angela Thirkell)
x Mr Avancen (Stella Gibbon)
x Absalom Goggs (Murder Death)
x Children of Children
The Nazarene
The Walls of Earth

... *Her publishers would send Agatha books to read, and
indeed the page above is headed 'From Collins'.*

or consider a murder weapon while compiling a reading list, or mull over a motive while transcribing travel directions. Throughout the Notebooks she is Agatha Christie, Queen of Crime while always remaining Agatha, the family member.

## Motive and Opportunity

One of her most personal creations, Ariadne Oliver, is generally accepted as Christie's own alter ego. Mrs Oliver is a middle-aged, successful and prolific writer of detective fiction and creator of a foreign detective, the Finnish Sven Hjerson. She hates literary dinners, making speeches, or collaborating with dramatists; she has written *The Body in the Library* and doesn't drink or smoke. The similarities are remarkable and there can be little doubt that when Mrs Oliver speaks we are listening to Agatha Christie.

In Chapter 2 of *Dead Man's Folly* Mrs Oliver shrugs off her ingenuity:

> *'It's never difficult to think of things,' said Mrs Oliver. 'The trouble is that you think of too many, and then it all becomes too complicated, so you have to relinquish some of them and that is rather agony.'*

And again, later in Chapter 17 she says:

> *'I mean, what can you say about how you write your books? What I mean is, first you've got to think of something, and then when you've thought of it you've got to force yourself to sit down and write it. That's all.'*

It was as simple as that and, for half a century, exactly what her creator did.

The process of production was, as we have seen, random and haphazard. And yet, this seeming randomness was transformed into an annual bestseller; and, for many years, into more than one bestseller. For more than half a century she delivered the latest 'Christie for Christmas' to her agent; for a quarter century she presented London's West End with one theatrical success after another; she kept magazines busy editing her latest offering. And all of them – novels, short stories and plays – flow with the fluid precision of the Changing of the Guard.

So although it is true that she had no particular method, no tried and true system that she brought with her down the long years of her career, we know this appearance of indiscriminate jotting and plotting is just that – an appearance. And eventually we come to the realisation that, in fact, this very randomness *is* her method; this is how she worked, how she created, how she wrote. She thrived mentally on chaos, it stimulated her more than neat order; rigidity stifled her creative process. And it explains how the Notebooks read from both ends, how they leap from one title to another on the same page, how different Notebooks repeat and develop the same ideas and why her handwriting can be impossible to read.

Notebook 15 and the plotting of *Cat Among the Pigeons* illustrate some of these points. She talks to herself on the page:

How should all this be approached? – in sequence?
Or followed up backwards by Hercule Poirot – from
disappearance . . . at school – a possibly trivial incident but
which is connected with murder? – but murder of whom
– and why?

She wonders and speculates and lists possibilities:

Who is killed?
Girl?
Games mistress?
Maid?
Foreign Mid East ?? who would know girl by sign?
Or a girl who ?

Mrs. U sees someone out of window – could be
  New Mistress?
    Domestic Staff?
    Pupil?
    Parent?

The Murder –
Could be    A girl (resembles Julia/resembles Clare?
    A Parent – sports Day
    A Mistress

Someone shot or stalked at school Sports?
Princess Maynasita there –
or – an actress as pupil
or – an actress as games mistress

She reminds herself of work still to be done:

Tidy up – End of chapter

Chapter III – A good deal to be done –

Chapter IV – A good deal to be worked over – (possibly end chapter with 'Adam the Gardener' – listing mistresses – (or next chapter)

Chapter V – Letters fuller

Notes on revision – a bit about Miss B

Prologue – Type extra bits

Chapter V – Some new letters

And for some light relief she breaks off to solve a word puzzle. In this well-known conundrum the test is to use all of the letters of the alphabet in one sentence. (Her answer omits the letter Z.)

A D G J L ~~M P S~~ V Y Z

THE QUICK BROWN FOX JUMPS over gladly

## Remembered Deaths

In *Cards on the Table* Mrs Oliver is asked if she has ever used the same plot twice.

> '*The Lotus Murder*,' murmured Poirot, '*The Clue of the Candle Wax*.'
>
> Mrs Oliver turned on him, her eyes beaming appreciation.
>
> '*That's clever of you – really very clever of you. Because, of course, those two are exactly the same plot – but nobody else has seen it. One is stolen papers at an informal weekend-party of the Cabinet, and the other's a murder in Borneo in a rubber planter's bungalow*.'
>
> '*But the essential point on which the story turns is the same*,' said Poirot. '*One of your neatest tricks*.'

So it is with Christie. She reused plot devices throughout her career; and she recycled short stories into novellas and novels, often speculating in the Notebooks about the expansion or adaptation of an earlier title. The Notebooks demonstrate how, even if she discarded an idea for now, she left everything there to be looked at again at a later stage. And when she did that, as she wrote in *An Autobiography*, 'What it's all about I can't remember now; but it often stimulates me.' So she used the Notebooks as an *aide-mémoire* as well as a sounding board.

The first example below dates from the mid-1950s and relates to the short stories 'Third Floor Flat' and 'The Mystery of the Baghdad Chest'; it is surrounded by notes for 'Greenshaw's Folly' and *4.50 from Paddington*. The second example, concerning 'The Adventure of the Christmas

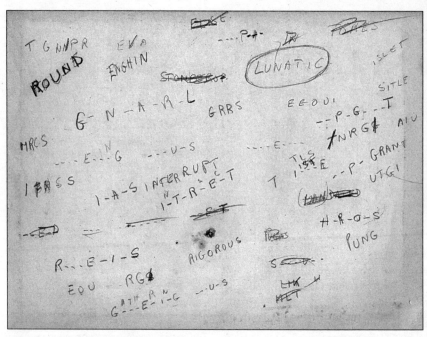

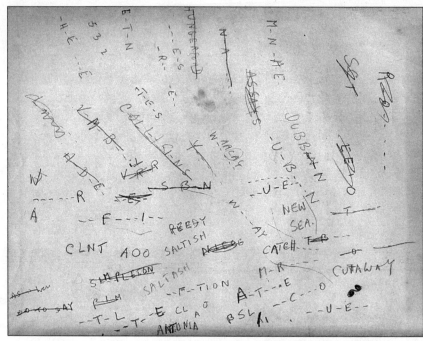

*Two pages of random word puzzles, probably the
rough work for a crossword.*

Pudding', is from early 1960 and the last one, concerning 'The Shadow on the Glass', probably from 1950:

Development of stories

3rd Floor Flat – murder committed earlier – return to get post and also footprints etc. accounted for – service lift idea? Wrong floor

Baghdad Chest or a screen?
Idea? A persuades B hide B
Chest or screen as Mrs B – having affair with C – C gives party – B and A drop in – B hides A – kills him – and goes out again

Extended version of Xmas Pudding – Points in it of importance

A Ruby (belonging to Indian Prince – or a ruler just married?) in pudding

A book or a play from The Shadow on the Pane idea? (Mr Q)

The following are examples of Christie's reworked ideas, many of which are discussed in this book. Some elaborations are obvious:

'The Case of the Caretaker/Caretaker's Wife'/*Endless Night*

'The Plymouth Express'/*The Mystery of the Blue Train*

'The Market Basing Mystery'/'Murder in the Mews'

'The Submarine Plans'/'The Incredible Theft'

'The Mystery of the Baghdad Chest'/'The Mystery of the Spanish Chest'

'Christmas Adventure'/'The Adventure of the Christmas Pudding'

'The Greenshore Folly'/*Dead Man's Folly*

In other cases she challenged herself when adapting and expanding by changing the killer:

*The Secret of Chimneys/Chimneys*

'The Second Gong'/'Dead Man's Mirror'

'Yellow Iris'/*Sparkling Cyanide*

'The Incident of the Dog's Ball'/*Dumb Witness*

Some stage versions differ from their source novels . . .

*Appointment with Death* presents a new villain with a compelling and daring solution.

*Chimneys* introduces many variations, including a new killer, on *The Secret of Chimneys*.

*And Then There Were None* unmasks the original killer within a very different finale.

Meanwhile, there are more subtle links between certain works:

*The Mysterious Affair at Styles, Death on the Nile* and *Endless Night* are all essentially the same plot.

*The Man in the Brown Suit, The Murder of Roger Ackroyd* and *Endless Night* all share a major plot device.

*Evil under the Sun* and *The Body in the Library* feature a common ploy.

*After the Funeral* and *They Do It with Mirrors* are both based on the same trick of misdirection.

*Murder on the Orient Express, At Bertram's Hotel* and, to a lesser extent, *The Hollow* are all built on a similar foundation.

*Three Act Tragedy, Death in the Clouds* and *The ABC Murders* all conceal the killer in similar surroundings.

And there are other examples that have, thus far, escaped notice:

'The Tuesday Night Club'/*A Pocket Full of Rye*

'A Christmas Tragedy'/*Evil under the Sun*

'Sing a Song of Sixpence'/*Ordeal by Innocence*

'The Love Detectives'/*The Murder at the Vicarage*

## The ABC of Murder

One system of creation that Christie used during her most prolific period was the listing of a series of scenes, sketching what she wanted each to include and allocating to each individual scene a number or a letter; this neat idea, in the days before computers with a 'cut and paste' facility, may have been inspired by her play-writing experience. She would subsequently reorder those letters to suit the purposes of the plot. In keeping with her creative and chaotic process, this plan was not always followed and even when she began with it, she sometimes abandoned it for a more linear approach (see *Crooked House*). And sometimes the pattern in the finished book would not exactly follow the sequence she had originally mapped out, perhaps due to subsequent editing.

The following, part of the plotting of *Towards Zero* from Notebook 32, is a perfect example of this method in practice.

E. Thomas and Audrey what's wrong? She can't tell him. He stresses I know, my dear – I know – But you must begin to live again. Something about 'died' a death – (meaning Adrian – somebody like N[evile] ought to be dead)
F. Mary and Audrey – suggestion of thwarted female – 'Servants even are nervous'
G. Coat buttons incident
H. Moonlight beauty of Audrey

Points

Mr T – A. Talk with Lady T – asks about Mary
     B. The story of murder led up to how?
     C. Royde and justice (after Mr T has said: Many
        murders known to police)
     D. Hotel – his rooms are on top floor

Work out sequence of evening
     G. H. A. D. C. B. ~~G. H.~~

It is notable how the E F G H scenes appear on an earlier page and the A B C D scenes on a later one. After they have all been tabulated, she then rearranges them to give the sequence she desires. At first, she intended the G and H scenes to follow A D C B but changed her mind, crossed them out and transposed them, squeezing them in, in front, at the left-hand margin of the page. A study of the relevant second section of the novel – 'Snow White and Red Rose' – will show that she followed this plan exactly:

| | |
|---|---|
| G. Coat buttons | V |
| H. Moonlight | V |
| A. Lady T | VI |
| D. Hotel | VI |
| C. Royde | VI |
| B. Lead up | VI |
| F. Mary and Audrey | VII |
| E. Thomas and Audrey | VIII |

Work out sequence of evening  G. H. A. D. C. B. ~~G. H.~~ [F E]

She follows this scheme in the plotting of, among others, *Sparkling Cyanide, One, Two, Buckle my Shoe* and *Crooked House*. But with her chaotic approach to creativity and creative approach to chaos, she sometimes abandons it.

Notebook 14 shows this scheme, up to a point, in use for

Middle Sequence.

Points

Mr T _ A/ Talk with Lady T _
Anna about Mary. She says
nn dealr ... free ...
B/ The story of murder
Led up to — How?

C/ Royde +Justice (after
Mr T has said: Mary
murder Known to police.)

D/ Hotel - His room are
on Top floor _

Work an Scene of Evening.

H.A. D .. C. B.
Drinks etc. Girl so to bed - Nevile Comes
M/ up. - He a Ted - Royde has some off _

*Detailed plotting for* Towards Zero *— see opposite page.*

*Crooked House* but with added complications – AA and FF. Ultimately she dispensed with the reordering of the letters and just reordered the scenes without the alphabetical guide-line. And the AA and FF were merely afterthoughts to be inserted at a later stage.

A. Inquires into Ass[ociated] Cat[ering] – discreet at first – Chartered Accountant will get us what we want [Chapter 10/11]

AA Also Brenda – femme fatale – are sorry for etc. [Chapter 9]

B. Later? – ~~On its~~ In Queer St. – Get Roger there – Roger – his story – etc. [Chapter 11]

C. Child's evidence – best evidence – there is – no good in court – children don't like being asked direct questions. To you she was showing off [Chapter 12]

D. Charles and Josephine – asks about letters – I was making it up – won't tell you – you shouldn't have told police [Chapter 13]

E. Charles and Eustace – (Listens outside door – really a boring teacher) Eustace – his views – scornful of Josephine [Chapter 16]

F. Charles and Edith – this side idolatry – asks Philip – you mustn't be deterred by his cold manner – really cared for his father – Philip is jealous of Roger [Chapter 14]

FF. Question as to saving Ass. Cat. Roger refuses – Clemency backs him up – Is very definite about it [Chapter 14. There are indications in Notebook 14 that she intended this to form part of H below]

G. Magda and Charles – Edith didn't hate him – in love with him – would have liked to marry him [Chapter 15]

H. Charles and Clemency – her total happiness in marriage – how Roger would have been happy away from it all – Josephine writing in her book [Chapter 14]

I. A.C. says – be careful of the child – there's a poisoner about [Chapter 12]

J. The weight over the door (if J) or definitely dies – little
   black book missing [Chapter 18]
K. Charles and Sophia Murder – what does murder do to
   anyone? [Chapter 4]

The notes for *Crooked House* also illustrate a seemingly contra-
dictory and misleading aspect of the Notebooks. It is quite
common to come across pages with diagonal lines drawn
across them. At first glance it would seem, understandably,
that these were rejected ideas but a closer look shows that the
exact opposite was the case. A line across a page indicates
Work Done or Idea Used. This was a habit through her most
prolific period although she tended to leave the pages, used
or not, unmarked in her later writing life.

### Ten Little Possibilities

In 'The Affair at the Bungalow', written in 1928 and collected
in *The Thirteen Problems* (1932), Mrs Bantry comes up with
reasons for someone to steal their own jewels:

> *'And anyway I can think of hundreds of reasons. She might have
> wanted money at once . . . so she pretends the jewels are stolen and
> sells them secretly. Or she may have been blackmailed by someone
> who threatened to tell her husband . . . Or she may have already
> sold the jewels . . . so she had to do something about it. That's done
> a good deal in books. Or perhaps he was going to have them reset
> and she'd got paste replicas. Or – here's a very good idea – and not
> so much done in books – she pretends they are stolen, gets in an
> awful state and he gives her a fresh lot.'*

In *Third Girl* (1966) Norma Restarick comes to Poirot and
tells him that she might have committed a murder. In
Chapter 2, Mrs Ariadne Oliver, that well-known detective
novelist, imagines some situations that could account for this
possibility:

*Mrs Oliver began to brighten as she set her ever prolific imagination to work. 'She could have run over someone in her car and not stopped. She could have been assaulted by a man on a cliff and struggled with him and managed to push him over. She could have given someone else the wrong medicine by mistake. She could have gone to one of those purple pill parties and had a fight with someone. She could have come to and found she'd stabbed someone. She . . . might have been a nurse in the operating theatre and administered the wrong anaesthetic . . .'*

In Chapter 8 of *Dead Man's Folly* (1956) Mrs Oliver again lets her imagination roam when considering possible motives for the murder of schoolgirl Marlene Tucker:

*'She could have been murdered by someone who just likes murdering girls . . . Or she might have known some secrets about somebody's love affairs, or she may have seen someone bury a body at night or she may have seen somebody who was concealing his identity – or she may have known some secret about where some treasure was buried during the war. Or the man in the launch may have thrown somebody into the river and she saw it from the window of the boathouse – or she may have even got hold of some very important message in secret code and not known what it was herself . . .' It was clear that she could have gone on in this vein for some time although it seemed to the Inspector that she had already envisaged every possibility, likely or unlikely.*

These extracts from stories, written almost 40 years apart, illustrate, via her characters, Christie's greatest strength: her ability to weave seemingly endless variations around one idea. There can be little doubt that these are Agatha Christie herself speaking and we can see from the Notebooks that this is exactly what she did. Throughout her career her ideas were consistently drawn from the world with which her readers were familiar – teeth, dogs, stamps (as below), mirrors, telephones, medicines – and upon these foundations she built

The A. B. C. Murder.                    13

Chapter I.

Hastings — his return from the
Argentine — Poirot — as young
as ever — Black hair. P. explains
false moustaches! P. replies - "dye
in honour."

not really working. my last case
task — slowly prepares itself.
The Letter.
    a robbery.
    he — a murder.

Chapter II.
Japp — the Commissioner.
the 14th notes beginning judicially.
telephone — an old woman —
for Andover — head bashed in —

---

*The opening of* The ABC Murders *(note the reference to a single 'Murder'), illustrating the use of crossing-out as an indication of work completed.*

her ingenious constructions. She explored universal themes in some of her later books (guilt and innocence in *Ordeal by Innocence*, evil in *The Pale Horse*, international unrest in *Cat among the Pigeons* and *Passenger to Frankfurt*), but still firmly rooted in the everyday.

Although it is not possible to be absolutely sure, there is no reason to suppose that listings of ideas and their variations were written at different times; I have no doubt that she rattled off variations and possibilities as fast as she could write, which probably accounts for the handwriting. In many cases it is possible to show that the list is written with the same pen and in the same style of handwriting. The outline of *One, Two, Buckle my Shoe* provides a good example as she considers:

Man marries secretly one of the twins
   Or
Man was really already married [this was the option adopted]
   Or
Barrister's 'sister' who lives with him (really wife)
   Or
Double murder – that is to say – A poisons B – B stabs A – but really owing to plan by C
   Or
Blackmailing wife finds out – then she is found dead
   Or
He really likes wife – goes off to start life again with her
   Or
Dentists killed – 1 London – 1 County

A few pages later in the same Notebook, also in connection with *One, Two, Buckle my Shoe*, she tries further variations on the same theme, this time introducing 'Sub Ideas'.

Pos. A. 1st wife still alive –
A.  (a) knows all – co-operating with him
     (b) does not know – that he is secret service

Pos. B 1st wife dead – someone recognises him – 'I was a great friend of your wife, you know –'

In either case – crime is undertaken to suppress fact of 1st marriage and elaborate preparations undertaken

C. Single handed

D. Co-operation of wife as secretary

Sub Idea C

The 'friends' Miss B and Miss R – one goes to dentist
Or
~~Does wife go to a certain dentist?~~
Miss B makes app[ointment] – with dentist – Miss R keeps it
Miss R's teeth labelled under Miss B's name

Also from Notebook 35, but this time in connection with *Five Little Pigs*, we find very basic questions and possibilities under consideration:

Did mother murder –
A. Husband
B. Lover
C. Rich uncle or guardian
D. Another woman (jealousy)

Who were the other people

During the planning of *Mrs McGinty's Dead*, the four murders in the past, around which the plot is built, provided an almost infinite number of possibilities and she worked her way methodically through them, considering every character living in Broadhinny, the scene of the novel, as a possible participant in the earlier murders. In this extract from Notebook 43 she tries various scenarios, underlining the possible killer in each case.

Which?

1. A. False – elderly Cranes – with daughter (girl – Evelyn)
   B. Real – Robin – son with mother <u>son</u> [Upward]
2. A. False Invalid mother (or not invalid) and son
   B. Real – dull wife of snob A.P. (Carter) <u>Dau</u>[ghter]
3. A. False artistic woman with <u>son</u>
   B. Real middle-aged wife – dull couple – or flashy Carters
   (daughter invalid)
4. A. False widow – soon to marry rich man
5. [A] False man with dogs – stepson – different name
   [B] Real – invalid mother and daughter – <u>dau</u>[ghter] does
   it [Wetherby]

And, later in the same Notebook, she considers which of her characters could fit the profiles of one of the earlier crimes, the Kane murder case:

Could be
Robin's mother    (E. Kane)
Robin      (EK's son)
Mrs Crane      (EK)
Their daughter    (EK's dau)
Mrs Carter    (EK's dau)
Young William Crane    (EK's son)
Mrs Wildfell    (EK's dau)

In Notebook 39 Christie rattles off six (despite the heading) plot ideas, covering within these brief sketches kidnapping, forgery, robbery, fraud, murder and extortion:

4 snappy ideas for short Stories

Kidnapping? [The Adventure of] Johnnie Waverley again
– Platinum blonde – kidnaps herself?

Invisible Will? Will written on quite different document

Museum robbery – celebrated professor takes things and examines them? – or member of public does

Stamps – Fortune hidden in them – gets dealer to buy them for him

An occurrence at a public place – Savoy? Dance? Debutantes tea? Mothers killed off in rapid succession?

The Missing Pekingese

The accurate dating of this extract is debatable. The reference 'missing Pekingese' is to 'The Nemean Lion', collected in *The Labours of Hercules* but first published in 1939. This, taken in conjunction with the reference to the 'Debutantes tea', probably indicates a late 1930s date when Christie's daughter, Rosalind, would have been a debutante. Only two of the other ideas appear in print ('Invisible Will' in 'Motive vs Opportunity' in *The Thirteen Problems* and 'Stamps' in 'Strange Jest' and *Spider's Web*), although not quite as they appear here.

In Notebook 47 Christie is in full flight planning a new short story, possibly a commission as she specifies the number of words. The following is all contained on one page and was probably written straight off:

Ideas for 7000 word story
A 'Ruth Ellis' . . . idea?
Shoots man – not fatally – other man (or woman) eggs her on

Say this 2nd person was –

A. Sister in law? Brother's wife – her son or child would get this money and not be sent to boarding school away from her influence – a gentle soft motherly creature
B. A mannish sister determined brother should not marry Ruby

C. Man (with influence over Ruby) works her up while
   pretending to calm her. X has some knowledge
   concerning him. He wants to marry X's sister
D. Man formerly Ruby's lover/husband – has it in for her
   <u>and</u> X

Unfortunately, she did not pursue this idea and no story resulted; she returned, four pages later, to plotting *The Unexpected Guest*, so the extract probably dates from the mid-1950s. (Ruth Ellis was the last woman to hang in the UK, in July 1955 after her conviction for the shooting of her lover David Blakely.)

### Destinations Unknown

When she sat down to consider her next book, even before she got as far as plotting, Christie would list possible settings. The following extract appears in Notebook 47 a few pages before notes for *4.50 from Paddington* ('seen from a train') and so would seem to date from the mid-1950s:

Book

Scene
Baghdad?
Hospital
Hotel [*At Bertram's Hotel*]
Flat    Third Floor Flat idea
     Baghdad Chest idea ['The Mystery of the Spanish
     Chest' and *The Rats*]
Small house in London husband and wife, children etc.
Park    Regent's Park
School    Girl's school [*Cat among the Pigeons*]
Boat    Queen Emma? Western Lady
Train    seen from a train? Through window of house or vice
versa? [*4.50 from Paddington*]

Beach    And Boarding house [possibly *Afternoon at the Seaside*]

Although difficult to date exactly, the following extract is probably from the very late 1940s. It is just after notes for *Mrs McGinty's Dead* (although with a totally different plot outline) and *They Do It with Mirrors* (ditto) and is followed by a list of her books in her own handwriting, the latest title of which is *The Hollow* (1946).

Ideas for Mise-en-scene?

Conditions like The White Crow. Start with the murder –
    a prominent person – such as a minister –
(Aneurin Bevan type?) – on holiday? Interrogation of his
    personnel – His wife – Female secretary
Male [secretary] – Difficulties as I don't know about
    Ministers
Chief pharmacist in a Hospital? Young medical man doing
    research on Penicillin?
A brains trust? Local one? BBC Mrs AC arrives to broadcast
    – Dies – not the real Mrs AC?
A big hotel? Imperial? No – done
Shop? Worth's during m uin parade – Selfridges – in a
    cubicle during Sale

Some of the references in this extract may need clarification. *The White Crow* is a 1928 detective novel by Philip MacDonald; it concerns the murder of an influential businessman in his own office (as in *A Pocket Full of Rye*). Aneurin Bevan was UK Minister of Health, 1945–51. The position of chief pharmacist was one with which Christie was familiar both from her early life and from her experience in the Second World War (*The Pale Horse* contains a gesture in this direction). 'Imperial' is a reference to *Peril at End House*, although the hotel is disguised as the Majestic. And Worth's, like Selfridge's, is a famous department store.

'Mrs AC arrives to broadcast' reminds us that although Christie refused countless requests throughout her career to broadcast on either radio or television, she did, at least once, take part in a *Desert Island Discs* type programme, *In the Gramophone Library*, broadcast in August 1946. And the rueful remark 'Difficulties as I don't know about Ministers' – my favourite comment from the entire Notebooks – shows that she abided by the old maxim: 'Write about what you know'.

### Surprise, Surprise!

But the biggest surprise in the Notebooks is the fact that many of the best plots did not necessarily spring from a single devastating idea. She considered all possibilities when she plotted and did not confine herself to one idea, no matter how good it may have seemed. In very few cases is the identity of the murderer a given from the start of the plotting.

The most dramatic example is *Crooked House*. By the mid-1940s she had experimented with the narrator-murderer, the policeman-murderer, the everybody-as-murderer and the everybody-as-victim gambits. With its startling revelation that the killer is a child, *Crooked House* remains one of the great Christie surprises, in the same class as *The Murder of Roger Ackroyd*, *Murder on the Orient Express*, *Curtain* and *Endless Night*. (To be entirely fair, at least two other writers, Ellery Queen in *The Tragedy of Y* and Margery Allingham in *The White Cottage Mystery* had already exploited this idea but far less effectively.) But a child-killer was not the *raison d'être* of this novel; the shattering identity of the murderer was only one element under consideration and not necessarily the key element. Even a cursory glance at Notebook 14 shows that Christie also considered Sophia, Clemency and Edith as well as Josephine when it came to potential murderers. It was not a case of arranging the entire plot around Josephine as the one unalterable fact.

Again, at no point in the notes for her last devastating

surprise, *Endless Night*, is there mention of the narrator-killer. It was not a case of simply repeating the Ackroyd trick; in fact, at only one point in the Notebook is there mention of telling the story in the first person. The inspiration for the shock ending came to her as she plotted rather than the other way round.

Arguably the last of the ingeniously clued detective novels, *A Murder is Announced*, would seem to allow of only one solution, and yet at one stage Letitia Blacklock is under consideration as the second victim of Mitzi, who has already murdered her own husband Rudi Sherz. It was not a case of deciding to write a novel featuring a supposed victim actually murdering her blackmailer during a carefully devised game. Nor did *Murder in Mesopotamia* always revolve around a wife-killing husband with a perfect alibi; Miss Johnston and, in fact, Mrs Leidner herself were also considered for the role of killer. The setting, the archaeological dig, would seem to have been the fixed idea for this novel and the rest of the plot was woven around it rather than vice versa.

Although this still seems surprising, it is in keeping with Christie's general method of working. Her strengths lay in her unfettered mental fertility and her lack of system. Her initial inspiration could be as vague as a gypsy's curse (*Endless Night*), an archaeological dig (*Murder in Mesopotamia*) or a newspaper advertisement (*A Murder is Announced*). After that, she let her not inconsiderable imagination have free rein with the idea and hey, presto! a year later the latest Christie appeared on the bookshelves. And some of the ideas that did not make it into that masterpiece might well surface in the one to be published the following year; or ten years hence.

Dotted throughout the Notebooks are dozens of phrases that show Agatha Christie the resourceful creator, Agatha Christie the critical professional, Agatha Christie the sly humorist at work. In many cases she 'thought' directly on to the page and there are many instances where she addresses herself in this way. Sometimes it is idle speculation as she toys with various ideas before settling on just one:

'How about this' . . . as she works out the timetable of 'Greenshaw's Folly'

'A good idea would be' . . . this, tantalisingly, is on an otherwise blank page

'or – a little better' . . . firming up the motive in *Hercule Poirot's Christmas*

'How about girl gets job' . . . from early notes for *A Caribbean Mystery*

'Who? Why? When? How? Where? Which?' . . . the essence of a detective story from *One, Two, Buckle my Shoe*

'Which way do we turn?' . . . in the middle of *Third Girl*

'A prominent person – such as a minister – (Aneurin Bevan type?) – on holiday? Difficulties as I don't know about Ministers' . . . rueful while looking for a new idea in the mid-1940s

When she has decided on a plot she often muses about the intricacies and possibilities of a variation:

'Does Jeremy have to be there then' . . . pondering on character movements for *Spider's Web*

'Contents of letter given? Or Not' . . . in the course of *Cat among the Pigeons*

'How does she bring it about . . . What drug' . . . while planning *A Caribbean Mystery*

'Yes – better if dentist is dead' . . . a decision reached during *One, Two, Buckle my Shoe*

'Why? Why??? Why?????' . . . frustration during *One, Two, Buckle my Shoe*

'He could be murderer – if there is a murder' . . . a possibility for *Fiddlers Three*

Like all true professionals she is self-critical:

'unlike twin idea – woman servant one of them – NO!!' . . . a decision during *The Labours of Hercules*

'NB All v. unlikely' . . . as she approaches the end of *Mrs McGinty's Dead*

'All right – a little elaboration – more mistresses?' . . . not very happy with *Cat among the Pigeons*

She includes reminders to herself:

'Look up datura poisoning . . . and re-read Cretan Bull' . . . as she writes *A Caribbean Mystery*

'Find story about child and other child plays with him' . . . probably her short story 'The Lamp'

'Possible variant – (read a private eye book first before typing)' . . . a reminder during *The Clocks*

'A good idea – needs working on' . . . for *Nemesis*

Things to line up' . . . during *Dead Man's Folly*

And there are the odd flashes of humour:

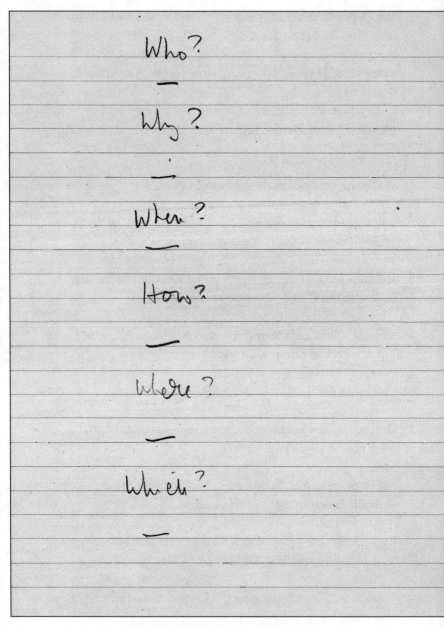

*From Notebook 35 and* One, Two, Buckle my Shoe – *the essence of detective fiction distilled into six words.*

'Van D. pops off' . . . during *A Caribbean Mystery*

'Pennyfather is conked' . . . a rather uncharitable description from *At Bertram's Hotel*

'Elephantine Suggestions' . . . from, obviously, *Elephants Can Remember*

'Suspicion of (clever!) reader to be directed toward <u>Nurse</u>' . . . a typically astute observation from *Curtain* when the nurse is completely innocent (note the use of the exclamation mark after 'clever')

We now have a clearer idea of Christie's approach to the construction of her stories. Using the Notebooks as a combination of sounding board and literary sketchpad, she devised and developed; she selected and rejected; she sharpened and polished; she revisited and recycled. And, as I hope to show by a more detailed analysis in the following chapters, out of this seeming chaos she produced a unique and immortal body of work.

# 4

# Rule of Three

'One of the pleasures in writing detective stories is that there are so many types to choose from: the light-hearted thriller . . . the intricate detective story . . . and what I can only describe as the detective story that has a kind of passion behind it . . .'

*An Autobiography*

‹o›

**SOLUTIONS REVEALED**

*The ABC Murders* • *After the Funeral* • *Appointment with Death* • *The Body in the Library* • *Curtain: Poirot's Last Case* • *Death in the Clouds* • *Death on the Nile* • *Endless Night* • *Evil under the Sun* • *4.50 from Paddington* • *Hercule Poirot's Christmas* • *The Hollow* • *Lord Edgware Dies* • *The Man in the Brown Suit;* • 'The Man in the Mist' • 'The Market Basing Mystery' • *The Mousetrap* • *The Murder at the Vicarage* • 'Murder in the Mews' • *The Murder of Roger Ackroyd* • *Murder on the Orient Express* • *The Mysterious Affair at Styles* • *One, Two, Buckle my Shoe* • *Ordeal by Innocence* • *A Pocket Full of Rye* • *Sparkling Cyanide* • *Taken at the Flood* • *They Came to Baghdad* • *They Do It with Mirrors* • *Three Act Tragedy* • 'The Unbreakable Alibi' • 'The Witness for the Prosecution'

‹o›

'Surely you won't let Agatha Christie fool you again. That would be "again" – wouldn't it?' Thus read the advertisement, at the back of many of her early Crime Club books, announcing recent and forthcoming titles from the Queen of Crime. The first Crime Club novel bearing the now-famous hooded gunman logo, was Philip MacDonald's *The Noose* in May 1930; Agatha Christie's first Crime Club title, *The Murder at the Vicarage*, followed in October of that year. By then Collins had already published, between 1926 and 1929, five Christie titles – *The Murder of Roger Ackroyd, The Big Four, The Mystery of the Blue Train, The Seven Dials Mystery* and *Partners in Crime* – in their general fiction list. As soon as The Crime Club was founded, her's was an obvious name to include and over the next half century she proved to be one of the most prolific authors – and by far the most successful – to appear under its imprint. This author/publisher relationship continued for the rest of her writing life, almost all of her titles appearing with the accompaniment of the hooded gunman.[2]

As the dustjacket on the first edition of *The Murder at the Vicarage* states, 'The Crime Club has been formed so that all interested in Detective Fiction may, at NO COST TO THEMSELVES, be kept advised of the best new Detective Novels before they are published.' By 1932 and *Peril at End House*, The Crime Club was boasting that 'Over 25,000 have joined already. The list includes doctors, clergymen, lawyers, University Dons, civil servants, business men; it includes two millionaires, three world-famous statesmen, thirty-two

---

2   Odhams Press first published *The Hound of Death* in 1933 and Collins reissued it in 1936 as a Crime Club title. Collins published two short story collections – *The Listerdale Mystery* and *Parker Pyne Investigates* – in 1934 but not as Crime Club titles, as the contents were not devoted exclusively to crime. For the same reason, although HarperCollins (as it had then become) published *Problem at Pollensa Bay* (1991) and *While the Light Lasts* (1997), neither appeared under the Crime Club imprint; after 1994 The Crime Club no longer existed.

# THE MURDER AT THE VICARAGE

## AGATHA CHRISTIE

Published for

# THE CRIME CLUB LTD.

*by*

W. COLLINS SONS & CO LTD

**LONDON**

*This is the first edition title page of* The Murder at the Vicarage,
*the first Agatha Christie title to appear under The Crime Club imprint
on 13th October 1930.*

knights, eleven peers of the realm, two princes of royal blood and one princess.'

And the advertisement on the first edition wrapper of *The ABC Murders* (1936) clearly states the Club's aims and objectives:

> The object of the Crime Club is to provide that vast section of the British Public which likes a good detective story with a continual supply of first-class books by the finest writers of detective fiction. The Panel of five experts selects the good and eliminates the bad, and ensures that every book published under the Crime Club mark is a clean and intriguing example of this class of literature. Crime Club books are not mere thrillers. They are restricted to works in which there is a definite crime problem, an honest detective process, with a credible and logical solution. Members of the Crime Club receive the Crime Club News issued at intervals.

As this suggests, not for nothing was the 1930s known as the Golden Age of detective fiction, an era during which the creation and enjoyment of a detective story was a serious business for reader, writer and publisher. All three took the elaborate conventions seriously. The civilised outrage that followed the publication of *The Murder of Roger Ackroyd* in 1926 showed what a serious breach of the rules its solution was considered at the time. So, while in many ways observing the so-called 'rules', and consolidating the image of a safe, cosy and comforting type of fiction, Agatha Christie also constantly challenged those 'rules' and, by regularly and mischievously tweaking, bending, and breaking them, subverted the expectations of her readers and critics. She was both the mould creator and mould breaker, who delighted in effectively saying to her fans, 'Here is the comforting read that you expect when you pick up my new book but because I respect your intelligence and my own professionalism, I intend to fool you.'

But how did she fool her readers while at the same time retaining her vice-like grip on their admiration and loyalty? In order to understand how she managed this feat it is necessary to take a closer look at 'The Rules'.

## THE RULES OF DETECTIVE FICTION – POE, KNOX, VAN DINE

### *Edgar Allan Poe: inventor of the detective story*

In April 1841 the American periodical *Graham's Magazine* published Edgar Allan Poe's 'The Murders in the Rue Morgue' and introduced a new literary form, the detective story. The unwritten ground-rules that distinguish detective fiction from other forms of crime writing – the thriller, the suspense story, the mystery story – were established in five Poe short stories. He pioneered:

* The brilliant amateur detective
* The less-than-brilliant narrator-friend
* The wrongly suspected person
* The sealed room
* The unexpected solution
* The 'armchair detective' and the application of pure reasoning
* The interpretation of a code
* The trail of false clues laid by the murderer
* The unmasking of the least likely suspect
* Psychological deduction
* The most obvious solution

All of Poe's pioneering initiatives were exploited by subsequent generations of crime writers and although many of those writers introduced variations on, and combinations of, them, no other writer ever established so many influential concepts. Christie, as we shall see, exploited them to the full.

The first, and most important, of the Poe stories, 'The Murders in the Rue Morgue', incorporated the first five ideas above. The murder of a mother and daughter in a room locked from the inside is investigated by Chevalier C. Auguste Dupin, who, by logical deduction, arrives at a most unexpected solution, thereby proving the innocence of an arrested man; the story is narrated by his unnamed associate.

Although Poe is not one of the writers she mentions in *An Autobiography* as being an influence, Agatha Christie took his template of a murder and its investigation when she began to write *The Mysterious Affair at Styles*, 75 years later.

## The brilliant amateur detective

If we take 'amateur' to mean someone outside the official police force, then Hercule Poirot is the pre-eminent example. With the creation of Miss Marple, Christie remains the only writer to create two famous detective figures. Although not as well known, the characters Tommy and Tuppence, Parker Pyne, Mr Satterthwaite and Mr Quin also come into this category.

## The less-than-brilliant narrator-friend

Poirot's early chronicler, Captain Arthur Hastings, appeared in nine novels (if we include the 1927 episodic novel *The Big Four*) and 26 short stories. After *Dumb Witness* in 1937, Christie dispensed with his services, though she allowed him a nostalgic swan song in *Curtain*, published in 1975. But she also experimented with other narrators, often with dramatic results: *The Man in the Brown Suit*, *The Murder of Roger Ackroyd*, *Endless Night*. The decision to send Hastings to Argentina may have had less to do with his mental ability than with the restrictions he imposed on his creator: his narration meant that only events at which he was present could be recounted. Signs of this growing unease can be seen in the use of third-person narrative at the beginning of *Dumb Witness* and intermittently throughout *The ABC Murders*, published the year before Hastings' banishment. Miss Marple has no permanent Hastings-like companion.

### The wrongly suspected person

This is the basis of some of Christie's finest titles, among them the novels *Five Little Pigs*, *Sad Cypress*, *Mrs McGinty's Dead* and *Ordeal by Innocence*, and the short story 'The Witness for the Prosecution'. The wrongly suspected may be still on trial as in *Sad Cypress* or already convicted as in *Mrs McGinty's Dead*. In more extreme cases – *Five Little Pigs*, *Ordeal by Innocence* – they have already paid the ultimate price, although in each case ill-health, rather than the hangman, is the cause of death. And being Agatha Christie, she also played a variation on this theme in 'The Witness for the Prosecution' when the accused suspect is shown to be the guilty party after all.

### The sealed room

The fascination with this ploy lies in the seeming impossibility of the crime. Not only has the detective – and the reader – to work out 'Who' but also 'How'. The crime may be committed in a room with all the doors and windows locked from the inside, making the murderer's escape seemingly impossible; or in a room that is under constant observation; or the corpse may be discovered in a garden of unmarked snow or on a beach of unmarked sand. Although this was not a favourite Christie ploy she experimented with it on a few occasions, but in each case – *Murder in Mesopotamia*, *Hercule Poirot's Christmas*, 'Dead Man's Mirror', 'The Dream' – the sealed-room element was merely an aspect of the story and not its main focus.

### The unexpected solution

Throughout her career this was the perennial province of Agatha Christie and the novels *Murder on the Orient Express*, *Endless Night* and *And Then There Were None*, as well as the short story 'The Witness for the Prosecution', are the more dramatic examples. But mere unexpectedness is not sufficient; it must be fairly clued and prepared. The unmasking of, for example, the under-housemaid's wheelchair-bound cousin from Australia, of whom the reader has never heard, may be unexpected but it is hardly fair. The unexpected murderer is dealt with below.

## The 'armchair detective' and pure reasoning

In 1842, Poe's story 'The Mystery of Marie Roget' was an example both of 'faction', the fictionalisation of a true event, and of 'armchair detection', an exercise in pure reasoning. Although set in Paris, the story is actually an account, complete with newspaper reports, of the murder, in New York some years earlier, of Mary Cecilia Rogers. In this story Dupin seeks to arrive at a solution based on close examination of newspaper reports of the relevant facts, without visiting the scene of the crime. The clearest equivalent in Christie is *The Thirteen Problems*, the collection in which a group of friends, including Miss Marple, meets regularly to solve a series of mysteries including murder, robbery, forgery and smuggling. Miss Marple also solves the murders in *The Mirror Crack'd from Side to Side* basing her solution on the observations of others, and visiting the scene of the crime only at the conclusion of the book. She undertakes a similar challenge in *4.50 from Paddington* when Lucy Eyelesbarrow acts as her eyes and ears. Poirot solves 'The Mystery of Hunter's Lodge', in *Poirot Investigates*, without leaving his sickbed; and in *The Clocks*, making what amounts to a cameo appearance, he bases his deductions on the reports of Colin Lamb. For the novels of Christie's most prolific and ingenious period (roughly 1930 to 1950), the application of pure reasoning applies. From the mid 1950s onwards there was a loosening of the form – *Destination Unknown, Cat among the Pigeons, The Pale Horse, Endless Night* – and she wrote fewer formal detective stories. But as late as 1964 and *A Caribbean*

*Mystery* she was still defying her readers to interpret a daring and blatant clue.

### The interpretation of a code

Poe's 'The Gold Bug', not a Dupin story, appeared in 1843, and could be considered the least important of his contributions to the detective genre. It involves the solution to a cipher in an effort to find a treasure. A variation on this can be found in the Christie short stories 'The Case of the Missing Will' and 'Strange Jest', both of which involve the interpretation of a deceased person's last cryptic wishes. Although the code concept was only a minor part of Christie's output it is the subject of the short story 'The Four Suspects' in *The Thirteen Problems*. On a more elaborate canvas, the interpretation of a code could be seen as the basis of *The ABC Murders*; and, more literally, it is the starting-point of Christie's final novel, *Postern of Fate*.

### The trail of false clues laid by the murderer

'Thou Art the Man', published in 1844, is not as well known as the other Poe stories but it includes at least two influential concepts: the trail of false clues and the unmasking of the most unlikely suspect. Although a minor theme in many Christie novels, the idea of a murderer leaving a trail of false clues is a major plot device in *The ABC Murders* and *Murder is Easy*; and in *Towards Zero* it is taken to new heights of triple-bluff ingenuity.

### The unmasking of the least likely suspect

Like its counterpart above, the unexpected solution, this was a career-long theme for Christie and appears at its most stunning in *The Murder of Roger Ackroyd*, *Hercule Poirot's Christmas*, *Crooked House* and *Curtain*. The double-bluff, a regular feature of Christie's output from her first novel onwards, also comes into this category.

*Psychological deduction*

Poe's 'The Purloined Letter' pioneered the ideas of psychological deduction and the 'obvious' solution. In this type of story, the deductions depend as much on knowledge of the human heart as on interpretation of the physical clues. In Poe's story Dupin's psychological interpretation of the suspect allows him to deduce the whereabouts of the eponymous letter. The Foreword to Christie's *Cards on the Table* explains that the deductions in that book will be entirely psychological due to the lack of physical clues apart from the bridge scorecards. And *Appointment with Death*, set in distant Petra, sees Poirot dependent almost entirely on the psychological approach. *Five Little Pigs* and *The Hollow* each have similar emotional and psychological content, although both novels also involve physical clues.

*The most obvious solution*

Poe's employment of the 'obvious solution' of hiding in plain sight (using a letter-rack as the hiding place of a letter) is adopted, though not as a solution, by Christie in 'The Nemean Lion', the first of *The Labours of Hercules*. The solutions to, for example, *The Murder at the Vicarage*, *Death on the Nile*, *Evil under the Sun* and *The Hollow*, among others, all unmask the most obvious culprits even though it seems that they have been cleared early in the story and have been dismissed by both detective and reader. In *An Autobiography*, Christie writes: 'The whole point of a *good* detective story is that it must be somebody obvious but at the same time, for some reason, you would find that it was *not* obvious, that he could not possibly have done it. Though really, of course, he *had* done it.'

So, Christie's output adhered to most of the conditions of Poe's initial model, while simultaneously expanding and experimenting with them. Although Poe created the template for later writers of detective fiction, early in the twentieth century two practitioners formalised the 'rules' for the construction of successful detective fiction. But these formalisations, by S.S. Van Dine and Ronald Knox, writing almost simultaneously on opposite sides of the Atlantic, merely acted as a challenge to Agatha Christie's ingenuity.

## S.S. Van Dine's 'Twenty Rules for Writing Detective Stories'

Willard Huntington Wright (1888–1939) was an American literary figure and art critic who, between 1929 and 1939, wrote a dozen detective novels under the pen name S.S. Van Dine. Featuring his detective creation Philo Vance, they were phenomenally successful and popular at the time but are almost completely – and deservedly, many would add – forgotten nowadays. Vance is an intensely irritating creation, with an encyclopaedic knowledge of seemingly every subject under the sun and with a correspondingly condescending manner.

In *The American Magazine* for September 1928 Wright published his 'Twenty Rules for Writing Detective Stories'. Christie knew of S.S. Van Dine; some of his novels can still be seen on the shelves of Greenway House and she mentioned him in Notebook 41, although it is doubtful if she was aware of his Rules until long after they were written. Van Dine's Rules are as follows:

1. The reader must have equal opportunity with the detective for solving the mystery.
2. No willful tricks or deceptions may be placed on the reader other than those played by the criminal on the detective.
3. There must be no love interest.
4. The detective himself, or one of the official investigators, should never turn out to be the culprit.

5. The culprit must be determined by logical deduction – not by accident, coincidence or unmotivated confession.
6. The detective novel must have a detective in it.
7. There simply must be a corpse in a detective novel.
8. The problem of the crime must be solved by strictly naturalistic means.
9. There must be but one detective.
10. The culprit must turn out to be a person who has played a more or less prominent part in the story.
11. A servant must not be chosen as the culprit.
12. There must be but one culprit no matter how many murders are committed.
13. Secret societies have no place in a detective story.
14. The method of murder, and the means of detecting it, must be rational and scientific.
15. The truth of the problem must be at all times apparent provided the reader is shrewd enough to see it.
16. A detective novel should contain no long descriptive passages, no literary dallying with side issues, no subtly worked-out character analyses, and no 'atmospheric' preoccupations.
17. A professional criminal must never be shouldered with the guilt in a detective novel.
18. A crime in a detective story must never turn out to be an accident or a suicide.
19. The motives for all the crimes in detective stories should be personal.
20. A list of devices, which no self-respecting detective story writer should avail himself of including, among others:

    ✳ The bogus séance to force a confession
    ✳ The unmasking of a twin or look-alike
    ✳ The cipher/code-letter
    ✳ The hypodermic syringe and the knockout drops
    ✳ The comparison of cigarette butts.

### Ronald Knox's Detective Story Decalogue

Monsignor Ronald Knox (1888–1957) was a priest and classical scholar who wrote six detective novels between 1925 and 1937. He created the insurance investigator detective Miles Bredon, and considered the detective story such a serious game between writer and reader that in some of his novels he provided page references to his clues. When he edited a collection of short stories, *The Best Detective Stories of 1928*, his Introduction included a 'Detective Story Decalogue'. These distilled the essence of a detective story, as distinct from the thriller, into ten cogent sentences:

1. The criminal must be someone mentioned in the early part of the story, but must not be anyone whose thoughts the reader has been allowed to follow.
2. All supernatural agencies are ruled out as a matter of course.
3. Not more than one secret room or passage is allowable.
4. No hitherto undiscovered poisons may be used, nor any appliance which will need long scientific explanation at the end.
5. No Chinamen must figure in the story.
6. No accident must ever help the detective, nor must he ever have an unaccountable intuition that proves to be right.
7. The detective must not himself commit the crime.
8. The detective must not light on any clues that are not instantly disclosed to the reader.
9. The stupid friend of the detective, the Watson, must not conceal any thoughts that pass through his mind; his intelligence must be slightly, but very slightly, below that of the average reader.
10. Twin brothers, and doubles generally, must not appear unless we have been duly prepared for them.

But as will be seen from a survey of Christie's output, many of the Rules laid down by both Knox and Van Dine were ingeniously ignored and often gleefully broken by the Queen of Crime. Her infringement was, in most cases, instinctive rather than premeditated; and her skill was such that she managed to do so while still remaining faithful to the basic tenets of detective fiction.

### Agatha Christie's Rule of Three

In order to examine these Rules, and Christie's approach to them, I have grouped together Rules common to both lists and have divided them into categories:

* Fairness
* The crime
* The detective
* The murderer
* The murder method
* To be avoided

### Fairness

Both lists are very concerned with Fairness to the reader in the provision of information necessary to the solution, and with good reason; this is the essence of detective fiction and the element that distinguishes it from other branches of crime writing. Van Dine 1 and Knox 8 are, essentially, the same rule while Van Dine 2, 5, 15 and Knox 9 elaborate this concept.

**Van Dine 1. The reader must have equal opportunity with the detective for solving the mystery.**

**Knox 8. The detective must not light on any clues that are not instantly disclosed to the reader.**

Christie did not break these essentially identical rules, mainly because she did not need to. She was quite happy to provide the clue, confident in the knowledge that, in the words of her great contemporary R. Austin Freeman, 'the reader would mislead himself'. After all, how many readers will properly interpret the clue of the torn letter in *Lord Edgware Dies*, or the bottle of nail polish in *Death on the Nile*, or the 'shepherd, not the shepherdess' in *A Murder is Announced*? Or who will correctly appreciate the significance of the smashed bottle in *Evil under the Sun*, or the initialled handkerchief in *Murder on the Orient Express*, or the smell of turpentine in *After the Funeral*?

**Knox 9. The stupid friend of the detective, the Watson, must not conceal any thoughts that pass through his mind; his intelligence must be slightly, but very slightly, below that of the average reader.**

It can be argued that the intelligence of the Watson character *has* to be below average because it is necessary for the Great Detective to explain his deductions to the reader *through* the Watson character. If the Watson were as clever as the detective there would be no need for an explanation at all. If Poirot were to look at the scene of the crime and announce, 'We must look for a left-handed female from Scotland with red hair and a limp,' and Hastings were to reply, 'Yes, I see what you mean,' the reader would feel, justifiably, more than a little exasperated. And, of course, this Rule overlaps with Knox 1 (see below) in the case of *The Murder of Roger Ackroyd* because Dr Sheppard in that famous case was acting as Poirot's Watson.

**Van Dine 2. No willful tricks or deceptions may be placed on the reader other than those played by the criminal on the detective.**

This Rule seems to negate the whole purpose of a good detective novel where, surely, the challenge is the struggle between reader and writer. In essence, the writer says: 'I present you with a challenge to spot the culprit before I am ready to reveal him/her. To make it easier for you, I will give you hints and clues along the way but I still defy you to anticipate my solution. However, I give you fair warning that I will use every trick in my writer's repertoire to fool you but I still promise to abide by the fair play rule.' As Dorothy L. Sayers said in the aftermath of the Roger Ackroyd controversy, 'It is the reader's business to suspect *everybody*.'

Into this category come Christie's greatest conjuring tricks, including *The Murder of Roger Ackroyd* and *Endless Night*. In both these novels the reader is fooled into accepting the bona fides of a character who is taken for granted but not 'seen' in the same way as other protagonists are. The narrator is a 'given' whose presence and veracity the reader accepts unquestioningly; and, indeed, the narrator's veracity in each case is above reproach. They do not actually *lie* at any stage, although there are certainly some ambiguous statements and judicious omissions whose significance is obvious only on a re-reading. In Chapter 27 of *The Murder of Roger Ackroyd* Dr Sheppard himself states:

> I am rather pleased with myself as a writer. What could be neater, for instance, than the following? *'The letters were brought in at twenty minutes to nine. It was just on ten minutes to nine when I left him, the letter still unread. I hesitated with my hand on the door-handle, looking back and wondering if there was anything I had left undone.'* All true, you see. But suppose I had put a row of stars after that first sentence! Would somebody then have wondered what exactly happened in that blank ten minutes?

All true; but not one reader in a thousand will stop to examine the details, especially not in the more innocent era of the 1920s, when the local doctor had a status just below that of the Creator.

Michael Rogers, in *Endless Night*, is also scrupulously fair in his account of his life. He tells us the truth but, as with Dr Sheppard, not the whole truth. But if we re-read Chapter 6, which recounts a telling conversation with his mother about 'his plan', what a new significance it all takes on when we know the truth. The 'plan', and even 'the girl', are no longer what we had originally supposed. This novel has much in common with *The Mysterious Affair at Styles* and *Death on the Nile*, as well as with *The Man in the Brown Suit* and *The Murder of Roger Ackroyd*. In the first two titles, two lovers collude, as in *Endless Night*, in the murder of an inconvenient wife, stage a dramatic quarrel and have seemingly foolproof alibis; *The Mysterious Affair at Styles* also features a poisoning which happens in the absence of the conspirators. In the latter two titles, the narrator (a diarist in *The Man in the Brown Suit*) is exposed as the villain.

**Van Dine 5. The culprit must be determined by logical deduction – not by accident, coincidence or unmotivated confession.**

An example of confession (albeit not unmotivated) as a solution in Christie's output is *And Then There Were None*, where the entire explanation is presented in the form of a letter of confession. In this most ingenious novel, Agatha Christie set herself an almost insoluble problem: how to kill off every character in the book and yet have an explanation at the end. The only solution would seem to be the one that she actually adopted: a confession. Confessions do feature in other novels – *Lord Edgware Dies*, *Why Didn't They Ask Evans?*, *Crooked House* – but only as confirmation of what has already been revealed, while *Curtain: Poirot's Last Case* contains one of the most shocking confessions in literary history.

**Van Dine 15. The truth of the problem must be at all times apparent – provided the reader is shrewd enough to see it.**

Although tautological, this is intended as an elaboration of the earlier Rules regarding fairness to the reader. One of the clearest examples of this in the Christie output is *Lord Edgware Dies* where a very audacious plot is, in retrospect, glaringly obvious. Other blindingly evident clues include the final words – '*Evil Eye . . . Eye . . . Eye . . .*' – of Chapter 23 of *A Caribbean Mystery*; or the description of Lewis Serrocold emerging from the study in Chapter 7 of *They Do It with Mirrors*; or the thoughts of Ruth Lessing in Chapter 2 of *Sparkling Cyanide* after her meeting with Victor; or, most controversially of all, Dr Sheppard's leave-taking of Roger Ackroyd in Chapter 4 of *The Murder of Roger Ackroyd*.

**Knox 6. No accident must ever help the detective, nor must he ever have an unaccountable intuition that proves to be right.**

There are, unfortunately, a few examples in Christie's oeuvre of 'deductions' not based on any tangible evidence. It must be conceded that they can only be accounted for only by intuition. How, for example, does Miss Marple alight on Dr Quimper in *4.50 from Paddington*? And only the 'Divine Revelation' forbidden by the Detection Club Oath can explain how Poirot knows that Lady Westholme from *Appointment with Death* spent time in prison in her early life.

### The crime

The crime itself did not feature strongly in the Rules, although Christie enjoyed the challenge of Van Dine 18 below.

**Van Dine 7. There simply must be a corpse in a detective novel.**

Although the first detective novel, Wilkie Collins' *The Moonstone* (1868), concerns a robbery rather than a murder, a mysterious death is the *sine qua non* of most detective novels. Although she broke this Rule often in her short story output, Christie almost never short-changed her readers in novel form, generously providing a multitude of corpses in *And Then There Were None, Death Comes as the End* and *Endless Night* – but there is no corpse discovered in *Five Little Pigs*.

**Van Dine 18. A crime in a detective story must never turn out to be an accident or a suicide.**

The rejection of this Rule could mean a huge disappointment for a reader who discovers, after 250 pages, that the death under investigation is not a crime at all. See how cleverly Agatha Christie overcomes this in *Taken at the Flood*, when none of the deaths is what it first seems. The seeming murder of 'Enoch Arden' is an accident, the death of Major Porter is suicide and the seeming suicide of Rosaleen Cloade is murder. In one brilliant plot she effortlessly breaks both aspects of Van Dine's Rule. In the Poirot cases 'The Market Basing Mystery' and 'Murder in the Mews' – both essentially the same story, the latter being a more elaborate version, of the former – we have not murder disguised to look like suicide but suicide disguised to look like murder. But there is another twist; the real murder plan is to get someone else hanged (and therefore murdered) for a crime they did not commit.

**Van Dine 19. The motives for all the crimes in detective stories should be personal.**

This Rule essentially outlawed murder committed for ideological reasons, with Van Dine suggesting that such murders should be confined to secret-service stories. Appropriately, this type of plot does feature in some of Christie's international thriller novels – *They Came to Baghdad, Destination Unknown, Passenger to Frankfurt* – as well as some of the early titles – *The Secret Adversary, The Secret of Chimneys* – but it is not a feature of her detective fiction. But into which category does the motive for the first murder in *Three Act Tragedy* fall?

### The detective

The figure of the detective occupied both writers: Van Dine 4 and Knox 7 are identical, although Van Dine added further embellishments in Rules 6 and 9. Some of Christie's greatest triumphs involve these Rules; she has joyously shattered all of them.

**Van Dine 4. The detective himself, or one of the official investigators, should never turn out to be the criminal.**

**Knox 7. The detective must not himself commit the crime.**

From the very beginning of the detective novel the unmasking of the official investigator was considered a valid ploy. *The Mystery of the Yellow Room* (1907) by Gaston Leroux, creator of *The Phantom of the Opera*, is credited in *An Autobiography* as being one of the two detective novels that Christie had enjoyed before embarking on *The Mysterious Affair at Styles*. It features one of the earliest examples of the criminal investigator, and in *The Clocks*, Poirot is unstinting in his praise for this groundbreaking novel. Some of Christie's most deftly plotted books featured this ploy. *Hercule Poirot's Christmas* was chosen by Robert Barnard, in his *Agatha Christie: A Talent to Deceive* (1980), as one of the three best novels of Dame Agatha's career, and indeed it is a classic Golden Age detective story: a snowbound country mansion, a murder, a group of suspects, a killer and a solution, breathtaking in its daring. An early foreshadowing of this ploy can also be found in 'The Man in the Mist' in *Partners in Crime*.

*The Mousetrap*, in both its stage and novella versions, and its earlier incarnation as the radio play *Three Blind Mice*, all unmask the investigator as the villain. Sergeant Trotter arrives like a *deus ex machina* in Monkswell Manor and is accepted unquestioningly both by its snowbound inhabitants and by the audience, although he is an imposter and not an actual policeman. In the late 1940s and early 1950s the policeman, like the village doctor, was perceived as un-corrupted and incorruptible, although modern audiences are more likely to spot this type of villain than their more innocent counterparts of an earlier age.

In *Curtain: Poirot's Last Case*, Agatha Christie played the last and greatest trick of all on her readers; and they admired her all the more for it. The ultimate sleight of hand from the supreme prestidigitator in the crime-writing pantheon, who but Agatha Christie would have thought of, and then carried out, this almost sacrilegious trick? After a half century of partnership, she unmasks Poirot as the killer. Certainly the book is contrived (which detective story is not?), but only the most churlish of readers would complain after such a dazzling culmination of two careers.

**Van Dine 6. The detective novel must have a detective in it.**

This is a perfectly reasonable Rule. But Agatha Christie made a career out of breaking the Rules, reasonable or otherwise, and she managed to demolish this one also. The most famous and best-selling crime novel of all time, *And Then There Were None*, has no detective, although, arguably, every character in the book is Victim, Murderer and Detective . . .; *Death Comes as the End* is also an example of a detectiveless detective novel. Its setting of Ancient Egypt 4,000 years ago does, however pre-date the Rules by some time.

**Van Dine 9. There must be but one detective.**

In the sense that Hercule Poirot and Miss Marple never meet between the covers of any of her books Agatha Christie abided by this Rule, but in many novels they work in close collaboration with the official investigators. And other titles feature an unofficial coming-together of, effectively, suspects in order to solve the crime. *Three Act Tragedy, Death in the Clouds* and *The ABC Murders* find Poirot working alongside some of those under suspicion in order to arrive at the truth. And in all three cases one of his group of collaborators is unmasked in the last chapter. Coincidentally or otherwise, these novels were all published in the same 12-month period between January 1935 and January 1936.

### *The murderer*

The other important figure, the murderer, also exercised both rule-makers. But Christie had broken most of these Rules before either Knox or Van Dine even compiled them.

**Knox 1. The criminal must be someone mentioned in the early part of the story, but must not be anyone whose thoughts the reader has been allowed to follow.**

While adhering to the former part of this injunction, the circumvention of the latter became almost a motif through-out Agatha Christie's writing life. As early as 1924 with *The Man in the Brown Suit* she neatly and unobtrusively breaks this rule, via Sir Eustace Pedler's diary. The most famous, or infamous, example is, of course, *The Murder of Roger Ackroyd*, her first for the publisher Collins. The book immediately ensured her fame and success and it is safe to assert that, even if she had never written another word, her name would still be remembered today in recognition of this stunning conjuring trick. Forty years later she replayed it but in such a different guise that most of her readers were not aware of the repetition. While a doctor in a small 1920s village narrates *The Murder of Roger Ackroyd*, a young, working-class, charming ne'er-do-well narrates *Endless Night*. But it is essentially the same sleight of hand at work. (See also 'Fairness' above.)

More subtly, we share the thoughts of a group of characters, which includes the killer, in *And Then There Were None*, but without identifying which thoughts belong to which character (Chapter 11). And in *The ABC Murders* we think we are sharing the thoughts of a serial killer when, in fact, he is the innocent dupe of the real killer. Less overtly, we are given an insight into the minds of the killer in *Five Little Pigs*, *Towards Zero* and *Sparkling Cyanide*.

**Van Dine 10. The culprit must turn out to be a person who has played a more or less prominent part in the story.**

Never one to cheat her readers, this is one of the Rules that Christie did not break. She never unmasked the second cousin of the under-housemaid as the killer in the last chapter. Taking her cue from 'The Purloined Letter', the Queen of Crime hid her murderers in plain sight.

**Van Dine 11. A servant must not be chosen as the culprit.**

This is not mere social prejudice (although there is plenty of that in the work of Van Dine himself) but a practical solution to the problem of the unmasking, in the last chapter, of a member of the domestic staff whose presence in the novel was fleeting at best. Consider how Christie overcame this stricture. Kirsten Lindstrom in *Ordeal by Innocence* is, strictly speaking, a domestic servant but her significance to the Argyle family can be interpreted as placing her outside this category. But it is as a servant that we meet, and continue to perceive, her. This same consideration applies to Miss Gilchrist in *After the Funeral*; witness the telling scene at the denouement when she bitterly recriminates the Abernethie family. Gladys, in *A Pocket Full of Rye*, is a clearer example of domestic servitude; indeed, it is her status as such that makes her a vital element of Lance's murderous plan. In defence of Christie's oft-criticised attitude to domestic servants, it is the subsequent death of Gladys that causes Miss Marple to arrive at Yewtree Lodge to avenge the death of a foolish and gullible former maid. And the closing pages of the book, as Miss Marple reads a letter from Gladys written just before her murder, are very affecting. The same plot device, and much of the same plot, can be seen in the earlier short story 'The Tuesday Night Club' in *The Thirteen Problems*.

**Van Dine 17. A professional criminal must never be shouldered with the guilt in a detective novel.**

Apart from brief – and not totally convincing – forays into organised crime in *The Big Four*, *The Secret of Chimneys* and *At Bertram's Hotel*, no use is made of a professional criminal in Christie's solutions.

**Van Dine 12. There must be but one culprit no matter how many murders are committed.**

Murderous alliances are a feature of Christie's fiction beginning with *The Mysterious Affair at Styles* and continuing with *The Murder at the Vicarage*, *Death on the Nile*, *One, Two, Buckle my Shoe*, *Evil under the Sun*, *The Body in the Library*, *Sparkling Cyanide* and *Endless Night*. *Cat among the Pigeons* and, to a lesser degree, *Taken at the Flood*, feature more than one killer working independently of each other; *The Hollow* features an unusual and morally questionable, collusion; and, of course, *Murder on the Orient Express* features the ultimate conspiracy.

## The murder method

Christie never resorted to elaborate mechanical or scientific means to explain her ingenuity, and much of her popularity and accessibility lies in her adherence to this simplicity. Many of her last-chapter surprises can be explained in a few sentences. Once you have grasped the essential fact that the corpse identified as A is, in fact, Corpse B and vice versa everything else falls into place; when you realise that all twelve suspects conspired to murder one victim all confusion disappears; when it dawns that the name Evelyn can mean a male or a female little further explanation is necessary.

**Van Dine 14. The method of murder, and the means of detecting it, must be rational and scientific.**

**Knox 4. No hitherto undiscovered poisons may be used, nor any appliance which will need long scientific explanation at the end.**

While Christie uses poisons as a means of killing characters more than most of her contemporaries, she uses only those that are scientifically known. But, that said, thanks to her training as a dispenser, she had more knowledge of the subject than many of her fellow writers and was familiar with unusual poisons and the more unusual properties of the common ones. Her first novel, *The Mysterious Affair at Styles*, depends for its surprise solution on knowledge of the properties of strychnine, but this is not unreasonable as the reader is fully aware of the poison used. In fact, there is a graphic description of the death of Mrs Inglethorpe and a discussion of the effects of, and the chemical formula for, strychnine. Taxine in *A Pocket Full of Rye*, ricin in 'The House of Lurking Death' from *Partners in Crime*, thallium in *The Pale Horse* and physostigmine in *Crooked House* are just some of the unusual poisons featuring in Christie. Fictitious drugs such as

Serenite in *A Caribbean Mystery*, Calmo in *The Mirror Crack'd from Side to Side* and Benvo in *Passenger to Frankfurt* also feature, but as the plot does not turn on their usage, they merely bend, rather than break, Knox's Rule.

## To be avoided

Some of these items are mere personal prejudice; there is no good reason why cigarettes or twins, for instance, cannot be a clue, or even a main plot device, provided that the reader has been properly prepared for them. With all of these the important point is the originality of the approach in utilising them – and this Christie had in full measure and overflowing.

**Van Dine 13. Secret societies have no place in a detective story.**

Many readers, including probably the author herself, would wish that *The Big Four* had never found its way between hard covers. Cobbled together at the lowest point in her life (after the death of her mother, the request for a divorce from her husband and her subsequent disappearance) with the help of her brother-in-law, Campbell Christie, this collection of linked short stories was re-edited into a novel. The 'secret society' bent on world domination that it features was, mercifully, a one-off aberration on Christie's part. *The Seven Dials Mystery* features an equally preposterous secret society, albeit one with a Christie twist. *The Pale Horse*, one of the best books of the 1960s, features a mysterious organisation, Murder Inc., that seems to specialise in remote killing, but a rational and horribly plausible scheme is revealed in the closing chapters.

**Knox 5. No Chinamen must figure in the story.**

This comment is not as racist as it may first appear. At the time of its writing Orientals in fiction were perceived, under the general heading of 'The Yellow Peril', as the personification of everything undesirable. A more detailed discussion of the subject can be found in Colin Watson's *Snobbery with Violence* (1971), an investigation of the social attitudes reflected in British crime fiction of the twentieth century, but suffice it to say that the white-slave trade, torture and other 'unspeakable acts' were the accepted fictional norms at the time for any character of Oriental extraction. This Rule was included to raise the literary horizon above that of the average opium den. Unfortunately, Christie succumbs to stereotype in *The Big Four* where, amid cringe-inducing scenes with Oriental characters and 'speech', the chief villain, 'the greatest criminal brain of all time', is Chinese. But these stories pre-dated Knox. Apart from *The Big Four*, and the more politically correct Poirot case 'The Lost Mine', no 'Chinamen' play a part in any of Christie's detective novels.

**Knox 3. Not more than one secret room or passage is allowable.**

This Rule is taken to mean that no solution may *turn* on the existence of a secret passage. It was designed to eliminate the possibility of an exasperated reader hurling his detective novel across the room as the detective explains how the killer gained access to his closely guarded victim through such a passage, the existence of which was unknown up to that point. Christie is not above introducing the odd secret passage almost as a challenge to the cliché, but their very introduction long before the solution is in keeping with the tenet of this Rule. *The Secret of Chimneys*, *Three Act Tragedy* and 'The Adventure of Johnnie Waverly' all feature, but openly and not covertly, a secret room or passage. The play *Spider's Web* features a sliding panel with a concealed cavity; and its use pokes gentle fun at this convention.

**Knox 10. Twin brothers, and doubles generally, must not appear unless we have been duly prepared for them.**

This Rule was formalised in an effort to avoid the disclosure that Suspect A, who had a cast-iron alibi for the night of the crime, was the guilty party because said alibi was provided by a hitherto unheard-of twin brother. Tongue firmly planted in literary cheek, Christie cocks a snook at this convention in 'The Unbreakable Alibi' in *Partners in Crime*. This is her take on the alibi-breaking stories of her contemporary Freeman Wills Crofts. And look at the ingenious double-bluff of *Lord Edgware Dies*. *The Big Four* also has an episode featuring a twin – one Achille Poirot . . .

**Van Dine 20. A list of devices, which no self-respecting detective story writer should avail himself of . . .**

*The bogus séance to force a confession*
At the end of *Peril at End House* Poirot arranges something very like a séance in End House, but it is really a variation on his usual 'all-the-suspects-in-the-drawing-room' ploy – although he does manage to elicit a confession. At the other end of a story is the séance in *The Sittaford Mystery*, where such an event is cleverly stage-managed in order to set a plot in motion.

*The unmasking of a twin or look-alike*
In *Partners in Crime*, Tommy and Tuppence tweak this Rule in 'The Unbreakable Alibi'.

*The cipher/code-letter*
'The Four Suspects', in *The Thirteen Problems*, features a very clever version of the code-letter and in the last book she wrote, *Postern of Fate*, Tommy and Tuppence find a hidden message that launches their final case.

*The comparison of cigarette butts*
'Murder in the Mews' features not just this idea but also the clue of the cigarette smoke, or, more accurately, the absence of cigarette smoke.

**Knox 2. All supernatural agencies are ruled out as a matter of course.**

**Van Dine 8. The problem of the crime must be solved by strictly naturalistic means.**

These two Rules are, in effect, the same and are more strictly adhered to, but Christie experiments on various occasions, especially in her short story output. The virtually unknown radio play *Personal Call* has a supernatural twist at the last minute just when the listener thinks that everything has been satisfactorily, and rationally, explained. *Dumb Witness* features the Tripp sisters, quasi-spiritualists, but apart from her collection *The Hound of Death*, which has a supernatural rather than a detective theme, most of Chritie's stories are firmly rooted in the natural, albeit sometimes evil, real world. *The Pale Horse* makes much of black magic and murder-by-suggestion but, like 'The Voice in the Dark' from *The Mysterious Mr Quin* and its seeming ghostly presence, all is explained away in rational terms.

**Van Dine 3. There must be no love interest.**

Although Van Dine managed this in his own books (thereby reducing them to semi-animated Cluedo), this Rule has been ignored by most successful practitioners. It is in the highest degree unlikely that, in the course of a 250-page novel, the 'love interest' can be completely excised while retaining some semblance of verisimilitude. Admittedly, Van Dine may have been thinking of some of the excesses of the Romantic suspense school, when matters of the heart take precedence over matters of the intellect; or when the reader can safely spot the culprit by pairing off the suspects until only one remains. Christie, as usual, turned this rule to her advantage. In some novels we confidently expect certain characters to walk up the aisle, instead of which one or more walk to the scaffold. In *Death in the Clouds,* Jane Grey gets as big a shock as the reader when the charming Norman Gale is unmasked as a cold-blooded murderer, in *Taken at the Flood,* Lynn is left pining after the ruthless David Hunter, and in *They Came to Baghdad,* Victoria is left to seek a replacement for the shy Edward. In some Christie novels the 'love interest' or, more accurately, the emotional element and personal interplay between the characters, is not just present but of a much higher standard than usual. In *Five Little Pigs, The Hollow* and *Nemesis* it is the emotional entanglements that set the plot in motion and provide the motivation; in each case it is thwarted love that motivates the killer.

**Van Dine 16. A detective novel should contain no long descriptive passages, no literary dallying with side-issues, no subtly worked-out character analyses, and no 'atmospheric' preoccupations.**

This Rule merely mirrors the time in which it was written: and it would be no bad thing to reintroduce it to some present-day practitioners. That said, character analysis and atmosphere can play an important part in a solution. In *The Moving Finger,* it is only when Miss Marple looks beyond the 'atmosphere' of fear in Lymstock that the solutions to both the poison-pen letters and the identity of the murderer become clear. In *Cards on the Table* the only physical clues are the bridge scorecards and Poirot has to depend largely on the character of the bridge-players, as shown by these scorecards, to arrive at the truth. In *Five Little Pigs,* an investigation into the murder committed sixteen years earlier has to rely almost solely on the evidence and accounts of the suspects, a procedure largely dependent on character analysis. In *The Hollow*, it is from his study of the characters staying for the weekend at The Hollow that Poirot uncovers the truth of the crime.

## RULE OF THREE: SUMMARY

The Knox Decalogue is by far the more reasonable of the two sets of Rules. Written somewhat tongue-in-cheek – 'Not more than one secret room or passage is allowable' – it is less repetitive and restrictive and shows less personal prejudice than does its American counterpart. A strict adherence to Van Dine's Rules would have resulted in an arid, uninspired and ultimately predictable genre. It would have meant forgoing (much of) the daring brilliance of Christie, the inventive logic of Ellery Queen, the audacious ingenuity of John Dickson Carr or the formidable intelligence of Dorothy L. Sayers. In later years it would have precluded the witty cunning of Edmund Crispin, the erudite originality of Michael Innes or the boundary-pushing output of Julian Symons. Van Dine's list is repetitive and, in many instances, a reflection of his personal bias: no long descriptive passages, no literary dallying with side-issues, no subtly worked-out character analyses, no 'atmospheric' preoccupations. It is somewhat ironic that while the compilers of both lists are largely forgotten nowadays, the writer who managed to break most of their carefully considered Rules remains the best-selling and most popular writer in history.

And so, from *The Mysterious Affair at Styles* in 1920 until *Sleeping Murder* in 1976, Agatha – Rule-Keeper and Rule-Breaker – produced at least one book a year and for nearly twenty of those years she produced two titles. The slogan 'A Christie for Christmas' was a fixture in Collins's publishing list and in

1935 it became clear that the name of Agatha Christie was to be a perennial best seller. That year, *Three Act Tragedy* sold 10,000 hardback copies and this figure trebled over the next decade. By the time of her fiftieth title, *A Murder is Announced*, she matched it with sales of 50,000; and never looked back. And all of this without the media circus that is now part and parcel of the book trade – no radio or TV interviews, no signing sessions, no question-and-answer panels and virtually no public appearances.

Although mutually advantageous, the relationship between Christie and her publisher was by no means free of controversy. The proposed jacket design for *The Labours of Hercules* horrified her ('Poirot going naked to the bath'), she considered that an announcement in 'Crime Club News' about 1939's *Ten Little Niggers* – its title later amended to the more acceptable *And Then There Were None* – revealed too much of the plot and in September 1967 she sent Sir William ('Billy') Collins a blistering letter for having received her so-called 'advance copies' of *Endless Night* only *after* she saw them herself on sale at the airport. And as late as 1968 she wrote her own blurb for *By the Pricking of my Thumbs*.

Thanks to her phenomenal sales and prodigious output, she became a personal friend of Sir William and his wife, Pierre, and conducted much of her correspondence through the years directly with him. They were regular visitors to Greenway, her Devon retreat, and Sir William was one of those who spoke at her memorial service in May 1976. A measure of the respect in which he held her can be gauged from his closing remarks, when he said that 'the world is better because she lived in it'.

# Crime Writers in the Notebooks

'Do you like detective stories? I do. I read them all and I've got autographs from Dorothy Sayers and Agatha Christie and Dickson Carr and H. C. Bailey.'

*The Body in the Library*, Chapter 6

Dotted through Christie's Notebooks are references to other crime novels and their writers. Many of these are fellow-writers, and their work known to her through her membership of the Detection Club. Proof that she was widely-read in her chosen *genre* is evident from passing references to the work of other writers not personally known to her. And, finally and intriguingly, there are references to her own work.

## The Detection Club in the Notebooks

The Detection Club, as its name suggests, is a club for writers of detective stories. Although the exact date is uncertain, it was probably founded in 1929. Anthony Berkeley and Dorothy L. Sayers were two of the founders and by the early 1930s all of the major writers of detective fiction of the day, including Agatha Christie, were members. Only writers of detective fiction, as distinct from crime writers in general, were eligible to join. It was not a professional body campaigning to improve the lot of crime writers; rather it was a glorified dining club with G.K. Chesterton, creator of Father Brown, as its first President, followed in 1936 by E.C. Bentley, author of the famous *Trent's Last Case*, and, from 1958 to her death in 1976, Agatha Christie. She agreed to this role on the understanding that she would never have to make a speech. Membership was by invitation only and all new members had to undergo an initiation ceremony, involving the President in ceremonial robes, a procession with candles and the initiate swearing an oath, while placing a hand on Eric the Skull, to uphold the club's rules.

Although these rules were unwritten and the ritual itself, designed by Sayers, light-hearted, the intentions behind them were serious and admirable. In an effort to raise the literary level of the detective story and to distinguish it from the thriller or 'shocker', candidates had to promise:

* to honour the King's English;
* never to conceal a vital clue from the reader;
* to adhere to detection as distinct from 'Divine Revelation, Feminine Intuition . . . Coincidence or Acts of God';
* to observe 'a seemly moderation in the use of Gangs, Death-Rays, Ghosts, Mysterious Chinamen and Mysterious Poisons unknown to Science';
* never to steal or disclose the plots of other members.

In the early days the Detection Club produced collaborative novels and, in more recent times, short story collections. In the early ventures different hands wrote succeeding chapters, each writer taking cognisance of the plot developments of his or her predecessor. Agatha Christie contributed to the three earliest publications, *Behind the Screen* in 1930, *The Scoop* the following year and the full-length novel *The Floating Admiral* in 1931. The first two shorter efforts were read in instalments on BBC radio and subsequently published in *The Listener*, finally appearing in book form in 1983.

In the case of *The Floating Admiral* each contributor, in an effort to prevent complications being introduced merely to make life difficult for the following contributor, had to include a proposed solution as well as a chapter. Christie's contribution is the shortest in the book, but her proposed solution is a typically ingenious one. However, she decided that the time and effort that went into such collaborations could be more profitably spent on her own writing and she politely declined to involve herself in further such ventures.

The main reference to the Detection Club in the Notebooks is in Notebook 41, the first page of which is headed 'Ideas 1931' (despite the uncertainty about its date of foundation, by the time of this note the club was well established):

The 13 at Dinner Detective story Club (?)

Miss Sayers and her husband – Poisons Mr Van Dine and Mr Wills Crofts and wife – Alibis Mrs Christie
Mr Rhode
Mr and Mrs Cole Mr Bentley
Miss Clemence Dane
Mr Berkeley and wife – fantastic writer

Although it is unlikely that this is what she had in mind when she wrote the note, the title *Thirteen at Dinner* was used in America two years later for *Lord Edgware Dies*. The US title refers to Chapter 15 of the book, where a character remarks that there were thirteen guests at the dinner table on the evening of Lord Edgware's death, thereby giving Lady Edgware an alibi with a dozen witnesses.

Of the 13 people she lists most were her Detection Club fellow-writers:

∗ 'Miss Sayers' is Christie's great contemporary Dorothy L. Sayers – writer, dramatist, anthologist, theologian and scholar. Although listed in Notebook 41 as 'Miss', Sayers had married Oswald Fleming in April 1926 but retained her maiden name for her professional activities.

* 'Mr Van Dine' was known to the reading public as S.S. Van Dine, creator of Philo Vance. The gap after his name would seem to indicate that Christie was not sure if he was married (he was), but his inclusion is odd. She certainly read his best-selling novels – some are on the shelves in Greenway House – but, as he lived in America, he was not a member of the Detection Club.

* 'Mr Wills Crofts' was Freeman Wills Crofts, creator of Inspector French of Scotland Yard, a painstaking and thorough policeman whose speciality (as indicated) is the unbreakable alibi. Like Christie his first novel, *The Cask*, appeared in 1920 and is still considered a classic. He continued to write until his death in 1955, producing over 40 novels.

* 'Mr Rhode' is John Rhode, whose real name was Major Cecil John Charles Street and who also wrote as Miles Burton. Like Christie he was a Crime Club author for much of his career and altogether he wrote almost 150 novels under both names.

* 'Mr and Mrs Cole' was the husband-and-wife team of G.D.H. and Margaret Cole, detective novelists and Socialists. Although the pair were prolific, with thirty novels to their credit, their books are verbose, lifeless and long out of print.

* 'Mr Bentley' was E.C. Bentley, whose reputation as a detective novelist rests almost entirely on one novel, *Trent's Last Case* (1913). He also issued a book of short stories and co-wrote another title, *Trent's Own Case*, both featuring Philip Trent.

* Clemence Dane is largely forgotten as a crime writer. *Enter Sir John*, filmed by Hitchcock as *Murder*, is her best known title.

* 'Mr Berkeley' is Anthony Berkeley, who also wrote as Francis Iles. A very influential writer, he foresaw the emergence of the crime novel, as distinct from the detective novel, and his contribution to both branches of

the genre is impressive. Alfred Hitchcock memorably filmed his Iles novel *Before the Fact* as *Suspicion*.

In addition to this list, Christie makes various allusions to her fellow Detection Club members in a range of works. *Partners in Crime*, Christie's 1929 Tommy and Tuppence collection of short stories, sees the Beresfords investigating their cases in the style of various detectives. She pastiches Berkeley in 'The Clergyman's Daughter' and Crofts in 'The Unbreakable Alibi' although, oddly, none of the other writers mentioned in Notebook 41 is featured.

An article Christie wrote for the Ministry of Information in 1945, 'Detective Writers in England', is also of note. Here the writers featured are John Dickson Carr, H.C. Bailey, Ngaio Marsh, Austin Freeman and Margery Allingham and Sayers, the only writer common to the article and Notebook 41, although all were members of The Detection Club. This may be due to the fact that Christie had more dealings with Sayers, mostly during the planning of the collaborative titles above, all of which were masterminded by Sayers. Chapter 6 of *The Body in the Library* also mentions Sayers, Bailey and Dickson Carr (as well as Christie herself); and 'The Flock of Geryon', the tenth *Labour of Hercules,* mentions Sherlock Holmes, Mr Fortune, the creation of Bailey, and Sir Henry Merrivale, the creation of Dickson Carr. Carr's *The Burning Court* is also a minor clue in *Evil under the Sun* and the same writer gets a further mention in *The Clocks*.

A single sentence each in Notebooks 18 and 35 also mentions the Detection Club, both with the same idea:

Guest night at the Det[ection] Club during ritual – Mrs. O[liver]'s 6 guests

Detection Club Murder – Mrs Oliver – her two guests – someone killed when the Ritual starts

Guest Night was, not surprisingly, an evening when members of the club could invite a guest for dinner. The 'ritual' was the initiation ceremony, involving the swearing of an 'oath' with Eric the Skull standing in for the Bible. As a detective novelist Mrs Oliver would, of course, have been a member of the club.

## Other Crime Writers in the Notebooks

Apart from the '13 at Dinner' list in Notebook 41, Agatha Christie makes other references to her fellow crime writers. The following is a selection of those mentioned:

✳   E.C. Bentley

Apart from his appearance in connection with the Detection Club, he is also referred to in Notebook 41. The following concerns a contribution to Bentley's anthology *A Second Century of Detective Stories*, published in 1938, where 'The Case of the Distressed Lady' from *Parker Pyne Investigates* represents Christie

A HP story for Bentley

✳   G.K. Chesterton

The creator of Father Brown, the immortal priest detective, and first president of the Detection Club, Chesterton contributed to their collaborative novel *The Floating Admiral*. The reference in Notebook 66 is a reminder to provide a short story for him, presumably for his 1935 anthology *A Century of Detective Stories*. She did not write a new one but instead provided 'Sing a Song of Sixpence'.

Ideas for G. K. C.

\*  John Creasey

In Notebook 52 there are two references, both very similar, to John Creasey, British crime writer of almost 600 books. Hugely prolific under a variety of pseudonyms, he was also a founder of the Crime Writers Association. In *The Clocks*, the typewriting agency, which is the focus of much of the novel, does some work for Creasey-like authors.

Miss M[artindale] is chief agent – Sec[retary] to Creasey
– who wrote spy stories

\*  Rufus King

Twice during the plotting of *Mrs McGinty's Dead* Christie mentions *Murder by Latitude*, a novel by this largely forgotten US writer. *Murder by Latitude* features a typical Christie setting, aboard a ship from which contact with land has been severed. Although not mentioned by name, there are a few of his novels in the library at Greenway House.

Atmosphere like Murder by Latitude – some people –
amongst them a Murderer

\*  A.E.W. Mason

Mason was the creator of Inspector Hanaud. The reference in Notebook 35 is to *At the Villa Rose*, published in 1910, a case involving the death of an elderly woman and the suspicion surrounding her companion. While plotting *One, Two, Buckle my Shoe* Christie reminds herself of it:

A murder discovered (woman? Elderly? Like Villa Rose) Clue
– a shoe buckle

✳ Edgar Allan Poe

The 'inventor' of the detective story when he published 'The Murders in the Rue Morgue' in 1841. 'The Purloined Letter', another famous case for his detective Auguste Dupin, turns on the idea of hiding in plain sight and Christie's reference is in connection with a fortune hidden not *in* but *on* an envelope, as stamps. She used this plot device in the short story 'Strange Jest' and in *Spider's Web*. The concept of hiding in plain sight is also used in 'The Nemean Lion'.

Stamps – fortune left in them – on old letters in desk – 'Purloined Letter' mentioned – they look in obvious envelope – really stamps on it

✳ Dorothy L. Sayers

Sayers' creation Lord Peter Wimsey made his debut in 1923 in *Whose Body?* and is mentioned in Notebook 41, as a model for Ronnie West in *Lord Edgware Dies*. It is also possible that the naming of Dr Peter Lord in *Sad Cypress* is homage to Christie's great contemporary.

Ronnie West (debonair Peter Wimseyish)

## Agatha Christie in the Notebooks

Christie several times references herself and her work in the Notebooks. For some reason she twice – in Notebooks 72 and 39 – lists some of her books, although the lists are not exhaustive nor is it obvious what the titles have in common; and she often refers to earlier titles as a quick reminder.

＊ Analysis of books so far
  Hotels – Body in Library, Evil under the Sun
  Trains Aeroplanes – Blue Train, Orient Express, Death in
  Clouds, Nile
  Private Life (country) Towards Zero, Hollow, Xmas, 3 Act
  Tragedy, Sad Cypress
  (village) Vicarage, Moving Finger Travel – Appointment
  with Death

This list appears just after notes for *Mrs McGinty's Dead*. The fact that *Taken at the Flood* does not appear in the list may mean that it was compiled in late 1946, after *The Hollow*, or early 1947, before *Taken at the Flood* was completed. From the headings it would seem that she was considering backgrounds previously used.

＊ Ackroyd
  Murder on Nile
  Death in Clouds
  Murder in Mesopotamia
  Orient Express
  Appointment with Death
  Tragedy in 3 Acts
  Dead Man's Mirror

And the above, squeezed into the corner of a page during the plotting of *Evil under the Sun*, is even more enigmatic. Apart from the fact that they are all Poirot stories, it is difficult to see what they have in common.

The next musing appears in the notes for *Towards Zero*. Wisely, she decided against it as another mysterious death at the hotel in the space of three years could look, in Oscar Wilde's famous phrase, like carelessness:

＊ Shall hotel be the same as Evil Under the Sun – N[eville]
  has to go across in trolley because high water

The following odd, and inaccurate, reference – Poirot was not involved in the case – to an earlier killer appears in the notes for *Elephants Can Remember*.

> ✳ Calls on Poirot – asks about Josephine (Crooked House)

This was among the last notes to appear, written just before the publication of *Postern of Fate*:

> ✳ Nov. 2nd 1973 Book of Stories The White Horse Stories First one – The White Horse Party (rather similar to Jane Marple's Tuesday Night Club)

Chapter 25 of *4.50 from Paddington* includes a brief, cryptic reference to *A Murder is Announced*, but without mentioning the title . . .

> ✳ Somebody greedy – bit about Letty Blacklock

. . . while this reference appears during the plotting of *Third Girl*:

> ✳ Poirot worried – old friend (as in McGinty) comes to tea

Finally, the idea of reintroducing Sergeant Fletcher from *A Murder is Announced* was briefly considered during the plotting of *A Pocket Full of Rye*:

> ✳ Chapter II – Crossways – Inspector Harwell – or Murder is Announced young man

# The First Decade 1920–1929

'It was while I was working in the dispensary that I first
conceived the idea of writing a detective story.'

*An Autobiography*

────────────◄O►────────────

**SOLUTIONS REVEALED**

*After the Funeral* • *Appointment With Death* • *Death in the
Clouds* • *The Man in the Brown Suit* • *The Mysterious Affair
at Styles* • *The Mystery of the Blue Train* • 'The Red Signal'
• *The Secret of Chimneys*

────────────◄O►────────────

*The Mysterious Affair at Styles* was published in the USA at the
end of 1920 and in the UK on 21 January 1921. It is a classic
country-house whodunit, a setting and form destined to
become synonymous with the name of Agatha Christie.
Ironically, over the following decade she wrote only one more
'English' domestic whodunit, *The Murder of Roger Ackroyd*
(1926). The other two whodunits of this decade are set abroad:
*The Murder on the Links* (1923) is set in Deauville, France and
*The Mystery of the Blue Train* (1928) has a similar South of
France background. With the exception of the last title, which
Christie, according to *An Autobiography*, 'always hated' and
had 'never been proud of', they are first-class examples of the

classic detective story then entering its Golden Age. Each title, with the same exception, displays the gifts that would later make Agatha Christie the Queen of Crime – uncomplicated language briskly telling a cleverly constructed story, easily recognisable and clearly delineated characters, inventive plots with all the necessary clues given to the reader, and an unexpected killer unmasked in the last chapter. These hallmarks would continue to be a feature of Christie's books until the twilight of her career, half a century later.

The rest of her novels of the 1920s consist of thrillers, both domestic – *The Secret Adversary* (1922), *The Secret of Chimneys* (1925) and *The Seven Dials Mystery* (1929) – and international – *The Man in the Brown Suit* (1924). While none of these titles are first-rate Christie, they all exhibit some elements that would appear in later titles. *The Secret Adversary*, the first Tommy and Tuppence adventure, unmasks the least likely suspect while *The Man in the Brown Suit* is an early experiment with the famous Roger Ackroyd conjuring trick. *The Seven Dials Mystery* subverts reader expectation of the 'secret society' plot device and *The Secret of Chimneys*, a light-hearted mixture of missing jewels, international intrigue, incriminating letters, blackmail and murder in a high society setting, shows early experimentation with impersonation and false identity.

Throughout the 1920s Christie's short story output was impressive, with three such collections published in the decade. The contents of *Poirot Investigates* (1924) first appeared in *The Sketch*, in a commissioned series of short stories, starting in March 1923 with 'The Affair at the Victory Ball'. By the end of that year two dozen stories had appeared and 50 years later the remainder of these stories had their first UK book appearance in *Poirot's Early Cases*. In 1953 Christie dedicated *A Pocket Full of Rye* to the editor of *The Sketch*, 'Bruce Ingram, who liked and published my first short stories.' In 1927, at a low point in Christie's life, after the death of her mother, the end of her marriage, and her own disappearance, *The Big Four* was published. This episodic

Poirot novel, consisting of a series of connected short stories all of which had appeared in *The Sketch* during 1924, can also be considered a low point in the career of Hercule Poirot as he battles international criminals intent on world domination. The last collection of the decade is the hugely entertaining *Partners in Crime* (1929). These Tommy and Tuppence adventures, most of which had appeared in *The Sketch* also during 1924, were pastiches of many of the crime writers of the time – 'The Man in the Mist' (G.K. Chesterton), 'The Case of the Missing Lady' (Conan Doyle), 'The Crackler' (Edgar Wallace) – and, while light-hearted in tone, contain many clever ideas.

Apart from her crime and detective stories, tales of the supernatural, romance and fantasy all appeared under her name in many of the fiction magazines that proliferated. The stories later published in the collections *The Mysterious Mr Quin*, *The Hound of Death* and *The Listerdale Mystery* were written and first published in the 1920s. And, of course, it was during the 1920s that Miss Marple made her first appearance, in the short story 'The Tuesday Night Club', published in *The Royal Magazine* in December 1927. With the exception of the final entry, 'Death by Drowning', the stories that appear in *The Thirteen Problems* were all written in the 1920s and appeared in two batches, December 1927 to May 1928, and December 1929 to May 1930. In 1924 her first poetry collection *The Road of Dreams* was published. And it seems likely that her own stage adaptation of *The Secret of Chimneys* was begun in the late 1920s, as was the unpublished and unperformed script of the macabre short story 'The Last Séance'.

The other important career decision taken in 1924 was to employ the services of a literary agent, Edmund Cork. The first task he undertook was to extricate Christie from her very one-sided contract with The Bodley Head Ltd and negotiate a more favourable arrangement with Collins, the publisher with which she was destined to remain for the rest of her life; as, indeed, she did with Edmund Cork.

Three of the best short stories Christie ever wrote were published during this decade. In January 1925 'Traitor Hands', later to achieve immortality as the play, and subsequent film, *Witness for the Prosecution*, appeared in *Flynn's Weekly*. The much-anthologised 'Accident' was published in the *Daily Express* in 1929; this was later adapted by other hands into the one-act play *Tea for Three*. And 'Philomel Cottage', which inspired a stage play and five screen versions as *Love from a Stranger*, appeared in *The Grand* in November 1924.

Finally, the first stage and screen versions of her work appeared during the 1920s. *Alibi*, adapted for the stage by Michael Morton from *The Murder of Roger Ackroyd*, opened in May 1928 while the same year saw the opening of films of *The Secret Adversary* – as *Die Abenteuer G.m.b.h.* – and *The Passing of Mr Quinn* [sic], based, almost undetectably, on the short story 'The Coming of Mr Quin'.

This hugely prolific decade shows Christie gaining an international reputation while experimenting with form and structure within, and outside, the detective genre. Although her first novel was very definitely a detective story, her output for the following nine years returned only twice to the form in which she was eventually to gain immortality.

ᗡᘂᗋ

### The Mysterious Affair at Styles
21 January 1921

◄○►

Arthur Hastings goes to Styles Court, the home of his friend John Cavendish, to recuperate during the First World War. He senses tension in the household and this is confirmed when Emily Inglethorp, John's stepmother, is poisoned. Luckily, a Belgian refugee, one Hercule Poirot, staying nearby is an old friend.

◄○►

As we saw in Chapter One 'The Beginning of a Career' one of the readers' reports on *The Mysterious Affair at Styles* mentioned the John Cavendish trial. In the original manuscript, Poirot's explanation of the crime is given in the form of his evidence in the witness box during the trial. In *An Autobiography* Christie describes John Lane's verdict on her manuscript, including his opinion that this courtroom scene did not convince and his request that she amend it. She agreed to a rewrite and although the explanation of the crime itself remains the same, instead of giving it in the course of the judicial process, Poirot holds forth in the drawing room in the kind of scene that was to be replicated in many later books.

Incredibly, a century later – it was written, in all probability, in 1916 – the deleted scene has survived in the pages of Notebook 37, which also contains two brief and somewhat enigmatic notes about the novel. Equally incredible is the illegibility of the handwriting, complicated by numerous deletions and insertions, many squeezed in, sometimes at an angle, above the original. And although the explanation of the crime is, in essence, the same as the published version, the published text was of limited help. The wording is often different and some names have changed. This exercise in transcription was the most challenging of the Notebooks but the fact that it is Agatha Christie's and Hercule Poirot's first case made the extra effort worthwhile.

In the version that follows I have amended the usual Christie punctuation of dashes to full stops and commas, and I have added quotation marks throughout. I use square brackets where an obvious, or necessary, word is missing in the original; a few illegible words have been omitted. Footnotes have been used to draw attention to points of particular interest.

Poirot returned late that night. I did not see him until the following morning. He was leaning, refreshed...

"Ah! my friend — All is well — All will now march —"

"Why?" I exclaimed. "You don't mean to say you have got —"

"Yes, Hastings — yes — I have found the missing link — Hush —"

On Monday the hearing was resumed & S. E. H.W. opened the case for the defence —

*Notebook 37 showing the beginning of the deleted chapter from*
The Mysterious Affair at Styles.

# THE MYSTERIOUS AFFAIR AT STYLES

*The story so far . . .*

*When wealthy Emily Inglethorp, owner of Styles Court, remarries, her new husband Alfred is viewed by her stepsons, John and Lawrence, and her faithful retainer, Evelyn Howard, as a fortune-hunter. John's wife, Mary, is perceived as being over-friendly with the enigmatic Dr Bauerstein, a German and an expert on poisons. Also staying at Styles Court, while working in the dispensary of the local hospital, is Emily's protégée Cynthia Murdoch. Then Evelyn, after a bitter row, leaves Styles. On the night of 17 July Emily dies from strychnine poisoning while her family watches helplessly. Hercule Poirot, called in by his friend Arthur Hastings, agrees to investigate and pays close attention to Emily's bedroom. And then John Cavendish is arrested . . .*

Poirot returned late that night.[3] I did not see him until the following morning. He was beaming and greeted me with the utmost affection.

'Ah, my friend – all is well – all will now march.'

'Why,' I exclaimed, 'You don't mean to say you have got—'

---

3  Chapter 11 ends with the words '"Well," said Mary, "I expect he will be back before dinner." But night fell and Poirot had not returned.' I suggest that it is at this point that the Notebook 37 extract would have appeared.

'Yes, Hastings, yes – I have found the missing link.[4] Hush . . .'

On Monday the hearing was resumed[5] and Sir E.H.W. [Ernest Heavywether] opened the case for the defence. Never, he said, in the course of his experience had a murder charge rested on slighter evidence. Let them take the evidence against John Cavendish and sift it impartially.

What was the main thing against him? That the powdered strychnine had been found in his drawer. But that drawer was an unlocked one and he submitted that there was no evidence to show that it was the prisoner who placed it there. It was, in fact, a wicked and malicious effort on the part of some other person to bring the crime home to the prisoner. He went on to state that the Prosecution had been unable to prove to any degree that it was the prisoner who had ordered the beard from Messrs Parksons. As for the quarrel with his mother and his financial constraints – both had been most grossly exaggerated.

His learned friend had stated that if [the] prisoner had been an honest man he would have come forward at the inquest and explained that it was he and not his step-father who had been the participator in that quarrel. That view was based upon a misapprehension. The prisoner, on return-ing to the house in the evening, had been told at once[6] that his mother had now had a violent dispute with her husband. Was it likely, was it probable, he asked the jury, that he should connect the two? It would never enter his head that anyone could ever mistake his voice for that of Mr. A[lfred] Inglethorp. As for the construction that [the] prisoner had destroyed a will – this mere idea was absurd. [The] prisoner

---

4  Chapter 12 is called 'The Last Link'. In the preceding chapter Poirot refers several times to 'the last link' in his chain of evidence.

5  John Cavendish's trial began on 15 September (Agatha Christie's birthday), two months after the poisoning of Emily Inglethorp.

6  The 'authoritatively told' of the published version is written over the original 'told at once' in Notebook 37.

had presented at the Bar and, being well versed in legal matters, knew that the will formerly made in his favour was revoked automatically. He had never heard a more ridiculous suggestion! He would, however, call evidence which would show who *did* destroy the will, and with what motive.

Finally, he would point out to the jury that there was evidence against other persons besides John Cavendish. He did not wish to accuse Mr. Lawrence Cavendish in any way; nevertheless, the evidence against *him* was quite as strong – if not stronger – than that against his brother.

Just at that point, a note was handed to him. As he read it, his eyes brightened, his burly figure seemed to swell and double its size.

'Gentlemen of the jury,' he said, and there was a new ring in his voice, 'this has been a murder of peculiar cunning and complexity. I will first call the prisoner. He shall tell you his own story and I am sure you will agree with me that he *cannot* be guilty. Then I will call a Belgian gentleman, a very famous member of the Belgian police force in past years, who has interested himself in the case and who has important proofs that it was *not* the prisoner who committed this crime. I call the prisoner.'

John in the box acquitted himself well. His manner, quiet and direct, was all in his favour.[7] At the end of his examination he paused and said, 'I should like to say one thing. I utterly refute and disapprove of Sir Ernest Heavywether's insinuation about my brother Lawrence. My brother, I am convinced, had no more to do with this crime than I had.'

Sir Ernest, remaining seated, noted with a sharp eye that John's protest had made a favourable effect upon the jury. Mr Bunthorne cross-examined.[8]

---

7  None of the questioning of John Cavendish by Sir Ernest appears in Notebook 37.

8  Mr Philips KC appears for the Crown in the published version.

'You say that you never thought it possible that *your* quarrel with your mother was identical with the one spoken of at the inquest – is not that very surprising?'

'No, I do not think so – I knew that my mother and Mr Inglethorp had quarrelled. It never occurred to me that they had mistaken my voice for his.'

'Not even when the servant Dorcas repeated certain fragments of this conversation which you *must* have recognised?'

'No, we were both angry and said many things in the heat of the moment which we did not really mean and which we did not recollect afterwards. I could not have told you which exact words I used.'

Mr Bunthorne sniffed incredulously.

'About this note which you have produced so opportunely, is the handwriting not familiar to you?'

'No.'

'Do you not think it bears a marked resemblance to your own handwriting?'

'No – I don't think so.'

'I put it to you that it *is* your own handwriting.'

'No.'

'I put it to you that, anxious to prove an alibi, you conceived the idea of a fictitious appointment and wrote this note to yourself in order to bear out your statement.'

'No.'

'I put it to you that at the time you claim to have been waiting about in Marldon Wood,[9] you were really in Styles St Mary, in the chemist's shop, buying strychnine in the name of Alfred Inglethorp.'

'No – that is a lie.'

That completed Mr Bunthorne's CE [cross examination].

---

9　Although *The Mysterious Affair at Styles* is set in Essex, there is an area called Marldon near Torbay, where Christie was living when she wrote the novel. The reference was replaced in the published novel by 'a solitary and unfrequented spot'..

He sat down and Sir Ernest, rising, announced that his next witness would be M. Hercule Poirot.

Poirot strutted into the witness box like a bantam cock.[10] The little man was transformed; he was foppishly attired and his face beamed with self confidence and complacency. After a few preliminaries Sir Ernest asked: 'Having been called in by Mr. Cavendish what was your first procedure?'

'I examined Mrs Inglethorp's bedroom and found certain . . .?'

'Will you tell us what these were?'

'Yes.'

With a flourish Poirot drew out his little notebook.

'Voila,' he announced, 'There were in the room five points of importance.[11] I discovered, amongst other things, a brown stain on the carpet near the window and a fragment of green material which was caught on the bolt of the communicating door between that room and the room adjoining, which was occupied by Miss Cynthia Paton.'[12]

'What did you do with the fragment of green material?'

'I handed it over to the police, who, however, did not consider it of importance.'

'Do you agree?'

'I disagree with that most utterly.'

'You consider the fragment important?'

'Of the first importance.'

---

10  The alternate, but crossed out, version in Notebook 37 reads, 'entered the box and was duly sworn. The little man was transformed.'

11  In Chapter 4, Poirot notes 'six points of interest': a coffee cup that was ground into powder; a despatch-case with a key in the lock; a stain on the floor; a fragment of some dark green fabric; and a large splash of candle grease on the floor. At first he withholds the sixth item, but later in the chapter he adds the bromide-powder box.

12  The surname is changed to Murdoch in the published version, although in some editions the name is spelt with a 'K' on the floor-plan in Chapter 3.

'But I believe,' interposed the judge, 'that no-one in the house had a green garment in their possession.'

'I believe so, Mr Le Juge,' agreed Poirot facing in his direction. 'And so at first, I confess, that disconcerted me – until I hit upon the explanation.'

Everybody was listening eagerly.

'What is your explanation?'

'That fragment of green was torn from the sleeve of a member of the household.'

'But no-one had a green dress.'

'No, Mr Le Juge, this fragment is a fragment torn from a green land armlet.'

With a frown the judge turned to Sir Ernest.

'Did anyone in that house wear an armlet?'

'Yes, my lord. Mrs Cavendish, the prisoner's wife.'

There was a sudden exclamation and the judge commented sharply that unless there was absolute silence he would have the court cleared. He then leaned forward to the witness.

'Am I to understand that you allege Mrs Cavendish to have entered the room?'

'Yes, Mr Le Juge.'

'But the door was bolted on the inside.'

'Pardon, Mr Le Juge, we have only one person's word for that – that of Mrs Cavendish herself. You will remember that it was *Mrs Cavendish* who had tried that door and found it locked.'

'Was not her door locked when you examined the room?'

'Yes, but during the afternoon she would have had ample opportunity to draw the bolt.'[13]

'But Mr *Lawrence* Cavendish has claimed that he *saw* it.'

There was a momentary hesitation on Poirot's part before he replied.

'Mr. Lawrence Cavendish was mistaken.'

---

13   At this point in Notebook 37 there is a reference to 'Other Book', possibly referring to another Notebook, no longer extant.

Poirot continued calmly:

'I found, on the floor, a large splash of candle grease, which upon questioning the servants, I found had not been there the day before. The presence of the candle grease on the floor, the fact that the door opened quite noiselessly (a proof that it had recently been oiled) and the fragment of the green armlet in the door led me at once to the conclusion that the room had been entered through that door and that Mrs Cavendish was the person who had done so. Moreover, at the inquest Mrs Cavendish declared that she had heard the fall of the table in her own room. I took an early opportunity of testing that statement by stationing my friend Mr Hastings[14] in the left wing just outside Mrs Cavendish's door. I myself, in company with the police, went to [the] deceased's room and whilst there I, apparently accidentally, knocked over the table in question but found, as I had suspected, that [it made] no sound at all. This confirmed my view that Mrs Cavendish was not speaking the truth when she declared that she had been in her room at the time of the tragedy. In fact, I was more than ever convinced that, far from being in her own room, Mrs Cavendish was actually in the *deceased's* room when the table fell. I found that no one had actually *seen* her leave her room. The first that anyone could tell me was that she was in Miss Paton's room shaking her awake. Everyone presumed that she had come from her own room – but I can find no one who *saw* her do so.'

The judge was much interested. 'I understand. Then your explanation is that it was *Mrs* Cavendish and not the prisoner who destroyed the will.'

Poirot shook his head.

'No,' he said quickly, 'That was not the reason for Mrs Cavendish's presence. There is only one person who *could* have destroyed the will.'

---

14  Hastings is Mr Hastings throughout *The Mysterious Affair at Styles*; he did not become Captain until *The Murder on the Links*.

'And that is?'

'Mrs Inglethorp herself.'

'*What?* The will she had made that very afternoon?'

'Yes – it must have been her. Because by no other means can you account for the fact that on the hottest day of the year [Mrs Inglethorp] ordered a fire to be lighted in her room.'

The judge objected. 'She was feeling ill . . .'

'Mr Le Juge, the temperature that day was 86 in the shade. There was only one reason for which Mrs Inglethorp could want a fire – namely to destroy some document. You will remember that in consequence of the war economies practised at Styles, no waste paper was thrown away and that the kitchen fire was allowed to go out after lunch. There was, consequently, no means at hand for the destroying of bulky documents such as a will. This confirms to me at once that there was some paper which Mrs Inglethorp was anxious to destroy and it must necessarily be of a bulk which made it difficult to destroy by merely setting a match to it. The idea of a will had occurred to me before I set foot in the house, so papers burned in the grate did not surprise me. I did not, of course, at that time know that the will in question had only been made the previous afternoon and I will admit that when I learnt this fact, I fell into a grievous error. I deduced that Mrs Inglethorp's determination to destroy this will came as a direct consequence of the quarrel and that consequently the quarrel took place, contrary to belief, *after* the making of the will.

'When, however, I was forced to reluctantly abandon this hypothesis – since the various interviews were absolutely steady on the question of time – I was obliged to cast around for another. And I found it in the form of the letter which Dorcas describes her mistress as holding in her hand. Also you will notice the difference of attitude. At 3.30 Dorcas overhears her mistress saying angrily that "scandal will not deter her." "You have brought it on yourself" were her words.

But at 4.30, when Dorcas brings in the tea, although the actual words she used were almost the same, the meaning is quite different. Mrs Inglethorp is now in a clearly distressed condition. She is wondering what to do. She speaks with dread of the scandal and publicity. Her outlook is quite different. We can only explain this psychologically by presuming [that] her first sentiments applied to the scandal between John Cavendish and his wife and did not in any way touch herself – but that in the second case the scandal affected herself.

'This, then, is the position: At 3.30 she quarrels with her son and threatens to denounce him to his wife who, although they neither of them realise it, overhears part of the conversation. At 4 o'clock, in consequence of a conversation at lunch time on the making of wills by marriage, Mrs Inglethorp makes a will in favour of her husband, witnessed by her gardener. At 4.30 Dorcas finds her mistress in a terrible state, a slip of paper in her hand. And she then orders the fire in her room to be lighted in order that she can destroy the will she only made half an hour ago. Later she writes to Mr Wells, her lawyer, asking him to call on her tomorrow as she has some important business to transact.

Now what occurred between 4 o'clock and 4.30[15] to cause such a complete revolution of sentiments? As far as we know, she was quite alone during the time. Nobody entered or left the boudoir. What happened then? One can only guess but I have an idea that my guess is fairly correct.

'Late in the evening Mrs Inglethorp asked Dorcas for some stamps and my thinking is this. Finding she had no stamps in her desk she went along to that of her husband which stood at the opposite corner. The desk was locked but one of the keys on her bunch fitted it. She accordingly opened the desk and searched for stamps – it was then she found the slip of

---

15 These timings are 30 minutes earlier than those in Chapter 12 of the novel.

paper which wreaked such havoc! On the other hand Mrs Cavendish believed that the slip of paper to which her mother [in-law] clung so tenaciously was a written proof of her husband's infidelity. She demanded it. These were Mrs Inglethorp's words in reply:

"'No, [it is out of the] question." We know that she was speaking the truth. Mrs Cavendish however, believed she was merely shielding her step-son. She is a very resolute woman and she was wildly jealous of her husband and she determined to get hold of that paper at all costs and made her plans accordingly. She had chanced to find the key of Mrs Inglethorp's dispatch case which had been lost that morning. She had meant to return it but it had probably slipped her memory. Now, however, she deliberately retained it since she knew Mrs Inglethorp kept all important papers in that particular case. Therefore, rising about 4 o'clock she made her way through Miss Paton's room, which she had previously unlocked on the other side.'

'But Miss Paton would surely have been awakened by anyone passing through her room.'

'Not if she were drugged.'

'Drugged?'

'Yes – for Miss Paton to have slept through all the turmoil in that next room was incredible. Two things were possible: either she was lying (which I did not believe) or her sleep was not a natural one. With this idea in view I examined all the coffee cups most carefully, taking a sample from each and analysing. But, to my disappointment, they yielded no result. Six persons had taken coffee and six cups were found. But I had been guilty of a very grave oversight. I had overlooked the fact that Dr Bauerstein had been there that night. That changed the face of the whole affair. *Seven, not* six people had taken coffee. There was, then, a cup missing. The servants would not observe this since it was the housemaid Annie who had taken the coffee tray in and she had brought in seven cups, unaware that Mr Inglethorp never took coffee.

Dorcas who cleared them away found five cups and she suspected the sixth [of] being Mrs Inglethorp's. One cup, then, had disappeared and it was Mademoiselle Cynthia's, I knew, because she did not take sugar in her coffee, whereas all the others did and the cups I had found had all contained sugar. My attention was attracted by the maid Annie's story about some "salt" on the cocoa tray which she took nightly into Mrs Inglethorp's room. I accordingly took a sample of that cocoa and sent it to be analysed.'

'But,' objected the judge, 'this has already been done by Dr Bauerstein – with a negative result – and the analysis reported no strychnine present.'

'There was no strychnine present. The analysts were simply asked to report whether the contents showed if there were or were not strychnine present and they reported accordingly. But I had it tested for a *narcotic*.'

'For *a narcotic?*'

'Yes, Mr Le Juge. You will remember that Dr Bauerstein was unable to account for the delay before the symptoms manifested themselves. But a narcotic, taken with strychnine, will delay the symptoms some hours. Here is the analyst's report proving beyond a doubt that a narcotic *was* present.'

The report was handed to the judge who read it with great interest and it was then passed on to the jury.

'We congratulate you on your acumen. The case is becoming much clearer. The drugged cocoa, taken on top of the poisoned coffee, amply accounts for the delay which puzzled the doctor.'

'Exactly, Mr Le Juge. Although you have made one little error; the coffee, to the best of my belief was *not* poisoned.'

'What proof have you of that?'

'None whatever. But I can prove this – that poisoned or not, Mrs Inglethorp never drank it.'

'Explain yourself.'

'You remember that I referred to a brown stain on the carpet near the window? It remained in my mind, that stain, for it was still damp. Something had been spilt there, therefore, not more than twelve hours ago. Moreover there was a distinct odour of coffee clinging to the nap of the carpet and I found there two long splinters of china. I later reconstructed what had happened perfectly, for, not two minutes before I had laid down my small despatch case on the little table by the window and, the top of the table being loose, the case had been toppled off onto the floor onto the *exact spot where the stain was*. This, then, was what had happened. Mrs Inglethorp, on coming up to bed had laid her untasted coffee down on the table – the table had tipped up and [precipitated] the coffee onto the floor – spilling it and smashing the cup. What had Mrs Inglethorp done? She had picked up the pieces and laid them on the table beside her bed and, feeling in need of a stimulant of some kind, had heated up her cocoa[16] and drank it off before going to bed. Now, I was in a dilemma. The cocoa contained no strychnine. The coffee had not been drunk. Yet Mrs Inglethorp had been poisoned and the poison must have been administered sometime between the hours of seven and nine. But what else had Mrs Inglethorp taken which would have effectively masked the taste of the poison?'

'Nothing.'

'Yes – Mr Le Juge – she had taken her *medicine*.'

'Her medicine – but . . .'

'One moment – the medicine, by a [coincidence] already contained strychnine and had a bitter taste in consequence. The poison might have been introduced into the medicine. But I had my reasons for believing that it was done another way. I will recall to your memory that I also discovered a box which had at one time contained bromide powders. Also, if

---

16  In *An Autobiography* Christie describes the trouble she had with the formidable Miss Howse at The Bodley Head, who insisted on the spelling 'coco' rather than, as here, 'cocoa'. The first edition uses the former, and incorrect, 'coco'.

you will permit it, I will read out to you an extract – marked in pencil – out of a book on dispensing which I noticed at the dispensary of the Red Cross Hospital at Tadminster. The following is the extract . . .'[17]

'But, surely a bromide was not prescribed with the tonic?'

'No, Mr Le Juge. But you will recall that I mentioned an empty box of bromide powders. One of the powders introduced into the full bottle of medicine would effectively precipitate the strychnine and cause it to be taken in the last dose. You may observe that the "Shake the bottle" label always found on bottles containing poison has been removed. Now, the person who usually poured out the medicine was extremely careful to leave the sediment at the bottom undisturbed.'

A fresh buzz of excitement broke out and was sternly silenced by the judge.

'I can produce a rather important piece of evidence in support of that contention, because on reviewing the case, I came to the conclusion[18] that the murder had been *intended* to take place the night before. For in the natural course of events Mrs I[nglethorp] *would* have taken the last dose on the previous evening but, being in a hurry to see to the Fashion Fete she was arranging, she omitted to do so. The following day she went out to luncheon, so that she took the actual last dose *24 hours later* than had been anticipated by the murderer. As a proof that it was expected the night before, I will mention that the bell in Mrs Inglethorp's room was found cut on Monday evening, this being when Miss Paton was spending the night with friends. Consequently Mrs Inglethorp would be quite cut off from the rest of the house

---

17  There are two blank lines in Notebook 37 at this point,
    presumably in order to check the chemical details as they appear
    in Chapter 12.

18  The alternative version in Notebook 37 is 'all the evidence points
    to the . . .'

_Notebook 37 showing the end of the deleted chapter from_
The Mysterious Affair at Styles. _See Footnote 19._

and would have been unable to arouse them, thereby making sure that medical aid would not reach her until too late.'

'Ingenious theory – but have you no proof?'

Poirot smiled curiously.

'Yes, Mr Le Juge – I have a proof. I admit that up to some hours ago, I merely *knew* what I have just said, without being able to *prove* it. But in the last few hours I have obtained a sure and certain proof, the missing link in the chain, a link *in the murderer's own hand*, the one slip he made. You will remember the slip of paper held in Mrs Inglethorp's hand? That slip of paper has been found. For on the morning of the tragedy the murderer entered the dead woman's room and forced the lock of the despatch case. Its importance can be guessed at from the immense risks the murderer took. There was one risk he did not take – and that was the risk of keeping it on his own person – he had no time or opportunity to destroy it. There was only one thing left for him to do.'

'What was that?'

'To hide it. He did hide it and so cleverly that, though I have searched for two months it is not until today that I found it. Voila, ici le prize.'

With a flourish Poirot drew out three long slips of paper.

'It has been torn – but it can easily be pieced together. It is a complete and damning proof.[19] Had it been a little clearer in its terms it is possible that Mrs Inglethorp would not have died. But as it was, while opening her eyes to *who*, it left her in the dark as to *how*. Read it, Mr Le Juge. For it is an unfinished letter from the murderer, Alfred Inglethorp, to his lover and accomplice, Evelyn Howard.'

◄○►

19  Notebook 37 reads: 'damning (2) and complete (1)', which I interpret as a reminder to reverse the adjectives; it is followed by 'for it is a letter from the [murderer]', which is crossed out and reinstated in the last sentence.

And there, like Alfred Inglethorp's pieced-together letter at the end of Chapter 12, Notebook 37 breaks off, despite the fact that the following pages are blank. We know from the published version that Alfred Inglethorp and Evelyn Howard are subsequently arrested for the murder, John and Mary Cavendish are reconciled, Cynthia and Lawrence announce their engagement, while Dr Bauerstein is shown to be more interested in spying than in poisoning. The book closes with Poirot's hope that this investigation will not be his last with '*mon ami*' Hastings.

The reviews on publication were as enthusiastic as the pre-publication reports for John Lane. *The Times* called it 'a brilliant story' and the *Sunday Times* found it 'very well contrived'. *The Daily News* considered it 'a skilful tale and a talented first book', while the *Evening News* thought it 'a wonderful triumph' and described Christie as 'a distinguished addition to the list of writers in this [genre]'. 'Well written, well proportioned and full of surprises' was the verdict of *The British Weekly*.

Poirot's dramatic evidence in the course of the trial resembles a similar scene at the denouement of Leroux's *The Mystery of the Yellow Room* (1907) – specifically mentioned in *An Autobiography* – where the detective, Rouletabille, gives his remarkable and conclusive evidence from the witness box. Had John Lane but known it, in demanding the alteration to the denouement of the novel he unwittingly paved the way for a half century of drawing-room elucidations stage-managed by both Poirot and Miss Marple. And although this explanation, in both courtroom and drawing room, is essentially the same, the unlikelihood of a witness being allowed to give evidence in this manner is self-evident. In other ways also *The Mysterious Affair at Styles* presaged what was to become typical Christie territory – an extended family, a country house, a poisoning drama, a twisting plot, and a dramatic and unexpected final revelation.

It is not a very extended family, however. Of Mrs

Inglethorp's family, there is a husband, two stepsons, one daughter-in-law, a family friend, a companion and a visiting doctor; there is the usual domestic staff although none of them is ever a serious consideration as a suspect. In other words, there are only seven suspects, which makes the disclosure of a surprise murderer more difficult. This very limited circle makes Christie's achievement in a debut detective novel even more impressive. The clichéd view of Christie is that all of her novels are set in country houses and/ or country villages. Statistically, this is inaccurate, as fewer than thirty (i.e. little over a third) of her books are set in such surroundings. And as Christie herself said, you have to set a book where people live.

Some ideas that feature in *The Mysterious Affair at Styles* would appear again throughout Christie's career. The dying Emily Inglethorp calls out the name of her husband, 'Alfred . . . Alfred', before she finally succumbs. Is the use of his name an accusation, an invocation, a plea, a farewell; or is it entirely meaningless? Similar situations occur in several novels over the next 30 years. One novel, *Why Didn't They Ask Evans?*, is built entirely around the dying words of the man found at the foot of the cliffs. In *Death Comes as the End*, the dying Satipy calls the name of the earlier victim, 'Nofret'; as John Christow lies dying at the edge of the Angkatells' swimming pool, in *The Hollow*, he calls out the name of his lover, 'Henrietta.' An extended version of the idea is found in *A Murder is Announced* when the last words of the soon-to-be-murdered Amy Murgatroyd, 'she wasn't there', contain a vital clue. In both *Murder in Mesopotamia* – 'the window' – and *Ordeal by Innocence* – 'the cup was empty' and 'the dove on the mast' – dying words indicate the method of murder. And the agent Carmichael utters the enigmatic 'Lucifer . . . Basrah' before he expires in Victoria's room in *They Came to Baghdad*.

The idea of a character looking over a shoulder and seeing someone or something significant makes its first appearance in Christie's work when Lawrence looks horrified at something he notices in Mrs Inglethorp's room on the night of her death. The alert reader should be able to tell what it is. This ploy is a Christie favourite and she enjoyed ringing the changes on the possible explanations. She predicated at least two novels – *The Mirror Crack'd from Side to Side* and *A Caribbean Mystery* – almost entirely on this, and it makes noteworthy appearances in *The Man in the Brown Suit*, *Appointment with Death* and *Death Comes as the End*, as well as a handful of short stories.

In the 1930 stage play *Black Coffee* – whose original title was to have been *After Dinner* – the only original script to feature Hercule Poirot, the hiding-place of the papers containing the missing formula is the same as the one devised by Alfred Inglethorp. And in an exchange very reminiscent of a similar one in *The Mysterious Affair at Styles*, it is a chance remark by Hastings that leads Poirot to this realisation.

In common with many crime stories of the period there are two floor-plans and no less than three reproductions of handwriting, all with a part to play in the eventual solution. And here also we see for the first time Poirot's remedy for steadying his nerves and encouraging precision in thought: the building of card-houses. At crucial points in both *Lord Edgware Dies* and *Three Act Tragedy* he adopts a similar strategy, each time with equally triumphant results. The important argument overheard by Mary Cavendish through an open window in Chapter 6 foreshadows a similar and equally important case of eavesdropping in *Five Little Pigs*.

In his 1953 survey of detective fiction, *Blood in their Ink*, Sutherland Scott describes *The Mysterious Affair at Styles* as 'one of the finest "firsts" ever written'. Countless Christie readers over almost a century would enthusiastically agree.

## *The Man in the Brown Suit*
### 22 August 1924

————————◄○►————————

When she is suddenly orphaned, Anne Beddingfeld[20] comes to London where she witnesses a suspicious death in a Tube station. A further death in the deserted Mill House convinces Anne to investigate and she boards a ship bound for South Africa, where she becomes involved in a breathless adventure.

————————◄○►————————

Christie's fourth novel drew extensively on her experiences with her first husband Archie when they both travelled the world in 1922. Although it starts in England, much of the novel is set on a ship travelling to South Africa and the climax of the novel takes place in Johannesburg. It is not a detective story but includes a whodunit element in tandem with murder, stolen jewels, a master criminal, mysterious messages and a shoot-out. It is an apprentice work before Christie found her true profession as a detective novelist and is hugely enjoyable, complete with a surprise solution which presages by two years her most stunning conjuring trick. And it also adopts the technique of using more than one narrator, a format that appears, in various guises, throughout her career in novels as diverse as *The ABC Murders, Five Little Pigs* and *The Pale Horse.*

The real-life Major Belcher, who employed Archie Christie as a business manager for the round-the-world trip, convinced Agatha Christie to include him as a character in her next novel. And he was not satisfied to be just any character; he wanted to be the murderer, whom he considered the most interesting character in any crime novel. He even suggested

---

20  Anne's surname appears in some editions as Beddingfield.

Myself – buying a giraffe

319

*This unpublished photograph, from her 1922 world tour with Archie, shows Agatha Christie buying a wooden giraffe beside a train, exactly as her heroine, Anne, does in Chapter 23 of* The Man in the Brown Suit.

a title, *Mystery at Mill House*, the name of his own house. In *An Autobiography* Christie admits that although she did create a Sir Eustace Pedler, using some of Belcher's characteristics, he was not actually the Major.

She also relates in *An Autobiography* that when the serial rights of *The Man in the Brown Suit* were sold to the *Evening News* they changed the title to *Anne the Adventuress*. She thought this 'as silly a title as I had ever heard' – although the first page of Notebook 34 is headed 'Adventurous Anne'.

The accuracy of the dozen pages in Notebook 34 suggests earlier, rougher notes, but as Christie wrote much of this book in South Africa it is understandable that they no longer exist.

Chapter I – Anne – her life with Papa – his friends . . . his death – A left penniless . . . interview with lawyer left with £95.

Chapter II – Accident in Tube – The Man in the Tube – Anne comes home.
     Announcement in paper 'Information Wanted' solicitor from Scotland Yard – Inspector coming to interview Anne – her calmness – Brachycephalic – not a doctor. Suggest about being a detective – takes out piece of paper – smells mothballs – realises paper was taken from dead man 17 1 22

III – Visit to Editor (Lord Northcliffe) – takes influential card from hall – her reception – if she makes good. The order to view – Does she find something? Perhaps a roll of films?

[There is no IV in the notebook]

V – Walkendale Castle – her researches – The Arundel Castle – Anne makes her passage

VI – Major Sir Eustace Puffin [Pedler] – changing cabins –
13 – to – 17 – general fuss – Eustace, Anne and Dr Phillips
and Pratt all laying claim to it

Or man rushes in to ask for aid – after stewardess has come
she finds he is stabbed in the shoulder – Doctor enters
'Allow me' – She is suspicious of him – he smiles – in the end
man is taken into doctor's cabin and Ship's doctor attends
him

The reference to Lord Northcliffe, the famous newspaper-
man, suggests that Christie intended to base Lord Nasby,
whom Anne visits in Chapter 5 to ask for a job, on him. And
both the alternative scenarios involving the changing of
cabins and the stabbed man featured in the novel.

❦

### *The Secret of Chimneys*
### 12 June 1925

A shooting party weekend at the country house
Chimneys conceals the presence of international
diplomats negotiating lucrative oil concessions with the
kingdom of Herzoslovakia. When a dead body is found,
Superintendent Battle's subsequent investigation
uncovers international jewel thieves, impersonation
and kidnapping as well as murder.

'These were easy to write, not requiring too much plotting
or planning.' *An Autobiography* makes only this fleeting reference to *The Secret of Chimneys*, first published in the summer
of 1925 as the last of the six books she had contracted to

produce for John Lane. In this 'easy to write' category she also included *The Seven Dials Mystery*, published four years later, which also features many of the same characters.

*The Secret of Chimneys* is not a formal detective story but a light-hearted thriller, a form to which she returned intermittently over the next quarter century. *The Secret of Chimneys* has all the ingredients, in generous profusion, of a good thriller of the period: missing jewels, a mysterious manuscript, compromising letters, oil concessions, a foreign throne, villains, heroes, and mysterious and beautiful women. It has distinct echoes of *The Prisoner of Zenda*, Anthony Hope's immortal swashbuckling novel that Tuppence recalls with affection in Chapter 2 of *Postern of Fate*: 'one's first introduction, really, to the romantic novel. The romance of Prince Flavia. The King of Ruritania, Rudolph Rassendyll ...' Christie organised these classic elements into a labyrinthine plot including a whodunit element.

The story begins in Africa, a country Christie had recently visited on her world tour in the company of her husband Archie. The protagonist, the somewhat mysterious Anthony Cade, undertakes to deliver a package to an address in London. This seemingly straightforward mission proves difficult and dangerous and before he can complete it he meets the beautiful Virginia Revel, who also has a commission for him: to dispose of the inconveniently dead body of her blackmailer. This achieved, they meet again at Chimneys, the country estate of Lord Caterham and his daughter Lady Eileen 'Bundle' Brent. From this point on, we are in more 'normal' Christie territory, the country house with a group of temporarily isolated characters, one of them of them a murderer.

But a major suspension of disbelief is called for when we are asked to believe that a young woman will pay a blackmailer £40 (roughly £1,500 today) for an indiscretion that she did not commit, just for the experience of being blackmailed (Chapter 6), and that two chapters later, when said blackmailer is found inconveniently, and unconvincingly, dead in her sitting room, she asks the first person who turns up on her doorstep (literally) to dispose of the body, while she blithely goes away for the weekend. By its nature this type of thriller is light-hearted, but *The Secret of Chimneys* demands much indulgence on the part of the reader.

The hand of Christie the detective novelist is evident in elements of the narration. Throughout the book the reliability of Anthony Cade is constantly in doubt and as early as Chapter 1 he jokes with his tourist group (and, by extension, the reader) about his real name. This is taken as part of his general banter but, as events unfold, he is revealed to be speaking nothing less than the truth. For the rest of the book Christie makes vague statements about Cade and when we are given his thoughts they are, in retrospect, ambiguous.

Anthony looked up sharply.

'Herzoslovakia?' he said with a curious ring in his voice. [Chapter 1]

'. . . was it likely that any of them would recognise him now if they were to meet him face to face?' [Chapter 5]

'No connexion with Prince Michael's death, is there?'

His hand was quite steady. So were his eyes. [Chapter 18]

'The part of Prince Nicholas of Herzoslovakia.'

The matchbox fell from Anthony's hand, but his amazement was fully equalled by that of Battle. [Chapter 19]

'I'm really a king in disguise, you know' [Chapter 23]

And how many readers will wonder about the curious scene at the end of Chapter 16 when Anchoukoff, the manservant, tells him he 'will serve him to the death' and Anthony ponders on 'the instincts these fellows have'? Anthony's motives remain unclear until the final chapter, and the reader, despite these hints, is unlikely to divine his true identity and purpose.

There are references, unconscious or otherwise, to other Christie titles. The rueful comments in Chapter 5 when Anthony remarks, 'I know all about publishers – they sit on manuscripts and hatch 'em like eggs. It will be at least a year before the thing is published,' echo Christie's own experiences with John Lane. The ploy of leaving a dead body in a railway left-luggage office, adopted by Cade in Chapter 9, was used in the 1923 Poirot short story 'The Adventure of the Clapham Cook'. Lord Caterham's description of the finding of the body in Chapter 10 distinctly foreshadows a similar scene almost twenty years later in *The Body in the Library* when Colonel Bantry shares this unwelcome experience. And Virginia Revel's throwaway comments about governesses and companions in Chapter 22 – 'It's awful but I never really look at them properly. Do you?' – would become the basis of more than one Christie plot, among them *Death in the Clouds*, *After the Funeral* and *Appointment with Death*. The same chapter is called 'The Red Signal', also the title of a short story from *The Hound of Death*, both sharing a common theme.

There are a dozen pages of notes in Notebook 65 for the novel, consisting mainly of a list of chapters and their possible content with no surprises or plot variations. But the other incarnation of *The Secret of Chimneys* makes for more interesting reading. For many years this title was one of the few Christies not adapted for stage, screen or radio. Or so it was thought, until it emerged that the novel was, very early in her career, one of Christie's first forays into stage adaptation. The history of the play is, appropriately, mysterious. It was scheduled to appear at the Embassy Theatre in London in December 1931 but was replaced at the last moment by a play called *Mary Broome*, a twenty-year-old comedy by one Allan Monkhouse.[21]

And that was the last that was heard of *Chimneys* for over 70 years, until a copy of the manuscript appeared, equally mysteriously, on the desk of the Artistic Director of the Vertigo Theatre in Calgary, Canada. So, almost three-quarters of a century after its projected debut, the premiere of *Chimneys* took place on 11 October 2003. And in June 2006, UK audiences had the opportunity to see this 'lost' Agatha Christie play, when it was presented at the Pitlochry Theatre Festival.

It is not known when exactly or, indeed, why Christie decided to adapt this novel for the stage, but it was probably done during late 1927/early 1928; a surviving typescript is dated July 1928. This would tally with the notes for the play, which are in the Notebook that has very brief, cryptic notes for some of the stories in *The Thirteen Problems*, the first of which appeared in December 1927. *The Secret of Chimneys* does not lend itself easily, or, it must be said, convincingly, to adaptation. If Christie decided in the late 1920s to dramatise one of her titles, one possible reason for choosing *The Secret of Chimneys* may have been her reluctance to put Poirot on the stage. She dropped him from four adaptations in later years: *Murder on the Nile*, *Appointment with Death*, *The Hollow* and *Go Back for Murder* (*Five Little Pigs*). The only play thus far to feature him was the original script, *Black Coffee*, staged the year before the proposed presentation of *Chimneys*. Yet, if she had wanted to adapt an earlier title, surely *The Mysterious Affair at Styles* or even *The Murder on the Links* would have been easier, set as they are largely in a single location and therefore requiring only one stage setting?

---

21  The complicated history of the initial staging of *Chimneys* is fully explored in Julius Green's account of Agatha Christie's contribution to stage drama in *Curtain Up: Agatha Christie – A Life in Theatre* (2015).

Perhaps with this in mind, the adaptation of *The Secret of Chimneys* is set entirely in Chimneys. This necessitated dropping large swathes of the novel (including the early scenes in Africa and the disposal, by Anthony, of Virginia's blackmailer) or redrafting these scenes for delivery as speeches by various characters, which tends to make for a verbose and static Act I. The remaining Acts are livelier with, eventually, revelations of multiple impersonations, as well as a 'new' murderer.

The solution in the stage version is the earliest example of Christie altering her own earlier explanation. She was to do this throughout her career, giving extra twists to dramatisations of *And Then There Were None*, *Appointment with Death* and *Witness for the Prosecution*. In *Chimneys* she makes even more drastic alterations to the original solution; the character unmasked as the villain at the end of the novel does not even appear in the stage adaptation. There are also sly references, to be picked up by alert Christie aficionados, to 'retiring and growing vegetable marrows' – a further indication of this being a post-*Murder of Roger Ackroyd* adaptation – and to the local town of Market Basing, a recurrent Christie location.

Some correspondence between Christie and Edmund Cork, her agent, in the summer of 1951 would seem to indicate that there were hopes of a revival, or to be strictly accurate, a first appearance of the play; but further developments in connection with a staging of the play, if any, remain unknown and it is clear that until Calgary in 2003 the script remained an 'unknown' Christie. The remote possibility that the script preceded the novel, which might have explained the unlikely choice for adaptation, is refuted by the reference in the opening pages of notes by the use of the phrase 'Incidents likely to retain'.

There are amendments to the original novel as the entire play is set in Chimneys, where a weekend house party, arranged in order to conceal an important international meeting, is about to begin, and by the opening of Act I, Scene

*The Cast of Characters and Scenes of the Play from
a 1928 script of* Chimneys.

ii the murder has been committed. In a major change from the novel, Anthony Cade and Virginia Revel – in a scence foreshadowing similar in *Spider's Web* and *The Unexpected Guest* – are the ones to find the body, although they say nothing and allow the discovery to be made the following morning. In effect, Act II opens at Chapter 10 of the book and from there on both follow much the same plan.

A major divergence is the omission of the scenes involving the discovery and disposal, by Cade, of the blackmailer's body. In fact, the entire blackmail scenario is substantially different. But whether written or staged, it is an unconvincing red herring and it could have been omitted entirely from the script without any loss. Other changes incorporated into the stage version include the fact that Virginia has no previous connection with Herzoslovakia, an aspect of the book that signally fails to convince. The secret passage from Chimneys to Wyvern Abbey is not mentioned, the character Hiram Fish is dropped and the hiding place of the jewels is different from, and not as well clued as, that in the novel.

The notes for *Chimneys* are all contained in Notebook 67. It is a tiny, pocket-diary sized notebook and the handwriting is correspondingly small and frequently illegible. In addition to the very rough notes for some of *The Thirteen Problems* the Notebook contains sketches of some Mr Quin short stories, including notes for a dramatisation of the Quin story 'The Dead Harlequin'. Overall, the notes for *Chimneys* do not differ greatly from the final version of the play, but substantial changes have been made from the original novel.

The first page reads:

People
Lord Caterham
Bundle
Lomax
Bill
Virginia

Tredwell
Antony
Prince Michael

Now what happens?

Incidents likely to retain – V[irginia] blackmailed

Idea of play
Crown jewels of Herzoslovakia stolen from assassinated
King and Queen during house party at Chimneys – hidden
there.

And twenty-five pages later an amended cast of characters:

Lord C
George
Bill
Tredwell
Battle
Inspector
Isaacstein
Bundle
Virginia
Antony
Lemaitre
Boris

The entire action of the play moves between the Library
and the Council Chamber of Chimneys. Chapter 16 of the
novel has a brief reference to visitors being shown over the
house and it is with such a scene that the play opens:

Act I Scene I – The Council Chamber

Lord C[aterham] in shabby clothes – Tredwell showing
party over. 'This is the . . . .' A guest comes back for his hat
tips Lord C. Bundle comes – 'First bit [of honest money]

ever earned by the Brents.' She and Lord C – he complains of political party Lomax has dragged him into. Bundle says why does he do it? George arrives and B goes. Explanation etc. about Cade – the Memoirs – Streptiltich . . . the Press – the strain of public life etc. Mention of diamond – King Victor – stolen by the Queen, 3rd rate actress – more like a comic opera – she killed in revolution

Despite the crossing-out and amended heading, the following passage appears in the script as Act I, Scene ii. It corresponds to Chapter 9 of the novel, although there it takes place in Virginia's house. I have broken up the extract and added punctuation to aid clarity.

~~Scene II   The Same (Evening)~~

Act II Scene I

That evening Antony arrives first – then V. He says about a poacher – shots – They do go to bed early – no light except in your window . . . – not this side of the house. Then she talks about the man – his queer manner – didn't ask for money – wanted to find out. Then discovery of body – she screams. He stops her – takes her to chair.
'It's all right my dear, it's all right.'
'I'm quite all right.'
'You marvellous creature – anyone else would have fainted.'
'I want to look.'
He goes, coming back with revolver.
'Yes – stay.'
He asks her to look.
'You are marvellous'
'Have you ever seen him before?'
'Have I – Oh! Why, it's the man – he's different. He had horn-rimmed glasses – spoke broken English.'
'This man wasn't . . . He was educated at Eton and Oxford'
'How do you know?'

'Oh, I know all right. I've – I've seen his pictures in the newspapers'

'Have you ever had a pistol?'

'No'

'It's [an] automatic.' Shows her.

'It's got my name on it.'

'Did you tell anyone – anyone see come down here?

'Go up to bed.'

'Shouldn't I shut the window after you?'

'No – no . . .'

'But . . .'

'No tell tale footprints'

V goes. A. comes round – examines body. A little earth – he sweeps it up – wipes fingerprints from handles inside. Then goes out, looking at pistol.

Christie reorganises her earlier listing of acts and scenes, although the sequence is somewhat confused:

Act II Scene I – The Library

[Act II] Scene II – The Council Chamber

Act III

Act II Scene I – The same (evening)

Scene II – The Library (next morning)

Act III The Council Chamber (that evening)

[Scene] II The same – the following evening

[Act II] Scene II The library next morning

Bundle and her father (the police and doctor)
Then begins – splutters – I've got Battle. Battle comes in, asks for information. Scene much as before – plenty of rope – gets him to look at body next door – watches him through crack – Antony slips out unnoticed

And the third act is sketched twice, the second time in a more elaborate version:

Act III Scene I The following evening

Assembled in library – George and Battle read code letter – Richmond – they wait – struggle in darkness. Lights go up – Antony holding Lemaitre – always suspected this fellow – colleague from the Surete

Act III That evening ~~Battle and George~~

Virginia, Lord C, Bundle go to bed. Lights out – George and Battle – the cipher – George 3 – man in armour. They [struggle] – door opens – the window – shadows. Suddenly outbreak of activity – they roll over and over – the man in armour clangs down. Suddenly door opens – Lord C. switches on light – others behind him. Battle in front of window – Antony on top of Lemaitre – 'I've got you.'

As the above extract might suggest, *The Secret of Chimneys* is, both as novel and play, a hugely enjoyable but preposterous romp; it is littered with loose ends, unlikely motivations and unconvincing characters. Suspects drop compromising notes; jewel thieves act with uncharacteristic homicidal responses; blackmail victims react with glee at a new 'experience' and bodies are disposed of with everyday nonchalance. And virtually nobody is who or what they seem. Why does Virginia not recognise Anthony if, as is reported in Chapters 15 and 24, she lived for two years in Herzoslovakia? Would someone really mistake a bundle of letters for the manuscript of a book? Would Battle accept Cade's bona-fides so easily? It is difficult not to have a certain amount of sympathy with the pompous George Lomax and to sympathise deeply with the unfortunate Lord Caterham.

There are glimpses of the Christie to come in the final surprise revelation and the double-bluff with King Victor (in a novel about a disputed kingdom, why use this name for a character unconnected with the throne?), but her earlier thriller, *The Man in the Brown Suit*, and the later *The Seven Dials Mystery*, are, if not more credible, at least far less incredible.

## The Mystery of the Blue Train
### 29 March 1928

The elegant train is the setting for the murder of wealthy American Ruth Kettering. Fellow passenger Katherine Grey assists Hercule Poirot as he investigates the murder as well as the disappearance of the fabulous jewel, the Heart of Fire, among the wealthy inhabitants of the French Riviera.

*The Mystery of the Blue Train* was written at the lowest point in Christie's life. In *An Autobiography* she writes, 'Really, how that wretched book came to be written I don't know.' Following her disappearance and her subsequent separation from Archie Christie, she went to Tenerife with her daughter Rosalind and her secretary, Carlo Fisher, to finish the already started book, the writing of which also represented an important milestone. She now realised that her status had advanced from amateur to professional: 'I was driven desperately on by the desire, indeed the necessity, to write another book and make money. [But] I had no joy in writing, no élan. I had worked out the plot – a conventional plot, partly adapted from one of my other stories ... I have always hated *The Mystery of the Blue Train* but I got it written and sent it off to the publishers. It sold just as well as my last book had done. So I had to content myself with that – though I cannot say I have ever been proud of it.'

The short story to which she refers is 'The Plymouth Express', published in April 1923. A minor entry in the Poirot canon, it is doubtful that it merited expansion into a novel. Extra complications in the shape of the history of the Heart of Fire are added in the novel and the inclusion of a new character, Katherine Grey, is significant. Katherine lives in St Mary Mead, although she does not seem to know a certain Miss Jane Marple, who had made her detective debut some three months earlier in 'The Tuesday Night Club'. A quiet, determined, sensible young woman seeing the world for the first time, Katherine is a sympathetic character who captivates Poirot.

Notes for *The Mystery of the Blue Train* are in two Notebooks: Notebook 1 has a mere five pages but Notebook 54 has over eighty, although the entries on each page are relatively short. They all reflect accurately the finished novel; no variations are considered, nor are there any discarded ideas, possibly because it was an expansion of a short story. Notes begin with Chapter 4 and then, twenty pages later, we find a listing of the earlier chapters, suggesting that those notes had been destroyed.

I include a dozen pages from towards the end of Notebook 54. They contain Poirot's explanation of the crimes, a passage so close to the published version in Chapter 35 that it merits reproduction in full. Although the published version is more elaborate, nowhere else in the plotting of her books is there anything else like this. Flowing handwriting covers the pages, elucidating a complex plot with a minimum of deletion. Much of the following passage is almost exactly as Agatha Christie wrote it in Tenerife in 1927; I have added only punctuation. The single most concentrated example of continuous text in the Notebooks, it is an impressive example of Christie's fluency, clarity and readability, all factors that play an important part in her continuing popularity.

'Explanations? Mais oui, I will give them to you. It began with 1 point – the disfigured face, usually a question of identity; but not this time. The murdered woman <u>was</u> undoubtedly Ruth Kettering and I put it aside.'

'When did you first begin to suspect the maid?'

'I did not for some time – one trifling [point] – the note case – her mistress not on such terms as would make it likely – it awakened a doubt. She had only been with her mistress two months yet I could not connect her to the crime since she had been left behind in Paris. But once having a doubt I began to question that statement – how did we know? By the evidence of your secretary, Major Knighton, a completely outside and impartial testimony, and by the dead woman's own ~~confession~~ testimony to the conductor. I put that latter point aside for the moment because a very curious idea was growing up in my mind. Instead, I concentrated on the first point – at first sight it seemed conclusive but it led me to consider Major Knighton and at once certain points occurred to me. To begin with he, also, had only been with you for a period of 2 months and his initial was also K. Supposing – just supposing – that it was <u>his</u> notecase. If Ada Mason and he were working together and she recognised it, would she not act precisely as she had done? At first taken aback, she quickly ~~fell in with him~~ gave herself time to think and then suggested a plausible explanation that fell in with the idea of DK's guilt. That was not the original idea – the Comte de la Roche was to be the stalking horse – but after I had left the hotel she came to you and said she was quite convinced on thinking it over that the man was DK – why the sudden certainty? Clearly because she had had time to consult with someone and had received instructions – who could have given her these instructions? Major Knighton. And then came another slight incident – Knighton happened to mention that he has been at Lady Clanraven's when there had been a jewel robbery there. That might mean nothing or on the other hand it might mean a great deal. And so the links of the chain –'

'But I don't understand. Who was the man in the train?'

'There <u>was</u> no man – don't you see the cleverness of it all? Whose words have we for it, that there was a man. Only Ada Mason's – and we believe in Ada Mason because of Knighton's testimony.'

'And what Ruth said . . .'

'I am coming to that – yes – Mrs. Kettering's own testimony. But Mrs Kettering's testimony is that of a dead woman, who cannot come forward to dispute it.'

'You mean the conductor lied?'

'Not knowingly – the woman who spoke to him he believed in all good faith to be Mrs Kettering.'

'Do you mean that it wasn't her?'

'I mean that the woman who spoke to the conductor was the maid, dressed in her mistress's clothes – ~~wearing her~~ very distinctive clothes remember – more noticeable than the woman herself – the little red hat jammed down over the eyes – the long mink coat – the bunch of auburn curls each side of the face. Do you not know, however, that it is a commonplace nowadays how like one woman is to another in her street clothes.'

'But he must have noticed the change?'

'Not necessarily, ~~he saw~~ The maid handed him the tickets – he hadn't seen the mistress until he came to make up the bed. That was the first time he had a good look at her and that was the reason for disfiguring the face – he would probably have noticed that the dead woman was not the same as the woman he had talked to. ~~M. Grey would~~ The dining room attendants might have noticed and M. Grey of course would have, but by ordering a dinner basket that danger was avoided.'

'Then – where was Ruth?'

P[oirot] paused a minute and then said very quietly 'Mrs Kettering's dead body was rolled up in the rug on the floor in the adjoining compartment.'

'My God!'

'It is easily understood. Major Knighton was in Paris – on your business. He boarded the train somewhere on its way round the *ceinture* – he spoke perhaps of bringing some message from you – then he draws her attention to something out of the window slips the cord round her neck and pulls . . . .It is over in a minute. They ~~roll up~~ put the body in the adjoining compartment of which the door into the corridor is locked. Major Knighton hops off the train again – with the jewel case. Since the crime is not supposed to be committed until several hours later he is perfectly safe and his evidence and the supposed Mrs. Kettering's words to the conductor will prove an alibi for her.

At the Gare de Lyon Ada Mason gets a dinner basket – then locks the door of her compartment – hurriedly changes into her mistress's clothing – making up to resemble her and adjusting some false auburn curls – she is about the same height. Katherine Grey saw her standing looking out of her window later in the evening and would have been prepared to swear that she was still alive then. Before getting to Lyons, she arranges the body in the bunk, changes ~~Her own~~ into a man's clothing and prepares to leave the train. ~~It must have been then that~~ When Derek Kettering enters his wife's compartment the scene had been set and Ada Mason was in the other compartment waiting for the train to stop so as to leave the train unobserved – it is now drawn into Lyons – the conductor swings himself down – she follows, unobtrusively however, to proceed by slouching inelegantly along as though just taking the air but in reality she crosses over and takes the first train back to Paris where she establishes herself at the Ritz. Her name has been ~~entered~~ registered as booking a room the night before by one of Knighton's female accomplices; she has only to wait for Mr. Van Aldin's arrival. The jewels are in Knighton's possession – not hers – and he disposes of them to Mr

Papapolous[22] in Nice as arranged beforehand, entrusting them to her care only at the last minute to deliver to the Greek. All the same she made one little slip . . .'

'When did you first connect Knighton with the Marquis?'

'I had a hint from Mr Papapolous and I collected certain information from Scotland Yard – I applied it to Knighton and it fitted. He spoke French like a Frenchman; he had been in America and France and England at roughly the same times as the Marquis was operating. He had been last heard of doing jewel robberies in Switzerland and it was in Switzerland that you first met Major K. The Marquis was famous for his charm of manner [which he used] to induce you to offer him the post of secretary. It was at that time that rumours were going round about your purchase of the rubies – the Marquis meant to have these rubies. In seeing that you had given them to your daughter he installed his accomplice as her maid. It was a wonderful plan yet like great men he has his weakness – he fell genuinely in love with Miss Grey. It was that which made him so desirous of shifting the crime from Mr Comte de la Roche to Derek Kettering when the opportunity presented itself. And Miss Grey suspected the truth. She is not a fanciful woman by any means but she declares that she distinctly felt your daughter's presence beside her one day at the Casino; she says she was convinced that the dead woman was trying to tell her something. Knighton had just left her – and it was gradually [borne in on her] what Mrs Kettering had been trying to convey to her – that Knighton was the man who had murdered her. The idea seemed so fantastic at the time that Miss Grey spoke of it to no one. But she acted on the assumption that it was true – she did not discourage Knighton's advances, and she pretended to him that she believed in Derek Kettering's guilt. . . .

---

22   Despite the spelling in the published version, this name is spelt Papapolous in Notebook 54.

'There was one thing that was a shocking blow. Major Knighton had a distinct limp, the result of a wound – the Marquis had no such limp – that was a stumbling block. Then Miss Tamplin mentioned one day that it had been a great surprise to the doctors that he should limp – that suggested camouflage. When I was in London I went to the surgeon who had ~~looked after~~ been in charge at Lady Tamplin's Hospital and I got various technical details from him which confirmed my assumption. Then I met Miss Grey and found that she had been working towards the same end as myself. She had the cuttings to add – one a cutting of a jewel robbery at Lady Tamplin's Hospital, another link in the chain of probability and also that when she was out walking with Major Knighton at St. Mary Mead, he was so much off his guard that he forgot to limp – it was only a momentary lapse but she noted it. She had suspicion that I was on the same track when I wrote to her from the Ritz. I had some trouble in my inquiries there but in the end I got what I wanted – evidence that Ada Mason actually arrived on the morning after the crime.'

# My Favourite Stories and 'The Man Who Knew'

'Looking back over the past, I become increasingly sure of one thing. My tastes have remained fundamentally the same.'

*An Autobiography*

———————◄◉►———————

What were Agatha Christie's own personal favourites of her output? In February 1972, in reply to a Japanese reader, she listed, with brief comments, her favourite books. But she makes an important point when she writes that her list of favourites would 'vary from time to time, as every now and then I re-read an early book . . . and then I alter my opinion, sometimes thinking that it is much better than I thought it was – or nor as good as I had thought'. Although the choices are numbered it is not clear if they are in order of preference; she adds brief comments and reiterates her earlier point at the outset:

At the moment my own list would possibly be:
*And Then There Were None* – 'a difficult technique which was a challenge . . .'
*The Murder of Roger Ackroyd* – 'a general favourite . . .'
*A Murder is Announced* – 'all the characters interesting . . .'
*Murder on the Orient Express* – '. . . it was a new idea for a plot.'
*The Thirteen Problems* – 'a good series of short stories.'

*Towards Zero* – '. . . interesting idea of people from different places coming towards a murder instead of starting with the murder and working from that.'

*Endless Night* – 'my own favourite at present.'

*Crooked House* – '. . . a study of a certain family interesting to explore.'

*Ordeal by Innocence* – 'an idea I had for some time before starting to work upon it.'

*The Moving Finger* – 're-read lately and enjoyed reading it again, very much.'

The list does not contain any great surprises and most fans would probably also select most of the same titles, perhaps replacing *The Thirteen Problems* and *The Moving Finger* with *The Labours of Hercules* and *The ABC Murders* respectively. Despite, or perhaps because of, Christie's lifelong association with Hercule Poirot, there are only two of his cases included, while Miss Marple is represented by three. Each decade of her writing career is represented and no less than five of the list are non-series titles.

A further insight, this time into some of her favourite short stories, came two years later. In March 1974 negotiations began between Collins and the author on the thorny subject of that year's 'Christie for Christmas'. 'Thorny' because the previous year's *Postern of Fate* had been a disappointment and, at the request of Christie's daughter Rosalind, the publisher was not pressing for a new book. The compromise was to be a collection of previously published short stories. Sir William ('Billy') Collins mooted the idea of a collection of Poirot short stories but, in a letter ('Dear Billy'), his creator felt that a book of stories entirely devoted to Hercule Poirot would be 'terribly monotonous' and 'no fun at all'. She hoped to persuade him that the collection 'could also include what you might describe as Agatha Christie's own favourites among her own early stories'. To this end she sent him a list described as 'my own favourite stories written soon after *The Mysterious Affair at Styles,* some before that'.

Before looking at this list it is important to remember that Dame Agatha was now in her eighty-fourth year, in failing health and a pale shadow of the creative genius of earlier years. She had not written a pure whodunit since *A Caribbean Mystery* in 1964 and the novels of recent years were all journeys into the past (both her own and her characters'), lacking the ingenious plots and coherent writing of her prime. If she had compiled a similar list even ten years earlier is it entirely possible that it would have been significantly different. Even the description of 'early stories' was, as we shall see, misleading.

Christie's 1974 list reads as follows:

The Red Signal
The Lamp
The Gipsy
The Mystery of the Blue Jar
The Case of Sir Andrew Carmichael
The Call of Wings
The Last Séance
S.O.S.
In a Glass Darkly
The Dressmaker's Doll
Sanctuary
Swan Song
The Love Detectives
Death by Drowning

Also included are two full-length novels, *Dumb Witness* and *Death Comes as the End,* although she acknowledges that the former is too long for inclusion. Perhaps significantly, in both these titles, like her recent publications, there are strong elements of 'murder in retrospect'; *Death Comes as the End* deals with murder in ancient Egypt and *Dumb Witness* finds Poirot investigating a death that occurred some months before the book begins. On her list the titles are numbered but there is no indication that the order is significant. I have regrouped them for ease of discussion.

The first eight titles are all from the 1933 UK-only collection *The Hound of Death*. As Christie suspected, many of them had been published prior to this in various magazines, the earliest (so far traced) as far back as June 1924 when 'The Red Signal' appeared in *The Grand*. The supernatural is the common theme linking these stories, with only 'The Mystery of the Blue Jar', published in *The Grand* the following month, offering a rational explanation. This type of story was on Christie's mind as, later in the accompanying letter, she explains that she was planning a 'semi-ghost story', adding poignantly, 'when I am really quite myself again.' Some of these titles are particularly effective – 'The Lamp' has a chilling last line and 'The Red Signal', despite its supernatural overtones, shows Christie at her tricky best. 'The Last Séance' (March 1927) is a very dark and, unusually for Christie, gruesome story, which also exists in a full-length play version among her papers; while 'The Call of Wings' is one of the earliest stories she wrote, described in *An Autobiography* as 'not bad'.

Of the remaining six titles, 'In a Glass Darkly' (December 1934) and 'The Dressmaker's Doll' (December 1958) are also concerned with supernatural events. The former is a very short story involving precognition while the latter is a late story that Christie felt that she 'had to write' while plotting *Ordeal by Innocence*. She passed it to her agent in mid-December 1957 and it was published the following year; in a note she describes it as a 'very favourite' story. 'Sanctuary' is also a late story, written in January 1954 and published in October of that year, and features a dying man found on the chancel steps while the sun pours in through the stained-glass window, this picture carrying echoes of similar scenes in the Mr Quin stories. Its setting is Chipping Cleghorn, featured four years earlier in *A Murder is Announced*, and that novel's Rev. Harmon and his delightful wife, Bunch, are the main protagonists alongside Miss Marple.

'Swan Song', published in *The Grand* in September 1926, is a surprising inclusion and appears probably due to Christie's lifelong love of music; despite its country house setting of an opera production, it is a lacklustre revenge story with neither a whodunit nor supernatural element. 'The Love Detectives', published in December of the same year, foreshadows the plot of *The Murder at the Vicarage* and features Mr Satterthwaite, usually the partner of Mr Quin but here making a solo appearance.

The final story, 'Death by Drowning', is the last of *The Thirteen Problems*, although its inclusion jars with the rest of the stories in that collection. Unlike the first twelve problems, 'Death by Drowning' (November 1931) does not follow the pattern of a group of armchair detectives solving a crime that has hitherto baffled the police. Miss Marple solves this case without her fellow-detectives and makes one of her very rare forays into working-class territory in a story involving a woman who keeps lodgers and takes in laundry. As an untypical Miss Marple story, it is another unpredictable inclusion.

Overall, the list is, like much of her fiction, very unexpected. Though the absence of Poirot can be explained by the fact that this list is an effort to persuade Collins to experiment with characters other than the little Belgian, there is, for instance, only one Mr Quin story, although she describes them in *An Autobiography* as 'her favourite'; and there are only two cases for Miss Marple, neither of which shows her at her best. Why, moreover, no 'Accident', no 'The Witness for the Prosecution', no 'Philomel Cottage'? And only three ('Sanctuary', 'The Love Detectives', 'Death by Drowning') can be described as Christie whodunits, albeit not very typical examples. The over-reliance on the supernatural is surprising, although this had been a feature of Christie's fiction from her early days – *The Mysterious Mr Quin*,

*The Hound of Death* – and is a plot feature, although usually in the red herring category, of such novels as *The Sittaford Mystery, Peril at End House, Dumb Witness, The Pale Horse* and *Sleeping Murder*.

In the event, the proposed book never came to fruition and, despite Christie's reservations, *Poirot's Early Cases* was published in November 1974.

Pre-dating both these lists, *An Autobiography* names yet another selection of 'favourites'. Here she describes *Crooked House* and *Ordeal by Innocence* as 'the two [books] that satisfy me best', and goes on to state that 'on re-reading them the other day, I find that another one I am really pleased with is *The Moving Finger*'. A *Sunday Times* interview with literary critic Francis Wyndham in February 1966 confirms these three titles as favourites, although the interview may have been contemporaneous with the completion of *An Autobiography* in October 1965 where the mention of the three titles comes in the closing pages. In the specially written Introduction to the Penguin paperback edition of *Crooked House* she wrote: 'This book is one of my own special favourites. I saved it up for years, thinking about, working it out, saying to myself "One day when I've plenty of time, and really want to enjoy myself – I'll begin it."'

Whatever her favourites, there seems little doubt about her least favourite title. Not only was *The Mystery of the Blue Train* difficult to compose but in *An Autobiography* she writes 'Each time I read it again, I think it commonplace, full of clichés, with an uninteresting plot.' In the Japanese fan letter she calls it 'conventionally written . . . [it] does not seem to me to be a very original plot.' She is even more disparaging in the Wyndham interview when she says, 'Easily the worst book I ever wrote was *The Mystery of the Blue Train*. I hate it.'

In view of the inclusion of 'The Red Signal' on the 1974 list above, it is appropriate to include 'The Man Who Knew', a very short short story – less than 2,000 words – from the

Christie Archive, and to compare and contrast it with its later incarnation, 'The Red Signal'.

The typescript is undated, the only guide a reference in the first paragraph to No Man's Land, suggesting that the First World War is over. In all probability, its composition pre-dates the publication of *The Mysterious Affair at Styles*; and this makes its very existence surprising. Very few short story manuscripts or typescripts, even from later in Christie's career, have survived, so one from the very start of her writing life is remarkable.

The only handwritten amendments are insignificant ones ('minute service flat' is changed to 'little service flat'), but some minor errors of spelling and punctuation have here been corrected.

# THE MAN WHO KNEW

Something was wrong . . .

Derek Lawson, halting on the threshold of his flat, peering into the darkness, knew it instinctively. In France, amongst the perils of No Man's Land, he had learned to trust this strange sense that warned him of danger. There was danger now – close to him . . .

Rallying, he told himself the thing was impossible. Withdrawing his latchkey from the door, he switched on the electric light. The hall of the flat, prosaic and commonplace, confronted him. Nothing. What should there be? And still, he knew, insistently and undeniably, that something was wrong . . .

Methodically and systematically, he searched the flat. It was just possible that some intruder was concealed there. Yet all the time he knew that the matter was graver than a mere attempted burglary. The menace was to *him*, not to his property. At last he desisted, convinced that he was alone in the flat.

'Nerves,' he said aloud. 'That's what it is. Nerves!'

By sheer force of will, he strove to drive the obsession of imminent peril from him. And then his eyes fell on the theatre programme that he still held, carelessly clasped in his hand. On the margin of it were three words, scrawled in pencil.

'Don't go home.'

For a moment, he was lost in astonishment – as though the

writing partook of the supernatural. Then he pulled himself together. His instinct had been right – there *was* something. Again he searched the little service flat, but this time his eyes, alert and observant, sought carefully some detail, some faint deviation from the normal, which should give him the clue to the affair. And at last he found it. One of the bureau drawers was not shut to, something hanging out prevented it closing, and he remembered, with perfect clearness, closing the drawer himself earlier in the evening. There had been nothing hanging out then.

His lips setting in a determined line, he pulled the drawer open. Underneath the ties and handkerchiefs, he felt the outline of something hard – something that had not been there previously. With amazement on his countenance, he drew out – a revolver!

He examined it attentively, but beyond the fact that it was of somewhat unusual calibre, and that a shot had lately been fired from it, it told him nothing.

He sat down on the bed, the revolver in his hand. Once again he studied the pencilled words on the programme. Who had been at the theatre party? Cyril Dalton, Noel Western and his wife, Agnes Haverfield and young Frensham. Which of them had written that message? Which of them *knew* – knew what? His speculations were brought up with a jerk. He was as far as ever from understanding the meaning of that revolver in his drawer. Was it, perhaps, some practical joke? But instantly his inner self negatived that, and the conviction that he was in danger, in grave immediate peril, heightened. A voice within him seemed to be crying out, insistently and urgently: 'Unless you understand, you are lost.'

And then, in the street below, he heard a newsboy calling. Acting on impulse, he slipped the revolver into his pocket, and, banging the door of the flat behind him, hurriedly descended the stairs. Outside the block of buildings, he came face to face with the newsvendor.

''Orrible murder of a well known physician. 'Orrible murder of a – paper, sir?'

He shoved a coin into the boy's hand, and seized the flimsy sheet. In staring headlines he found what he wanted.

### HARLEY STREET SPECIALIST MURDERED.
### SIR JAMES LAWSON FOUND SHOT THROUGH
### THE HEART.

His uncle: Shot!

He read on. The bullet had been fired from a revolver, but the weapon had not been found, thus disposing of the idea of suicide.

The weapon – *it was in his pocket now*: why he knew this with such certainty, he could not have said. But it was so. He accepted it without doubt, and in a blinding flash the terrible peril of his position became clear to him.

He was his uncle's heir – he was in grave financial difficulties. And only that morning he had quarrelled with the old man. It had been a loud bitter quarrel, doubtless overheard by the servants. He had said more than he meant, of course – used threats – it would all tell against him! And as a culminating proof of his guilt, they would have found the revolver in his drawer . . .

*Who had placed it there?*

It all hung on that. There might still be time. He thought desperately, his brain, keen and quick, selecting and rejecting the various arguments. And at last he saw . . .

A taxi deposited him at the door of the house he sought.

'Mr Western still up?'

'Yes, sir. He's in the study.'

'Ah!' Derek arrrested the old butler's progress. 'You needn't announce me. I know the way.'

Walking almost noiselessly upon the thick pile of the carpet, he opened the door at the end of the hall and entered the room. Noel Western was sitting by the table, his back to the door. A fair, florid man; good looking, yet with a something in his eyes that baffled and eluded. Not till Derek's hand touched his shoulder, was he aware of the other's presence. He leaped in his chair.

'My God, you!' He forced a laugh. 'What a start you gave me, old chap. What is it? Did you leave something behind here?'

'No.' Derek advanced a step. 'I came to return you – *this*!'

Taking the revolver from his pocket he threw it on the table. If he had had any doubts, they vanished now before the look on the other's face.

'What-what is it?' stammered Western.

'The revolver with which you shot James Lawson.'

'That's a lie.' The denial came feebly.

'It's the truth. You took my latchkey out of my overcoat pocket this evening. You remember that your wife and I went in the first taxi to the theatre. You followed in another, arriving rather late. You were late because you had been to my rooms to place the revolver in my drawer.'

Derek spoke with absolute certainty and conviction. An almost supernatural fear showed upon Noel Western's face.

'How – how did you know?' he muttered, as it were in spite of himself.

'*I* warned him.'

Both men started and turned. Stella Western, tall and beautiful, stood in the doorway which connected with an adjoining room. Her fairness gleamed white against the sombre green of the window curtains.

'I warned him,' she repeated, her eyes full on her husband. 'Tonight, when Mr Lawson mentioned casually something about returning home, I saw your face. I was just beside you, although you did not notice me, and I heard you mutter between your teeth "There'll be a surprise for you when you do get home!" And the look on your face was – devilish. I was afraid. I had no chance of saying anything to Mr Lawson, but I wrote a few words on the programme and passed it to him.

I didn't know what you meant, or what you had planned – but I was afraid.'

'Afraid, were you?' cried Western. 'Afraid for *him*! You still may be! That's why I did it! That's why he'll hang – yes, hang – hang – hang! Because you love him!' His voice had risen almost to a scream, as he thrust his head forward with blazing eyes. 'Yes – I knew! You loved him! That's why you wanted me to see that meddling old fool, Lawson, who called himself a mental specialist. You wanted to make out I was mad. You wanted me put away – shut up – so that you could go to your lover!'

'By God, Western,' said Derek, taking a step forward with blazing eyes. He dared not look at Stella. But behind his anger and indignation, a wild exultation possessed him. She loved him! Only too well he knew that he loved her. From the first moment he had set eyes on her, his doom was sealed. But she was another man's wife – and that man his friend. He had fought down his love valiantly, and never, for one moment, had he suspected there was any feeling on her side. If he had known that – he struggled to be calm. He must defend her from these raving accusations.

'It was a conspiracy – a great conspiracy.' The high unnatural voice took no heed of Derek. 'Old Lawson was in it. He questioned me – he trapped me – found out all about my mother having died in an asylum (Ha ha! Stella, you never knew that, did you?). Then he spoke about a sanitorium – a rest cure – all lies! Lies – so that you could get rid of me and go to your lover here.'

'Western, you lie! I've never spoken a word to your wife that the whole world couldn't hear.'

Noel Western laughed, and the laugh frightened them both, for in it was all the low cunning of a maniac.

'You say so, do you? *You* say so!' Carried away by fury, his voice rose higher and higher, drowning the protests of the other, drowning the sound of the opening door. 'But I've been too clever for you! Old Lawson's dead. I shot him. Lord!

what fun it was – knowing who'd hang for it! You see, I'd heard of your quarrel, and I knew you were in pretty deep financial water. The whole thing would look ugly. I saw it all clearly before me. Lawson dead, you hung, and Stella – pretty Stella – all to myself! Ha ha!'

For the first time, the woman flinched. She put up her hands to her face with a shivering sob.

'You say you saw it all clearly before you,' said Derek. There was a new note in his voice, a note of solemnity. 'Did you never think that there was something *behind* you?'

Quelled in spite of himself, Noel Western stared fearfully at the man before him.

'What – what do you mean?'

'Justice.' The word cut the air with the sharpness of steel.

A mocking smile came to Western's lips.

'The justice of God, oh?' he laughed.

'And the justice of men. *Look behind you!*'

Western spun round to face a group of three standing in the doorway, whilst the old butler repeated the sentence that his master's words had drowned before.

'Two gentlemen from Scotland Yard to see Mr Lawson, sir.'

An awful change came over Noel Western's face. He flung up his arms and fell. Derek bent over him, then straightened himself.

'The justice of God is more merciful than that of men,' he said. 'You do not wish to detain me, gentlemen? No? Then I will go.' For a moment his eyes met Stella's, and he added softly: 'But I shall come back . . .'

—◦—

The expansion of 'The Man Who Knew' into 'The Red Signal' suggests that Christie rewrote this after some experience in plotting a detective story. 'The Red Signal' was first published in June 1924, so it was written probably the previous year and, therefore, after the publication of *The Mysterious Affair at Styles* and *The Murder on the Links*, both novels with carefully constructed plots and unsuspected denouements. By the beginning of 1924 she had also published a dozen Poirot short stories, so technically she was now more adept at laying clues, both true and false, misdirecting the reader and springing a surprise.

Plot-wise both versions of the story are identical, the later one merely longer and more elaborate than the earlier. Some elements remain exactly the same: the description of Stella's husband as 'florid', the ominous words 'Don't go home', the revolver found in the handkerchief drawer. But 'The Red Signal' has a larger cast of characters, a greater emphasis on the supernatural and a more unexpected final revelation. Unlike the earlier version, the reader is encouraged to trust the character unmasked as the villain; in the earlier version Noel Western is unknown to the reader until his unmasking. The cunning hand of Christie the detective novelist can be seen in some of the plot expansion: the ambiguous conversation between Dermot and his uncle when we are mistakenly confident, after subtle misdirection, that the subject of the conversation about insanity is Clair; the red signal of the title and the warning 'Don't go home', which applies equally to Sir Arlington and to Dermot; and the ruse of Dermot masquerading as his own servant, which would become one of Christie's favourite stratagems for hoodwinking her readers. On a more mundane note however, is it likely that a newsboy would sell newspapers and shout headlines at close to midnight? If the party has just returned from the theatre it cannot be much earlier.

While by no means a typical Christie tale, we can see how, after writing a mere handful of detective stories, Agatha Christie was able to transform a slight short story such as 'The Man Who Knew' into a clever exercise in misdirection.

# II

## The Second Decade 1930–1939

'The funny thing is that I have little memory of the books
I wrote just after my marriage.'

*An Autobiography*

—◆◇◆—

**SOLUTIONS REVEALED**

*After the Funeral* • *Appointment With Death* • *Black Coffee* •
*Curtain: Poirot's Last Case* • 'Dead Man's Mirror' • *Death in
the Clouds* • *Death on the Nile* • 'Death on the Nile' • 'The
Dream' • *Evil under the Sun* • *Endless Night* • 'Greenshaw's
Folly' • *Hercule Poirot's Christmas* • 'How Does Your Garden
Grow?' • *Lord Edgware Dies* • 'The Love Detectives' • 'The
Market Basing Mystery' • *The Mirror Crack'd from Side to Side*
• *The Murder at the Vicarage* • *Murder in Mesopotamia* •
'Murder in the Mews' • *A Murder Is Announced* • *The
Mysterious Affair at Styles* • 'The Mystery of the Baghdad
Chest' • *The Mystery of the Blue Train* • *One, Two, Buckle My
Shoe* • *Peril at End House* • 'Problem at Sea' • *Sad Cypress*
• 'The Second Gong' • *The Sittaford Mystery* • *Sparkling
Cyanide* • *Taken at the Flood* • *Three Act Tragedy* • 'Triangle
at Rhodes' • *Why Didn't They Ask Evans?*

—◆◇◆—

The years 1930 to 1939 were undoubtedly Agatha Christie's
Golden Age, in terms of ingenuity, productivity and diversity.

In 1930 she published the first Miss Marple novel, *The Murder at the Vicarage*, and the first Mary Westmacott, *Giant's Bread*. By the end of the decade she had produced a further sixteen full-length novels and six short story/novella collections (seven if the 1939 US-only *The Regatta Mystery* is included). Most of her classic titles appeared in this decade. She experimented with the detective story form in *And Then There Were None* (1939), she broke the rules in *Murder on the Orient Express* (1934), she pioneered an early example of the serial killer in *The ABC Murders* (1936) and made a brief return to the light-hearted thriller with *Why Didn't They Ask Evans?* (1934). Reflecting her own love of travel, she sent Poirot abroad in *Murder in Mesopotamia* (1936), *Death on the Nile* (1937) and *Appointment with Death* (1938), for the type of detective experience not shared by most of his literary crime-solving contemporaries.

As well as an impressive output of detective novels, she also published short stories: crime fantasy with *The Mysterious Mr Quin* (1930), the supernatural in *The Hound of Death* (1933), a mixture of crime, romance and light-hearted adventure in *The Listerdale Mystery* and *Parker Pyne Investigates* (both 1934); and mastered the difficult novella form in *Murder in the Mews* (1937). Despite the first appearance of Miss Marple in a full-length book and the publication of some of Poirot's best cases, she also published non-series titles: *The Sittaford Mystery* (1931) and *Murder is Easy* (1939). In addition, she wrote the scripts for *Black Coffee* (1930), her only original Poirot play, and *Akhnaton* (written 1937), a historical drama set in ancient Egypt. She contributed to the round-robin detective stories of the Detection Club, *Behind the Screen* in 1930 and *The Floating Admiral* and *The Scoop* in 1931; and she wrote her first radio play, *Yellow Iris* (1937).

She would never again – perhaps not surprisingly – equal this productivity; the second half of the following decade saw her slow down to a mere one title a year. But the truly astonishing aspect of this output is not just the volume but also the consistency. None of the titles produced in these years fall below the level of excellent. All of them display her talents – ingenuity and readability, intricacy and simplicity – at the height of their powers and many are now recognised classics of the genre, representing a standard which other crime writers strove to match.

Her work was in demand for the lucrative magazine market in the UK and North America and for translation throughout Europe. She was one of the first writers to be chosen, in 1935, for publication in the new Penguin paperbacks; and her hardback sales for each new title entered the five-figure category. From *Three Act Tragedy* (1935) onwards her first-year sales never fell below 10,000. Film versions of her work – *Alibi* (based on *The Murder of Roger Ackroyd*) and *Black Coffee,* both in 1931, and *Lord Edgware Dies* in 1934 – were released, although all three featured a seriously miscast Austin Trevor, a six foot tall Irishman, in the role of Poirot; and *Love from a Stranger,* adapted from the short story 'Philomel Cottage', appeared in 1937 with Joan Hickson (who would achieve international fame almost 50 years later as the definitive TV Miss Marple) in a small role. *Black Coffee* and *Love from a Stranger* had been produced as stage plays earlier in the decade; and *Chimneys,* her own stage adaptation of her 1925 novel, was scheduled – but mysteriously failed – to appear in 1931. The first Christie, and Poirot, on television came in June 1937 with the broadcast of *Wasp's Nest.*

It is entirely possible that Christie's happy personal life was, at least in part, responsible for this productive professional life. In September 1930 she had married Max Mallowan, thus ending the profoundly unhappy period of her life which began with the death of her mother in 1926 and culminated in her divorce from Archie Christie in 1928. Secure in a stable marriage, with a happy and healthy daughter, and spending some months of every year cheerfully working on an archaeological dig alongside her husband, she produced new books with enviable ease. And to judge from the evidence of the Notebooks, plot ideas for future books were not in short supply. The early 1930s coincide with the most indecipherable pages of the Notebooks, when her handwriting could hardly keep pace with her ingenuity. By the mid 1930s, reading the latest Agatha Christie had become not just a national but an international pastime.

### 'The Bird with the Broken Wing'
April 1930

---

Mr Satterthwaite is summoned by the mysterious Mr Quin to a house party where he saves one life but fails to save another.

---

In a specially commissioned Introduction for the 1953 Penguin edition of *The Mysterious Mr Quin* Christie wrote that she considered Mr Quin 'an epicure's taste'; he was 'a figure invisible except when he chose, not quite human, yet concerned with the affairs of human beings'. His companion in all of the stories is elderly Mr Satterthwaite, 'the gossip, the looker-on at life' who 'recognises drama when he sees it'. Harley Quin, who takes his name and his appearance from the *Commedia dell'arte* Harlequin figure in the china cabinet from Christie's childhood home, Ashfield, magically appears when there is a problem – frequently, but not invariably, a mysterious death – to be solved.

The first Mr Quin story, 'The Coming of Mr Quin', was published in March 1924 and between that date and April 1930, when the collection *The Mysterious Mr Quin* was published, a further ten stories appeared. An earlier publication of 'The Bird with the Broken Wing' has not yet been traced and it is very possible that its book appearance was its first.

It is an oddly perfunctory tale in which, unlike most of the other stories, Mr Quin makes only a cameo appearance on the last page; his name is 'spelt' during the table-turning with which the story opens and the appearance in nearby woods of a Harlequin-like figure is mentioned by one of the characters.

Notebooks 33 and 59 have brief notes for the story. Immediately following in the latter are extended notes for *The Sittaford Mystery*, published the following year, lending strength to the theory that the story was written later than the others, possibly in order to bring the tally for a collection to an even dozen. Both sets of notes contain reference to 'The Black Swan' and it would seem that this was under consideration as the title.

Notebook 33 summarises the main plot elements, although names and details were to change:

> Table turning. Mr S present – a message for you – name of Quin.
> Black Swan
> Mrs McCrane – she has gone to stay with some people – at Laidel. Mr S hurries off there – as it is near at hand – met by distraught husband – Isabel hanged herself on back of door – The police are there – ~~Inspector~~ Chief Constable – a friend of Mr S's. Didn't do it herself – they didn't get on – far away from anywhere

Notebook 59 contains more detail and the accurate name of the victim, although Kerslake will change to Graham:

> ~~The Black Swan~~
> Bird with Broken Wing
> Mabelle hangs on the door – the Black Swan – so many of that family queer. Husband says she had not come up to bed when he retired – host says she did – only room along that passage.

> Mr Kerslake – he denies she ever went in there – his mother
> – Mrs Kerslake opposite – white haired – inflexible – papers
> burnt – fragments of letter – ~~to her~~ from her son

The clue that is the key to the solution of the case is noted:

> Then someone puts [the ukele] back. Housemaid asked –
> she says thinks in early morning – he asks someone to play
> yuke – they say not in tune – tune it up – string snaps.
> Examines it – not an A string at all

Despite the inclusion of Mr Satterthwaite on the first page of these notes brief consideration is given to:

> Either Miss Marple...or Poirot? or Mr Quin?

Perhaps this musing gave rise to the presence of Mr Satterthwaite alongside Poirot a few years later in *Three Act Tragedy* and, briefly, 'Dead Man's Mirror'?

And, finally, the brief closing scene with Mr Quin is also sketched:

> 'I might have saved her –
> Mr Q says – Is death the greatest evil?

It should be remembered that the following year's book, *The Sittaford Mystery*, opened with a similar pivotal scene of table-turning; and the first page of 'The Bird with the Broken Wing' also contains, serendipitously, the title of a novel from a decade later: *N or M?*

## *'Manx Gold'*

May 1930

Cousins Juan and Fenella race to find a treasure as they match wits with their dead uncle – and a killer.

A full history of this story can be found in the 1997 collection *While the Light Lasts,* thanks to sterling detective work by its editor Tony Medawar. Briefly, the chairman of a tourism committee in the Isle of Man approached Christie, in late 1929, with a view to her creating a treasure hunt on the island to boost tourist numbers. After a visit in April 1930 she wrote 'Manx Gold', for a fee of £65 (approx. £1,300 today), and it was published in five instalments, complete with clues, in the *Manchester Daily Dispatch,* in the third week of May of that year, and in a booklet distributed throughout the island. The 'treasure' was four snuffboxes hidden in separate locations around the island. (It is at an exhibition of snuff-boxes that Hercule Poirot meets Mr Shaitana in *Cards on the Table.*)

Notebook 59 has twenty pages of notes for this unusual commission. Unfortunately those pages contain some of the most indecipherable notes of any Notebook, with much crossing out, doodling and rough diagrams. The story is a minor effort, remarkable mainly for the uniqueness of its creation and for the number of ideas that were to resurface in a book four years later. A snapshot and a dying man's last words as well as a villainous doctor are all features of *Why Didn't They Ask Evans?*. And, indeed, Juan and Fenella, a couple joining forces to elucidate a mystery, could be seen as fore-runners of Bobby Jones and Lady Frances Derwent from that novel. (Oddly, Juan and Fenella are both fiancés and first cousins.) The invisible ink idea first surfaced in 'Motive Vs.

Opportunity' two years earlier and as a minor plot element in Chapter 20 of *The Secret Adversary*.

The notes accurately reflect the story as it appeared. There were however some name changes – Ronald and Celia become Juan and Fenella and Robert becomes Ewan – while the cliff fall and cuff-link clue were eventually discarded:

> Story
> Ronald and Celia – first cousins – letter from deceased uncle. Her annoyance about uncle – they arrive – the housekeeper – 4 snuff boxes missing. Letter left – with doggerel rhyme – call at lawyers. Then they start off – get it – on their return – meet the others – Dr ~~Crook~~ [Crookall was the name of the chairman of the Tourism Committee!] MacRae – Alan – Robert Bagshawe . . . doesn't like his smile. They decide to pool with others. Next day – the clues – housekeeper goes to get them – stolen – she admits that they asked her and she refused – a cuff link – it was Robert.
>    They dash out – find R in grounds – dying – murdered – hit on head or in hospital – has fallen over cliff. They lean near him – may be conscious at end – opens eyes says 'D'ye ken – ?' – dies

The 'doggerel rhyme' referred to above appears in Notebook 59 in two forms, the one that actually appeared and the following, an earlier unused draft:

> 4 points of the compass so there be, South and West North and East
> A double S – No East for me Fare forth and show how clever you be.

Two of the other clues also appear:

> Excuse verbosity – I am all at sixes and sevens and Words brought out by heat of fire

*A rough sketch (and even rougher handwriting!) of a clue in the search for* Manx Gold, *from Notebook 59.*

Another point of interest in this Notebook is a rough drawing of the clue that falls out of the map of the island – a cross,
a circle and an arrow pointing down to the detail of the little
lines on one side of the circle, as noticed by Fenella.

### The Murder at the Vicarage
13 October 1930

When unpopular churchwarden Colonel Protheroe is
found shot in the vicar's study in St Mary Mead, the vicar's
neighbour identifies seven potential murderers. Two
confessions, an attempted suicide and a robbery confuse
the issue but Miss Marple understands everything when
she realises the significance of the potted palm.

*The Murder at the Vicarage* was the first Agatha Christie title
issued under the new Crime Club imprint, and the first book-
length investigation for Miss Marple. It appeared in serial
form in the USA three months before its UK publication,
leading to the conclusion that the bulk of the novel was
completed during 1929. Disappointingly, Christie writes in
*An Autobiography* that she 'cannot remember where, when or
how I wrote it, why I came to write it or even what suggested
to me that I should select a new character – Miss Marple.'
She goes on to explain that the enjoyment she got from the
creation of the Caroline Sheppard character in *The Murder
of Roger Ackroyd* was a factor in the decision to re-create an
'acidulated spinster, full of curiosity, knowing everything,
hearing everything; the complete detective service in the
home'.

Jane Marple made her first appearance in print in a
series of six short stories published between December 1927

and May 1928 in the *Royal Magazine,* beginning with 'The Tuesday Night Club'. A further six stories were published between December 1929 and May 1930 in *The Story-Teller* and all twelve were published, with the addition of 'Death by Drowning', as *The Thirteen Problems* in June 1932. In the first story Miss Marple sits in her house in St Mary Mead, dressed completely in black – black brocade dress, black mittens and black lace cap – in the big grandfather chair, knitting and listening and solving crimes that have baffled the police. She is described as 'smiling gently' and having 'benignant and kindly' blue eyes. But the first description we receive of her, from the vicar's wife, Griselda, in *The Murder at the Vicarage* is 'that terrible Miss Marple . . . the worst cat in the village'. The vicar himself, while describing her as 'a white-haired old lady with a gentle, appealing manner', also concedes that 'she is much more dangerous' than her fellow parishioner, the gushing Miss Wetherby. He captures the essence of Miss Marple when he states in Chapter 4 that 'There's no detective in England equal to a spinster lady of uncertain age with plenty of time on her hands.' By 1942 and *The Body in the Library*, Miss Marple has cast off, temporarily at least, both St Mary Mead and her black lace mittens to accompany Dolly Bantry to the Majestic Hotel in Danemouth to solve the murder of Ruby Keene. And thereby to join the company of the Great Detectives.

*The Murder at the Vicarage* has its origins in the Messrs Satterthwaite and Quin short story 'The Love Detectives', published in December 1926 in *The Story-Teller* magazine. Here two adulterous lovers commit murder and then confess separately, confident in the knowledge that if they make the 'confessions' incredible enough (they each claim to have used different and incorrect weapons), neither of them will be believed. In both short story and novel the victim is the husband, and the killers are his wife and her lover. Significantly, in each case a stopped clock causes confusion as to the time of death. The novel adapts the motive, the means and the device of false confessions, adds extra suspects and replaces the duo of Satterthwaite and Quin with Miss Marple; but they are, essentially, the same story.

The notes for *The Murder at the Vicarage* are all contained in Notebook 33 and consist of 70 very organised pages that closely follow the progress of the novel. For the early chapters the chapter number is included; thereafter the remainder of the notes follow the novel in chronological order with little in the notebook that is not included in the published version. Two maps of St Mary Mead are included and the rest of Notebook 33 contains the draft for *Three Act Tragedy*.

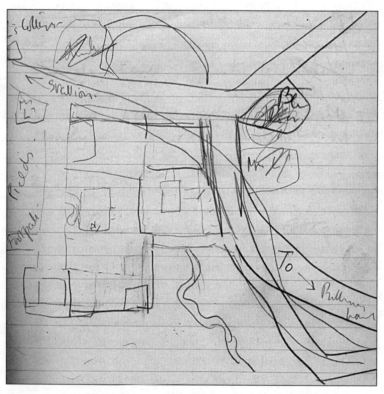

*From Notebook 33 Christie's own sketch of St Mary Mead for* The Murder at the Vicarage *showing most of the locations that appear in that novel.*

Inexplicably, the notes begin at Chapter 3 with nothing for the first two chapters. The extracts below have been edited for clarity.

Chapter III
Griselda and Vicar – Vicar meets Mrs L[estrange] at Church
– shows her round. Studio – he goes to it to see picture
– Anne and Lawrence. Anne comes to him in Study – taps
on window
Chapter IV
Dinner that night – Lawrence there – Dennis – afterwards
Lawrence with vicar. Dennis comes in after Lawrence has
gone – wants to tell things. Says 'What a rotten thing
gossip is.' Where does Mrs Lestrange go to at night.
Chapter V
Vicar called away – returns and discovers body.

Although the next extract is labelled 'Chapter VII' in the Notebook, it appears in the published novel as Chapter 6. From here on the Notebook does not specify chapter headings but I have added the actual chapter numbers to preserve the chronology:

Chapter VII [actually Chapter 6]
Inspector shuts up room and window and leaves word
no-one is to go in. Learns from Mary next morning Mr
Redding has been arrested – Griselda says 'What' –
incredulous – couldn't be Lawrence. What earthly motive.
Vicar does not want to say about Anne. Entrance of Miss
Marple – very terrible business – discusses it with them. Of
course one knows who one thinks – one might be wrong.
They tell her L arrested. She is suspicious – he has
confessed. Oh! Then – I see I was wrong – I must have been
wrong. Explain about clock – Griselda says again he knew.
Miss M pounces on note – 'Yes that is curious.' Mary says
Col. Melchett.

[Chapter 7]
A sad business – young Redding came in to the police
station, threw down the pistol, a Mauser 25, and gave
himself up. Declined to give motive. One thing I am amazed
– the shot not heard. Vicar explains where kitchen is – still,
I feel it would have been heard – silencer. They go to
Haydock. They tell him Redding has confessed – Haydock
looks relieved – that saves us all a lot of anxiety. Say 6.30
not later than that – the body was cold, man. Redding
couldn't have shot him then. He looked worried – but if the
man says so he's lying. But why on earth should he lie?

[Chapter 8]
The clock – what about the clock – it stopped at 6.22. Oh!
I put it back. Note [from Anne] to Vicar. 'Please – please –
come up to see me. I have got to tell someone.' Hands it to
Col Melchett – they go up – Slack, Col and vicar. They go up.
Anne – Want to ask you a few questions – she looks at him.
Have you told them? I shook my head. I've been such a
coward – such a coward – I shot my husband – I was
desperate. Something came over me – I went up behind him
and fired. The pistol? It – it was my husband's – I took it out
of a drawer. Did you see anyone? No – Oh! yes – Miss Marple.

[Chapter 9]
They go to see Miss Marple. They ask her. Yes – I saw Mrs
Protheroe at about a quarter past six. No – not flustered at
all. She said she had come to walk home with her husband.
Lawrence came from wood path and joined her. They went
into the studio – then left and walked off that way. She
must have taken the pistol with her. Miss M says no pistol
with her. Slack says concealed on her person – Miss M says
'quite impossible.'

[Chapter 10]
Vicar goes home – Miss Cram with Griselda – about Guides
– really curious – she goes. Vicar and Mary – about shot.

What time – she is amazed. Griselda says about Archer the poacher. Colonel and Slack arrive. They go into study.

[Chapter 11]
Miss Marple with Griselda – Miss M says it reminds her of things etc. etc. – the washerwoman and the other woman – hate. I wish you would tell me the 7 [suspects]. She shook her head. The note – the curious point about it.

[Chapter 12]
They go to interview Lawrence. He tells – arrived there to say I couldn't leave after all – found him dead. Pistol – it was mine – I picked it up and rushed. I felt demented. You were sure it was Anne? He bowed his head. I thought that after we had parted that afternoon she had gone back and shot him. No, he had never touched the clock. Mrs P, we know you didn't do it. Now – will you tell me what you did? She does. If anyone else confesses to the murder, I will go mad.

[Chapter 13]
Miss Hartnell [actually changed to Mrs Price-Ridley] indignant complaint about being rung up – a degenerate voice. It threatened me – asked about shot. Yes, I did hear something down in the wood – just one odd shot – but I didn't notice it particularly

[Chapter 14]
Haydock says about Hawes – Encephalitis lethargica. Mention of Dennis age by Haydock.

Although the novel is narrated by the vicar, it is not until Chapter 15 that 'I', the narrator, appears. Note the fluctuation thereafter between first and third person narrative:

Note from Mrs. Lestrange – I go there. Has hardly greeted her before the Inspector arrives – she asks vicar to stay – questions. She refuses information.

[Chapter 16]
It was after tea time that I put into execution a plan of my own – whoever committed the murder etc. Goes into wood – meets Lawrence with large stone in his hands. He explains – for Miss Marple's rock garden

[Chapter 18]
Inquest that morning [afternoon] – Vicar and doctor and Lawrence give evidence. Anne Protheroe – her husband in usual spirits – Mrs Lestrange – Dr Haydock gave medical certificate. Murder by person or persons unknown.

[Chapter 19]
Then drops into Lawrence's cottage. He describes how he got on at Old Hall – a tweenie overheard something – wasn't going to tell the police.

[Chapter 20]
Vicar goes home – finds Lettice has been there – Mary very angry – has come home and found her searching in study – yellow hat.

[Chapter 21]
After dinner – Raymond West – the crime – Mr Stone. Raymond says it wasn't him. Great excitement – tell the police. Another peculiar thing – I told him about the suit case.

[Chapter 22]
Letter from Anne – Vicar goes up to see her – a very extraordinary occurrence. Takes me to attic – the picture with the slashed face. Who is it? The initials E.P. on trunk.

[Chapter 23]
Vicar on way back knows police are searching barrow – his sudden brain wave – finds suitcase – takes it to police station – old silver.

[Chapter 24]
Vicar goes home – Hawes there – says will vicar preach –
reference to headache powder. Notes 3 by hand – one in
box – anonymous one.

[Chapter 25]
Mrs Price Ridley – her maid, standing at gate, saw
something or heard somebody sneeze. Or a tennis racquet
in a hedge – on the way back along footpath.

Near the end of the notes is a draft of the schedule that
appears in Chapter 26. Although it tallies in general with the
published version, minor details – the date of the month and
a difference of minutes in some of the timetable – change.

Occurrences in connection with the death of Colonel
Protheroe
To be explained [and] arranged in chronological order
~~Wednesday~~ Thursday – 20th
11.30 Col. Protheroe alters time of appointment to 6.15 –
easily overheard
12.30 Mrs Archer says pistol was still at Lawrence Redding's
cottage – but has previously said she didn't know
5.30 Fake call put through to me from East Lodge – by
whom?
5.30 Col and Mrs P leave Old Hall in car and drive to village
6.14 Col. P arrives at my house Vicarage and is shown into
study by maid Mary
6.20 Anne Protheroe comes to study window – Col P not
visible (writing at desk)
6.23 L and A go into studio
6.30–6.35 The shot
6.30–6.35 Call put through from LR's cottage to Mrs PR
6.45 L.R. visits vicarage finds body
6.50 I find body

The attempted murder of Hawes and the text of the ambiguously worded but apparently incriminating letter of Chapter 29 are sketched in the closing stages of the notes, which end abruptly with the revelation of the guilty names:

> [Chapters 27/28]
> The call – I – I want to confess. Can't get number. Goes there – finds letter on table.

> [Chapter 29]
> Dear Clement
> It is a peculiarly unpleasant thing I have to say – after all I think I prefer writing it. It concerns the recent peculations. I am sorry to say that I have satisfied myself beyond any possible doubt of the identity of the culprit. Painful as it is for me to have to accuse an ordained priest of the Church . . .

The Notebook has no mention of Miss Marple's explanation, although her casual mention of the names of the guilty is reflected in the book:

> Melchett arrives – Hawes ill – they send for Haydock – overdose of sulphanol.
> Miss M says Yes – that's what he wants you to think – the confession of the letter – the overdose – that he took himself. It all fits in – but it's wrong. It's what the murderer wants you to think.
> The murderer?
> Yes – or perhaps I'd better say Mr Lawrence Redding

> [Chapter 30]
> They stare at her.
> Of course Mr R is quite a clever young man. He would, as I have said all along, shoot anyone and come away looking distraught.
> But he couldn't have shot Col Protheroe.

No – but <u>she</u> could.
Who?
Mrs Protheroe.

As the first Marple novel, the place of *The Murder at the Vicarage* in crime fiction history is an important one. Miss Marple is the most famous, and arguably the most able, of the elderly female detectives. She was not the first; that honour goes to Miss Amelia Butterworth, who solved her first case in *The Affair Next Door* in 1897. Created by Anna Katharine Green, sometimes called the Mother of the Detective Story, Amelia's career – like Miss Marple's – was predicated on a combination of leisure and curiosity, as distinct from the professional female whose motivation was mainly economic. Other well-known female sleuths of the era included spinster schoolteacher Hildegarde Withers, the creation of Stuart Palmer; mystery writer Susan Dare, the creation of M.G. Eberhart; Gladys Mitchell's psychologist Mrs Bradley; and Patricia Wentworth's private enquiry agent Miss Maud Silver. All of these were contemporaries of Miss Marple, although only the heroine of St Mary Mead can be classified as a complete amateur.

*The Murder at the Vicarage* is a typical village murder mystery of the sort forever linked with the name of Agatha Christie; although, with ten books already published, it was only the second such novel she had produced, the other being *The Murder of Roger Ackroyd*. Its central ploy – the seemingly impregnable alibis of a pair of murderous adulterers – was one to which Christie would return throughout her career. It had already featured in *The Mysterious Affair at Styles*; *Death on the Nile*, *Evil under the Sun* and *Endless Night* are other prime examples.

## *The Sittaford Mystery*
### 7 September 1931

————————◄o►————————

During a séance at Sittaford House the death of
Captain Trevelyan is foretold. The prediction comes true
when his friend Major Burnaby finds the Captain's body,
murdered in his own home, six miles away. Inspector
Narracott investigates with the unsought help of Emily
Trefusis, whose fiancé has been arrested.

————————◄o►————————

Despite the full-length debut of Miss Marple in *The Murder at
the Vicarage* the previous year and the absence of Hercule
Poirot since *The Mystery of the Blue Train* in 1928, Christie
submitted a non-series novel to The Crime Club in 1931. *The
Sittaford Mystery* had a six-part serialisation in the USA, as
*Murder at Hazelmoor*, six months prior to its UK appearance.

The small bungalows, each with a quarter-acre of ground,
described in Chapter 1 of *The Sittaford Mystery* owe their
inspiration, according to an early draft of *An Autobiography*,
to the granite bungalow in Throwleigh, Dartmoor purchased
for £800 by Christie and her sister Madge for their brother
Monty on his return from Africa in 1923. The Dartmoor
background, and the sub-plot of the escaped convict, inevitably recalls Sherlock Holmes and *The Hound of the Baskervilles*
(1902), which uses the same evocative and atmospheric
setting as well as a similar sub-plot. Conan Doyle himself is
referenced in Chapter 11 of *Sittaford* when Charles Enderby
plans to write to him for an opinion on séances; this is
a reference to Conan Doyle's enthusiasm for spiritualism
during the last years of his life. Despite the passing reference
in Chapter 7 to Trevelyan's will, dated 13 August 1926,
and written 'five or six years ago', the mention of Conan
Doyle indicates that *The Sittaford Mystery* was written, at the

latest, in early 1930, as Conan Doyle died in July of that year.

As a plot device, the supernatural appeared sporadically throughout the works of Agatha Christie. Two years after *The Sittaford Mystery* the supernatural dominated *The Hound of Death*, a collection of short stories, most of them published years earlier in various magazines. It includes stories about a psychic in 'The Hound of Death', second sight in 'The Gipsy', a ghost in 'The Lamp', possession in 'The Strange Case of Sir Arthur [sometimes Andrew] Carmichael'; and in 'The Last Séance' and 'The Red Signal' a séance, also the main plot device of *The Sittaford Mystery*. In the later novels *Dumb Witness* and *The Pale Horse*, the supernatural plays a part; and in *Taken at the Flood* it is her psychic 'gift' that directs Katherine Cloade to approach Hercule Poirot. However, in the novels the paranormal is usually a smokescreen to camouflage a clever plot; and so the table-turning in *The Sittaford Mystery*, proves to be not merely atmospheric.

All of the notes for *The Sittaford Mystery* are contained in forty very organised pages of Notebook 59. Most of the chapters are sketched accurately and even some of the chapter headings are included, although the chapter numbers in the Notebook do not correspond exactly with those of the published novel. Unusually, most of the characters' names, with the exception of the Inspector, are also as published, and there are no shopping lists, no breaking off to plan a stage play, no digressions to a different novel. The year 1931 was also the last of that decade in which Christie had only one title published. Starting in 1932 with *Peril at End House* and *The Thirteen Problems*, Collins Crime Club published more than one Christie title per year. This increased rate of production is probably one of the reasons for more chaotic subsequent Notebooks.

Following in the footsteps of Tuppence Beresford in *The Secret Adversary* and more recently, *Partners in Crime*, Anne Beddingfeld from *The Man in the Brown Suit* and 'Bundle' Brent from *The Secret of Chimneys*, Emily Trefusis in *The*

*Sittaford Mystery* is another young Christie heroine with an independent mind and a yearning for adventure. She also foreshadows Lady Frances (Frankie) Derwent in *Why Didn't They Ask Evans?* and, twenty years later, Victoria Jones in *They Came to Baghdad*.

The first four chapters of the novel are accurately reflected in the early notes, although the time of death in the novel is amended to 5.25. Oddly, the secret of the novel upon which the alibi is based, is not mentioned at this stage and the brief summary below, while the truth, is not the whole truth.

> The séance
> Burnaby insists on going off to see his friend. Starts in the snow, goes up to house, rings and then goes in. Finds body, rings up doctor. Hit by sand bag (put under door for draughts). Dead two hours; could he have died at 6.15? Yes – very probably.
> Inquest – Scotland Yard
> Inspector – he questions Major Burnaby: Why did you say 6.15? Hums and haws – at last explains. Goes to see friend who is scientific.

Following this, Christie rather chaotically considers possible suspects before returning to the beginning of the novel. She confidently heads page 26 . . .

> Chapter I At Mrs Willet's
> Major Burnaby put on his gum boots, took his hurricane lantern. Goes through snow to Mrs. Willets. Arrive at house – description. Captain Trevelyan – his qualities – 6 bungalows – first for his old friend and crony and lets the others.
> Major B – Ronnie Garfield – young ass staying with invalid Aunt for Xmas
> Mr Rycroft – entomologist dried up little man
> Mr Duke – big square man

The conversation – the glasses – mention of it being the first Friday for two years he hasn't gone down to Midhampton to Capt. Trevelyan. 'I walk. What's twelve miles – keep yourself fit.' Looks at Violet . . . they said curves were coming in again – all for curves

Young man (journalist) arrives at hotel, accosts Major Burnaby. I'm on the staff of the Daily Wire. Overheard – young man explains – presents with cheque – No 1 The Cottages. Then gets into ~~cottage~~ conversation – goes out and wires to his paper. Comes back and talks loudly. Tells Burnaby he wants to photograph his cottage. Mr Enderby then goes out and finds Batman. So then things <u>are</u> square after all. Explains how the late captain used his name.

In April 1926 Colonel A. Christie of Styles, Sunningdale was listed as a winner of a Consolation Prize in a *Daily Mirror* competition in which readers were asked to predict the solution to Anthony Berkeley's *The Wintringham Mystery*. Was the prize-winning explanation actually Agatha's, and could this have inspired her plot? (I am grateful to Tony Medawer for this intriguing fact.)

Each person at séance must have connection
Violet Wilton and a ne'er do well
Captain Trevelyan
Mary Trevelyan married a man called Archer – 3 sons?
Bill [Brian Pearson] the ne'er-do-well – nothing much known of him, supposed to be in Australia, really in Newton [Abbot] seeing Violet.
John, the good stay-at-home, in Town for a literary dinner. He is married – really having an intrigue with an actress. [Martin Dering?]
Another was at the theatre with a girl (Story changes – girl agrees) they give wrong theatre – play has moved there – or

different actor in it yes, better – Gielgud instead of Noel Coward.

Ronald Payne, in love with Mary Archer, has come down here to persuade old uncle to do something.

Batman has married – living with wife 2 cottages away – comes in to do for him. A prize of new books has arrived for him at Batman's.

Brief sketches of potential chapters cover eight pages and while some of the descriptions below tally with published chapters, as the list progresses the matches become less faithful. It is entirely possible, of course, that the original manuscript followed this pattern and that subsequent editing resulted in the book we now know. I have added chapter numbers where the descriptions seem to tally but in some cases this is not feasible.

I Afternoon at Sittaford [Chapter 1]

II Round the Table [Chapter 2]

III Discovery at Midhampton [Chapter 3]

IV Inspector Pollock [Narracott] takes over [Chapter 4]

V At Mr and Mrs Evans [Chapter 5]

VI Inspector P and B visit lawyer – the will [Chapter 7]

VII The journalist bit [Chapter 8]

VIII Exeter and Jennifer Gardiner, Nurse – husband – names of nephews and nieces [Chapter 9]

IX James Pearson – facts about detained during his Majesty's pleasure [Chapter 10]

X She decides on taking counsel of Mrs Belling. You poor dear girl – the young gentleman – the attraction between [Chapter 11 and 12]

XI Sittaford – photograph of Major Burnaby's cottage – Sittaford House – Mrs and Miss Willett [Chapter 13/14]

XII The Professor on Psychical Research consents to be interviewed [Chapter 16]

XIII Prolonged interview at Exeter – alibis examined

XIV Mrs Grant – her husband, Ambrose Grant – author – literary dinner

XV Looking up AG's alibi [Chapter 24]

XVI The four – Major B out of it – the three others

XVII The Willets – nothing to be got out of them [Chapter 18]

XVIII Duke and Pollock – Duke indicates doubt of what has happened

XIX His story – engaged to Violet on way home

At the very end of the notes Christie reverts to her alphabetical method of cut and paste – assigning letters to a series of short scenes and then rearranging these letters to suit the purposes of her plot. I list the alphabetical sequence first and then her rearrangement, with comments:

A. Mrs C[urtis] full of ~~death~~ convict [Chapter 15]

B. Enderby and his interview with Emily – eye of God etc. [Chapter 25]

C. Young Ronald comes along – wants Emily to come and see his aunt [Chapter 17]

D. Miss Percehouse – acid spinster – Emily feels some kinship with her etc. Emily arranges with her to get a message . . . . to talk to Willetts – or Ronald goes with her. Label business. [Chapter 17]

E. She sees Violet Willett – evidently very nervous. Emily goes back for umbrella – creeps up stairs – the door. My God, will the night never come [Chapter 18]

F. Captain Wyatt and bulldog – eyes her up and down [Chapter 18]

G. Duke's house – Inspector Pollock comes out of door [Chapter 19]

H. Emily's interview with him [Chapter 19 and 27]

I. Enderby's theory – before [Chapter 19]

J. Emily's interview with Dr. Warren [Chapter 20]

K. The trunk label [Chapter 17]

L. The watch by night – Brian Pearson [Chapter 22]

M. Pollock at Exeter – Brian's movements checked up to Thursday [Chapter 24]

N. Since then? Since then – I don't know [This cryptic reference remains a mystery]

O. Enderby says Martin Dering not at dinner. Says he knows because Harris [Carruthers] was there – had one empty place – one side of him [Chapter 19]

P. Pollock clears up Martin Dering – the wire – answer comes all right [Chapter 27]

Q. Jennifer – either Emily or Inspector [Chapter 20]

R. Investigates her alibi – possible [Chapter 20]

S. Rycroft – name in book [Chapter 24]

T. Letter from Thomas Cronin about boots [Chapter 28]

U. Interview with Dacre the solicitor [Chapter 20]

Z. Emily interviews Mr Duke [Chapter 29]

Below are the regroupings as they appear in Notebook 59, with the relevant chapters added. The rearrangement does not follow the novel exactly but the broad outline is accurate, although inexplicably the letters H, K, N and R do not appear at all. The scene F obviously gave trouble as it appears twice, each time with a question mark.

A   B   C   F?   D   E [Chapters 15/17/18, apart from B which is Chapter 25]

I   O   G   O   F? [Chapters 18/19]

J   Q   U   L [Chapters 20/22]

M   S   P   T   Z [Chapters 22/24/27/28]

An interesting question in connection with the three novels published between 1931 and 1934 arises from a brief note in Notebook 59 and a later anecdote. In the lengthy Introduction to *Passenger to Frankfurt* (1970), Christie explained how sometimes a title was settled even before any story was in mind. She gave as an example the time that she visited a friend whose brother was just finishing the book he was reading; he tossed it aside and said, 'Not bad, but why on earth didn't they ask Evans?' She immediately decided that this would be the title for an as yet unwritten novel but, she wrote, she did not worry about the plot or the question of who Evans might be. That, she was sure, would come to her; as, indeed, it did – but when?

During the plotting of *The Sittaford Mystery*, page 24 of Notebook 59 reads:

'The Inspector killed – concussion confirmed Why Didn't they ask Evans? Ada Evans – also name of gardener.'

During the plotting of *Lord Edgware Dies*, page 53 of Notebook 41 reads:

'Chapter XXVI Why didn't they ask Evans.'

And earlier in Notebook 41 she also wrote a note to herself:

'Can we work in Why Didn't they ask Evans.'

When plotting *The Sittaford Mystery*, could Christie have possibly toyed with the idea of killing the Inspector? Perhaps she intended that the Inspector be attacked and concussed, uttering the significant words as he collapsed? This theory gains some support from the fact that up to this point in the plotting the Inspector is the only investigator. Emily is not mentioned in the notes until twenty pages later, when Christie had gone back to the beginning of the novel and begun to draft individual chapters. Captain Trevelyan's manservant Evans is 'asked' more than once and it is Emily's final questioning of him that is responsible for drawing her attention to the missing boots; and thereby to the solution. When Christie did eventually incorporate a not-questioned Evans into a novel (one for which there are no notes) called, not surprisingly, *Why Didn't They Ask Evans?*, the witnessing of a will was the very event that caused Evans not to be asked; and Sittaford's Evans receives a modest inheritance under Captain Trevelyan's will. For further speculation upon this intriguing enigma see *Lord Edgware Dies*.

⌒⌒⌒

### 'The Mystery of the Baghdad Chest'
January 1932

### 'The Mystery of the Spanish Chest'
September 1960

---◄○►---

When a stabbed corpse is found in a large chest the assumption is that the murderer hid it there to avoid discovery. Poirot, however, thinks otherwise . . .

---◄○►---

It is difficult to imagine that Christie's involvement in the Detection Club collaborative radio serial, *Behind the Screen*, broadcast on BBC June–July 1930, did not influence, or even inspire, the writing of 'The Mystery of the Baghdad Chest'. In each a body, inside a chest behind a screen, is stabbed in a room in which a group of people is gathered. In both stories the victim, hiding in the chest for purposes of his own, has been drugged earlier; and in each the corpse's blood, seeping onto the floor, leads to the discovery of the crime. The further detail of a slammed door, as indication of someone leaving the house, is also a feature of both and in each it is a red herring.

Christie worked on *Behind the Screen* in 1929, her instalment (Chapter 2 'Something is Missing') was broadcast in June 1930 and Notebook 41 is headed:

Ideas 1931

It is not unreasonable to assume that this means 'January 1931' and a few pages later notes for 'The Mystery of the Baghdad Chest' appear, just before those for *Lord Edgware Dies*. After its initial appearance in *The Strand* magazine in January 1932 this version of the story was not published in the UK until 1997, when it was collected in *While the Light Lasts*. Over twenty-five years after its first publication the story was completely re-written as 'The Mystery of the Spanish Chest', with a magazine appearance in September 1960, just prior to its inclusion in *The Adventure of the Christmas Pudding* a month later. The plot in each version is identical, although names are changed and Hastings, who narrates the earlier version, is absent in the later.

Perhaps frustration at having to follow someone else's plot and make allowances for the writer to follow (Dorothy L Sayers) created a desire in Christie to weave her own variation on the plot? This may account for the detailed accuracy of the 1931 notes:

Man stabbed in room – everyone there – behind screen – gagged first

Man induced to hide in other man's rooms (his wife coming there) – has tea first (drugged)

Later – a suspect comes in and later all there

Man hides in chest – (but bores hole to see through) has previously had a dinner with friend Major Curtis who was one of last people to see him alive – then goes to Albany – valet knows him – admits him – he says he wants to write letter. Valet leaves him – presently hears bang of door

Later party

Major Curtis
Mrs Anstey

Sir Arthur Wanger (flat owner)
Mr and Mrs Sikes
They all go off – the Sikes first

Anyway
Curtis kills him in chest – idea being that Antony came in
later and surprised his wife and Major – Wanger killed him
and put him in chest...but P[oirot] detects by holes found in
back of chest for air – not to see – fresh

With only minor changes – 'gagged' to 'drugged' and some
names – the printed version follows these notes closely.

When considering, in the late 1950s, short stories for possible expansion Christie wrote a brief synopsis of the plot:

Development of stories...
Baghdad Chest or a screen?
Idea?
A persuades B hide behind chest or screen as
Mrs B having affair with C – C gives party – B and A drop in
– B hides – A kills him and goes out again

These are followed by notes for 'Greenshaw's Folly', also
included in *The Adventure of the Christmas Pudding*, the title
story of which is itself an expansion of 'The Theft of the
Royal Ruby'.

But she was not yet finished with variations on Baghdad/
Spanish chests. A few years after the appearance of the
'Spanish' version of the story, a large chest became, once
again, a pivotal element in a Christie plot. In *The Rats*, the
first of three one-act plays included in *Rule of Three*, a body is
found in a chest – described variously in the notes as being
from either Kuwait or Baghdad – which effectively dominates
the set of the play and the attention of the main characters,
the eponymous rats.

And now the (probable) inspiration for all three incarnations can be admired by visitors in the hallway of Greenway House, Dame Agatha's Devon home.

## *Peril at End House*
### 7 February 1932

While holidaying in St Loo Poirot and Hastings meet Nick Buckley, the impoverished owner of End House. When she tells them that she has had three close brushes with death, Poirot investigates, but is unable to avert a real tragedy at End House.

*Peril at End House* was published on both sides of the Atlantic in early February 1932 with a serialisation in both places some months earlier. This, in turn, would mean that it was written most probably during late 1930/early 1931. The plotting for it is contained in two Notebooks, 59 and 68. The latter is a very small pocket-diary sized notebook and, apart from a detailed listing of train times from Stockport to Torquay, is devoted entirely to this novel. Notebook 59 also contains extensive notes for the Mr Quin story 'The Bird with the Broken Wing', first published in *The Mysterious Mr Quin* in April 1930, and for 'Manx Gold' in May 1930.

*Peril at End House* is a magnificent example of the Golden Age detective story. It is rarely mentioned in any discussion of Christie's best titles and yet it embodies all of the virtues of the detective story in its prime: it is told with succinct clarity, enviable readability and scrupulous fairness in clueing. Every single fact the reader needs in order to arrive at the correct solution is given with superb sleight of hand. And like all of the best detective stories the secret of the plot (a mistake in names) is, in retrospect, simple.

On page 3 of Notebook 59 Christie uses a telling phrase – 'conversation without having a point', referring to the early conversation between Poirot and Hastings in the garden of the hotel. At this point in her career virtually every conversation in a novel has a 'point': the delineation of an important character trait (the silk stockings episode in *Cards on the Table*), a hint about motivation (Major Burnaby gruffly discussing crosswords and acrostics in Chapter 1 of *The Sittaford Mystery*), a major clue (the difficulty, established in Chapter 2, of getting a sleeping berth on the normally half-empty Orient Express) or the confirmation of a previously suspected fact (the picnic in *Evil under the Sun*). And although she refers to a conversation without having a point, there is a mention of the missing airman (the motive) in the actual conversation to which the notes allude.

As usual some of the names change – Lucy Bartlett becomes Maggie Buckley, while Walter Buckhampton is Charles Vyse and the Curtises become the Crofts – but much of the notes tally with the finished novel, leading once more to the suspicion that earlier notes have not survived. Interestingly, in Notebook 59 the character of Nick Buckley is referred to throughout as Egg – the future nickname of Mary Lytton-Gore in *Three Act Tragedy*; although it is odd that the surname Beresford, already in use for Tommy and Tuppence, is chosen.

Poirot and Hastings sitting in Imperial Hotel – H reads from paper about Polar expedition – a letter from Home Secretary begging Poirot to do something. H urges him to do so – P refuses – no longer any wish for kudos. The garden – girl – someone calls 'Egg' – Poirot goes down stairs – falls – girl picks him up – she and Hastings assist him to verandah – he thanks her suggests cocktail. H is sent to get them – returns to find pair firm friends

People in this story

Egg Beresford – owner of End House

Cousin Lucy – a distant cousin – 2nd or 3rd cousin – Lucy Bartlett

Egg's cousin Walter Buckhampton – son of her mother's sister – he works in a solicitor's office in St. Loo – he loves Egg

Mr and Mrs Curtis – old friends who live next door – he is an invalid who came down there years ago – they seem pleasant and jovial

Freddie – Frederica Rice – a friend – parasite who lives on Egg and admits it frankly

Lazarus – has a big car – often down there – a member of an antique firm in London

The hotel where Poirot and Hastings stay is the Imperial, an actual Torquay hotel, complete with a verandah overlooking Torquay Bay; in the book it is re-imagined as the Majestic Hotel in St Loo. The opening of the book follows the above plan exactly and the characters are recognisable.

The plot is developed further in Notebook 68; I have indicated the chapters in which each scene occurs:

At End House they pass Lodge and cottage – man gardening – bald head old fashioned spectacles – stares – admitted to End House – they wait for Nick – old pictures – gloom – damp – decay. Nick enters – slight surprise – Poirot talks to her – shows her bullet [Chapter 2]

They return to Hotel – Freddie Rice talks to Poirot – suggests Nick is an amazing little liar – likes to invent things. Poirot presses her – such as – she talks about brakes of car [Chapter 2]

P asks her if she will send for a woman friend – she suggests 'My cousin Maggie' – she was to come to me next month –

I could ask her to come now – second cousin really – there's a large family of them – Maggie is the second – she's a nice girl – but perhaps a bit dull [Chapter 3]

A call upon Mr Vyse – a reference to legal advice – P mentions he called yesterday at 12 – but Mr. Vyse was out – Mr Vyse agrees [Chapter 6]

The fireworks – they go over to the Point – Nick and Maggie are to follow – they all watch – they're a long time. Poirot and H go back – fall over body in scarlet shawl – then see Nick coming – it's Maggie – Nick with traces of tears on her face [Chapter 7]

*Peril at End House* is significant not just because of its own virtues but also because of the number of themes and ideas that Christie went on to exploit in later stories:

* The murder in *Peril at End House* takes place during a fireworks display which camouflages the gunshot. This idea is also an important plot feature of the 1936 novella 'Murder in the Mews'. In fact, it is one of the refinements added to the original version of that story, 'The Market Basing Mystery' (see below).
* The use of names as a device to fool the reader makes an early appearance in this novel. It was to reappear in *Dumb Witness, Mrs McGinty's Dead, A Murder is Announced* and, with an international twist, in *Murder on the Orient Express.*
* A murder method that involves sending poisoned chocolates to a patient in hospital resurfaces three years later in *Three Act Tragedy*, when it is used to despatch the unfortunate Mrs de Rushbridger.
* A vital and poignant clue from the contents of a letter posted by the victim shortly before her death and subsequently forwarded by the recipient to Poirot

appears again (and even more ingeniously) the following year in *Lord Edgware Dies*.

✳ The use of cocaine by the 'smart set' of the 1930s is revisited in *Death in the Clouds* when Lady Horbury is found to have cocaine in her dressing-case.

✳ As in *Lord Edgware Dies* an attractive and ruthless female draws Poirot, for her own purposes, into the case.

✳ Subterfuge concerning wills was also to be a feature of *Sad Cypress, A Murder is Announced, Taken at the Flood* and *Hallowe'en Party*.

∽↶↷∽

## 'The Second Gong'
### July 1932

――――――◄○►――――――

Hubert Lytcham Roche is found shot dead in his locked study, but luckily one of his dinner guests is Hercule Poirot.

――――――◄○►――――――

Although first published in the UK in the July 1932 *Strand* magazine it was not until the posthumous 1991 UK collection *Problem at Pollensa Bay* that 'The Second Gong' appeared between hard covers. The re-written and expanded version, 'Dead Man's Mirror', was one of the four novellas comprising *Murder in the Mews*.

Notes appear in three Notebooks, 30, 41 and 61, although the reference in Notebook 30 is merely to the possibility of elaboration. Notebook 41 has, unusually for a short story, ten pages of notes neatly summarising the main plot at the outset, the only difference being the smashing of a window rather than a mirror. The notes reflect accurately the progress of the story with the usual changes of names and minor plot details (I have included the published names):

Bullet passed through him and out to gong. Then door was locked on inside and body turned so that shot would have gone through window.

Second Gong

Girl coming down stairs late – meets boy – they ask butler – No, Miss – first gong. Secretary joins them (or girl anyway) – murderer – the shot fired from library just when he joins them

Dinner 8.15 – First gong 8.5. At 8.12 Joan comes down with Dick – butler says 1st gong (shot!). ~~Geor~~ Jervis joins them. Exeunt

At 7 Diana picks flowers – stain on dress. At 8.10 Diana hurries out – gets rose – tries window – is going away when shot is heard from road

Murderer shoots [victim] at 8.6 – shuts and locks door, goes out through window – bangs it and it shuts, smoothes over footprints – is in library when shot is fired.

Mrs Mulberry [No equivalent]

Diana Cream [Cleves] clever (adopted daughter)

Calshott – the agent – a one-armed man – ex-soldier [Marshall]

Geoffrey Keene (secretary)

John Behring – old friend – rich man [Gregory Barling]

They go in to drawing room. Diana joins them – Mrs Lytcham Roche – vague – spectral – John Behring – 2nd gong – M. Poirot. No L[ytcham] R[oche] – an extraordinary thing. Butler says still in his study. Diana mentions that he's been very queer all day – yes, he may do something dreadful. P watches her – they go to study – locked.

Break down door – dead man – mirror – window locked – (reopened by John Behring) pistol by hand – 'Gong' – key in his pocket. Inspection of window – he opens it – ground – no footprints. Police sent for – questions.

John Behring

Mrs LR [Lytcham Roche]

Miss Cleves
[Geoffrey] Keene (pick[s] up from hall)
Butler [Digby]
Police satisfied – doctor a little uncertain as to mirror.
Poirot goes out with torchlight – comes back – asks Joan for
shoes – comes out – J with him (and Dick) Diana –
Michaelmas daisies. Come, mes enfants, Shows them
window (gong then?). Asks butler about Michaelmas daisy
– Yes – then a few words with him.

As can be seen, the notes, telegrammatic in style, include even the details of the Michaelmas daisies and the stain on Diana's dress. The novels immediately preceding 'The Second Gong' – *The Murder at the Vicarage, The Sittaford Mystery, Peril at End House* – all appear in the Notebooks more or less as they eventually appeared in print. Rough work, if any, may have been done elsewhere and the Notebooks represented an outline as distinct from the working out of details of the plot.

'The Second Gong' one of the few experiments that Christie made with that classic situation of detective fiction – the locked room problem, where the victim is found in a room with all the doors and windows locked from the inside, making escape for the killer seemingly impossible. *Why Didn't They Ask Evans?, Murder in Mesopotamia* and *Hercule Poirot's Christmas* also have similar situations. Fascinating though these situations can be, Christie never makes them a major aspect of her plot, and the solution in 'The Second Gong' is disappointingly mundane.

In both 'The Second Gong' and *Hercule Poirot's Christmas* a killer fakes the time of the murder more significantly in both a character picks up something; obviously an important clue as it gets its own note – 'Picks-up from hall' – and when confronted proffers a different object in the hope of avoiding detection. And there is a thematic connection with *Black Coffee*, the only stage play to feature Poirot, and premiered the year before the short story: in each case Poirot answers a summons too late to avert tragedy and the killer proves to be the male secretary of a wealthy man.

There are no notes for the elaboration of 'The Second Gong' into 'Dead Man's Mirror', apart from the appearance of the names Miss Lingard and Hugo Trent on a single page of Notebook 61. The plot is almost identical and although a different killer is unmasked, their position in the household is essentially the same as in the original.

◈

### 'Death on the Nile' (short story)
#### July 1933

—◄◊►—

Aboard *SS Fayoum* Lady Grayle approaches
Parker Pyne with a story of being poisoned by
her husband. But is it just a story?

—◄◊►—

Notes for 'Death on the Nile' are contained in Notebook 63:

Wife confides to P (. . . or clergyman)
    That she thinks her husband is poisoning her. She has
money – apparently duel between husband and P – really
husband is victim – wife is dupe – young man paying
attention to niece is engineering it all – making love to auntie

While the death scene in this short story has strong echoes of *The Mysterious Affair at Styles* and the overall plot has distinct similarities with another Poirot case, 'The Cornish Mystery'. The resemblance is so marked that this extract could indicate 'The Cornish Mystery'; but the wife in 'Death on the Nile' is wealthy whereas her Cornish counterpart is not.

Note that Christie intended the story to involve Hercule Poirot ('P.' was her shorthand for Poirot; 'P.P.' for Parker

Pyne) but the published version featured Parker Pyne; Poirot was eliminated possibly because of his earlier involvement in 'The Cornish Mystery'.

Two further pages of notes in Notebook 63 also reveal that Christie considered a dramatisation of the story:

Play    PP version Death on the Nile

Lady Grayle – hard boiled – 45
   Sir George – 50 good fellow – sportsman
Miss McNaughton – hospital nurse
Pam – lovely, nice
Michael – Sir G's secretary
Dr. Crowthorne

Act II
She is poisoned – Miss M thinks it is Sir G – Doctor takes
   charge – strychnine found on Sir G – Miss M loses her head
Act III
Young people – Pam says Miss M did it – puts it up to
   doctor – he gets to work on her – Michael and Doctor

These notes follow the story closely, with no indication of the elaboration which would have been necessary to transform a ten-page short story. The reason for this may be deduced from the surrounding pages of the Notebook, where Christie experimented with other possible dramatic scenarios. On either side of this sketch there are similar brief outlines for stage adaptations (none of which were pursued) of *Three Act Tragedy*, 'Triangle at Rhodes' and 'The House at Shiraz', as well as an original, *Command Performance*. And earlier, and later, in the same Notebook there are detailed notes for the dramatisation of the novel *Death on the Nile*. Interestingly, with the exception of *Three Act Tragedy*, all of the titles share a foreign setting.

## Lord Edgware Dies
### 4 September 1933

◄○►

When Lord Edgware is found stabbed in his study it
would seem that his wife, actress Jane Wilkinson, has
carried out her threat. But her impeccable alibi forces
Poirot to look elsewhere for the culprit. Two more
deaths follow before a letter from the dead
provides the final clue.

◄○►

*Lord Edgware Dies*, set amongst the glitterati of London's West
End, began life in Rhodes in the autumn of 1931 and was
completed on an archaeological dig at Nineveh on a table
bought for £10 at a bazaar in Mosul. It was dedicated to Dr
and Mrs Campbell Thompson, who led the archaeological
expedition at Nineveh, and a skeleton found in a grave
mound on site was christened Lord Edgware.

The inspiration for the book and for the character of
Carlotta Adams came from the American actress Ruth
Draper, who was famed for her ability to transform herself
from a Hungarian peasant to a Park Lane heiress in a matter
of minutes and with a minimum of props. In *An Autobiography*
Christie notes, 'I thought how clever she was and how good
her impersonations were . . . thinking about her led me to
the book *Lord Edgware Dies*.'

Although never mentioned in the same reverent breath as
*The Murder of Roger Ackroyd* or *Murder on the Orient Express*,
*Lord Edgware Dies*, despite its lack of a stunning surprise solution, is a model of detective fiction. The plot is audaciously
simple and simply audacious and, like many of the best
plots, seems complicated until one simple and, in retrospect,
obvious, fact is grasped; then everything clicks neatly into
place. Every chapter pushes the story forward and almost

every conversation contains information to enable Poirot to answer the question, 'Did Lady Edgware carry out her threat to take a taxi to her husband's house and stab him in the base of the skull?'

Lord Edgware himself is in the same class as the victims from both 1938 novels, Mrs Boynton from *Appointment with Death* and Simeon Lee from *Hercule Poirot's Christmas*; he is a thoroughly nasty individual whose family despises him and whose passing few mourn. There are also subtle suggestions of a relationship between himself and his Greek god-like butler, Alton.

The progress of *Lord Edgware Dies* was mentioned sporadically by Christie to her new husband, Max Mallowan, in letters written to him from Grand Hotel des Roses, Rhodes in 1931.

Tuesday Oct. 13th [1931]
I've got on well with book – Lord Edgware is dead all right – and a second tragedy has now occurred – the Ruth Draper having taken an overdose of veronal. Poirot is being most mysterious and Hastings unbelievably asinine.
. . . breakfast at 8 . . . meditation till 9. Violent hitting of the typewriter till 11.30 (or the end of the chapter – sometimes if it is a lovely day I cheat to make it a short one!)

Presumably there were 'lovely days' at the time of writing Chapters 8 and 16!

Oct. 16th
Lord Edgware is getting on nicely. He's dead – Carlotta Adams (Ruth Draper) is dead – and the nephew who succeeds to the property is just talking to Poirot about his beautiful alibi! There is also a film actor with a face like a 'Greek God' – but he is looking a bit haggard at present. In fact a very popular mixture I think. Just a little bit cheap perhaps . . .

> Oct. 23rd
>
> True, I have got to Chapter XXI of Lord Edgware which is
> all to the good . . . I should never have done that if you had
> been there . . . I must keep my mind on what the wicked
> nephew does next . . .

All of the notes for this novel are spread over almost fifty
pages of a pocket-diary sized Notebook 41. They outline the
novel very closely with few deletions or variations. It would
seem that the writing of this novel went smoothly with the
plot well established beforehand. The notebook is headed
'Ideas – 1931' and the first ten pages, prior to the notes for
*Lord Edgware Dies*, contain brief notes for 'The Mystery of
the Baghdad Chest' (1932) and an even briefer note for *Why
Didn't They Ask Evans?*, as well as a one-sentence outline of the
crucial idea behind *Three Act Tragedy*.

There are also two references to *Thirteen at Dinner*, the title
under which *Lord Edgware Dies* appeared in the USA, but it is
not clear if these two references are coincidental or if the
idea of 13 guests at a dinner (as mentioned in Chapter 15)
was an earlier idea that Christie subsumed into *Lord Edgware
Dies*. The first reference lists thirteen members of the Detection Club in connection with this plot (see The Detection
Club in the Notebooks), and five pages later the idea of
'Thirteen at Dinner as a short story?' is considered though
not pursued.

Two jottings, a dozen pages apart, accurately reflect the
first two chapters of the book; and in between these, in the
last extract below, Christie summarises the murder plot. As
can be seen, the only details to change are minor ones: the
name Mountcarlin changes to Edgware, the secretary Miss
Gerard becomes Miss Carroll and Martin Squire becomes
Bryan Martin, although at this stage he is merely an admirer
rather than a fellow actor. The Piccadilly Palace Hotel, the
door ajar, the waiter and the corn knife all appear in the
book.

An actress Jane W comes to see Poirot – engaged to Duke of Merton – her husband – not very bright – best way would be to kill him she drawls – Hastings a little shocked. But I shouldn't like to be hanged. Door is then seen to be a little ajar. Martin Squire [Bryan Martin] – pleasant hearty young fellow – an admirer of Miss Wilkinson's. He is seen next evening having supper with Carlotta

Sequence
At theatre – CA's performance – H's reflections – Is JW really such a good actress? Looks round – JW – her eyes sparkling with enthusiasm. Supper at Savoy – Jane at next table – CA there also (with Ronnie Marsh) – rapprochement – JW and Poirot – her sitting room – her troubles. I'll have to kill him (just as waiter is going out) Enter Bryan (and CA). JW has gone into bedroom. B asks what did she say – means it – amoral – would kill anyone quite simply

Plot
Jane speaks to Carlotta – bribes her – a thousand pounds – to go to Mr? Jefferson's dinner. Rendezvous at Piccadilly Palace at 7.30. They change clothes – C goes to dinner. At 9.15 J. rings her up. C. says quite alright. J goes to Montcarlin House – rings – tells butler (new) that she is Lady Mountcarlin goes in – Hullo John. Secretary (Miss Gerard) sees her from above. ~~Shoot~~? Or stab? Ten minutes later she leaves. At 10.30 butler goes to room – dead. Informs police – they come. Go to Savoy – Lady M came in ~~at~~ half an hour ago <u>or</u> following morning. J kills him with corn knife belonging to her maid Eloise

Christie then considers her suspects, although this list is much shorter than the eventual cast of characters:

People
Lord Mountcarlin [Edgware]

Other man Duke? Millionaire?
Bryan Martin – actor in films with her
Lord Mountcarlin's nephew Ronnie West – debonair Peter
Wimseyish
Miss Carroll – Margaret Carroll – Middle-aged woman – a
Miss Clifford

The reference to 'debonair Peter Wimsey' is to Lord Peter Wimsey, the detective creation of Christie's crime-writing contemporary Dorothy L. Sayers and the hero of (at that point) a half-dozen novels and a volume of short stories. The Clifford reference is, in all likelihood, to a member of the Clifford family at whose home the young Agatha attended social evenings.

The vital letter written by Carlotta and forwarded from her sister in Canada (Chapters 20 and 23) is sketched, but only the crucial section, containing the giveaway clue:

Arrival of a letter
he said 'I believe it would take in Lord Mountcarlin himself.
Now will you take something on for a bet. Big stakes,
mind.' I laughed and said 'How much' but the answer fairly
took my breath away. 10,000 dollars, no more no less. Oh,
little sister – think of it. Why, I said, I'd play a hoax on the
King in Buckingham Palace and risk lese majeste for that.
Well, then we got down to details.

And the Five Questions of Chapter 14 are listed in cryptic form:

Then Points?
A. Sudden change of mind
B. Who intercepted letter
C. Meaning of his glare
D. The pince-nez – nobody owns them – except Miss Carroll?
E. The telephone call (they will go to Hampstead)

The Notebook does include one intriguing sequence, not reflected in the book:

> . . . or says I have been used as a tool – I feel ill. I didn't know what I ought to do – letter to Superintendent of police (rang up) – letter to Bryan Martin. A telephone number Victoria 7852 . . . No, no, I forgot – he wouldn't be there. Tomorrow will do.
> A letter she writes but does not post? Or a friend comes to see her?

These would seem to be the actions of Carlotta Adams as described by her maid in Chapter 9, so perhaps the original intention was to report the abandoned phone call directly. And the second reference is to the vital letter to her sister, the facsimile of which, in Chapter 23, gives Poirot the clue that eventually solves the case.

Page 53 of Notebook 41 throws a further intriguing side-light on *Why Didn't They Ask Evans?*. The following note appears under a heading:

> Chapter XXVI
> Why didn't they ask Evans
> Ah! I can see it all now – Evans comes. Questions about BM [Bryan Martin]. She answers – pince-nez left behind

This refers to Chapter 28 of *Lord Edgware Dies* and the questioning of the maid, Ellis. At the end of the previous chapter Poirot has a revelation when, passing a cinema-goer in the street, he overhears the observation, 'If they'd just had the sense to ask Ellis . . .'; or, in other words, 'Why didn't they (have the sense to) ask Ellis?' It is entirely possible that the writing of *Why Didn't They Ask Evans?* followed closely on the completion of *Lord Edgware Dies*. Although there are no notes – apart from the phrase itself – for *Why Didn't They Ask Evans?* its serialisation began the same month, September

1933, in which *Lord Edgware Dies* was published. Christie possibly felt that the questioning of Evans/Ellis, and the intriguing reason for that lack of questioning, deserved a more elaborate construction than the one given in *Lord Edgware Dies*. And so she wrote *Why Didn't They Ask Evans?*, where the identification and questioning of Evans is the entire *raison d'être* of the book. Is it entirely coincidental that the Evans of the later novel is also a maid? For further discussion of the Ellis/Evans enigma see the notes on *The Sittaford Mystery*.

❧

## Three Act Tragedy
### 7 January 1935

---◄○►---

Who poisoned Reverend Babbington at Sir Charles's cocktail party? And, more bafflingly, why? What became of Sir Bartholomew's mysterious butler Ellis? What secret did Mrs de Rushbridger hide? In the last act Poirot links these three events to expose a totally unexpected murderer – and an even more unexpected motive.

---◄○►---

*Three Act Tragedy* is based on one of the most original ideas in the entire Christie output. A single sentence in Notebook 41 shows the inspiration for the novel and from it Christie produced a perfectly paced and baffling whodunit, full of clever and original ideas. Apart from the brilliant central concept we also find a victim murdered not because of what she knows but on account of what she *doesn't* know; a new conjuring trick in a clever poisoning gambit; a witty yet chilling closing line; and, unwittingly, a foreshadowing, in the final chapter title, of a famous case to come. Mr Satterthwaite, normally the partner in crime of the mysterious

Mr Quin, here makes an appearance alongside Hercule Poirot.

*Three Act Tragedy* shares much with *Lord Edgware Dies* from two years earlier. Both are set firmly among the glittering classes and include a clothes designer and an observant playwright among the suspects; both feature a murderous member of the acting profession and a deadly masquerade; and both feature Hercule Poirot. Oliver Manders' motorcycle 'accident' on the night of Sir Bartholomew's death is the same as that engineered by Bobby and Frankie in the previous year's *Why Didn't They Ask Evans?*. A variation on the impersonation at the centre of the plot was also to appear in the following year's book, *Death in the Clouds*, and, more light-heartedly, was the basis for the 1925 short story 'The Listerdale Mystery'.

It is also possible that this novel is Christie's version, tongue somewhat in cheek, of a well-known cliché of classic detective fiction. In *Three Act Tragedy* she provides a solution in which The Butler Did It – and at the same time, The Butler Didn't Do It. And the other old chestnut, the secret passage, also gets an airing, although almost as an aside.

The notes for *Three Act Tragedy* are the last to outline the course of a novel accurately with little extraneous material or discarded ideas. From *Death in the Clouds* onwards notes contain speculation and changes of mind, but the notes for titles up to, and including, *Three Act Tragedy* are relatively organised and straightforward.

Notebooks 33 and 66 contain forty pages, but the brilliantly original basis for the book was sketched, four years before publication, in Notebook 41. On a page headed 'Ideas – 1931' we read the following:

Idea for book
Murder utterly motiveless because dead man and murderer unacquainted. Reason – a rehearsal

This unique idea was left to mature for two years before the bulk of the novel was written during 1933. Almost inevitably, the background would have to be somewhat theatrical, so from the first page of the book Sir Charles Cartwright's ability to assume a role onstage is emphasised. Mr Satterthwaite watches him walk up the path from the sea and observes 'something indefinable that did not ring true' about his portrayal of 'the Retired Naval man'; and this is, in effect, the foundation on which the novel is built.

Appropriately, Notebook 33 sketches, in cryptic notes, this opening scene. This is followed by a list of the characters and, apart from the mysterious Richard Cromwell, who may be the forerunner of Oliver Manders, the names listed are close to those in the published book.

> The Manor House Mystery
> Ronald [Sir Charles] Cartwright walks up – shiplike rolling gait – clean shaven face – not have been sure [if he actually was a sailor]. Mr Satterthwaite smiling to himself
> Egg/Ray Lytton Gore
> Lady Mary Lytton Gore
> Richard Cromwell
> Mr and Mrs Babbington
> Sir Bartholomew Frere [Strange]
> ~~Capt. and Mrs Dakers~~
> Angela Sutcliffe
> Satterthwaite
> Captain Dacres – bad lot – little man like jockey
> Mrs Cynthia Dacres runs dress shops (Ambrosine)
> Anthony McCrane [Astor] – playwright
> Miss Hester [Milray] – secretary – dour ugly woman of forty-three

The title at the top of the page – 'The Manor House Mystery' – is a generic and inadequate one and does not appear again. 'Three Act Tragedy' is more dramatic and is in keeping with the theatrical theme: an actor, a playwright, a dress designer, a masquerade and 'a rehearsal'.

The all-important discussion of Ellis, the butler, and his mysterious disappearance is sketched, as is the possible connection between the two fatal dinner-parties:

Bit about butler
Chapter II
Interview with Johnson – mellow atmosphere. Then it must be this fellow, Ellis; tells all about butler – not there a fortnight – questioned by police – not seen to leave house but be left – looks fishy. Says Miss Lytton Gore told him about other death. Must be some connection but was likely to be the butler. Why did the fellow disappear if he hadn't got a guilty conscience?
Port analysed – found correct. Inspector comes in – talks about nicotine poisoning. [Second Act, Chapter 2]

London – Egg arrives over to dine with them – pale, wounded looking. The position – the three of us – questions. Are the deaths of Sir B[artholomew] and B[abbington connected?]
Yes
If so, what people were at one and which at the other
Miss Sutcliffe, Captain and Mrs Dacres, Miss Wills and Mr Manders
You can wash out Angela and Mr Manders
Egg says can't wash out Miss Sutcliffe. I don't know her
Mr S says can't wash out anybody
She has washed out Mr Manders
Egg agrees [Second Act, Chapter 7]

Notebook 66 opens when the investigation is well under way and the interviews with the suspects are divided between the self-styled detectives. The first page is headed:

Division of work
P suggests Egg should tackle Mrs Dacres; C[harles
Cartwright] Freddie D[acres] and A[ngela] S[utcliffe];
S[atterthwaite] Miss Wills and O[liver] M[anders]. Says
Miss Wills will have seen something. C. says S. do AS – will
do the Wills woman. P suggests S. should do OM [Third
Act, Chapter 5]

Miss W[ills]
Sir C. – birthmark on butler's arm. She gets him to hand her
the dish. As he goes out looks back – her smile was
disquieting in the extreme. She writes in a little book.
[Third Act, Chapter 9]

An experiment – I will give the party. Charles stays behind
– the glasses etc. Miss Will's face – P appeals for anyone to
tell anything they know [Third Act, Chapter 11]

The third death, that of Mrs de Rushbridger, and the revelatory discussion of the play rehearsal are also sketched briefly.

Mr Satterthwaite and Poirot go to Yorkshire. Mrs R dead –
a small boy got it from a man who said he got it from a
loony lady – 'Bit loony she was.' She cannot speak now, says
Poirot. This must be stopped – then is someone else in
danger [Third Act, Chapter 13]

Happy families – I ask for a pack of cards – I get them. Mrs
Mugg – the Milkman's wife – Egg explains. P says he hopes
she will be very happy. She goes off to dress rehearsal of
Angela Sutcliffe's play by Miss Wills – Little Dog Laughed.
Tiens – I have been blind – the motive for the murder of Mr
Babbington [Third Act, Chapter 14]

There are two further points to consider. The first is a variation on the Evans/Ellis issue. As discussed in *The Sittaford*

*Mystery* and *Lord Edgware Dies*, the cryptic note in Notebook 41 – 'Can we work in Why Didn't They Ask Evans?' – could conceivably also apply to *Three Act Tragedy*. Ellis/Evans in *Lord Edgware Dies* and Evans in *The Sittaford Mystery* both provide vital clues that lead to the solution of the mystery. And if Poirot had been able to question the missing Ellis of *Three Act Tragedy*, he would almost certainly have prevented the death of Mrs De Rushbridger. But because he doesn't actually exist, it is obvious Why They Didn't Ask Ellis.

The second, and little remarked upon, enigma is The Mystery of the Altered Motive. While the US and UK texts of *The Moving Finger* and *Murder is Easy/Easy to Kill* are considerably different, in *Three Act Tragedy* the disparity is more significant. In the UK edition of the book, during Poirot's explanations in the final chapter, the motive attributed to Sir Charles, the supposed bachelor, is that he is actually married: 'And there is the fact that in the Haverton Lunatic Asylum there is a woman, Gladys Mary Mugg, the wife of Charles Mugg' (Sir Charles' real name). And, Poirot explains, Sir Bartholomew Strange as 'an honourable, upright physician . . . would not stand by silent and see [him] enter into a bigamous marriage with an unsuspecting young girl' (Egg). During Chapter 12 of the Third Act, Sir Charles tells Egg about his real name but otherwise the reader has no reason to suspect that he already has a wife, albeit one confined to an asylum.

In the US edition, however, it is Sir Charles, and not his wife, who is insane and as Poirot clarifies, 'In Sir Bartholomew he saw a menace to his freedom. He was convinced that Sir Bartholomew was planning to put him under restraint. And so he planned a careful and extremely cunning murder.' And, as he is being led away, Sir Charles breaks down: 'His face . . . was now a leering mask of impotent fury. His voice rang shrill and cracked . . . *Those three people had to be killed . . . for my safety.*' Melodramatic exits aside, of the two potential motives, the latter is by far the more compelling.

The amended denouement means that certain passages in the book which foreshadow the altered motive are significantly different. The most crucial changes occur in Chapters 7 and 26 of the US edition. In Chapter 7 Sir Charles and Mr Satterthwaite interview the Chief Constable, Colonel Johnson. In the course of this conversation Sir Charles says, 'I've retired from the stage now, as you know. *Worked too hard and had a breakdown two years ago*'; and extracts from Sir Bartholomew's diary are quoted, including one significant one: '*Am worried about M . . . don't like the look of things*' (my emphasis). Chapter 26 includes a lengthy conversation between Poirot and Oliver Manders. None of these passages appear in the equivalent chapters of the UK edition. The first two changes provide the clues to Sir Charles' breakdown: Sir Bartholomew's 'M' referring to Cartwright's real name, Mugg, and his concern over Sir Charles' mental health. The third prepares the way for Manders to replace Sir Charles in Egg's affections, although this scenario could apply in either case.

However, as the book was published (both as a magazine serial and in book form) in the USA in advance of its UK publication it is likely that it was the latter edition that was altered. But the question remains: why?

In a letter (undated, as usual, but from internal evidence probably late 1972/early 1973) to her agent, Christie herself briefly refers to the problem and states, 'I am studying the problem of *Three Act Tragedy* . . . in the Dodd Mead [the US edition] Sir Charles goes mad . . . I have a feeling that was what I originally wrote.' But this is by no means conclusive; and the Notebooks throw no light on this intriguing mystery.

### *Death in the Clouds*
### 1 July 1935

————————◄○►————————

The mysterious and silent death of Madame Giselle high over the English Channel on a flight from Paris challenges Hercule Poirot – especially as he is a suspect. His investigation involves a visit to Paris, a blowpipe, a detective novelist and a wasp.

————————◄○►————————

All of the notes for this title are included in Notebook 66 and comprise thirty pages with some fascinating diagrams. The notes accurately reflect the novel, with some minor deviations mentioned below. Oddly, the all-important list of the passengers' possessions, which contains the main clue in the novel and which first draws Poirot's attention to the killer, is not included in the notes.

The first page succinctly states the plot:

Aeroplane Murder – A special knife with thin pointed blade. Man gets up – goes into lavatory (blue pullover) comes back in white coat – darting like a steward – leans over talks about menu card stabs man – gives low sneeze at same time – goes back – returns in blue pullover and sits down again

From the beginning of the notes the killer is a man and, perhaps surprisingly, even the detail of his blue pullover is retained. The idea of a low sneeze (an echo of *The Murder at the Vicarage*) was, however, discarded and the victim changed to a woman.

In later pages the plot is further elaborated:

Chapter II

The steward – discovers the body – asks for doctor.
   B[ryant] comes
HP at his elbow – the ways – the Duponts suggest it –
   Mr Ryder agrees – mark on neck – P picks up thorn –
   Mr Clancy – blowpipe – arrow poison.
Arrival at Croydon – everyone kept in first car – Inspector
   – in plain clothes – another Inspector – Japp –
Why, it's Mr Hercule Poirot – Or asks stewards who he is
   – they say they know him by sight etc.

Some pages earlier the idea of a blowpipe or an arrow as a murder weapon was considered. But, with typical Christie ingenuity, they were both to be used as a weapon for stabbing:

Stabbed by an arrow
   ”   by dart (poison) from blow pipe

This appears as Idea C on a list of plot ideas, in which Idea H is 'Aeroplane murder'. She settled on the blow-pipe for *Death in the Clouds*, while the arrow idea was used many years later in 'Greenshaw's Folly'. In *Mrs McGinty's Dead*, Mrs Oliver complains bitterly about pedantic readers who write to her pointing out mistakes in her books. She instances the blow-pipe she used in her novel *The Cat it was who Died*, 'where I made a blow-pipe a foot long and it's really six feet' (Chapter 12). This sounds very like a rueful Agatha Christie!

Most of the characters were also settled from early on although names were to change:

People on the plane
Mr Salvey and Mr Rider – Business acquaintances [James
   Ryder and, possibly, Daniel Clancy]
Mr Ryder Long – a dentist [Norman Gale]

Lady Carnforth – a gambler – husband won't pay her debts
[Countess of Horbury]

Jane Holt – a girl who has a humdrum career who has won
a prize in the Irish Sweep [Jane Grey]

M. Duval – pere et fils – Archaeologists [the Duponts]

Venetia Carr (who wants to marry Carnforth) [Venetia
Kerr]

James Leslie younger brother of Carnforth [possibly
replaced completely by Dr. Bryant]

Madeleine Arneau – maid to Lady Carnforth ['Madeleine']

Plot developments are considered, although not their eventual sequence:

Then Lady Carnforth – Japp and P – P stays behind and
gets her to suggest his staying behind – tells her the truth
and frightens her [Chapter 19]

Venetia Carr – P and J? – P plays on her dislike of Lady C
[apart from a brief appearance in Chapter 12 Venetia
Kerr does not feature again]

Mr Ryder – all fairly straightforward – business difficulties
etc. [Chapter 18]

The Duponts – M. Dupont is to lecture at Antiquarian
Society but perhaps they see them in Paris [Chapter 22]

Bryant – Japp interviews him – P goes as patient – may be
a drug supplier – or someone who has done an Illegal
operation – or guilty of non-professional conduct
[Chapter 20/23]

Clancy – received the little man very hospitably – very
chatty [Chapter 15]

Oddly, Venetia Kerr is not questioned either by Poirot or
any of his fellow-investigators. Note also her address, Little

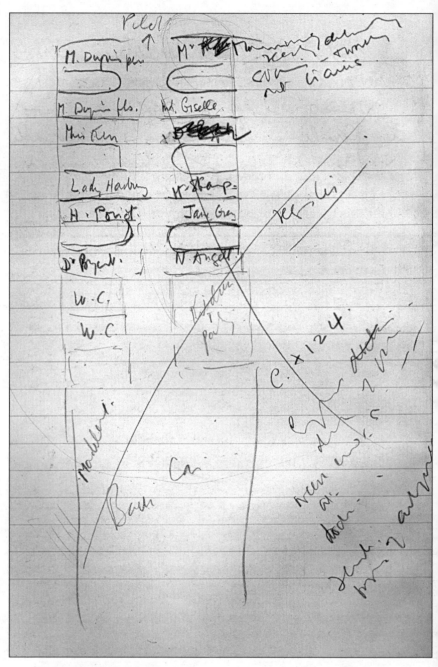

*These sketches from consecutive pages of Notebook 66 show great attention to detail during the plotting of* Death in the Clouds. *Vitally, Norman Angell's seat in the earliest two sketches is beside the WCs . . .*

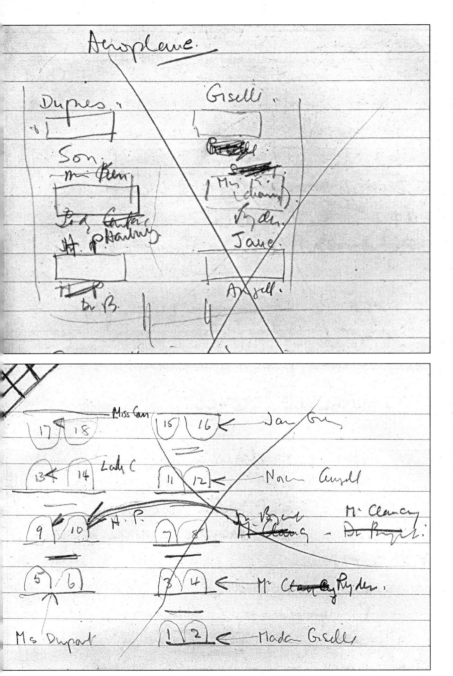

*. . . but he is subsequently moved to the opposite end of the cabin, as dictated by the plot. Note the inclusion of the pilot's cabin, the kitchen and pantry, the WCs, and the fact that some seats face each other.*

Paddocks, the scene, fifteen years later, of a dramatic killing in *A Murder is Announced*. And the subterfuge adopted by the Countess of Horbury to disguise her cocaine, by labelling it 'Boracic powder', is the same as that adopted by the criminal twenty years later in *Hickory Dickory Dock*.

With her customary plot fertility, Christie came up with a few possibilities for Gale's partner in crime:

Motive

Inheritance of money by daughter Anne

A. Anne is Jane Holt – Jane Holt and Angell [Norman Gale] plan the murder
B. Anne is Jane Holt – she is unaware of this – but Angell determines to marry her
C. Angele Morisot is Anne – she is in it with Angell – creates disturbance by coming in and speaking to her mistress at moment of murder – also gives damaging evidence against her
D. Angele Morisot is Anne – but is not guilty – she is engaged to Angell but never sees him on liner. He gets engaged to her under a false name – James Clare – a novelist – has a flat in London
E. ~~Real~~ False Angele Morisot presents herself with full proofs of identity to recover fortune (Real one Jane)

The most striking is the idea of Jane Grey as a fellow criminal, which would have provided an undoubted surprise. It was however abandoned in favour of Idea C, the maid.

The notes also include diagrams illustrating the disposition of the passengers in the plane seats. Both from these and the novel itself, it is clear that the interior of a plane cabin in the 1930s was very different to that of a modern plane. The sketches show only 18 seats and a mere 11 passengers, and of the possible nine aisle seats, only two are occupied. And a feature common to all three sketches is the arrangement of Jane and Angell (as Norman Gale was known at that stage). They are always shown sitting opposite each other in window seats, away from the aisle, as dictated by the plot. The chances of Gale being identified on his admittedly daring walk through the plane on the way to and from his commission of the crime are remote; as he reasonably guessed, Jane was likely to spend the interim checking her appearance. A greater danger, and one that has not been commented upon, was from the other stewards; it was much more likely that they would have spotted an 'extra' steward.

The plot of *Death in the Clouds* depends on a device that has garnered adverse criticism. The accusation is that the killer, and by extension the author, takes it for granted that 'nobody looks at a servant'. This ploy, and its reverse – a servant masquerading as an employer – is used in many Christie titles: *The Mystery of the Blue Train, Appointment with Death, One, Two, Buckle my Shoe, Sparkling Cyanide, Taken at the Flood* and *After the Funeral*, as well as the long short story 'Greenshaw's Folly'. Christie somewhat defuses this accusation with the following exchange from Chapter 24 ii of *After the Funeral*:

'I ought to have seen it sooner – I felt in a vague kind of way
    I had seen you before somewhere – but of course one
    never looks much at –' He stopped.
'No, one doesn't bother to look at a mere companion-help
    . . . a drudge, a domestic drudge! Almost a servant.'

## *'How Does Your Garden Grow?'*
### August 1935

———————◄○►———————

A plea for help to Poirot is too late to save Amelia Barrowby, but he is determined to get to the truth.

———————◄○►———————

> *Mary, Mary, quite contrary*
> *How does your garden grow?*
> *With silver bells and cockle-shells*
> *And pretty maids all in a row.*

This short nursery rhyme features no less than five times throughout the Notebooks, even though it provides the title of just one short story. This story's connection to the nursery rhyme is stronger than 'Sing a Song of Sixpence' or 'Four and Twenty Blackbirds', as it includes the shells, the garden and the killer's name. Mary Delafontaine poisons her aunt and hides the shells of the fatal oysters among the other cockle shells used as decoration in her garden. She tries, unsuccessfully, to incriminate the foreign companion:

The old lady – the foreign girl – Mary – the 'weak' husband

The final plot is encapsulated in Notebook 20:

Oyster story – Man dies after dinner – strychnine in oyster – swallowed – shells out in garden or in shell box – food analysed – nothing. Possibly some complication about a cachet he took – or someone gave him – if so, unjustly accused

It is another example of one of Christie's favourite early plot devices – the summoning of Poirot to the scene of a suspected crime and his consequent discovery that he is too late. As early as 1923 she first used this idea in *The Murder on the Links*, and subsequently in 'The Cornish Mystery', *Dumb Witness* and 'The Incident of the Dog's Ball'. The device has both an emotional and a practical impact. The summoner, who has promised to explain the situation in detail, is now unable to do so and Poirot has a moral, as well as a practical, imperative to solve the crime. The appearance of any foreigner (including Poirot) is always viewed with suspicion by the inhabitants of small villages throughout the Christie canon, and in 'How Does Your Garden Grow?', the appearance of a Russian character allows Christie to subvert, yet again, reader prejudice. As she was to do even more comprehensively two years later in *Dumb Witness*.

The main character, Mary Delafontaine, became a byword in Christie's shorthand, appearing in abbreviated form in the course of plotting *Third Girl* and *Ordeal by Innocence* respectively, even though she was used in the final plot of neither novel:

Mary Del. – Arthur (innocent husband) – Katrina –
suspicious, passionate – for money looks after old boy

Olivia (The Mary Delafontaine wife)

The name was actually used for one of the victims, a friend of Mrs Oliver's, in *The Pale Horse*.

### *The ABC Murders*
### 6 January 1936

◄○►

A series of letters to Hercule Poirot challenges him to a deadly game. Despite these forewarnings, the letter-writer manages to kill Alice Ascher in Andover, Betty Barnard in Bexhill, and Sir Carmichael Clarke in Churston. As the entire country watches, can Poirot prevent the D murder?

◄○►

In Notebook 13, in the course of a fifteen-page travel diary, we find an exact date for the writing of this novel.:

Tuesday November 6th [1934] Started *The A.B.C. Murders*.

Featuring a hugely imaginative concept – an alphabetical series both of murder victims and locations, chosen apparently at random – that was carried off with consummate skill and daring, *The ABC Murders* was destined to become one of the top three Christie titles. And it is now forgotten that it was one of the earliest versions of the 'serial killer', a ploy that is now a staple of both the bookshelf and the screen. When this book was written the phrase did not even exist and is yet another example of Christie anticipating, without even realising it, motifs that were to dominate crime fiction in later years. (The other major anticipation was *Death Comes as the End*, set in Ancient Egypt and foreshadowing another current trend for crime novels set in various eras of the past.)

Sadly there are only fifteen pages of notes for *The ABC Murders*, scattered over three Notebooks. I suspect that there were earlier and rougher notes that have not survived, because the book's intricate premise needed detailed planning and the notes we have are relatively straightforward and organised.

The earliest jotting would seem to be Notebook 66, as item E on a list that includes the plot outlines for 'Problem at Sea', 'The Dream', *Death in the Clouds, Dumb Witness* and *Sad Cypress,* and also includes the rudimentary germ of what was to become, almost 20 years later, *A Pocket Full of Rye*:

> Series of murders – P gets letter from apparent maniac.
>
> First – an old woman in Yorkshire – Second – a business man – Third – a girl (tripper?) – Fourth – Sir McClintock Marsh (who isn't killed – but escapes) – Fifth – Muriel Lavery
>
> Analysis of his house party – one person knows girl but has absolute cast iron alibi.
>
> Idea of book is to prove alibi false but really Sir MM – murdered ~~second v~~ third victim for reasons of his own – 1st and 2nd camouflage – idea being to fasten guilt on cast iron alibi man

It is interesting to note several points of similarity, even in this early jotting, with the finished novel. These include the retention of the 'old woman' as the first victim, although the novel's second victim is a young girl – 'tripper?' – at a seaside resort, reflecting the Notebook's third victim. The device of two earlier murders as camouflage for a third – 'for reasons of his own' – is retained while the owner of the 'cast-iron alibi' would seem to be the forerunner of Alexander Bonaparte Cust, with this cast-iron alibi for the 'B' murder.

In contrast, the most surprising divergence from the finished novel is the unmasking of the fourth supposed 'victim' as the killer. This 'victim as killer' idea had already been used to great effect by Christie in *Peril at End House,* it would be used again, to equally surprising effect, in *One, Two, Buckle my Shoe, A Murder is Announced* and *The Mirror Crack'd from Side to Side.*

The reference to 'his house party' is also puzzling. There is no house party setting in *The ABC Murders,* although the idea does have echoes of the analysis of Sir Bartholomew Strange's fatal house party in *Three Act Tragedy*. And, of course, there is no mention of the alphabetical sequence, which is the whole *raison d'être* of the novel; if the fifth victim is Muriel Lavery then the sequence is certainly not alphabetical.

Notebook 20 also has a brief outline of the plot and here the alphabetical sequence has been established. The details of the significant 'C' murder have moved nearer to those in the novel, but there are still major differences:

> Aberystwyth – old woman Mrs. Ames – husband suspected
> Bexhill – Janet ~~Taylor~~ Blythe
> Cottersmarch – Sir Morton ~~Carmichael~~ Clarke – also a very
>     wealthy man – his brother Rudolph – anxious to help –
>     Janet Taylor's friend or sister also keen
> Doncaster – James Don – killed in a cinema
> P. gets a telegram – E. – sends it himself – man is released
>     – R[udolph] says this must be another murder

Much of the detail of the first four murders here is retained. The A murder features an old lady whose husband is suspected; the location, however, is different (perhaps because Andover is easier to spell and/or pronounce than Aberystwyth!). The B murder is the same location although the victim's name is different – note the change from a 'T' to a 'B' initial – although Barnard is the surname eventually chosen. The C murder has the same set-up – a wealthy Sir Morton Clarke (note that the name as it appears in the book, Carmichael, is, interestingly, deleted here). The brother and sister of two of the victims are anxious to help, an idea pursued in Poirot's band of helpers. The D murder does take place in Doncaster and in a cinema, although in the novel it is actually a victim with the surname initial E.

A major surprise, however, and one that is, unfortunately, left unexplained, is the reference to the E murder. I would hazard a guess that in sending an ABC letter to himself Poirot was stage-managing the release from prison of a suspect (possibly Alexander Bonaparte Cust) he knows to be innocent. He could also have been forcing the killer's hand, thereby precipitating a more dramatic unmasking in the last chapter.

Notebook 66, some fifty pages after the first reference, again takes up the novel beginning with possible locations for the murders. It goes on to consider two theories, both of which contain some elements – the existence of a 'real' victim, with an avaricious legatee, in a sequence of 'camouflage' victims – that Christie eventually adopted. Finally, it lists the questions that Poirot asks his five helpers in Chapter 32 of the novel:

A.B.C. Murder

Poirot gets letter
To Aberystwyth

Brixham or Bexhill
~~Cheadle~~ or Croydon
~~Dartmouth~~ Daneshill

Theory A
Intended victim Sir ~~Lucas~~ Oscar Dane –
It causes a stir – his fortune goes to his brother Lewis Dane

Theory B
Intended victim Janet King
3rd victim is Sir Oscar Dane – <u>but</u> he is only stabbed – not fatally injured – her will leaves everything to her cousin Vera who is the nurse attending Oscar – Vera and Oscar are attracted to each other

Only one of the possible locations, Bexhill, was actually used in the book. Dartmouth and both of the C suggestions are rejected in favour of Churston, a location well known to Christie. It is still possible to get the train, like Poirot and Hastings, to Churston and walk from there to Greenway House, although at this point, 1934, Christie did not yet own the house.

Theory A was the eventual choice as the main plot, although Theory B had some interesting possibilities. Sir Oscar Dane faking an attack on himself in order to kill another victim and inherit, through marriage, a fortune is a very Christie-an concept but it does have more than an echo, from two years earlier, of *Peril at End House* (where Nick Buckley fakes attacks on herself in order to kill her cousin and inherit a fortune) and this is possibly the reason for its rejection.

The biggest surprise at this point is that the victims are not chosen alphabetically despite the fact that a few pages earlier Christie is listing Brixham/Cheadle/Dartmouth. The third 'victim' is Dane and the fourth is King. While some connection between the victims would have been necessary, the alphabetical sequence was brilliant and – like many Christie ploys – brilliantly simple. We will never know who or what inspired it, but perhaps Christie remembered *Why Didn't They Ask Evans?*, published two months before she began *The ABC Murders*, where an open ABC Guide is mentioned in Chapter 24 and used as a clue to a character's whereabouts?

Finally, the five questions of Chapter 32 all appear in the Notebook as they appear in the book, apart from a different initial ('J') for the Mary Drower question and the substitution of the shorter and subtler 'Ascot hat' one for the Franklin Clarke.

P asks a question of all of them
Megan – a passion for truth – want the truth? – NO – You
    may not want the truth but you can give a truthful
    answer!
Thora – would you have married Sir C if his wife had died

F[ranklin] Do you remember the news in the paper the day
　　you landed or [a question about] Ascot hats
J. Have you got a young man?
D[onald] When did you take your holiday

And one of the main themes of Chapters 32 and 35, a murderer hunted like a fox, is captured in a last cryptic note:

Bit about the fox

### 'Problem at Sea'
### February 1936

————————◄○►————————

Mrs Clapperton is found dead in her cabin
during a holiday cruise and Poirot's solution
depends on his most unusual witness ever.

————————◄○►————————

The first note for this story, dated January 1935, appears in
Notebook 66 and the elaboration later in the same Notebook
includes much of the detail of the completed story:

Ventriloquist – on boat . . . Col C. very good with cards –
says he has been on music hall stage etc. Wife dies in cabin
but her voice heard inside after she has been killed

Man tells steward to lock cabin – body already inside –
later comes back and ~~Cabin lock~~ Calls to wife – she answers
apparently (ventriloquist). Hypodermic beside her – and
pricks on her bare arm

One point of difference between the notes and the finished
story is that the hypodermic idea is replaced by stabbing.

While the ventriloquism plot device is clever it would not have carried a novel; how right Christie was to use it for a short story.

ᴓᴝᴓ

## *'Triangle at Rhodes'*
### May 1936

Despite warning the protagonists, Hercule Poirot is unable to prevent a murder in his Rhodes holiday hotel. But he can solve it by correctly interpreting the fatal triangle.

The genesis of this short story is complicated. There are variant texts in the US and the UK appearances, and there are copious notes for its dramatisation. And as it was expanded and altered for the novel *Evil under the Sun*, some of the notes overlap and intersect. It is not possible to date the Notebooks accurately, but the following in Notebook 20 succinctly summarises the plot:

> The triangle – Valerie C. loved by Commander C. and Douglas Golding

It went through a few changes before arriving at the version we know. These notes, complete with Christie's sketches of the various 'eternal triangles', are on either side of those for 'Problem at Pollensa Bay'. To complicate matters even more, two separate and totally different settings and sets of characters are listed:

> Soviet Russia

Room at hotel –
In train –

The Triangle

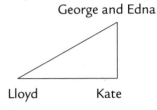

George and Edna

Lloyd        Kate

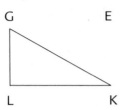

G                    E

L                    K

Anna and Ivan
The Gordons – Lloyd and Jessica

Rhodes – Bathing – Emily Renault (Joan Heaslip)

The Courtneys – beautiful – faded – empty-headed
The Goldings arrive – man – plain wife – a shock to discover
they are on honeymoon – his devotion to Mrs C – bowled
over – antagonism between him and C – a quarrel at dinner
– everyone talking about it.
    Quiet woman comes to PP . . . what shall she do? He
says leave the island at once – you are in danger – (PP says
to himself where has he seen her – remembrance of murder
trial). Lee a chemist – Golding has his usual drink – gin and
ginger tonic – Mrs Golding drinks it instead and dies

The setting of Soviet Russia (perhaps inspired by a brief foray
there while returning from Ur in 1931) would have been
unique for Christie and very unusual for detective fiction
in general at the time. It is perhaps not surprising that this
version was never developed. The second scenario is nearer
to the published version although as a case for Parker Pyne.
    Eventually in Notebook 66 we arrive at the 'real' version.
The short précis below of the plot is in the middle of the
notes for *The ABC Murders*, a position which tallies with the

publication dates of each. That this plot and setting should suddenly appear, fully formed, while Christie was plotting one her greatest novels is yet another example of her creative fertility.

> Poirot story – Chantries – she beautiful, empty headed, he a strong silent man of personality – The Goldings – G infatuated with Mrs C – Mrs G in despair comes to Poirot – you are in danger. Various scenes if book – actually Chantries and Mrs G are lovers – the gin and tonic – Gold – is supposed to want to kill C – Mrs C drinks it instead – and dies

Note the words in the middle of this jotting – 'Various scenes if book'. Christie obviously thought, and correctly, that this situation had great potential for elaboration. And she did just that a few years later in *Evil under the Sun*, although the plots are quite different. Both feature a triangle situation in a beach setting although in each case the triangle is cleverly presented in such a way as to confound reader expectation. There is also a distinct similarity to the method of poisoning adopted by the killer in *The Mirror Crack'd from Side to Side*, over 25 years later.

Finally, the following from Notebook 58 may seem like a rough note for 'Triangle at Rhodes', although it actually occurs in the middle of the jottings for *A Caribbean Mystery*:

> Triangle idea (Rhodes)
> Lovely siren – her husband – devoted, dark, cynical – little brown mouse, nice little woman, wife – plain stupid husband – dark husband really has liaison with mouse. They plan to do away with siren – stupid husband is to be suspected

There are similarities between the two – the quartet of two husbands and wives in an exotic beach setting. But in fact

Christie included it as a plot resumé to herself as she considered possibilities for her Caribbean quartet.

## 'The Regatta Mystery'
### June 1936

'The Regatta Mystery' is unique in the Christie output: it exists in two versions, one with Parker Pyne and a second with Hercule Poirot. The story was first published in the US in the *Chicago Tribune* in May 1936 and in the UK the following month in *The Strand* magazine. The US version featured Parker Pyne but Poirot investigated in the UK, possibly because he was better known to *Strand* readers than Parker Pyne. The first post-*Strand* UK publication of the story was in the omnibus *Hercule Poirot: The Complete Short Stories* (2008). The plot in both versions is identical although there are minor textual differences consequent on the change of character.

Surviving notes confirm that Parker Pyne was the detective in the original version. The first page of Notebook 20 is headed:

The Reminiscences of Mr P P told by himself

The ideas for potential reminiscences include:

The strangulation story...
The Infra-Red photograph...
Mr P P and his niece...meeting with a financier...
At restaurant in Soho – beautiful girl...

And, intriguingly:

The Adventure of the Victorian Whatnot

The most extensive Parker Pyne notes are those for 'The Regatta Mystery' and they include a brief mention of another Christie character:

> Mrs Oliver sent to Mr. P.P.
> Can you think up a new Adventure story?
> Mrs Oliver trots out all the old chestnuts

Detective novelist Ariadne Oliver, before she appeared alongside Poirot, worked for Parker Pyne, where her job was to create suitable plots to solve problems brought by clients. In 'The Case of the Discontented Soldier', she devises a scenario utilising the 'old chestnut' of characters trapped in a cellar with rising water; and she is name-checked in 'The Case of the Rich Woman'.

The notes follow closely the course of the story, apart from the usual name changes:

> A bet – that if I am a thief I could hide a thing and you could not find it. Game checked for a minute – as the waiter removed the plates – then went on – it was passed round + round.

> Newsboy on rounds – calling – man throws down a penny to him – catches newspaper. He is therefore suspected – comes to Mr P. P.

> Characters
> Mr Leonard (diamond merchant)
> Mr. Griffin          ”
> Miss Eve Keen (Canadian girl)
> Mr and Mrs Harrington – smart live by their wits couple
> Miss Gloria King (actress)
> George Earle

The girl says I've dropped it – then she's searched – but
she has really got it – bit of plasticine – stuck into ring of
bag

The story is set in Dartmouth, a short journey across the
river from Greenway House, and the description of the
dining-room in which it takes place tallies exactly with that
of the Royal Castle Hotel at Dartmouth harbour. Although
lighter in tone than her murder mysteries, the plot is replete
with clever Christie ideas and one of the main devices was
re-cycled twenty-five years later, in *Cat among the Pigeons*.

## *Murder in Mesopotamia*
### 6 July 1936

When Amy Leatheran accepts a nursing job on
an archaeological dig looking after the neurotic
Mrs Leidner she little suspects that she will be involved
in the investigation of her patient's murder. But how
did the killer gain access to his victim when the
room was under constant observation?

From the time of her marriage to Max Mallowan, Christie
accompanied him annually to Iraq on his archaeological
expeditions. These travels gave her background for her
foreign travel novels but the one that most closely matches
her own experiences is *Murder in Mesopotamia*. The setting
is an archaeological dig and, apart from the detective plot,
there is much detail of day-to-day living, written from first-
hand knowlege.

The surviving notes are not extensive, less than fifteen
pages in total scattered over four Notebooks. Notebook 66

has a one-line jotting in a list dated January 1935; she wrote the novel during that year with hardback publication in July 1936:

Dig murder 1st person Hospital Nurse?

A list of characters given in Notebook 20 tallies with the published novel (although some of the men are not definitely recognisable), as does the basic situation outlined immediately following:

The People
1. Dr. L[eidner]
2. Mrs L[eidner]
3. Architect B. man of 35 taciturn attractive [Richard Carey]
4. Epigraphist P. moody man – hypochondriac or Priest (not really a priest!) [Fr. Lavigny]
5. Young man R. inclined to be garrulous or naïve [David Emmott]
6. Miss Johnson – middle aged – devoted to L.
7. A wife – not archaeological – pretty – frivolous [Mrs. Mercado]
8. A dour young man G. [Carl Reiter]

The wife – very queer – Is she being doped against her own knowledge? Atmosphere gradually develops of intensity – a bomb may explode any minute

Sadly, there are no detailed notes for the plot mechanics, especially in view of Christie's reminder to herself at the start of this extract:

Can we work in/on [?] the window idea?

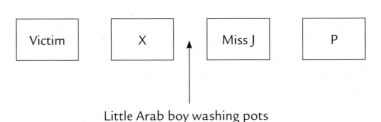

Little Arab boy washing pots

The 'window idea' is undoubtedly one of her most ingenious, and like all of her best plots it is simple – in retrospect. That said, when, in Chapter 23, Miss Johnson stands on the roof and says 'I've seen how someone could come in from outside – and no one would ever guess,' she is not being strictly accurate. It would have been more truthful to say 'I've seen how someone could commit this murder – and no one would ever guess.' The murderer did not come in from outside – he was already present – and Miss Johnson suddenly realised how he had managed to commit the murder without ever leaving the roof.

And despite the reference to the vital 'window idea', the accompanying diagram is not really relevant to it as it represents part of the ground floor plan of the Expedition House, although a different one to that included in the finished novel.

Although Christie experimented briefly with other possible killers, the front-runner always seems to have been Dr Leidner:

Possible gambits – Mrs. L's past life – Some man she has injured – husband or someone she betrayed – hate her – pursued her – she gets more and more nervous

Development
A. Mrs. L is killed
B. Somebody else is killed in mistake for her – really she engineers it and persecution story is an invention

Dr. L murders Mrs. L
Then a second murder – someone who knew something –
  Miss Johnson?

Miss J original wife – her revenge?
Or – a trumped up story by wife – and husband killed?
Or Dr. L the villain

Finally, Notebook 47 reveals that Christie considered using *Murder in Mesopotamia* as the basis for a play. However, she rejects the idea of using the novel's characters or plot as a basis (despite the 'troublemaking attractive woman', a similar character to Mrs Leidner) and sketches an alternate scenario:

Play on a dig? Possible characters from Murder in Mesopot[amia]

Director American – ~~with a troublemaking wife~~ – in love with a troublemaking attractive woman – widow of an inventor – or atom scientist – imprisoned for Communist activities – (after Hiss idea?) Ten years ago – he's in prison – she has divorced him – in love with Deirdre? Married to him – is ~~Really~~ on point of having affair with middle-aged architect – two doctors from medical conference Baghdad come along – one a friend of expedition – the other a plastic surgeon – he gets killed – then she does

Alger Hiss was a US State Department official accused of spying and jailed in 1950, but for perjury. His guilt or innocence of the spying accusation is still a matter of debate. He died in 1992. This outline seems an unlikely subject for a stage play, but some of these ideas were adapted for *Destination Unknown*.

Despite a highly ingenious murder, a unique setting, a dramatic situation and an unexpected murderer, *Murder in Mesopotamia* cannot qualify as first-class Christie. The story behind the motive for Mrs Leidner's murder beggars the reader's belief; how Christie (or her editor) ever thought this was a likely, or even a credible, scenario is difficult to imagine. Apart from the intrinsic dissatisfaction, it also spoils one of the few examples of Christie's use of the 'impossible crime' device. This is a sub-genre of the detective novel where the interest lies not only in the identity of the killer (Who?) but also in the means by which the crime is committed (How). In the 'impossible crime' detective novel victims are found in the middle of snow-covered lawns with no footprints, in a room under constant observation (as here) or a room with all the doors and windows locked from the inside (as in *Hercule Poirot's Christmas* or 'The Second Gong').

### 'Murder in the Mews'
December 1936

◄○►

A quill pen, a dressing case, a game of golf
and a cuff link all combine to make Hercule Poirot
suspicious of a Guy Fawkes Night suicide.

◄○►

With customary ingenuity Christie plays a neat variation on 'murder disguised as suicide' by turning the concept on its head in the novella 'Murder in the Mews', an early proof of her ingenuity at ringing the changes on a clichéd plot device. This ploy first appeared over ten years earlier in the short story 'The Market Basing Mystery', and when she came to elaborate it a decade later she retained the original idea and added some refinements. Despite flaunting the main clue – the green quill pen – she still leads the reader, and Inspector Japp, a merry dance of misdirection.

As the Notebooks reveal, the 5 November background was

originally to have been a very different plot. Among a list of plot ideas in Notebook 20 that included *Sad Cypress*, 'Triangle at Rhodes' and 'Problem at Sea' we find the following:

> Murderer leaves body just before he finds it (officially)!
> It has been dead for two hours so he has alibi
> > Nov. 5th – fireworks going off. Book?

But the only aspect of this jotting that she subsequently used was in 'Murder in the Mews', where she adopted this Guy Fawkes connection; echoing *Peril at End House* four years earlier, fireworks are used as a camouflage for a gunshot. Most of the plotting is in Notebook 30:

> Adaptation of Market Basing Mystery
> Mrs Allen – young woman living in Mews – engaged to be married – her friend, Jane Petersham – quiet dark girl

> The Mews Murder
> P and Japp Guy Fawkes day – little boy – back to Japp's
> > room – a call – young woman shot – in Mayfair
> Mrs. Allen – Miss Jane Plenderleith – she arrived home that
> > morning – found her friend dead

> Locked cupboard (with golf clubs in) tennis balls – and a
> > couple of empty suitcases.
> Pistol in hand too loose – wrist watch on right wrist –
> > blotting paper torn off – stubs of two different
> > cigarettes

Typically, the pages are scattered throughout the Notebook and are interspersed with ideas for stories with a British Museum and National Gallery background, the death of a fortune-teller and much of the plotting for *Dumb Witness*. Not surprisingly in a novella more than six times the length of the original, most of the material above is new; only the wristwatch clue and the cigarettes are retained from the earlier story. And the characters and background in the two versions are totally different.

∞↶↷∞

### Dumb Witness
5 July 1937

————————————◂○▸————————————

Emily Arundell writes to Hercule Poirot on 17 April but he does not receive the letter until 28 June. And by then she is dead. Poirot goes to Market Basing to investigate her death, where the case involves spiritualism, a brooch, a dog's ball – and another death.

————————————◂○▸————————————

Most of the notes for *Dumb Witness,* are contained in Notebook 30 together with notes for *Death on the Nile* and the short story 'The Incident of the Dog's Ball'. *Dumb Witness* was published at the end of 1936 in the US as a *Saturday Evening Post* serial called *Poirot Loses a Client,* and as *Mystery at Littlegreen House* in a UK serialisation beginning in February 1937.

In connection with the US serialisation, a surviving letter dated June 1936 from Edmund Cork to Christie thanks her for the revised version sent to the *Saturday Evening Post* magazine (who paid $16,000 for it, $2,000 more than *Cards on the Table*). Cork considered the revisions a 'tremendous improvement' and suggested 'using it for Collins also'. This most probably refers to the first four chapters, in which the 'little English village' setting is told in the third person, with the rest of the book being narrated by Hastings.

*Dumb Witness* is the archetypal Christie village mystery – a mysterious death in a well-to-do household, a collection of impecunious relatives, the village doctor and solicitor, and the arrival of Poirot whose questioning sets village tongues wagging. Once again the red herring of spiritualism is dragged across the investigation. As far back as 'The Adventure of the Egyptian Tomb' in 1923 Christie murderers used this ploy to cover their tracks. And as late as 1961 and *The Pale Horse*, with a more sinister version of *Dumb Witness*'s Tripp sisters, spiritualism is a major plot device.

Reader prejudice is toyed with, and yet again subverted, with the introduction of suspicious foreigner, Dr Tanios. Four previous killers are mentioned – *Death in the Clouds*, *The Mysterious Affair at Styles*, *The Murder of Roger Ackroyd* and *The Mystery of the Blue Train* – and there is an oblique reference to *Murder on the Orient Express* in Chapter 25.

Unusually, we know from internal evidence – the ending of Chapter 7 – the exact timeline of the novel; Emily Arundell died on 1 May 1936 and Poirot's investigation began on 28 June, although for most of that investigation there is nothing to show that murder has been committed. The description of Market Basing in Chapter 6 corresponds to that of Wallingford where Christie had, some years earlier, bought Winterbrook House.

The notes, headed with a working title, list the family members and background, although names and details – Charles is not married and his sister is Teresa, not Bella – were to change:

Death of Martha Digby [Emily Arundell]

The Digbys – their family history
Miss Martha – Miss Amelia – Miss Jane – Miss Ethel and
    Mr Thomas
Marriage of Mr Thomas – to a barmaid?
Mr John [Charles] and Miss Daphne (T's children)
John – stock exchange – married – his wife clever woman
Daphne [Bella] marries an Armenian? Dr. Mendeman
    [Tanios] – charming man – his wife quiet, cold

The early chapters of the novel are accurately sketched with only minor differences: the chemist is delayed until Chapter 21 and there is a cryptic reference to painting in connection with Theresa:

General Plan
P. receives letter – he and H[astings] – he writes – then he tears it up – No, we will go – Market Basing – The Lamb . . . Board to be let or sold. Visit to house agents – an order to view – Ellen conversation – rap – rap – rap – a ball drops down staircase terrier wagging his tail

The chemist – his remembrances – they pretend that are writing up a history of the town – he is an amateur archaeologist – the history of the family. P goes to doctor – as a patient (and an archaeologist) doctor comes to dine – a good deal of local gossip – some little mystery about that death? Doctor indignant – perfectly natural causes – he says – well, I should think you'd be satisfied now. P. says 'But she died'

Theresa – flat in Chelsea – painting – her engagement to Dick Donaldson – latter wants to specialise – infection – liver – serum therapeutics

Oddly, there are references to Peggy, rather than (Ara)Bella, in both of the following extracts. This was probably an early name choice for the character, as the clue of the symmetrical letter seen in the mirror, M for Margaret, would still apply. As we will see, this device was considered in conjunction with the plotting for *Death on the Nile*.

Another visit to the terrier – to the Tripps – hallucinations etc. – evidence of the cook – Miss Theresa on stairs that night – a piece of thread – yes, Ellen had found it. Miss Lawson again – money missing from drawer – knew who

Dr Seles — very ill man — had known her at St John's poisons.

Pfeiffer mentions his researches.
The Castor oil plant.
Then A. *who* killed her?
B. Why?

Miss Van Schuyler —

Mrs Pf. says — a woman in her cabin ill and was sick. Oh! I'm sorry. Says it was Mrs Pleur.

H. M. A. W. I. O. T. U. V. Y.

Helen.
Nellie.
Margaret. Mary
Peggy. Polly.
Greta.
Henrietta
Etta.
Ettie.
Antoinette
Nelly

Wilhelmina
Billie
Mina.
Winifred
Freda.
Isabel
Belle.
Augusta
Gussy.
Theodora
Dora.
Anne
NAN—

*This* **Dumb Witness** *of experimentation with symmetrical letters and corresponding names is from Notebook 30. Note the inclusion here of 'Wilhelmina/ Mina', the first name of Miss Lawson. The all-important 'Arabella' and 'Teresa' are arrived at later in the same Notebook.*

took it. P. bullies her a bit – she gets rattled – talks about
poor Peggy – who has left her husband

Peggy again – about husband – she refuses to say – P. says
tell me – I'm going to be in danger – she refuses to say
anything. H. says 'she knows something' – asked about
dressing gown – says yes – she has a dark blue silk one –
Theresa gave it to her. When? When we were all down
that weekend, Which day? I can't remember

And a page of letters and names experimenting with symmetrical letters, the vital clue as misinterpreted by Miss
Lawson, eventually arrives at the required one:

ARABELLA        A.T.
   BELLA        T.A. Arundell

# The Incident of the Dog's Ball

Although it was not published until 2009 – over seventy years after *Dumb Witness* – it seems appropriate, because of the intertwined genesis of novel and short story, to include here discussion of 'The Incident of the Dog's Ball'.

In this story we have a recognisable and typical Christie setting: a small village, a wealthy old lady and her avaricious relatives. It is immediately apparent, even from the title, that there are strong links to *Dumb Witness* with a a similar basic situation and the germs of ideas subsequently expanded: the brief mention of the Pym spiritualists, the all-important accident on the stairs. But unlike some other occasions when she reused an earlier idea or short story (e.g. 'The Mystery of the Baghdad/Spanish Chest'), here Christie gives us a different murderer and explanation.

The plot device of Poirot receiving a plea for help from someone who dies before he can talk to them is one that she had used previously. As early as *The Murder on the Links* (1923) his correspondent is already dead when Poirot arrives in France. And 'The Second Gong', 'The Cornish Mystery' and 'How Does Your Garden Grow?' feature the device

## When was it written?

Of the Poirot and Hastings short stories, all with the exception of 'Double Sin' (September 1928) and 'The Mystery of the Baghdad Chest' (January 1932) were published in

1923/24. All the short stories after 1932 feature Poirot alone. No notes for any of those early stories survive and where Christie refers to them in the Notebooks, it is only as speculation on expanding or reusing them. In many ways 'The Incident of the Dog's Ball' is similar in style, setting and tone to many other short stories dating from the early 1920s and published in *Poirot Investigates* and *Poirot's Early Cases*. But if it was written early in Christie's career, this in turn raises the question of why it would have languished for almost twenty years without appearing in print. It does not appear in her agent's records of work received by them and offered for sale. I hope to show that it dates from later in her career.

In Notebook 30 it is included in a list which may help to establish more accurately its date of composition:

Ideas
A. Dog's Ball
B. Death on the Nile
C. Strychnine absorbed through skin?
D. Double Alibi e.g. A and B murder C but – A is accused of trying to murder B at same time.
E. Figurehead woman. Man back from Africa.
F. Second Gong elaborated
G. Mescaline
H. Illegitimate daughter – apomorphine idea?
Ideas to be incorporated
   Brownie camera idea
   Brooch with AO or OA on it AM. MA

If we apply some of Poirot's own methods we may be able to arrive at a timetable.

*Clue No. 1*
There are a number of immediately recognisable stories in this list: *Dumb Witness* or 'The Incident of the Dog's Ball' (A), *Death on the Nile* (B), *They Do it with Mirrors* (D) and *Sad Cypress*

Ideas

A. Paris Ball.

B. Death on the Nile.

C. Strychnine absorbed through skin?

D. Double alibi e.g. A & B murder C. but – A is accused of trying to murder B. at same time.

E. Figure... woman. Man back from Africa.

F. Second Gong elaborated.

G. Mescual.

H. Hysterical daughter. gramophone idea?
Ideas to be incorporated

Brownie Camera idea.

Brown nr. AO or OA or it AM. HA

Wife of (Dr Herter?) herself is thief or murderess etc – makes up story that someone has stolen ring or poison etc. + hood... A.M. seen in glass. She knows that

*This Dog's Ball from Notebook 30 is part-transcribed on the previous
page. Note the three intertwined fish logo in the top right-hand corner.*

(H). 'The Second Gong' (F) was first published in June 1932 and both *Dumb Witness* and *Death on the Nile* in 1937, the former in July and the latter in November of that year. So it is reasonable to assume that the list was written between those dates, i.e. after (if it was to be elaborated) 'The Second Gong' in June 1932 and before *Dumb Witness* in July 1937.

*Clue No. 2*
Unlike Item F on the list, 'Second Gong elaborated', there is no mention of elaboration in connection with 'Dog's Ball', lending support to the theory that it did not then exist as a short story.

*Clue No. 3*
In the Christie Archive there are two letters from her agent Edmund Cork. One, dated 26 June 1936, acknowledges receipt of a revised version of *Dumb Witness*; another, dated 29 April 1936, expresses delight at her news that *Death on the Nile* was finished. We now have a new later limit for the creation of the list: after June 1932 and before April 1936.

*Clue No. 4*
It is not unreasonable to suppose that the writing of *Death on the Nile* and *Dumb Witness*, both of them among her longest books, took over a year, which would bring our latest date back to April 1935. Our new dates are now June 1932 and April 1935. And if we add two items of conjecture to the equation . . .

*Clue No. 5*
In the change from 'The Incident of the Dog's Ball' to *Dumb Witness*, the setting moves from Little Hemel, in the county of Kent, to Market Basing, Berkshire:

> General Plan P. receives letter – he and H – he writes – then
> he tears it up – No, we will go – Market Basing – The Lamb

Market Basing is commonly assumed to bear more than a passing resemblance to Wallingford where Agatha Christie lived. She bought her house there in 1934 and this may account for the change of setting for the novel. There is evidence for this in the reference to The Lamb, a Wallingford pub, in Notebook 63. This is, admittedly, conjecture but as Poirot would say, 'It gives one furiously to think, does it not?'

*Clue No. 6*
Miss Matilda Wheeler writes to Poirot on 12 April, a Wednesday, according to Poirot's exposition: 'Consider the dates, Hastings' (section *v*). The 12th of April 1933 fell on a Wednesday.

*Conclusion?*
'The Incident of the Dog's Ball' was written, in all likelihood, in 1933.

## Why was it never published?

By the mid-1930s Agatha Christie was a household name, selling 10,000 hardbacks in the first year of a new title. She was one of the first writers to appear in paperback and her books had been dramatised and filmed. Why would any magazine not publish a new Poirot story, with its guarantee of increased sales? If it was offered to them . . . Again, we are in the realms of speculation, but I think the reason it never appeared in print is disappointingly mundane: it was never published because Agatha Christie never offered it to her agent. Because, in turn, she decided to turn it into a novel. Consider the evidence:

*Clue No. 1*
Her production of short stories had decreased from the multiple appearances of earlier years – 27 in 1923 and 34 in 1924 – to a mere half-dozen in 1933 and seven the following year. As she said when she declined to contribute to further

Detection Club collaborations, 'the energy to devise a series is much better employed in writing a couple of books'. She may well have thought the same about 'Dog's Ball' and decided to turn it into a complete new Poirot book.

## Clue No. 2

The Edmund Cork letter referred to above, dated 26 June 1936, acknowledges receipt of a revised version of *Dumb Witness*. This probably refers to the addition of the first four chapters, a domestic English village setting, which were added to help ensure a US serialisation in the *Saturday Evening Post* in November and December 1936. This in turn lends support to the idea that the novel was an expansion of 'The Incident of the Dog's Ball'. In the novel Hastings begins his first-person narration only at Chapter 5; the first four chapters are told in the omniscient third person with the assurance from Hastings that he did not witness the earlier events personally but that he 'has set them down accurately enough'. And, possibly significantly, the opening scenes of both the short story and Chapter 5 are, apart from the month of the year, identical.

## Clue No. 3

This not-offered-for-sale theory may also account for the major oversight involving the dates within the story. In section *i* Poirot says 'No, April the 12th is the date [on which the letter was written] assuredly' but in section *iv* he refers to August as the month when Miss Wheeler wrote the letter. An agent and/or an editor would surely have noticed a mistake of this magnitude, and one so germane to the plot?

## Conclusion

It is entirely possible that 'The Incident of the Dog's Ball' was written in 1933 and never offered for publication but, instead, transformed, in 1935/36, into the novel *Dumb Witness*.

The story is referred to in two Notebooks, but in Notebook 30 it is mentioned only in passing as Idea A in the list above. In Notebook 66 we find more detail with resemblance to the short story rather than the novel:

Dog's Ball    People

Mrs Grant – typical old lady
Miss Lawson – twittery companion
Mollie Davidson – Niece – earns living in a beauty parlour
Her young man – a ne'er do well
Journalist – Ted Weedon – has been in prison for forgery
    – forged uncle's name in City office –
owing to girl pressing him for money – some actress
James Grant – prim . . . respectable gentleman –
Engaged to hospital nurse – Miss O'Gorman
Ellen
Cook

The niece's name – Mollie Davidson – remains the same, as does her occupation; and that name appears nowhere else in the notes for *Dumb Witness*. The nephew's is amended only slightly to Graham, although that of the victim changes substantially from Mrs Grant to Miss Wheeler. Neither Mollie's young man or James Grant's fiancée features in the short story although Ted Weedon's proclivity for forgery is transferred to Charles Arundell, the rechristened nephew in the novel.

# THE INCIDENT OF THE DOG'S BALL [23]

*(From the notes of Captain Arthur Hastings O.B.E.)*

## i

I always look back upon the case of Miss Matilda Wheeler with special interest simply because of the curious way it worked itself out – from nothing at all as it were!

I remember that it was a particularly hot airless day in August. I was sitting in my friend Poirot's rooms wishing for the hundredth time that we could be in the country and not in London. The post had just been brought in. I remember the sound of each envelope in turn being opened neatly, as Poirot did everything, by means of a little paper-cutter. Then would come his murmured comment and the letter in question would be allotted to its proper pile. It was an orderly monotonous business.

And then suddenly there came a difference. A longer pause, a letter not read once but twice. A letter that was not docketed in the usual way but which remained in the recipient's hand. I looked across at my friend. The letter now lay on his knee. He was staring thoughtfully across the room.

'Anything of interest, Poirot?' I asked.

'*Cela dépend.* Possibly you would not think so. It is a letter

---

23　The exact wording of the title appears, more than once, in Chapter 9 of *Dumb Witness* and also in Miss Arundell's letter in Chapter 5.

from an old lady, Hastings, and it says nothing – but nothing at all.'

'Very useful,' I commented sarcastically.

'*N'est ce pas?* It is the way of old ladies, that. Round and round the point they go! But see for yourself. I shall be interested to know what you make of it.'

He tossed me the letter. I unfolded it and made a slight grimace. It consisted of four closely written pages in a spiky and shaky handwriting with numerous alterations, erasions, and copious underlining.

'Must I really read it?' I asked plaintively. 'What is it about?'

'It is, as I told you just now, about nothing.'

Hardly encouraged by this remark I embarked unwillingly on my task. I will confess that I did not read it very carefully. The writing was difficult and I was content to take guesses on the context.

The writer seemed to be a Miss Matilda Wheeler of The Laburnums, Little Hemel. After much doubt and indecision, she wrote, she had felt herself emboldened to write to M. Poirot. At some length she went on to state exactly how and where she had heard M. Poirot's name mentioned. The matter was such, she said, that she found it extremely difficult to consult anyone in Little Hemel – and of course there was the possibility that she might be completely mistaken – that she was attaching a most ridiculous significance to perfectly natural incidents. In fact she had chided herself unsparingly for fancifulness, but ever since the incident of the dog's ball she had felt most uneasy. She could only hope to hear from M. Poirot if he did not think the whole thing was a mare's nest. Also, perhaps, he would be so kind as to let her know what his fee would be? The matter, she knew, was very trivial and unimportant, but her health was bad and her nerves not what they had been and worry of this kind was very bad for her, and the more she thought of it, the more she was *convinced* that she was right, though, of course, she would not *dream* of saying anything.[24]

That was more or less the gist of the thing. I put it down with a sigh of exasperation.

'Why can't the woman say what she's talking about? Of all the idiotic letters!'

'*N'est ce pas?* A regrettable failure to employ order and method in the mental process.'

'What do you think she does mean? Not that it matters much. Some upset to her pet dog, I suppose. Anyway, it's not worth taking seriously.'

'You think not, my friend?'

'My dear Poirot, I cannot see why you are so intrigued by this letter.'

'No, you have not seen. The most interesting point in that letter – you have passed it by unnoticed.'

'What is the interesting point?'

'*The date, mon ami.*'

I looked at the heading of the letter again.

'April 12th,' I said slowly.

'*C'est curieux, n'est ce pas?*' Nearly three months ago.'[25]

'I don't suppose it has any significance. She probably meant to put August 12th.'

'No, no, Hastings. Look at the colour of the ink. That letter was written a good time ago. No, April 12th is the date assuredly. But why was it not sent? And if the writer changed her mind about sending it, why did she keep it and send it now?'

He rose.

'*Mon ami* – the day is hot. In London one stifles, is it not so? Then how say you to a little expedition into the country? To be exact, to Little Hemel which is, I see, in the County of Kent.'

---

24  This letter is very similar to that sent by Miss Amelia Barrowby, another elderly lady living in a small village who is subsequently poisoned, in 'How Does Your Garden Grow?'

25  If the letter was written on 12 April and received by Poirot in early August, this should read 'nearly four months ago'.

I was only too willing and then and there we started off on our visit of exploration.

## *ii*

Little Hemel we found to be a charming village, untouched in the miraculous way that villages can be when they are two miles from a main road. There was a hostelry called The George, and there we had lunch – a bad lunch I regret to say, as is the way at country inns.

An elderly waiter attended to us, a heavy breathing man, and as he brought us two cups of a doubtful fluid called coffee, Poirot started his campaign.

'A house called The Laburnums,' he said. 'You know it? The house of a Miss Wheeler.'

'That's right, sir. Just past the church. You can't miss it. Three Miss Wheelers there were, old-fashioned ladies, born and brought up here. Ah! well, they're all gone now and the house is up for sale.'

He shook his head sadly.

'So the Miss Wheelers are all dead?' said Poirot.

'Yes, sir. Miss Amelia and Miss Caroline twelve years ago and Miss Matilda just a month or two ago. You thinking of buying the house, sir – if I may ask?'

'The idea had occurred to me,' said Poirot mendaciously. 'But I believe it is in a very bad state.'

'It's old-fashioned, sir. Never been modernised as the saying goes. But it's in good condition – roof and drains and all that. Never grudged money on repairs, Miss Wheeler didn't, and the garden was always a picture.'

'She was well off?'

'Oh! very comfortably off indeed, sir. A very well-to-do family.'

'I suppose the house has been left to someone who has no use for it? A niece or nephew or some distant relative?'

'No, sir, she left it to her companion, Miss Lawson. But

Miss Lawson doesn't fancy living in it, and so it's up for sale. But it's a bad time for selling houses, they say.'

'Whenever one has to sell anything it is always a bad time,' said Poirot smiling, as he paid the bill and added a handsome tip. 'When exactly did you say Miss Matilda Wheeler died?'

'Just the beginning of May, sir – thank you, sir – or was it the end of April? She'd not been in good health for a long time.'

'You have a good doctor here?'

'Yes, sir, Dr Lawrence. He's getting on now, but he's well thought of down here. Always very pleasant-spoken and careful.'

Poirot nodded and presently we strolled out into the hot August sunshine and made our way along the street in the direction of the church.

Before we got to it, however, we passed an old-fashioned house set a little way back, with a brass plate on the gate inscribed with the name of Dr Lawrence.

'Excellent,' said Poirot. 'We will make a call here. At this hour we shall make sure of finding the doctor at home.'

'My dear Poirot! But what on earth are you going to say? And anyway what are you driving at?'

'For your first question, *mon ami*, the answer is simple – I shall have to invent. Fortunately I have the imagination fertile. For your second question – *eh bien*, after we have conversed with the doctor, it may be that I shall find I am not driving at anything.'

### *iii*

Dr Lawrence proved to be a man of about sixty. I put him down as an unambitious kindly sort of fellow, not particularly brilliant mentally, but quite sound.

Poirot is a past master in the art of mendacity. In five minutes we were all chatting together in the most friendly fashion – it being somehow taken for granted that we were old and dear friends of Miss Matilda Wheeler.

'Her death, it is a great shock to me. Most sad,' said Poirot. 'She had the stroke? No?'

'Oh! no, my dear fellow. Yellow atrophy of the liver. Been coming on for a long time. She had a very bad attack of jaundice a year ago. She was pretty well through the winter except for digestive trouble. Then she had jaundice again the end of April and died of it. A great loss to us – one of the real old-fashioned kind.'

'Ah! yes, indeed,' sighed Poirot. 'And the companion, Miss Lawson – ?'

He paused and rather to our surprise the doctor responded promptly.

'I can guess what you're after, and I don't mind telling you that you've my entire sympathy. But if you're coming to me for any hope of "undue influence" it's no good. Miss Wheeler was perfectly capable of making a will – not only when she did – but right up to the day of her death. It's no good hoping that I can say anything different because I can't.'

'But your sympathy –'

'My sympathy is with James Graham and Miss Mollie. I've always felt strongly that money shouldn't be left away from the family to an outsider. I daresay there might be some sort of case that Miss Lawson obtained an ascendency over Miss Wheeler owing to spiritualistic tomfoolery – but I doubt if there's anything that you could take into court. Only run yourself in for terrific expense. Avoid the law, wherever you can, is my motto. And certainly medically I can't help you. Miss Wheeler's mind was perfectly clear.'

He shook hands with us and we passed out into the sunlight.

'Well!' I said. 'That was rather unexpected!'

'Truly. We begin to learn a little about my correspondent. She has at least two relatives – James Graham and a girl called Mollie. They ought to have inherited her money but did not do so. By a will clearly not made very long ago, the whole amount has gone to the companion, Miss Lawson. There is also a very significant mention of spiritualism.'

'You think that significant?'

'Obviously. A credulous old lady – the spirits tell her to leave her money to a particular person – she obeys. Something of that kind occurs to one as a possibility, does it not?'

### *iv*

We had arrived at The Laburnums. It was a fair sized Georgian house, standing a little way back from the street with a large garden behind. There was a board stuck up with For Sale on it.

Poirot rang the bell. His efforts were rewarded by a fierce barking within. Presently the door was opened by a neat middle-aged woman who held a barking wire-haired terrier by the collar.

'Good afternoon,' said Poirot. 'The house is for sale, I understand, so Mr James Graham told me.'

'Oh! yes, sir. You would like to see over it?'

'If you please.'

'You needn't be afraid of Bob, sir. He barks if anyone comes to the door, but he's as gentle as a lamb really.'

True enough, as soon as we were inside, the terrier jumped up and licked our hands. We were shown over the house – pathetic as an empty house always is, with the marks of pictures showing on the walls, and the bare uncarpeted floors. We found the woman only too ready and willing to talk to friends of the family as she supposed us to be. By his mention of James Graham, Poirot created this impression very cleverly.

Ellen, for such was our guide's name, had clearly been very attached to her late mistress. She entered with the gusto of her class into a description of her illness and death.

'Taken sudden she was. And suffered! Poor dear! Delirious

at the end. All sorts of queer things she'd say. How long was it? Well, it must have been three days from the time she was took bad. But poor dear, she'd suffered for many years on and off. Jaundice last year she had – and her food never agreed with her well. She'd take digestion tablets after nearly every meal. Oh! yes, she suffered a good deal one way or another. Sleeplessness for one thing. Used to get up and walk about the house at night, she did, her eyesight being too bad for much reading.'

It was at this point that Poirot produced from his pocket the letter. He held it out to her.

'Do you recognise this by any chance?' he asked.

He was watching her narrowly. She gave an exclamation of surprise.

'Well, now, I do declare! And is it you that's the gentleman it's written to?'

Poirot nodded.

'Tell me how you came to post it to me?' he said.

'Well, sir, I didn't know what to do – and that's the truth. When the furniture was all cleared out, Miss Lawson she gave me several little odds and ends that had been the mistress's. And among them was a mother of pearl blotter that I'd always admired. I put it by in a drawer, and it was only yesterday that I took it out and was putting new blotting paper in it when I found this letter slipped inside the pocket. It was the mistress's handwriting and I saw as she'd meant to post it and slipped it in there and forgot – which was the kind of thing she did many a time, poor dear. Absent-minded as you might say. Well, I didn't know what to do. I didn't like to put it in the fire and I couldn't take it upon myself to open it and I didn't see as it was any business of Miss Lawson's, so I just put a stamp on it and ran out to the post box and posted it.'

Ellen paused for breath and the terrier uttered a sharp staccato bark. It was so peremptory in sound that Poirot's attention was momentarily diverted. He looked down at the dog who was sitting with his nose lifted entreatingly towards the empty mantelpiece of the drawing-room where we were at the time.

'But what is it that he regards so fixedly?' asked Poirot.

Ellen laughed.

'It's his ball, sir. It used to be put in a jar on the mantelpiece and he thinks it ought somehow or other to be there still.'

'I see,' said Poirot. 'His ball . . .' He remained thoughtful for a moment or two.

'Tell me,' he said. 'Did your mistress ever mention to you something about the dog and his ball? Something that perturbed her greatly?'

'Now it's odd your saying that, sir. She never said anything about a ball, but I do believe there was something about Bob here that was on her mind – for she tried to say something just as she was dying. "The dog," she said. "The dog –" and then something about a picture ajar – nothing that made sense but there, poor soul, she was delirious and didn't know what she was saying.'

'You will comprehend,' said Poirot, 'that this letter not reaching me when it should have done, I am greatly intrigued about many things and much in the dark. There are several questions that I should wish to ask.'

By this time Ellen would have taken for granted any statement that Poirot had chosen to make. We adjourned to her somewhat overcrowded sitting-room and having pacified Bob by giving him the desired ball which he retired under a table to chew, Poirot began his interrogations.

'First of all,' he said, 'I comprehend that Miss Wheeler's nearest relations were only two in number?'

'That's right, sir. Mr James – Mr James Graham whom you mentioned just now – and Miss Davidson. They were first cousins and niece and nephew to Miss Wheeler. There were five Miss Wheelers, you see, and only two of them married.'

'And Miss Lawson was no relation at all?'

'No, indeed – nothing but a paid companion.'

Scorn was uppermost in Ellen's voice.

'Did you like Miss Lawson, Ellen?'

'Well, sir, she wasn't one you could dislike, so to speak. Neither one thing nor the other, she wasn't, a poor sort of creature, and full of nonsense about spirits. Used to sit in the dark, they did, she and Miss Wheeler and the two Miss Pyms. A sayance, they called it. Why they were at it the very night she was taken bad. And if you ask me, it was that wicked nonsense that made Miss Wheeler leave her money away from her own flesh and blood.'

'When exactly did she make the new will? But perhaps you do not know that.'

'Oh! yes, I do. Sent for the lawyer she did while she was still laid up.'

'Laid up?'

'Yes, sir – from a fall she had. Down the stairs. Bob here had left his ball on top of the stairs and she slipped on it and fell. In the night it was. As I tell you, she used to get up and walk about.'

'Who was in the house at the time?'

'Mr James and Miss Mollie were here for the weekend. Easter it was, and it was the night of Bank Holiday. There was cook and me and Miss Lawson and Mr James and Miss Mollie and what with the fall and the scream we all came out. Cut her head, she did, and strained her back. She had to lie up for nearly a week. Yes, she was still in bed – it was the following Friday – when she sent for Mr Halliday. And the gardener had to come in and witness it, because for some reason I couldn't on account of her having remembered me in it, and cook alone wasn't enough.'

'Bank holiday was the 10th of August,'[26] said Poirot. He looked at me meaningfully. 'Friday would be the 14th. And what next? Did Miss Wheeler get up again?'

'Oh! yes, sir. She got up on the Saturday, and Miss Mollie

---

26 This should read 'April'.

and Mr James they came down again, being anxious about her, you see. Mr James he even came down the weekend after that.'

'The weekend of the 22nd?'

'Yes, sir.'

'And when was Miss Wheeler finally taken ill?'

'It was the 25th, sir. Mr James had left the day before. And Miss Wheeler seemed as well as she'd ever been – bar her indigestion, of course, but that was chronic. Taken sudden after the sayance, she was. They had a sayance after dinner, you know, so the Miss Pyms went home and Miss Lawson and I got her to bed and sent for Dr Lawrence.'

Poirot sat frowning for a moment or two, then he asked Ellen for the address of Miss Davidson and Mr Graham and also for that of Miss Lawson.

All three proved to be in London. James Graham was junior partner in some chemical dye works,[27] Miss Davidson worked in a beauty parlour in Dover Street. Miss Lawson had taken a flat near High Street, Kensington.

As we left, Bob, the dog, rushed up to the top of the staircase, lay down and carefully nosed his ball over the edge so that it bumped down the stairs. He remained, wagging his tail, until it was thrown up to him again.

'The incident of the dog's ball,' murmured Poirot under his breath.

*v*

A minute or two later we were out in the sunshine again.

'Well,' I said with a laugh. 'The dog's ball incident did not amount to much after all. We now know exactly what it was. The dog left his ball at the top of the stairs and the old lady tripped over it and fell. So much for that!'

'Yes, Hastings, as you say – the incident is simple enough.

---

27  Oddly, this very specific occupation, suspicious in the context of a poisoning mystery, is never mentioned again.

What we do not know – and what I should like to know – and what I *mean* to know – is why the old lady was so perturbed by it?'

'Do you think there is anything in that?'

'Consider the dates, Hastings. On Monday night, the fall. On Wednesday the letter written to me. On Friday the altered will. There is something curious there. Something that I should like to know. And ten days afterwards Miss Wheeler dies. If it had been a sudden death, one of these mysterious deaths due to "heart failure" – I confess I should have been suspicious. But her death appears to have been perfectly natural and due to disease of long standing. *Tout de même –*'

He went off into a brown study. Finally he said unexpectedly:

'If you really wished to kill someone, Hastings, how would you set about it?'

'Well – I don't know. I can't imagine myself –'

'One can always imagine. Think, for instance, of a particularly repellent money-lender, of an innocent girl in his clutches.'

'Yes,' I said slowly. 'I suppose one might always see red and knock a fellow out.'

Poirot sighed.

'*Mais oui*, it would be that way with you! But I seek to imagine the mind of someone very different. A cold-blooded but cautious murderer, reasonably intelligent. What would he try first? Well, there is accident. A well staged accident – that is very difficult for the police to bring home to the perpetrator. But it has its disadvantages – it may disable but not kill. And then, possibly, the victim might be suspicious. Accident cannot be tried again. Suicide? Unless a convenient piece of writing with an ambiguous meaning can be obtained from the victim, suicide would be very uncertain. Then murder – recognised as such. For that you want a scapegoat or an alibi.'

'But Miss Wheeler wasn't murdered. Really, Poirot –'

'I know. I know. *But she died*, Hastings. Do not forget – *she died*. She makes a will – and ten days later she dies. And the only two people in the house with her (for I except the cook) both benefit by her death.'

'I think,' I said, 'that you have a bee in your bonnet.'

'Very possibly. Coincidences do happen. But she wrote to me, *mon ami*, she wrote to me, and until I know what made her write I cannot rest in peace.'

#### *vi*

It was about a week later that we had three interviews.

Exactly what Poirot wrote to them I do not know, but Mollie Davidson and James Graham came together by appointment, and certainly displayed no resentment. The letter from Miss Wheeler lay on the table in a conspicuous position. From the conversation that followed, I gathered that Poirot had taken considerable liberties in his account of the subject matter.

'We have come here in answer to your request, but I am sorry to say that I do not understand in the least what you are driving at, M. Poirot,' said Graham with some irritation as he laid down his hat and stick.

He was a tall thin man, looking older than his years, with pinched lips and deep-set grey eyes. Miss Davidson was a handsome fair-haired girl of twenty-nine or so. She seemed puzzled, but unresentful.

'It is that I seek to aid you,' said Poirot. 'Your inheritance it has been wrested from you! It has gone to a stranger!'

'Well, that's over and done with,' said Graham. 'I've taken legal advice and it seems there's nothing to be done. And I really cannot see where it concerns *you*, M. Poirot.'

'I think James, that that is not very fair to M. Poirot,' said Mollie Davidson. 'He is a busy man, but he is going out of his way to help us. I wish he could. All the same, I'm afraid nothing can be done. We simply can't afford to go to law.'

'Can't afford. Can't afford. We haven't got a leg to stand upon,' said her cousin irritably.

'That is where I come in,' said Poirot. 'This letter' – he tapped it with a finger-nail – has suggested a possible idea to me. Your aunt, I understand, had originally made a will leaving her property to be divided between you. Suddenly, on the 14th April she makes another will. Did you know of that will, by the way?'

It was to Graham he put the question.

Graham flushed and hesitated a moment.

'Yes,' he said. 'I knew of it. My aunt told me of it.'

'What?' A cry of astonishment came from the girl.

Poirot wheeled round upon her.

'You did not know of it, Mademoiselle?'

'No, it came as a great shock to me. I thought it did to my cousin also. When did Auntie tell you, James?'

'That next weekend – the one after Easter.'

'And I was there and you never told me?'

'No – I – well, I thought it better to keep it to myself.'

'How extraordinary of you!'

'What exactly did your aunt say to you, Mr Graham?' asked Poirot in his most silky tone.

Graham clearly disliked answering the question. He spoke stiffly.

'She said that she thought it only fair to let me know that she had made a new will leaving everything to Miss Lawson.'

'Did she give any reason?'

'None whatever.'

'I think you ought to have told me,' said Miss Davidson.

'I thought better not,' said her cousin stiffly.

'*Eh bien*,' said Poirot. 'It is all very curious. I am not at liberty to tell you what was written to me in this letter, but I will give you some advice. I would apply, if I were you, for an order of exhumation.'

They both stared at him without speaking for a minute or two.

'Oh! no,' cried Mollie Davidson.

'This is outrageous,' cried Graham. 'I shall certainly not do anything of the sort. The suggestion is preposterous.'

'You refuse?'

'Absolutely.'

Poirot turned to the girl.

'And you, Mademoiselle? Do you refuse?'

'I – No, I would not say I refused. But I do not like the idea.'

'Well, I do refuse,' said Graham angrily. 'Come on, Mollie. We've had enough of this charlatan.'

He fumbled for the door. Poirot sprang forward to help him. As he did so a rubber ball fell out of his pocket and bounced on the floor.

'Ah!' cried Poirot. 'The ball!'

He blushed and appeared uncomfortable. I guessed that he had not meant the ball to be seen.

'Come on, Mollie,' shouted Graham now in a towering passion.

The girl had retrieved the ball and handed it to Poirot.

'I did not know that you kept a dog, M. Poirot,' she said.

'I do not, Mademoiselle,' said Poirot.

The girl followed her cousin out of the room. Poirot turned to me.

'Quick, *mon ami*,' he said. 'Let us visit the companion, the now rich Miss Lawson. I wish to see her before she is in any way put upon her guard.'

'If it wasn't for the fact that James Graham knew about the new will, I should be inclined to suspect him of having a hand in this business. He was down that last weekend. However, since he knew that the old lady's death would not benefit him – well, that puts him out of court.'

'Since he knew –' murmured Poirot thoughtfully.

'Why, yes, he admitted as much,' I said impatiently.

'Mademoiselle was quite surprised at his knowing. Strange that he should not tell her at the time. Unfortunate. Yes, unfortunate.'

Exactly what Poirot was getting at I did not quite know, but knew from his tone that there was something. However, soon after, we arrived at Clanroyden Mansions.

### *vii*

Miss Lawson was very much as I had pictured her. A middle-aged woman, rather stout, with an eager but somewhat foolish face. Her hair was untidy and she wore pince-nez. Her conversation consisted of gasps and was distinctly spasmodic.

'So good of you to come,' she said. 'Sit here, won't you? A cushion. Oh! dear, I'm afraid that chair isn't comfortable. That table's in your way. We're just a little crowded here.' (This was undeniable. There was twice as much furniture in the room as there should have been, and the walls were covered with photographs and pictures.) 'This flat is really too small. But so central. I've always longed to have a little place of my own. But there, I never thought I should. So good of dear Miss Wheeler. Not that I feel at all comfortable about it. No, indeed I don't. My conscience, M. Poirot. *Is it right?* I ask myself. And really I don't know what to say. Sometimes I think that Miss Wheeler meant me to have the money and so it must be all right. And other times – well, flesh and blood is flesh and blood – I feel very badly when I think of Mollie Davidson. Very badly indeed!'

'And when you think of Mr James Graham?'

Miss Lawson flushed and drew herself up.

'That is very different. Mr Graham has been very rude – most insulting. I can assure you, M. Poirot – there was no undue influence. I had no idea of anything of the kind. A complete shock to me.'

'Miss Wheeler did not tell you of her intentions?'

'No, indeed. A complete shock.'

'You had not, in any way, found it necessary to – shall we say, open the eyes – of Miss Wheeler in regard to her nephew's shortcomings?'

'What an idea, M. Poirot! Certainly not. What put that idea into your head, if I may ask?'

'Mademoiselle, I have many curious ideas in my head.'

Miss Lawson looked at him uncertainly. Her face, I reflected, was really singularly foolish. The way the mouth hung open for instance. And yet the eyes behind the glasses seemed more intelligent than one would have suspected.

Poirot took something from his pocket.

'You recognise this, Mademoiselle?'

'Why, it's Bob's ball!'

'No,' said Poirot. 'It is a ball I bought at Woolworth's.'

'Well, of course, that's where Bob's balls do come from. Dear Bob.'

'You are fond of him?'

'Oh! yes, indeed, dear little doggie. He always slept in my room. I'd like to have him in London, but dogs aren't really happy in town, are they, M. Poirot?'

'Me, I have seen some very happy ones in the Park,' returned my friend gravely.

'Oh! yes, of course, the Park,' said Miss Lawson vaguely. 'But it's very difficult to exercise them properly. He's much happier with Ellen, I feel sure, at the dear Laburnums. Ah! what a tragedy it all was!'

'Will you recount to me, Mademoiselle, just what happened on that evening when Miss Wheeler was taken ill?'

'Nothing out of the usual. At least, oh! of course, we held a séance – with distinct phenomena – distinct phenomena. You will laugh, M. Poirot. I feel you are a sceptic. But oh! the joy of hearing the voices of those who have passed over.'

'No, I do not laugh,' said Poirot gently.

He was watching her flushed excited face.

'You know, it was most curious – really *most* curious. There was a kind of halo – a luminous haze – all round dear Miss Wheeler's head. We all saw it distinctly.'

'A luminous haze?' said Poirot sharply.

'Yes. Really most remarkable. In view of what happened,

I felt, M. Poirot, that already she was *marked*, so to speak, for the other world.'

'Yes,' said Poirot. 'I think she was – marked for the other world.' He added, completely incongruously it seemed to me, 'Has Dr Lawrence got a keen sense of smell?'

'Now it's curious you should say that. "Smell this, doctor," I said, and held up a great bunch of lilies of the valley to him. And would you believe it, he couldn't smell a thing. Ever since influenza three years ago, he said. Ah! me – physician, heal thyself is so true, isn't it?'

Poirot had risen and was prowling round the room. He stopped and stared at a picture on the wall. I joined him.

It was rather an ugly needlework picture done in drab wools, and represented a bulldog sitting on the steps of a house. Below it, in crooked letters, were the words '*Out all night and no key!*'[28]

Poirot drew a deep breath.

'This picture, it comes from The Laburnums?'

'Yes. It used to hang over the mantelpiece in the drawing-room. Dear Miss Wheeler did it when she was a girl.'

'Ah!' said Poirot. His voice was entirely changed. It held a note that I knew well.

He crossed to Miss Lawson.

'You remember Bank Holiday? Easter Monday. The night that Miss Wheeler fell down the stairs? *Eh bien*, the little Bob, he was out that night, was he not? He did not come in.'

'Why, yes, M. Poirot, however did you know that? Yes, Bob was very naughty. He was let out at nine o'clock as usual, and he never came back. I didn't tell Miss Wheeler – she would have been anxious. That is to say, I told her the next day, of course. When he was safely back. Five in the morning it was.

---

28  This picture (it changes to a jar with similar wording in Chapter 8 of the novel) can be seen in Greenway House and may have been part of Christie's inspiration. She was a dog-lover and lifelong dog-owner.

He came and barked underneath my window and I went down and let him in.'

'So that was it! *Enfin!*' He held out his hand. 'Goodbye, Mademoiselle. Ah! Just one more little point. Miss Wheeler took digestive tablets after meals always, did she not? What make were they?'

'Dr Carlton's After Dinner Tablets. Very efficacious, M. Poirot.'

'Efficacious! *Mon Dieu!*' murmured Poirot, as we left. 'No, do not question me, Hastings. Not yet. There are still one or two little matters to see to.'

He dived into a chemist's and reappeared holding a white wrapped bottle.

### *viii*

He unwrapped it when we got home. It was a bottle of Dr Carlton's After Dinner Tablets.

'You see, Hastings. There are at least fifty tablets in that bottle – perhaps more.'

He went to the bookshelf and pulled out a very large volume. For ten minutes he did not speak, then he looked up and shut the book with a bang.

'But yes, my friend, now you may question. Now I know – everything.'

'She was poisoned?'

'Yes, my friend. Phosphorus poisoning.'

'Phosphorus?'

'Ah! *mais oui* – that is where the diabolical cleverness came in! *Miss Wheeler had already suffered from jaundice. The symptoms of phosphorus poisoning would only look like another attack of the same complaint.* Now listen, very often the symptoms of phosphorus poisoning are delayed from one to six hours. It says here' (he opened the book again) '"*The person's breath may be phosphorescent before he feels in any way affected.*" That is what Miss Lawson saw in the dark – Miss Wheeler's phosphorescent breath – "a luminous haze". And here I will read you again. *"The jaundice having thoroughly pronounced itself, the system may be considered as not only under the influence of the toxic action of phosphorus, but as suffering in addition from all the accidents incidental to the retention of the biliary secretion in the blood, nor is there from this point any special difference between phosphorus poisoning and certain affections of the liver – such, for example as yellow atrophy."*[29]

'Oh! it was well planned, Hastings! Foreign matches – vermin paste. It is not difficult to get hold of phosphorus, and a very small dose will kill. The medicinal dose is from 1/100 to 1/30 grain. Even .116 of a grain has been known to kill. To make a tablet resembling one of these in the bottle – that too would not be too difficult. One can buy a tablet-making machine, and Miss Wheeler she would not observe closely. A tablet placed at the bottom of this bottle – one day, sooner or later, Miss Wheeler will take it, and the person who put it there will have a perfect alibi, for she will not have been near the house for ten days.'

'She?'

'Mollie Davidson. Ah! *mon ami*, you did not see her eyes when that ball bounced from my pocket. The irate M. Graham, it meant nothing to him – but to her. "I did not know you kept a dog, M. Poirot." Why a *dog*? Why not a child? A child, too, plays with balls. But that – it is not evidence, you say. It is only the impression of Hercule Poirot. Yes, but everything fits in. M. Graham is furious at the idea of an exhumation – he shows it. But she is more careful. She is afraid to seem unwilling. And the surprise and indignation she cannot conceal when she learns that her cousin has known of the will all along! He knew – and he did not tell her. Her crime had been in vain. Do you remember my saying it was unfortunate he didn't tell her? Unfortunate for the poor Miss Wheeler. It meant her death sentence and all the good

---

29  This scientific explanation appears verbatim in Chapter 29 of *Dumb Witness*.

precautions she had taken, such as the will, were in vain.'

'You mean the will – no, I don't see.'

'Why did she make that will? The incident of the dog's ball, *mon ami*.

'Imagine, Hastings, that you wish to cause the death of an old lady. You devise a simple accident. The old lady, before now, has slipped over the dog's ball. She moves about the house in the night. *Bien*, you place the dog's ball on the top of the stairs and perhaps also you place a strong thread or fine string. The old lady trips and goes headlong with a scream. Everyone rushes out. You detach your broken string while everyone else is crowding round the old lady. When they come to look for the cause of the fall, they find – the dog's ball where he so often left it.

'But, Hastings, now we come to something else. Suppose the old lady earlier in the evening after playing with the dog, puts the ball away in its usual place, and the dog goes out – *and stays out*. That is what she learns from Miss Lawson on the following day. She realises that *it cannot be the dog who left the ball at the top of the stairs*. She suspects the truth – but she suspects the wrong person. She suspects her nephew, James Graham, whose personality is not of the most charming. What does she do? First she writes to me – to investigate the matter. Then she changes her will *and tells James Graham that she has done so*. She counts on his telling Mollie though it is James she suspects. They will know that her death will bring them nothing! *C'est bien imaginé* for an old lady.

'And that, *mon ami*, was the meaning of her dying words. I comprehend well enough the English to know that it is a *door* that is ajar, not a *picture*. The old lady is trying to tell Ellen of her suspicions. The dog – the picture above the jar on the mantelpiece with its subject – 'Out all night' and the ball put away in the jar. That is the only ground for suspicion she has. She probably thinks her illness is natural – but at the last minute has an intuition that it is not.'

He was silent for a moment or two.

'Ah! if only she had posted that letter. I could have saved her. Now –'

He took up a pen and drew some notepaper towards him.

'What are you going to do?'

'I am going to write a full and explicit account of what happened and post it to Miss Mollie Davidson with a hint that an exhumation will be applied for.'

'And then?'

'If she is innocent – nothing –' said Poirot gravely. 'If she is not innocent – we shall see.'

### ix

Two days later there was a notice in the paper stating that a Miss Mollie Davidson had died of an overdose of sleeping draught. I was rather horrified.[30] Poirot was quite composed.

'But no, it has all arranged itself very happily. No ugly scandal and trial for murder – Miss Wheeler she would not want that. She would have desired the privacy. On the other hand one must not leave a murderess – what do you say? – at loose. Or sooner or later, there will be another murder. Always a murderer repeats his crime. No,' he went on dreamily 'it has all arranged itself very well. It only remains to work upon the feelings of Miss Lawson – a task which Miss Davidson was attempting very successfully – until she reaches the pitch of handing over half her fortune to Mr James Graham who is, after all, entitled to the money. Since he was deprived of it under a misapprehension.'

He drew from his pocket the brightly coloured rubber ball.

'Shall we send this to our friend Bob? Or shall we keep it on the mantelpiece? It is a reminder, *n'est ce pas, mon ami*, that nothing is too trivial to be neglected? At one end, Murder, at the other only – the incident of the dog's ball . . .'

---

30  This somewhat questionable procedure, with Poirot taking the law into his own hands, is also adopted in the novel.

### *Death on the Nile (novel)*
1 November 1937

───────────◄○►───────────

When Simon Doyle marries wealthy Linnet Ridgeway,
and not Jacqueline de Bellefort, the consequent train
of events culminates in triple murder aboard a Nile
steamer. Hercule Poirot, also travelling on SS *Karnak*,
has observed the tragedy unfolding and investigates
one of his most famous cases.

───────────◄○►───────────

Although published late in 1937, this classic Poirot title was
written almost two years earlier. A letter from Edmund Cork
dated 29 April 1936 expressed delight at Christie's news that
*Death on the Nile* was finished. Unfortunately, there are few
notes for the plot of this famous title. We do, however, have,
in Notebook 30, a list of potential characters – including
one very significant one – and a brief note about possible
plot development. Most of the ideas originally intended for
inclusion were waylaid into other titles.

Plans

Death on the Nile

Miss Marple?
Mrs P (ex wardress of American prison)
Mathew P son – nice
Mrs Mathew P – nice
Miss P nervy hysterical girl
Master P Boy of 20 – excitable
Dr. Pfeiffer – doctor and toxicologist
Mrs Pfeiffer – recently married to him – 35 – attractive –
    with past
Marc Tierney – archaeologist – a little apart from the rest

Mrs Van Schuyler – boring American woman elderly
   snobbish
Mrs Pooper cheap novelist[31]
Miss Harmsworth – girl companion to Miss Van Schuyler
Miss Marple
Rosalie Curtis sickly girl
Mrs Gibson – non stop talker

The biggest surprise in this list is the (double) inclusion of Miss Marple: at first with, and than without, a question mark. Prior to this, the only novel in which Miss Marple had appeared was *The Murder at the Vicarage* in 1930, and her next novel appearance, *The Body in the Library*, was still a further five years away. Moreover, the 1932 short story collection *The Thirteen Problems*, set firmly in the parlours of St Mary Mead, could hardly be seen as a preparation for an exotic Egyptian adventure. For in 1937 the Nile was as exotic to the majority of Christie readers as Mars is to her current audience: very few travelled abroad for holidays, if, in fact, they took holidays at all. So to transport Miss Marple from the (admittedly relative) safety of St Mary Mead to the banks of the Nile and subsequently to the Temple of Karnak, Abu Simbel and Wadi Haifa may have been seen as a journey too far; and so Poirot was substituted. Miss Marple eventually gets to solve her own 'foreign' case, but not until almost 30 years later, when her nephew Raymond sends her on a holiday to the fictional island of St Honore, there she solves *A Caribbean Mystery*.

In contrast, at this stage Poirot was a seasoned traveller; and, of course, a foreigner to begin with. Since his arrival in Britain he had solved cases in a variety of distant locations: France (*The Murder on the Links*, *The Mystery of the Blue Train*, *Death in the Clouds*), Yugoslavia (*Murder on the Orient Express*) and Italy (*The Big Four* and 'Triangle at Rhodes'). His most

---

31  'Mr and Mrs Puper' were pet names for each other that Agatha
    and Max used in private correspondence.

recent case had involved solving a *Murder in Mesopotamia* and he had already visited Egypt and the Valley of the Kings while solving 'The Adventure of the Egyptian Tomb' in 1923. All things considered, Poirot was a much more likely sleuth to board SS *Karnak* for a particularly blood-soaked journey down the Nile.

Some of the remaining names also provide material for speculation:

Mrs P (ex wardress of American prison)
Mathew P son – nice
Mrs Mathew P – nice
Miss P nervy hysterical girl
Master P Boy of 20 – excitable

In these five characters can be seen the seeds of the Boynton family from 1938's *Appointment with Death*. Mrs P is described as a wardress in an American prison exactly as, two years later, the monstrous Mrs Boynton would be; the 'nice' son, Mathew and his wife Mrs Mathew, are the forerunners of Lennox and Nadine Boynton, while the 'nervy and hysterical' Miss P corresponds to Ginevra. Raymond is the last remaining male of the Boynton family although he could hardly be described as an 'excitable boy'. It is interesting that, although Christie decided against using this family in *Death on the Nile*, when she did utilise them she placed them in another foreign setting, Petra.

Mrs Van Schuyler – boring American woman elderly
snobbish

And in a later note:

Mrs Van Schuyler – a well known confidence trickster
Miss Harmsworth – girl companion to Miss Van Schuyler

The only character to remain as described – with a modification from Mrs to Miss – is Miss Van Schuyler, although her idiosyncrasy changes from confidence trickery to kleptomania. Miss Harmsworth became Cornelia Robson, her unfortunate niece.

Mrs Pooper cheap novelist

The unhappily named Mrs Pooper (see above) eventually became Salome Otterbourne, who specialised in outspoken novels of love and sex. One of her titles, 'Snow upon the Desert's Face', is almost the same as the early, unpublished non-crime novel written by Agatha Christie herself, *Snow upon the Desert*. This was probably a personal joke inserted by Christie for the amusement of her family.

Rosalie Curtis sickly girl

Rosalie Curtis may well have changed to Rosalie Otterbourne, daughter of the ill-fated Salome.

Some possible plot developments are sketched on the pages following the cast list. Note that 'P', i.e. Poirot ('but P proves that . . .'), has now firmly replaced Miss Marple:

Dr. Pfeiffer's wife has been recognised – he decides to do away with Mrs. Oger

Wife of (Dr. Pfeiffer) herself is thief or murderer etc. – makes up story that someone has stolen ring or poison etc. and brooch A.M. seen in glass. She knows that A.M. is in lounge with others at that time but P proves that M.A. is real lettering
    or
M.A. idea and yellow dress M.A. has not yellow dress – woman with yellow dress has not initial A.M.

Dr. Elbes – very ill man – had known her at St. John's prison
Pfeiffer mentions his researches the castor oil plant
Now then A. Who killed her?
          B. Why?


Although the Pfeiffers were never to feature in any Christie work, some of these ideas were to resurface in other books: a stolen ring in *Hickory Dickory Dock* and the prison wardress in *Appointment with Death*.

But the main idea is the symmetrical letters of the alphabet and how confusion can arise depending on whether they are seen directly or through a mirror. A half page of Notebook 30 lists all such letters, 'H M A W I O T U V Y', and a further list of possible female names starting with each one. (X is omitted presumably on the basis that names beginning with X are rare.) Christie finally settled on Isabel Oger, hence the reference to Mrs Oger above. This idea was eventually incorporated into *Dumb Witness*, published four months earlier, although with completely different names. Whether it was ever in fact intended as a plot device for *Death on the Nile* is debatable, despite the fact that the scenario Christie sketched involved the Pfeiffers from the list of characters for that novel. Adding to this doubt is the fact that there are no names on the original list with either the initials AM or MA.

Almost the final note for this title in Notebook 30 reads:

The Plan
Nellie is heard saying 'I wish she were dead – will never be
free till she's dead.


Nellie is one of the names appearing on the list of reversible initials ('Helen, Wilhelmina') but the words she utters are very similar to the opening line, overheard by Hercule Poirot, of *Appointment with Death*. 'You do see, don't you, that she's got to be killed?' This, taken in conjunction with Mrs P's former profession and the make-up of her family, can be seen to form the basis of the later novel.

### 'The Dream'
### February 1938

————————————◄○►————————————

Poirot is summoned by eccentric millionaire
Benedict Farley who is haunted by a terrifying dream.
Can Poirot prevent the dream coming true?

————————————◄○►————————————

This clever short story preceded Christie's writing of Poirot's greatest short cases, *The Labours of Hercules*. It is a neat, and almost unrecognisable, re-telling of *Murder in Mesopotamia*, shorn of the exotic archaeological trappings and transferred to central London. The first page of Notebook 66 reads:

> Ideas
> For G.K.C.

This, most probably, refers to her possible contribution to G. K. Chesterton's 1935 anthology *A Century of Detective Stories*. The next twelve pages of the Notebook contain preliminary notes for 'Problem at Sea', *Death in the Clouds, The ABC Murders, Sad Cypress, Dumb Witness* and *They Do It With Mirrors*. And on the list of possible short stories Idea B reads:

> Head out of window by some trick – horse or queer sight
> – shot from window next door – body put in client's home
> later by man who discovers body – he not suspected
> because death takes place an hour ago or the window
> above man is drawn up by hook – brought back into study
> in packing case

As these notes were probably written in 1934 it is entirely possible that this short note also inspired 1936's *Murder in Mesopotamia*. Because the plot device in short story and novel is exactly the same: a victim lured into putting his/her head out of a window by dangling something mysterious in their line of vision, and a murderer with a perfect alibi until they 'discover' the body. The note suggests a window in a next-door house but the plot works equally well – if not better – if both windows are part of the same building, while 'the window above' is a variation on *Murder in Mesopotamia*.

Twenty pages later we read an intriguing note:

Re-ordering of [Idea] B
Alibi
The man in the next room
Raymond – Now then Aunt Jane – a mystery for you

When, twenty-five years later, Christie plotted 'Greenshaw's Folly' (See 'The Fourth Decade') she referenced 'The Dream' in her notes in Notebook 47 with a synopsis of its plot as a starting point for her new Miss Marple story.

The Dream
Wrong man interviews woman. Girl gives her instruction
– she goes into next room to type. Then finds apparently
same woman dead. Really dead before – has said secretary
is out or faithful companion

And when her nephew Raymond West brings his aunt the intriguing problem he uses very similar words to those jotted, a quarter century earlier, in Notebook 66:

'Tell us, Aunt Jane,' said Raymond. 'Will there be a murder or won't there?'

Further, both 'Greenshaw's Folly' and 'The Dream' share the ideas of servant/master impersonation, as well as the use of a window as misdirection. The camouflage of the paranormal (the dream that 'foresees' the future) is an echo of *The Sittaford Mystery*, from seven years earlier, while Dr Stillingfleet will re-appear almost thirty years later in *Third Girl*; and *Little Dog Laughed*, the play written by Muriel Wills/Anthony Astor from *Three Act Tragedy*, provides the alibi for the victim's wife and daughter. And the closing exchange between Dr Stillingfleet and Poirot foreshadows Poirot's final case. . .

❧

### Appointment with Death
2 May 1938

◄○►

The appalling Mrs Boynton terrorises her family
even while they are on holiday in Petra. When she is
found dead at their camp more than one person is
relieved. Hercule Poirot, while sympathising with
the family, has 24 hours to find the killer.

◄○►

There are notes for both the novel and stage versions of this title. Over sixty pages of notes for the latter are contained in four Notebooks and twenty for the novel in Notebook 61, just ahead of preliminary notes for *Hercule Poirot's Christmas* and extended notes for *Akhnaton*. Although published in May 1938, there was an earlier serialisation that January in the *Daily Mail*, heralded by an essay, 'How I Created Hercule Poirot', specially written by Agatha Christie and reprinted following this discussion.

In *Appointment with Death* Christie sets herself another technical challenge. The investigation takes place in just 24 hours (although the set-up takes considerably longer) in the spectacular setting of Petra, far removed from the facilities of Scotland Yard. There are no fingerprints, no outsiders, no Hastings; just Hercule Poirot and the suspects. That said, parts of the solution can be explained only by divine intervention: how can Poirot know about the earlier life of the killer? Tellingly, when Christie adapted this for the stage she completely changed the ending and presented the audience with a more plausible and psychologically compelling solution.

The first page of Notebook 61 is headed 'The Petra Murder'. This is immediately followed by a list of characters and brief descriptions, whose forerunners can clearly be detected in the notes for *Death on the Nile*. The name Boynton does not appear at this stage, and the family are referred to throughout as Platt:

Characters
Roy – young, neurotic (26?)
Nadine            (22?)
Lucia – Mrs P's own daughter?
Jefferson – eldest son
Prunella (his wife – clear, balanced hair
Sarah Grant (Sybil Grey) a young doctor – interested in
    mental psychology [Sarah King]
Lady Westholme M.P. (a possible future Prime Minister)
Dr Gerard (French?)
Mrs Gibson (very distraught talker)? [Miss Price]

Six pages later (after a quick detour to jot down notes for 'Dead Man's Mirror', *Sad Cypress* and *Curtain*), Christie amends her characters – as usual, some are later renamed, while others do not appear in the novel – and proceeds with her system of assigning letters to scenes. She plots A to L without hesitation or deviation (which may indicate that she had already worked on this elsewhere), even though the order will change quite considerably. The novel's opening sentence, the most arresting of any Christie novel ('You do see, don't you, that she's got to be killed'), does not appear until Scene L in the notes. The fact that Poirot is mentioned in conjunction with this statement may account for its being brought forward.

Petra Murder

The Platt family at Mena House – then on boat to Palestine

People
Mrs Platt [Mrs Boynton]
Jefferson Platt [replaced by Lennox]
Nadine his wife
Marcia [Carol]
Lennox [becomes Raymond in the novel]
Ginevra
Sarah Grey [Sarah King]
Amos Cope (in love with Nadine) [becomes Jefferson Cope in the novel]
Lady Westholme M.P.
Dr Gerard – French doctor
Sir Charles Westholme [does not appear]

A. Sarah Grey and Gerard discuss Mrs Platt – S says sadistic [Part I Chapter 6]
B. Marcia and Lennox – 'It can't go on – Why shouldn't it? It always has – She'll die some day – There's no one to help us. [Part I Chapter 1]
C. Mrs Platt and Ginevra – you're tired tonight my dear – ill – she forces her to be ill [Part I Chapter 4]
D. Nadine and Amos – Why are you here? Leave it all [Part I Chapter 5]
E. Nadine and Jefferson – she begs him – he cries Don't leave me [Part I Chapter 8]
F. Nadine and Mrs Platt – She does not feel spell [Part I Chapter 8]

G. N and Marcia who has overheard conversation –
   I wouldn't blame you if you did go
H. Amos and Mrs P – latter says she is ill – can only have her
   own family – a snub [Part I Chapter 5]
I. Marcia and Sarah Grey [Part I Chapter 7]
J. Lennox and Sarah – she tells him to leave – I can't – I'm
   weak – I'm no good to you [Part I Chapter 9]
K. Sarah and Gerard she admits I've fallen for him [Part I
   Chapter 9]
L. Lennox and Marcia – we've got to kill her – It would – it
   would set us all free – HP overhears that last sentence
   [Part I Chapter 1]

There is much speculation in the notes as to the method of
murder, lending strength to the argument that this was a
character-driven, rather than a plot-driven, book. And it is
not insignificant that in the stage version there is not only a
different villain but also a different method. As can be seen,
Christie considered quite a few poisons before settling on
digitoxin:

Method of Crime etc.

Sarah's drug stolen

Abricine – Sarah's stolen – sudden violent illness of Mrs Pl[att]
Prussic acid in smelling salts?
Digitalin
Narcotic at lunch
One servant takes up genuine drink (tea?) – One Lady M
   who takes false tea
If poison – Coniine – Digitoxin – Coramine
If coniine or coramine – did Lady MacMartin and Miss
   Pierce go up and speak to her – she did not answer
If insulin Mrs P injected herself
Point of coniine (or coramine) the muscular paralysis

The old woman sits – each of family goes up and speaks to
her – they all see she is dead – but no one says so

The stage adaptation, up to the denouement, is largely the
same as the novel. However, as with some of the other stage
plays – *The Hollow, Death on the Nile, Go Back for Murder/Five
Little Pigs* – Poirot is dropped. The major difference is the
new ending but there is also a discussion in Act II, Scene I of
Mrs Boynton's previous career as a wardress. Both of these
are discussed in the notes. And it is the seemingly insignificant Miss Price who supplies the vital information leading to
the solution, as Christie sketches the revelatory dialogue:

Do you know – have you done perhaps done rescue work?
A wardress. Miss P uncomfortable – gets up goes away.
Sarah who is sitting nearby – then breaks in – 'That explains
a lot of things – you didn't give up your job when you
married – you've carried on with it. The need to dominate
etc.'

To be a drug addict – so very sad for the family
S: Miss Pierce what are you saying
Miss P: Nothing – nothing at all
S: Are you saying that Mrs. Boynton took drugs
Miss P: I found out – quite by accident – of course. I knew it
    was far worse
S: But that means . . . Mrs. Boynton was a drug addict
Miss P: Yes dear, I know
S: Tell me – you've got to tell me
Miss P: No, I shall say nothing. The poor woman is dead
    and . . .
S: Tell me – what did you see or hear –
Miss P tells what she saw – put into stick. Sarah calls Col.
    Carbury – all come – takes out from stick

✴

# 'How I Created Hercule Poirot'

'Why not make my detective a Belgian?'
*An Autobiography*

———————◄○►———————

**SOLUTIONS REVEALED**
*Death on the Nile*

———————◄○►———————

Agatha Christie wrote the article that follows to introduce the *Daily Mail*'s serialisation of *Appointment with Death* (or, as they renamed it, *A Date with Death*) on 19 January 1938, prior to the May publication of the novel.

The appearance of the 'latest Agatha Christie' in a newspaper or magazine was mutually advantageous. Both author and periodical enjoyed a boost in sales and publicity. Although not every novel had a pre-publication appearance, as early in her career as *The Mysterious Affair at Styles* and as late as *Sleeping Murder* Christie was regularly serialised on both sides of the Atlantic. Changes to the title and often to the text were tolerated, as the financial rewards were significant. But the enterprise was not without its pitfalls. A competition to accompany the serialisation of *The ABC Murders*, in which readers were invited to send in their solutions, was won by a reader who got every detail of the plot correct.

Although republished in the *Agatha Christie Centenary Celebration* book in September 1990, and again in *Little Grey Cells: The Quotable Poirot* a further 25 years later, the following version is reproduced from the pages of Notebook 21 and I have left intact many of the original deletions, made by Christie herself. This will help to show how fluently she could produce 1,400 words with a minimum of cutting and re-arrangement. Unusually, the text in Notebook 21 is continuous and, apart from the slightly amended drafts of the final paragraphs, would seem to have been completed at one sitting; it is all written with the same ink and, until the final stages, in the same handwriting on a dozen consecutive pages. The published version was shorter and slightly different; some paragraphs were rearranged to create a more coherent structure but I include here the entire text exactly as it was first written.

> How did the character of Hercule Poirot come into being?
> Difficult to say – ~~he came perhaps about accidentally that is~~ I realise that he came into being not at all as he himself would have wished ~~it~~. 'Hercule Poirot first,' he would have said. 'And then a plot to display his remarkable talent to the best advantage.' But it was not so. The ~~idea often~~ plot of the story, *The Mysterious Affair at Styles*, was roughed out and then came the dilemma: a detective story – now what kind of detective? It was ~~wartime~~ in the early autumn ~~days~~ of 1914 – Belgian refugees were in most country places.[32] Why not have a Belgian refugee, ~~for a~~

---

32  Germany invaded Belgium in early August 1914, so the arrival of refugees would probably have been nearer to late than early autumn 1914. This chronology is at variance with her own *Autobiography*, where she writes that she first conceived of writing a detective story while working at the hospital dispensary (1915–16). And a key point in the plot of *The Mysterious Affair at Styles* is dependent on knowledge of the properties of poisons, gained through her experience there.

~~detective,~~ a former shining light of the Belgian Police force.

What kind of man ~~he~~ should he be? A little man perhaps, with a somewhat grandiloquent name. Hercule – something – Hercule Poirot – yes, that would do. What else about him? He should be very neat – very orderly (Is that because I was a wildly untidy person myself?)[33]

Such was the first rough outline – mostly, you will note, externals – but certain ~~fad~~ traits followed almost automatically. Like many small dandified men, he would be conceited and he would, of course, (why 'of course?') have a ~~luxuriant~~ handsome moustache. That was the beginning. Hercule Poirot emerged from the mists and took concrete shape and form. ~~but he was a particularly~~ Once ~~he was~~ that had happened he took charge, as it were, of his own personality – there were all sorts of things about him that I did not know, but which he proceeded to ~~develop~~ show me. There was more in this little man than I had ever suspected. There was, for instance, his intense interest in the psychology of every case. As early as *The Murder on the Links* he was showing his appreciation of the mental processes of ~~the~~ a murderer – and insisting that ~~planning of a~~ every crime had a definite signature.[34]

Method and order still meant much to him – but not nearly so much as before. In *The Murder of Roger Ackroyd* he was at his best investigating a crime in a quiet country village and using his knowledge of human nature to get at

---

33  As if to emphasise this point, the page immediately preceding this essay has a heading 'Ideas 1940', obviously written at least two years afterwards; one of the ideas listed would become, later again, *The Moving Finger*. Presumably, the 12 pages needed for this essay were, conveniently, blank at the back of Notebook 21 when Christie went in search of a suitable gap.

34  In Chapter 9 of *The Murder on the Links* Poirot lectures the examining magistrate Hautet, and the policeman Giraud, on the psychology of the criminal.

the truth. For the terrible death on the Blue Train ~~he was~~ I have always suspected ~~not I have always thought he was not, I think, quite~~ he was not at his best but the solution of Lord Edgware's death was, I consider, a good piece of work on his part, though he gives some of the credit to Hastings.[35] *Three Act Tragedy* he considers one of his failures though most people do not agree with him – his final remark at the end of the case has amused many people [but] Hercule Poirot cannot see why![36] He considers that he merely stated an obvious truth.

And now, what of the relation between us – between the creator and the created? Well – let me confess it – there has been at times a coolness between us. There are moments when I have felt 'Why, why, did I ever invent this detestable, bombastic tiresome little creature? Eternally straightening things, forever boasting, always twirling his moustaches and tilting his 'egg-shaped head.' Anyway, what is an egg-shaped head? Have I ever seen an egg-shaped head? When people say to me, 'Which way up is the egg? – do I really know[?] I don't, because I never do see pictorial things clearly. But nevertheless, I know that he has an egg-shaped head covered with black, suspiciously black, hair[37] and I know that his eyes occasionally shine ~~and some~~ with a green light. And ~~once or~~ twice in my life I have

---

35   This is a reference to the chance remark that Hastings makes in Chapter 27, and which is acknowledged by Poirot at the end of Chapter 29, concerning the ill-fated Donald Ross. It is immediately followed by the equally vital and chance remark made by a cinema-goer and overheard by Poirot as they cross the Euston Road.

36   Why Poirot should consider *Three Act Tragedy* one of his failures is not clear, unless it is the fact that two further people die before he spots the vital point that motivated the first murder. His remark in the very last line of the book – 'It might have been ME!' – would not surprise anyone who knew him well.

37   In the first chapter of *The ABC Murders* Poirot extols the virtues of Revivit, a hair dye.

actually seen him – once on a boat going to the Canary Islands[38] and once having lunch at the Savoy. I have said to myself, 'Now if you had only had the nerve you ~~would~~ could have snap-shotted the man in the boat and then when people have said "Yes, but what is he like? I could have produced that snap shot and said 'This is what he is like.' And in the Savoy perhaps I would have gone and explained the matter but life is full of lost opportunities. If you are doubly burdened – first by acute shyness and secondly by only seeing the right thing to do or say twenty-four hours late – what can you do? ~~Except~~ only write about quick-witted men and resourceful girls whose reactions are like greased lightning!

Yes, there have been moments when I have disliked M. Hercule Poirot very much indeed –when I have rebelled bitterly against being yoked to him for life (usually at one of these moments that I receive a fan letter saying 'I know you must love your little detective by the way you write about him.)[39] But now, I must confess it, Hercule Poirot has won. A reluctant affection has sprung up for him. He has become more human, less irritating. I admire certain things

---

38  The mention of 'seeing' Hercule Poirot while in the Canary Islands is most probably a reference to the holiday Christie spent there with Rosalind and Carlo in 1927 after the trauma of 1926. It was here that she worked on *The Mystery of the Blue Train*.

39  The arrival of a fan letter extolling the virtues of her detective rouses the same reaction in Agatha Christie as it does some years later in Ariadne Oliver in Chapter 14 of *Mrs McGinty's Dead*. 'Why all the idiotic mannerisms he's got? These things just happen. You try something – and people seem to like it – and then you go on – and before you know where you are, you've got someone like that maddening Sven Hjerson tied to you for life. And people even write to you and say how fond you must be of him. Fond of him? If I met that bony, gangling, vegetable-eating Finn in real life, I'd do a better murder than any I've ever invented.'

about him – his passion for the truth, his understanding of human frailty and his kindliness. ~~I did not understand suspect before that he felt so strongly so strictly not for the punishment of the guilty but for the vindication of the innocent.~~ And he has taught me something – to take more interest in my own characters; to see them more as real people and less as pawns in a game. In spite of his vanity he often chooses deliberately to stand aside and let the main drama develop. He says in effect, 'It is their story – let them show you why and how this happened.' He knows, of course, that the star part is going to be his all right later. He may make his appearance at the end of the first act but he will take the centre of the stage in the second act and his big scene at the end of the third act is a mathematical certainty.

He has his favourite cases. *Cards on the Table* was the murder which won his complete technical approval;[40] the *Death on the Nile* saddened him.[41] Since *Appointment with Death* is *sub judice* he must not comment on it here; let me only say that three points in it appealed to him strongly. Firstly the fact that desire for truth on the part of another man coincided with his own strong feelings on that point. [Secondly] the limitations of his investigation also appealed to him – the necessity of getting at the truth in twenty four hours with no technical evidence, post-mortems or the usual facilities of his background resources And thirdly he was fascinated by the peculiar psychological interest of the case and ~~particularly~~ by

---

40   In the 'Foreword by the Author' to *Cards on the Table* Christie confirms that 'it was one of Hercule Poirot's favourite cases'; and in the final chapter Poirot calls it 'one of the most interesting cases I have ever come across'.

41   At the end of *Death on the Nile* Jacqueline de Bellefort asks Poirot, 'About me, I mean. You do mind, don't you?' And he answers, 'Yes, Mademoiselle.'

the strong malign personality of the dead woman.[42]

Well, I have told you all I can of Hercule Poirot – it is possible he has not finished with me yet – there may be more of him – facts to know which I have not fathomed.

Having drawn a line, literally, under the essay at this point Christie then decides to redraft the last paragraph and expand it slightly, although she omits the third reason for including *Appointment with Death* among Poirot's favourite cases:

Firstly that he undertook the case at the express desire of a man whose passion for truth was equal to his own.[43] Secondly the technical difficulty of the investigation ~~put him on his mettle~~ made a special appeal to him and the necessity of reaching the truth in twenty four hours without the help of expert ~~brilliance~~ evidence of any kind

Well, I have given you some of my impressions of Hercule Poirot – they are based on an acquaintance of many years standing. We are friends and partners. I must admit that I am considerably beholden to him financially. Poirot considers that I could not get along without him <u>but</u> on the other hand I consider that but for me Hercule Poirot would not exist.

There are times when I, too, have been tempted to

---

42  Oddly, both books of 1938, *Appointment with Death* and *Hercule Poirot's Christmas*, feature two of the most detestable characters in the entire Christie output: Mrs Boynton in *Appointment with Death* and Simeon Lee in *Hercule Poirot's Christmas*. A monstrous character automatically provides motive, although in neither case is their sheer detestability the reason for their murder. But it seems unlikely that this, and not the stunning and unique Petra setting, should be one of the characteristics of the case that appealed to Poirot.

43  This is a reference to Colonel Carbury, the man who asks Poirot to investigate the death of Mrs Boynton. In Part II, Chapter 15 Poirot says, 'The truth, I have always thought, is curious and beautiful.'

commit murder.[44] I am beholden to him financially. On the other hand, he owes his very existence to me. In moments of irritation I point out that by a few strokes of the pen (or taps on the typewriter) – I could destroy him utterly. He replies grandiloquently 'Impossible to get rid of Hercule Poirot like that – he is much too clever! ~~To permit such a thing to happen~~ And so, as usual, the little man has the last word!

### *Hercule Poirot's Christmas*
19 December 1938

Simeon Lee is a wealthy and horrible old man who enjoys tormenting his family. When he gathers them together for Christmas he sets in motion a train of events that culminates in his own murder. Luckily Hercule Poirot is staying with the Chief Constable and is on hand to investigate.

Published originally during Christmas week, with a serialisation on both sides of the Atlantic a month earlier, this is Christie at her most ingenious. Expert misdirection, scrupulous clueing, an unexpected murderer all coalesce to produce one of the all-time classic titles. Despite its title and publication date, however, there is no Christmas atmosphere whatever, even before the murder occurs. 'The Adventure of

---

44  This telling phrase, 'tempted to commit murder', may have been the musing that led, eventually, to *Curtain: Poirot's Last Case*. The chronology fits. This article would have been written, in all likelihood, at the end of 1937 or the very beginning of 1938 and page 7 of Notebook 21, the source of this essay, is headed 'Poirot's Last Case'; and there are a further four pages in the same Notebook with more detailed notes.

the Christmas Pudding', an inferior story from every view-point, is far more festive. An earlier case, *Three Act Tragedy*, is discussed in Part III, 'December 24th', and a foreshadowing of *They Do It with Mirrors* appears in Part VI, 'December 27th', while the biblical reference to Jael two pages later is the basis for the radio play *Butter in a Lordly Dish*.

There are two pages of Notebook 61 with rough notes for what was to become *Hercule Poirot's Christmas*. The pages follow immediately after the notes for *Appointment with Death*, published six months earlier:

Blood Feast

Inspector Jones – comes to see old Silas ~~Faraday~~
Chamberlayne – diamond king from S.A.

Characters

A family such as
Arthur – the good stay at home one
Lydia – clever nervy wife
Mervyn – son still at home dilettante artist
Hilda – his very young wife – rather common
David – very mean – sensitive
Dorothy – his articulate wife
Regina – unhappy woman – separated from husband
Caroline – her daughter – fascinating – reportedly bad
Edward – her devoted husband – bad lot

Although some names are accurate – Lydia, Hilda, David – the personality traits are not reflected in the eventual characters; and the last three listed have no equivalents. The policeman's name changes although Simeon Lee did make his fortune in South Africa.

Christie opens with the beginning of a quotation from Shakespeare's *Macbeth*, which may have been intended as a title, and quickly follows this with sketches of the Lee family. She breaks off to write brief notes for what were to become

*Curtain* and *Sad Cypress* and then returns to *Hercule Poirot's Christmas*. The first draft of the characters is immediately recognisable, apart from the Nurse, who does not appear in the novel:

A. Who would have thought [the old man to have had so much blood in him?]

Old Simeon Lee – A horrid old man

Alfred – the good son – (a prig) bores his father
Lydia – Alfred's clever well-bred bitter wife – she makes
    gardens
Harry? – The Prodigal son – he comes home and the old
    man likes him
Stephen Fane – A young man from S. Africa – son of
    Simeon's partner – (he cheated him!) – S. is really
    Simeon's son
Juanita Simeon's grand-daughter [Pilar] – back from Spain –
    his daughter ran away with a Spaniard and J. is really not
    grand-daughter – latter was killed in revolution – J was
    her friend
The Nurse – says old man was going to leave her all his
    money – wanted to marry her. She was married already
    – her husband is in New Zealand

The course of the story is outlined in the extract below, the novel following this synopsis closely:

Possible course of story

1. Stephen in train going up to Midcourt – this drab people
   – his impatience – the sun he comes from – then his first
   sight of Pilar – exotic – different – ~~reads label~~
2. Pilar in train – thinking – keyed up – her nervousness
   – handsome looking man – conversation – about Spain
   – the war – finally he reads label

3. Alfred and Lydia – conversation – she is like a greyhound
   – mention of her gardens – telephone call – Patterson
   – Horbury – she doesn't like that man

4. George and Magdalene – or David and Hilda strong
   motherly woman
   If G and M – his pomposity – and earnestness – his wife's
   impatience – her vagueness at some point about a letter
   (she has a lover) – he says better off when my father dies
   – they must go for Xmas important not to offend old
   man – he has written saying he would like to have all his
   children round him at Xmas – sounds quite sentimental

5. David and H
   He gets letter – nervous – neurotic passionately fond of
   his mother – won't go to the house – she, wise and
   motherly, persuades him – he goes off and plays piano
   violently

6. Harry Hugo arrives – cheery word to old Patterson – the
   prodigal – I could do with a drink – greeting from Lydia
   – she likes him

7. Old man himself – Horbury – he asks about his family –
   then goes and gets out diamonds – his face devilish
   glee

Interview with Alfred

Interview with Harry

Talk about prodigal son to Horbury

There were still significant clues to be inserted, while she also paid attention to the description, given by various characters, of the 'scream' establishing the (supposed) time of death:

Scenes to work in
(A) Portrait of old Lee P looks at it – found by someone
(B) Passport dropped out of window
(C) Statues in recess

(D) P. buys moustache
(E) Balloon

Screams
Alfred  A man in mortal agony
Lydia Like a soul in hell
Harry Like killing a pig
David Like a soul in hell

Although the plotting follows closely the course of the novel with relatively few deviations, Christie did try a few variations, the main ones being the presence of a conniving nurse or a criminal husband-and-wife. At this stage 'Drew' is the fore-runner of Sugden, the investigating officer, but there is no mention of his being a policeman:

Who is murderer?

~~Nurse   a fairly good-looking young woman of thirty (actually his daughter)   her desire for revenge~~

Drew is the man – Why? Illegitimate son – then Nurse is his sister – the two of them planned it

or – like Macbeth – a man and his wife do this – son of an earlier marriage?
    Possibly his second marriage was illegal – he makes a will so worded that the children of his second marriage inherit even if not legitimate – that will is destroyed – a draft is prduced by Nurse leaving it to her.

A new idea – is Nurse married to one of the sons? – the gay prodigal? – he manages to pull a string at the right moment

As suggested by her crossing-out of the idea here, Christie did not utilise the nurse in this novel. But the homicidal nurse was to resurface two years later in *Sad Cypress*.

## *And Then There Were None*
### 6 November 1939

———————◄○►———————

Ten strangers are invited to a weekend on an
island off the coast of Devon. Their host fails to
appear and a series of deaths among their fellow-
guests make them realise that one of them is a
killer following the macabre nursery rhyme
that hangs in each bedroom.

———————◄○►———————

*And Then There Were None* (originally published as *Ten Little
Niggers*) is Agatha Christie's most famous novel, her greatest
technical achievement and the best-selling crime novel of all
time. Of all the 'nursery rhyme' titles this is the one that most
closely follows the original:

*Ten little nigger boys went out to dine*
*One choked his little self and then there were nine;*
*Nine little nigger boys sat up very late*
*One overslept himself and then there were eight;*
*Eight little nigger boys travelling in Devon*
*One said he'd stay there and then there were seven;*
*Seven little nigger boys chopping up sticks*
*One chopped himself in half and then there were six;*
*Six little nigger boys playing with a hive*
*A bumble bee stung one and then there were five;*
*Five little nigger boys going in for law*
*One got in Chancery and then there were four;*
*Four little nigger boys going out to sea*
*A red herring swallowed one and then there were three;*
*Three little nigger boys walking in the Zoo*
*A big bear hugged one and then there were two;*
*Two little nigger boys sitting in the sun*

> *One got frizzled up and then there was one;*
> *One little nigger boy left all alone*
> *He went and hanged himself and then there were none.*

Frank Green's rhyme from 1869 and its implications – and the manner of each death – are a constant theme throughout the novel, most chillingly when the characters realise its deadly significance. Although Christie adopted the 'He got married and then there were none' ending for the stage adaptation, she used the original ending for the climax of the novel.

With the writing of this book Christie set herself a challenge and in *An Autobiography* she describes how the difficulty of the central idea attracted her: 'Ten people had to die without it becoming ridiculous. I wrote the book after a tremendous amount of planning . . . It was clear, straightforward, baffling and yet had a perfectly reasonable explanation . . . the person who was really pleased with it was myself, for I knew better than any critic how difficult it had been.'

When Collins began to advertise the book in *Booksellers Record* in July 1939, they called it, quite simply, 'the greatest story Agatha Christie has ever written'. But their item in the *Crime Club News* incurred the wrath of the writer herself and she wrote from Greenway House on 24 July to William Collins to protest. She felt that too much of the plot was revealed, pointing out that 'any book is ruined when you know exactly what is going to happen all the way along'. She also includes a veiled threat when she reminds him that she is just about to sign a contract for her next four books and is unwilling to do so unless they can guarantee that this error of judgement will not be repeated. Despite the fact that Collins declared it to be 'certainly the greatest detective story that the Crime Club has ever published and probably, we believe, the world will declare it the greatest detective story ever written', they included too many revelation: the island, the rhyme, the disappearing china figures, the realisation that the killer is among them and, most damning of all, the fact that the last one to die is not necessarily the villain. One's sympathies are entirely with Agatha Christie; all they omitted was the name of the killer.

The 'tremendous planning' is not evident from Notebook 65, the only one to feature this novel. This Notebook does, however, include interesting details of various characters that did not make it into the completed book. And, on the evidence of the Notebooks alone, it would seem to be the characters themselves that gave most trouble. At no stage are ten characters listed. At first there are eight (I have added probable names to both lists, although Vera Claythorne, Emily Brent, Philip Lombard and General MacArthur appear in the novel as listed in the Notebook, with minor background details altered):

Ten Niggers

Doctor – drunk at op – or careless [Dr Armstrong]
Judge – unjust Summing Up [Judge Wargrave]
Man and Wife – Servants (did in old lady) [Mr and Mrs Rogers]
Girl – whose lover shot himself [Vera]
Husband and wife – Blackmailing
Allenby – Youngish man – dangerous alert [Lombard]

At a later stage, to judge from the change from pencil to pen and the slightly different handwriting, she tries again. This time she includes twelve characters:

1. Vera Claythorne – Secretary at school – has applied at agency for holiday post
2. Mr Justice Swettenham in first class carriage [Judge Wargrave]
3. Doctor – telegram from Gifford – Can you join us – etc. [Dr Armstrong]
4 5. Capt and Mrs Winyard – Letters – mutual friend Letty Harrington – Come for weekend

6.  Lombard – visited by solicitor or confidential agent
    – offered one hundred guineas – take it or leave it
7.  University student who runs over children – a bit
    tight – arrives in car [Anthony Marston]
8.  Llewellyn Oban – Committed perjury in murder case
    – man executed [Blore]
9.  Emily Brent – turned out maidservant – later drank
    oxalic acid – letter from someone starting guest
    house and is a friend of hers – free stay
10 11.  Man and wife servant [Mr and Mrs Rogers]
12.  General MacArthur – killed 30 men unnecessarily
    in war

Each of the lists includes a husband-and-wife combination, Capt. and Mrs Winyard in the latter list, and these were the ones to be dropped. The second listing is much nearer to that of the novel although it is possible to discern the germ of the characters in the first tentative listing.

Two further refinements to the plot are included between characters 8 and 9 in the Notebook. Most of the guests to the island are lured by arrangements or invitations made by a Mr or Mrs Owens, sometimes with the initials 'U.N.' or, as Justice Wargrave says at the end of Chapter 3, 'by a slight stretch of fancy: UNKNOWN'. The initials undergo a few variations and the first note below is probably the seed of this idea. The second note refers to the diminishing collection of china figurines on the dining-room table:

Ulick Noel Nomen

Ten Little Niggers on dinner table

After a blank page the notes begin with Chapter 8 and, over the next eight pages, trace the course of the rest of the novel including the scene at Scotland Yard. This means that the last seven murders (from Rogers onwards) are all covered in this relatively short space, lending further support to the theory that the plotting for the book was done elsewhere and Notebook 65 represents the almost-finished plot.

Chapter VIII
The Search
Passing General Macarthur
They separate there? Go different ways –
Then house (A sudden scare Rogers? In his wife's room? They had seen him in garden a moment or two before – Inference he moves very quietly)

No-one on island

Suspecting each other – All go for a wash for lunch
(?) Blore goes to fetch General – Dead – life preserver

Chapter IX
Judge takes charge – exhibits a good deal of quickwittedness [sic] – Armstrong and Wargrave – Judge has an idea.
The storm comes on – all of them huddled into a room – nerves crackling. Next morning – no Rogers – no sign of him – breakfast not laid. Men search island – at breakfast – suddenly Vera sees – ~~Seven~~ Six niggers. Growing suspicion of Emily – a face watches her – a wasp stings her – dead bee on floor. Everyone terrified – all keep together. Where's old Wargrave – they find him dressed up in red robe and wig. He and Blore carry him up – the dining room – still 5 niggers. The 3 of them – criminal must be Armstrong. Finally: body washed up Armstrong! Blore crushed by falling rock. Vera and Lombard – one of us – her fears – self preservation – she gets his revolver – finally she shoots him – at last – safe – Hugo

The investigation –
The other deaths Owen? V and L last? Mrs R[ogers] and
    AM [Marston] all dead –

Morris dead too – he did all arrangements – committed
    suicide – dead –
Young man suggests Wargrave – Edward Seton was guilty
    – Old Wargrave was queer

Epilogue – Letter in bottle – he describes how it was done

One idea that was abandoned was that of a 'watcher' through-out the action. After the death of Emily Brent we read in the Notebook that 'A face watches her'; and at the climax of the story, when Vera goes up to her room the notes read 'Goes up to her bedroom – the noose – man steps out of darkness'. In retrospect the reader can imagine the killer 'watching' the unfolding of his plan, both before and after his supposed death, but it appears from these brief references that Christie toyed with the idea of mentioning the nameless 'watcher'. Far more effective and less melodramatic, however, is the concept she adopted at the end of Chapter 11, and again in Chapter 13, when she allows us to share the thoughts of the six remaining characters, including the killer's, but without identifying the thinker.

An interesting footnote is provided by the American crime-writer Ellery Queen. In his *In the Queen's Parlor* (1957) he discloses how, twice during his writing career, he had to abandon a book-in-progress when he read the latest Agatha Christie. Francis M. Nevins in his study of Queen, *Royal Bloodline*, confirms that one of these was a plot based on the same idea as *And Then There Were None*.

# The Third Decade 1940–1949

'I never found any difficulty in writing during the war . . . '
*An Autobiography*

◀○▶

**SOLUTIONS REVEALED**

*The ABC Murders* • 'The Affair at the Bungalow' •
*After the Funeral* • *And Then There Were None* • *Appointment
with Death* • *At Bertram's Hotel* • *The Body in the Library* • 'The
Case of the Caretaker/Caretaker's Wife' • *Cat among the
Pigeons* • 'The Companion' • *Crooked House* • *Curtain* •
*Death in the Clouds* • *Elephants Can Remember* • *Endless Night*
• *Evil under the Sun* • *Five Little Pigs* • *The Hollow* •
*The Labours of Hercules* • *The Moving Finger* • *The Murder at
the Vicarage* • *The Murder of Roger Ackroyd* • *Murder on the
Orient Express* • 'The Mystery of Hunter's Lodge' • *The
Mystery of the Blue Train* • *N or M?* • 'The Regatta Mystery'
• *Sad Cypress* • *Sparkling Cyanide* • 'Strange Jest' •
*Taken at the Flood* • *Three Act Tragedy* • *Towards Zero*

◀○▶

During the Blitz of the Second World War Agatha Christie
lived in London and worked in University College Hospital
by day; and, as she explains in *An Autobiography*, she wrote
books in the evening because 'I had no other things to do.'

She worked on *N or M?* and *The Body in the Library* simultaneously and found that the writing of two totally different books kept each of them fresh. During this period she also wrote the final adventure of Hercule Poirot, *Curtain: Poirot's Last Case.* Although it was always asserted that Miss Marple's last case, *Sleeping Murder,* was written at around the same time, I hope to show that the date of composition of that novel is much later in the decade. And it was at this time too that she worked on *Come, Tell Me How You Live* (1946), her 'meandering chronicle' of life on an archaeological dig.

Production slowed down during the 1940s, but only slightly. Thirteen novels, all but one, *N or M?* (1941), detective stories, were published; and a collection of short stories appeared towards the end of the decade. But if the quantity decreased, the quality of the writing increased. While still adhering to the strict whodunit formula Christie began, from *Sad Cypress* (1940) onwards, to take a deeper interest in the creation of her characters. For some of her 1940s titles, the characters take centre stage and the detective plot moves further backstage than heretofore. The central triangle of *Sad Cypress* is more carefully portrayed, and the emotional element is stronger, than most of the novels of the 1930s, with the possible exception of *Death on the Nile.* Similarly *Five Little Pigs* (1943), *Towards Zero* (1944), *Sparkling Cyanide* (1945) and especially *The Hollow* (1946) all contain more carefully realised characters than many previous novels.

In 1945 Christie wrote an essay, 'Detective Writers in England', for the Ministry of Information. In it she discusses her fellow writers in the Detection Club – Dorothy L. Sayers, Margery Allingham, Ngaio Marsh,[45] John Dickson Carr, Freeman Wills Crofts, R. Austin Freeman, H.C. Bailey, Anthony

---

45  Ngaio Marsh did not become a member of the Detection Club until 1974. This was solely for reasons of geography; because she lived in New Zealand it was impossible for her to attend regular meetings.

Berkeley. She then adds a few modest words about herself, including this interesting remark: 'I have become more interested as the years go on in the preliminaries of crime. The interplay of character upon character, the deep smouldering resentments and dissatisfactions that do not always come to the surface but which may suddenly explode into violence.' *Towards Zero* is an account of the inexorable events leading to a vicious murder at the zero hour of the title; *Five Little Pigs*, her greatest achievement, is a portrait of five people caught in a maelstrom of conflicting emotions culminating in murder; *Sparkling Cyanide*, adopting a similar technique to *Five Little Pigs*, is a whodunit told through the individual accounts of the suspects, many of them caught in the fatal consequences of an adulterous triangle. And the 'deep smouldering resentments' of her essay are more evident than ever in the prelude to the sudden explosion of violence at a country-house weekend in *The Hollow*. This novel, which could almost be a Mary Westmacott title, features Poirot, although when Christie dramatised it some years later, she wisely dropped him. For once, his presence is unconvincing and the detection element almost a distraction, although the denouement is still a surprise. Through all of this, she managed the whodunit factor though with less emphasis on footprints and fingerprints, diagram and floor plans, and initialled handkerchiefs and red kimonos.

And still she experimented with the detective novel form: *Death Comes as the End* (1945), set in Ancient Egypt in 2,000 BC, is a very early example of the crime novel set in the past; *N or M?* is a wartime thriller; *The Body in the Library* (1942) takes the ultimate cliché of detective fiction and dusts it off; and for *Crooked House* (1949) she devised an ending so daring that her publishers asked her to change it. Her only short story collection of this decade, *The Labours of Hercules* (1947), is also her greatest.

Apart from her detective output she also published two Westmacott novels. One of them, *Absent in the Spring* (1944), was written in 'a white-heat' over a weekend; this was followed three years later by *The Rose and the Yew Tree*. As further proof of her popularity, she made publishing history in 1948 when she became the first crime writer to have a million Penguin paperbacks issued on the same day, 100,000 each of ten titles.

After a lacklustre stage adaptation, by other hands, of *Peril at End House* in 1940, she wrote her own stage adaptation of *And Then There Were None* in 1943, thoroughly enjoying the experience; and dramatisations of two of her 'foreign' novels, *Appointment with Death* and *Death on the Nile*, followed in 1945 and 1946 respectively. And Miss Marple's stage debut, *Murder at the Vicarage*, not adapted by Christie herself, appeared in 1949. One of the best screen versions of a Christie work, René Clair's wonderful film *And Then There Were None*, appeared in 1945 and was followed two years later by an inferior second version of *Love from a Stranger*, the inaptly titled film of the excellent short story 'Philomel Cottage'.

Her most enduring monument, *The Mousetrap*, began life in May 1947 as the radio play *Three Blind Mice*, written as a royal commission for Queen Mary's eightieth birthday. In October of that year it also received a one-off television broadcast. The following year another play written directly for radio, *Butter in a Lordly Dish*, was broadcast.

During her third decade of writing Agatha Christie consolidated her national and international career, attracted the attentions of royalty and Hollywood, and experimented with radio. In continuing to extend the boundaries of detective fiction she graduated from a writer of detective stories to a detective novelist.

## *Sad Cypress*
### 4 March 1940

───────────◀◉▶───────────

Elinor Carlisle is on trial for the murder of Mary Gerard.
The case against her seems foolproof as only she had the
means, motive and opportunity to introduce poison at
the fatal lunch. Dr Lord thinks there is more to it than
meets the eye and approaches Hercule Poirot.

───────────◀◉▶───────────

*Come away, come away, death*
*And in sad cypress let me be laid*
*Fly away, fly away breath!*
*I am slain by a fair, cruel maid.*

Shakespeare, *Twelfth Night*

Although published in March 1940, *Sad Cypress* had appeared
in serial form in the USA at the end of the previous year. It is
a novel of carefully drawn characters with a clever plot device
at the core, although less emphasis on clues and timetables
and the minutiae of detection. And as other commentators
have pointed out there are some flaws in the plot ...

Notebooks 20 and 66 state the main plot device and as
early as this 1935 note that the murderer was to be female:

Rose without thorns – a thornless white rose mentioned by
front door – later apomorphine injected by murderer into
herself

Jan 1935
A. Rose without thorn mentioned by front door – later
murderess injects apomorphine into herself – draws
attention to prick as having been caused by thorn

*This sketch appears, inexplicably, in Notebook 35 during the plotting of* Five Little Pigs *(1943) but is unmistakably the cover design for* Sad Cypress *(1940). Alongside the tree is, possibly, a coffin – of cypress wood? – as per the quotation?*

Four pages later in Notebook 66 a second reference shows that, two years later, it was still in the planning process:

Feb 1937
A (as before)
A. Illegitimate daughter – Begins hospital nurse attending
~~old~~ wealthy woman – (she learns about daughter
supposedly d[aughter] of gardener) then kills off patient by
sweets sent from niece – later niece and Mary antagonistic
over a young man – nurse poisons Mary – Evelyn (niece)
thought to have done it.

Notebook 21 adds some detail, while item G on an alphabetical list in Notebook 66 also includes a similar plot device – but in a very different setting:

Retired hospital nurse – apomorphine stunt – Evelyn Dane
– inherits from Aunt – Mary is really daughter – actually
companion – Jeremy is cousin who has loved Evelyn and
now loves Mary – Nurse pretends to be surprised to see
Mrs. D's picture – she attended her for the birth of a
child etc.

Poison – man injects apomorphine after sharing some
dish – small tube with morphia on it found later – really
apomorphine. Family reunion – old father killed – who did
it? – he has whisky and soda for tea – others have tea –
~~fresh tea~~

The family reunion mentioned in the latter extract was changed but the idea of disguising the poison in freshly brewed tea was retained.

As with other books, the notes contain little that is different from the finished novel, leading to the suspicion that there were earlier discarded notes. Apart from some name changes – Roger becomes Roddy, Mrs Dacres is changed to

Mrs Welman and the first Nurse becomes O'Brien – the notes closely follow the course and detail of the novel:

Beginning
Elinor in London – anonymous letter – accusing undue influence – Elinor about to destroy it – then rings up Roger

Old Mrs. Dacres very ill – nurses in charge of case – gossip Mrs. Nurse Chaplin – a local nurse – Nurse Hopkins – they talk together – A photograph Mrs. D – asks for – signed Lewis – her husband's name was Roger Henry

Somewhat sudden death of old lady – suspicious absence of morphine? – Nurses not sure – she dies intestate

The characters were settled and the eternal triangle was defined from the beginning:

The relations – in house
    Mary Dane [Gerrard] – daughter of gardener – acted as companion
    Evelyn her niece arrives – and Roger Dacres – nephew by marriage
    She is a real character – hard up – fascinating – antagonism between her and Mary

Roger falls in love with Mary – Eve gives her a sum of money – Mary comes to life – Nurse Chaplin advises her to make a will

Dr. Lord – good-looking young man – fall in love with Elinor?

The nurses – Moira O'Brien resides in house – Nurse Hopkins from village – comes every morning to give a hand. As Nurse C leaves – Mary accompanies her – says her

Auntie in Australia is a hospital Nurse

Mary's death? She is at cottage – Elinor asks her to come up to the house for lunch – a cold lunch – Sandwiches – Nurse offers to make them a nice cup of tea – (apomorphine in kitchen) – the sandwiches – Mary to have salmon ones as she is a Catholic – gets her excited and then drowsy – Nurse Hopkins doesn't like the look of her – sends for doctor – difficult to get him – morphine poisoning

One of the flaws in the plot of *Sad Cypress* is that at the fatal lunch the killer cannot know that Elinor Carlisle will not also drink the poisoned tea along with Mary. The short note in Notebook 21 to the effect that 'Mary to have salmon ones as she is a Catholic' may have been an early solution to this problem of ensuring that only the intended victim ingested the poison, by attempting to guarantee that Mary would be limited in the type of sandwich (assumed erroneously to be the means of poisoning) she could eat. However, as the murder occurs on a Thursday (Chapter 7), Mary would not, in fact, be limited in her choice; the restriction on eating meat applied only to Fridays. And, in the event, the killer did not prepare the supposedly poisoned sandwiches anyway, so could not have stage-managed that aspect of the scene.

But there is a further problem, also of a practical nature: how could Nurse Hopkins have known that Elinor would call herself and Mary from the Lodge to the house for the fatal lunch? And how did she have a hypodermic and apomorphine with her? Her original plan to poison Mary in her own (Hopkins') cottage, as surmised by Poirot in the final chapter, does not answer the question either, as that scenario, even if it were to include Elinor, would be so unlikely as to be suspicious. Unfortunately the Notebooks give no indication as to whether Christie considered this difficulty.

The aftermath of the murder is also accurately reflected in Notebook 21, with little deviation from the finished novel:

Death of old lady – no will – her fortune goes to Elinor as next of kin

E and Roger – a little stiffness – she says it doesn't matter which of us has it – he again feels there is a coolness between them.

R. and Mary – incipient love affair – she is pleased – Mary's young man Edmund is angry – they quarrel

Elinor sees them together – R. is ringing her

Elinor gives Mary £1000 pounds – she accepts

And ultimately . . .

Dr. Lord comes to Poirot – insists it wasn't her – can't be Hopkins she had nothing to do with sandwiches – just made tea which they both drank – little bit of paper with morphine under the stove – the kitchen – it was open – someone could have got in there while the others were down in the Lodge

## One, Two, Buckle my Shoe
### 4 November 1940

Shortly after a much-dreaded appointment with his dentist, Poirot is recalled to the surgery to investigate Mr Morley's unexpected death. Two more of that morning's patients are found dead before Poirot can say 'Nineteen, twenty, my plate's empty.'

> *One, two, buckle my shoe*
> *Three, four, shut the door*
> *Five, six, pick up sticks*
> *Seven, eight, lay them straight*
> *Nine, ten, a big fat hen*

*Eleven, twelve, men must delve*
*Thirteen, fourteen, maids are courting*
*Fifteen, sixteen, maids in the kitchen*
*Seventeen, eighteen, maids in waiting*
*Nineteen, twenty, my plate's empty . . .*

The notes for this novel are contained in four Notebooks with the majority (over 75 pages) in Notebook 35, where they alternate with the notes for *Five Little Pigs*. *One, Two, Buckle my Shoe* is Christie's most complicated novel, with a triple impersonation underpinning a complex murder plot with roots in the distant past. The novel centres on the identity of a dead body but, unlike *4.50 from Paddington*, it is a tantalising, rather than an aggravating, question.

The only questionable aspect of this novel is, ironically, the use of the nursery rhyme. It is strained and unconvincing and, apart from the all-important shoe buckle, the rhyme has little or no significance other than providing chapter titles. This is confirmed by the following extract from Notebook 35 where Christie jots down the rhyme and tries to match ideas to each section. As can be seen, they are not very persuasive and in fact few of them, apart from the shoe buckle, went into the novel:

One Two Buckle my Shoe – the Shoe Buckle – think of it
– the start of this case

The Closed Door – something about a door – either room locked or something not heard through closed door when it should have been.

Picking up sticks – assembling clues

Lay them Straight – order and method

A good fat hen – the will – read – rich woman it was who died – murdered woman – fat elderly – two girls – man recently coming to live with rich relative?

Men must Delve – Digging up garden – another body – discovered buried in garden – wrong owner of shoe buckle?

Maids a courting – 2 girls – heiresses of Fat Hen? Or would have been connected by husband of fat hen – in collusion with maid servant

Maids in the kitchen – servant's gossip

Maids in Waiting?

My Plate is Empty
End

Clue – a shoe buckle

An example of the type of organised listing that occurs throughout the Notebooks, the plot of *One, Two, Buckle my Shoe* occurs as Idea H on a list from A to U. This list looks to have been written straight off with three or four ideas to a page in the same handwriting and with the same pen. Some of them include minor elaboration, but the possibility of combining Idea H with the twins or chambermaid idea was not pursued).

Ideas
  A. Poirot's Last Case – history repeats itself – Styles now a guest house [*Curtain*]
  B. Remembered Death – Rosemary dead [*Sparkling Cyanide*]
  C. Dangerous drug stolen from doctor's car. [A suggestion in *Hickory Dickory Dock*]
  D. Legless man – sometimes tall – sometimes short
  E. Identical twins (one killed in railway smash)
  F. Not identical twins
  G. A murderer is executed – afterwards is found to be innocent [*Five Little Pigs/Ordeal by Innocence*]
  H. Dentist Murder Motive? Chart substitution? Combine with E? or F? or J?

   I. Two women – arty friends – ridiculous – one is crook
   J. Chambermaid in hotel accomplice of man
   K. Stamps – but stamps <u>on</u> letter ['Strange Jest']
   L. Prussic acid
   M. Caustic potash in cachet
   N. Stabbed through eye with hatpin
   O. Witness in murder case – quite unimportant – offered
      post abroad
   P. Third Floor Flat idea
   Q. Figurehead of ship idea
   R. Prussic acid – 'Cry' in bath
   S. Diabetic idea – insulin (substitute something else)
      [*Crooked House*]
   T. Body in the Library – Miss Marple [*The Body in the*
      *Library*]
   U. Stored blood idea, wrong blood

A few pages later, the germ of the plot emerges although, as can be seen from the question marks, the idea was hazy. As she frequently did, Christie considered a multitude of possibilities in working out the details, but apart from a name change this short note is the basis of the novel:

> Dead woman supposed to be actress? Rose Lane – (really is Rose Lane) but body shown to be <u>someone else</u> –
> Why?
> Why???
> Why?????

From the (admittedly unscientific) evidence that the word 'dentist' occurs 65 times in the Notebooks against a mere 13 appearances for the word 'buckle', it would seem that the background came before the all-important clue, or even the nursery rhyme. But this combination of dentist – his family, patients, surgery and, vitally, files – together with the rhyme and its accompanying main clue, gave Christie the ideal situation for creating confusion about the identification of a body. She could now pursue serious plot development:

Dentist Murder
H.P. in dentist's chair – latter talking while drilling
Points:
  (1)  Never forget a face – patient – can't remember where I saw him before – it will come back to me
  (2)  Other angles – a daughter – engaged to a rip of a young man – father disapproves
  (3)  Professional character – his partner


Much hinges on evidence of <u>teeth</u> (death of dentist)

Dentist murdered – H.P. in waiting room at time – patients charts removed or substituted

Dentist – HP in waiting room – sent away

Rings Japp – or latter rings him

Do you remember who was in waiting room?

She begins to develop the novel's characters, sketching in tentative notes about names and backgrounds, in a well-ordered list of the scenes – 'silhouettes' – introducing them:

Latest dentist ideas

Little silhouettes of the people going to Mr Claymore that day

1  Mr Claymore himself at breakfast
2  Miss D – mentions a day off or just gets telephone call
3  Miss Cobb or Miss Slob at breakfast – Miss C saying much better – not aching

4  Mr Amberiotis – talk of his landlady – about his tooth – careful English
5  Caroline – (young swindler?) or Mr Bell (dentist's daughter lover – American? Trying to see father)
6  Dentist's partner – rings – can he come up to see him – a service lift – unprofessional conduct?
7  Mr. Marron Levy – a board meeting – a little snappy – admits at end – toothache – gets into Daimler – 29 Harley St.
8  H.P. His tooth – his conversation with dentist – meets on the stairs – woman with very white teeth?
Later Japp – suspicious foreigner

Not all of the characters that she sketched made it into the novel and some that did appeared under different names. The dentist victim became Morley instead of Claymore, Miss D became Gladys Neville, and Marron Levy became Alistair Blunt. Mr Bell possibly became Frank Carter, the boyfriend of Gladys, and Miss Cobb's conviction that her toothache is improving is similar to our eventual introduction to Miss Sainsbury Seale. Miss Slob and Caroline were abandoned after this listing. Oddly, the shoe buckle is not mentioned at all here and the white-toothed woman mentioned in item 8 has replaced or, more likely, foreshadowed, Miss Sainsbury Seale.

Throughout the notes Christie continued trying to fit her ingenious plot into the plan of the nursery rhyme:

1 – 2
Miss S going to dentist
Mr Mauro
Miss Nesbit
Mr Milton
H.P. in waiting room – shoe buckle – loose – annoys him

3 – 4
Japp comes – P. goes with him – interview partner's wife?
– secretary etc.

5 – 6
The body – evidence of identity destroyed – but identified
from clothes. Mrs Chapman's flat – the shoes – either a
buckle missing or one found there

(7–8 does not get separate attention.)

9 – 10
Julia Olivera – married not in love – Aunty Julia – 'the
daughter is attractive'

11 – 12
Men Must Delve – dentist's secretary had been crying
because young man has lost his job. In garden next
morning – the gardener – P goes round a bush – Frank
Carter – digging

13 – 14
Mrs Adams – that conversation – then – in park Jane and
Howard

15 – 16
Final Maids in the Kitchen touch – one of the maids
upstairs looked over – saw Carter – watched Carter went
in – saw dentist dead

17 – 18
Miss Montressor – dark – striking – gardening – her
footprint in bed

19 – 20
P outlines case – smart patent new shoe – foot and ankle
strap – buckle torn off. Later woman found – shoe and
buckle sewn on. It was a woman's shabby shoe – other
was new

But I am not persuaded. The early sections – the buckle, picking up sticks (clues) and laying them straight (interpreting them) – are acceptable. But the gardening motif ('men must delve') and the maids looking over the banisters are simply unconvincing. The dauntingly clever plot does not need this window-dressing and the book can stand, without any references to the rhyme, as a superb example of detective fiction.

If, however, any further proof were necessary of the ingenuity and fertility of Agatha Christie, a glance at almost any page of Notebook 35 would supply it. The following ideas are scattered throughout the notes for *One, Two, Buckle my Shoe*. None of them was used.

> Idea of two women – one criminal working with man goes to dentist – simply in order to give man alibi

> Harvey – rich, unscrupulous – married to young wife – a widow when he married her – had she murdered first husband?

> Or Double suicide man and woman – one of them not the person – therefore suicide not murder – dentist could have identified her

> M. wants to get rid of someone – (his wife?) therefore he kills his wife and another man but it proves not to be his wife but another woman

### 'Four and Twenty Blackbirds'
### March 1941

─────────◄○►─────────

Poirot investigates the mysterious death of an elderly man
when his suspicions are aroused – by the man's diet.

─────────◄○►─────────

*Sing a song of sixpence, a pocket full of rye,*
*Four and twenty blackbirds, baked in a pie . . .*

The title of 'Four and Twenty Blackbirds' appears for the first
time in Notebook 20:

4 and 20 blackbirds

Located ahead of Christie's reminder to herself ('To be
added – Sketch of Leatheran career – Chapter II') to amend
*Murder in Mesopotamia*, this dates it to the mid-1930s, at least
six years before the story first appeared. A rough sketch of
the story itself appears in Notebook 66 just ahead of a sketch
for 'Triangle at Rhodes':

Impersonation of old man – he eats a different meal on
the Tuesday – nothing else noticed. Died later.

Mr P Parker Pyne – They talk – points out elderly man
with a horn beamed ~~and spectacles~~ eye-glass – bushy
eyebrows

Old fellow hasn't turned up – waiter says he is upset –
first noticed it a fortnight ago – when he wouldn't have
his jam roll – had blackberry tart instead. Sees body –
teeth – no blackberry tart. Empty house – fell downstairs –
dead – open letter

These notes contain one surprise: the allocation of this case to Parker Pyne instead of Hercule Poirot. In fact this change could be quite easily imagined; this is not one of the more densely plotted Poirot stories, and it is probable that market forces dictated the substitution of the Belgian. And as we shall see, this is not an isolated example of the interchangeability of characters.

It has to be said that the connection to the nursery rhyme is very tenuous. For the purposes of the story the blackbirds of the rhyme become blackberries: the main clue is the lack of discoloration of the victim's teeth. A more fitting title is that used on the story's first US appearance in *Colliers Magazine* in November 1940, 'The Case of the Regular Customer'.

## Evil under the Sun
### 9 June 1941

Beautiful Arlena Marshall is murdered while
staying at the same glamorous hotel on Smuggler's Island
where Hercule Poirot is holidaying. He investigates her
murder, which involves a typewriter, a bottle of suntan
lotion, a skein of wool and a packet of candles.

*Evil under the Sun* was written during 1938 and delivered to Edmund Cork by 17 February 1939. It had first appeared, in the USA, as a serial towards the end of 1940. At first glance *Evil under the Sun* and 'Triangle at Rhodes' appear to be the same story. Both feature Hercule Poirot, a beach setting and two couples as the main protagonists. In each case, one couple consists of a vamp and a quiet husband, the other a charmer and a 'mouse' (in Christie's own word). And both stories exemplify perfectly Christie's fertility of plot invention because, despite these not insignificant similarities, the solutions and killers are completely different. In each case the triangle the reader is encouraged to envisage is completely wrong and also completely different. In both cases clever stage-management forces the reader to look in the wrong direction despite, in the case of the novel, abundant clues to the truth.

There are 60 pages of Notebook showing its origins, and we can see the detailed working-out that went into one of Christie's most ingenious plots. The setting exists in reality as Burgh Island, off the coast of Devon, a venue well known to Christie as she stayed at the hotel there on a few occasions. The island is cut off from the mainland twice a day at high tide and is reached by a sea-tractor. She utilises its geography to suit her purposes in creating a perfect alibi.

That storehouse of plot devices, *The Thirteen Problems*, yet again provided the rough basis for this novel. 'A Christmas Tragedy' features two people, the murderer and a witness (in this case Miss Marple herself), finding a 'dead' body before it has been murdered, thereby providing the killer with an impeccable alibi. In the case of the short story the body is the result of a natural death, conveniently dead two hours earlier, but in the novel it is the live body of the killer's accomplice. Both plots also feature a large and camouflaging hat (also a feature of *Dead Man's Folly*). Many refinements were obviously possible in the course of a novel: a larger cast of suspects, the added complication of a triangle situation, a warm beach to confuse the time of death and a more elaborate alibi for the killer. But it is essentially the same plot.

From the first page of Notebook 39 Christie seems to have the plot, the main characters and the setting already well advanced. This may be because she was developing an earlier short story. Names were to change but this description was to form the basis of the book:

Seaside Mystery

H.P. is at seaside – comments on bodies everywhere – makes old-fashioned remarks. Main idea of crime – G an ordinary rather 'simple' man is apparently bowled over by a well-worn siren. His wife is very unhappy about it – shows distinct jealousy. He has alibi all morning (with H.P.) goes with a woman for a walk and discovers body of siren – distinctive bathing dress – Chinese 'hat' – and red auburn curl. Suggest to woman to stay with body – she flinches – he finally says he will and she goes for police. Part of 'dead woman' is acted by (wife?) or (woman he really cares about?). Immediately after woman has gone for help – siren appears from other direction – he kills her (strangled?) and places her in same position

Therefore characters are:
George Redfern – quiet bank manager etc.
Mary Redfern – white skin / not (tanned) dark
Gloria Tracy – Siren very rich – mad on men
Edward Tracy – Husband
Rosemary Weston – in love with Edward

Scene Hotel on island – Bigbury [Burgh Island]

If the names were not exactly the same as those in the published novel – the first names of the Redferns became Patrick and Christine, while Gloria and Edward Tracy became Arlena and Kenneth Marshall, and Rosemary Weston is Rosamund Darnley – the differences are not significant enough to prevent recognition.

A few pages later, several details have been established:

Beginning

House – built by a sea captain sold first when bathing came in

Hercule Poirot – with whom?

The American in Appointment with Death  [Jefferson Cope]

Major Blount [Barry] or Miss Tough [Brewster] looking at everyone

Arlena King – red haired lovely – husband – an author and playwright – Arlena left a fortune a year or two previously

Jean [Linda] – her daughter – athletic girl – hates stepmother

Middle aged spinster – sister of Arlena's husband – says she's a bad lot

People?

Kenneth ~~Leslie~~ Marshall

Arlena ~~Leslie~~ Marshall

Linda ~~Leslie~~ Marshall

Patrick ~~Desmond Redfern~~ –

Cristina      "      or McGrane

Mr and Mrs Gardener (Americans)

Or (Bev) (gone with Desmond) [Possibly Irene, the Gardeners' far-off daughter]

Rosemary Darley

H.P.

Or Mrs Barrett   [not used]

The Reverend Stephen Mannerton [Lane]

Horace Blatt (red faced magnate)

Miss Porter [Miss Brewster]

Mrs Springfelt [not used]

Major Barry

The reference to *Appointment with Death* above is slightly mystifying; there is no reference to this book in *Evil under the Sun* and no character in common, apart from Poirot. Christie may have toyed with the idea of introducing Jefferson Cope from the earlier novel and perhaps abandoned it in case it spoiled the reader's enjoyment of *Appointment with Death*. The Gardeners, the compromise American characters she instead created, provide light relief throughout the novel.

She also utilises her alphabetical sequencing, working out short scenes of encounters rather than plot development. Although she does not follow the sequence exactly, the only scene not to appear in any form is E. Scene B is the all-important one that Poirot remembers in Chapter 11 ii when he muses on five significant remarks:

Beginning

A. House built by etc. [Chapter 1 i]

B. H.P. watches bodies – Mrs Gardener – reciting Beverly etc. – her husband says Yes, darling – Mr Barrett, Miss Porter and Miss Springer. Arlena – pushes off on her float. Major Barry – these red-headed gals – I remember in Poonah [Chapter 1 ii and iv]

C. The Marshalls arrive – Kenneth and Rosemary – an encounter

D. Linda thinks – her face – breakfast [Chapter 2 ii]

E. Miss Porter and Miss Springer – latter tells her friend what she overheard. You were with Desmond and Cristina and H.P. and Mrs Kane

F. Rosemary and H.P. – taste in wives [Chapter 2 i]

G. Christine Redfern and Desmond

H. Rosamund and Kenneth [Chapter 3 i]

One particularly intriguing element of the notes concerns the complicated alibis Christie provided for most of the characters. This caused much crossing-out and rearranging and she changed the details quite considerably before she arrived at a version that pleased her. Two of her favourite unused ideas, the dishonest, collusive chambermaid and the two 'arty' friends, surfaced briefly before being discarded and returned to the 'unused' category, while she also experimented with other solutions before returning to the thoughts she had initially set out:

Alternative Plan

Arlena dies Christine disappears
   Desmond and Christine go out on a float – early – or in their boat – Japanese sunshade. You do believe me, darling, when I tell you there's nothing in it at all. No one sees them come back

Alternatives

A. Desmond kills Christine
   First arranges body – then drowns her – gets rid of other woman – puts C's body on rocks as though fallen from above – right spot indicated by stone (peculiar colour marking etc.) the night before.

B. Desmond and Gladys Springer do murder – (Christine is, perhaps, only fiancée?). Gladys and 'friend' are at Gull Cove – latter sketching – forever looking for flowers (or shells?). Goes through cave – acts the part of 'the body' and returns

C. Christine and Desmond are a pair of crooks. Money – banked in her name – her story of blackmail coming out when questioned by the Police

D. Is the chambermaid Desmond's wife? ALL her stories false – about blackmail – about seeing Christine etc. – alters Linda's watch

Where is everyone?
Blatt – out in boat – later sails found in a cave
Major Barry – drive his car into Lostwitch – business – market day – early closing – lots of people on beach

*This sketch from Notebook 39 shows the mainland and the island (complete with compass points) and the route between the two. Also shown are the Hotel and Tennis Court, the Bathing Beach as well as Pixy Cove and Gull Cove. Note the change of mind about the last two locations.*

The Gardeners – on beach (she goes up to get wool or he
gets it for her)
Babcock – to church – signs book – but it could be previous
day
Kenneth? Typing in room
Rosamund? Bathing? On float
Tennis – Christine, Rosamund, Kenneth, Gardener

And many of the clues that feature in the novel (the bath
that no one will admit taking, the candles, the sun-tan lotion
bottle) appear in the Notebooks:

About Linda – Packet of candles – calendar – other things
she remembers – green?
Bath?
Kenneth – typing at middle table
Bottle thrown from window

♈

## *N or M?*
### 24 November 1941

---

Which of the guests staying at the Sans Souci
guest house is really a German agent? A middle-aged
Tommy is asked to investigate and although Tuppence's
presence is not officially requested, she is determined
not to be left out. Which is just as well, because
Tommy disappears . . .

---

*N or M?* marked the return of Tommy and Tuppence. We last
met them in *Partners in Crime* (1929) and they are now the
parents of twins Derek and Deborah, although the chronology of their lives does not bear close scrutiny. At the end of

*Partners in Crime* Tuppence announces that she is pregnant, which – even allowing for the fact that the individual stories were written up to six years earlier – would make her eldest child a teenager, at most; and yet both children are involved in the war effort. Like Miss Marple's age and the timescale of *Curtain*, the dubious chronology should not interfere with our enjoyment.

*N or M?* was serialised six months ahead of book publication in UK and two months earlier again in the USA. This tallies with a November 1940 letter from Christie to her agent, Edmund Cork, wondering if she should rewrite the last chapter. It was her intention to set it in a bomb shelter where Tommy and Tuppence find themselves after their flat has been bombed. As she explains in *An Autobiography*, she worked on this book in parallel with *The Body in the Library*, alternating between the two totally different books, thereby ensuring that each one remained fresh. This combination is mirrored in the brief mention – very formally as 'Mr and Mrs Beresford' – below, from Notebook 35.

As a couple, Tommy and Tuppence have not lost their sparkle and the subterfuge undertaken by Tuppence in the early chapters, which enables her to overcome the reluctance of Tommy and his superiors to involve her in events, is very much in keeping with earlier manoeuvres in both *The Secret Adversary* and *Partners in Crime*. In the novel Christie manages to combine successfully the spy adventure and the domestic murder mystery. There is the overriding question of the fifth-column spy but also the more personal mystery of the kidnapped child. With customary ingenuity Christie brings them both together.

Notebook 35 considers the as-yet-unnamed novel:

3 Books

Remembered death [published in the UK as *Sparkling Cyanide*]

The Body in the Library
Mr and Mrs Beresford

And six pages later she sketches in the opening of the book. It would seem from the notes that the fundamentals of the plot were clear before she began it. Most of the notes in Notebooks 35 and 62 are in keeping with the completed novel, with the usual minor name changes. In the middle of the notes there are some pages of 'real' spy detail culled, presumably, from a book. It is a fascinating glimpse into a relatively unknown area of the Second World War, and somewhat surprising that Christie was able to access this information while the war was still in progress:

Holy figures of Santa containing Tetra (explosive)
Man in telephone booth – are numbers rearranged
Cables on bottom of Atlantic – submarines can lay wires
and copy messages
Mention of 'illness' means spying is under observation.
Recovery is at risk

An experiment with code creation makes a brief appearance in Notebook 35, where she sketches the notes of the musical scale and the lines and spaces of the musical stave. She adds words – CAFE, BABE, FACE – all composed from the notes of the scale, ABCDEFG. And she outlines a possible character combining a musical background and a workplace with musical-scale initials: 'A pianist at the BBC'.

Christie next considers potential characters, most of them very cryptically.

T and T
T (for Two)

Tommy approached by MI – Tuppence on phone – really listens – when T turns up at Leahampton – first person he sees is Tuppence – knitting!

Possible people
Young German, Carl – mother a German?
Col Ponsonby – old dug out [Major Bletchley]
Mrs Leacock (who keeps guest house) [Mrs Perenna]
Mr Varney [Mr Cayley]
Mrs Varney [Mrs Cayley]
Daughter with baby comes down to stay [Mrs Sprot]

Later in the same Notebook, she considers the 'main idea' of the book, though this description is only partly reflected in the novel itself:

Main idea of T and T
Woman head of espionage in England?

In fact, in the opening chapter we read of the 'accidental' death of the agent Farquhar who, with his dying breath, managed to say 'N or M,' confirming the suspicion that two spies, a male, N, and a female, M, are at work in England. The psychology behind the concealment of this dangerous female is as clever as anything in Christie's detective fiction.

Notebook 13 has a concise and accurate outline of the book. Details were to change but this is the essence of the plot and would seem to be the first jottings. Not all of these details were to be included and others, not listed here, were to appear. The alternative title indicates that she possibly considered the book as a 'second innings' for Tommy and Tuppence:

N or M

2nd innings

Possible course of plot
T and T walk – meet – plan of campaign – T's sons
[Chapter 2]
Following incidents

Sheila and Carl together [Chapter 2]
Tuppence and Carl [Chapter 2]
Golf with Major Quincy (Bletchley) 'too many omen' –
Commander Harvey [Haydock] has house on cliff – a coast
watcher [Chapter 3 ii]
Mrs. O'Rourke [Chapter 4]
Mildred Skeffington – 'Betty' [Chapter 2]
Mr. and Mrs. Caley – (Varleys?)
Miss Keyes [Minton] [Chapter 3]
Mrs. Lambert and son

The foreign woman – speaks to Carl in German [Chapter 5
iii]
Kidnapping of child [Chapter 7 ii]
Carl tries to gas himself
Does T hide in Commander's house?
Is he kidnapped on golflinks? Or go to Commander's house
– and be drugged there – the sailing boat [Chapter 9 ii]
A reference to 'Little Bo Peep' – 'Mary has a little lamb' Jack
Warner Horner [Chapter 14 i]
Mrs. O'Rourke – her voice loud and fruity – really drugged
teas with Mrs Skeffington

Notebook 35 has more about Carl and the foreign woman as
well as the first mention of the death of the child's mother,
although nothing more about the subterfuge around that
aspect of the plot. And it is in this Notebook that Christie
identifies the two killer spies.

Possible plots

T and T established – Carl immediate object of suspicion
– unhappy – nervy – he and Margaret Parotta – Mrs P –
sinister. Tommy and Col Lessing – play golf together – Col
tells him something suspicious about someone (Mrs P?)
also very much against German boy.

Tup meets foreign looking woman hanging round

Tup has letters – from her 'sons' – leaves them in drawers –
they have been tampered with.
Child kidnapped – found alive – woman dead – documents
planted on her

Information thus sent is true to inspire confidence – Col. L
[Haydock] and Mrs Milly ~~Turnbull~~ Saunders [Sprott] are N
and M

Notebook 62 lists a few more scenes. Scene B appears in the
book despite its deletion in the notes:

A. Tommy – supper Haydock – discovery – hit on head
   – imprisoned [9 ii]
B. ~~Deb and young man   about mothers Leamouth~~ [10 iv]
C. Tup finds Tommy disappeared. Mrs B says never came
   back last night. Rung up a day later – young man says all
   right – not to worry. Penny plain and Tuppence coloured
   – Deborah – Derek [10 iii and 11 iii]

And this short final extract from the same Notebook encapsulates quite an amount of plot, although in such cryptic
style that it would be impossible to make sense of it –
especially the final phrase – as it stands:

The kidnapping of Betty – Mrs Sprott shoots Polish woman
– with revolver taken from Mrs Keefe's drawer – arrest of
Karl – incriminating papers – invisible ink on bootlaces

An accusation often levelled against Christie's writing is that
it never mirrors reality and is set in 'Christie-time'. This
adventure of the Beresfords is very much rooted in reality
and features the war as part of the plot more than any other
title. It is also sobering to remember that when she wrote

this book the war still had five years to run. *N or M?* has many clever touches and the interplay between Tommy and Tuppence remains as entertaining as it was on their two previous appearances. Sadly, it was the last we were to read of Tommy and Tuppence until *By the Pricking of my Thumbs*, over 25 years later.

# Miss Marple and 'The Case of the Caretaker's Wife'

'Miss Marple insinuated herself so quickly into my life that I hardly noticed her arrival.'

*An Autobiography*

————————————◄o►————————————

'The Case of the Caretaker' was first published in the UK in *The Strand* in January 1942, followed by 'Tape-Measure Murder' in February and 'The Case of the Perfect Maid' in April. These short stories can be seen as preludes to Miss Marple's looming investigation of *The Body in the Library* in May 1942. Between *The Thirteen Problems* in 1932 and the publication, in quick succession, of these three short stories UK readers had seen the elderly detective in action only in the slight 'Miss Marple Tells a Story' in 1935. In the USA the *Chicago Sunday Tribune* published 'The Case of the Caretaker' in July 1942.

Apart from being a very typical Marple murder-in-a-village case – the 'big house', the local doctor, gossiping neighbours, the post office – this short story is important in the Christie output as it is the precursor of the last great novel that she was to write over a quarter-century later, *Endless Night*. The similarities are remarkable – wealthy heiress marries ne'er-do-well charmer, builds a house in the country and is menaced by a peculiar old woman. Her death, following a horse-riding 'accident', is shown to have been orchestrated by her husband and his lover. What distinguishes the plot in the novel is the manner of its telling, the characterisation of the main protagonists and the shock ending.

In common with many short stories, there is little Notebook material relating to 'The Case of the Caretaker'. The first brief note below, reflecting the theme and the final poignant words of the story, appears in Notebook 60 and its accompanying page contains notes for the companion story, 'The Case of the Perfect Maid'. The surrounding pages of this Notebook contain early notes for what would become *The Moving Finger* (1943) and *Curtain*, so a composition date of 1940/41 is confirmed.

> Poor little rich girl
> Old Mr Murgatroyd turned out – shakes fist etc. – really is
> <u>paid</u> by husband – accident at home – she is called in. Miss
> M tells Haydock what to look for

The second, slightly elaborated note below is from Notebook 62. There, the inspiration is one of a list of one-sentence short story ideas, many of which remained undeveloped. The list is followed by the detailed notes for *N or M?* (1941) and then a page headed 'Books 1941', so it is reasonable to assume that the following was also written during 1940.

> A. Poison Pen
> B. A Cricket story
> C. Committee crime
> D. Infra Red photograph
> E. 'Facing up' story
> F. District Nurse
> G. Charwoman comes to Miss M.
> H. Arty spinster friends
> I. Poor little rich girl
> J. Lady's maid and parlour maid
> K. Stamp story

L. Dangerous drugs stolen
M. Legless man
N. Extra gong at dinner

Idea A became *The Moving Finger*, K became 'Strange Jest', G and J were combined in 'The Case of the Perfect Maid', and I became 'The Case of the Caretaker'. Idea N remains a mystery; both versions of this idea – 'The Second Gong' (1932) and the more elaborate 'Dead Man's Mirror', in (1937) – had already been solved by Poirot. At a later date, to judge from the different pen and less sprawling handwriting, Christie begins to expand ideas I, G, C and J and then added ideas K, L, M and N. This expansion is an accurate sketch of 'The Case of the Caretaker/Caretaker's Wife':

> I.
> Esme Harley, rich heiress, married to self serving man
> (politician? younger son ne'er-do-well?) unused to country
> life – old woman (or man) curses her when she is out riding
> – horse swerves. Horse shot with air gun – bolts – Esme is
> thrown. Clare Wright (doctor's daughter?) comes up to her
> – injects digitalin? Heart gives out as she is taken home.
> Or
> Husband does it – the clock tower gives time. Yes, but he
> winds it or butler winds it (like 'Sign in the Sky')

This draft is very similar to the published version – an heiress, a ne'er-do-well son, a bolting horse and an injection – but there also differences. As frequently happens, the names change, but there is also uncertainty about the sex of the caretaker, and the doctor's daughter is sketched in as the villain of the piece. The second possibility, the clock tower, contains an explicit reference to the Mr Quin story 'The Sign in the Sky', in which the murderer alters the time of the clocks in his house in order to create an alibi. But altering the domestic clocks is far removed from changing the tower clock and thereby attempting to fool an entire population, which seems a very impractical and unconvincing idea. Wisely, Christie abandoned it.

The 'doctor's daughter' as murderer idea is more complicated. In the published version it is the chemist's wife, a former lover of the husband, who conspires with him by supplying the poison, although she does not actually administer the injection. In the Notebook at this stage the husband is not the first choice for murderer, but arranging the innocent-seeming presence of the doctor's daughter in order that she administer an injection is perhaps one of the reasons for her replacement with Esme's husband.

Dr Haydock's niece – not daughter – Clarice is one of the main characters in the story; and she also, unsuspectingly, provides a subsidiary motive for the murder. But as Dr Haydock appears throughout Miss Marple's detective career, it would hardly be fitting for her to identify his daughter as the killer. Hence the name 'Clare Wright' and the question mark in the Notebook.

Both the UK and US versions of the short story are identical. But among Christie's papers is a second, significantly different version.

Why this second version should exist is open to speculation. Most Christie short stories were originally published in magazines and many of her novels appeared, prior to book publication, in newspapers and periodicals. Editors were notorious for their predilection for changing stories and cutting novel serialisations, often for reasons of space. Christie complained about this when asked to change *Dumb Witness* and a 1944 letter from her agent talks about the 'serial version' of *Towards Zero* that Christie had prepared 'in accordance with their [*Colliers Magazine*] instructions'. I have discussed the different versions of *Three Act Tragedy*, also accounted for, in all likelihood, by an editor. So the different versions of 'The Case of the Caretaker/Caretaker's Wife' may well be explained away that simply. But if so, it means that the edited version was the one submitted for US publication, although the newly discovered version is more straightforward and logical.

One of the main differences between the known version (Version A) and the new version (Version B) is the method of narration. In A the story is told in the form of a manuscript prepared, for reasons never made clear, by Dr Haydock and given to Miss Marple to read while recovering from flu; B tells a similar story directly, without the device of the manuscript, and this certainly makes for a more convincing narration. But the differences are not merely in the manner of telling.

The setting of St Mary Mead is firmly established by the second sentence of B, but in A we have to wait until four pages from the end for confirmation of this, despite the fact that 'the village' is mentioned but unnamed on the second page. B features Miss Marple's neighbours, familiar to readers from their appearances in *The Murder at the Vicarage* and the soon-to-be-published *The Body in the Library* – Mrs Price Ridley, Miss Hartnell and Miss Wetherby; A has the vaguely analogous Mrs Price, Miss Harmon and Miss Brent. These changes are not only completely inexplicable in themselves but it is very difficult to see how they were explained or justified to Christie and/or her agent. Adding further confusion, Julia Harmon is the vicar's wife in *A Murder is Announced*, as well as the later Marple short story 'Sanctuary'.

B finds Miss Marple playing a much more central role; she talks to Mrs Murgatroyd, and Clarice and the doctor, and generally acts as the observant old lady that she is. While reading the doctor's manuscript and then propounding her solution is similar to the plan of the short stories in *The Thirteen Problems*, it seems cumbersome and unnecessary compared to B.

Finally, the title of B is more logical and accurate. Mrs Murgatroyd's husband was the caretaker and he has been dead for two years in both versions; so why 'The Case of the

Caretaker'? Notebook 62, as we have seen, vacillates about this point.

The following has had some minor errors of spelling and punctuation corrected.

# THE CASE OF THE CARETAKER'S WIFE

'And where is the bride?' asked old Miss Hartnell genially.

The village of St Mary Mead was all agog to see the rich and beautiful young wife that Harry Laxton had brought back from abroad. There was a general indulgent feeling that Harry, wicked young scapegrace, had all the luck! Everyone had always felt indulgent towards Harry. Even the owners of windows that had suffered from his indiscriminate use of a catapult had found their just indignation dissipated by young Harry's abject expressions of regret. He had broken win-dows, robbed orchards, poached rabbits, and later ran into debt, got entangled with the local tobacconist's daughter, been disentangled, and sent off to Africa – and the village as represented by various ageing spinsters had murmured indulgently:

'Ah well. Wild oats! He'll settle down.'

And now, sure enough, the prodigal had returned – not in affliction, but in triumph. Harry Laxton had 'made good' as the saying goes. He had pulled himself together, worked hard, and had finally met and successfully wooed a young Anglo-French girl who was the possessor of a considerable fortune.

Harry might have lived in London, or purchased an estate in some fashionable hunting county – but at least he was a faithful soul. He came back to the part of the world that was home to him. And there, in the most romantic way, he purchased the derelict estate in the Dower House of which he had passed his childhood.

Kingsdean House had been unoccupied for nearly seventy years. No repairs were ever done to it and it had gradually fallen into decay and abandon. It was a vast unprepossessing grandiose mansion, the gardens overgrown with rank vegetation, and as the trees grew up higher around it, it seemed more and more like some gloomy enchanter's den. An elderly caretaker and his wife lived in the habitable corner of it.

The Dower House was a pleasant unpretentious house and had been let for a long term of years to Major Laxton, Harry's father. As a boy, Harry had roamed over the Kingsdean estate and knew every inch of the tangled woods, and the old house itself had always fascinated him.

Major Laxton had died some years ago, so it might be thought that Harry would have had no ties to bring him back. But on his marriage, it was to St Mary Mead that he brought his bride. The ruined old Kingsdean House was pulled down. An army of builders and contractors swooped down upon the place and in an almost miraculously short space of time, (so marvellously does wealth tell!) the new house rose white and gleaming amongst the trees.

Next came a posse of gardeners and after them a procession of furniture vans. The house was ready. Servants arrived. Lastly a Rolls Royce deposited Harry and Mrs Harry at the front door.

St Mary Mead rushed to call, and Mrs Price Ridley who owned the large house near the Vicarage and who considered herself to lead society in the place sent out cards of invitation for a party to 'meet the bride.'

It was a great event in St Mary Mead. Several ladies had new frocks for the occasion. Everyone was excited, curious, anxious to see this fabulous creature. It was all so like a fairy story.

Miss Hartnell, weather beaten hearty spinster, threw out her question as she squeezed her way through the crowded drawing room door. Miss Wetherby, a thin acidulated spinster, fluttered out information.

him. And there, in the most romantic way, he purchased the derelict
estate in the ~~B~~ower ~~H~~ouse of which he had passed his ~~childish life~~ *childhood.*

Kingsdean House had been *un*occupied for nearly seventy years.
~~The property of a ruined owner,~~ (it had gradually fallen into
~~decay and abandon.~~ *and decay & abandon)* No repairs wer~~e~~ ever done to it~~.~~ *And* ~~elderly~~
~~caretaker and wife lived in the one habitable corner of it.~~ It
was *a* vast unprepossessing gradiose mansion ~~and~~ *as* the gardens ~~fell~~
~~to overgrow~~ *with rank* vegetaion *as* and the trees grew up higher *& darker*
around it, it seemed more and more like some gloomy enchanter's den.
*An elderly caretaker & his wife lived in the one habitable corner of it*

~~The~~ ~~B~~ower ~~H~~ouse, ~~n ar its western boundary, had been kept in~~
~~repair. It~~ was a pleasant unpretentious house and had been let
for a lon~~g~~ term of years to Major Laxton, Harry's father. As a
boy, Harry had roamed over the *Kingsdean* ~~neglected~~ estate and knew every inch
of the tangled woods, and the *old* house itself had always fascinated him.
~~Major Laxton had died leaving a bare pittance to his son.~~ *some years ago, so it might be thought*
*that Harry would have had no tie bring him back*
But on his marriage, it was to St ~~M~~ary Mead that ~~Harry~~ *he* brought
his bride~~, and it was soon learned that the whole estate had been~~
bought by them ~~and that~~ The ruined old ~~building~~ *Kingsdean House* was ~~to be~~ pulled
down ~~and a new house erected on the site.~~ And ~~almost at once~~
an army of b~~uild~~ ers and con~~tr~~ actors swooped down upon the place
and in an almost miraculously short space of time, (so marvellously
does wealth tell,) the new house rose white and gleaming amongst
the trees.
~~Then~~ *Next* came a ~~posse~~ of gardners and ~~finally~~ *after them* a procession of
furniture vans. The house was ready. Servants arrived. Lastly

'Oh my dear, *quite* charming. Such pretty manners. And quite young. Really, you know, it makes one feel quite *envious* to see someone who has *everything* like that. Good looks and money, and breeding – (*most* distinguished, nothing in the least *common* about her) and dear Harry *so* devoted.'

'Ah,' said Miss Hartnell, 'It's early days yet.'

Miss Wetherby's thin nose quivered appreciatively.

'Oh my dear, do you really think—?'

'We all know what Harry is,' said Miss Hartnell.

'We know what he *was*. But I expect *now*—'

'Ah,' said Miss Hartnell. 'Men are always the same. Once a gay deceiver, always a gay deceiver. *I* know them.'

'Dear, dear. Poor young things!' Miss Wetherby looked much happier. 'Yes, I expect she'll have trouble with him. Someone ought really to *warn* her. I wonder if she's heard anything of the old story?'

The eyes of the two ladies met significantly.

'It seems so very unfair,' said Miss Wetherby, 'that she should know *nothing*. So awkward. Especially with only the one chemist's shop in the village.'

For the erstwhile tobacconist's daughter was now married to Mr Edge, the chemist.

'It would be so much nicer,' said Miss Wetherby, 'if Mrs Laxton were to deal with Boots in Much Benham.'

'I daresay,' said Miss Hartnell, 'that Harry Laxton will suggest that *himself*.'

Again a significant look passed between them.

'But I certainly think,' said Miss Hartnell, 'that she ought to *know*.'


## ii

'Beasts!' said Clarice Vane to old Miss Marple. 'Absolute beasts some people are!'

Miss Marple looked at her curiously.

Clarice Vane had recently come to live with her Uncle, Dr

Haydock. She was a tall dark girl, handsome, warm hearted and impulsive. Her big brown eyes were alight now with indignation.

She said:

'All these *cats* – *saying* things – *hinting* things!'

Miss Marple asked:

'About Harry Laxton?'

'Yes, about his old affair with the tobacconist's daughter.'

'Oh *that*!' Miss Marple was indulgent. 'A great many young men have affairs of that kind, I imagine.'

'Of course they do. And it's all over. So why harp on and bring it up years after? It's like ghouls feasting on dead bodies.'

'I daresay, my dear, it does seem like that to you. You are young, of course, and intolerant, but you see we have very little to talk about down here and so, I'm afraid, we do tend to dwell on the past. But I'm curious to know why it upsets you so much?'

Clarice Vane bit her lip and flushed. She said in a curious muffled voice: 'They look so *happy*. The Laxtons, I mean. They're young, and in love, and it's all lovely for them – I hate to think of it being spoilt – by whispers and hints and innuendoes and general beastliness!'

Miss Marple looked at her and said: 'I see.'

Clarice went on:

'He was talking to me just now – he's so happy and eager and excited and – yes, *thrilled* – at having got his heart's desire and rebuilt Kingsdean. He's like a child about it all. And she – well, I don't suppose anything has ever gone wrong in her whole life – she's always had everything. You've seen her, don't you think—'

Miss Marple interrupted. She said:

'As a matter of fact I haven't seen her yet. I've only just arrived. So *tiresome*. I was delayed by the District Nurse. Her feelings, you know, have been hurt by what—'

But Clarice was unable to take an interest in the village

drama which Miss Marple was embarking upon with so much zest. With a muttered apology she left.

Miss Marple pressed onwards, full of the same curiosity that had animated everyone in St Mary Mead, to see what the bride was like.

She hardly knew what she expected, but it was not what she saw. For other people Louise Laxton might be an object of envy, a spoilt darling of fortune, but to the shrewd old lady who had seen so much of human nature in her village there came the refrain of a popular song heard many years ago.

'*Poor little rich girl . . .*'

A small delicate figure, with flaxen hair curled rather stiffly round her face and big wistful blue eyes, Louise was drooping a little. The long stream of congratulations had tired her. She was hoping it might soon be time to go . . . Perhaps, even now, Harry might say—? She looked at him sideways. So tall and broad shouldered with his eager pleasure in this horrible dull party.

Oh dear, here was another of them! A tall grey haired fussily dressed old lady bleating like all the rest.

'This is Miss Marple, Louise.'

She didn't understand the look in the old lady's eyes. She would have been quite astonished if she had known what it was:

'*Poor little rich girl . . .*'

### iii

'Ooph!' It was a sigh of relief.

Harry turned to look at his wife amusedly. They were driving away from the party. She said:

'Darling, what a frightful party!'

Harry laughed.

'Yes, pretty terrible. Never mind, my sweet. It had to be done, you know. All these old pussies knew me when I lived here as a boy. They'd have been terribly disappointed not to have got a good look at you close up.'

Louise made a grimace. She said:

'Shall we have to see a lot of them?'

'What? Oh no – they'll come and make ceremonious calls with cardcases and you'll return the calls and then you needn't bother any more. You can have your own friends down or whatever you like.'

Louise said after a minute or two:

'Isn't there anyone *amusing* living down here?'

'Oh yes. There's the country set, you know. Though you may find them a bit dull too. Mostly interested in bulbs and dogs and horses. You'll ride, of course. You'll enjoy that. There's a horse over at Eglinton I'd like you to see. A beautiful animal perfectly trained, no vice in him, but plenty of spirit.'

The car slowed down to take the turn into the gates of Kingsmead. Harry wrenched the wheel and swore as a grotesque figure sprang up in the middle of the road and he only just managed to avoid it. It stood there, shaking a fist and shouting after them.

Louise clutched his arm.

'Who's that – that horrible old woman?'

Harry's brow was black.

'That's old Murgatroyd – she and her husband were caretakers in the old house – they were there for thirty years.'

'Why did she shake her fist at you?'

Harry's face got red.

'She – well, she resented the house being pulled down. And she got the sack, of course. Her husband's been dead two years. They say she got a bit queer after he died.'

'Is she – she isn't – starving?'

Louise's ideas were vague and somewhat melodramatic. Riches prevented you coming into contact with reality.

Harry was outraged.

'Good Lord, Louise, what an idea! I pensioned her off, of

course – and handsomely, too. Found her a new cottage and everything.'

Louise asked bewildered:

'Then *why* does she mind?'

Harry was frowning, his brows drawn together.

'Oh how should I know? Craziness! She loved the house.'

'But it was a ruin, wasn't it?'

'Of course it was – crumbling to pieces, roof leaking, more or less unsafe. All the same I suppose it – *meant* something to her. She'd been there a long time. Oh! I don't know! The old devil's cracked I think.'

Louise said uneasily:

'She – I think she cursed us . . . Oh Harry, I wish she hadn't.'


### iv

It seemed to Louise that her new home was tainted and poisoned by the malevolent figure of one old crazy woman. When she went out in the car, when she rode, when she walked out with the dogs there was always the same figure waiting. Crouched down on herself, a battered hat over wisps of iron grey hair, and the slow muttering of imprecations.

Louise came to believe that Harry was right, the old woman *was* mad. Nevertheless that did not make things easier. Mrs Murgatroyd never actually came to the house, nor did she use definite threats, nor offer violence.

Her squatting figure remained always just outside the gates. To appeal to the police would have been useless and in any case Harry Laxton was averse to that course of action. It would, he said, arouse local sympathy for the old brute. He took the matter more easily than Louise did.

'Don't worry yourself about it, darling. She'll get tired of this silly cursing business. Probably she's only trying it on.'

'She isn't, Harry. She – she *hates* us! I can *feel* it. She – she's ill wishing us.'

'She's not a witch, darling, although she may look like one! Don't be morbid about it all.'

Louise was silent. Now that the first excitement of settling in was over, she felt curiously lonely and at a loose end. She had been used to life in London and the Riviera. She had no knowledge of, or taste for, English country life. She was ignorant of gardening, except for the final act of 'doing the flowers.' She did not really care for dogs. She was bored by such neighbours as she met. She enjoyed riding best. Sometimes with Harry, sometimes, when he was busy about the estate, by herself, she hacked through the woods and lanes, enjoying the easy paces of the beautiful horse Harry had bought for her.

Yet even Prince Hal, most sensitive of chestnut steeds, was wont to shy and snort as he carried his mistress past that huddled figure of a malevolent old woman . . .

One day Louise took her courage in both hands. She was out walking. She had passed Mrs Murgatroyd, pretending not to notice her, but suddenly she swerved back and went right up to her. She said a little breathlessly,

'What is it? What's the matter? What do you want?'

The old woman blinked at her. She had a cunning dark gypsy face, with wisps of iron grey hair, and bleared suspicious eyes. Louise wondered if she drank.

She spoke in a whining and yet threatening voice.

'What do I want, you ask? What indeed? That which has been took away from me. Who turned me out of Kingsdean House? I'd lived there girl and woman for near on forty years. It was a black deed to turn me out and it's black bad luck it'll bring to you and him.'

Louise said:

'You've got a very nice cottage and—' she broke off.

The old woman's arms flew up. She screamed!

'What's the good of that to me? It's my own place I want,

and my own fire as I sat beside all them years. And as for
you and him I'm telling you there will be no happiness for
you in your new fine house! It's the black sorrow will be
upon you – sorrow and death and my curse! May your fair
face rot . . .'

Louise turned away and broke into a little stumbling run.
She thought:

'*I must get away from here*. We must sell the house. We must
go away . . .'

At the moment such a solution seemed easy to her. But
Harry's utter incomprehension took her aback. He exclaimed:

'Leave here? Sell the house? Because of a crazy old
woman's threats? You must be mad!'

'No, I'm not. But she – she frightens me . . . I know
something will happen.'


*v*


A friendship had sprung up between Clarice Vane and young
Mrs Laxton. The two girls were much of an age, though dissimilar both in character and in tastes. In Clarice's company
Louise found reassurance. Clarice was so self reliant, so sure
of herself. Louise mentioned the matter of Mrs Murgatroyd
and her threats but Clarice seemed to regard the matter as
more annoying than frightening.

'It's so stupid, that sort of thing,' she said. 'But really very
annoying for *you*!'

'You know, Clarice, I – I feel quite frightened sometimes.
My heart gives the most awful jumps.'

'Nonsense, you mustn't let a silly thing like that get you
down. She'll soon get tired of it.'

'You think so?'

'I expect so. Anyway don't let her see you're frightened.'

'No. No, I won't.'

She was silent for a minute or two. Clarice said:

'What's the matter?'

Louise paused for a moment, then her answer came with a rush.

'I hate this place! I hate being here! The woods, and this house, and the awful silence at night, and the queer noise owls make. Oh and the *people* and everything!'

'The people? What people?'

'The people in the village. Those prying gossiping old maids.'

Clarice said sharply:

'What have they been saying?'

'I don't know. Nothing particular. But they've got nasty minds . . . when you've talked to them you feel you wouldn't trust anybody . . . not *anybody* at *all*!'

Clarice said:

'Forget them. They've nothing to do but gossip. And most of the muck they talk they just invent.'

Louise said:

'I wish we'd never come here . . . but Harry adores it so – Harry.'

Her voice softened. Clarice thought, 'How she adores him!'

She said abruptly:

'I must go now.'

'I'll send you back in the car. Come again soon.'

Clarice nodded. Louise felt comforted by her new friend's visit. Harry was pleased to find her more cheerful and from then on urged her to have Clarice often to the house.

Then one day he said:

'Good news for you, darling.'

'Oh, what?'

'I've fixed the Murgatroyd! She's got a son in America, you know. Well, I've arranged for her to go out and join him. I'll pay her passage.'

'Oh Harry, how wonderful! I believe I might get to like Kingsdean after all.'

'*Get* to like it? Why, it's the most wonderful place in the world!'

'To *you* darling, not to me!'

'You wait!' said Harry confidently.

Louise gave a little shiver. She could not rid herself of her superstitious fears so easily.

## *vi*

If the ladies of St Mary Mead had hoped for the pleasure of imparting information about her husband's past into the ears of the bride, they were disappointed by Harry Laxton's own prompt action.

Miss Hartnell and Clarice Vane were both in Mr Edge's shop, the one buying mothballs and the other a packet of indigestion lozenges, when Harry Laxton and his wife came in.

After greeting the two ladies, Harry turned to the counter and was just demanding a toothbrush when he stopped in mid speech and exclaimed heartily:

'Well, *well*, just see who's here! Bella, I do declare!'

Mrs Edge, who had hurried out from the back parlour to attend to the congestion of ladies, beamed back cheerfully at him showing her big white teeth. She had been a dark handsome girl and was still a reasonably handsome woman, though she had put on weight and the lines on her face had coarsened, but her large brown eyes were full of warmth as she replied:

'Bella it is, Mr Harry, and pleased to see you after all these years.'

Harry turned to his wife.

'Bella's an old flame of mine, Louise,' he said. 'Head over ears in love with her, wasn't I, Bella?'

'That's what *you* say,' said Mrs Edge.

Louise laughed. She said:

'My husband's very happy seeing all his old friends again.'

'Ah,' said Mrs Edge, '*we* haven't forgotten you, Mr Harry. Seems like a fairy tale to think of you married and building up a new house instead of that ruined old Kingsdean House.'

'You look very well and blooming,' Harry said, and Mrs Edge laughed and said there was nothing wrong with her and what about that toothbrush?

Clarice, watching the baffled look on Miss Hartnell's face, said to herself exultantly:

'Oh well *done*, Harry! You've spiked their guns!'

Indeed, though Miss Hartnell did her best, with mysterious hints of having seen Harry Laxton and Mrs Edge talking together on the outskirts of the village, to revive a bygone scandal, she met with no success, and had to fall back upon vague hints as to the general depravity of men.

### *vii*

It was Dr Haydock who said abruptly to Miss Marple:

'What's all this Clarice tells me about old Mrs Murgatroyd?'

'Mrs Murgatroyd?'

'Yes. Hanging about Kingsdean and shaking her fist and cursing the new regime.'

Miss Marple looked astonished.

'How extraordinary. Of course Murgatroyd and his wife were always a queer couple, but I always thought the woman was devoted to Harry – and he's found her such a nice new cottage and everything.'

'Just so,' said the doctor drily. 'And by way of gratitude she goes up and makes a nuisance of herself and frightens his wife to death.'

'Dear dear,' said Miss Marple. 'How peculiar. I must have a word with her.'

Mrs Murgatroyd was at home this afternoon and was smoking a pipe. She received Miss Marple without undue deference.

'I thought,' said Miss Marple reproachfully, 'that you were fond of Mr Laxton.'

Mrs Murgatroyd said:

'And who told you that?'

'You used to be when he was a boy.'

'That's a long time since. He hadn't pulled down house then.'

'Do you mean you'd rather be living there in that lonely ruined place than here in this nice cottage?'

'What I feel's my own business.'

'Do you mean that it's really true that you go up there and frighten young Mrs Laxton with curses?'

A strange film came over the dirty old woman's eyes. She said, and there was dignity and menace in her voice:

'I know how to curse, I do. I can do it proper. You'll see.'

Miss Marple said:

'What you are doing is cruel and uncivilised and – and I don't understand it. What harm has Harry Laxton ever done you?'

'That's for me to say.' She leaned forward nodding her head triumphantly. 'I can hold my tongue, I can. You won't get anything out of me.'

Miss Marple came away looking puzzled and worried. She met the doctor just outside his own gate.

He said, 'Well?'

'Oh dear, I am very much upset. There is – I am convinced there is – something very dangerous going on. Something that I don't understand.'

'Get anything out of the old woman?'

'Nothing at all. She – I can't understand her.'

Haydock said thoughtfully:

'She's not crazy, you know. She's got *some* idea at the back of her mind. However, I'm glad to say Laxton is shipping her off to America next week.'

'She's consented to go?'

'Oh yes, jumped at it. I wondered – well, she's an artful old devil. I wondered if she had been playing for just this to happen? What do *you* think?'

Miss Marple said, 'I don't know what to think. But I wish – I wish she were gone . . .'

The next morning Louise Laxton was thrown from her horse and killed.

### *viii*

Two men in a baker's van had witnessed the accident. They saw Louise come out of the big gate, saw the old woman spring up and stand in the way waving her arms and shouting, saw the horse start, swerve and then bolt madly down the road throwing Louise Laxton over his head . . .

One of them stood over the unconscious figure, not knowing what to do next, while the other rushed to the house to get help. Harry Laxton came running out, his face ghastly. They took off a door of the van and carried her on it to the house. But when the doctor arrived she had died without regaining consciousness.

The author of the catastrophe had slunk away. Frightened, perhaps, at what she had done, she slipped into her cottage and packed her belongings and left. She went straight off to Liverpool.

'And the law can't touch her,' said Haydock bitterly.

He was speaking to Miss Marple who had paid him an unexpected visit.

He went on, his tone reflecting the deep anger and discouragement of his mood.

'You couldn't make out a case against her. A clever counsel would tear her to pieces. She didn't even threaten. She never touched the horse. It's a case of malevolent will power, that's all. She terrified that poor child, and she scared the horse and he bolted with her. It's an *accident* – that's all. But in my opinion, Louise Laxton was murdered as truly as I stand here talking to you.'

Miss Marple nodded her head.

'I agree with you.'

'And that half witted malevolent old crone commits murder and gets away with it! And all for no reason as far as I can see . . .'

Miss Marple was twisting her fingers nervously.

She said:

'You know, Dr Haydock, I don't think she did murder her.'

'Not legally, perhaps.'

'Not at all.'

Haydock stared.

'But you just said—'

'You see, we are talking at cross purposes. I do think Louise was murdered – but not by the person you think.'

Haydock stared. He said:

'My dear old friend, are you mad, or am I?'

'Oh I know it may sound *quite* ridiculous to you, and of course it is entirely an *idea* on my part, only, if it *is* so, it is most important that the truth should come out, because one doesn't want to see another young life ruined and it might be – in fact, it probably would be. Oh dear, how incoherent I sound, and it is necessary, I know, to be calm and *businesslike* in order to convince you.'

Haydock looked at her attentively. He said:

'Tell it your own way.'

'Oh, *thank* you. Well, you see, there are certain facts that seem so at variance with the whole thing. To begin with – Mrs Murgatroyd always hated Kingsdean House – they only stayed there because Murgatroyd drank and couldn't keep any other job. So you see it seems very unlikely that she'd feel leaving so keenly. Which means, of course, that somebody *paid* her to act that way she's done . . . *putting on an act*, they call it nowadays.'

Haydock drew a deep breath.

'What are you trying to say?'

'Poor little rich girl,' said Miss Marple unexpectedly. 'Gentlemen, so I have noticed, are nearly always attracted by the same *type*. Not always in the same class of life, of course, but there's usually physical resemblance. Bella Edge, for instance, was a tall dark handsome girl with white teeth and a lot of spirit. Rather like your niece Clarice. That's why when I saw Louise I was quite sure that Harry wasn't the least bit in love with her. He married for money. And after that he planned to get rid of her.'

Haydock said incredulously:

'You think he paid that old woman to come and curse in order to scare his wife and finally induce her horse to run away with her. My dear woman, that's a tall order!'

'Oh yes, yes, put like that. Did she die of the fall?'

'She had a fractured arm and concussion, but she actually died of the shock.'

'You've not done an autopsy, have you? And has anyone examined the horse?'

'What's the idea?'

Miss Marple said:

'I'm suggesting, absurd or not, that it wasn't Mrs Murgatroyd who caused the horse to bolt. That was only the *apparent* cause – for the onlookers. Harry was always very good with a catapult. A stone may have struck the horse just as it came through the gate. Then it bolted and threw Louise. The fall might have killed her but when Harry came out she was still alive. I think that then, before you got there, he may have injected something to make certain.'

Haydock said: 'You terrifying woman![46] I suppose you'll tell me what he injected next?'

'Oh, really I have not the least idea. Probably some very swift heart poison.'

'Such things aren't easy to get hold of.'

Miss Marple said sharply:

---

46  This handwritten addition to the typescript is, apart from 'Haydock' and 'you', illegible. This transcription seems the most likely exchange.

'Bella Edge could have got it for him.'

'Well – er yes – perhaps, but why should *she* do such a thing?'

'Because, poor woman, she's always been crazy about Harry Laxton. Because I've no doubt he's been playing her up and telling her after Louise was dead he'd take her away from her husband and marry her.'

'Marry Bella Edge!'

'He wouldn't, of course! But afterwards she couldn't give him away. She'd be too afraid for herself. Actually Harry plans to marry your niece Clarice. She's no idea. He fell in love with her at that party. That's why you've got to do something if you can. She's in love with him and you don't want her married to a murderer.'

'Not if *I* can help it,' said Haydock grimly.

Satisfied, Miss Marple went out into the clear sunshine of the morning.

She said under her breath:

'Poor little rich girl . . .'

———————————◄○►———————————

Two interesting amendments that appear in the original typescript merit mention. The first time the name Clarice appears, in section ii, it has been inserted in handwriting and the following has been deleted: 'Griselda Clement, the young and pretty wife of the vicar . . .' This is the only appearance in the typescript of Griselda and by the top of the next page, and thereafter, 'Clarice' has been typed. Possibly as she wrote Christie decided to make Clarice part of the motive, something that she could not have done with happily married mother Griselda, whom her readers knew from *The Murder at the Vicarage*. The second change was to the scene in the chemist's shop (section vi), when Bella and Harry's conversation is witnessed by Clarice and Miss Harmon/Hartnell. Here again, 'Clarice' is inserted in handwriting and 'Miss Marple' is deleted. And the closing paragraph of this section, here reinstated, is omitted in Version A, to the detriment of the plot; the information given here is an indication of collusion between Harry and Bella.

Version A has the totally incredible account, given by Dr Haydock in the closing scene, in which Harry, the newly widowed murderer, drops a hypodermic syringe out of his trouser pocket. No murderer, regardless of circumstance, would resort to this probably painful, not to mention potentially fatal, method of concealment. I cannot believe that Agatha Christie ever envisioned such a scene; this *must* be the invention of a (poor) magazine editor.

Despite her last-minute substitution and insertion in the two instances mentioned above, Clarice plays a more pivotal role in Version B. Although in both versions she provides part of the motive, it is more unequivocal and less covert in Version B than in the earlier version, where her interest in Harry is peripheral.

Overall, this newly discovered version is longer, more convincing and more coherent than its predecessor. The awkward, not to mention unmotivated, manuscript ploy is replaced by a more straightforward narration in which Miss Marple takes centre stage – where she belongs.

## *The Body in the Library*
### 11 May 1942

---◄○►---

When the body of a glamorous blonde is found
on Mrs Bantry's library rug in Gossington Hall,
she decides to call in the local expert in murder,
Miss Marple. Together they go to the Majestic
Hotel where Ruby Keene was last seen alive.
And then a second body is found . . .

---◄○►---

As we have seen, the writing of *The Body in the Library* was done in parallel with that of *N or M?*. Thus two very dissimilar novels, one a classical whodunit, the other a wartime thriller, would remain fresh. This experiment was, in all likelihood, during 1940; *N or M?* appeared as a serial in the USA in March 1941; *The Body in the Library* was serialised in the USA in May/June 1941 and published as a novel there in February 1942. It is probable that *N or M?* was completed before *The Body in the Library* as the timescale in the latter for Basil Blake's injuries (mentioned in Chapter 16 ii) in the Blitz, which began in September 1940, would seem to place the completion of the Marple title well into 1941.

There are references to previous Miss Marple cases. In Chapter 1 iv she mentions that her 'little successes have been mostly theoretical', an allusion to *The Thirteen Problems*, the last time she had featured in a Christie title. A few pages later Inspector Slack ruefully recalls his earlier encounter with the elderly sleuth in *The Murder at the Vicarage*; and Mrs Bantry reminds Miss Marple (as if she needed it) that the earlier murder had occurred next door to her. Sir Henry Clithering recalls her perspicuity in 'Death by Drowning', the last of *The Thirteen Problems*, in Chapter 8.

Unusually for Christie, the social reaction to the discovery of a body in Colonel Bantry's library is remarked upon. Playful at first, with exaggerated reports circulating in St Mary Mead in Chapter 4, more serious discussion ensues in Chapter 8 ii when Miss Marple considers the potential long-term effect of social ostracism. Some years earlier in *Death in the Clouds* Poirot had questioned Jane Grey and Norman Gale about the practical effects on their lives, and businesses, of involvement in a murder, but he was considering motive and not social reaction.

The main plot device of this novel – the interchangeability of bodies – is very similar to that of the previous year's *Evil under the Sun*. In that novel, in order to establish an alibi a live body masquerades as a dead one; in *The Body in the Library* one dead body is intentionally misidentified as another, again in order to establish an alibi. Despite its light-hearted beginning there is a genuinely dark heart to *The Body in the Library*, with its use of a totally innocent schoolgirl as a 'decoy' body, chosen solely on the basis of her similarity to the 'real' victim, Ruby Keene. This is the earliest example in Christie's output of the murder of a child (apart from the almost incidental murder of Tommy Pierce in *Murder is Easy*) and unlike later examples – *Dead Man's Folly* and *Hallowe'en Party* – the victim is cold-bloodedly selected solely to provide a corpse.

Notes for this novel are contained in six Notebooks, the bulk of them in Notebook 62. The plot variations are minimal, confirming Christie's remarks in *An Autobiography*, that she had been thinking about the plot for 'some time'. One note, in Notebook 35, is however at strange variance with the finished novel; the 'disabled' reference could have inspired Conway Jefferson, but otherwise the only similarity is 'Killed somewhere else?'

Body in Library
Man? Disabled? Sign of power? No name on clothes
Inhaling Prussic acid vapour (glucose) Manager of a
disinfecting process. Killed somewhere else?

An earlier draft, from Notebook 13, outlines the basic plot device – the switch of the bodies and the misidentification – but many of the surrounding details are different. Oddly, one of the conspirators in this first draft is Ruby Keene, the victim in the published novel. At this stage in the planning there is no mention of Conway Jefferson, who provides the motive, and his extended family, which provides most of the suspects. The Girl Guide, the buttons, the bleached blonde – all these plot elements are in place, though as yet the background is not filled in:

> Body in Library
> Mrs. B – awaiting housemaid etc. – telephone to Miss Marple. Peroxide blonde connected with young Paul Emery [Basil Blake] – rude young man who has fallen out with Bantry and who had a platinum blonde down to stay (scandal). Paul is member of set in London – real murderer has it in for him – dumped body on him – Paul takes it up to Bantry's house or real blonde girl knew Paul's blonde girl and about cottage – so decoyed Winnie there (with key from friend). Body is really Girl Guide decoyed by Mavis who pretends she has film face. She and man make her up after she is dead. Paul proves he was in London at party at 11 pm. Really arrives home about 3 – finds dead girl – is a bit tight – thinks we'll push her onto old Bantry.
> Now – <u>why</u>?
> Idea is that Mavis de Winter, night club dancer, is dead.
> Say: Ruby Keene, Mavis de Winters, were friendly in Paris – come over here – live separately <u>or</u> share flat. Ruby Keen goes to the police – her friend disappeared – went off with man. She identifies body as Mavis – Mavis was fond of Mr Saunders. Mr. S has alibi because he was seen with Mavis <u>after</u> certain time. Later ~~Body of~~ Mavis is killed and burnt in car – girl guides uniform found.
> Why variants
> Idea being to kill Ruby Treves

This is followed by a bizarre variation, presumably taking the name Ruby as inspiration:

A. Is Ruby Rajah's friend?
He gave her superb jewels – young man – Ivor Rudd – attractive – bad lot – takes her to England – tells her there's been an accident – girl guide dead – fakes body – drives it down to Paul Seton's. Later identifies it as Ruby's body – later takes Ruby out in car and sets fire to it – girl guide buttons and badge found

Notebook 31 is headed confidently on the first page and followed by a list of characters to which I have added the probable names from the book. Then the main timetable is sketched, with a further paragraph filling in some of the details:

The Body in the Library
People
Mavis Carr [Ruby Keene]
Laurette King [Josie Turner]
Mark Tanderly [Mark Gaskell]
Hugo Carmody – legs taken off in last War – very rich [Conway Jefferson]
Step children    Jessica Clunes
                Stephen Clunes
                Edward
Man (Mark or Steve) takes her [Mavis] to Paul's cottage. Leaves her there – carefully asks way or draws attention to car? Body left there at (say) 9.30 – Mavis seen alive last at 9.15 in hotel. Both girls had drink. W[innie] doped at 6.30 or 7. Pansied up after being killed at 9 pm – driven ½ hours drive by Mark 9.~~30~~ to 10 – Mavis in hotel 9 to 10 – goes upstairs at 10 (killed). Mark dancing 10–12. Body in empty bedroom – [body] taken out and put in car between 12 and 1 – covered with rug. Driven off early morning – set on fire

(time fuse) in wood. Mavis last seen 10 pm – did not come on and dance – car found missing, later found abandoned in St. Loo.

One of the dangers inherent in writing two books at the same time is shown in the extract below from Notebook 35, which has another possible sketch of the plot. This summary includes a Milly Sprott, a character from *N or M?*. Presumably she was to be the Girl Guide character, as the list of characters that follows includes a Winnie Sprott. This extract may be the very first musings on the book.

Body in the Library        Suggestions
Body immature – yellow bleached hair – extravagant make-up – (really girl guide – lost – ~~or a VAD~~ – adenoidy). Suggestion is <u>actress</u> – handbag with clippings of theatrical news – revue – chorus – foreign artist. Body planted on young artist who has had row with Col B – (in war – military service etc.) and who has had blonde girl friend down. He plants her on Col B with help of real blonde friend. She can turn up later alive and well. Does girl in London come down and identify dead girl as Queenie Race. Really QR is alive – later Queenie killed and body dressed in Guide's clothes.
Why was Milly Sprott killed – she saw too much – or overheard it? She is identified by Ruby – Ruby is accomplice of villain

Body L[ibrary]
Calling the Bantry etc.
Platinum blonde – everything points to young Jordan
Body
Blonde girl
Young Jordan's friend
Winnie Sprott – girl guide
Mrs Clements – Brunette

Ruby Quinton – actress
Identified by ~~best fr~~ sister or friend or gentleman friend
Why?
Real Ruby engineers whole story – she – young man – life
insurance?

Notebook 62 lists individual chapters and although the chapter headings do not tally, the material covered is as it appears in the novel. The names too are mostly retained, although Col. Melrose becomes Melchett, and Michael Revere and Janetta transform into Basil Blake and Dinah Lee:

The Body in the Library
Chapter I
Mrs B housemaid etc. Miss Marple comes up and sees body
Chapter II
Col Melrose – his attitude to Col B – Michael Revere and his
blonde. Col M goes down there – M[ichael] in very bad
temper – got down after party. Arrival of Janetta ['his
blonde']
Chapter III
Melrose in his office – Inspector Slack – missing people.
Who came down by train the night before? Lot of people at
station. Bantrys – Mrs B went to bed early – Col B out at
meeting of local Conservative Association
Chapter IV
Arrival of Josie – she is taken to the hall – sees body – Oh
Ruby all right. Story begins to come out – Conway Jefferson
– Mrs Bantry knows him
Chapter V
At hotel – Jefferson – Adelaide – Mark – Raymond (the pro)
– evidence about girl
Chapter VI
Mrs B finds Jefferson – old friend – Miss M with her
Chapter VII
Adelaide and Miss M and Mrs B – Josie and Raymond

In the middle of these listings Christie sketches what she refers to as the 'real sequence', the mechanics of the murder plot, as well as a list of the characters. The deletions suggest that she amended this afterwards to reflect the eventual choices:

Real sequence – Winnie King leaves rally 6.30 – goes with Josie to hotel – drugged in tea – put in empty bedroom. After dinner 9.30 Mark takes girl to car and drives her to bungalow (Friday night). Strangles her 10 and puts her in – drives back – Ruby is on view 10 to 10.30 – then killed with veronal or chloral – put in room by Josie's. 5 am – Mark and Josie take her down to car – (pinched from small house in street . . . young man's car) ~~Josie~~ Mark drives her out to wood – leaving trail of petrol – gets away – walks back – arrives in time for breakfast or his bathe?

People
(Josie!) Josephine Turner
Ruby Keene
Raymond Clegg [Starr]
Conway Jefferson
Adelaide Jefferson – Rosamund?
Peter Carmody
Mark Gaskell
Then
Bob Perry (car trader)
~~Michael Revere~~ Basil Blake
Diane Lee Dinah Lee
Mrs ~~Revere~~ Blake
Hugo ~~Trent~~ Curtis McClean (Marcus)
Pam Rivers [Reeves]
~~Basil Penton~~
George Bartlett

Reason why Miss Marple knows
Bitten nails

Teeth go down throat (mentioned by Mark). 'Murderers always give themselves away by talking too much' [Chapter 18]

Abandoning her list of chapters, Christie briefly sketches some scenes all of which appear in the second half of the novel, although the combination of characters sometimes varies:

A. Interviewing girls – Miss M present [14 ii]
B. Col Clithering interviews Edwards [14 i]
C. Col C and Ramon [13 iii but with Sir Henry]
D. Addie and Miss M [12 ii but with Mrs. B]
E. Mark and Mrs B or Miss M [12 iv but with Sir Henry]
F. Mrs B and Miss M [13 iv]
G. Doctor and Police [13 i]

In her specially written Foreword for the 1953 Penguin edition of *The Body in the Library*, Christie explains that when she tackled one of the clichés of detective fiction – the body in the library – she wanted to experiment with the convention. So she used Gossington Hall in St Mary Mead and Colonel Bantry's very staid, very English library but made her corpse a very startling one – young and blonde, with cheap finery and bitten fingernails. But, as so often happens in a Christie novel, what may seem to be mere dramatics is actually a vital part of the plot. *Three Act Tragedy, Death on the Nile, Sparkling Cyanide, A Murder is Announced* – all feature a dramatic death, but in each case the scene in question is part of an artfully constructed plot; and so it is with *The Body in the Library*. Christie also considered the opening of this novel – Mrs Bantry's dream of winning the Flower Show is interrupted by an hysterical maid with the early morning tea – the best she had written; and it is difficult not to agree.

## Five Little Pigs
### 11 January 1943

<o>

Carla Lemarchant approaches Hercule Poirot and asks him to vindicate her mother, who died in prison sixteen years earlier while serving a sentence for the murder of her husband. Poirot contacts the five other suspects and asks them to write accounts of the events of the fatal day.

<o>

*This little piggy went to market*
*This little piggy stayed at home*
*This little piggy ate roast beef*
*This little piggy had none*
*This little piggy cried wee-wee-wee all the way home.*

Published in the UK in January 1943, having already appeared in the US six months earlier, *Five Little Pigs* represents the apex of Christie's career as a detective novelist; it is her most perfect combination of detective and 'straight' novel. The characters are carefully drawn and the tangle of relationships more seriously realised than in any other Christie title. It is a cunning and scrupulously clued formal detective novel, an elegiac love story and a masterly example of story-telling technique with five individual accounts of one devastating event. And the use of the rhyme is not forced; each of the five main characters is perfectly reflected in the words of the verse. But, as the Notebooks reveal, the journey to the book we now know was neither straightforward nor obvious.

From the technical point of view the challenge that Christie sets herself in this novel is daunting. As well as the 16-year gap between the crime and Poirot's investigation she limits herself to just five possible murderers. Seven years earlier she had first experimented with the device of a small circle of suspects; in *Cards on the Table* there are just four bridge-players. With *Five Little Pigs* she attempts something similar, although this time she allows herself some physical clues in the shape of a glass, a beer bottle and a crushed pipette.

It is also the greatest of Christie's 'murder in the past' plots. In fact if we don't count *Dumb Witness* – the investigation of a two-month-old murder – it is also the first of such plots. Alderbury, the scene of the crime, is based closely on Christie's own Greenway House and the geography of the story corresponds exactly with its grounds. The Battery, where Elsa poses on the battlements and watches her lover die, looks out over the River Dart and the path where the crushed pipette is found leads back up to Greenway House.

The nursery rhyme is quoted in full in Notebook 35, heralding 75 pages of notes:

5 Little Pigs
One Little Piggy went to Market (Market Basing)
1 little    ”    stayed at home
1 little    ”    had roast beef
1 little    ”    had none
1 little    ”    wa-wa-wee-wee

But it was a long and frustrating process before she arrived at the masterly plot. It is not until sixty pages into the notes that the plot she eventually used took serious shape. Before that, she had considered a different murder method, a different murderer and different suspects; in fact, a different story altogether.

Her 'five little pigs' are successful businessman Philip Blake and his stay-at-home brother Meredith, both childhood friends of the victim, artist Amyas Crale; Elsa Greer, Amyas's model and mistress; Angela Warren, sister of the convicted Caroline; and Miss Williams, Angela's governess.

*This map from Notebook 35 shows the murder scene in* Five Little Pigs *with the Boathouse on the left (also the scene of a murder in* Dead Man's Folly*), Greenway House in the top right-hand corner, and the positions of Miss W(illiams) and C(aroline). The photo of the Battery from the time of writing shows the wall where Elsa posed.*

At the start of the notes we can clearly see the forerunners of these five main characters, although, as yet, Christie had not decided on the victim, let alone the villain:

> Girl – (New Zealand) learns her mother has been tried and condemned for murder – possibly convicted to penal s[ervitude] – for life and then died
> Great shock – she is an heiress uncle having left her all his money – gets engaged – tells man her real name and facts – sees look in his eye – decides then and there to do something about it – her mother not guilty – comes to H.P.
> The past – 18 years ago? 1920–24
>
> If not guilty who was?
>
> 4 (or 5) other people in house (a little like Bordens?)
>
> Did mother murder
> A. Husband
> B. Lover
> C. Rich uncle or guardian
> D. Another woman (jealousy)
>
> Who were the other people – Possibilities
>
> Servant – Irish girl rather dumb – Ellen
> Housekeeper – woman – reserved – practical – another Carlo
> Girl – 15 at time (now 30 odd) (a Judy?)
> Man – English gentleman – fond of gardening etc.
> Woman – Actress?

The early notes are a relatively accurate plan of what was to follow, but there are differences. Carla Lemarchant ('the Girl') is a Canadian rather than a New Zealander; and of the five sketches for possible characters one of them, 'the dumb Irish servant girl Ellen', is completely dropped. The 'Girl' and the 'Man' eventually became Angela and Meredith respectively; the 'housekeeper' is the prototype for Miss Williams and the 'woman' becomes Elsa Greer – although not a professional actress, she is in many ways the consummate performer.

There are three references that may require explanation. The reference to 'Bordens' is to the infamous Lizzie Borden murder case in Fall River, Massachusetts in August 1892 when Mr and Mrs Borden were hacked to death in the family home while their daughter Lizzie and the Irish maid Bridget were in the house. Although Lizzie was tried for the brutal murders, she was acquitted and no one was ever convicted. To this day her guilt or innocence is still a matter of debate and argument. 'Carlo' is Carlo Fisher, Agatha Christie's personal secretary from 1924 and, ultimately, friend. 'Judy' is in all probability Judith Gardner, the daughter of Agatha's friend Nan Gardner (née Kon).

A major problem with this initial set-up is evident: there are four female characters and only one male. Subsequent attempts bring it closer to the final arrangement:

The 5 people

Miss Williams elderly Caro – devoted to Caroline

Mrs Sargent – Caro's elder half-sister – married money – etc.

Lucy – husband's sister – violently anti-Caro

A. (Idea) – Caro has injured a sister or brother when a child owing to her ungovernable temper – she believes this s[ister] or b[rother] did crime – therefore feels that she is expiating and gains content

Is s[ister] or b[rother] No 5 – Wee-Wee

And eventually she arrives at the five suspects in the novel itself. The following brief notes reflect accurately, apart from a name change of Carslake to Blake, the 'five little pigs' and their inter-relationships:

> Philip Carslake – George's Hill – Prosperous – his best friend – Amyas – virulent against Caro – Describes how the injured step sister – as instance of her temper – induced to write an account –

> Meredith – his home – takes P up to house – (now a hostel for youth) ghosts – he explains – will write – hedges about Elsa – shares picture of her – I did find she could have done it – her daughter

> Elsa – rich woman – Changed from picture – frozen – virulent against Caro – vindictive – talks a little – sends her account. You want truth? You shall have it (says drama to vent spleen)

> Miss Williams – elderly – room in London – Violently pro Caro – but admits she <u>knows</u> – about Angela – P persuades her truth is best – She agrees – will write –

> Wee Wee woman of brains – character – successful archaeologist – welcomes P's intervention – quite convinced – explains why Caro couldn't have done it – because of what she did to her

All of the details of the crime were arrived at only after numerous attempts. Through much of the notes the murder method was to be a shooting rather than a poisoning, and even though this was not pursued it is interesting to see how much of the attendant detail was retained:

> A. Pistol – (Amyas's) wiped clean of prints except his – but they are wrong – also her prints in blood on table – Miss W

covers for Angela? – saw her doing this – Angela in boat? But is returning)

Did someone pretend to be Wee-wee – steal up to him from behind and use her voice – press pistol against his head and fire – C thinks it is W[ee-wee] has heard voice – picks up pistol and wipes it

Caro heard Angela – speaking to Amyas pressed revolver into his back – sporty playacting – (she had peashooter) . . . she got there found him dead. Picked up pistol – wiped it – put it in his hand – but suicide not possible and one of her fingerprints on butt

Caroline went down to call Amyas for lunch – shot – but before she got there – Caro seen to take pistol from drawer of desk

Caro comes – Elsa springs up, snatches revolver – and shoots him – then rushes away – Caroline – sees her – thinks it is Angela – horrified – stunned at find – Elsa goes up to house – drops jersey on path – Miss Williams comes down – picks up jersey – then hears shot – she goes on – sees Caro – pressing his hand over revolver

In the novel the vital clue that convinces Poirot of Caroline's innocence is her wiping of the beer bottle and the subsequent superimposition of Amyas's fingerprints on it, as witnessed by Miss Williams. As can be seen in four of the extracts, this wiping was originally intended for a gun. And the detail of Caroline being seen taking a pistol is retained in the novel by her being seen taking the poison from Meredith's laboratory. In three of these extracts we also see the vital factor of Caroline's mistaken belief that the culprit is Angela, thereby paving the way for her ultimate sacrifice.

The rejection of a gun in favour of poison is no surprise, as Christie knew little about the former but had a professional knowledge of the latter. She used poison more than any other murder method and more than most of her contemporaries, resorting to firearms infrequently. When Christie does decide on poison her fertility of invention is once again very evident in both the type of poison and its method of administration:

Nucleus – poison in port – husband had a glass in his room (analysed and full of it) – Caro seen washing out port decanter (by maid)

Poison – Sherry – One person poured it out, Caro took glass to Am – later cyanide found in glass, or belladonna

Possibilities of poison
A – Poison put into sherry at time when 'shut your eyes etc' is done – C has brought sherry to him – she finds him (having heard WW) later dead – wipes glass – puts dead man's fingers on it – (seen by Miss W)

B – Sherry pure – cyanide in strawberry – Caro still does her act – murderer adds cyanide to sherry – dregs with pipette – latter is found

C – Medicine – HCN – added to sherry by Caro – capsule is already taken

D – Capsule altered to AC from PC

Coniine – in capsule?
Result – he appears drunk – staggers about – double vision – (P's evidence) – E. sits down and watches him die – somebody comes – she gets up and speaks to him – joins other person – he shakes his head – or – seen sitting behind a table

A decanter – port? – Caroline washed it out afterwards

Box of cachets – <u>before</u> meals

HCN and bismuth mixture – extra HCN? Beer?

It is notable that even when she decides on coniine, the capsule idea in the above list is not used.

Other important plot points, and clues, are mentioned. The mistaken interpretation of overheard remarks is emphasised in the first two extracts; the final moving letter written by Caroline from her prison cell to her sister, in the third extract, is another example of misinterpretation. Angela's penchant for practical jokes, as evidenced by the slug and, later, the valerian, is an important factor in Caroline's supposition of her guilt. And the all-important wiping of the glass (beer bottle in the book) surfaces again:

Case against Caroline – Quarrelled with husband that morning – said 'I'd love to kill you. Someday I will'

Don't you worry – I'll see to her packing (send her packing) heard between Caro and Amyas

A's – including parting note from C in prison my darling I am quite content – going to Amyas – also important about C's lover – Meredith?

Miss W – re Angela and slug

Miss W <u>saw</u> Caro wipe glass or cleaning revolver prints

After an admonition to herself, Christie eventually arrives at the plot we know:

Go over the morning again

Dinner with Meredith night before – the drugs – Valerian – coniine etc. – Caroline takes coniine – Elsa sees her – Talk between Meredith and Amyas – one more day – row between Angela and Amyas – School – next day Meredith discovers coniine has been taken – rings up Philip – (? Is Philip somewhere and Elsa with him – she hears?) Elsa is sitting ~~With~~ to M – says she is cold – goes up to house (gets coniine) – (Did Caroline and Amyas have row after breakfast – ? Did Elsa hear them – did she say to Philip 'conjugal quarrel') – sits – come out – presently A comes out and says come down and sit.

Elsa tests him – Caroline comes down – Elsa is cold – goes to get jersey (gets coniine) – Caro and Amyas have row – some of it overheard by P and M (But their evidence – I'll kill you etc. – heard by Philip and E). 'Haven't I told you I'll send her packing' – Comes out – sees them and says school – Angela etc. – Elsa reappears this time <u>has</u> jersey – he drinks off beer – Says (after looking down to sea) – they turn round – Elsa is there – He drinks off beer – says hot and disgusting – Caro ~~goes away~~ says she'll bring him some down iced – she goes to get it – finds Angela at refrigerator – doing something to beer – Caro takes bottle from her – Caro goes down with it – she pours it out and gives it to him – he drinks it off.
~~Miss Williams~~ – Meredith looks at Elsa – sitting there – her eyes – once or twice she speaks – (she has put some coniine in dregs of glass – not bottle) – We're going to be married aren't we? – looks up and sees Meredith – acts her part. M sees A from door – queer expression – doesn't say anything – one of his moods – M says I hear you were over at my place this morning – A says Yes – I wanted – something?

Caroline and Miss W find him – C sends Miss W for ~~police~~ doctor – she then smashes his beer bottle and replaces it by another. Findings – beer in glass had coniine in it – and his fingers superimposed on hers – but not as they could have been

Oddly, there is little of Poirot's final scene, the explanation of the events of 16 years earlier and the revelation of the real killer of Amyas Crale. For all practical purposes, the necessary detail for that scene is included in the above extract and Christie probably felt confident of writing the closing chapter without the need for further detailed notes. Even though Poirot is certain he has arrived at the truth, he realises that there is no proof . . .

Last Scene

Ph and M are there – Angela comes in – then W – finally Lady D – M is a little dismayed. Caroline had motive – she had means – now to hand takes coniine and it seems quite certain she <u>did</u> take it – has questioned Meredith if person could handily take it if 5 people in room – but she was last and M in doorway had his back to room – so we take it as proved that she took it

⌒⌒⌒

## *The Moving Finger*
### 14 June 1943

Shortly after Jerry Burton and his sister move to the idyllic village of Lymstock, a series of anonymous letters horrifies the inhabitants and culminates in the death of the local solicitor's wife. The vicar's wife decides to send for an expert in wickedness – Miss Marple.

*The Moving Finger writes; and, having writ moves on*
*The Rubaiyat of Omar Khayyam*

*The Moving Finger* is the third Christie novel narrated by a male. Apart from the Hastings novels, seven other titles (*The*

*Murder of Roger Ackroyd, The Murder at the Vicarage, The Moving Finger, Crooked House, Endless Night*; and partly *The Pale Horse* and *The Clocks*) have male narrators while only two (*Murder in Mesopotamia* and, for the most part, *The Man in the Brown Suit*) have female ones. While it is by no means extraordinary for a female writer to write as a male, this may have been dictated from the beginning of Christie's career when, having created Hastings as Poirot's chronicler, she grew accustomed to the idea of telling the story as a male. It would have been inconceivable for Poirot to have a close female friend with whom he lived and shared his cases. And equally inconceivable, but for different reasons, is the possibility that they would be recounted by his wife! In *The Moving Finger* it is also odd that Jerry Burton narrates the entire story without ever telling us anything about his background or that of his sister. Apart from the fact that he was a pilot and that Joanna has a busy social life we learn nothing about them.

Although Lymstock is the typical English village associated with Agatha Christie and very much Miss Marple teritory, the sleuth's absence until Chapter 10 (of the UK edition), and her presence for a mere ten pages, makes it almost a cameo appearance.

*The Moving Finger* also has the most unusual denouement of any Christie novel as we learn the killer's identity before Miss Marple's explanation. The ploy to trap the murderer is known to the reader as we watch him attempt another killing. This is at variance with similar ruses in, for example, *The Body in the Library, Cards on the Table* and *Towards Zero*, where the reader is unaware of the identity of the victim of the trap.

There are only fifteen pages of notes for *The Moving Finger* most of them in Notebook 62. The plotting progresses smoothly, with the usual technique of assigning letters to scenes. An initial note is dated, although not very precisely:

> Ideas (1940)
> Poison pen – letters in village – 'repressed spinster'
> indicated – really plot by someone to discredit her –
> (a resourceful mother?)   Miss Marple

Although a 'repressed spinster' as the source of the anonymous letters is much discussed in Lymstock as, indeed, the killer hoped, the 'discrediting' idea was abandoned; perhaps it had too many echoes of the recent *Murder is Easy*. In a typical piece of Christie misdirection the minor crime of anonymous letters is merely camouflage for the major crime of murder, a plot device similar to that of *The ABC Murders*. Christie began work on the novel the following year and the town, the people and their names, the events and the first murder all appear in the book as they do in Notebook 62:

> Anonymous letters – deliberate – finally woman commits
> suicide as a result of letter – really killed (by husband?)

> Books 1941 Miss M? or told in 1st person
>     Poison Pen – all round village – unhappiness etc. – wife of
> lawyer (?) gets one – kills herself – really is killed by husband
> – and he then puts letter in her pocket – its subject matter
> is untrue

> Suspected of writing letters – Vicar's ~~sister~~? wife –
> schoolmistress – doctor's ~~wife~~ sister? – Hearty spinster –
> maidservant – maidservant is next killed because she saw
> something or knew something

> Description of town – market town known better days –
> they take bungalow – the letters come – not sister – wonders
> if there is much of this sort of thing about – what about if a
> shot in the dark hits the bulls eye?

> Resume of people they meet

Dr. Thomas – his sister – dark fierce 'manly looking' woman
– little Mr Pye – Vicar – his wife – goes home to find Mrs.
Symmington calling

Once again we see the method of assigning letters to scenes,
although in this case no rearrangement of them is specified:

Progress　Moving Finger　Points

A. J[erry] discovers book of sermons cut out pages
   [Chapter 9 v]
B. Megan goes home [Chapter 7 ii]
C. Maid knows something – scene between her and Elsie
   H[olland] – Joanna overhears comes back and tells J?
   Did she come back that afternoon? Does she come and
   ask advice from Partridge? She is killed – deliberate
   [Chapter 7, but not exactly as described here]
D. Tea with Miss Emily – big raw-boned dragon looks after
   her [Chapter 7 iv]
E. Vicar? His wife – vague – slightly bats? Hits nail on head
   – poor Aimee very unhappy woman [Chapter 5 i]
F. Institute? Someone typing – J goes in – finds Aimee who
   'heard' someone leave [Chapter 10 ii]
G. J going off to sleep 'No S[moke] W[ithout] F[ire]'
   – smoke – smoke screen – War – 'scrap of paper' Nurse
   told him as little boy – etc [Chapter 8 i]
H. Spiteful rumour about – Elsie means to be No. 2
   [Chapter 9 ii]
I. The posted letters – Aimee's written at Institute – one of
   them is IT – substituted – (did she drop them and pick
   them up in High St. – S[ymmington] there) (E[mily]
   B[arton] at Institute too) [Chapter 13 ii]

As can be seen, the order changed considerably – the muti-
lated book of sermons (scene A) is not discovered until
Chapter 9 – and the scenes are scattered through the book.

Scene C is an ingenious twist on the person who 'knows something' and then becomes the next victim. Here, the fact that the maid saw *nothing* when she should have seen *something* seals her fate.

*The Moving Finger* is another title that Christie considered dramatising. Notebook 45 consists of rough preliminary notes including a list of the characters of the novel and tentative settings. The multiple potential settings, as shown by the note below, created immediate problems in devising a successful dramatisation:

> Scene?
> Maisonette or divided house?
> Garden of same used by both
> Room in police station
> Symmington's house

Not only was *The Moving Finger* published almost a year earlier in the USA but the US and UK editions are significantly different, a fact that did not come to light until 1953 when Penguin Books published the title. Correspondence between Edmund Cork and Christie's US agent in July 1953 concluded that the copy supplied to Penguin had been the US edition, as the UK file copy had been a war casualty. The most likely explanation, according to them, was that the US publishers had worked from the *Colliers Magazine* serialisation, which had 'cut' the manuscript, deleting some minor characters and altering some passages, including the opening scene. Apart from puzzling references to characters who do not (seemingly) exist the overall effect is to leave the US edition a shorter book.

The same situation, and probable explanation, also applies to *Murder is Easy.*

## *Towards Zero*
### 3 July 1944

—————————◄○►—————————

Before murder interrupts a holiday weekend in Lady
Tressilian's house in Gull's Point, we meet a disparate
group of people. All of their destinies are inextricably
linked as zero hour approaches. Superintendent
Battle investigates a case where the solution
seems obvious. But is it too obvious?

—————————◄○►—————————

Sharing a plot device from *The Murder at the Vicarage* and
more recently 'Murder in the Mews', *Towards Zero* is a dark
and emotional crime novel as well as a very clever detective
story with subtle clueing and better-than-usual characterisa-
tions. The plot resembles a series of Russian dolls with the
reader offered one solution within which is another, and
beyond that yet another.

The plotting is in two Notebooks, the majority in Notebook 32 and with a further ten pages in Notebook 63. Its
genesis seems to have been painless and clear from the start;
the notes follow the finished book very closely, although
Christie toyed with a few ideas that did not appear.

On the first page the all-important story that Mr Treves
tells is clearly stated. Apart from the importance of the
homicidal tendency of its main protagonist, it also includes
the important clue of the (unspecified) 'physical trait', a
distinction shared by all the suspects:

Story about 2 children – bows and arrows – one kills the
other – or shotgun?
One child practiced – narrator – old man – says he would
know that child again by a physical trait

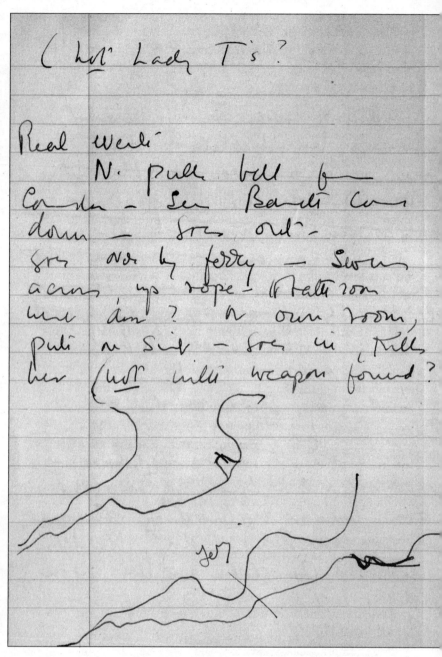

*This page from Notebook 32 shows both Neville's actions on the night of the murder in* Towards Zero, *and a rough diagram of the local geography.*

Yes, so many people all converging from different points –
    all Towards Zero

There is an alphabetical list of scenes, although it does not tally exactly with the novel. It would seem that there was to be a Sir Marcus and a Mr Trevelyan; in the novel they are amalgamated into Mr Treves. None of the members of the house party are included. The listing of 'The Cleaners' is at first puzzling until we remember that a dry-cleaning firm with mixed-up suits provides one of the main clues. Its inclusion in the opening scenes would have presented a fascinating puzzle for the reader.

A. MacWhirter – suicide – his rescue – fall off cliff – arrested
    by tree
B. Sir Marcus – holding forth in his chambers after
    acquittal of client
    [There is no C in the Notebook]
D. The murderer – his mind – the date
E. Superintendent Battle
F. Mr. Trevelyan – looking at hotel folders
G. The Cleaners

As usual names were to change, although not as totally as other novels (Nevil, Judy and Clare/Audrey Crane become Nevile, Kay and Audrey Strange):

People
Lady Tressillian
Mary Aldin or Kate Aldin
Barrett (lady's maid)
Thomas Royde
Adrian Royde
Nevil Crane – well known tennis player and athlete
Judy Crane – formerly Judy Rodgers
Ted Latimer – wastrel – lives on his wits

Clare Crane or Audrey Crane – formerly Audrey Standish
MacWhirter

Towards Zero
Nevill (or Noel) Crane – tennis player – athlete sportsman
Audrey his first wife 'Snow White' – frozen – fractured –
    hysterical childhood etc.
Judy his second wife – a glamorous girl – suffused with
    vitality – pagan – Rose Red

The events of the fatal night are worked out:

Night of Tragedy

Neville and Lady T – quarrel overheard by butler – then he
goes – rings bell for Barret (old maid). He has also put
narcotic in her milk – she sees him go out – goes to Lady T
who denies ringing bell. B feeling very confused and queer
gets back to bed and passes out. Lady T discovered in
morning.

A few interesting ideas were not included although the series
of dated vignettes that opens the novel could be seen, in
retrospect, as sketches of eventual witnesses. The victim is
not related to Judy/Kay and Audrey has not remarried, thus
paving the way for a romance at the end of the novel:

Towards Zero

Series of vignettes of various people – witnesses at murder
trial which takes place in last chapter?

Who is victim? Judy's stepmother? Her father – very rich
man – left the money to 2nd wife (chorus girl or shop girl)
she has it for life – Judy wants the money

Audrey quickly remarries her quiet doctor – a biologist – or archaeologist – they are happy but poor – she wants stepmother's money for research

But one of the most tantalising notes concerns a 'new end' to *Towards Zero*. The page references are, presumably, to those of the publishers' proofs, and one interesting point is that in the novel it is McWhirter who carries out all of the actions here attributed to Thomas Royde. Unfortunately we will never know what the original draft was – the Notebook then continues to list the events that appear in the published novel just before the section 'Zero Hour':

New End to Zero starting P. 243

Thomas and little girl acquaintance – Dog and fish – Goes to cleaner – (lost slip) quarrel about suit – Royde – ever so sorry – thought you said Boyd – Easthampton Hotel – gets suit – takes it home – smell on shoulder – takes it back – or rings up. Goes to Easthampton Hotel – no Boyd staying there – goes up to cliff – Audrey – afraid of being hanged.

P. 255 the police come – Battle talks to the others ending with Royde – then goes to house – Mary comes across him in attic – Or Kay? Wet rope

269? Royde speaks to B privately – B comes out – A taken off – then B looks over house – finds rope – Mary? Or Kaye? Finds him there – it would be strong enough to hang a man!

## *'Strange Jest'*
### July 1944

―――――――◆○▶―――――――

When wealthy Uncle Mathew dies and leaves very little in
his will, his legatees approach Miss Marple in an attempt
to uncover the whereabouts of his missing fortune.

―――――――◆○▶―――――――

This Miss Marple short story was first published in the USA
in November 1941 but did not appear in the UK until almost
three years later. It is a slight non-crime story built around a
single device, the interpretation of clues to a missing fortune.
Its brevity, a mere ten pages, confirms its similarity to a rebus
or literary acrostic.

The interpretation of a will appears in a few Christie
short stories. Poirot deals with 'The Case of the Missing
Will', Tommy and Tuppence tackle 'The Clergyman's Daughter'/'The Red House'; 'Strange Jest' is one of the Miss Marple
versions, the other being 'Motive vs. Opportunity' in *The
Thirteen Problems.*

A page in Notebook 62 headed 'Short Marple Stories' lists
ideas that eventually appeared as 'The Case of the Perfect
Maid', 'The Case of the Caretaker', 'Tape-Measure Murder',
*The Moving Finger* and, oddly, *Endless Night.* There are also
some unused ideas, including two that appear again and
again, the twins and the chambermaid. Some pages later,
there are three pages of notes on 'Strange Jest' including a
full outline of the plot:

Found on love letters from abroad – cryptogram in letter?
No – stamps on it.
    Old Uncle Henry – died – had money but hid it
somewhere – Gold? Diamonds? Bonds? Last words – taps
his eye – (glass eye like Arsene Lupin). They look through

desk – secret drawer found by furniture expert – love letters
from Sierra Leone signed Betty Martin

The idea of unrecognised and valuable stamps on an
envelope appears again in *Spider's Web* nearly 15 years later.
The reference to Arsène Lupin is to the crime story 'The
Crystal Stopper' featuring that character by Maurice Leblanc.

Also of note is the glass eye idea itself. Christie decided not
to use it in this story, instead adopting the idea of Uncle
Henry (Mathew in the published version) tapping his eye.
But it is entirely possible that the glass eye, which formed a
key plot device in *A Caribbean Mystery*, almost 25 years later,
had its origins here.

☙❦❧

## *Death Comes as the End*
### 29 March 1945

---◄○►---

In Egypt in 2000 BC, wealthy landowner Imhotep
shocks his family by marrying a new young wife, who
antagonises everyone. Murder follows, but the evil in the
family is not satisfied by a single death and the killer
strikes again . . . and again . . . and again.

---◄○►---

Long before the current vogue for mysteries set in the past,
Agatha Christie was a pioneer. *Death Comes as the End*, written
in 1943, was an experiment suggested by Stephen Glanville,
professor of Egyptology and a friend of Max Mallowan. He
provided much of the basic information as well as research
material. Most of the usual crime fiction ingredients – police
resources and post-mortem analyses, telephones and telegrams, fingerprints and footprints, formal investigation and
inquests – and the clueing of her other books, had to be

abandoned. So, while not a first-class Christie, it is nonetheless a major achievement.

Part of the difficulty interpreting the Notebooks for this title is the fact that the names of the characters change throughout the 80-odd pages of the five different Notebooks. At various times the character that appears in the novel as Nofret is also called Ibunept, Nebet, Ibneb and Tut. And, of course, it is not possible to be sure if names refer to male or female characters.

Christie writes in *An Autobiography* that 'Houses were far more difficult to find out about than temples or palaces.' And in Notebook 9 we find sixteen pages of notes on 'Life and Customs in Ancient Egypt' with details of everyday life (the page references are to some of the volumes borrowed from Stephen Glanville):

Bead bracelets or gold rings with green glazed scarabs P.110
   P.46 also

Embalming 21$^{st}$ D. P.111 and 55

The making of papyrus paper P.114

Description of bow and arrow P.127

Description of Scribe outfit P.14

Description Foundation dynasty P. 51

Description mummification etc. P.55 and P.57

Notebook 46 contains the initial sketch for the family. Despite name changes, the characters are all recognisable:

Middle Kingdom Setting   Characters

Ipi – (old mother) Tyrant? Devil? Wise? [Esa]

Father – old fusser – kindly – a nuisance [Imhotep]

Meru – (elder son) Good boy of family – a bit dull – inwardly resentful? [Yahmose]

S – ? Bad boy of family – not at home – Troublemaker [Sobek]

H – Spoilt young son – precocious [Ipy]

Concubine – Victim? Beautiful in danger or Evil – full of power [Nofret]

M's wife – a shrew [Satipy]

S's wife – gentle creature or an Emilia? [Kait]

A daughter – energy – resolve [Renisenb]

N – family friend – shrewd – lawyer like maybe tell in 1st person [Hori – but the '1st person' idea was not pursued]

Hepshut – mischief maker [Henet]

The basic situation is described in Notebook 13:

Nofret arrives – everyone cruel to her – she is fierce to them – her tales of foreign cities – the way she stirs up strife – Hori says always there underneath. She writes by scribe to Imhotep – Imhotep replies furious to family – he returns – settlement of land on her. She dies – scorpion stung her – everyone knew – Rensenb troubled – then remembers a scene between Nebet and Seneb

The notes for this novel include another example of Christie's letter-allocation system. Although it is headed Chapter 15, these scenes are in fact scattered through Chapters 15, 16 and 17. But her final decision ('A.C.D. – then BB') is followed through and I have added the relevant chapter headings:

Chapter XV

A  Esa and Henet [15 iii]

B  Henet and Imhotep [16 i]

C  Renisenb and 'Everything is Fear' – meets Aapene –
   Why do you look at me strangely? Then sees Yahmose –
   discusses it with him – who could it be? [15 iv]

D  ~~Renisenb~~ Yahmose and his father – Y. more authority [15 v]

E  Kait and Renisenb [15 vii]

F  Renisenb. Teti and Kameni – his eyes on her – strong
   children [15 vii]

G  Renisenb and her father – marriage [17 i]

H  Ren. and Kameni – love talk – the amulet – broken – she
   goes home – looks in box – Henet finds her with it –
   H's hints [17 ii and iii]

Who dies next?

A.A. Esa – from unguent – or perfumed oil

B.B. Aahene [Ipy]

Yes, B.B. after cheeking Henet [15 vi] who complains to
   Imhotep

So: A.C.D. – then B.B.

And this is the order as it appears in the published novel:

A  Esa and Henet [15 iii]

C  Renisenb and 'Everything is Fear' – meets Aapene –
   Why do you look at me strangely? Then sees Yahmose –
   discusses it with him – who could it be? [15 iv]

D  ~~Renisenb~~ Yahmose and his father – Y. more authority
   [15 v]

B.B.  Aahene [Ipy]. Yes, B.B. after cheeking Henet [15 vi]

The Notebooks offer a possible solution to a tantalising
puzzle. In *An Autobiography*, Christie writes:

*Stephen [Glanville] argued with me a great deal on one point of my denouement and I am sorry to say that I gave in to him in the end . . . If I think I've got a certain thing right in a book – the way it should be – I'm not easily moved from it. In this case, against my better judgement, I did give in. It was a moot point, but I still think now, when I re-read the book, that I would like to re-write the end of it . . . but I was a little hampered by the gratitude I felt to Stephen for all the trouble he had taken and the fact that it had been his idea in the first place.*

It is not entirely clear what is meant by 'the end of it': the identity of the killer or the manner of revelation? If she means a more dramatic final scene we shall never know, although this would seem unlikely as the setting of the denouement clearly echoes the earlier murders of both Nofret and Satipy. But if she had a different killer in mind, she had already considered a few candidates:

Henet – hated wife – and all children – eggs on Ibneb – then kills her

Henet – loves old boy – killed first wife – and second 'sister' – determined to destroy Ibneb – pretends to suck up to her

Hori – in league with Ib? She is to gain ascendancy over old woman – Hori has speculated – blame is to be put on Meru

Hori and Ibneb are buddies – he arranges for her to meet old boy – puts him up to deed of settlement by pretending to object – she then rats or is going to – he kills her – then pretends – she is revenging herself on family – final scene with Renisenb – you Hori – young cousin rescues her

Son (bad lad) comes in – speaks to concubine – he likes her – idea is they are in it together

And there was another fascinating idea that never made it to the printed page at all. In Notebook 13 the idea of having a modern parallel running alongside the historical one is considered. It is possible to see, even in these brief notes, similarities between the ancient and modern characters. The old professor and his young wife are Imhotep and Nofret, Julie is obviously Henet, Regina is a latter-day Renisenb and Edward and Silas could be Sobek and Ipy:

> Modern start – Old professor or Chancellor – his young wife – he brings out son and son's wife – widowed daughter and child
>
> Julie (ancient Mademoiselle who has stayed with them) – young archaeologist who has stayed with them
>
> Discovery of Tomb Letters – Including one ~~from~~ to dead wife who is accused of killing Tut
>
> Author's second wife died suddenly – she took drug by mistake
>
> Young wife dies – quarrel between father and son and wife – F[ather] says new will – all to Ida
>
> Julie and portrait of Eleanor (first wife) who was going to come back
>
> Elaborated
>
> Dr. ~~Elinor Solomon~~ Oppenheim
> Ida – his young wife
> Julie the faithful maid and companion ex-governess
> Edward Mervyn Oppenheim – dependent on father – is he archaeologist
> Charlotte – sculptress – or musician (pianist) – or historical – or political writer
> Charlotte's brother – Richard – the archaeologist
> Regina Oppenheim a widow with children –

~~Oscar Walsh~~ – Jeremy Walsh – a young writer – psychic –
deductive – knows too much about people
other son Silas

From the phrase 'Young wife dies', paralleling the death of 'young wife' Nofret, it would seem that the parallels were to extend to further than merely relationships. However, the idea was not pursued any further than these short notes; perhaps because it would have meant shorter stories within each period.

These two aspects – the alternative ending and the parallel narrative – make this an even more fascinating novel than heretofore suspected, even without considering the ground-breaking historical setting. Seemingly complete and inter-locking as it is, it would seem that Christie was ready to embroider a few more threads through her narrative. It is entirely probable that, had she pursued her present-day parallel, she would have revealed yet another solution; if both branches of the story had arrived at the same destination, a distinct sense of anticlimax would have resulted. So a unique background produced one actual solution, another intended one and a possible third.

### *Sparkling Cyanide*
3 December 1945

An elegant restaurant, a glamorous birthday party
and beautiful Rosemary Barton is poisoned during the
toast. A year later, in a macabre reconstruction at the
same restaurant and with an almost identical party, there
is another death. But who was the intended victim?
Colonel Race investigates.

Although published in December 1945, *Sparkling Cyanide* was serialised six months earlier in the UK and more than a year earlier in the USA. A copy of the typescript had already been sent to Christie's US agents by January 1944, so this title was completed by the end of 1943. It is a very elaborated version of the short story (and subsequent radio play) 'Yellow Iris', which was first published in July 1937. The basic plot in both is the same but a different murderer is unmasked at the end of the novel.

Here the dramatic unexpectedness of a poisoning during a social occasion recalls a similar scene in *Three Act Tragedy* and foreshadows another in *The Mirror Crack'd from Side to Side*. However, some reservation remains as to the feasibility of the scheme. Is it really likely, especially in view of the subsequent investigation, that no one notices the incorrect seating arrangement that is vital to the success of the plot? The preparation and mechanics are masterly and the telling of it is very daring (re-read Book I, Chapter 2 and admire the audacity of the killer's name) but while the concept is undoubtedly clever, its practical application is somewhat doubtful.

There are structural similarities to *Five Little Pigs* with the reminiscences of six possible murderers, although, unlike the earlier novel, they are not in the form of written accounts. We discover Rosemary Barton through the eyes of the suspects, including her killer, with a different picture emerging in each account. Through individual memories, in the first 70 pages of the book, we see her as wife, sister, niece, lover, friend, adulterer and, finally, victim.

Notes for *Sparkling Cyanide* are scattered over ten Notebooks, the most concentrated appearing in Notebooks 13 and 63 with eighteen pages each. The remaining eight have anywhere between one and six pages of disjointed notes, including a few false starts and some repetition. Despite name changes the characters as sketched in Notebook 35 below are immediately recognisable. As can be seen, the alternative title (under which it was published in the USA) emphasises the 'murder in retrospect' aspect of the novel:

Remembered Death 'Here's Rosemary – that's for
  Remembrance'
Book I
'Sweet as remembered kisses after death'
What must I do to drive away remembrance from my eyes?


Beginning of In Memoriam
Rosemary
Iris . . . shadows – the beginning of it all


Book
Remembered Death – girl's name is Rue

Remembered Death
Rosemary (dead) – husband – George Barton – acts very
  suspiciously – he is a businessman
Stephen Fane [Faraday] – R's lover
Lady Mary Fane – his wife – cold proud clinging jealous
Tony Getty [Tony Morelli aka Anthony Browne] – former
  lover of R's apparently in love with Viola [Iris]
Ruth Chambers [Lessing] – George Barton's sec[retary]
  – efficient girl – may be in love with him
Lucilla Drake – old pussy – cousin – lives with them – has a
  son in S. America – ne'er do well
Murder (of George or V[iola]?) by son who is secretly
  married to Ruth
Col. Race on job


In Notebook 63 we see the novel beginning to take shape, with six characters thinking about Rosemary:

Remembered Death    Six people are remembering
Rosemary Blair [Barton] who had died last November

Sandra – R. her hatred of her – her suspicion that St. doesn't care for her

Iris – puzzling it out – letters etc. – George's manner – Anthony's coming – the Faraways [Faradays]

Stephen – his life – meeting S – calculated advance – the marriage – Rosemary – shock – infatuation – the awakening – her attitude – after the birthday

Anthony Browne – thinking of R – wondering how he could ever have been attracted – her facile loveliness. His name – 'a nice name' – eminently respectable – borne by chamberlain to Henry VIII

Ruth
It all began with Victor – interview in office with George. Her . . . undesirable relation – my wife – tender-hearted – girlish affection for him – he's got to get out of the country – Argentine cash.

George
Thinking of his wife – (drinking?) – maudlin – what a pretty thing she was – always knew he wasn't young enough. He'd made up his mind to it – all the same when he'd first had an inkling – the letter – blotting paper – written to whom – that fellow Browne? or that stick Stephen Faraday.

Notebook 21 has a sketch of the table of the first party (Rosemary is included) and, as in the passing reference in the short story version, seems to be set in New York rather than London. It is possible that Boyd Masterson was a forerunner of Colonel Race:

George has had letter – 'Your wife was murdered'

His oldest friend Boyd Masterson – latter consults with Iris

– Iris meets Tony – staying with Stephen Fane M.P. and Lady Mary Fane.

The Party
* George Barton
* Iris
* Tony
* Stephen
* Mary [Sandra]
? Carolyn Mercer (R's girlfriend) [dropped, possibly in favour of Ruth]
? Boyd Masterson
? Lucilla Drake (elderly cousin)

N .Y.

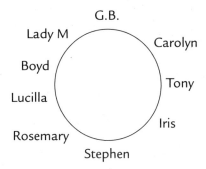

Oddly, the following single page is in the middle of the plotting of *Five Little Pigs*, giving the impression that it was dashed down as Christie thought of it. There are two years between publications, but it must be remembered that a blank page was all Christie needed; chronology was not a factor.

Remembered Death   Possible developments

Black out – snapdragon? At Savoy – performers – indecent song – everyone listens breathlessly – not to miss words. Waiter and drinks – Lights go up – Viola [Iris] gets up to

*Sparkling Cyanide's fatal seating plan –*
*see opposite page.*

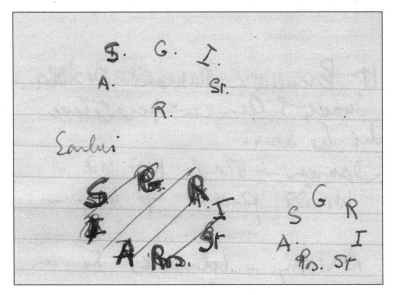

*These three cramped drafts, from Notebook 25, of the table from* Sparkling Cyanide *show 'Rosemary' in two of them, indicating the first fatal dinner-party.*

dance – drops bag – young man replaces it on table – on next seat – therefore – a man dies – George Barton

Although Ruth and Victor were always the front-runners for villains, other characters were also considered. In the final extract below, Charles is George Barton and Pauline is Iris Marle:

A. George – kills Rosemary – keep control of money – she is going to leave him. Then Iris because she too will demand money – Lucilla Drake will leave it in her hands. He manufactures letter – work up the 'murdered' idea – ropes in Race

B. Victor Drake – arranges it with Ruth – Ruth to marry George – R. slips cyanide in R's handbag. Victor as waiter puts it in her glass. Iris inherits money – <u>not</u> George – is

keen on Gerry – Ruth and Victor (married) decide to act
– Victor <u>ostensibly</u> in S. America. Ruth puts cyanide in
Stephen's pocket – letter in Iris's bag (from Stephen to
Rosemary) – bag replaced wrongly on table – therefore Iris
sits down wrong place – George drinks the poison

C. Victor is the man and he is also Gerry Wade [Anthony
Browne] – in with Ruth – plot laid between them

Killer could be
Charles – (first death suicide) – has misappropriated P's
[Pauline, later Iris] money
   Or
Anthony (really V's lover?) – killed her – Charles finds out –
means to separate them – Charles is killed
   Or
Pauline? Killed her sister

## The Hollow
### 25 November 1946

---

Poirot is not amused by the scene at the swimming
pool – the sprawled man and the woman with the revolver
standing over him. He assumes that it has been arranged
for his benefit until he realises that it is not a tableau;
he is looking at a dying man . . .

---

*I hate the dreadful hollow behind the little wood*
*Its lips in the field above are dabbled with blood red heath,*
*The red ribb'd ledges drip with a silent horror of blood*
*And Echo there, whatever is ask'd her, answers 'Death'.*

Tennyson, *Maud*

Although it is more blood-drenched than the novel, Poirot quotes the Tennyson poem in Chapter 18. Interestingly, the last line of the poem also appears in Notebook 3 in an entry dated October 1972, when Christie was planning what was to be her final novel.

The very earliest glimmering of the plot of *The Hollow* can be seen in a throwaway line in Notebook 13 – 'Poirot asked to go down to country – finds a house and various fantastic details' – hidden among an A–Z list of other ideas. The very fact of Poirot going 'down to country' is the first clue but the fantastic details are those found in the tableau awaiting him when he calls to The Hollow: the dying man with his blood dripping into the pool, the woman standing over him holding the revolver, and the other onlookers in the drama, one holding a basket of eggs and another holding a basket of dahlia heads.

Described unenticingly on the original blurb as 'a human story about human people', *The Hollow* is almost a Mary Westmacott title. It resembles a 'straight' novel more than a detective story and, indeed, has less in the way of clues and detection than almost any other Poirot title. In an article for the Ministry of Information in 1945 Christie wrote: 'Naturally one's methods alter. I have been more interested as the years go by in the preliminaries of crime. The interplay of character upon character, the deep smouldering resentments and dissatisfactions that do not always come to the surface but which may suddenly explode into violence.' This is the template of *The Hollow* – a weekend of smouldering and complicated emotions erupting into murder. *Five Little Pigs* and *Sad Cypress* paved the way but in *The Hollow*, her powers of characterisation reached full flower. *Five Little Pigs* is the most perfect example of the fusion of character and detection, *Sad Cypress* still has a distinct detective plot with clues and alibis; but in *The Hollow*, the detection is minimal and Poirot is almost surplus to requirements.

It is inconceivable that he would have bought a house in

the country and at no subsequent time is it even mentioned. And as this case involves little in the way of physical clues, he is almost entirely dependent on the characters. When Christie says in *An Autobiography* that Poirot doesn't fit, she is quite right. It was probably pressure from her publishers that caused her to insert him into this milieu after a three-year absence. He doesn't appear until almost a hundred pages in and, even more peculiarly, his French idioms are almost completely absent. When, some years later, Christie came to dramatise *The Hollow*, she excluded him; and it is difficult not to agree with this decision.

The notes in Notebook 13 are preceded by *Death Comes as the End* and followed by *Taken at the Flood*, a sequence reflected in the order of publication. The first point of interest is the fact that two alternate titles were under consideration for *The Hollow*, both reflecting elements of the finished novel. The events take place over what proves, indeed, to be a tragic weekend and the poignant memories of happier early days – a motif that runs throughout the novel – dominate the lives of many of the characters:

Tragic Weekend
Return Journey

Elizabeth Savarnake [Henrietta]
Lucy Angkatell
Gwenda – her niece [Midge]
John Christow/Ridgeway
Gerda Ridgeway
Veronica Cray
Edward
Henry Angkatell

Lady Angkatell in early morning – Gwenda – poor Gerda etc [Chapter I]

H.P. next door

Note that the niece's name, Gwenda, was abandoned (perhaps because of its similarity to Gerda) in favour of Midge. But it is also possible that there is a connection with Gwenda from *Sleeping Murder*, in view of the new timeline for the writing of that novel (q.v.). And the alternative that was considered for (Dr) John Christow's name, Ridgeway, became the name of the disease which he was studying.

The salient elements of the plot are succinctly captured in a half-dozen pages of Notebook 13:

> John at consulting desk – gear changing – annoyance with
> G. – E. and her wonderful knack with cars
> E. in studio
> Edward – his nervousness – sly, clever creature
>
> Points
>
> Gerda in straightforward fashion because discovers liaison
> of John
> Lady A – sheer vagueness
> Edward – in love with Eliz.
> Eliz. [Henrietta] – very cleverly tries to shield G
> Bit of clay pointing to herself
> Ends by Gerda trying to kill Eliz.

More practical details are teased out in Notebook 31:

> Now strict mechanics
> G. takes revolvers – shoots John – puts revolver in knitting
> bag – or puts revolver in fox cape and purse down below
> settee. Henrietta finds it – puts it back in collection
>     Inspector comes to Sir Henry – asks about revolver.
> Is another missing?
>     Sir H. stalls – finally says it is
>     Was it in a holster?
>     Yes
>     Holster found in road near V's cottage – in bush?

Gerda takes out 2 revolvers – shoots him with one puts holster in V's fur then shoots him – drops it in knitting bag and other by John's body or follows John to cottage – drops holster – comes back after him to pool – shoots him – back at home hides revolver?

Recovers it at inquest? Gudgeon takes revolver from eggs – puts it in study

Henrietta does indeed try to shield Gerda, although she doesn't resort to the piece-of-clay gambit. Nor is there an attempt to incriminate Veronica Cray by placing the gun in her fur cape, although in the stage adaptation the gun is found in her handbag. Christie sketches a few possible scenarios for the disposal of the incriminating gun and holster, elements from each of which – the two revolvers, Sir Henry's missing revolver, Gudgeon and the eggs – appear in the novel.

Notebook 32 has an already reordered alphabetical sequence (but without, for some reason, any F, G or I) although it is not followed exactly in the novel. Note that here she is referring to the story as 'Echo', reflecting the last line of the Tennyson quotation:

End of Echo
H.P. on seat around pool – Inspector's men crashing about
– Grant comes to him – making a monkey of him

A. Must find pistol fired just before – Mrs. C no time to hide it – must have hidden it near [Chapter 26]
B. All of them with motive – Lady A and David – Edmund and Henrietta. P. says solution – away not towards – from not to. G[rant] says sometimes I think they all know – P says They do know. [Chapter 26]
C. Lady A – about truth – would be satisfied [Chapter 27]
H. Midge breaks off engagement [Chapter 27]
D. P. at home – Inspector – they find pistol [Chapter 26]

E. Midge and Edward and gas [Chapter 28]

J. P and Henrietta find leather holster [Chapter 29]

*The Hollow* features strong echoes of Greenway in the descriptions of Ainswick, the Angkatell family home that dominates both the book and the lives of many of the characters. It is described in Chapter 18 as 'the white graceful house, the big magnolia growing up it, the whole set in an amphitheatre of wooded hills'; and in Chapter 6: 'the final turn in through the gate and up through the woods till you came out into the open and there the house was – big and white and welcoming'.

### *Three Blind Mice*
(Radio 30 May 1947; Short Story 31 December 1948;
Play 25 November 1952)

—————————◄o►—————————

Monkswell Manor Guest House welcomes its first
visitors, including the formidable Mrs Boyle and the
mysterious Mr Paravacini, as well as amusing Christopher
Wren and enigmatic Miss Casewell. But Sergeant Trotter
arrives to warn them of a potential killer in their midst,
just before one of the guests is murdered.

—————————◄o►—————————

> *Three blind mice, three blind mice*
> *See how they run, See how they run*
> *They all ran after the farmer's wife*
> *She cut off their tails with a carving knife*
> *Did you ever see such a thing a thing in your life*
> *As three blind mice*

As usual, *An Autobiography* is maddeningly vague about dates, so when Christie writes 'About then the B.B.C. rang me up and asked me if I would like to do a short radio play for a pro-gramme they were putting on for some function to do with Queen Mary', we must assume it was in 1946 as the 'function' was the eightieth birthday of Queen Mary on 30 May 1947. She duly presented them with *Three Blind Mice*, a half-hour radio play. The following 21 October it was broadcast as a 30-minute television play with the same title and script. She then reworked it as a long short story, published in December 1948, which was collected, but only in the USA, in *Three Blind Mice and other Stories* in 1950. When the collection that ultimately appeared only in the UK as *The Adventure of the Christmas Pudding* was in the planning stage, Christie made it clear that she did not want 'Three Blind Mice' to be included, in order not to spoil the enjoyment of the 'masses of people [who] haven't seen it yet'.

In *An Autobiography* she continues, 'The more I thought about *Three Blind Mice*, the more I felt that it might expand from a radio play lasting twenty minutes to a three act thriller.' So she re-wrote it as a stage play, but when it came to presenting it a new title had to be found as the original was already the name of a play. Her son-in-law, the erudite Anthony Hicks, came up with *The Mousetrap* (from Act II, Scene ii of *Hamlet*) and it opened in London on 25 November 1952. The rest is history . . .

The main differences between the various versions are in the opening scenes. The radio and television versions include the scene of the first murder; the stage version includes it only as sound effects in the dark. An early draft of the script included an opening scene with two workmen sitting round a brazier asking a passer-by for a match. This passer-by transpires to be the murderer on his way from killing Mrs Lyon in nearby Culver Street and it is here that he drops the notebook containing the address of Monkswell Manor. Replacing this scene in the novella version is one set in Scotland Yard where the workmen describe the events of that evening.

3

*An amusing rebus in Notebook 56 heads the top of the first of
only two pages to feature the most famous play in the world –*
Three Blind Mice (*later* The Mousetrap).

There is almost nothing showing the genesis of this most famous work as a radio play. Notebook 56 does, however, have two pages headed, amusingly, 3 (an eye crossed out) (a mouse). As the following passage indicates, these few notes refer to either the novella or the stage version:

> Arrival of Christopher Wren – his muffler – his dark
> overcoat – his light hat (throw on bench) – weight of
> suitcase – nothing in it? Some significant word between him
> and Molly. Police in London – Sergeant Dawes – the
> workmen – man was indistinct. The notebook – brought to
> S.Y. by one of them? The identification – Monkswell Manor.
> H'm – get me the Berkshire police. Mrs Bolton arrives –
> My dear, a formidable woman – very Memsahib

A reference to Christopher Wren's suspicious suitcase appears in the novella, as does the 'get me the police' phrase; the combination of these two ideas would lend support to the theory that it is the novella version to which the Notebook refers. Also notable is the odd reference to Mrs Bolton rather than Mrs Boyle, the name by which the character is known in every version.

## The Labours of Hercules
### 8 September 1947

As he plans his retirement, Hercule Poirot is
attracted to the idea of a few well-chosen cases as
his swan song. He will accept only cases similar to those
undertaken by his mythological namesake, emphasising
that his will be metaphorical equivalents.

*The Labours of Hercules* is not just Agatha Christie's greatest short story collection; it is one of the greatest collections in the entire crime fiction genre. It is brilliant in concept, design and execution.

All but one of the stories were published originally in *The Strand* magazine over a period of almost a year. 'The Nemean Lion' appeared in November 1939 and the rest of the tales followed in the same order as the book until 'The Apples of the Hesperides' in September 1940. The final story, 'The Capture of Cerberus', did not appear in *The Strand* and has, as will be seen, a more complicated history.

In August 1948 Penguin Books made publishing history when they issued one million Agatha Christie paperbacks on the same day – 100,000 copies each of ten titles. The venture was such a success that it was repeated five years later. This time they were titles of her own choosing, and for each she wrote a special Foreword giving some background information. One of this second batch was *The Labours of Hercules* and in its Foreword Christie explains that Poirot's Christian name was the inspiration behind these stories. She reveals that some of the tales – 'The Lernean Hydra' and 'The Cretan Bull' – were straightforward and typical Poirot cases. 'The Erymanthian Boar' and 'The Girdle of Hyppolita' gave more trouble, while 'The Capture of Cerberus' almost defeated her.

The metaphors throughout are inspired: wagging tongues represent the multi-headed viper in 'The Lernean Hydra', a sleazy tabloid newspaper stands for the polluted Augean Stables and 'The Apples of the Hesperides' are those on a priceless Cellini chalice. The stories themselves range from the domestic mystery in 'The Lernean Hydra' and the nostalgic love story, albeit with a Christie twist, in 'The Arcadian Deer', to the brutal thriller in 'The Erymanthian Boar'. Amusing scenes – Poirot suffering in a hotel in the west of Ireland – alternate with terrifying scenes – Poirot helpless at the approach of a razor-wielding criminal – and poignant ones – Poirot convincing a terminally ill ballerina to return to her true love.

In many of the stories Christie manages to work in a second example of symbolism apart from the main one. 'The Erymanthian Boar' features a dangerous criminal in snowy surroundings, mirroring the physical setting as well as the metaphorical animal; 'The Cretan Bull' has a man of magnificent physique as well as, literally, basinfuls of blood; in 'The Apples of the Hesperides' Poirot is helped by the tipster Atlas who, like his famous namesake, takes a great weight on his shoulders; and the clamouring schoolgirls at the end of 'The Girdle of Hyppolita' are compared to the Amazons of the fable. Hercules' castanets of bronze in the original are replaced by the modern telegraph in 'The Stymphalean Birds'; the golden horns of 'The Arcadian Deer' appear as the golden hair of Katrina and in the mythical version Hercules does not kill the deer but returns it safely, as does Hercule Poirot with the love of Ted Williamson's life.

Unlike most Christie short stories, there are copious notes, possibly because they were conceived as a collection and because research into the originals was involved. Most of these notes are included in Notebook 44 with some minor notes scattered over three others, Notebooks 28, 39 and 62.

Notebook 44 contains background to the Greek myths:

Hydra of Lernea – 9 heads burnt out in flames – last head cut off and buried

The Deer with feet of bronze – horns of gold – feet of bronze – dedicated to Artemis – a year to find her

Boar of Erymanthe – Combined with centaurs of Pholoe – trapped on precipice of snow and captured alive

Augean Stables – River through breach in wall

Birds of Stymphalia – Birds of prey eat human flesh. H drives them out with bronze castanets and shoots them

Cretan Bull – mad bull

Horses of Diomedes (Mares) – savage – chained to mangers – H tames them

Girdle of Hyppolita – Hera spreads rumour and Amazons revolt

Troupeau of Geryon – giant with 3 bodies or with 3 heads – guarded by 2-headed dog Ortho and Eurython

Apples of Hesperides – H holds up sky while A[tlas] gets apples – A wants table then H asks for cushion for shoulder – hands back to A and goes off. Golden apples given by Immo to Jupiter for nuptials – apples delivered – are given back to Hesperides

Cerberus – Descent into underworld – no weapon – Cerberus returns to underworld

She listed ideas, many of which were incorporated. Notice, though, how the two stories that she admitted gave her trouble, 'The Erymanthian Boar' and 'The Girdle of Hyppolita', change quite considerably and the one that 'almost defeated' her, 'The Capture of Cerberus', is totally different in the published collection:

Lion of Nemea – Peke dog kidnapped

Hydra of Lernea – Poison Pen – or scandal in country place – one person at bottom of it
   Lernean Hydra – Woman suspected of killing husband – (verdict was accident!)

Deer of Arcadia – Dancer who disappears – young man – could P find her

Erymanthian Boar – Criminal traced and taken – race gang?

Stymphalean Birds – Young man blackmailed . . . by two women

Augean Stables – Political scandal – HP to distract attention – gets medical student to produce dead body Sham murder? Party funds or archaeological theft?

Cretan Bull – Mad killer?

Horses of Diomedes – taming of his children – boys? By introducing them to police work

Girdle of Hyppolita – a head mistress? Oxford don? A priceless manuscript?

Geryon Cattle – Strange sect – leader unmasked – perhaps the flock of some pastor – a new sect – religious enthusiast Geryon from Orient – eastern Religion

Apple of Hesperides – Treasure in a convent – disappeared many years ago – stolen – given by thief to convent

Cerberus – A dog story? Or somebody dead – brought back from the dead – or been murdered?

### 'The Nemean Lion'

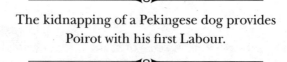

The kidnapping of a Pekingese dog provides Poirot with his first Labour.

As can be seen, the notes for 'The Nemean Lion', the longest story in the collection, are extensive and follow closely the published version. It may well have been the case that, as the first story in the series, Christie gave it careful consideration. A lone note in Notebook 39 foreshadows elements of the plot:

Companion left Peke – she goes as housemaid – gives
different names alternate places? She and friend – latter
gets reward

Notebook 44 has an accurate precis:

HP summoned by Joseph Hoggin – old boy very upset – his
wife lost her Pekingese – received a demand for £200, which
she paid and dog was returned. HP has interview with Mrs J
and Miss Carnaby – the companion – foolish talkative
woman. Facts are as follows – Amy and Ching went to park
– A saw baby in his pram – just speaking to Nurse but Ching
gone – lead cut – she fetches lead – HP admits it is cut – the
women look at him breathlessly – then letter comes – the
money to be sent in £1 notes.

In the end P instructs Georges to find flat between
certain limits – he asks Sir J – remind him of manufacturer
in Liege who poisoned his wife to marry a blonde secretary.
P's visit to flat on Miss A's day out – Augustus barks and
tries to keep him out. The invalid sister – P knows all – her
defence – no pension – old age – no home and no
education – a trade union. Ching left at flat – Augustus
taken – can always find his way home. How often? Ten
times.

The plot, a very clever one, is also particularly rich for a
twenty-page short story. There is the main plot involving the
Pekinese dog/Nemean Lion but also a sub-plot involving the
soap manufacturer poisoner in Belgium years earlier. Amy
Carnaby's situation – elderly untrained companion facing a
bleak future in her old age – is similar to that of Dora Bunner
in *A Murder is Announced*. Poirot considers Amy 'one of the
most successful criminals that I have ever encountered', and
mentions this case in Chapter 14 of *The Clocks*. And it is not
fanciful to see, in the switch-of-dogs idea, the forerunner of
*Evil under the Sun*, which appeared two years later.

### 'The Lernean Hydra'

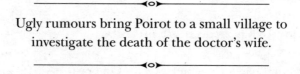

Ugly rumours bring Poirot to a small village to
investigate the death of the doctor's wife.

The plot is contained on two pages in Notebook 44, the only
difference being the change of name from Nurse Carpenter
to Harrison:

> Doctor comes to P – embarrassed – no good going to
> police – wife dead – rumours – practice falling off – doesn't
> know how to combat it. P asks – who is the woman?
> Doctor angry – leaves – P says must have truth. Girl
> dispenser – admits will marry her – wife a difficult invalid –
> details of her death consistent with poisoning arsenic.
> P warns him – I shall get at truth. P sees girl – honest –
> frank – says old Miss L is worst. P. sees Miss L – etc. etc.
> Tracked down to Nurse – Handsome middle-aged woman –
> Nurse Carpenter? – She did it. He finds nurse – her
> Madonna face – he presses her – autopsy – she says no –
> no indeed – she <u>was</u> murdered – morphia pills

And ten pages later . . .

> Lernean Hydra Cont.
> P talks of Home Office – she says yes – because Mrs O was
> murdered. P gets them to announce engagement – Jean gets
> abusive letter. The morphia pills – v – opium pills – Doctor
> called in – orders opium pills – which Jean supplies

The intervening pages include preliminary notes for four of
the other Labours as well as two pages of chemical formulae,
possibly of potential poisons. This outline is generally in
keeping with the published story; note however that the idea,

in the second extract, of announcing an engagement and a consequent abusive letter is not pursued. In many ways this is the most typically Christiean of all the Labours – Poirot goes to a small village to investigate a mysterious death, in this case the possible poisoning of a wife, whose widower is under suspicion. The short stories 'The Cornish Mystery' and 'How Does Your Garden Grow?', and the novels *Dumb Witness* and *Mrs McGinty's Dead*, as well as the Marple novel *The Moving Finger*, all have similar set-ups. And this short story has distinct parallels with the earlier story 'The Blue Geranium' from *The Thirteen Problems*.

## 'The Arcadian Deer'

---◄○►---

Poirot penetrates an impersonation as he
reunites two lovers before it is too late.

---◄○►---

'The Arcadian Deer' is an idyllic story, as befits one set in Arcady, and does not feature a crime. There is however a Christiean twist in the final words of the first extract, and one that she uses a few times elsewhere in her work, although usually for a sinister purpose. The impersonation of an attendant (maid, butler, waiter, steward) is used here for non-criminal reasons, unlike its use in *Death in the Clouds*, *Appointment with Death*, *Three Act Tragedy*, *Sparkling Cyanide*, *Elephants Can Remember* and *At Bertram's Hotel*. And its reverse (the impersonation by a domestic of a 'real person') is a feature of *Taken at the Flood*, *The Mystery of the Blue Train*, *After the Funeral* and *Murder on the Orient Express*. Short stories 'The Affair at the Bungalow' and 'The Companion' from *The Thirteen Problems* and 'The Mystery of Hunter's Lodge' from *Poirot Investigates* also feature this ploy.

There are two sketches for the opening scene of this story,

the second of which is the more detailed. Both versions are accurate, although Ted's beloved, Mary Brown in the first draft, has become in the second the more romantic Marie and, ultimately, 'Nita – Incognita – Juanita':

> Young man in country village – car breaks down – appeals to him – find his sweetheart Mary Brown – gone to London and vanished – if in trouble will see her through. Was MB down there with a rich lady – MB was servant – really the dancer herself (kept by Lord Masterfield?) or wife of a rich polo playing young American. P sees her – a hard faced Young woman – she tells him she has not maid's address. The maid – a coarse looking girl. P knows it is the girl herself

> Begging your pardon Sir – the young man – simple – handsome as a god – his persistence. Recognised HP from photo in Tatler – couldn't be another moustache like that – P softens. P has dinner at Inn – young man comes up there – find this girl – Marie – doesn't know other name. Switzerland – the girl – he hardly remembers her – so changed – her maid – Yes – remembers her – that other – do you mean Juanita – replaced maid when latter was away – P says Yes – what happened to her – she died young – Arcady. P explains – mystery about maid – blackmailed Sir George – his wife – Nita – Incognita – Juanita

### 'The Erymanthian Boar'

◄○►

A violent criminal and an isolated setting combine to make Poirot's fourth Labour a very dangerous one.

◄○►

As befits its origins, this is the most bloodthirsty of the Labours and is a very atypical Christie story; gangsters arranging a rendezvous on a Swiss mountaintop is not a regular feature of her output. The image of Hercule Poirot hopping out of bed to relieve three thugs of their firearms while someone else holds them at bay is one that sits badly with the great detective of the square eggs and the black-currant *sirop*. That said, the story has a twisting plot with multiple impersonations crammed into a mere twenty pages. This is also a use of the plastic surgeon idea, mentioned a few times in the Notebooks, including the early, unused notes for *Sleeping Murder*, as well as those for *Crooked House* and the tentative dramatisation of *Murder in Mesopotamia*.

The following notes accurately reflect, if somewhat cryptically, the course of a complex story:

Switzerland – HP leaves World's End – goes to Zermatt and up from there to hotel at top – something happens to funicular. Has HP first received telegram – or note – from M. Belex who saw him – the notorious Marascaud – believed to be up there – Inspector Drouet – certain people went up in funicular with him.

    Schwab – lonely American

    Dr. Karl Lutz (~~nervous physician~~) or Austrian Jewish doctor – facial surgeon

    3 horsey men – cardsharpers

    Nervous English doctor

    Already there?

    The waiter – Gustave – introduces himself to HP as Inspector Drouet

    Manager – terribly nervous – has been bribed by Gust[ave]

Mysterious patient

    Marascaud bookmaker – took cash – share out in this lonely place. Gustave said 'It's one of them' – G is 'attacked' in night – doctor attends on him – speaks to P. P sees him – his face smothered in bandages. Who attacked him – 3 men – they get drunk – attack P – Schwab – saves him with pistol

The notes are partly utilised as the criminal Marrascaud is 'traced and taken' alive, an important point, as Poirot underlines in the last line of the story; the 'race gang' element, however, is not pursued.

### 'The Augean Stables'

————————◄○►————————

The fifth Labour presents Poirot with one of
the most unusual cases of his entire career.

————————◄○►————————

The plot – involving some elements from Christie's preliminary notes, though not the 'dead body' – is summarised in Notebook 62:

> Hercule Poirot and Prime Minister – P looks at him – as
> old Scotch chemistry Professor has said he's a good man.
> P explains why Dagmar always hated her father – clean up
> the Augean stables – P sees Mrs NP – still beautiful woman
> – her reaction – P says certain cryptic things to her.
> P and Dashett (young newspaper man) – says you have
> to turn the Thames and wash out Houses of Parliament.
> Sydney Cox – editor of This Week's Garbage – nasty little
> man – HP comes to them – pleads – threatens – finally begs.
> Paragraph – The Honey Bee – in Little Bedchester – in the
> Tube – Mrs NP leaves London for Scotland. Libel trial –
> Miss Greta Handersohn – a waitress in a café in
> Copenhagen – approached by a journalist. P says a very old
> idea – Queen's Necklace – to discredit Marie Antoinette.

This story follows the notes very closely, but there is one puzzling feature – the use of the initials 'NP' throughout in reference to the Prime Minister. There is no equivalent in the story, where the Prime Minister is Edward Ferrier.

Although an enjoyable story with an inspired symbolism, it is one that is in the highest degree unlikely both in its mechanics and in its outcome. One can't help wondering if Christie's unpleasant experiences in the aftermath of her 1926 disappearance were, to some degree, responsible for this swipe at the tabloid newspaper industry. This case is mentioned in the 'Maids in the Kitchen' chapter of *One, Two, Buckle My Shoe* when Poirot refers to it as 'ingenious'.

## 'The Stymphalean Birds'

◄o►

A good deed has horrifying consequences
for an innocent abroad.

◄o►

The first attempt at this story, with its domestic setting, does not figure at all in the published version although it is possible to discern the germ of the subsequent idea: two women, an abusive husband, a young man emotionally blackmailed into helping.

> Mrs Garland and Mrs Richardson – latter married –
> terrified of husband – latter gets a gun out – young woman
> parks herself in Gary's apartment – he is young, married, a
> solicitor. Husband comes and browbeats him – threatens
> divorce – a womanish creature – Or – mother pleads also
> – an aging creature

A second outline, however, is followed almost exactly with Poirot making a very belated appearance in just the last four pages. The change of setting to a fictional foreign country, Herzoslovakia (scene of *The Secret of Chimneys*), is in keeping with other Labours:

> Harold – his friendship with Nora Raymond – two women
> – Poles – look like birds. Her husband is studying
> architecture – her mother – worried – anxious. She comes
> into his room – for help – husband rushes in – swings
> something at her – she dodges – rushes out – man rushes
> after her – into her room – she fires – he falls – she gets him
> out of room – someone might come. Mother comes – says
> he's dead. Advices [sic] HP – he speaks to him – or – hotel
> manager – kept quiet – he goes out and wires for money –
> gives it to them – police come – everything hushed up –
> then mother in agony again – the women in room next door
> have heard

Even here, though, there are differences. In the published version there is no mention of Nora Raymond and a paperweight achieves the 'death', not the gun suggested by the notes; a gunshot in a hotel would make the plot unworkable.

## 'The Cretan Bull'

Is Poirot's seventh Labour merely a case of bad
heredity or is it something more sinister?

There are relatively few notes for the seventh Labour, 'The Cretan Bull'. The main problem seems to have been the choice of poison; Christie finally settled on atropine (also the poison of choice in 'The Thumb Mark of St Peter' from *The Thirteen Problems*). The story shares an untypical emphasis on blood – the 'mad killer' idea – with 'The Erymanthian Boar'. But as in other Christie titles – *Hercule Poirot's Christmas* and 'The Importance of a Leg of Mutton' from *The Big Four* – this is an important part of the plot:

P asked down – country squire and old friend fear that
squire's boy is mad – madness in family – boy has been in
Navy – (got out of that) – squire never got over wife's
death – boating accident or car accident –
(Does HP enquire about that as though he thinks car
had been tampered with by crony? Wife only with him
by afterthought says husband – asked, friend blusters –
said first he had heard of that – make him sound
suspicious. Boy marvellously handsome – girl there in love
with him – he himself believes he is mad. Drug – eyes?
Scopolamine – hyoscyamine – atropine – or aconite –
ointment smeared on – hallucinations. Final attempt to
kill girl

This story shares a plot device with *A Caribbean Mystery* and is
in fact referenced during the plotting of that novel. The
most interesting words in the above extract are undoubtedly
'make him sound suspicious'. This was the strategy on which
Christie built her career: the presentation of a story so as to
make the innocent seem guilty and, more importantly, the
guilty innocent. Few people reading this story will not single
out George Frobisher as the villain of the piece, which is
exactly what Christie intended.

## 'The Horses of Diomedes'

------------◄○►------------

Poirot tackles the scourge of drug-pushers.

------------◄○►------------

There are two distinct sets of notes for this eighth Labour.
Despite the fact that Notebook 44 contains the 'correct' notes
for most of the other Labours, the relevant notes for this
story are those from Notebook 62:

P on trail of drug racket – County place – (not county) – rich manufacturers etc –

Old General Boynton – Gout – choleric – swollen leg. Daughters – wild girls – one gets herself into a mess – not daughter at all?

Gang – Old Boy the head of the racket – Girls turn on him

Stillingfleet – calls on Poirot – the drug racket – turns decent people into wild beasts – you asked me to keep my eyes open – girl in a fire – mews – hashish – he got girl out of it. The other sister – used to be decent kids – father an Old General. P sees them – sullen girl – hard boiled – says Stillingfleet is a good sort. P says will look her father up – look of alarm in her eyes – P says will be discreet. S[tillingfleet] and P – says very young – 18 – damned shame they aren't better looked after – P goes down to Norfolk – the General – Gout – temper – worried about his girls. P says: Who are their friends?

Dalloway – man like a horse – slow etc. – Mrs Larkin – at her house P sees the others – dartboard etc. –

Hylda – vague girl – Cummings – young doctor – assistant to older man – sandwich box (belonging to Dalloway) in hall – P gets note (look in S. Box) – he does

There are minor changes – Dr Stillingfleet (possibly of 'The Dream' and *Third Girl*) changes to Dr Stoddart, the sandwich box becomes a hunting flask and there is no mention of a dartboard.

There are also notes in Notebook 44, but they present different, and in one case, rather outlandish speculations:

The Mares of Diomedes

Old racing man – his 'gals' very wild – what can P do? – Bloomsbury – one of them shoots someone – (Mrs Barney?) – unlike twin idea – woman servant one of them – NO!!

OR

P pays a young man to be 'killed' by one of them – Or –
Secret service – Jacinta?

The idea of 'the old General and his wild girls', from the
first extract, is retained (note the change from 'boys', in the
preliminary notes, to 'girls' here) but the bizarre idea of
Poirot paying someone to allow himself to be killed, presumably as a ruse, was abandoned. The reference to Mrs Barney
is to an infamous London murder case when the glamorous
Elvira Barney was tried, and subsequently acquitted, for
the shooting of her lover Michael Scott Stephen in May
1932.

The potent symbolism of the mythical horses that feed
on human flesh transmuting into dope peddlers who carry
out a similar loathsome trade is undeniable. But there is an
element of sermonising in the story that tends to detract
from its plot. Once again Christie trades on our mis-
perception, this time of the seemingly typical retired army
stereotype, a not infrequent character in her fiction: Colonel
Protheroe in *The Murder at the Vicarage*, Major Porter in *Taken
at the Flood*, Major Palgrave in *A Caribbean Mystery*, General
Macarthur in *And Then There Were None* and Major Burnaby
in *The Sittaford Mystery*. And there are many more examples,
not all of them trustworthy . . .

The allusion to the unlike twin is to an idea that crops up
again and again throughout the Notebooks. As shown by its
constant reappearance, Christie never successfully tackled
this idea and here was no exception. A certain amount of
exasperation is detectable in the exhortation, 'NO!!', to
herself.

## 'The Girdle of Hyppolita'

◄o►

Two seemingly disparate cases, an art
robbery and a missing schoolgirl, are brought
together in the ninth Labour.

◄o►

This is another story that is considerably changed from
Christie's early conception of it, although traces of the 'head
mistress' idea are still evident. In plotting this story Christie
gave free rein to her considerable inventiveness as she considered metaphors for the original myth: a manuscript, an
archaeological find, a picture. And even after the picture was
adopted, she still considered some other scenarios:

P at Oganis or Lestranges – very super girl's finishing school
– the frightening Miss Beddingfeld

Is girl there really a crook? Or is she missing millionaire's
daughter who is being hunted for everywhere?

A precious manuscript? A picture? An archaeological find?
A stolen picture? Painted over by one of the girls (crook)
and presented to Head Mistress – latter therefore taken it
into the right country – custom's Pass – etc.

Kidnapped schoolgirl – she is new – delivered over to Miss
Nortress – dull with plate [plaits?] – wire on teeth –
miserable skinny looking object – they go to Paris – girl
disappears on train – (really emerges from lavatory and
joins man – all made up – very actressy – in mink coat. On
way back from lunch – slips into lavatory – man comes out
– hat found on line. Girl found a day later at Amiens –
unhurt – dazed.
  Theft of famous picture (G of H). It is to be smuggled

into France – to dealer there? – crook? Acc[tress] takes
employment with 'elder sister' – meets child – and takes her
to Victoria – knock out drops – false actress becomes kid
– once in France changes in lavatory – arrives with man –
very smart.

Pictures in exhibition with other girls work – P as
conjuror – wipes it off with turpentine – exposes the Girdle
of Hyppolita

A Labour that is rich in plot when two seemingly separate
storylines nearly converge. The smuggling of a valuable item
in a schoolgirl's luggage reappears twenty years later in *Cat
among the Pigeons*. The masquerade of an adult as a young girl
is also a plot feature of that book, as well as of the short story
'The Regatta Mystery'.

## 'The Flock of Geryon'

<o>

A protagonist from 'The Nemean Lion' returns to
help Poirot investigate a series of odd deaths.

<o>

'The Flock of Geryon' is the weakest of the Labours, and
this is reflected in the paucity of notes; those that exist are
vague enough to have been developed in almost any way. The
following is from Notebook 44, and the sect suggested in
the preliminary notes is one of the starting-off points:

P is visited by Miss? (Amelia) – little annuity – exercises
people's dogs – has been reading German book – criminal
impulses – sublimation. Could she work for P? A case – her
friend – strange sect – down in Devon. Young millionaire's
son – there? Or middle-aged daughter of very rich man?
Or rich man's widow?

There is no particular ingenuity in either the story or the symbolism. The story is rescued by the presence of the enterprising and entertaining Amy Carnaby from 'The Nemean Lion'. Oddly, there is no mention in the notes of Carnaby's name. 'Miss? (Amelia)' may be Christie's own shorthand (although it is not very short!) or it may simply be that she had no copy of *The Strand* to hand to check the earlier name. There is a brief reference to Hitler in this story (see also the original 'The Capture of Cerberus').

### 'The Apples of the Hesperides'

————————◄○►————————

A remote setting provides Poirot with the final clue
in a case that really began centuries earlier.

————————◄○►————————

There are fewer notes for 'The Apples of the Hesperides' than for any other Labour. The plot is not involved and required little in the way of planning once the main clue of the nun was planted. The basic outline reflects the final version:

> Millionaire – gold chalice stolen from him – no clue. P talks
> to American detective – Pat Ryan – a wild fellow – a decent
> wife – but wouldn't get him to run straight – she went back to
> Ireland – or daughter – a nun. Ireland – the convent – P arrives
> there – tramp with bottle of brandy – world in my hands

> Little tipster in bar in Ireland – 'Atlas' is his pseudonym –
> HP says doesn't look it (horse to back – 'The World' by
> Greek Hero out of Geography). You have not to hold up the
> World – only Hercule Poirot

Some minor details are different – the horse to back is Hercules rather than the more elaborate one of the notes; and there is no tramp.

Like the earlier 'The Erymanthian Boar', this case takes Poirot to a remote and beautiful location, this time on the west coast of Ireland. Apart from mentioning a coach tour holiday of Irish gardens in Chapter 11 of *Hallowe'en Party*, this is his only visit to Ireland and is memorable to him for all the wrong reasons.

Like Sir Joseph Hoggin in 'The Nemean Lion', Emery Power loses financially as a result of Poirot's investigation although in his case there is a spiritual benefit. (There is a minor error of fact when Poirot promises him that 'the nuns will say Masses for your soul'. Nuns can't say Mass and Mass for the soul is celebrated only after a person's death.) The final scene, in the isolated convent on the edge of the Atlantic, is a particularly poignant.

## 'The Capture of Cerberus'

Is the Countess Vera's nightclub the scene of
more than just harmless revelry?

The following extracts refer to the version of the story collected in *The Labours of Hercules* in 1947. It is further proof of Christie's fecundity with plot that she was able to imagine a second allegorical interpretation of the last Labour of Hercules. In the myth Hercules has to pass into Hell, overcoming the ferocious hound that guards the gates; in the Poirot Labour Hell is a nightclub with a large dog at the entrance foyer. The steps down into the club are labelled 'I meant well' and 'I can give up any time I like', an amusing take on the old saying 'The path to Hell is paved with good intentions'. And the hound, originally intended as a nightclub 'gimmick', plays a vital part in the plot.

Name changes aside, the following outline is an accurate summary:

Cerberus

Raid – blackout for 2 minutes – has it happened? And J tells
    P?
Combed the place inside out – jewels – no, drugs – no
    jewels but 5 or 6 people noticed weren't there –
Secret exit – whole grill moves out – house next door –
    Cabinet Minister etc.
We were in the clear – Jimmy Mullins – wanted – Battersea
    Murderer – has given the place a write up –
But this time we've got to succeed –
P talks to dog man –
The fatal evening – Is P there? – Or does he hear?


He comes over wall – black out etc. – how many people
    come out
Mr Vitamian Crusoe –
Miss Sylvia Elkins
~~Giuseppe~~ Martacendi – cook's boy
Paul Varesco
Two packets – the emeralds – the other – cocaine

This is a more light-hearted interpretation of the myth than the original unpublished version, and we get a glimpse of Miss Lemon's hitherto unsuspected feminine instincts in the closing lines. On 'the fatal evening' Poirot is at the club but leaves early and Christie adopts the idea of Japp recounting the details to him ('or does he hear?'). None of the early part of this story – Poirot's meeting with the Countess in the London Underground and his subsequent visit to her night-club – features in the Notebooks.

# 'The Capture of Cerberus' (1939)

◄○►

In 'The Capture of Cerberus' Poirot once more
looks for a missing person, and in this respect his twelfth
Labour resembles similar missions in 'The Arcadian Deer'
and 'The Girdle of Hyppolita'. But this final task has
an unprecedented aspect – his quarry is dead.

◄○►

Labours one to eleven were first published in the UK in *The
Strand* magazine beginning in November 1939 ('The Nemean
Lion') and culminating in September 1940 ('The Apples of
the Hesperides'). It has always been a mystery to Christie
scholars why 'The Capture of Cerberus' did not appear at
the same time. My discovery, in 2006, of a hitherto unknown
and unpublished version of the story, with a completely
different setting and plot, offers a possible solution.

Although Collins Crime Club eventually published *The
Labours of Hercules* on 8 September 1947, with Christie providing a rewritten twelfth case and adding an introductory
Foreword to explain the rationale for Poirot's undertaking,
the final story's earlier rejection by *The Strand* remained
puzzling. The magazine had always provided a ready
market for Christie short stories throughout the 1930s and
into the 1940s, with her name emblazoned on the cover as a
selling point.

Christie herself explicitly mentions this story in the specially written Foreword to the 1953 Penguin edition of *The Labours of Hercules* when she explains that in the writing of the stories, 'over the final *Capture of Cerberus* I gave way completely to despair'. She left it aside for six months and 'then suddenly, one day coming up on the escalator on the Tube the idea came. Thinking excitedly about it, I went up and down on the escalator about eight times.' But, as we shall see, while this may be the truth, it is not the whole truth . . .

## When was it written?

On 12 January 1940 Edmund Cork wrote to Christie about 'The Capture of Cerberus', explaining that he thought that *The Strand* would not publish it (at this stage they had already published the first three Labours) and suggesting that she think about writing a replacement for eventual book publication. *The Strand* had already paid £1,200 for the stories as written and if they decided not to publish one of them – as they may have indicated to Edmund Cork – they were not entitled to look for a replacement. On 12 November 1940 (after *The Strand* had appeared without the final Labour) Christie wrote to Cork asking for the return of 'the Cerberus story' in order 'to do a new one'. But it was not until 23 January 1947 (i.e. early in the year of the book's publication) that the second version was finally submitted.

Notebook 44 contains most of the notes for all twelve of the stories. At first glance it seems that they were all plotted and finished together, as most of the notes tally with the published stories. But a closer examination, in light of the discovery of the alternative version and this correspondence, shows a potentially different story. The initial notes for the last half-dozen stories all begin, and in some cases finish, on a right-hand page of Notebook 44 with the left-hand page left blank; and they follow the sequence of the book. Notes for the rejected version of 'Cerberus' follow this pattern. But the notes for the collected version are inserted, in different ink and slightly different writing, on a left-hand page, sand-wiched, out of sequence, between those for 'The Horses of Diomedes' and 'The Flock of Geryon'. It is not unreasonable to suppose that, when inspiration for the revamped story struck, Christie went back to her original notes and inserted her new idea as near as she could to the original. Also, these later notes are written in biro, while the original notes are, like those for all the other Labours, in pencil.

## Why was it never published?

There can be little doubt that the political situation of the time and the poorly disguised picture of Adolf Hitler in section *iii* was the main (and probably only) reason for the rejection of the story. Unusually for Christie, it is blatantly political from the first page, with its mention of not just the impending war but also the previous one: 'The world was in a very disturbed state – every nation alert and tense. At any minute the blow might fall – and Europe once more be plunged in war.' Later in the story we read of 'August Hertzlein . . . [who] was the dictator of dictators. His warlike utterances had rallied the youth of his country and of allied countries. It was he who had set Central Europe ablaze . . .' And in case there is any lingering doubt he is later described as having 'a bullet head and a little dark moustache'.

This surely was too close to the actual state of the world and one particular inhabitant in 1939 to be considered escap-ist reading? Why Christie chose to exploit this theme will never be known, as there is little evidence elsewhere in her work that she was particularly political.

In an interview for her Italian publishers, Mondadori, con-ducted soon after the publication of *Passenger to Frankfurt* in 1970, she admits: 'I have never been in the least interested in politics.' So why did she not simply tone down the portrait and change the name? Well, in a way, she did . . .

The story's assassination scenario is utilized in the 'Good

Cerberus.

Read — blackout for 2 minutes
Has it happened? Are J. tells P.?
Combed the place inside out — Jewels
in the soup? No drugs No drugs
No jewels — but 5 or 6 people
hustled were in there —

Secret Societ — while girl moves
out — house next door — Cabinet
Minister etc  we were in the
Clear — Jury Mullins — wanted —
Battersea Murderers — Has given the
place a write up —

But this time we've got to
Suceed —

P. talks to Dog man —
then rings up Japp.
The fatal evening
Is P there?
or does he hear?

*Two pages showing the two sets of notes for 'The Capture of Cerberus'.
The left-hand page (Notebook 44) refers to the version published in* The
Labours of Hercules, *and the right-hand page (Notebook 62) . . .*

Cerberus-

Punk + Vera Ronattoff -
Says he ... "He brings
people back from the dead."

Dr Hershattz-
Hitler made a marvellous
speech - I am willing to die -
And fall shot - A boy -
has been each side of him - Shoots
him - revolver in hand -
The Boy was my Son.
I want him brought back to life -

Father Lavallois
His convert - He planned to open
Great Meeting - To propose
International Disarmament -

*. . . to the newly-discovered earlier version included in the Appendix.
Note the difference in handwriting over the almost 10-year period.*

Fat Hen' chapter of *One, Two, Buckle My Shoe* (1940) and the Countess Vera is fondly recalled by Poirot in the 'Maids Are Courting' chapter of the same novel. The writing of that novel and the short story would have been contemporaneous. And Chapter 17 of *Passenger to Frankfurt* contains more than a passing reference to the main idea of the short story. Is it possible that, 30 years after it had been rejected, Agatha Christie unearthed her idea and inserted it into a very different book? And that, long after *The Strand* had ceased publication, she had the last laugh?

There are notes for the rejected version of the story in Notebooks 44 and 62:

> Cerberus
> Does Poirot go to look for 2 friends supposedly dead
> ~~Lenin   Trotsky   Stalin~~
> ~~George II   Queen Anne~~
> Must go unarmed (like Max Carrados in room story)

> Poirot and Vera Rossakoff – says to a friend – 'he brings people back from the dead'
>     Dr Hershaltz
>     Hitler made a marvellous speech – I am willing to die
> – and falls shot – a boy. Two men each side of him – surprise him – revolver in hand. The boy was my son – I want him brought back to life.
>     Father Lavallois – his convert – he planned to speak – a great meeting – to propose International Disarmament.
> Dr Karl Hansberg – compiles stastistics – letter of introduction from . . . medical authorities in Berlin – doctor in charge lured away by religion – nurse tries to prevent him. Herr Hitler – hands him a card.

While the similarities to Hitler are quite clear in the story, there is no mention of the actual name until we read Notebook 62. But the 'hands him a card' at the end is mystifying, as are some of the other references. If, as is almost certain, this was written in 1939 why are Lenin, Trotsky and Stalin listed? Lenin died in 1924 but Trotsky lived until 1940 and Stalin until 1953; and the other two historical figures were long dead. Moreover, none of them could be considered friends. All the names are crossed out in Notebook 44 but their presence at all is inexplicable. The Max Carrados reference is to the blind detective created by Ernest Bramah and the story 'The Game Played in the Dark'.

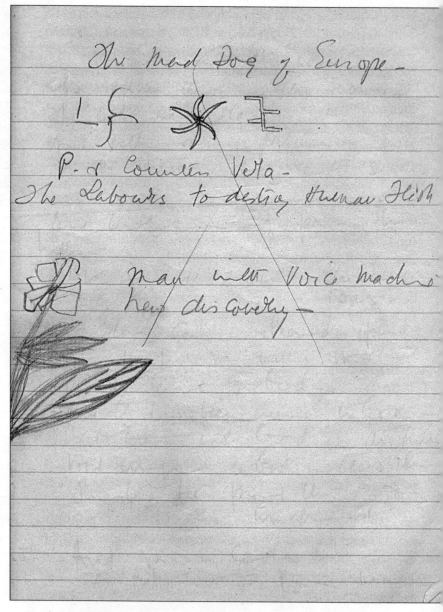

The Mad Dog of Europe –

P. & Countess Vera –
The Labours to destroy human Flesh

man with Voice machine
new discovery –

*This page from Notebook 62, during the original plotting of 'The Capture of Cerberus' (despite the reference to 'destroy human flesh' and its echo of 'The Horses of Diomedes'), may represent Christie's doodles of a variation on the Swastika.*

# THE CAPTURE OF CERBERUS

## i

Hercule Poirot sipped his *apéritif* and looked out across the Lake of Geneva.[47]

He sighed.

He had spent his morning talking to certain diplomatic personages, all in a state of high agitation, and he was tired. For he had been unable to offer them any comfort in their difficulties.

The world was in a very disturbed state – every nation alert and tense. At any minute the blow might fall – and Europe once more be plunged into war.

Hercule Poirot sighed. He remembered 1914 only too well. He had no illusions about war. It settled nothing. The peace it brought in its wake was usually only the peace of exhaustion – not a constructive peace.

He thought sadly to himself:

'If only a man could arise who would set enthusiasm for peace flaming through the world – as men have aroused enthusiasm for victory and conquest by force.'

Then he reflected, with Latin commonsense, that these

---

47  Unlike the collected version, which is set unequivocally in London, the previously unpublished version has, like many other Labours, an international flavour. From the first sentence we are 'abroad' and, for the third time in the Labours, in Switzerland (perhaps significantly a neutral country). Poirot has already visited the country during 'The Arcadian Deer' and 'The Erymanthian Boar'.

ideas of his were unprofitable. They accomplished nothing. To arouse enthusiasm was not his gift and never had been. Brains, he thought with his usual lack of modesty, were his speciality. And men with great brains were seldom great leaders or great orators. Possibly because they were too astute to be taken in by themselves.

'Ah well, one must be a philosopher,' said Hercule Poirot to himself. 'The deluge, it has not yet arrived. In the meantime this *apéritif* is good, the sun shines, the Lake is blue, and the orchestra plays not badly. Is that not enough?'

But he felt that it was not. He thought with a sudden smile:

'There is one little thing needed to complete the harmony of the passing moment. A woman. *Une femme du monde* – *chic*, well-dressed, sympathetic, *spirituelle!*'[48]

There were many beautiful and well-dressed women round him, but to Hercule Poirot they were subtly unsatisfactory. He demanded more ample curves, a richer and more flamboyant appeal.

And even as his eyes roamed in dissatisfaction round the terrace, he saw what he had been hoping to see. A woman at a table nearby, a woman so full of flamboyant form, her luxuriant henna-red hair crowned by a small round of black to which was attached a positive platoon of brilliantly feathered little birds.

The woman turned her head, her eyes rested casually on Poirot, then opened – her vivid scarlet mouth opened too. She rose to her feet, ignoring her companion at the table, and with all the impulsiveness of her Russian nature, she surged towards Hercule Poirot – a galleon in full sail. Her hands were outstretched, her rich voice boomed out.

'Ah, but it is! It *is*! *Mon cher Hercule Poirot*! After how many years – how many years – we will not say how many! It is unlucky.'

Poirot rose to his feet, he bent his head gallantly over the

---

48 A most unlikely and almost unique thought for Poirot!

Countess Vera Rossakoff's hand. It is the misfortune of small precise men to hanker after large and flamboyant women. Poirot had never been able to rid himself of the fatal fascination the Countess had for him. Now, it was true, the Countess was far from young. Her makeup resembled a sunset, her eyelashes dripped with mascara. The original woman underneath the makeup had long been hidden from sight. Nevertheless, to Hercule Poirot, she still represented the sumptuous, the alluring. The bourgeois in him was thrilled by the aristocrat. The old fascination stole over him. He remembered the adroit way in which she had stolen jewellery on the occasion of their first meeting, and the magnificent aplomb with which she had admitted the fact when taxed with it.[49]

He said:

'*Madame, enchanté –*' and sounded as though the phrase were more than a commonplace politeness.

The Countess sat down at his table. She cried:

'You are here in Geneva? Why? To hunt down some wretched criminal? Ah! If so, he has no chance against you – none at all. You are the man who always wins! There is no one like you – no one in the world!'

If Hercule Poirot had been a cat he would have purred. As it was he twirled his moustaches.

'And you, Madame? What is it that you do here?'

She laughed. She said:

'I am not afraid of you. For once I am on the side of the angels! I lead here the most virtuous of existences. I endeavour to amuse myself, but everyone is very dull. Nichevo?'

The man who had been sitting with the Countess at her table had come over and stood hesitating beside them. The countess looked up.

---

49  This is a reference to the first meeting of Vera Rossakoff and Poirot
    in 'The Double Clue', published in December 1923, when he
    unmasked her as a jewel thief. They subsequently met four years
    later in *The Big Four*.

'Bon Dieu!' she exclaimed. 'I forgot you. Let me present you. Herr Doktor Keiserbach – and this – this is the most marvellous man in the world – M. Hercule Poirot.'

The tall man with the brown beard and the keen blue eyes clicked his heels and bowed. He said:

'I have heard of you, M. Poirot.'

Countess Vera overbore Poirot's polite rejoinder. She cried:

'But you cannot possibly know how wonderful he is! He knows everything! He can *do* anything! Murderers hang themselves to save time when they know he is on their track. He is a genius, I tell you. He never fails.'

'No, no, Madame, do not say that.'

'But it is *true*! Do not be modest. It is stupid to be modest.' She turned to the other man. 'I tell you, he can do miracles. He can even bring the dead back to life.'[50]

Something leaped – a startled flash – into the blue eyes behind the glasses. Herr Keiserbach said:

'So?'

Hercule Poirot said:

'Ah, by the way, Madame, how is your son?'

'The beloved angel! So big now – such shoulders – so handsome! He is in America. He builds there – bridges, banks, hotels, department stores, railways – anything the Americans want.'

Poirot looked slightly puzzled. He murmured:

'He is then an engineer, or an architect?'

'What does it matter?' demanded the Countess Rossakoff. 'He is adorable. He is wrapped up in iron girders and things called stresses. The kind of things I have never understood nor cared about. But we adore each other.'[51]

Herr Keiserbach took his leave. He asked of Poirot:

---

50  This is a reference to *The Big Four* when Poirot arranges the return to the Countess of the small son she had thought long dead.

51  The passage about the Countess's son is almost word-for-word the same as in the collected version of the story.

'You are staying here, M. Poirot? Good. Then we may meet again.'

Poirot asked the lady:

'You will have an *apéritif* with me?'

'Yes, yes. We will drink vodka together and be very gay.'

The idea seemed to Hercule Poirot a good one.[52]

## ii

It was on the following evening that Dr Keiserbach invited Hercule Poirot to his rooms.

They sipped a fine brandy together and indulged in a little desultory conversation together.

Then Keiserbach said:

'I was interested, M. Poirot, by something that our charming friend said about you yesterday.'

'Yes?'

'She used these words. *He can even bring the dead back to life.*'

Hercule Poirot sat up a little in his chair. His eyebrows rose. He said:

'That interests you?'

'Very much.'

'Why?'

'Because I feel those words may have been an omen.'

Hercule Poirot said sharply:

'Are you asking me to bring the dead to life?'

'Perhaps. What would you say if I did?'

Hercule Poirot shrugged his shoulders. He said:

'After all, death is death, Monsieur.'

'Not always.'

Hercule Poirot's eyes grew sharp and green. He said:

'You want me to bring a person who is dead to life again. A man or a woman?'

'A man.'

---

52  It seems odd that Poirot would look forward to drinking vodka.

'Who is it?'

'You do not appear appalled by the task?'

Poirot smiled faintly. He said:

'You are not mad. You are a sane and reasonable individual. Bringing the dead to life is a phrase susceptible of many meanings. It may be treated figuratively or symbolically.'

The other said:

'In a minute you will understand. To begin with, my name is not Keiserbach. I adopted that name so that I should pass unnoticed. My own name is too well-known. That is, it has been too well-known for the last month.

'Lutzmann.'

He spoke it significantly. His eyes searched Poirot closely. Poirot said sharply:

'Lutzmann?' He paused and then said in a different tone. 'Hans Lutzmann?'

The other man said in a hard dry voice:

'*Hans Lutzmann was my son . . .*'

### iii

If, a month previously, you had asked any Englishman who was responsible for the general condition of European unrest, the reply would almost inevitably have been 'Hertzlein'.

There was, it was true, also Bondolini,[53] but it was upon August Hertzlein that popular imagination fastened. He was the dictator of dictators. His warlike utterances had rallied the youth of his own country and of allied countries. It was he who had set central Europe ablaze and kept it ablaze.

On the occasion of his public speeches he was able to set huge crowds rocking with frenzied enthusiasm. His high strangely tuned voice had a power all its own.

People in the know explained learnedly how Hertzlein was

---

53  Although he sounds like a character from the world of operetta, it is difficult not to think of Mussolini.

not really the supreme power in the Central Empires. They mentioned other names – Golstamm, Von Emmen. These, they said were the executive brains. Hertzlein was only the figurehead. Nevertheless it continued to be Hertzlein who loomed in the public eye.

Hopeful rumours went about. Hertzlein had an incurable cancer. He could not live longer than six months. Hertzlein had valvular disease of the heart. He might drop down dead any day. Hertzlein had had one stroke already and might have another any moment. Hertzlein after violently persecuting the Catholic Church had been converted by the famous Bavarian monk, Father Ludwig. He would shortly enter a monastery. Hertzlein had fallen in love with a Russian Jewess, the wife of a doctor. He was going to leave the Central Empires and settle down with her in Sweden.

And in spite of all the rumours, Hertzlein neither had a stroke, nor died of cancer, nor went into a monastery, nor eloped with a Russian Jewess. He continued to make rousing speeches amidst scenes of the greatest enthusiasm and at judicious intervals he added various territories to the Central Empires. And daily the shadow of war grew darker over Europe.

Desperately people repeated all the hopeful rumours even more hopefully. Or demanded fiercely:

'Why doesn't someone assassinate him? If only he were out of the way . . .'

There came a peaceful week when Hertzlein made no public utterances and when hopes of each of the separate rumours increased tenfold.

And then, on a fateful Thursday, Herr Hertzlein addressed a monster meeting of the Brothers of Youth.

People said afterwards that his face was drawn and strained, that even his voice held a different note, that there was about him a prescience of what was to come – but there are always people who say such things afterwards.

The speech began much as usual. Salvation would come

through sacrifice and through the force of arms. Men must die for their country – if not they were unworthy to live for it. The democratic nations were afraid of war – cowardly – unworthy to survive. Let them go – be swept away – by the glorious force of the Young. Fight – fight and again fight – for Victory, and to inherit the earth.

Hertzlein, in his enthusiasm stepped out from behind his bulletproof shelter. Immediately a shot rang out – and the great dictator fell, a bullet through his head.

In the third rank of the listening people, a young man was literally torn to pieces by the mob, the smoking pistol still grasped in his hand. That young man was a student named Hans Lutzmann.

For a few days the hopes of the democratic world rose high. The Dictator was dead. Now perhaps, the reign of peace would come. That hope died almost immediately. For the dead man became a symbol, a martyr, a Saint. Those moderates whom he had failed to sway living, he swayed dead. A great wave of warlike enthusiasm swept over the Central Empires. Their Leader had been killed – but his dead spirit should lead them on. The Central Empires should dominate the world – and sweep away democracy.

With dismay, the peace lovers realised that Hertzlein's death had accomplished nothing. Rather it had hastened the evil day. Lutzmann's act had accomplished less than nothing.

### iv

The dry middle-aged voice said:

'*Hans Lutzmann was my son.*'

Poirot said:

'I do not yet understand you. Your son killed Hertzlein –'

He stopped. The other was slowly shaking his head. He said:

'My son did *not* kill Hertzlein. He and I did not think alike. I tell you he loved that man. He worshipped him. He believed in him. He would never have drawn a pistol against him. He was a Nazi[54] through and through – in all his young enthusiasm.'

'Then if not – who did?'

The elder Lutzmann said:

'That is what I want you to find out.'

Hercule Poirot said:

'You have an idea . . .'

Lutzmann said hoarsely:

'I may be wrong.'

Hercule Poirot said steadily:

'Tell me what you think.'

Keiserbach leaned forward.

*v*

Dr Otto Schultz readjusted his tortoiseshell rimmed glasses. His thin face beamed with scientific enthusiasm. He said in pleasant nasal accents:

'I guess, Mr Poirot, that with what you've told me I'll be able to go right ahead.'

'You have the schedule?'

'Why, certainly, I shall work to it very carefully. As I see it, perfect timing is essential to the success of your plan.'

Hercule Poirot bestowed a glance of approval. He said:

'Order and method. That is the pleasure of dealing with a scientific mind.'

Dr Schultz said:

'You can count on me,' and wringing him warmly by the hand he went out.

*vi*

George, Poirot's invaluable manservant, came softly in.

He inquired in a low deferential voice:

---

54  Despite the unavoidable allegory throughout the story, this is the only unequivocal reference to the Nazis.

'Will there be any more gentlemen coming, sir?'

'No, Georges, that was the last of them.'

Hercule Poirot looked tired. He had been very busy since he had returned from Bavaria the week before. He leaned back in his chair and shaded his eyes with his hand. He said:

'When all this is over, I shall go for a long rest.'

'Yes, sir. I think it would be advisable, sir.'

Poirot murmured:

'The Last Labour of Hercules.' Do you know, Georges, what that was?'

'I couldn't say, I'm sure, sir. I don't vote Labour myself.'

Poirot said:

'Those young men that you have seen here today – I have sent them on a special mission – they have gone to the place of departed spirits. In this Labour there can be no force employed. All must be done by guile.'

'They seemed very competent looking gentlemen, if I may say so, sir.'

Hercule Poirot said:

'I chose them very carefully.'

He sighed and shook his head. He said:

'The world is very sick.'

George said:

'It looks like war whichever way you turn. Everybody's very depressed sir. And as for trade it's just awful. We can't go on like this.'

Hercule Poirot murmured:

'We sit in the Twilight of the Gods.'

## vii

Dr Schultz paused before a property surrounded by a high wall. It was situated about eight miles from Strasbourg.

He rang the gate bell. In the distance he heard the deep baying of a dog and the rattle of a chain.

The gate-keeper appeared and Dr Otto Schultz presented his card.

'I wish to see the Herr Doktor Weingartner.'

'Alas, Monsieur, the doctor has been called away only an hour ago by telegram.'

Schultz frowned.

'Can I then see his second in command?'

'Dr Neumann? But certainly.'

Dr Neumann was a pleasant-faced young man, with an ingenuous open countenance.

Dr Schultz produced his credentials – a letter of introduction from one of the leading alienists in Berlin. He himself, he explained, was the author of a publication dealing with certain aspects of lunacy and mental degeneracy.

The other's face lighted up and he replied that he knew Dr Schultz's publications and was very much interested in his theories. What a regrettable thing that Dr Weingartner should be absent!

The two men began to talk shop, comparing conditions in America and Europe and finally becoming technical. They discussed individual patients. Schultz recounted some recent results of a new treatment for paranoia.

He said with a laugh:

'By that means we have cured three Hertzleins, four Bondolinis, five President Roosevelts and seven Supreme Deities.'

Neumann laughed.

Presently the two men went upstairs and visited the wards. It was a small mental home for private patients. There were only about twelve occupants.

Schultz said:

'You understand I'm principally interested in your paranoiac cases. I believe you have a case admitted quite recently which has some peculiarly interesting features.'

## *viii*

Poirot looked from the telegram lying on his desk to the face of his visitor.

The telegram consisted simply of an address. Villa Eugenie Strasbourg. It was followed by the words 'Beware of the Dog'.

The visitor was an odoriferous gentleman of middle-age with a red and swollen nose, an unshaven chin and a deep husky voice which seemed to rise from his unprepossessing looking boots.[55]

He said hoarsely:

'You can trust me, guv'nor. Do anything with dogs, I can.'

'So I have been told. It will be necessary for you to travel to France – to Alsace.'

Mr Higgs looked interested.

'That where them Alsatian dogs come from? Never been out of England I 'aven't. England's good enough for me, that's what I say.'

Poirot said:

'You will need a passport.'

He produced a form.

'Now fill this up. I will assist you.'

They went laboriously through it. Mr Higgs said:

'I had my photo took, as you said. Not that I liked the idea of that much – might be dangerous in my profession.'

Mr Higgs' profession was that of a dog stealer, but that fact was glossed over in the conversation.

'Your photograph,' said Poirot, 'will be signed on the back by a magistrate, a clergyman, or a public official who will vouch for you as being a proper person to have a passport.'

A grin overspread Mr Higgs' face.

'That's rare, that is,' he said. 'That's rare. A beak saying as I'm a fit and proper person to have a passport.'

---

55  The dog handler is called Mr Higgs, and described as 'odoriferous' in both versions of the story.

Hercule Poirot said:

'In desperate times, one must use desperate means!'

'Meaning me?' said Mr Higgs.

'You and your colleague.'

They started for France two days later. Poirot, Mr Higgs, and a slim young man, in a checked suit and a bright pink shirt, who was a highly successful cat burglar.

### ix

It was not Hercule Poirot's custom to indulge in activities in his proper person, but for once he broke through his rule. It was past one in the morning when, shivering slightly in spite of his overcoat, he was laboriously hoisted to the top of a wall by the help of his two assistants.

Mr Higgs prepared to drop from the wall into the grounds inside. There was a violent baying of a dog and suddenly an enormous creature rushed out from under the trees.[56]

Hercule Poirot ejaculated:

'*Mon Dieu*, but it is a monster! Are you sure –?'

Mr Higgs patted his pocket with complete assurance.

'Don't you worry, guv'nor. What I've got here is the right stuff. Any dog'll follow me to hell for it.'

'In this case,' murmured Hercule Poirot, 'he has to follow you out of hell.'

'Same thing,' said Mr Higgs, and dropped off the wall into the garden.

They heard his voice.

'Here you are, Fido. Have a sniff of this . . . That's right. You come along of me . . .'

His voice died away into the night. The garden was dark and peaceful. The slim young man assisted Poirot down

---

56   Such is the political flavour, the eponymous Hound is almost forgotten and he plays a much smaller role than his counterpart in the collected story.

from the wall.[57] They came to the house. Poirot said:

'That is the window there, the second to the left.'

The young man nodded. He examined the wall first, smiled in satisfaction over a convenient pipe, and then easily and seemingly without effort he disappeared up the wall. Presently, very faintly, Poirot heard the sound of a file being used on the barred window.

Time passed. Then something dropped at Poirot's feet. It was the end of a silk ladder. Someone was coming down the ladder. A short man with a bullet head and a little dark moustache.

He came down slowly and clumsily. At last he reached the ground. Hercule Poirot stepped forward into the moonlight.

He said politely:

'*Herr Hertzlein, I presume.*'


*x*


Hertzlein said:

'How did you find me?'

They were in the compartment of a second class sleeper bound for Paris.

Poirot, as was his fashion, answered the question meticulously.

He said:

'At Geneva, I became acquainted with a gentleman called Lutzmann. It was his son who was supposed to have fired the shot that killed you and as a result young Lutzmann was torn to death by the crowd. His father, however, was firmly

---

57  In the course of this story we see a different Poirot, one who longs for the company of a woman, drinks vodka and now climbs over a wall, although this is a feat he has already performed in the course of the eleventh Labour, 'The Apples of the Hesperides'. Indeed, the tracking down and eventual discovery of August Hertzlein is reminiscent of a similar procedure involving the Cellini chalice in that story.

convinced that his son had never fired that shot. It seemed therefore as though Herr Hertzlein had been shot by one of the two men who were on either side of Lutzmann and that the pistol was forced into his hand and those two men had fallen upon him at once crying out that he was the murderer. But there was another point. Lutzmann assured me that in these mass meetings the front ranks were always packed with ardent supporters – that is to say by thoroughly trustworthy persons.

'Now the Central Empire administration is very good. Its organisation is so perfect that it seemed incredible that such a disaster could have occurred. Moreover there were two small but significant points. Hertzlein, at the critical moment, came out from his bulletproof shelter and his voice had sounded different that evening. Appearance is nothing. It would be easy for someone to carry out an impersonation on a public platform – but the subtle intonation of a voice is a thing more difficult to copy. That evening Herr Hertzlein's voice had lacked its usual intoxicating quality. It was hardly noticed because he was shot only a very few minutes after he had started to speak.

'Suppose, then, that it was *not* Herr Hertzlein speaking, and consequently *not* Herr Hertzlein who had been shot? Could there be a theory that would account for those very extraordinary happenings?

'I thought that that was possible. Amongst all the various rumours that circulate in a time of stress, there is usually a foundation of truth beneath at least one of them. Supposing that that rumour was true that declared that Hertzlein had lately fallen under the influence of that fervent preacher, Father Ludwig.'

Poirot went on, speaking slowly:

'I thought it possible, Excellency, that you, a man of ideals, a visionary, might have come suddenly to realise that a new vista, a vista of peace and brotherhood, was open to humanity, and that you were the man to set their feet upon that path.'

Hertzlein nodded violently. He said in his soft husky thrilling voice:

'You are right. The scales fell from my eyes. Father Ludwig was the appointed means to show me my true destiny. Peace! Peace is what the world wants. We must lead youth forward to live in brotherhood. The youth of the world must join together, to plan a great campaign, a campaign of peace. And *I* shall lead them! *I* am the means appointed by God to give peace to the world!'

The compelling voice ceased. Hercule Poirot nodded to himself, registering with interest his own aroused emotion.

He went on drily:

'Unfortunately, Excellency, this vast project of yours did not please certain executive authorities in the Central Empires. On the contrary it filled them with dismay.'

'Because they knew that where I led, the people would follow.'

'Exactly. So they kidnapped you without more ado. But they were then in a dilemma. If they gave out that you were dead, awkward questions might arise. Too many people would be in the secret. And also, with you dead, the warlike emotions you had aroused might die with you. They hit instead upon a spectacular end. A man was prevailed upon to represent you at the Monster meeting.'

'Perhaps Schwartz. He took my place sometimes in public processions.'

'Possibly. He himself had no idea of the end planned for him. He thought only that he was to read a speech because you yourself were ill. He was instructed at a given moment to step out from the bulletproof shelter – to show how completely he trusted his people. He never suspected any danger. But the two storm troopers had their orders. One of them shot him and the two of them fell on the young man standing between them and cried out that it was his hand that had fired the shot. They knew their crowd psychology.

'The result was as they had hoped. A frenzy of national

patriotism and a rigid adherence to the programme of force by arms!'

Hertzlein said:

'But you still do not tell me how you found me?'

Hercule Poirot smiled.

'That was easy – for a person, that is, of my mental capacity! Granted that they had not killed you (and I did not think that they could kill you. Someday you might be useful to them alive, especially if they could prevail upon you to readopt your former views). Where could they take you? Out of the Central Empires – but not too far – and there was only one place where you could be safely hidden – in an asylum or a mental home – the place where a man might declare tirelessly all day and all night that he was Herr Hertzlein and where such a statement would be accepted as quite natural. Paranoics are always convinced that they are great men. In every mental institution there are Napoleons, Hertzleins, Julius Caesars – often many examples of *le bon Dieu* himself!'

'I decided that you would most probably be in a small institution in Alsace or Lorraine where German speaking patients would be natural; and probably only one person would be in the secret – the medical director himself.

'To discover where you were I enlisted the services of some five or six *bona fide* medical men. These men obtained letters of introduction from an eminent alienist in Berlin. At each institution they visited the director was, by a curious coincidence, called away by telegram about an hour before the visitor's arrival. One of my agents, an intelligent young American doctor, was allotted the Villa Eugenie and when visiting the paranoic patients he had little difficulty in recognising the genuine article when he saw you. For the rest, you know it.'

Hertzlein was silent a moment.

Then he said, and his voice held once again that moving and appealing note:

'You have done a greater thing than you know. This is the beginning of peace – peace over Europe – peace in all the world! It is my destiny to lead mankind to Peace and Brother-hood.'

Hercule Poirot said softly:

'Amen to that . . .'

### xi

Hercule Poirot sat on the terrace of a hotel at Geneva. A pile of newspapers lay beside him. Their headlines were big and black.

The amazing news had run like wildfire all over the world. HERTZLEIN IS NOT DEAD.

There had been rumours, announcements, counter-announcements – violent denials by the Central Empire Governments.

And then, in the great public square of the capital city, Hertzlein had spoken to a vast mass of people – and there had been no doubt possible. The voice, the magnetism, the power . . . He had played upon them until he had them crying out in a frenzy.

They had gone home shouting their new catchwords.

*Peace . . . Love . . . Brotherhood . . . The Young are to save the World.*

There was a rustle beside Poirot and the smell of an exotic perfume.

Countess Vera Rossakoff plumped down beside him. She said:

'Is it all real? Can it work?'

'Why not?'

'Can there be such a thing as brotherhood in men's hearts?'

'There can be the belief in it.'

She nodded thoughtfully. She said:

'Yes, I see.'

Then, with a quick gesture she said:

'But they won't let him go on with it. They'll kill him. Really kill him this time.'

Poirot said:

'But his legend – the new legend – will live after him. Death is never an end.'

Vera Rossakoff said:

'Poor Hans Lutzmann.'

'His death was not useless either.'

Vera Rossakoff said:

'You are not afraid of death, I see. I am! I do not want to talk about it. Let us be gay and sit in the sun and drink vodka.'

'Very willingly, Madame. The more so since we have now got hope in our hearts.'

He added:

'I have a present for you, if you will deign to accept it.'

'A present for me? But how charming.'

'Excuse me a moment.'

Hercule Poirot went into the hotel. He came back a few seconds later. He brought with him an enormous dog of singular ugliness.

The Countess clapped her hands.

'What a monster! How adorable! I like everything large – immense! Never have I seen such a big dog! And he is for me?'

'If it pleases you to accept him.'

'I shall adore him.' She snapped her fingers. The large hound laid a trusting muzzle in her hand. 'See, he is as gentle as a lamb with me! He is like the big fierce dogs we had in Russia in my father's house.'

Poirot stood back a little. His head went on one side. Artistically he was pleased. The savage dog, the flamboyant woman – yes, the tableau was perfect.

The Countess inquired:

'What's his name?'

Hercule Poirot replied, with the sigh of one whose labours are completed:

'Call him Cerberus.'

### Butter in a Lordly Dish
### 13 January 1948

———◄◦►———

Luke Enderby K.C is a dedicated philanderer and,
after a successful prosecution, arranges to meet his latest
conquest for an illicit weekend at her country cottage.
Where a surprise awaits him . . . and the listener.

———◄◦►———

*'He asked water, and she gave him milk; she brought forth butter
in a lordly dish'*

*Judges* 5: 25

Throughout her long career Agatha Christie's relationship
with radio was mutually advantageous; she benefited from a
medium that was the mainstay of family entertainment and
BBC listenership increased by featuring a hugely popular
writer. In 1930 and 1931, respectively, she contributed to the
collaborative Detection Club radio serials *Behind the Screen*
and *The Scoop*, reading her own contributions live on air. In
1937 she wrote her first play for radio, an adaption of the
Poirot short story, 'Yellow Iris'. Her husband-and-wife detective team, Tommy and Tuppence were brought to radio life,
in the persons of real-life couple Richard Attenborough and
Sheila Sim, in a 1953 series, *Partners in Crime*. In January/Feb-
ruary 1956 BBC radio broadcast an Agatha Christie season
which featured a documentary celebrating her achievements
and six dramatisations: *The ABC Murders, The Mysterious Affair
at Styles, Murder in Mesopotamia*, 'Death by Drowning', 'The
Adventure of the Clapham Cook', 'The Case of the Kidnapped Dog' ('The Nemean Lion'). Since 1984 BBC Radio 4 has
broadcast dramatisations of all of the Marple and many of the
Poirot and non-series novels. And, of course, the most famous theatrical production of all time, *The Mousetrap*, began

life as a half-hour radio drama, *Three Blind Mice*, in 1947.

Christie's relatively unknown contributions to radio drama were two original scripts, *Personal Call* and *Butter in a Lordly Dish*, written specifically for broadcast. Both involve miscarrages of justice, a theme that appeared throughout her career: *Murder on the Orient Express, Cards on the Table, And Then There Were None, Five Little Pigs, Ordeal by Innocence*. Neither a typical Christie whodunit, their common theme is revenge; in each case absolute and, unusually for Christie, dreadful.

*Butter in a Lordly Dish* was originally broadcast as the first in a series of six plays, with the overall title 'Mystery Playhouse', written specially for BBC Radio by members of the Detection Club. The history of this short work can be traced back to a very early unpublished short story, 'The Wife of the Kenite', which features a gruesome revenge exacted by a woman who, many years earlier, suffered a terrible loss at the hands of a stranger. With customary economy, Christie changed the original South African setting and nationalities of the main protagonists but retained the plot. The cryptic title is from the Biblical tale of Jael and Sisera in the *Book of Judges* and its significance becomes clear as the play proceeds. Suffice it to say that radio is the perfect medium for a play culminating in a climax of shocking sound effects, aided by a vivid imagination. One of the most unusual murder methods in the entire crime fiction genre is revealed after thirty minutes of suspenseful dialogue.

There are only two pages of sparse notes in Notebook 14 for *Butter in a Lordly Dish*, whose title seems to have been decided from the outset. The 'man' in question is Sir Luke and, when it finally reached the radio, the woman's name had changed to Julia Keene.

B. B. C. Play Butter in a Lordly Dish

Woman, Mrs Adare, has made acquaintance with man on purpose. ~~They arrive at a hotel~~ – at her country cottage

Butter in a Lordly Dish – sounds quite Biblical

Tell me about some of your cases – Danny freed – suspected before – but alibi – his wife

### *Taken at the Flood*
12 November 1948

---

Gordon Cloade is killed in an air raid and his new young wife, Rosaleen, inherits a fortune. When a mysterious death brings Hercule Poirot to Warmsley Vale he realises that the Cloade family, badly in need of money, has good reason to kill her. So why was it not Rosaleen who died?

---

> *There is a tide in the affairs of men,*
> *Which, taken at the flood, leads on to fortune . . .*
>
> Shakespeare, *Julius Caesar*

Like *4.50 from Paddington* and *Ordeal by Innocence*, the title of *Taken at the Flood* gave trouble. *The Incoming Tide* or *There is a Tide* were under consideration until it was discovered that Taylor Caldwell's new novel was called *There Was a Time*. The eventual title, a quotation from *Julius Caesar*, is mentioned in the body of the novel in Book II, Chapter 16. Tantalisingly, in a letter dated September 1947 Christie's agent refers to a 'revised' version of the novel and the 'marvellous job in altering it'. But this remains a mystery, as there is nothing in either the Notebooks or the surviving correspondence to clarify it.

The plot of *Taken at the Flood* is one of Christie's most

intricate. To begin with, none of the deaths are as they initially seem. The first death, presumed a murder, is an accident; the second, presumed a suicide, is in fact a suicide (although seasoned Christie readers will suspect murder); and the third, presumed suicide, is a murder. This combination of explanations is unique in the Christie output.

Furthermore, both Frances and Rowley Cloade, independently of each other, complicate the real killer's plan with sub-plots of their own, each of which ends with the violent death of their conspirators. Then there is confusion about the identity of the first corpse. Is he Enoch Arden? Is Robert Underhay still alive? Is he the man found dead in the Blue Boar? And if he isn't, who is that corpse? This plot device is shared, brilliantly, in *One, Two Buckle my Shoe*, and much less successfully in *4.50 from Paddington*.

Some of this complexity is mirrored in the notes, due mainly to the fact that they are intertwined for much of the time with those for *They Do It with Mirrors* and *Sleeping Murder*. In the notes, Christie's working title for the book hovered between 'Cover Her Face', the one-time title for *Sleeping Murder*, and 'Mirrors', shorthand for *They Do It with Mirrors*. Each is used three times but in all cases with the character names and plot of *Taken at the Flood*. It is worth remembering that none of the three titles is very specific; all could, with minimal tweaking, apply to any Christie title.

In the opening pages of Notebooks 19 and 30 we find the genesis of the Cloade family situation:

Cover her Face

Characters

The Cloades

Nathaniel – solicitor – embezzling money [Jeremy]
Frances – His wife daughter of – Lord Edward Hatherly
father Lady Angarethick – says her family are all crooks

Jeremy – ex-pilot – lawless – daring [probably the origin of David Hunter]

Jane Brown – Girl of character engaged to Jeremy? [Lynn]

Susan Cloade – (or a widow?) Cool – discerning [Adela or Katherine]

Rosaleen Hunter
Nathaniel Clode [sic]
Frances Clode – (aristocratic wife)
Susan Ridgeway
A Cloade – war widow – breeds dogs

The above, from Notebook 30, is the only use of the name 'Rosaleen' anywhere in the notes and it is used with her Hunter, rather than Cloade, surname. Throughout the notes she is referred to as Lena, itself a diminution of Rosaleen. The 'Cloade war widow' who breeds dogs may have been inspired by Christie's own daughter Rosalind, a devoted dog lover and breeder, whose first husband, Hubert Prichard, perished in the war.

Notebook 13 illustrates Christie's frequently adopted alphabetical system:

A. Mrs. Marchmont asks Lena for money – (gets it?) [Book I Chapter 5]

B. Frances asks – David interrupts – her reaction – for the moment he feels afraid

    David and Lena look out of window – sees Lynn. Lena sees too?

    He goes off – interview with Lynn – then him and Lena again [Book I Chapter 6]

C. Hercule Poirot – Aunt Kathie – spirit guidance [Prologue]

D. The farm – Lena and Rowley – he looks at it just as he looks at her – (planning its death?) she goes away – stranger comes – asks way to (?) Furrowtown – goes passed it – face is familiar to Rowley [Book I Chapter 8]

E. Rowley goes up to White Hart – Beatrice the barmaid
   photo of L. and Edmund – Frances and Jeremy – photo
   – to get H.P's address [Book I Chapters 11 and 12]

F. David reading letter – get your things packed – go
   up to London – stay there – I'll deal with this [Book I
   Chapter 10]

G. David and E.A. – veiled blackmail – D. says get out of
   here [Book I Chapter 9]

H. Where is money to be paid? London? Tube? Poirot
   – seat? etc. – Bessie overhears (David goes to London
   – to see Lena Tube – Rowley in crowd) [not used]

I. Rowley visits Poirot – urges him to come to Warmsley
   Heath [Book II Chapter 1]

J. Death of E.A. – David suspected – arrested? – button in
   dead man's hand [Book II Chapter 5]

K. Lena and the Church [Book II Chapter 6]

L. Poirot and Lynn – people much the same – don't change
   [Book II Chapter 12]

Although most of these, slightly rearranged, appear in the published novel, there are a number of minor differences: scene H does not feature at all; Furrowtown in scene D becomes Furrowbank in the book; it is not a button (scene J) that is found in the room but a cigarette lighter with the initials DH; and scene C in the novel precedes much of the action.

Rosaleen's religion, apart from being a major factor in her personality, is also an important plot device. Her Roman Catholicism, and its attendant guilt, haunts all of her conversation with David. Read again their scenes in light of the solution and much of the dialogue takes on a different meaning. And it is the scene at the church that gives Poirot one of his clues:

Lena – depressed – says – very worried I've been – wants to
see priest – asks him – doesn't go to confession

Priest – Lena – (or clergyman) Go to confession – I'm in mortal sin

Lena gets conscience – her letter – ~~planning of death~~ – wickedness – I want to make what reparation I can

Girl and R[oman] C[atholic] church – P sees her

*Taken at the Flood* is another novel for which quite a few intriguing ideas were rejected:

Lena in London – D. telephones her – goes to station – sees station master – Swings out of express as it leaves – returns to White Hart though window – Knifes E.A. – leaves as clue something he has already missed (lighter?) – goes to call box
L. telephones Anne 9.18
D.    ″        ″    ″  (London wants you)

Here we see the set-up of the faked telephone call that establishes Hunter's alibi. But he doesn't knife 'E.A.' (Enoch Arden) as he finds him already dead from a head wound when he gets there. For much of the notes, meanwhile, Rowley is the villain:

Rowley arranges L's suicide (in London) has to go to see a bull etc
Does Rowley play the part of Underhay in London – with Lena

While he is not indictable at the end of the novel, Rowley does have two deaths on his conscience. But his playing the part of Underhay in London could be seen as a complication too far. Another suggestion was that Rowley and Frances should work together:

Rowley – jealous of David – has plans – he and Frances

> agree to blackmail – but Rowley's idea is to inherit – so
> Lena must die

In fact Rowley and Frances work independently in the novel, although without any idea of killing Rosaleen.

> Possibly button from Lena's dress found by E.A.'s body – or does Rowley take it away. Shot heard as Anne and R and D are approaching house. Suggested that R could have laid timing fuse to cartridge

A timing fuse to fake a gunshot, thereby confusing the time of death, is a plot device in *The Murder at the Vicarage*, but otherwise Christie depended only rarely on mechanical means to achieve her effects (*The Murder of Roger Ackroyd* being a notable exception).

Although it is preceded by a number of rejected ideas – Nathaniel/Jeremy does not resort to blackmail and murder – the last line of the following note does reflect the reality of the novel. Major Porter, a poignant portrait, agrees, through poverty, to perjure himself but later, in a final futile attempt to regain his self-respect, kills himself:

> Cover her Face

> Nathaniel who has embezzled a lot of trust funds – wife is Rose – 'county' – shrewd – fond of him but knows his weakness – gallant and sticks to sinking ship. Says at last 'Of course I always knew he was a crook' . . . Family all rather crooked – but Rose is straight – (nice!). Enoch is steady character he has come across – conversation in club inspires him to hire Enoch to sound out Lena and levy blackmail. Enoch turns screws on him – he kills Enoch –
> (a) tries to fasten crime on Lena – or (b) suicide – then goes to Porter – gets him to identify dead man as Underhay Porter desperately poor agrees.

The following, while an interesting plot twist, would have been a difficult one to carry off:

> U. is alive – reads inquest – arrives at Doon – sees – Lena – falls in love with her?

It would mean Underhay falling in love with the woman masquerading as his dead wife and robbing his fortune.

But the most intriguing of the ideas Christie rejected concern the book's possible title:

> Cover her ~~eyes~~ face – mine eyes dazzle – she died young – outburst by David. Why?

Exactly – why? Why would David Hunter have exclaimed these words? The quotation 'Cover her face – mine eyes dazzle – she died young' is from *The Duchess of Malfi*, and concerns the murder of a sister by a brother. Presumably David would have used it upon the death of Rosaleen, his 'sister'? Now we understand why *Cover Her Face* was considered as a title. Whatever is the case, echoing, as it does, the critical scene in Chapter 3 of *Sleeping Murder*, it can be seen as further confirmation that *Sleeping Murder* was written later than formerly assumed.

## *Crooked House*
### 23 May 1949

―――――――――◄o►―――――――――

Charles Hayward falls in love with Sophia Leonides during the war and is fascinated by her family, who live together in a 'crooked house' ruled over by her wealthy grandfather. When he is poisoned, it becomes clear that a member of the family is crooked in the criminal sense.

―――――――――◄o►―――――――――

*There was a crooked man and he went a crooked mile,*
*He found a crooked sixpence beside a crooked stile,*
*He had a crooked cat which caught a crooked mouse,*
*And they all lived together in a little crooked house.*

*Crooked House* remains one of the great Christie shock endings. So shocking was it considered that Collins wanted her to change the ending (*Sunday Times* interview, 27 February 1966), but she refused. It would be reasonable, therefore, to suppose that this solution was the book's *raison d'être*. But as we saw in Chapter 3, several characters were considered as possible murderers before Christie arrived at her shocking solution.

In her specially written Foreword to the Penguin 'Million' edition of *Crooked House* Agatha Christie writes: 'This book is one of my own special favourites. I saved it for years, thinking about it, working it out, saying to myself "One day when I have got plenty of time, and want to really enjoy myself – I'll begin it." I should say that of one's output, five books are work to one that is real pleasure. Writing *Crooked House* was pure pleasure.'

If, indeed, she spent years thinking and working it out, none of those notes have survived. Notebook 14, which contains most of the notes for this title, also contains, un-usually, two dates. A few pages before the *Crooked House* outline the dates 'Sept. 1947' and '20th Oct [1947]' appear. The novel first appeared in an American serialisation in October 1948 and was published in the UK in May 1949. From internal evidence (a reference to Aristide's will being drafted 'last year' in November 1946) and from the evidence of the Notebooks below, the book was completed late in 1947 or early in 1948. So the years spent 'thinking about it and work-ing it out' are, in all probability, those spent in the mental process before pen was put to paper. The twenty-plus pages of notes cover the entire course of the novel.

The first page of notes in Notebook 14 is headed 'Crooked House' so that seems to have been the title from the  outset; and, indeed, it is difficult to think of a better one. But Note-book 56 lists, on its opening page, the germ of *A Pocket Full of Rye*, with a distinct reference to a crooked house – although it is possible that the intention was to have a crooked, in the sense of dishonest, businessman and no reference to the novel of that name is intended.

> Sing a song of sixpence – the crooked sixpence found
>   (a Crooked man Crooked wife Crooked house)
> Coming home – Parlourmaid – maid and son – collusion
>   – maid killed to prevent her telling

Some pages before the detailed plotting are two references:

> Crooked House
> Crippled soldier – with scarred face – old man is treating him for war wounds – but <u>not</u> war wounds – really a murderer

> Plans Sept. 1947
> ~~Crooked House (The Alt[erations]).~~ Done

It is not possible to date the first entry as this 'crippled soldier' scenario does not appear in any Christie title, but the second, a page later, is headed unambiguously, showing that the bulk of the novel, if not the entire novel, was completed by this date with only the alterations to attend to. But the crossing out of words is Christie's usual indication that something has been completed; here, in the same ink, we have the word 'Done' added.

Two pages later the plotting begins. The family is set out in some detail, as is the Sophia/Charles set-up:

Old Aristide Kriston – Gnome but attractive – vitality – a restaurant keeper – then marries the daughter of a fox hunting squire – good looks – very fair and English.

Roger – Greek – clever – devoted to father

Clemency – woman scientist

Leo – fair handsome [possibly a forerunner of Philip]

Penelope – good humoured – motivated [possibly a forerunner of Magda]

Sophia

His second wife – Dorcas (Tabitha) [Brenda]

Laurence – the crippled tutor

[Told in] First person – Charles(?) in Foreign office – Sophia Alexander is in his department – her talk – attraction – Oh, we all live together in a little crooked house – he looks up nursery rhyme – sees her in London – or arranges so to do – murder of Grandfather. She refuses to marry him – because of murder – because I don't know which of us did it? – anyone of us might. His father is A.C. [Assistant Commissioner] – Charles goes into it all – the old man – his marriage

There is a succinct, initial assertion on the second page of notes that 'Harriet kills the old man'. However, consideration is subsequently given to five other characters: Brenda, the second wife; Clemency, Roger's wife; the tutor Laurence; the formidable Edith de Haviland, Aristide's sister-in-law; and Sophia. The idea 'Laurence – really no legs' is not pursued, despite Christie's fascination with this as a plot device (see 'Unused Ideas'), and Laurence remains crippled only in the emotional sense. And although the killer was eventually named Josephine, this name does not appear until the thirteenth page of notes. She is earlier (as above) referred to as Harriet and/or Emma:

> Dorcas – No [Brenda]
> Clemency? Yes her motive – Fanatical – slightly mad
> Or shall it be Clemency – No gain – they will be out on
>     the world
> Does Laurence do it – a cripple – Laurence – really no legs –
>     therefore always different heights
> Edith – Yes – possible
> Sophia Possible Lack of moral fibre

Christie explores this idea further, although it is possible to infer – 'Yes – interesting' in the first extract and '(if J)', five pages later, in the second – that at this stage she had not definitely settled on Josephine (as she has now become) as the killer:

> Emma [Josephine] – Yes – interesting – not normal – wants
> power – hated her grandfather for something particular
> – (wouldn't let her do ballet dancing and you must start
> young?): Motive – adjust for <u>her</u> method – an abnormally
> high intelligence. If so is there a second murder – Yes – the
> old nurse (if Emma)

> The weight over the door (if J) or definitely dies – little black
>     book nursery.
> Child's ending – best evidence there is – no good in court –

> children don't like being asked direct questions – to you
> she was showing off.
> Charles and Josephine – asks about letters – I was making it
> up – won't tell you – you shouldn't have told police.
> Josephine writing in her book. A.C. says – be careful of the
> child – there's a poisoner about

Although there is no mention of Josephine in the early pages, when she is mentioned she is given a page to herself and her detective work. Throughout the novel we are told of her ghoulish curiosity, her eavesdropping, her knowledge of detective fiction, and, poignantly, her little black book containing, supposedly, her detective notes:

> Does Harriet know that Uncle Roger has been doing this?
> An odious child who always knows what's going on
> Josephine – the ghoul – she knows – I've been doing
> detective work
> Finds Roger was going away – because I think because he'd
> embezzled money
> And Edith hates Brenda – they wrote to each other – I know
> where they kept the letters
> I didn't like grandfather – ballet – dancing nono.

Although it a major Christie title, due to its shocking denouement, *Crooked House* is not a formally clued detective story. The answer is very evident in retrospect – Josephine's confident claim of her knowledge of the killer, her lack of fear, the dents on the wash-house floor from the experiments with the marble door-stop – but it is not possible to arrive at the solution by logical deduction. Despite this, the novel shows that even after a 30-year career Christie still retains her ability to surprise and entertain.

# IV

## *The Fourth Decade 1950–1959*

'So I was happy, radiantly happy, and made even more so by the applause of the audience.'

*An Autobiography*

While she still produced her annual 'Christie for Christmas', the 1950s was Agatha Christie's Golden Age of Theatre. Throughout this decade her name, already a constant on the bookshelf, now became a perennial on the theatre marquee as well. In so doing she became the only crime writer to conquer the stage as well as the page; and the only female

playwright in history to have three plays running simultaneously in London's West End. Other playwrights – Frederick
Knott or Francis Durbridge – wrote popular stage thrillers
and some of her fellow crime writers wrote stage plays –
Dorothy L. Sayers' *Busman's Honeymoon*, Ngaio Marsh's *Singing
in the Shrouds* – but Christie is still the only crime writer to
achieve equal fame and success in both media.

The decade began with the publication, in June, of her
fiftieth title, *A Murder is Announced*, one of her greatest detective novels and Miss Marple's finest hour. Elements of its plot
depend on food rationing, identity cards, fuel shortages, and
a new social mobility. Likewise, many of her 1950s novels
reflected this new social order in a post-war Britain.

*They Do It with Mirrors* (1952) is set in a reform home for
delinquents; *Mrs McGinty's Dead* (1952) finds Poirot staying at
an unspeakable guest-house while he solves the murder of a
charwoman. *Hickory Dickory Dock* (1955) is set in a student
hostel and *Ordeal by Innocence* (1958) is a dark novel about a
miscarriage of justice. The female protagonist of *4.50 from
Paddington* (1957) makes a living, despite a university degree,
as a short-term domestic help; *Cat among the Pigeons* (1959)
combines a murder mystery with international unrest and
revolution. And two titles – *They Came to Baghdad* (1951) and
*Destination Unknown* (1954) – represent a return, 30 years
after *The Man in the Brown Suit*, to the foreign thriller.

In this decade the final Mary Westmacotts were published,
*A Daughter's a Daughter* in 1952 and *The Burden* in 1956.
And in April 1950 Agatha Christie began to write *An Autobiography*, a task that would take over fifteen years, although
it would not appear in print until after her death. Despite
this impressive range of projects, throughout the 1950s her
output remained steady, although 1953, with *After the Funeral*
and *A Pocket Full of Rye*, was the last year that saw more than
one 'Christie for Christmas'. During the 1950s, to the probable chagrin of Collins Crime Club, Christie concentrated
her literary efforts on the stage.

Exactly a year after her fiftieth title became a best-seller, *The Hollow*, her 1946 Poirot novel, made its debut as a play, despite the prognostications of Christie's daughter Rosalind, who tried to dissuade her mother from adapting what she saw as unsuitable dramatic material. The play was a success and, buoyed by its reception, Christie began in earnest to turn her attention to the stage. In *An Autobiography* she explains that writing a play is much easier than writing a novel because 'the circumscribed limits of the stage simplifies things' and the playwright is not 'hampered with all that description that . . . stops [the writer from] getting on with what happens'.

In 1952 *The Mousetrap* began its unstoppable run. Originally a radio play, written at the express request of Queen Mary, who celebrated her eightieth birthday in 1947, Christie subsequently adapted it as a long short story and, finally, as a stage play. After tryouts in Nottingham, it opened at London's Ambassadors Theatre on 25 November 1952. By the mid 1960s it had broken every existing theatrical record and it still sailed serenely on. The following year her greatest achievement in theatre, *Witness for the Prosecution*, opened and confirmed Agatha Christie's status as a crime dramatist. The year after that the play duplicated its London success on Broadway, earning for its author an Edgar award from the Mystery Writers of America.

The previous three plays had been her own adaptations of earlier titles, but she now began producing original work for the stage. *Spider's Web* (1954) was the first, followed by *Verdict* and *The Unexpected Guest* (both 1958). Although all three contained a dead body, something audiences had come to expect from a Christie play, in most other respects they were surprises. *Spider's Web* was another commission, this one written at the request of the actress Margaret Lockwood, and was a light comedy with a whodunit element. *Verdict*, the only failure of the decade, was, despite its title and the presence of a murdered body, not a whodunit at all; and *The Unexpected Guest* was a brooding will-they-get-away-with-it – or so it seems until the final surprise. In between these titles *Towards Zero*, an adaptation of her 1943 novel, opened to a lukewarm reception in 1956.

On radio Tommy and Tuppence, played by *The Mousetrap*'s husband-and-wife team of Richard Attenborough and Sheila Sim, appeared in a 13-part adaptation of *Partners in Crime* beginning in April 1953. The following year the BBC broadcast an original radio play, *Personal Call*. The artistically and critically acclaimed Billy Wilder version of *Witness for the Prosecution* arrived on screen in 1957 and remains the best film version of any Christie material. And in 1956 US television cast (the unlikely) Gracie Fields in the role of Miss Marple in *A Murder is Announced*.

The 1950s saw The Queen of Crime expanding her literary horizons from phenomenally successful crime novelist to equally impressive crime dramatist. And in 1956, in recognition of her exceptional contribution to both, Agatha Christie was awarded a CBE.

### *A Murder is Announced*
5 June 1950

An advertisement in the local paper announcing a
murder brings many of the inhabitants of Chipping
Cleghorn to Little Paddocks, the home of Miss Blacklock,
where the ensuing game of Murder turns deadly.
Miss Marple, who is visiting the local vicar,
investigates a triple killing.

*A Murder is Announced* was publicised as Agatha Christie's fiftieth title (although a 1939 US collection, *The Regatta Mystery*, had to be included in order to reach this significant number) and was the occasion of a major launch and celebration party in London's Savoy Hotel in June 1950. The author happily posed for photographs, with Sir William Collins, beside a cake iced with the jacket design. Other guests included fellow crime writer Ngaio Marsh and the actress Barbara Mullen, then appearing in the West End as Miss Marple in *The Murder at the Vicarage.*

*A Murder is Announced* remains one of the best detective novels Christie ever wrote. It qualifies effortlessly for the Top Ten and it is easily the best of the Marple titles. Ingeniously constructed, daringly clued and perfectly paced, it is a wonderful half-century title. It shares a major plot device with both 'The Companion' in *The Thirteen Problems* and 'The House at Shiraz' in *Parker Pyne Investigates*. A mere ten pages of notes include interesting ideas that were considered before settling on the final plot. The following, from in Notebook 35, is idea J in an alphabetical list, dated 1947:

> J. A Murder has been (combine with H)
>     People going to meet in a Country house ~~Or at a dinner party in London~~ – Like [Ten Little] Niggers – each of them thinking beforehand – about 6 people – they all have motive for killing a certain man – that is <u>why</u> they are asked – victim turns up last – host and hostess (a Mrs North) – it is often let – for parties or a London house – street numbers repainted
>
> A death has been arranged and will take place on Monday Feb 6th at 20 Ennerly Park Gardens – friends accept this, the only intimation – no flowers by request

As we shall see, the setting changed a few times before arriving at Chipping Cleghorn, as did the wording of the invitation. And in the finished novel we do indeed meet a group of people going to a house in the country, although not all with a motive for murder. 'Mrs North' is possibly Christie's friend Dorothy North (the dedicatee of *One, Two, Buckle my Shoe*). The reference 'combine with H' is to an earlier jotting about a plot, never pursued, involving a divorced mother of two daughters whose first husband inherits a fortune. The children are Primrose and Lavender and the subsequent murders were to involve flowers left by the bodies; hence the 'no flowers by request' instruction.

In Notebook 31 we can see the plot taking shape in notes inserted on four pages – in the middle of the plotting for *They Came to Baghdad* – dated, some pages earlier, 'May 24th'. This is, in all likelihood, 1948; on 8 October 1948 Edmund Cork, Christie's UK agent, wrote assuring her American agent that, although she had not written a word that year, she was shortly to start on a Miss Marple story. In fact she worked on it in 1949.

Argument I, below, is the plot with which we are familiar although some fine-tuning was necessary: Harry (Patrick Simmons in the novel) is not the victim nor is he in possession of knowledge dangerous to Miss Blacklock. Apart from other name changes, as indicated, this is the plot as it finally appeared.

The really interesting passage, however, is Argument II. Here we are presented with a totally different plot and murderer with Letitia as victim rather than perpetrator:

A M[urder] has been arranged

Letitia Bailey at breakfast reading out [Letitia Blacklock]
Amy Batter – someone calls her Lottie [Dora Bunner]
young man Harry Clegg – son or nephew of old school
    friend? [Patrick Simmons]
Phillipa Hedges lodger [Phillipa Haymes]
Col and Mrs Standish [Col. and Mrs Easterbrook]
'Hinch' and 'Potts' [Hinchcliffe and Murgatroyd]
Edmund Darley and his mother [Edmund and Mrs.
    Swettenham]

Mitzi – maid?

The events

Argument I
L[etitia] is Deus ex Machina – Sister 'Charlotte' is really her
. . . . . . Sister 'consumptive' acting I[n] P[lace]

Clue
1 Belle gives this away
2 Called Lotty by Amy instead of Letty

[therefore] L. has to remove – Harry? He knows by
snapshot – (seen it in album?) – (tie up with disappearance
of album?) – (or blank space in it) later – ostensibly photos
of P and E – or their mother – Phillipa is 'Pip' Recognised by
L. who is however quite beneficent towards her and
advances theory that H. is Pip. L. shoots ~~Pip~~ H – Later
poisoning – Amy dies instead of her – Circle narrows to look
for Emma or Emma's husband – or Phillipa's husband
(missing) – Point anonymous letter from 'Pip' (written by L)
sent to Belle.

   3rd excitement is the danger to someone who has found
out something (Phillipa?) her boy friend (love interest?)
Edmund or Edmund's rather mysterious friend

Argument II

Mitzi is prime mover – she is 'Emma' – Shot young man is
her husband – this comes out later – she sticks to it – Harry
and Phillipa arranged ambush together – second murder is
Letitia – ~~(Mitzi very ill?) Poisoning~~ – Mitzi suspected –
persecuted Polish Girl – sulky – persecution complex – then
she nearly dies – Does Leticia make new will?

In an undated note to Collins, Christie draws attention to
the galley proofs with the *correct* spellings of 'Lotty' and
'enquiries', reminding them of the importance of ensuring

that they are printed *incorrectly* sometimes – 'Plot depends on this'. There is just a single reference to this in Notebook 30:

> Idea
> inquire enquire – both in same letter (part of it forgery)

When she incorporated this into *A Murder is Announced* we can see how she used it more subtly. By including the different spellings, on almost consecutive pages in Chapter 18, in documents supposedly written by the same character, she defies her readers to spot the anomaly and, thereby, a major indication of the killer's identity. It remains one of her most daring clues.

Although notes for *A Murder is Announced* are sparse, we are fortunate to have an early typewritten draft – one of the few known to exist – with copious handwritten notes. One toys with the name of the village – 'Chipping Burton? Chipping Wentworth?' – instead of the original Chipping Barnet; and the names of the Inspector – 'Cary? Craddock?' – instead of the original Hudson, and of the victim – 'Wiener?' – instead of the original Rene Duchamps. The original wording of the advertisement was also amended from 'A Murder has been arranged and will take place on Friday Oct. 13th at Little Paddocks at 6.p.m. Friends please accept this, the only intimation.' Also, the title on this draft is the slightly more cumbersome *A Murder has been Arranged*. Puzzlingly, the name 'Laetitia' appears throughout and every example has been amended, by hand, to plain, and accurate, 'Miss (Blacklock)', leading to the assumption that this switch was a late inspiration despite its appearance in the notes – 'Sister "Charlotte" is really her' – as above.

The only jarring note in this otherwise near-perfect detective novel is the unlikely denouement in the kitchen of Little Paddocks when Miss Marple displays a hitherto unknown gift for ventriloquism. A feature common to almost all of the Marple titles is a dramatic closing chapter. Like

*A Murder is Announced, The Body in the Library, The Moving Finger, They Do It with Mirrors, 4.50 from Paddington, A Caribbean Mystery, At Bertram's Hotel, Nemesis* and *Sleeping Murder* all culminate in a scene where the killer incriminates him or herself, usually in a misguided attempt at another murder. In most cases this is because Miss Marple's solution is usually short on verification and largely dependent on her intuition, which, however unerring, is not the same as legal proof. Ironically, in *A Murder is Announced*, above all her other cases, proof is abundant with numerous clues to complement Miss Marple's gifted insight. As Robert Barnard has pointed out in his masterly study of Dame Agatha, *A Talent to Deceive*, Miss Marple's reputation as a Great Detective is not improved by her emergence from a broom cupboard at the climax of the novel. This short two-page scene could have been easily amended to omit this embarrassment.

Apart from its superlative detective plot *A Murder is Announced* is also a convincing picture of an England stumbling out of post-war austerity. We are no longer in the world of butlers and cocktail receptions; there is no dressing for dinner or questioning the lady's-maid; no weekend guests or alibis provided by nights at the opera. The shadow of rationing and bartering, deserters and foreign 'help', ration books and identity cards hovers over the book. In fact, some of the clues come from that very milieu: the seemingly extravagant use of the central heating, the note with the incriminating spelling, the ease of access to houses to assist bartering. Chapter 10 iii also includes a telling conversation between Miss Marple and Inspector Craddock on the changing of the old order: 'Fifteen years ago one knew who everybody was . . . But it's not like that anymore . . . nobody knows anymore who anybody is.' And this, with customary Christie ingenuity, is also subsumed into the plot.

Another aspect of this novel that merits attention is the understated presence of the lesbian couple, Miss Hinchcliffe and Miss Murgatroyd. Heretofore, the few examples of gay characters scattered through the novels have been either figures of fun (Mr Pye in *The Moving Finger* or Mr Ellsworthy in *Murder is Easy*) or menace (Lord Edgware's Greek-godlike butler or, some years later, Alec in *The Rats*). The picture of the Chipping Cleghorn couple is matter of fact and, as far as the villagers are concerned, unremarkable; and after the murder of Murgatroyd, moving. This is a distinct improvement on the representation of Christopher Wren in *Three Blind Mice,* three years earlier. He is one of her campest creations and is described in the original script as having a 'pansy voice'; and he is not toned down in *The Mousetrap,* two years after *A Murder is Announced,* where he remarks on the attractiveness of policemen (Act I, Scene ii). Shortly after the appearance of *A Murder is Announced,* when Christie was planning *Mrs McGinty's Dead,* she considered the inclusion of '2 young men who live together'.

## They Came to Baghdad
### 5 March 1951

---◄○►---

After losing her job and falling for a young man she meets in a London park, Victoria Jones travels to Baghdad, where she becomes involved, not entirely unwillingly, in murder, mystery and international intrigue.

---◄○►---

'It is difficult to believe that Mrs Christie regards this as more than a joke.' This was the verdict from the first person at Collins to read *They Came to Baghdad.* Phrases such as 'far-fetched and puerile . . . not worthy of Mrs Christie . . . wildly improbable' pepper the report, but it goes on to admit that 'it is eminently readable' and that 'its sheer vitality and humour and the delightful . . . Victoria Jones carry it through.' It should be remembered that this book followed *Crooked House* and *A Murder is Announced*, both first-class Christie detective novels. *They Came to Baghdad*, the first foreign adventure story since *The Man in the Brown Suit* a quarter of a century earlier, was obviously a shock.

The manuscript was received by Collins in late July or early August 1950 and published the following March with a serialisation in *John Bull* in January. Edmund Cork wrote to Christie on 21 August asking for clarification, for the Collins reader, of two small points: why does Carmichael use the name 'Lucifer' instead of 'Edward', when he is dying in Chapter 13; and a question about the scar on Grete Harden's lip early in Chapter 23 resulted in the insertion of the sentence beginning 'Some blotchily applied make-up . . .' In the USA, a radio and TV version were broadcast in September 1951 and on 12 May 1952 respectively. For such an atypical Christie title it is surprising that it should have been adapted so quickly for other media.

The notes for this novel are contained in three Notebooks – 31, 49 and 56, which has 95 pages, the opening page of which reads:

The House in Baghdad
A. A 'Robinson' approach. Disgruntled young man – turned down – by girl – light hearted
B. T and T
C. Woman about to commit suicide in Baghdad
D. Smell of fear

As can be seen, the working title of the book was *The House in Baghdad* and the planning of it, to judge from a letter dated 3 October of that year, went back as far as October 1947. The 'Robinson' reference is puzzling but the first notes otherwise reflect the basic set-up. The biggest surprise in this list is the inclusion of Tommy and Tuppence, who also feature in the more detailed notes later in the same Notebook, as all of their published adventures (both in novel and short story form) are firmly British based. Idea C is clearly the forerunner of *Destination Unknown*, which was to follow three years later, and throughout the notes for *They Came to Baghdad*, the name Olive, the main protagonist of *Destination Unknown*, appears frequently, together with some of the plot of the later novel. The phrase 'smell of fear' appears like a motif throughout the notes, where it occurs 17 times, and it appears in the novel in Chapter 6.

Notebook 31 continues the Tommy and Tuppence idea:

Baghdad Mystery May 24th
T and T – went into Consulate – didn't come out
Points
At Consulate – Kuwait chest – Tup. looks inside – nothing – but something showing that gunman had been there. He hid in the chest?
Sir Rupert Stein – great traveller – was to meet S. He came from Kashmir – found dead in Baghdad later – really kidnapped before?
They went to Baghdad
Beginning in Basrah – the hunted man – into the Consulate – the man through – up the stairs – meets man coming down – through door to bedroom.
Miss Gilda Martin – attention paid to her – goes to the Zia hotel – she has a little red book.
Archaeologists – including Mrs. Oliver and her brother – latter is learned gentleman horrified by her inaccurate Professor Dorman. A question of poison arises – Mrs O. tries to get it – finally does get it – then it disappears – she is very upset.

The 'May 24th' reference, less definite than might at first seem, is most likely 1949. If Christie was correcting the text in September 1950, after the manuscript had been considered by Collins, it is unlikely that the rough notes for the novel had been first sketched a mere three months earlier. And a page of Notebook 56 is dated unequivocally 'Oct. 1949'. At this point Tommy and Tuppence are still under consideration and there are certainly some similarities between Victoria and Tuppence: resourcefulness, courage, determination and a sense of humour.

There is a definite foreshadowing of Sir Stafford Nye from *Passenger to Frankfurt* in the sketch of Sir Rupert Stein and, indeed, in the eventual Sir Rupert Crofton Lee in the novel. Both characters, each with an international reputation, make their appearance in airports and both favour the dramatic look by wearing long cloaks with hoods. Sir Stafford survives his airport adventure but Sir Rupert is not so lucky.

Another surprise is the inclusion of Mrs Oliver and her hitherto unknown brother. This could have been an entertaining pairing, affording Christie an opportunity to vent her spleen on some of the nit-picking observations of critics and readers. The 'question of poison' would suggest a more traditional whodunit rather than a spy adventure.

The 'Kuwait chest' has echoes of the earlier Poirot short story 'The Mystery of the Baghdad Chest' and its later and more elaborate form 'The Mystery of the Spanish Chest', and *The Rats*, the one-act play from *Rule of Three*. In each case a body is discovered in such a chest. Gilda Martin may have been an early version of Victoria.

To judge from the amount of notes (over 100 pages, more than for any other title) and the amount of repetition in those notes, this book gave more trouble than other, more densely plotted whodunits. Again and again in Notebook 56 the opening chapters are sketched, each time with only minor differences. Uniquely these are not alternatives but repetitions of just one scene, which remains substantially the same throughout, as the examples below illustrate. Victoria Jones does not appear until 50 pages into the planning, at which point Olive is put aside until *Destination Unknown*.

The following nine examples are some of the notes for the opening of the book, all with only minor differences.

They Went to Baghdad
Quotation from girl's book – Western approach – Olivia in plane – Sir Rupert Crofton Lee – great traveller and orientalist – his traveller's cape and hood

Olive in the plane – behind Sir Rupert – his cape slips back – boil on neck – (perhaps he is flown on by RAF plane to Basrah)

Sketch (rough) – Olive arrives in Baghdad

Approaches
A. Olive – plane – Crofton Lee – boil
Tentatives
Olive arrives in Basrah – welcome by Mr. D – ordinary life – Sir Rupert – does not recognise her – supercilious she thinks

Start with A
Olive leaving England – Heathrow – Sir Rupert in plane – her thoughts – divorce – future – Baghdad – sensible – happy free life – uneasy feeling of something she doesn't want to remember – then sees back of Sir R's neck

Victoria Jones – a plain girl with an amusing mouth – can do imitations – is doing one of her boss – gets sack – finds young man – also sacked? Edward – ex-pilot – given me a job in an office

Parts settled – Victoria Jones in London and Edward

Vic. – Journey out – Sir Rupert – Cairo? Air hostess? – arrival in Baghdad

(A) Journey out – Victoria Mrs HC Sir R changes at Heliopolis – arrive Baghdad Aerodrome

Running alongside the Olive/Victoria approach was what Christie called the Eastern approach, the events leading up to the scene in the consulate that sets the plot in motion:

> Eastern approach – in the Market – Arabs – young man's feelings – goes to Souk. In Consulate's office waiting room – smell of fear – Richard knows it well – in war – looks around waiting room
>
> 2. Carmichael ~~Stewart~~ in Marshes – with Arabs – coming into civilisation
>
> B. Carmichael – with Arabs – bazaar – something wrong
>
> Approach B. Carmichael gets to Basrah – everything as planned – to South – passwords – all OK – to Consulate – fear – then along passage – upstairs – Richard watches him go – last time ever seen alive. Idea is for false Rupert to extract information from him
>
> Richard – off boat at Basrah – waiting room – smell of fear – ~~man stumbles puts in his pocket   What~~?
>
> Start
>
> A. Richard off boat – smell of fear – somehow or other something is passed to him (washing bag) – finds afterwards wonders what it is
> B. In from Marshes – something wrong – does he put half – Message in Kuwait chest – specially made secret drawer – has been a conjurer – goes up steps – vanishes

Notebook 56 speculates about bringing the various strands of the plot together, although Janet McCrae does not feature in the novel. The illustration below, from the same Notebook, is similar to that drawn by Dakin in the first chapter of the book and is also the idea behind the well-known Tom Adams Fontana paperback cover from the late 1960s.

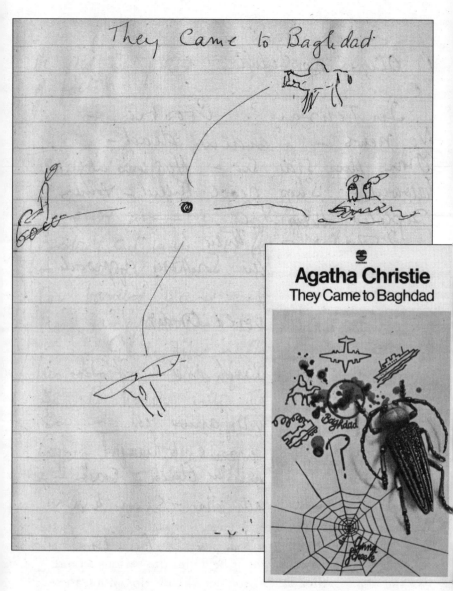

*At the end of Chapter 1 of* They Came to Baghdad *Dakin doodles*
*a sketch like this but the above is Christie's own interpretation of the title*
*from Notebook 56. The Tom Adams painting for the 1970's Fontana*
*paperback edition is a more elaborate and sinister version.*

4 people bringing four parts of the puzzle
Schute's [Scheele] evidence from America
Carmichael's from Persia(?) Kashgar(?)
Sir Rupert's from China
Janet McCrae's from the Bahamas

1. Olive in the plane – behind Sir Rupert – his cape slips
back – boil on neck (perhaps he is flown on by RAF plane to
Basrah)
2. Carmichael ~~Stewart~~ in Marshes – with Arabs – coming
into civilisation
3. Richard lands from ship – goes to Consulate – smell
of fear
4. Crooks? In train? At Alep – Damascus? Stamboul –
agents everywhere

Notebook 56 also considers the identity of the villain:

Is Crosbie real villain? Does he send Olive (or Vic) to Basrah
on his own account?
Can Edward be young (Nazi) villain – uses Victoria. V.
resembles Anne Schepp – that is why Edward picks her up

A. Does Edward (IT!) deliberately select Victoria
Or
B Edward and Victoria allies
If A, Victoria pairs with Richard? Deakin ?
If B, is villain Mrs Willard (plaster on arm?)

Overall, as the Collins reader rightly noted, the novel has
great pace and readability and, if not taken seriously or
examined in any detail, is an entertaining read. But it must
be asked why Edward, in Chapter 2, should draw attention
to 'something fishy' in the Baghdad set-up (thereby setting
the whole novel in motion) when he is the (very surprising)
villain of the piece. He could easily have invented another
reason to persuade Victoria to follow him. This very basic

flaw in the plot is, possibly, a reflection of the problems the book seems to have given in its creation. But as the Collins reader observed, the character of Victoria, as well as the depiction of life in Baghdad and on an archaeological dig, more than compensate.

### Mrs McGinty's Dead
### 3 March 1952

---

At the request of Superintendent Spence, Poirot agrees to reinvestigate the murder of charwoman Mrs McGinty, found battered to death two months earlier. Although James Bentley has been convicted of her murder, someone in Broadhinny is ready to kill again. And yet, they are all very nice people . . .

---

> *Mrs. McGinty's dead, how did she die?*
> *Down on one knee just like I*
> *Mrs. McGinty's dead, how did she die?*
> *Holding her hand out just like I*
> *Mrs. McGinty's dead, how did she die?*
> *Like THIS!*

Along with 'The Adventure of the Clapham Cook' in 1923, *Mrs McGinty's Dead* is one of Poirot's rare ventures into the working class. Continuing a pattern set two years earlier by *A Murder is Announced*, the novel is decidedly unglamorous, reflecting post-war social adjustment. The murder of a charwoman, appalling accommodation, an attempt on Poirot's life and a completely uncharismatic defendant all combine to make *Mrs McGinty's Dead* a particularly dark case.

There are more than 70 pages of notes with names, motives,

suspects, the earlier cases and the current possibilities all appearing in chaotic profusion. The permutations and combinations of the four vitally important early cases and their possible incarnations as current inhabitants of Broadhinny are almost limitless; and all of them are considered.

On the first page Christie sets out the premise of the novel, leaving only the name of the 'old friend' to be decided:

> Inspector ?[sic] old friend retiring worried about case just ending at the Old Bailey (or just ~~sentenced~~ sent for trial). Not right – evidence all there – motive – opportunity and clues – but all wrong – his duty to get the facts – sent them to Public Prosecutor – there his responsibility ended. He can't do any more . . . Can P do something?
>
> <u>Facts?</u>
>
> No facts. No-one else with motive – as a matter of fact, they're all very nice people

The cover of the first edition of *Mrs McGinty's Dead* was emblazoned 'Poirot is Back!' and he works alongside Superintendent Spence, his 'old friend' from their previous case, *Taken at the Flood*, four years earlier.

It would seem that the title was already decided, possibly because it is the name of a children's game, albeit not a very well known one. It is quoted and described in Chapter 1 but only the title is utilised and there is no attempt to follow the rest of the verse. This was the one unalterable fact around which Christie effortlessly wove these ideas, any one of which would have made an acceptable plot. And over thirty years after her first novel, her powers of invention show no signs of deserting her and she sketches at least seven possible scenarios. As can be seen, preliminary notes first emerged as early as 1947, five years before the book's appearance:

> Mrs McGinty's Dead
> Mrs M is charwoman – middle aged office cleaner –

because of something in wastepaper basket – she pieced
together letters? Had taken something home

Morphia in the morning tea –

Flats! Lawn Road – only super – Mrs M is one of the cleaners

1947

A. Mrs McGinty's Dead

Start Charwoman found dead in office – Lifted to sofa –
later discovered strangled

Someone goes to break news at her home – real Mrs M is
dead 6 months ago – this one is known to other cleaners
as her sister in law

Why?

Who?

A woman of 50–60 – Hands calloused – feet manicured –
good underclothes

Mrs McGinty's Dead

A. Mrs M is a charwoman. When investigated, it is found
that she has no past history – she bribed former woman
and took her place – her references were forged – 17
Norton St. Birmingham – an accommodation address.
What was she doing in Eleanor Lee's office . . . Evidence
for blackmail?

B. Mrs M is a char – 'does for' the Remington family – lives
in a little house by P.O. – takes a lodger – (James
McBride) her savings broken open – Or hit on head –
blood on James's clothes – he tries to burn them in
boiler.

C. Mrs M ~~elderly~~ middle-aged woman – lived with elderly
husband James McGinty. Found killed – JM tells very
peculiar story – (like Wallace) or is he nephew inherits
money. Really young man cultivates her acquaintance –
flatters her up – finally kills her in such a way J is bound
to be suspected – Why?

Ideas for HP (Mrs McGinty)
4 or 5 people in household – one dangerous – P's only clue
   – he is pushed at race meeting under horse's hoof or train
   etc. by one of them. Mrs McGinty – (housekeeper?) leaves
   – is sent away – why? Later he finds her – she is dead

'Wallace' in item C above is a reference to the infamous 1931 Liverpool murder case. Like Mrs McGinty, Julia Wallace was found in her own sitting room with fatal head injuries. Her husband, whose alibi could never be substantiated, was convicted of her murder, although subsequently released.

All of the clues that appear in the book feature in Notebook 43: the bottle of ink and the letter, the newspaper cutting with its all-important mistake, the coffee cup, the sugar-cutter and Maureen Summerhayes's very daring remark during the party:

Inkstain on the dead woman's finger. Bought bottle of ink that afternoon at PO – no letter found. Newspaper – Daily Newshound or Evening Paper

Sugar cutter – Judge and wife brought them back – Vicarage sale of work

Real clue Robin
E. Kane changed her name to Hope – Evelyn Hope – girl – but not girl – boy. Robin's 'mother' is not his mother – he got her name by deed poll – she was paid to give her name to him – later he kills her – does not want her to tell about past story

Robin's method for second murder – has coffee cup with dregs and lipstick

The slip in paper – child not yet born – therefore sex not – known

Don't like being adopted, do you? (A remark by Maureen Summerhayes at party)

And then the suspects . . .

Now consider each likely household

1. Married couple in late thirties – very vague – like R and A [Rosalind and Anthony, Christie's daughter and son-in-law] – do market gardening – (he is son – or she is daughter of X) [possibly the Summerhayeses]

2. Invalid woman with son – son is artist – or does painted furniture or a writer – (detective stories?) [Mrs Upward and Robin]

3. Vaughans – unstable husband (banker or solicitor) quiet self-effacing wife – children? – one (son) hers by former marriage?

4. ~~Rich woman  wife very flashy~~ – 2 young men – live together – (one is son of X) has told stupid rich girl he is son of Russian Grand Duke

Details of the previous cases differ slightly between Notebook and novel:

Edith Kane [Eva Kane/Evelyn Hope]

Went out that day – he poisoned Wife – a lot of gup in paper – all about that innocent child – betrayed – she and her child – the child born later – a daughter – the little daughter who never knew her father's name. The new life for Edith Kane – went to Australia – or S. Africa – a new life in a new world.

   She went – yes – but she came back 25 years ago

Janice Remington – acquitted of killing her husband or her
   lover like Madeleine Smith [Janice Courtland]

Little Lily Waterbrook – took chopper to aunt – detained
  – only fifteen – released later – Harris? [Lily Gamboll]

Greenwood Case – daughter – changed name – her evidence
  saved father – thirtyish

Newspaper suspects – Age now
55  Eva Kane (? changed name to Hope – went abroad
  – had s[on] or d[aughter]
45  Janice Crale – or The Tragic Wife – husband died of
  morphia – or bath – lover did it – unpleasant man –
  perverse – took drugs [Janice Courtland]
30  Lily Gamboll – killed aunt

The reference to 'Madeleine Smith' is to the woman tried
for poisoning her lover Emile L'Engelier in Glasgow in 1857.
The verdict was 'Not Proven'; in reality, an acquittal. Like the
Wallace case above, it is still the focus of keen speculation.

Appearing together on just one page of Notebook 43, the
following would have been added when the plot was well
advanced. All these occur in Chapters 13 and 14:

Points to be worked in
A. Mrs Upward sees photo – familiar
B. Mrs Rendell came down to see Mrs Upward that night
  – couldn't make her hear
C. Maureen talks about being adopted
D. Mrs O sums up Maureen's age and appearance
E. Mrs Rendell asks P about anonymous letters – untrue
F. Poirot told by Mrs O – it was Dr Rendell

In particular, Point C is the main clue that incriminates the
killer – although few readers will notice it, so subtly is it inserted. And Point A sets up the second murder in Broad hinny
as Mrs Upward plays a very dangerous game with Poirot.

### They Do It with Mirrors
17 November 1952

—◄○►—

Miss Marple goes to Stonygates, the reform
home for young delinquents run by the husband
of her childhood friend Carrie Louise. Although
the atmosphere is tense, when murder is committed
the victim is totally unexpected. More deaths
follow before Miss Marple penetrates the
murderer's conjuring trick.

—◄○►—

*They Do It with Mirrors* was serialised six months before book
publication in both the UK and the USA and was Christie's
second title of 1952, following a few months after *Mrs McGinty's
Dead*. Leaving aside the unlikely background – a reform home
for juvenile delinquents – the underlying conjuring trick is
clever although the subsequent killings are, like similar deaths
in later novels of the 1950s – *4.50 from Paddington*, *Ordeal by
Innocence* – unconvincing and read suspiciously like padding.
The misdirection involving Carrie Louise's tonic is similar to
that in *After the Funeral* the following year. Having successfully
deceived her readers for over thirty years, Agatha Christie
could still devise new and infuriatingly simple tricks and her
presentation of clues remained as devious and daring as ever:
the description of Lewis Serrocold opening the door of the
locked study after the quarrel.

Most of the notes, almost thirty pages, are contained in
Notebook 17, with brief references to the main plot device in
another seven. The central idea, the fake quarrel, was one that
Christie nursed for a long time before finally incorporating it
into a book. Over the years she considered numerous variations and settings and the plotting was entangled, at different
times, with both *Taken at the Flood* and *A Pocket Full of Rye*.

Jan 1935
A and B alibi A has attempted to murder B – really they
both murdered C

Ideas for G.K.C.
Alibi by attempted murder. A tries murder B and fails
(Really A and B murder C or C and D)

They do it with Mirrors
Combine with Third Floor Flat – fortune telling woman
dead, discovered by getting into wrong flat

Plans Nov. 1948 Cont.
Mirrors
Approach – Miss M. on jury – NAAFI girl[58] – Japp or equal
unhappy about case – goes to Poirot. The fight between
two men – (maisonette) – one clatters down – goes up
again in service lift and through door – shouts for help –
badly wounded – thereby they prove an alibi

Mirrors
Basic necessity – two enemies who give each other alibi.
Brothers – Cain and Abel

A split B's head open once – A bad tempered cheerful ne'er
do well; B Cautious stay at home

Mirrors
The antagonism between two people providing the alibi for
one. Sound of quarrel overheard – struggle and chairs –
finally he comes out – calls for doctor

---

58  Navy, Army and Air Force Institute, founded in 1921 to run
    recreational establishments needed by the armed forces, and to
    sell goods to servicemen and their families.

Mirrors

The trick – P and L fake quarrel – overheard below (actually
P. does it above) L. returns and stuns him – calls for help

The 'fake quarrel' trick extends back as far as Christie's first
book, *The Mysterious Affair at Styles*, where Alfred Inglethorp
and Evelyn Howard feign an argument in order to allay
suspicion. *Death on the Nile* and *Endless Night* also feature
this deception. In *They Do It with Mirrors* the trick depends,
like that of a conjuror, on the misdirection of an audience's
attention while the murder is actually committed elsewhere.
As can be seen in the first example above, this 1935 note may
well have inspired *Death on the Nile* two years later; and the
'G.K.C.' note was for a 1935 anthology *A Century of Detective
Stories*, edited by G.K. Chesterton. The reference to 'Third
Floor Flat' is to the 1929 Poirot short story; its possible
combination with the 'mirrors' idea is echoed again in
the example following, with the mention of the service lift.
This dated extract is from Notebook 14, directly after the
main notes for 1949's *Crooked House*. The 'Cain and Abel'
note is from the early 1950s; it appears a few pages before
the rough notes for the adaptation of *The Hollow* as a play.
The final example shows the connection with *A Pocket
Full of Rye*, with the initials of Percival and Lancelot from that
novel.

Notebook 63 confirms that Christie considered the title a
promising one and shows an elaboration of the idea as she
experiments with various combinations of male/female and
A/B. The reference to 1941's *Evil under the Sun* shows that
this version postdates 1937's *Death on the Nile*.

They Do it with Mirrors (Good title?)

Combine with AB alibi idea – A and B, apparently on bad
terms, quarrel

(a) Man and Woman (?) Jealousy? He pays attention to

someone else? or she does? or married couple? (too like Evil under Sun)

(b) Two men or two women quarrelled about a man (or woman) according to sex

Result – clever timing – B phones police or is heard by people in flat or being attacked by A (A is really killing C at that moment!). C's death must be synchronised beyond any possible doubt.

A stabbed by B – then B goes off to kill X – A does double act of quarrel – ending with great shout – 'he's stabbed me.'

A has alibi (given by the attacked B) – B has alibi (given by injury and A's confession) – [therefore] suspicion is narrowed to D E or F

Then she tries out completely different plots, while retaining the promising title. The first one has echoes – sisters masquerading as 'woman and maid' – of the 1942 Miss Marple story, 'The Case of the Perfect Maid', and the second is somewhat similar to the Poirot case *Mrs McGinty's Dead*. The third is a resumé of 'Triangle at Rhodes', with the addition of a quarrel and the substitution of Miss Marple for Poirot; and the final one is an original, and confusing, undeveloped scenario:

They do it with Mirrors

Idea?
Adv[ertisement] for identical twins. Really put in by twins – crooks who are not identical. Woman and maid (really sisters). The maid gives alibi etc. and talks for the first one

Mirrors

Starting Inspector (?) The Moving Finger or one of the others. Calls on Miss M – retiring – his last case – doesn't like it – puts it to her – evidence to the P[ublic] P[rosecutor] overwhelming but he isn't satisfied

Could Mirrors be triangle idea
Valerie – rich, immoral, man mad
~~Michael~~ Peter – Air ace – married to her
Marjorie – brown mouse
Douglas – her husband – rather anxious – keen on Valerie
Miss Marple
V[alerie] poisoned – it was meant for P[eter]. Could there be quarrel overheard – M and D really M and P (pretending to be D)

Mirrors
Randal and ~~Nicholas~~ Harvey Derek – brothers – violent quarrel – over woman? N marries Gwynneth. Old lady killed by H and R during time when R is attacking H or by R and G

In Notebook 17 Christie arrives at the plan that she eventually adopted. She drafts the set-up twice in three pages and then proceeds to a list of characters remarkably close to that of the finished work:

Mrs. Gordon, old friend of Miss Marple at Ritz – asks her to come. Same age but Mrs. Gordon all dolled up etc. – vague curious woman. Worried about Loulou – married that man – all efficiency and eye glasses. Fuss over young man who attacked him – said he was his father – had previously said to several people that Churchill was his father.

Mirrors

Miss M summoned by rich friend (at school together in Italy? France?). 2 sisters – both married a good deal Mrs. B

and Mrs. E. Former vague but shrewd – knows how to
manage men – with Louie, Mrs. E. men know how to
manage her. She is committed to this cultural scheme – by
first husband. 2nd selfish artist. She has various children by
first husband; by second – selfish pansy young man [and] by
third. E. is hard headed character, accountant. A big trust
(by D) – E. is one of principal trustees – others being old
lawyer – old Cabinet Minister – later dead lawyer replaced
by son – C[abinet] M[inister] replaced by Dr's son, young
man – has come to college – taken and accepted by E.

People in Mirrors

Carrie Louise – friend of Gulbrandsen
Lewis Serrocold
Emma Westingham [Mildred Strete] – daughter – plain –
married Canon W. now a widow come home)
Gina – daughter of Gulbrandsen's adopted daughter, Joy,
who married unsatisfactory Italian Count, name of San
Severiano – daughter back to Gulbrandsen
Walter – her young American husband – good war record –
but obscure origin
Edgar – a psychiatric 'case' young research worker? Or
secretary? a bastard and a little insane
Dr. Maverick – Resident physician under Sir Willoughby
Goddard leading psychiatrist
Jeremy Faber [Stephen Restarick] – Stepson of Carrie
Louise by second husband 'bad Larry Faber', a scenic
designer in love with Gina
'Jolly' Bellamy [Bellever] – a Carlo [Carlo Fisher, Christie's
devoted secretary and friend], devoted to Carrie Louise –
or is she?
Christian Gulbrandsen

The arrival of Miss Marple and her introduction to the
inhabitants of Stonygates is sketched in Notebook 17:

Miss M arrives – met at station by Edgar – introduces himself – his statement – Winston [Churchill] is his father – C[arrie] L[ouise] – charming greeting. They see Gina out of window – with handsome dark man. 'What a handsome couple' says Miss M – C-L looks disturbed – not her husband – Mike – gives acting classes to boys – gets up plays etc.

Telegram from Christian

Mike or Wally to Miss M about Edgar being Montgomery's son. Talk about Edgar – illegitimate of course – served a short prison sentence

Earlier in the same Notebook, and while Lance and Percival were still possible characters in *They Do It with Mirrors*, she sketched the following scenes, remarkable for their similarity to the all-important scene in the published version:

Procedure
P. asks Renee to come into room – study – they start quarrelling – not married etc. Conversation continues – her voice high and clear, he goes out by window, kills father and comes back. She stabs him – shoots him etc.
Or
Same with two brothers – violent quarrel. P's voice heard first, then L's – L's continues – then P. knocked out. 'Oh God, I think I've killed him'

In Notebook 43 Christie outlines the events of Chapter 7 iii with only minor differences – in the published version Dr Maverick leaves before the quarrel and returns after the shooting; and it is Miss Bellever who discovers the body.

After dinner, Gulbrandsen goes to his room – 'I have some typing to do.' Lewis takes medicine away from Louise – powder – calc. Aspirin – for arthritis – moment of strain. Tel[ephone] – Jolly goes – 'Alexis has arrived at station

– can we send a car.' Lewis goes to his room – Edgar comes
through window – 'My father' – makes scene. Goes into
Lewis's room – shuts door behind him, locks it – voices
raised. Ought to break down door – Carrie Louise very calm
'Oh, no dear, Edgar would never harm Lewis.'

Maverick says very important not to apply force – Maverick
goes. Jolly rather violent about it – leaves hall. Then – 'You
didn't know I had a revolver' – presently sound of shot –
somebody screams – no, not here – it's outside – far away.
Edgar shouting – things falling over. Then, shot inside room
– Edgar calling out – 'I didn't mean it, I didn't mean to.'
'Open this door' – Edgar unbolts it – Lewis ~~shot~~ not shot –
missed, two holes in parapet. Then Edgar breaks down.
Lewis asks Stephen to fetch Gulbrandsen or ask him for
some figures. They go – Gulbrandsen shot. Then Alexis
walks in.

A page of Notebook 43 is headed with a straightforward
question. The possibilities are then considered, with those
characters ostensibly in the clear and those still under
suspicion listed separately. But as we – and the police –
discover, things are not always as they seem:

Who could have shot Christian Gulbrandsen

Miss Bellever
Alexis
Gina
Stephen
Clear    Gina and Stephen – off
Lewis
Edgar
Dr. Maverick
Carrie Louise
Miss Marple

And the clue of the typewriter letter is drafted later on the same page:

> Bottom bit left in typewriter – or just left
>
> Dear David
> You are my oldest friend. Beg you will come here to advise us on a very grave situation that has arisen. The person to be considered and shielded is father's wife Carrie-Louise. Briefly I have reason to believe . . .

As usual, Christie sketched some undeveloped ideas. In the extract below, E is Lewis Serrocold, but none of this sketch is used, apart from the clever adaptation of the well-known phrase, 'Abandon hope all ye that enter here.' Note also the possibility of using Abney, her sister's home, as a setting; which she does six months later in *After the Funeral*.

> Scene Abney
> E's a fanatic about delinquent children – they take them
>
> 'Recover hope all ye that enter here' [Chapter 5]
>
> Secret training school for thieves and embezzlers. Director E. – under David clever master with forged credentials
>
> C. Gulbrandsen finds out about it and goes to police – then says he made a mistake. Then shot. Police suggest young man Walters – a bit balmy – someone tells him E is his father – incites him to attack him – so as to help as cover – they do it with mirrors

## *After the Funeral*
### 18 May 1953

───────────◄○►───────────

At the family reunion following the funeral of Richard
Abernethie, Cora Lansquenet makes an unguarded
remark about his death: 'But he was murdered, wasn't
he?' When she is savagely killed the following day
it would seem that her suspicions were justified.

───────────◄○►───────────

*After the Funeral* appeared in the USA, as *Funerals Are Fatal*,
two months before its UK publication and in both countries
book publication was preceded by an earlier serialisation.
*After the Funeral* is typical Christie territory – an extended
family in a large country house, and the death of a wealthy
patriarch with impecunious relatives hoping for an inheritance. That family is also her most complicated, resulting
in the inclusion of a family tree.

The dedication reads 'For James in memory of happy days
at Abney.' 'James' was Christie's brother-in-law James Watts,
the husband of her sister Madge. They lived in Abney, a vast
Victorian house built in the Gothic style, exactly as Enderby
Hall is described on the first page of the novel. It was to
Abney that Christie retired in 1926 to recover from the
trauma of her disappearance. The house is also mentioned
in the Author's Foreword to *The Adventure of the Christmas
Pudding*: 'Abney Hall had everything! The garden boasted a
waterfall, a stream and a tunnel under the drive!' In Chapter
23 of *After the Funeral* Rosamund has a conversation with
Poirot seated by such a waterfall in the garden.

There is a reference to *Lord Edgware Dies* in Chapter 12, and
the same chapter also contains two (coincidental) references,
in the space of four pages, to a *Destination Unknown* (the
following year's book). The distinctiveness and recognisability

of backs is discussed in Chapter 16 and this would also feature in *4.50 from Paddington*. And the attempted murder of Helen Abernethie, overheard down a phone line, in Chapter 20 has distinct similarities to the actual murder of Donald Ross 20 years earlier in *Lord Edgware Dies*, and to that of Patricia Lane in *Hickory Dickory Dock*, two years later.

The death of Cora is one of Christie's most brutal and bloody murders, rivalling those of Simeon Lee in *Hercule Poirot's Christmas* and Miss Sainsbury Seale in *One, Two, Buckle my Shoe*. But, unlike the murders in these novels, the reason for the savagery of the killing in *After the Funeral* is not justified by the plot and it is difficult to understand why this method was adopted by the killer or, indeed, by Christie. There is never any question about the identity of the corpse as there was in *One, Two, Buckle my Shoe* and there is no subterfuge about the time of death as there was in *Hercule Poirot's Christmas*.

*After the Funeral* also includes one of Christie's most daring examples of telling readers the truth and defying them to interpret it correctly. At the end of Chapter 3 we fondly imagine we are sharing the thoughts of Cora Lansquenet but, on closer examination, her name is never mentioned; the description of 'a lady in wispy mourning' applies equally well to her impersonator. Although the thoughts we share are perfectly believable as those of a sister in mourning, they are also capable of a more sinister interpretation when we later realise whose thoughts they actually are. This subterfuge is shared in an equally daring, and yet perfectly truthful, manner in Chapter 2 of *Sparkling Cyanide*.

All of the notes are in Notebook 53, where they alternate with those for *A Pocket Full of Rye*, published later the same year. Along with the title, the basic plot appears on the first page of notes exactly as it does in the novel, with no crossings out or alternatives. The only point to change is that the 'somebody' who speculates about the murder of Richard is, in fact, 'Cora'.

Throughout the notes it would seem that the plotting of

this book went smoothly. Apart from one major deviation – the quick-change impersonation of housekeeper and house-holder – the notes accurately reflect the entire plot, proceeding chronologically and with very little deleting or revising or list-ing of alternatives. The concise encapsulation of the plot on the first page of Notebook 53 even includes the name of the artist of the concealed painting that provides the motive.

The underlying misdirection of *After the Funeral* also featured in the previous year's novel, *They Do It with Mirrors*.

> After the Funeral
> Family returning from cemetery – a meal – deceased's
> younger sister – not been seen for many years or at all by his
> grandchildren etc. – Cora Lansquenet – (Somebody says –
> of course – he was murdered) Cora L murdered the next
> day. Really the CL of funeral is not CL – CL is already dead
> [actually drugged]. Companion kills C – Why? Contents of
> house are left to her including a picture? A Vermeer – she
> paints it over with another

As usual, names were to change:

> Characters
> Cora Lansquenet – youngest ~~daughter~~ sister of old ~~Mrs~~ Mr
> Dent (like James). Married a rather feckless painter – lived
> abroad a lot
> Pam and husband (actor)
> Jean – Leo's widow (2nd wife?)
> Judy and Greg (photographer)
> Andrea – (Miles's wife) he doesn't come – too delicate
> George – (Laura's son) in City

A look at the family tree shows minor differences in the eventual make-up of the Abernethies. Leo's wife becomes Helen and the '2nd wife' idea was discarded; Andrea and Miles, the hypochondriac, become Maude and Timothy; Pam

Helen Leo's wife.
Timothy & Maude — Stansfield Grange —?
Yorkshire?

George Denman? Crosfield.
Michael Shane
Rosamond "
Gregory Banks ?
? Susan Banks.
? Elizabeth
? Jane

Cornelius Abernethie — Coralie Bassington

Richard—Elinor Wells  Timothy m Maude Fox  Gordon m Paula Isdus  Laura m Henri Cro
Mortimer                                        Susan m Gregory  George
(d.)                                            Banks.

Geraldine m Antony Cassns        Cora m Pierre Lansquant

Rosamund m Michael Shane

Lytchett St Mary.

*The family tree (with a few question marks) of the Abernethies from* After
the Funeral, *one of the most complicated families in all of Christie.*

becomes Rosamund with an actor husband, Michael Shane; and Judy becomes Susan, while Greg has a change of profession to chemist's assistant. Although the comment 'like James' (Christie's brother-in-law) appears after Mr Dent (the forerunner of Richard Abernethie), there is nothing to show that the character was, in fact, anything like James Watts.

It is not until some pages into the notes that Poirot is mentioned, although in the novel it is Mr Entwhistle, the family lawyer, who actually brings him into the case:

> HP is got into case by doctor attending old Larraby – exhumation requested – cannot see how it can be anything but a natural death – only, of course, it <u>could</u> be an alkaloid etc

Christie again employs her alphabetical sequence but this time there is little rearranging. The main reordering, as it appears in the book, is the poisoning of Miss Gilchrist *before* she gets to Timothy's rather than afterwards. In fact, it is partly because of the poisoning that she agrees to go to Timothy's.

A. Mr E gets telephone call from Maude – agrees to go up [Chapter 5]

B. Before goes up – calls on George – Tony and Rosemary [Michael and Rosamund] [Chapter 5]

C. Visits Timothy and Maude [Chapter 6]

D. HP and Ent[whistle] Whole thing rests on E's belief in Cora's hunches – she thought it was murder – she had some basis for thinking it so she was quite willing to hush it up – therefore – murder [Chapter 7]

E. Susan finds a wig in Cora's drawer [Chapter 11]

F. Susan arranges for Miss G to go to Tim's [Chapter 10]

G. HP receives reports [Chapter 12]

H. HP goes to Enderby – meets Andrea [actually Helen] – her story of something wrong – (Point here is was looking at Cora) – HP represents himself to be taking a house for foreign refugees – Andrea [Maude] speaks of paint smell upsetting Timothy [Chapter 14]

I. At Timothy's Miss G gets into her stride – gossip with daily women – nun? Miss G very surprised – same nun she is almost certain who was at Cora's – ? Then wedding cake? To Miss G – she is delighted – taken ill – but not fatal [Chapter 15]

J. They all assemble at Enderby to choose anything from sale – some comedy? Miss G says something about wax flowers? Or something that she could not have seen [Chapter 19]

Points in conversation

A. Nuns – what they were like – same one – a moustache [Chapter 19]

B. R[osamund] asks about wax flowers on malachite table – Miss G says looked lovely there [Chapter 19]

C. Susan says Cora didn't really sketch Polperro – from a postcard [Chapter 18]

D. Talk about seeing yourself [Chapter 19]

One major sequence in Notebook 53 does not appear in the finished novel. Christie referred to it as the Hunter's Lodge idea:

> Idea like Hunter's Lodge? Housekeeper doubles with someone else made up glamorous

This is a reference to one of Poirot's early cases, 'The Mystery of Hunter's Lodge'. The plot device, which bears more than a passing resemblance to *After the Funeral,* depends on the ability of the murderer to effect a quick change and to appear both as housekeeper and householder within minutes of each other.

Although in Chapter 15 this idea is briefly considered, it is never a serious possibility as a solution. But the underlying subterfuge is very much the same: a domestic successfully masquerades as both mistress and maid, fooling the family and the police (and the reader) into believing someone alive when they have already been murdered. The impersonation in *After the Funeral* is played over a longer period and is more elaborate. And as the reader is told very early in the novel that Cora had lived abroad for over twenty-five years, the masquerade is perfectly feasible. Lanscombe the butler 'would hardly have known her'; Mr Entwhistle, the family lawyer, was 'able to see little resemblance to the gawky girl of earlier days'; and none of the younger generation of Abernethies knew her at all. At first it seems as if Christie toyed with the idea of the quick-change routine and in Chapter 15 there is an opportunity for this when Miss Gilchrist answers the door in response to a bell that nobody else hears and a caller that no one else sees. Pages 26–7 of the notes consider the ramifications of such a development. But this was subsequently subsumed into the nun motif and the impersonation took on a more leisurely aspect.

Does Helen, while with Jean, see woman who collects subscriptions – herself – and immediately after appear as herself – quick change owing to geography of house – such as appearing at front door and in Hall – just calling to ask you – one moment please – two voices. Helen hurries into room where Jean is upstairs – she is in morning room. Jean rings up police – then goes down – visitor is there
Or
Visitor coming in – J says will you wait – get my purse – goes to phone tells police – comes out finds Helen. H goes down to keep him in play – gone.
Appearance of all the people
Cora – blonde hair faded curls like a bird's nest – make up – big? plump? or a hennaed bang
Miss Earle [Gilchrist] – grey hair brushed back – Pince nez or iron-grey bob – very thin

The caller – blue grey hair well dressed – (transformation)
slight moustache – dark eyes (belladonna) deep voice – well
cut tweeds – large sensible feet. When Jean sees her –
difference in costume wig – coat and street shoes – all
removed – thrown in closet – overall and slippers – Gone!
What did she come for? Things have to be got rid of – taken
away in suitcase – left in train

Finally, most of Chapter 20 is sketched:

P goes to bed – feels something significant said – odd
business about Cora's painting – paint – Timothy – smell of
paint. Something else – something connected with
Entwhistle – something Entwhistle had said – significant –
and something else – a malachite table and on it wax
flowers only somebody had covered the malachite table
with paint. He sat up in bed. Wax flowers – he remembers
that Helen had arranged them that day. A rough plan –
Mr Entwhistle – the smell of paint – the wax flowers.

Although the necessary clues are here paraded for the reader,
how many will appreciate their significance?

Immediately following, the scene where Helen realises the
implication of what she noticed at the funeral is sketched,
although this is broken into two scenes in the book (Chapter
20 iii and iv):

Helen – in the room – to see ourselves – she looks – my right
eye goes up higher – no it's my left – she made an
experimental face – she put her head on one side and said it
was murder wasn't it? And with that it came back to her –
of course – that was what was wrong – excited – goes down
to telephone – (or in early morning) – Mr E – do you see –
she didn't – CONK

## A Pocket Full of Rye
9 November 1953

———————◄o►———————

Rex Fortescue is poisoned in his counting
house; his wife is poisoned during afternoon tea
of bread and honey; and the maid is strangled
while hanging out the clothes. A macabre
interpretation of the nursery rhyme brings
Miss Marple to Yewtree Lodge to investigate
the presence of blackbirds.

———————◄o►———————

*Sing a song of sixpence, a pocket full of rye,*
*Four and twenty blackbirds, baked in a pie,*
*When the pie was opened, the birds began to sing,*
*Was not that a dainty dish to set before the king?*

*The king was in his counting-house, counting out his money,*
*The queen was in the parlour, eating bread and honey,*
*The maid was in the garden, hanging out the clothes*
*When down came a blackbird and pecked off her nose.*

*A Pocket Full of Rye* first appeared in October 1953 as a *Daily
Express* serial. The official reader's report from Collins, dated
April 1953, described it as 'highly readable, exciting, baffling
and intelligent; it is plotted and handled with a skill that
makes most current detective fiction look like the work of
clumsy amateurs'. Although he considered the means of the
first murder too far-fetched, overall he rated it as a 'good'
Christie, a verdict which seems a little lukewarm after such
an effusive description.

The notes for the novel are contained in five Notebooks,
the bulk of them in Notebook 53, with shorter references in
the other four. The following cryptic reference in Notebook

56 gives the origins of the plot: the first story, 'The Tuesday Night Club' (1927), *The Thirteen Problems*:

General pattern like hundreds and thousands

A housemaid, at the behest of her married lover, sprinkles 'hundreds and thousands' (the coloured sugar confection used to decorate trifles), liberally doped with arsenic over a dessert in order to eliminate an inconvenient wife. As if to clinch the matter, the maid in both short story and novel is called Gladys.

As can be seen from the following note in Notebook 14, the plots of *A Pocket Full of Rye* and *They Do It with Mirrors* were intertwined in the early stages of plotting (this note would seem to date from the late 1940s as it appears with notes for *Crooked House*):

Mirrors
Percival and Lancelot brothers – P good boy – L bad lad
– violent antagonism between them – actually they get
together to put Father out of the way and his young wife?
The trick – P and L fake quarrel – overheard below (actually
P. does it above) L. returns and stuns him – calls for help

The faked quarrel became the main plot device of *They Do It with Mirrors* while the brothers Lancelot and Percival remained with *A Pocket Full of Rye*.

A few pages later Christie sketches a plot:

The King was in his Counting House
Pompous magnate dead in (a) Office (b) Suburban house
– Blackbirds Mine
Good son Percival – bad son Lance – deadly enemies (really
in cahoots?) Motive – swindle by one of the sons? Servant
(N.A.A.F.I. girl) in league with Lance – she could alter all
clocks. Girl takes father's coffee to study – comes out

screaming? Lance first to get to him (kills him then) others coming up. Old man drugged first – must have been at dinner (Lance not there). Girl suspected – could have doped him and stabbed him and put rye in man's pockets. They argue – she is found dead – with clothes pin

This is much nearer to the actual plot, although details were to change: there is no altering of clocks or stabbing in the finished novel and the brothers are not 'in cahoots'. Here also is the first mention of Blackbird Mines, the supposedly worthless mines which prove to be a source of uranium, thereby providing the killer's motivation. This aspect of the plot is very reminiscent of the swindle perpetrated on his partner by Simeon Lee, the victim in *Hercule Poirot's Christmas*. The reference to a 'N.A.A.F.I. girl' also appears in notes for *They Do it With Mirrors*.

But it is in Notebook 53 that we find most of the detailed plotting. Although this follows the pattern of the novel closely, we can see here that various other possibilities were considered before their eventual rejection. Both Percival and his wife, and Lance and Adele, were considered as the murderers; Lance might have been either a 'good boy' or a 'bad lot'; and Christie proposed the use of strychnine or arsenic as a poison rather than taxine:

Percival married to a girl (crook) abroad. She comes down to stay with other brother Lancelot – posing as his wife – she and Percival are the ones who do the murder

Lance in it with Adele – Adele is engaged to father – gets her to kill father – then arrives just in time to poison her tea

Lance is on plane returning from East. He is good son – his wife is Ruby Mackenzie

Good son Percival – bad son Lance – deadly enemies (really in cahoots?)

Strychnine and arsenic found later in cupboard in hall on top shelf or in dining room alcove in soup tureen on top shelf

After these speculations the plot begins to emerge. The material in the following extracts, all from Notebook 53, appears in the novel:

Lance (bad boy) is returning on plane – father has sent for him. Before he can get home father dies – [Perci]Val's wife is Ruby Mackenzie – Lance has got together with Marlene at holiday camp. Gives her powder to put in early morning tea – says it will make his father ill – he will be sent for – Marlene is in terrible state – Lance arrives home – in time to poison Adelaide – (in tea?) then adds it to honey

Chapter I
Tea during 11 – the newest typist makes it
Office – blond secretary – takes in the boss's tea
'Mr Fortescue is in conference – '
Scream – ill – blond rushes in – out – call for doctor –
    phone – Hospital

Tea – A[dele] eats honey off comb – son gives it to her in tea – dies. Or son poisons her by putting stuff in meal before he comes back officially – girl meets him outside

Maid in garden – clothes peg on nose. Miss M points out later you wouldn't go out and hang up clothes at that time? But you would meet young man

After death of girl Gladys – Miss M arrives in hall – sergeant baffled – Inspector remembers her – Miss M very positive

about girl Gladys – dead – must be stopped – nose and
clothes peg – human dignity

### *Personal Call*
### 31 May 1954

―――――――――◄○►―――――――――

When James Brent receives a phone call from his
former wife, Fay, he is mystified; Fay has been dead for
over a year. Further calls reveal a murderous history –
but whose? As the calls persist, he agrees to meet
this mysterious woman at a railway station . . .
with fatal consequences.

―――――――――◄○►―――――――――

*Personal Call*, like *Butter in a Lordly Dish*, was also a Detection
Club play. It was completed in Iraq and posted to Anthony
Gilbert, then the Club's secretary, on 19 April 1952, although
it was not broadcast, for reasons unknown, until two years
later. It was subsequently re-broadcast with a new cast in
November 1960. Inspector Narracott investigates and, as the
crime takes place in Devon, he may well be the same Inspector Narracott who investigated the Dartmoor-set *The Sittaford
Mystery*.

Notebook 53 contains seven pages of Notes and they
follow directly after the final notes for *After the Funeral*, also
drafted in 1952 for publication the following year. As with
*Butter in a Lordly Dish*, the title seems to have been settled
before the plotting began and, as if in confirmation, it also
appears at the start of the second batch of notes within the
Notebook. Although the earliest jottings contain the essence
of the finished version, Christie also toyed with no less than
six different scenarios, all of which were rejected, although
some of them were adapted for later titles. Thirty years into

her career this is Christie at full creative stretch, plotting a half-hour radio play.

At three points in the notes the idea of a phone call interrupting a cocktail party is mentioned; this starting point seems to have been fixed and over the course of seven pages she experiments with possible developments, before eventually returning to the one with which she began. And from these brief notes it is possible to discern that not only was she using a different plot but also a different type of story.

> [1] Janet is there and so is he but neither sent for the other – telephone rings. A dead body in the cupboard – Janet identifies body as husband.
>
> [2] They meet – each has had a call – neither sent them. Caretaker tells them story of the Personal Call – I went up to him – he took the receiver – and shot himself
>
> [3] Or – hotel room – it has been booked in their name
>
> [4] Grand Guignol type of story? Dead body in room girl screams. Neighbour explains – murder in this room some years ago – since then – haunted
>
> [5] Young man – lured away by girl – she is in danger. Regular Buchan Bulldog Drummond type of story – really she is in with a gang of crooks – like Stympahalean Birds? or Edward Robinson? Commoner setting – such as Rajah's Emerald – young man – girl bickering – he has adventure
>
> [6] Personal Call in the middle of cocktail party – Husband? Wife? Girl blackmailed – tells her friend Rosamund – Nonsense, I'll go with you or instead of you.

Ideas 1- 3 are all sketched on the same page of Notebook 53 and show Christie's fertility of plot on the basis of just two words. Each contains the germ of what was to become *The Rats*, the first of the *Rule of Three* plays (qv): an adulterous couple each receive a phone call summoning them to a flat where the dead body of the woman's husband is concealed. Here, as in the finished stage script ten years later, a will-they-get-away-with-it plot is indicated. Nothing similar to the caretaker's story appears anywhere in Christie.

Idea 4, from later in the same Notebook, has a slight foreshadowing of what was to become, a decade later, *The Clocks* – 'Dead body in room girl screams' – but otherwise contains nothing subsequently used. A tale of the supernatural seems indicated from the mention of 'haunting'.

Idea 5 mentions three of her own short stories, 'The Stymphalean Birds' from *The Labours of Hercules* and 'The Manhood of Edward Robinson' and 'The Rajah's Emerald', both from *The Listerdale Mystery*, all of which feature a young man embroiled in a series of bewildering and potentially criminal events. Also mentioned are two other crime writers, John Buchan, creator of Richard Hannay, hero of, among other titles, *The 39 Steps* (1915); and Sapper (pen-name of H.C. McNeile), the creator of Bulldog Drummond, a long-forgotten action character. A tale of a strong silent type rescuing a fair maiden seems to have been the idea behind this sketch.

Idea 6 could have been the Christie version of 'the biter bit' with the no-nonsense Rosamund taking charge of her more reticent friend. This name is also that of one of the suspects of *After the Funeral*, written at the same time.

All of the above were rejected in favour of those below. Again the cocktail party is the starting point and the notes then outline the finished script closely. Although she used a railway station with which she was familiar, Newton Abbot in Devon, she explained in the accompanying letter to Anthony Gilbert that this setting was not absolutely necessary; in fact, the first notes name 'Marchington' station. A railway station allowed her to exploit fully the potential for sound effects: phone-calls, disembodied voices, public announcements and through-trains, all specified in the Notes.

Personal Call

Cocktail Party – noises of same – maid fetches James Brent

Hullo
Don't you know? It's Fay speaking. I want you to meet me
What do you mean – where are you
I'm at Marchington Junction
God
Wife – What's the matter?
Cruel practical joke – asks Exchange – no call put through
from Newton Abbot

A personal call to Mr James Brent
Can Mr ~~Abbot~~ Brent take a personal call from Newton
Abbot?
Playing Bridge – goes out. Wife says is going to listen on
phone.
Hullo
Hullo darling – it's Fay. I'm at Newton Abbot – that's where
you left me. I'm still there – waiting for you. Train noises
('Stopping train to Plymouth on No. 3 platform') That's the
boat train from Plymouth – it doesn't stop. You see, I wasn't
lying – you must come, I'll be expecting you on Tuesday 21st

Hullo – hullo – Can Mrs James Brent
This is Mrs Brent
Hullo
Who are you
I'm Fay Mortimer – I know who you are. Don't travel into
town by train – I'm warning you.
Is something going to happen

Newton Abbot – noise – 'Change for Plymouth and
Cornwall – Change for Plymouth and Cornwall'

## *Destination Unknown*
1 November 1954

―――――――――◀◉▶―――――――――

In order to solve the mystery of his disappearance,
Hilary Craven agrees to impersonate the dead wife
of scientist Thomas Betterton. She joins a mysterious
group aboard a plane bound for an unknown destination
and when it lands in the middle of nowhere she
needs all her courage and wits.

―――――――――◀◉▶―――――――――

The UK serialisation of *Destination Unknown* preceded book publication by two months, while US readers had to wait until 1955, when it was published as *So Many Steps to Death*. From this year onwards Christie produced only one title per year, but it must be remembered that the 1950s was her Golden Age of Theatre.

Following only four years after *They Came to Baghdad*, *Destination Unknown* is another adventure-cum-travel story, and an even more unlikely one. Like all Christie titles, even the weakest, it has a compelling premise, but one that is not credibly developed or resolved. The opening section dealing with the state of mind of Hilary Craven as she considers suicide could have been more profitably extended at the expense of some of the interminable travel sequences, which merely pad out the novel. Unlike other one-off heroines in earlier titles – Anne Beddingfeld in *The Man in the Brown Suit*, Victoria Jones in *They Came to Baghdad*, and, in a more domestic setting, Emily Trefusis in *The Sittaford Mystery* and Lady Frances Derwent in *Why Didn't They Ask Evans?* – Hilary is not looking for either adventure or a husband. It is the loss of her husband through divorce and the death of her child that causes her to agree to the challenging suggestion that she change her method of suicide from sleeping pills to a potentially fatal impersonation. *Destination Unknown* contains none of the light-hearted scenes of the earlier *They Came to Baghdad*, mainly due to the fact that Victoria and Hilary are totally different characters.

There are a mere dozen pages of notes, scattered over Notebooks 12, 53 and 56; and Notebook 12 has a page dated 'Morocco Cont[inued]. Feb 28th'.

The year is, in all likelihood, 1954. Collins were anxious as that year progressed and no book reached them. If Christie was still plotting it in February in the year of publication, this would indeed be a cause for alarm. This is somewhat reflected in Notebook 12, which has four scattered attempts to get to grips with the plot. The dated page goes on to discuss possible plot developments when Hilary has already arrived at her final destination, so it is safe to assume that most of the plotting was complete at that stage.

The notes for *Destination Unknown* are inextricably linked with those of *They Came to Baghdad* from three years earlier. Much of the sketching of *They Came to Baghdad* features a character named Hilary/Olive and it would seem that, to begin with, the ideas that were to be included in one novel eventually generated two. The earliest indication of this comes in Notebook 56, where four possible ideas for *The House in Baghdad* (an early title for *They Came to Baghdad*) were noted. As we have seen in the discussion of that novel, one of the four became the basis of *Destination Unknown*.

Notebook 12 contains notes mainly for the first half of the book although sketchy, most of the following ideas appear in the novel with only the usual name changes:

Morocco – Hospital – Olive dying says 'Warn him – Boris – Boris knows – a password – Elsinore?
Ou sont les neiges – The snows of yesteryear. The Snow Queen – Little Kay – Snow, Snow beautiful snow you slip on lump and over you go. [Chapter 4]
She is vetted by Dalton . . . The instructions – tickets etc.

She goes to hotel – her conversation with people. Miss
Hetherington – stylish spinster; Mrs. Ferber [Baker?] –
American [Chapter 5]
Hilary – goes to Marrakesh. Then to fly to Fez – small plane
– or plane to Tangier. Comes down – forced landing – petrol
poured over it – bodies
Fellow travellers
Young American – Andy Peters
Hilary
Olaf ~~Ericsson~~ [Torquil Ericsson]
Madame Depuis – elderly Frenchwoman
Carslake – business man – or could be German
Dr. Barnard [Dr Barron]
Mrs Bailer [Mrs Baker]
Nun [Helga Needham] [Chapter 8]

Morocco Cont. Feb 28th

The arrival
Start from a point or little later. Hilary is finishing toilet?
Dresses – her panic – no escape. 'That's not my wife' – sits
on bed – fertile brain thinking out plans – injure her face?
Story about wife – couldn't come? Dead? That journalist is
it Tom Betterton – the hostess comes for her – meeting with
Tom – 'Olive' [Chapter 11]

Notebook 53 contains the background that the reader learns
only at the end of the novel. Unlike her detective novels, the
reader is not given the information necessary to arrive at this
scenario independently. In these extracts Henslowe is the
Betterton of the novel and the American professor is Caspar
instead of the Mannheims of the novel. Confusingly, in the
book the real wife is Olive and Hilary is the impersonator,
but in the Notebook Olive appears as the impersonator.

Morocco
Henslowe – young chemist – protégé of Professor Caspar –

(a world famous Atom scientist – refugee to USA). H marries
C's daughter Eva Caspar – Eva dies a couple of years after
the marriage. Argument – Eva inherits her father's genius – is
a first-class physicist and makes a discovery in nuclear
fission. H. murders her and takes discovery as his.

The idea of a plastic surgeon altering fingerprints is an interesting but unexplored possibility:

This disappearance business is an agency run by an old
American – a kind of Gulbenkian[59] – he pays scientists good
sums to come to him – also plastic surgeons – who also
operate on finger prints. A suspicion gets about that
Henslowe is not Henslowe because he is not brilliant

And the devious Christie can be seen in the last note
('Because he is <u>not</u> Henslowe?'). The obvious explanation is
not the one she adopts: it is not that 'Henslowe' is really
someone else, but that he is not the scientist that he purports
to be, because his reputation was built on the genius of his
dead first wife:

Olive sees real wife dying in hospital – dying words –
enigmatic – but they mean something. Olive and Henslowe
meet – he recognises her as his wife – why? Because he is
<u>not</u> Henslowe?

Christie also toyed with a more domestic variation concerning the earlier murder that set most of the plot in motion:

Conman finds out about murder [of Elsa] and has a hold
over him

---

59  Calouste Gulbenkian, an Armenian businessman and
    philanthropist, founder of The Gulbenkian Foundation for
    charitable educational, artistic, and scientific purposes.

Communist Agent?
A woman?
Just an ordinary blackmailer?

Henslowe marries again
Deliberately a communist?
Just a devoted woman?

His disappearance and journey to Morocco is planned
deliberately by him. [Therefore] Olive when on his trail will
eventually discover that the dead body they come across
(actually the blackmailer) is a private murder by Henslowe
and all the Russian agents stuff is faked by Henslowe

After four very traditional whodunits in the previous two
years *Destination Unknown* is a disappointment. Despite a
promising opening the novel ambles along to a destination
that is more unbelievable than unknown, with little evidence
of the author's usual ingenuity. The denouement of *They
Came to Baghdad* unmasked an unexpected (if somewhat
illogical) villain but there are no surprises at the climax of
*Destination Unknown*. It is undoubtedly the weakest book of
the 1950s.

### Spider's Web
14 December 1954

---◄○►---

When she discovers a murdered body in her drawing
room shortly before her diplomat husband is due home
with an important politician, Clarissa devises a plan to
fool the police. She enlists the help of three houseguests,
unaware that the murderer is closer to home than
she could possibly think.

---◄○►---

There are twenty pages of notes for *Spider's Web*, all contained in Notebook 12. The character of Clarissa, created specifically for the actress Margaret Lockwood, is Christie's finest comic creation. The play itself is a comedy thriller with sufficient of both to make it a winning combination. It is also a successful blend of whodunit and will-they-get-away-with-it, with a surprise killer unmasked in the closing minutes, maintaining Christie's reputation for shock revelations. The will-they-get-away-with-it scenario was not a regular feature of Christie's output but it is also exploited in her next three plays: *The Unexpected Guest*, *Verdict* and *The Rats*.

The first page of notes is headed:

Act III Spiders Web  Laura Finds a Body?

Christie adopts her usual method of assigning letters to the various plot points that follow but, despite the heading, not all refer to Act III. Some of them, as marked, appear in Act II, Scene ii, leading to the suspicion that the acts were rearranged, possibly in the course of rehearsal. There are no surprises in the notes and no unexpected plot developments. With the exception of Sir Rowland Delahaye, who appears in the notes as Sir M, even the names remain the same.

### Points

A. Miss Peake is on spare room bed
B. Miss Peake appears – 'the body's disappeared' – she winks
C. Sir M says – 'never grown up' [Act I]
D. Inspector and Sir M – Latter puts forward idea of narcotics [Act II, Scene ii]
E. Inspector suggests he had actually found something in desk [Act II, Scene ii]
F. Clarissa (to Sir M) did one of you move it? No – all herded together in dining room

G. Cl. asks Sir M (or Hugo) name of antique dealers

H. The book – Sir M says 'What's the Inspector consulting
   – Who's Who' [Act II, Scene ii]

I. Sir M. says story about friend and stamps or envelope
   with autographs

J. Clarissa asks Elgin about references [Act II, Scene ii]

K. Pippa comes in – terrible yawns – hungry

L. Clarissa accuses Miss Peake of being Mrs. Brown

The main preoccupation for the scenes involving Pippa was
the presence or absence, in retrospect for obvious reasons, of
Jeremy. These scenes appear in Act I.

The Pippa bits

1. Recipe book candles, Can you eat it? Present (Sir M
   Jeremy? Clarissa?)

2. Priest's Hole – Place to put a body. Present Jeremy and ?
   ? ? [sic]

3. The autographs – Pippa shows them – puts them away in
   shell-box

4. Then bit about stamps – Present <u>not</u> Jeremy – others ad
   lib

Among Christie's papers is a suggested screen treatment,
dated 1956, for a possible film version of this play. It is not
entirely certain that it is by Christie herself but it looks 'unofficial', i.e. as if done by someone not directly involved in
the subsequent 1960 film. It sketches out the events that
have taken place prior to the start of the play: Clarissa meeting Henry, Miranda desperate for drugs, the subsequent
divorce and remarriage and Pippa's acceptance of Clarissa;
it also includes the sale of a stamped envelope to Mr
Sellon.

*Spider's Web* is full of ideas from earlier works:

✳ Miss Peake hides the body across the top of the spare-room bed under the bolster, as does the villain in 'The Man who was No. 16', the final story in *Partners in Crime.*

✳ The missing playing card is a plot device of 'The King of Clubs'.

✳ The idea of valuable stamps on an envelope appears in 'Strange Jest'.

✳ Pippa's creation of a wax doll is the same course of action as Linda Marshall followed in *Evil under the Sun.*

✳ Clarissa taking responsibility for the murder when it seems as if Pippa is responsible has echoes of Caroline Crale's actions on behalf of her sister, Angela, in *Five Little Pigs.*

✳ 'The Adventure of the Cheap Flat' also has the ploy of a property made available at a discount price to the right person.

✳ There is also yet another clever variation on a clue involving names (see *A Murder is Announced, Mrs McGinty's Dead* and *Peril at End House*).

✳ There are sly references to *Ten Little Nigger Boys* [sic] in Act II, Scene ii, and to a 'body in the library' in Act I.

### *Hickory Dickory Dock*
31 October 1955

A series of mysterious thefts in the student hostel run by Miss Lemon's sister in Hickory Road culminates in the death of one of the students. The incongruity of the objects stolen attracts the attention of Hercule Poirot, who visits the hostel – just before the first death.

> *Hickory Dickory Dock*
> *The mouse ran up the clock*
> *The clock struck one*
> *The mouse ran down*
> *Hickory Dickory Dock*

The notes for *Hickory Dickory Dock* are scattered over fifty pages of Notebook 12, with two brief and unsuccessful attempts to come to grips with it in Notebooks 31 and 35. Despite the rejection of these other ideas Christie did not give up on utilising the rhyme, although it supplies only the title and even that is tenuous. Apart from the address (which itself was changed from Gillespie Road) there is no attempt in the novel to follow the verse, although Poirot quotes briefly from it in the closing lines.

The following shows that the book had been largely finished early in the year prior to publication:

Suggestions to enlarge and improve Hic. Dic. Doc. May
1954

Some motifs from earlier novels recur. Mrs Nicoletis has a conversation with her unnamed killer much as Amy Murgat-royd did in *A Murder is Announced*; and Patricia Lane's telephone call to the police-station as the killer attacks her recalls Helen Abernethie's in *After the Funeral* and Donald Ross's in *Lord Edgware Dies*. And there is an unlikely relation-ship, akin to similar in *4.50 from Paddington* and *The Mirror Crack'd from Side to Side* revealed towards the end of the novel.

The incongruity of the stolen objects presents Poirot, and the reader, with an intriguing puzzle and the explanations are satisfying. But there are arguably too many characters and some of the foreign students are little more than stereotypes.

Each of the first five pages of notes for this book is headed

'Holiday Task', suggesting that it was written at a time when Christie should have been relaxing. It would seem that the plotting did not come easily, as endless permutations and much repetition is included. The first page of the notes has the glimmering of a plot, much of which remained, although there were to be many changes before she was happy with it. By the end of the first page a possible starting point, with echoes – 'one thing needed others camouflage' – of *The ABC Murders*, emerges:

> Things have disappeared – a rather stupid girl 'Cilly' (for Celia or Cecelia) – very enamoured of dour student – going in for psychiatry – he doesn't notice her. Valerie, a clever girl puts her up to stealing 'He'll notice you through silly things or rather – one really good thing'
>
> Stealing – things keep disappearing – really just one thing needed others camouflage

Some early ideas were, thankfully, not pursued . . .

> Hickory Dickory Dock
> Complex about the word Dock – a terror story – danger – girl in job – finds out something
>
> H.P. in train – girl gets him to go stealing
>
> Holiday Task (Cont.) 23 Gillespie Road
> Does Miss Lemon decide to go as Matron? Bored by retirement – asks Poirot's advice

. . . and some later ones that sounded more promising were also abandoned.

> ~~Hickory Dickory Dock~~
> First death at one o'clock – Second at 2 o'clock

Important – 2 murders
[First] happens quite soon after P's lecture

1. Mrs. Nicoletis? Why? Blackmails? One of the gang and slipping?
2. Johnston? – Her trained mind has made certain deduction – etc. – possibly finds after what's [the] matter – a warning hold your tongue –
3. Aka bombo?
4. Nigel?
5. Patricia

Although Christie toyed with the idea of other characters as the eventual villain, Valerie was always a front-runner, either alone or with various combinations of other students:

1. Valerie – Master mind of racket – uses students – puts C up to it – Nigel in it with her? Or blackmails her or later N. one of victims
2. Nigel – finds out about racket – or in it with Valerie – childish excitable

Basic to the plot is a bet about obtaining poison and some of the tactics suggested are, for the mid-1950s, horribly plausible. The 'doctor's car' idea was one that surfaced a few times throughout the Notebooks and the white coat used in the novel as camouflage (echoes of *Death in the Clouds*) to access a hospital drug cupboard is one obviously inspired by Christie's personal experiences in University College Hospital during the Second World War:

The 4 methods – a bet is made – Argument
Nigel
Valerie
Len
Angus

They bring back
D[angerous]D[rugs] from car – Tube of morphine
Hosp. Patient – Phenobarbitol
Poison cupboard – Strych. Or Digi?

Bicarbonate bottle taken to put powder in – and
bicarbonate substituted?

Then drugs destroyed but not one of them – the hospital
one?

By page 50 of Notebook 12 the plot is under control:

Main arguments

V. an organiser of smuggling into this country (jewels?)
(drugs?) by means of students. Mrs. N is in it – buys houses
for students – also a shop on corner nearby – where rucksacks
are sold – which have false bottoms (stones imbedded in
glue (or powdered heroin in rouleau [roll] of canvas).
Police are on V's track – she passes something to Nigel –
Bath salts – he examines this – finds heroin – replaces it
with bicarbonate – and puts stuff in his bicarbonate bottle.
Police come to house – V. destroys rucksack cuts it up –
afterwards works on Celia.

And a few pages later some refinements are considered,
although the saccharine and rucksack ideas and the involvement of Elizabeth Johnson are subsequently rejected:

Points to be resolved

Morphine (Acetate?) replaced by <u>boracic acid</u> – latter
shows green flame when burned (Recognised by <u>Celia</u>?)
[therefore] C. knows boracic was taken to replace
morphia.

Pat found morphia – took B.[oracic] A[cid] from bathroom.

Saccharine? Did C. use this in coffee? Morphia tablets exchanged for sacchar

Val. runs smuggling racket (Killed C?)

E[lizabeth] J[ohnson] in with Val on smuggling

Akibombo – saw – what? to do with boracic? – to do with rucksack?

Smuggling Gems? Dope? Mrs. Nic V's mother? Just figurehead?

Although Nigel's back-story – he was responsible for the death of his mother and his father has left a letter to this effect to be opened after his death – plays a vital part in the plot, it is not until approaching the end of the notes that it is sketched in:

Argument

N. bad lot – needs money – tries to get it from his mother – forges her name – or gives her sleeping draught – she dies – he inherits – inquest – overdose – accident. But father turns him out – he cashes in on his mother's money. (Goes through it?) Pals up with Valerie – in smuggling racquet – has by then taken another name – archaeological diplomat – friends with students etc. Police come – he thinks for him – father dead? – letter left with lawyer – takes out bulbs – (or are bulbs – new ones – stolen – and one taken out in hall)

Nigel gives mother poison (Money) – Father a chemist – tests it or finds it – turns Nigel out – signs a deposition – at bank in case of his death – or if Nigel does anything dishonourable – N. is to change his name

One of the 'Suggestions to enlarge and improve' the novel noted above is Patricia's murder:

> Nigel goes to police station . . . Pat (?) rings up – speaks to
> Nigel – breathless scared voice – Nigel – I think I know –
> who must have taken the morphia because I remember it
> was there that night . . . I don't want to say . . . Right . . .
> Nigel and Police go – Pat dead. Nigel cries like a small boy

Coming so late in the novel, however, this feels somewhat superfluous, an idea that enlarges rather than improves. In fact, a sketch of it had already appeared ten pages earlier:

> End sequence
> After Nigel and Pat scene Nigel goes round to Police Station.
> Pat (ostensibly) – really Valerie – rings up – knows who took
> it. They go there – Pat dead – Nigel's grief – real – H.P.
> arrives.

This murder is similar to the late murders in *4.50 from Paddington* and *Ordeal by Innocence,* in the following years. Mrs Oliver, in Chapter 8 of *Cards on the Table,* says: 'What really matters is plenty of bodies! If the thing's getting a little dull, some more blood cheers it up. Somebody is going to tell something – and then they're killed first. That always goes down well. It comes in all my books . . .' And in Chapter 17 of the same novel: 'when I count up I find I've only written thirty thousand words instead of sixty thousand, and so then I have to throw in another murder . . .' It is difficult not to think of these remarks, tongue-in-cheek though they may be, when reading *Hickory Dickory Dock.*

Both, Janet Morgan and Charles Osborne refer to the fact that there were plans, in the early 1960s, to turn this book into a musical. Unlikely as this may seem, some of the music was written and a title – 'Death Beat' – had been decided upon, but the project eventually came to nothing.

## *Dead Man's Folly*
### 5 November 1956

———————◄○►———————

Mrs Oliver organises a Murder Hunt in the
grounds of Nasse House. When the 'body' turns
out to be only too real, Hercule Poirot is on hand
to discover who killed schoolgirl Marlene Tucker
and what happened to Lady Folliat.

———————◄○►———————

Although it was published in November 1956, *Dead Man's Folly*
had a complicated two-year genesis. Two years previously
Agatha Christie wrote a novella, 'The Greenshore Folly',
which proved difficult to sell for magazine serialisation. Her
agent withdrew it and Christie expanded and elaborated it
into *Dead Man's Folly*. The original novella was published in
2014 as *Hercule Poirot and the Greenshore Folly*, complete with a
detailed history of its genesis and subsequent expansion to
novel length.

Notes relating to *Dead Man's Folly* are contained in Notebooks 45 and 47. As a result of its history, it is difficult to tell
from the Notebooks whether the notes refer to the novella
or the novel version, but it seems likely that Notebook 47,
with a discussion of basic points, is the original novella
and Notebook 45 the elaborated version. In fifteen pages
Christie sketched the entire plot of 'The Greenshore Folly' so
when it came to expanding it, she had only to elaborate individual scenes – the plot was already entire from the novella
version.

Notebook 47 sketches some ideas, all of which, with minor
changes – garden fete rather than 'Conservative Fete', Girl
Guide victim rather than Boy Scout – were to be included in
the story:

Mrs Oliver summons Poirot – she is at Greenway –
professional job – arranging a Treasure Hunt or a Murder
Hunt for the Conservative Fete, which is to be held there

'Body' to be boy scout in boat house – key of which has to
be found by 'clues'

or a <u>real</u> body is buried where tree uprooted and where
Folly is to go

Some ideas
Hiker (girl?) from hostel
Next door – really Lady Bannerman [Stubbs]

It is significant that, from the start, the story was to be set
at Greenway. Although she had used the grounds of her
house before in *Five Little Pigs*, and would use the ferry at the
bottom of the garden in *Ordeal by Innocence*, *Dead Man's Folly*
represents an extended and detailed use of her beloved
Greenway. Apart from the house itself, and its history as told
by Mrs Folliat, also featured in the story are the Gate Lodge,
Ferry Cottage, the Boathouse, the Battery, the Tennis Court
and the Youth Hostel next door; and the internal geography
of the house reflects reality even down to Poirot's bedroom
and the bathroom across the corridor. The magnolia tree
near the front door where Mrs Folliat and Hattie stand
to talk, the winding drive ending at the big iron gates, the
winding and steep path connecting the Battery and the Boathouse – all these exist to this day.

The notes that follow, all from Notebook 47, form the basis
of *Dead Man's Folly*. Christie decided on a version of B below
as the motivation although nobody called Lestrade features
in either version:

Who wants to kill who
A. Wife wants to kill rich P Lestrade has lover – both
    poor

B. Young wife recognised by someone who knows she is married already – blackmail?

C. P Lestrade – has a first wife who is not dead – (in S. America?) – it is wife's sister who recognises him
   Czech girl at hostel? P mentions meeting a hostel girl 'trespassing' – angry colloquy between them seen (but not heard) by someone – he decides to kill her

D. Mrs Folliat – a little balmy – or young Folliat at hostel?

Mrs Folliat of original family who built it – now belongs to Sir George Stubbs with beautiful young wife – Chilean girl? – Italian mother – Creole? – Rich sugar people – girl is feeble minded. Spread about that Sir G made his money in Army Contracts – really Sir G (a pauper) is planning to kill wife and inherit her money

The references to 'Greenshore' in the following extract would seem to confirm that Notebook 47 contains the original novella notes:

Does Sir George marry Hattie Deloran – she is mentally defective – he buys place 'Greenshore' and comes here with his wife – the night a folly has been prepared – she is buried. The Folly goes up the next day – another Lady Dennison [Stubbs] takes her place – servants see nothing – they go out for a stroll – other girl comes back (from boathouse). Then for a year Sir George and Lady Dennison are well known for guests. Then the time comes for Lady D to disappear – she goes up and down to London – doubles part with pretending to be a student

Sally Legge remains in the novel; the reason for the change of first name from Peggy was highlighted by Christie herself below. Definitely a good idea!

Points to be decided

A. Who first chosen for victim? Peggy Legge? Something about Old Peg Leg

B. What did Maureen [Marlene] know or do – heard grandfather talk about body and Sir George really being James?

Or

Does she snoop? Intending to snoop on events? Really sees Lady S change into hiker?

Or

See Sir George and his partner together?

What does Maureen write on Comic

Mrs O's clue?

Boat house?

House boat?

Maureen's scribble on the comic – G[eorge] S[tubbs] goes with a girl from the YHA

The following extracts, from Notebook 45, have page references, presumably to the proofs of 'The Greenshore Folly'. The accompanying remarks are reminders to Christie herself, as she expands the original story. She also experiments with the details of Mrs Oliver's Murder Hunt and clarifies, for herself, the timetable of the fatal afternoon:

P.119 – Elaborate Mrs F's remembering

P.21 – A much elaborated scene in the drawing room at tea

P.24 Go on to Legges after 'Hattie'

Recast order of next events

P.38 elaborate breakfast party –

P.47 Perhaps an interview with Michael Weyman at tennis Pavilion

Clear up point about Fortune teller's tent

p.61 much more detail after discovery of body

Mrs Oliver's plan

The Weapons
Revolver
Knife
Clothes Line

Footprint (in concrete)
Rose Gladioli or Bulb catalogue? Marked?
Shoe
Snap shot

Who?        Victim
Why?        Weapon
How?        Motive
Where?       Time
When        Place


Scheme of afternoon –

4 pm P[eggy] L[egge] leaves tent
4.5 pm H[attie] tells Miss B to take tea
4.10 pm H goes into tent – out of back into hut – dresses as
    girl – goes to boat house
4.20 Calls to Marlene – strangles her then back and arrives
    as herself Italian girl – talks to young man with turtles
    [turtle-shirted competitor]
4.30 leaves with Dutch girl and pack on back or with turtle
    – Dutch girl goes to Dartmouth – Italian girl to Plymouth

### *'Greenshaw's Folly'*
### December 1956

————————◄○►————————

Miss Marple uses her gifts for armchair detection to
solve the brutal murder of Miss Greenshaw, owner of the
monstrous Greenshaw's Folly. In doing so she uses her
knowledge of theatre, gardening – and human nature.

————————◄○►————————

'Greenshaw's Folly' was written as a replacement for 'The
Greenshore Folly', which, in turn, had been written as a gift
for the Diocesan Board of Finance in Exeter. Embarrassingly,
it had proved impossible to sell the story (due, probably, to
its unusual length) and Christie recalled the original and
replaced it with one bearing a similar-sounding title: 'Greenshaw's Folly'. It was published in the UK in the *Daily Mail* in
December 1956; in the USA, *Ellery Queen's Mystery Magazine*
published it in March of the following year, referring to it as
Christie's 'newest story'.

Unusually for a short story, there are twenty-five pages of
notes in two Notebooks. Those in Notebook 3 are alongside
notes for *4.50 from Paddington* and *The Unexpected Guest*.

Many themes and ideas from earlier stories make brief,
and partly disguised, appearances in 'Greenshaw's Folly'. The
mistress/housekeeper impersonation appeared thirty-five
years earlier in 'The Mystery of Hunter's Lodge' and more
recently in *After the Funeral*. The weapon normally used from
a distance but employed at close quarters featured in *Death
in the Clouds*, the fake policeman appeared in *The Mousetrap*
and 'The Man in the Mist' from *Partners in Crime*, and unsuspected family connections had been a constant element
of Christie's detective fiction for years. And below, we see the
reappearance of an old reliable idea: no one looks properly at
a parlour maid or, in this case, a policeman.

The main plot device, as well as the choice of detective, is briefly outlined at the beginning of Notebook 3, while Notebook 47 sketches the opening pages as well as unequivocally stating the title:

Miss M
Hinges on policeman – not really a policeman – like parlourmaid one does not really look at policemen. Man (or woman) shot – householder rushes out – Policeman bending over body tells man to telephone – a colleague will be along in a moment

Greenshaw's Folly
Conversation between Ronald [Horace] who collects monstrosities and Raymond West – photograph – Miss Greenshaw

Notebook 47 considers two possible plot developments. The first is clearly the seed of the Poirot novel *The Clocks*, to be written five years later. 'The Dream' is a Poirot short story from 1938 which contains elements of 'Greenshaw's Folly': the impersonation, by the killer, of the victim and the consequent faking of the time of death.

Typist sent from agency to G's Folly alone there – finds body – or blind woman who nearly steps on it. Clocks all an hour wrong. Why? So that they will strike 12 instead of 1.

The Dream
Wrong man interviews woman – girl gives her instruction – she goes into next room to type. Then finds apparently same woman dead – really dead before – has said secretary is out or faithful companion – faithful companion seen walking up path. Combine this with policeman – girl is typing – looks up to see police constable silhouetted against light.

The Notebooks show vacillation between Alfie and the nephew as murderer or, at least, conspirator. As can be seen, much thought and planning went into the timetable of the murder and impersonation, and this element of the plot is undoubtedly clever.

Are Mrs C. and Alfie mother and son?
Are Mrs C. and nephew mother and son?

Mrs C. and Alf do it. Get Miss G. to make will – then one of them impersonates Miss G.

A.  Alfie then is seen to leave just before real policeman appears
e.g.    11.55 Alfie leaves whistling or singing
        12    Alfie as policeman arrives. Fake murder – Mrs C. yells Help etc.  Alfie then in pub
        12.5    Alfie as policeman

B. Nephew is the one who does it.  An actor in Repertory – Barrie's plays
        Alfie leaves ~~11.55~~ 12 o'clock. Nephew steals in, locks doors on Lou and Mrs. C, kills Aunt, then strolls, dressed as Aunt, across garden – asks time.

Mrs C. and N[at or nephew]
        12.15 – Fake murder – with Mrs C.
        12.20 – Policeman
        12.23 – Real police
        12.25 – Nephew arrives
Alfred gets to lunch – so he is <u>just</u> all right – or meets pal and talks for a few minutes
Or
Mrs C. and Alfred
Fake murder Mrs C. 12.45 (Alfred in pub)
Policeman (Alfred)    12.50
Real police          12.55
Alfred returns        12.57

Nephew                    1 o'clock    (has been given misleading
directions)

The following very orderly list has a puzzling heading; why
'things to *eliminate*'? Few of them actually are eliminated;
most of them remain in the finished story:

Things to eliminate

Will idea (Made with R[aymond] and H[orace] as witness)
left to Mrs C. or Alfie too
Policeman idea
Alfie is nephew
Alfie Mrs C.'s son
Alfie is not nephew but pretends to be – Riding master and
Mrs C.'s son)
Nephew and policeman's uniform ( Barries' plays)
Nephew and Alfie are the same
Mrs C. plays part of Miss G.

As we have seen, Christie toyed with alternative versions of
the plot and solution before she eventually settled on one that
is, sadly, far from foolproof; the mechanics of the plot do not
stand up to rigorous scrutiny. Would the 'real' police, for
example, not query the presence and identity of the first
'policeman', despite Miss Marple's assertion that 'one just
accepts one more uniform as part of the law'? And we have to
accept that someone would work for nothing on the basis of
expectations from a will. The will itself poses further problems. The conspirators assume it leaves the money to them,
either to the housekeeper, as promised, or to the nephew, as
inheritance. But, in reality, the estate is left to Alfred, thereby
ensnaring him in the fatal trio of means, motive and opportunity. But if the conspirators knew this they had no motive; and
if they didn't know it, framing Alfred was never a possibility.

### *4.50 from Paddington*
4 November 1957

———————◄○►———————

While travelling to visit her friend Miss Marple,
Elspeth McGillicuddy witnesses a murder committed on
a train running parallel with hers. During the search
for the body, attention focuses on Rutherford Hall,
home of the Crackenthorpe family. Miss Marple
and her agent Lucy Eylesbarrow investigate.

———————◄○►———————

*4.50 from Paddington* was received at Collins in late February
of 1957 and went through more title changes than any
other book. At various times it was 4.15, 4.30 and 4.54, before
eventually becoming *4.50 from Paddington*. One typescript is
headed '4.54 from Paddington', mainly because, as Christie
explained in a letter to her Edmund Cork dated 8 April
(1957), there was no actual train at that time. She agreed
that 'Four-Fifty from Paddington' or even '5 o'clock from
Paddington' were better titles.

The story opens on 20 December (1956) – 'It was quite
dark now, a dark dreary, misty December day – Christmas
was only five days away' (Chapter 1) – but apart from Miss
Marple attending Christmas dinner at the Vicarage there is
no further mention, or atmosphere, of the holiday season.

All the notes for this title, almost 40 pages, are in four
Notebooks: 3, 22, 45 and 47. The extract below is from Notebook 47 and a few pages later notes for 'Greenshaw's Folly'
and *The Unexpected Guest* are pursued and the 'train idea' is
shelved.

Train – seen from a train? Through window of house. Or
vice versa?
   Train idea

> Girl coming down by train to St. Mary Mead sees a
> murder in another train drawn up alongside – a woman
> strangled. Gets home – talks about it to Miss Marple –
> Police? Nobody strangled – no body found.
>     Why – 2 possible trains one to Manchester – one a slow
> local. Where can you push a body off a train

Notebook 3 sketches the basic idea (with Mrs Bantry in place
of Mrs McGillicuddy) but Notebook 45 has a succinct and
accurate version of the opening chapter of the novel:

> The Train
>
> Mrs McGillicuddy – a friend of Miss Marple's – going to stay
> with her – in train from Paddington – another train on other
> line – but same direction – that's overtaken – hang together
> for a moment, through window of compartment level with
> hers – a man strangling blonde girl – then – train goes on.
>     Mrs MG very upset – tells ticket collector – Station
> master? Oh! Jane I've seen a murder

Uniquely among Christie's books, we are informed from the
outset that the murderer is a man. A mere four pages into
Chapter 1 the reader is told: 'Standing with his back to the
window and to her was a man. His hands were round the
throat of a woman who faced him and he was slowly, remorse-
lessly, strangling her.' With such an unequivocal statement
the possibility that the figure seen could have been a woman
in disguise is never seriously considered and Christie knew
her readers would feel totally cheated if that transpired
to be the solution. Therefore, with the exception of Emma
Crackenthorpe (the motive) and Lucy Eylesbarrow (the investigator), all the main characters are male. The problem this
presented was to make the men broadly similar as physical
beings while distinguishing them as characters. She reminds
herself of this in Notebook 22:

Must get clear on men

Three dark men – all roughly 5ft 10 to 6 ft Loose jointed
People    Cedric eldest?
        Harold married no children
        Alfred
        Bryan Eastley Ex pilot – Husband of Edith (dead)
        Father of Alistair or stepfather?

2 sons of old man – good boy (in Bank) Artist – or scene
designer or producer

Cedric – a Robert Graves – rolling stone, uninhibited –
(eventually to marry Lucy Eylesbarrow)

Sir Harold Crackenthorpe – busy man – director of
Crackenthorpe Ltd. Well to do – not really? On rocks?

Bryan? R.A.F. Wing Command D? At a loose end

Alph[red] Dark slender – the crooked one – black market in
war – Ministry of Supply

The 'Robert Graves' reference is to Christie's friend and Torquay neighbour – the author of *I, Claudius* among others – who
was a critical fan and the dedicatee of *Towards Zero*. This reference also clarifies the question left unanswered at the end of
the novel: which of her admirers will Lucy eventually marry?

There were seemingly minor points to consider but ones
that impacted on the plot: how to ensure the necessary darkness for the commission of the crime and how to account for
the presence in the house of two young boys. The question of
possible dates is considered in two Notebooks:

Points to settle

Date of journey possibly Jan 9th or thereabouts
Points to take in – holidays (boys) New Year (Cedric)
Time of getting dark (train)

Dates
Holidays? April – Stobart-West and Malcolm there
So murder end of February? Say – ~~24th~~ 26th

The eventual decision to place the murder just before, and the investigation just after, Christmas answered all the concerns.

But the biggest problem about *4.50 from Paddington* is the identity of the corpse. It is a problem for Miss Marple, the police, the reader and, I suspect, for Agatha Christie herself. We do not know for certain until the novel's closing pages whose murder is actually under investigation, thus making what would otherwise have been a first-class 'Christie for Christmas', something of a disappointment. It also raises the question of how, divine intervention aside, Miss Marple can possibly know the story behind the murder. When the original reader at Collins, reporting on the manuscript, admits that 'unless I am being very stupid I cannot see how anyone could have known that murderer's motive', it is difficult not to sympathise.

The following note shows that Christie had two ideas about the possible identity of the corpse – Anna the dancer or Martine – and, reluctant to abandon either, eventually used aspects of both:

Is dead woman Anna the dancer or not?
Is Anne = Mrs Q – or is Anna red herring arranged by Q
Is woman killed because she is Martine and has a son or
     because she is Q's wife and he plans to marry

### The Unexpected Guest
12 August 1958

————————◄○►————————

When Michael Starkwedder stumbles out of the
fog and into the Warwick household, he finds Richard
Warwick shot dead and his wife, Laura, standing nearby
holding a revolver. Between them they concoct a plan
to explain the situation before ringing the police.
But who really shot Richard Warwick?

————————◄○►————————

During the 1950s Agatha Christie reigned supreme in London's West End. *The Hollow* led off the decade in June 1951, followed by *The Mousetrap* in November 1952. October 1953 saw the curtain rise on *Witness for the Prosecution*; *Spider's Web* opened in December of the following year and *Towards Zero* (co-written with Gerald Verner) in September 1956. In 1958 two new Christie plays appeared: *Verdict* in May and *The Unexpected Guest* in August. With the exception of *Verdict* all were major theatrical successes, two of them at least, *The Mousetrap* and *Witness for the Prosecution*, assuring Agatha Christie's eternal fame as a playwright.

Spider's Web had been the first original Christie stage play since *Black Coffee* in 1930. *Verdict* and *The Unexpected Guest* continued this trend for new, as distinct from adapted, material, although both of these scripts are considerably darker in tone than *Spider's Web*. To some extent all three feature attempts to explain away a mysterious death with less emphasis than usual on the whodunit element. And in *The Unexpected Guest* Christie sets herself the added challenge of portraying a mentally disturbed 19-year-old. On a more personal note, the description of the victim, Richard Warwick, has distinct similarities to Christie's brother, Monty. Both spent part of their adult life in Africa, both needed an attendant when they returned to live in England and both had the undesirable habit of taking pot-shots at animals, birds and, unfortunately, passers-by. *An Autobiography* describes Monty's account of a 'silly old spinster going down the drive with her behind wobbling. Couldn't resist it – I sent a shot or two right and left of her'; this is exactly Laura's description in Act I, Scene i of Richard's behaviour. There, it must be emphasised, all similarities ended, as Richard Warwick is portrayed as a particularly despicable character.

*Verdict*, after a critical mauling due, in part, to a mistimed final curtain, lasted only one month but in August 1958, spirit unquenched, the curtain rose on the next offering from the Queen of Crime. *Verdict* was an atypical Christie stage offering; despite its title it is not a whodunit and has no surprise ending, but *The Unexpected Guest* returned to more recognisable fare. Although partly a will-they-get-away-with-it type of plot, it also has a strong whodunit element and a last-minute surprise.

Christie had, presumably, spent summer 1958 writing a new play to overcome the disappointment of *Verdict*. Or so it seemed. But Notebook 34 shows, with an unequivocal date, that the earliest notes for this play had been drafted even before *The Mousetrap* had begun its unstoppable run. Three pages of that Notebook show that almost the entire plot of the play already existed. A more likely scenario, and one borne out by further notes below, is that the plotting of the play was already well advanced before *Verdict* even opened.

1951 Play
Act I
Stranger stumbling into room in dark – finds light – turns it on – body of man – more light – woman against wall – revolver in hand (left) – says she shot him.
'There's the telephone –
Uh?
'To ring up the police'

Outsider shields her – rings police – rigs room

People  Vera

Julian (lover?)

Benny (Cripple's brother)

Act II

Ends with S[tranger] accusing V[era] of lying. Julian killed him – you thought I'd shield you – (she admits it) or led up to by his realising she is left handed; crime committed by right handed person

Curtain as –

'Julian did it'

She – 'You can't prove it – you can't alter your story'

'You ingenious devil'!

Act III

Suspicion switches to Benny having done it. But actually it is woman. Ends with her preferring S[tranger] to Julian

Characters could be

Vera (Sandra)

Julian

Mrs Gregg    mother of victim

Stepmother

Barny    feeble minded boy

Rosa        "        "    girl

Miss Jennson – Nurse

Julian's sister

Lydia or niece of Julian's – hard girl

This is, in rough outline, the plot and characters of *The Unexpected Guest*. The only element missing is the vital part played by 'the Stranger', who does not even figure in the list of characters, despite his 'stumbling' entrance at the beginning of the play. The explanation for this may be simply that the final twist had not occurred to Christie when she began drafting the play. This is in keeping with other titles; the shock endings to both *Crooked House* and *Endless Night* do not form a large part of the plotting of either novel and would seem to have emerged during, rather than inspiring, the writing. But even without the final twist *The Unexpected Guest* is still an entertaining whodunit.

Notebook 53 also has a concise summation of the plot, this time including a list of possible murderers. These three pages appear, unexpectedly, during extended plotting for *After the Funeral* and *A Pocket Full of Rye*, both completed in the early 1950s and published in 1953. These notes reflect the finished play, although neither victim nor killer has yet been decided. The new-named 'stranger' has taken on a more important aspect and is under consideration as the murderer.

Plan      The Unexpected Guest
Act I
Trevor blundering in – in fog or storm – Sandra against wall – pistol. He and she – he rigs things – rings police.
Scene between them
Curtain – end of scene
Scene II
People being questioned by police
Julian Somers MP
Sandra
Nurse Eldon
Mrs Crawford
David Crawford – invalid
Or
David Etherington Sandra's brother
Act II
Further questions
Julian and Sandra – Trevor's suspicions. He accuses her – having tricked her with revolver
Damned if I'll shield him
What else can you do – now? etc.
Act III
Mrs Crawford takes a hand. 'Who really did it' – (brightly)
Now who did?

1. Trevor the enemy from the past – his idea is to return and find body
2. Nurse? Told him about wife and Julian – his reaction is that he knew all about it – is brutal to her – she shoots him
3. Governess to child? Or to defective?
4. Defective has done it – or child
5. Mrs Crawford?

The following clearly dated extract appears in Notebook 28, between notes for *By the Pricking of my Thumbs* and *Endless Night*, both published in the late 1960s. This decade-long gap illustrates again the unpredictable chronology of the Notebooks.

Some confusion is evident in the naming of the main female character, referred to here as Vera, but in the course of the notes she is also referred to as Ruth and/or Judith:

FOG
Nov 1957
M enters – R dead
V. revolver in hand – admits – the build up – tells her of MacGregor – dead man displayed in bad light – letter written – printed – left – <u>then</u> (M. rings up police?) V goes up stairs – paper bag trick – they come down – M. enters – discovery – M rings up police. Does Ruth – make some remark about lighter (Julian's)
Scene II
Police – then family
Julian comes – lighter – he picks it up etc.
Act II
Police again or a police station – or his hotel and V. comes there?
Ends with Julian and V
His saying 'You did not kill him – didn't know even how to fire a revolver'

Act III
(Cast?)  V[era]
      M[ichael and/or MacGregor]
      Jul[ian]
      Police Insp.
        "   S[ergeant]
      Mrs Warwick
      Judith Venn [no equivalent]
      Bernard Warwick [possibly Jan]
      Crusty [possibly Miss Bennett]
      Angell – Manservant (Shifty)
Crusty works on Bernard or Judith or Bernard begins talking
Points to decide
Judith (angry because R. chucks her out). If so, Bernard is
induced by her to confess or even boast. He is taken away.
M. clears him and breaks down J. [M] says to V. (good luck
with J.) he is M[acGregor]
Or
Bernard boasts to killing him – he is killed – cliff? window?
etc.
Case closed. Then M springs his surprise

At this point the play is referred to as 'Fog'; and the same
title appears in other Notebooks, once with the addition of
'The Unexpected Guest' in brackets. As a title 'Fog' has its
attractions, as, in both the physical and metaphorical sense,
fog plays a role in the play. 'Swirls of mist' are described in
the stage directions and fog is necessary to lend credence to
Starkwedder's story of crashing his car; and the other characters, as well as the audience, are in a fog of doubt throughout.
Unusually for a UK-set Christie play the scene is specifically
set near the Bristol Channel, with a fog-horn sounding a
melancholy note periodically. In fact, the stage directions
specify that 'the fog signal is still sounding as the Curtain falls'.

## *Ordeal by Innocence*
3 November 1958

———————◄○►———————

Jacko Argyle died in prison while serving a
sentence for the murder of his stepmother. His alibi
for the fatal night was never substantiated – until now.
Arthur Calgary arrives at the family home and
confirms Jacko's alibi. But the real killer is still
among the family, ready to kill again.

———————◄○►———————

On 1 October 1957 Agatha Christie wrote to Edmund Cork, asking him to check on the following legal situation: if person A were tried and convicted of murder despite his claim that he was with person B at the crucial time of the killing; person B is never found and A dies in prison six months into his incarceration; then B, who has been abroad for a year, turns up and approaches the police to confirm A's story and provide the alibi. Christie wanted clarification on the situation with regard to a 'free pardon' and the possible reopening of the case. She assured Cork that an early reply would enable her to get to work 'industriously on this projected new book'. The date 'Oct 6th' appears on page 20 of Notebook 28, confirming that the novel was planned and written the year before publication.

'This is easily the best non-branded [i.e. non-Poirot or Marple] Christie we have had for some time . . . *The Innocent* [as it was then called] is close to achieving a successful blend of the classical detective story and the modern conception of a crime novel.' This was the enthusiastic verdict on 1 May 1958 when Collins received the latest Christie. The reader considered that it could benefit from cutting and mentioned that Agatha Christie proposed to do that. His other reservation was about the title and he suggested some alternatives:

'Viper's Point', 'A Serpent's Tooth', 'The Burden of Innocence' and, prophetically, 'Cat among the Pigeons', the title of the following year's book.

The short story 'Sing a Song of Sixpence', collected in *The Listerdale Mystery*, contains distinct similarities to this novel. Although the story first appeared in December 1929, almost thirty years earlier, the parallels to *Ordeal by Innocence* are too many to be mere coincidence: the outsider detective, the elderly matriarch bludgeoned to death for money, the gnawing suspicion and distrust, the eventual disclosure of an unsuspected emotional and criminal partnership.

*Ordeal by Innocence* remains one of the best of the latter-day Christies. It is a crime novel, as distinct from a classical detective story, with deeply held convictions about truth and justice, guilt and innocence. It is marred only by the inclusion, in the last twenty pages, of two perfunctory crimes, an actual and an attempted murder. Coming so near the end of the novel, they do not convince either as an illustration of the killer's panic or as a suspense-building exercise; the Notebooks, however, give some insight into the inclusion of these murders.

Notebook 28 contains almost forty pages of notes, with the earliest jottings accurately reflecting the opening of the novel, even to the amount of the fare paid to the boatman. The ferry used by Arthur Calgary still operates at the end of Greenway Road just past the imposing gates of Dame Agatha's summer residence.

Arthur Calgary – Crossing ferry – begins

The ferry came to a grinding halt against the shelving pebbles – A.C. paid fourpence and stepped ashore

Well, this was it – he could still, he supposed, turn back etc

An early page sketches an accurate account of the crime, although at this point the character Jacko is still appearing in the Notebook as Albert:

Violent quarrel between Albert and Mrs A – he attacks her
– she is nearly dead – K. sends him off to obtain an alibi.
At 8 o'clock – with her again and kills her or he sticks her
with a knife – she gets up – tells about him.

Possible course of real events –

Albert – determined to get money out of Mrs. Argyle makes
up to Lindstrom – wants her to marry him – she agrees –
Mrs. A – won't help – Leo won't help – he works on her – the
sandbag from under the door – at 8.15 a form she does not
understand – Mrs A bends over it – K socks her

The family members underwent name changes but are still
recognisable, while Mr Argyle, Kirsten and Maureen are
substantially the same as the finished novel. The calculation
of Tina's age confirms that these notes were written in 1958:

Tina half-caste girl – (5 in 1940 – 23 now) married to local
postman? Builder's mason? farmer

Linda – married to a man since paralysed – she lives there
[Mary]

Johnnie – a job in Plymouth comes over quite often

Albert – bad lot – unstable ~~hanged~~ convicted of murder of
Mrs. Argyll [Jacko]

Mr Argyll – a scholar

Mr Argyll – (or Mr Randolph) Randolph Argyle? Ambrose
Randolph?
    Thin – ethereal – surrounded by books

Kirsten?
    Her homely face – pancake flat – ~~nose~~ surrounded by
bleached permanent w[ave] hair
    How much better a nun's coif and wimple? – not a

contemplative lay sister – the kind who inspected you
through a grille before admitting you to the visitor's parlour
– or Mother Superior's presence

Calgary goes and sees – Maureen – (married to him?) – Silly
common little girl – but shrewd – went to family when he
was arrested – they didn't know ~~she~~ he was married.

Mary – Tenement in New York – hatred of it all – mother
out in street – car passed – Mrs A – adoption – then hotel
life – nursery growing up – plans for her – meeting with
Philip – no background – goes off marries him – he sets up
in business – Fails – then polio – Mrs. Argyle – wants them
there – he is quite ready to go – goes into hospital – Mary
goes to stay at Sunny Point

The two subsequent victims are also considered, although
the original intention was that *either* Philip or Tina would be
the victim:

Who is killed? Philip poisoned – doesn't wake up or Tina
stabbed – she walks from Kirsty to Mickey – collapses

The poisoning of Philip was discarded in favour of stabbing.
And a possible reason for the unsuccessful attempt on Tina
is that, in the absence of any other evidence, it provides
proof. For readers who doubt the medical likelihood of Tina's
stabbing, there are two editions of the *British Medical Journal*,
dated 28 January and 18 February 1956, among Christie's
papers with pages dealing with just this situation; and both
articles are marked. A careful reading of a very daring
Chapter 22 should be enough to dispose of any accusations
of cheating.

There were also ideas that never got further than Notebook 28:

Forged will – forged in favour of real murderer – but forged very badly? Or forged badly in favour of Albert.

Husband dislikes wife and hated the children. Wanted to marry someone? Or had son of his own.

She was going to alter will in favour of a foundation for orphans – which cut out husband.

And, finally, two intriguing ideas, both actually variations on the same theme . . .

Or was Albert her [i.e. Mrs Argyle's] son

Is Kirsten Albert's real mother?

Both of these would have worked and would, moreover, have made psychological sense. The former would have made a profoundly affecting scenario; the latter would perhaps have been more effective as a motivation for Kirsten (as it did for her counterpart in 'Sing a Song of Sixpence') than the one actually used. However, the possibilities of unacknow-ledged parenthood as both plot device and motivation are fully explored in *Hercule Poirot's Christmas*, *Sad Cypress* and *Mrs McGinty's Dead* among others, so perhaps it was simply a case of avoiding repetition.

With customary ingenuity, Agatha Christie resolved the thorny question of legal justice and moral justice. With the death in prison of Jacko while serving a sentence for a crime he did not commit, Christie could be accused of a disservice to both natural and legal justice. Fifteen years earlier in *Five Little Pigs*, Caroline Crale, wrongly convicted, but with her own collusion in expiation for an earlier mis-demeanour, dies in prison. And in *Mrs McGinty's Dead* (1952) the unsympathetic James Bentley is also wrongly convicted but is saved by Poirot before his execution. But in *Ordeal by Innocence* Jacko is finally shown to have been morally responsible, even if his was not the hand that struck the fatal blow.

## *Cat among the Pigeons*
2 November 1959

---◀○▶---

As the headmistress, Miss Bulstrode, welcomes the
pupils for the new term at exclusive Meadowbank School
she little realises that before term ends a pupil will be
kidnapped, four staff will be dead and a murderer
will have been unmasked. It's just as well that
Julia Upjohn called in Hercule Poirot.

---◀○▶---

With a serialisation beginning the previous September, *Cat among the Pigeons* was the 1959 'Christie for Christmas'. It is a hugely readable mixture of domestic murder mystery and international thriller with a solution that reflects both situations. In this, the unmasking of two completely independent killers, it is a unique Christie. It was the first Poirot since 1956 and there would not be another one until *The Clocks*, four years later. The reader's report on the manuscript, dated June 1959, was enthusiastic ('highly entertaining') rather than ecstatic ('not a dazzling performance'). Described as having 'enough of the crossword puzzle element towards the end to satisfy the purists, even though the solution shows that plot to be rather far-fetched' and to be 'more saleable than *Ordeal by Innocence*', the reader recommended including the book in a new contract. Although Collins was considering the manuscript in purely commercial terms, few Christie aficionados would agree that it outshines *Ordeal by Innocence*, a far superior crime novel.

As will be seen, Christie toyed with the idea of having

Miss Marple solve the murders at Meadowbank and this is more credible than a school-girl 'escaping' to consult Poirot. That said, Miss Marple had already had a busy decade with one minor and four major investigations; and she would not, perhaps, have been as adept with the international element.

In the opening chapter there is a variation on the ploy of a character seeing something momentous – '"Why!" exclaimed Mrs Upjohn, still gazing out of the window, "how extra-ordinary!"' – that has an important bearing on subsequent events. This has often taken the form of seeing something over the shoulder of another character – see discussion of *The Mysterious Affair at Styles* – just before a mysterious death and the unidentified sight forms part of the solution. If Miss Bulstrode had been listening properly to Mrs Upjohn, much of the ensuing mayhem might have been avoided. Two further examples would appear within the next five years: when Marina Gregg, in *The Mirror Crack'd from Side to Side*, looks down her own staircase and sees something that transfixes her, and when the unfortunate Major Palgrave, in *A Caribbean Mystery*, recognises a killer over Miss Marple's shoulder, just before his own murder. As with other novels from Christie's later period – *Hickory Dickory Dock*, *4.50 from Paddington*, *Ordeal by Innocence*, *The Mirror Crack'd from Side to Side* – there is a last-minute murder in the closing stages, featuring the victim talking to an unnamed killer.

There are over eighty pages of notes devoted to *Cat among the Pigeons* in three Notebooks, most of them in Notebook 15. The intricacy of the plot, with an unusually large cast of characters, two separate plot strands and scenes set in Ramat and Anatolia, as well as Meadowbank, account for these extensive notes.

The first page of Notebook 15 is headed 'Oct. 1958 Projects', and goes on to list the ideas that would become *The Pale Horse*, *Passenger to Frankfurt* and *Fiddlers Five/Three*, along with the possibility of plays based on either *Murder is Easy* (or, as it appears in the Notebook, 'Murder Made Easy') or 'The Cretan Bull', from *The Labours of Hercules*. Idea C on this list became *Cat among the Pigeons*.

The earliest notes consider which detective to use and at this stage also the princess/schoolgirl impersonation is under consideration, carrying echoes of a similar plot device in 'The Regatta Mystery'.

> Book
> Girl's school? Miss Bulstrode (Principal)
> Mrs. Upjohn – or parent – rather like Mrs. Summerhayes in
> Mrs. McGinty, fluffy, vague but surprisingly shrewd
> Miss Marple? Great niece at the school?
> Poirot? Mrs. U sits opposite him in a train?
> Someone shot or stalked at school sports?
> Princess Maynasita there or an actress as pupil or an
> actress as games mistress

There were two contenders for the book's title. The rejected one is briefly mentioned at the start of Chapter 8, when the two policemen first hear of the murder:

> Death of a Games Mistress
> Cat among the Pigeons

A list of characters in Notebook 15 is remarkably similar to those in the published novel, although the number of characters would increase considerably:

> Possible characters
> Bob Rawlinson
> Mrs. Sutcliffe (his sister)
> Frances [Jennifer] Sutcliffe (her daughter)
> Angele Black
> Fenella (pupil at school)
> Mademoiselle Amelie Blanche

Miss Bolsover [Bulstrode] Principal of School
'Meadowbank'
Miss Springer – Gym Mistress
Mrs. Upjohn (rather like Mrs. Summerhayes)
Julia Upjohn
Mr Robinson

It seems likely that Angele Black and Amelie Blanche were amalgamated into Angele Blanche and that 'Fenella' was intended to be another agent, masquerading as a pupil, possibly alongside Ann Shapland. The comparison of Mrs Upjohn with Maureen Summerhayes refers to Poirot's inefficient landlady in his disreputable guest house in *Mrs McGinty's Dead*, and it is an apt one. Both are disorganised, voluble and immensely likeable; and each is the possessor of a valuable piece of information which imperils their safety.

The set-up on the opening day of the new term is sketched, including the all-important Mrs Upjohn and her sighting, although at this stage what, or more strictly, whom she sees is still undecided:

Likely opening gambit
First day of summer term – mothers etc. – Mrs. U sees someone out of window. Could be New Mistress? Domestic Staff? Pupil? Parent?

The letters that constitute Chapter 5, and that contain much that is later significant, are considered in Notebook 15:

Letters

Julia
Jennifer
Angele Blanche
Chaddy
Eleanor Vanstittart

Anonymous to ??
Well, I've settled in all right – you'd have laughed like a drain
to see the reception committee. I've settled in – in this I
look the part all right. Anyway, nobody seems to have any
doubts of my bona fides – then we shall see what we shall
see – I hope!

The letter from Miss Chadwick ('Chaddy') did not material-
ise and although there is an anonymous one it is clear to the
reader that the writer is Adam, the gardener. The inclusion
of the one sketched here would have been tantalisingly mysterious.

Christie devotes a lot of space to the progress of the tennis
racquet:

History of Racquet
A. Brought home by Mrs. Sutcliffe by sea (Does she see
A[ngele] B[lanche] at Tilbury?)
B. Her husband meets her – drives them straight down to
country or they go down by train and it is left in train?
C. House is entered – tennis racquets taken and a few other
things, later recovered by police

It is this unlikely object that sets the plot in motion, carrying
echoes of the ninth Labour of Hercules, 'The Girdle of Hip-
polita', where Poirot investigates the disappearance of the
schoolgirl Winnie King, also an unwitting smuggler of con-
traband in her luggage. The initial swapping of the tennis
racquets is acceptable but the scene in Chapter 12 ii, when a
total stranger approaches Jennifer and asks to exchange
them (again), is less than convincing. Christie considers and
discards the use of a lacrosse stick; note also her practical
concerns about how long lost property offices retain items:

Motive? Motive? Jewels bound for Near East country – prior
to abdication – perhaps shirks plan turns back. Pilots sister

The 3rd weekend of term –

About what happens.

Miss Bullstrode – goes for weekend to Duchess of Arlington – to meet Professor Banikow

Leave school in Steam? Cheque – Jm & Chaddy

Jewella – your uncle has an ? in London will call for you out to-morrow

Mary Greg – Elizabeth – Princess Gulund. Veronica –

28 girls – Ann Shapland

off – Miss Johnson – his sister home from Kenya –

~~Can Call for Jewell~~

Vans Morton & Chaddy – dreadful – words –

Can Call for Jewella.

Then 2nd one –

Cartner Sees Bob — etc.

Meets Crooks at Savoy —
A name & address —

Found drowned — ?

Ann sent on job — examining
Sports Pavilion — Miss S interrupts —
Shot —

who is other woman? Who Calls for
Jacquet?

takes them out of country concealed in schoolgirl's 'kit.'
Lacrosse stick?
Tennis racquet? Where they lie concealed. Mother (or
aunt?) killed – her room at the hotel ransacked – dies of
shock?
Racquets swopped by girls – Jennifer? Julia?
Woman who comes – New lamps for old. Exchange tennis
racquet for new one <u>but</u> it has already been swopped. Lost
property office – how long – find out

She then sketches the scene more or less as it appears in the
book:

A lady calls – tweedy, county, vague – asks girl 'Can you tell
me where I can find Janet McGrane? It's Janet McGrane.
What a coincidence' Story about bringing a new tennis
racquet 'As I was coming here anyway to ask about the
school for my niece.' Takes old racquet to be restrung etc. J.
gives her old tennis racquet <u>but</u> it's <u>not</u> really hers – she has
done a swap (with Julia?). Hers wasn't 'balanced.' She
exchanges it for one that needs restringing. Does woman
say 'It needs restringing – that's what your aunt said.' <u>But</u>
her's <u>had</u> been restrung for going abroad – a sort of 'New
lamps for old' touch

The enterprising Julia brings Hercule Poirot into the case in
Chapter 17, and Notebook 15 summarises her efforts:

Julia leaves French class – goes to London – contacts
Hercule Poirot – Maureen Summerhayes (from Mrs
McGinty) is her godmother. Tells about Mrs. U's letter and
her own observations. HP takes it seriously – goes to
school. Interview with Miss B – they get on well – Miss B
tells about Mrs. U and HP tells her about Mrs. U's letter to
India.

And the killer appears in Notebook 15 with a change of name. An earlier note shows some indecision, but no lack of ideas, about the possible identity of this killer:

> Games Mistress, school maid, parent recognised by Mrs. U[pjohn] as espionage agent.
> Ann Shelbourne [Shapland] – a criminal by choice – as a girl wild – gives herself an alibi. In studying her career – a double life – like a drunk who has occasional 'benders.' Very able – good jobs – first on stage – then sec. to Sir Dawson Kops – over Oil Company? or Industrial Magnate, in between other things

There was always going to be more than one murder; in the Notebooks the second murder seems to have been definite from the early stages. Although most Christie novels feature more than one death, the later deaths are usually as a result of the earlier one. Here, because of the two separate plot strands, the second murder is independent of the first; but, of course, the reader is unaware of this until the explanation. And the setting of the Games Pavilion seems to confirm the connection, as was Christie's intention. But the identity of her third victim was still undecided at this stage:

> 3 deaths
> 1. Miss Springer's games mistress (she surprises someone in sports pavilion)
> 2. Miss   ?   Miss Bulford's probable successor
> 3. ?
> 1st murder because of jewels. 'Angelina' is in Springer part – interrupted by Games mistress – kills her. Then Chaddy kills Rich
>
> Miss Bulstrode retiring. Going to take someone into partnership. Chadwick? Margaret Rich (Mathematical mistress?). But really Mary Templar – young – only there a few terms. But the stuff that's needed.

Second murder is committed by Miss Chadwick – sees
light in Sports pavilion and finds Miss V there – also sees
light – Chaddy has taken sandbag with her as weapon.
Tempted – hits

She lists alternative scenarios, some of which – Miss Springer
in Ramat, the art room attack – were rejected and others
– Julia and her missing mother, Miss Rich in Ramat –
incorporated into the novel.

One possible sequence
B [Ann Shapland] does not recognise Mrs. U[pjohn] until
Sports Day – does not know Mrs. U has seen her before.
Manages an attack from behind (in the Arts Display
Room?) Mrs. U concussed badly – taken to hospital

Alternative
(A) Rich is school teacher in Ramat. Pregnant – absent that
term – not the woman who sees Bob [therefore] Dancer is
the woman on balcony – Either Fenella Angele or Fenella or
Ann
B. Springer was schoolteacher in Ramat she saw Bob – got
job at M[eadowbank]. Goes out to Pav[ilion] followed by ?
Ann – member of organisation who shoots her
Points to be fitted in and retained
A. Julia comes to consult Poirot – mother missing? in
hospital with concussion? Gone abroad – E. Africa?
Safari?
B. Recognition by Mrs. U of somebody at school. Is that
somebody the victim or the murderer. Does an incident
happen at some other school?
C. 3 people on the job – (1) Knows about racquet (2) Relies
on Fenella – (impersonates?). Believes Mrs. S. – has been
instructed to give jewels to Fenella. (3) A woman who is put
on to following whoever knows about racquet (S.T. or D)
[school teacher or domestic]

Overall, the two distinct strands of *Cat among the Pigeons*, the international and the academic, coalesce convincingly. And what seems like cheating, the transition between Chapter 14 i and ii, is shown in retrospect to be perfectly fair and acceptable. And perhaps as a counter-balance to the excess of male characters in *4.50 from Paddington*, here we have an excess of female characters. Apart from Adam, the gardener, all the other male characters – even Poirot! – are somewhat peripheral

# The Fifth Decade 1960–1969

'After all, to be able to continue writing at the age of 75 is very fortunate.'

*An Autobiography*

───────────◄○►───────────

**SOLUTIONS REVEALED**

*After the Funeral* • *At Bertram's Hotel* • *By the Pricking of my Thumbs* • *A Caribbean Mystery* • *The Clocks* • 'The Cretan Bull' • *Dead Man's Folly* • *Endless Night* • *Hallowe'en Party* • *Lord Edgware Dies* • *The Man in the Brown Suit* • *The Mirror Crack'd from Side to Side* • *The Murder of Roger Acknoyd* • *The Pale Horse* • *Rule of Three* • *Third Girl* • *Three Act Tragedy* • 'The Witness for the Prosecution'

───────────◄○►───────────

As she entered her fifth decade of crime writing Agatha Christie continued experimenting with her chosen genre. The 1960s began inauspiciously with a collection of short stories, the title story of which, 'The Adventure of the Christmas Pudding', was a reworking of the 1923 Poirot case, 'A Christmas Adventure'; but the elaboration, unlike similar earlier experiments, added only words. 'The Mystery of the Spanish Chest', in the same collection, was a far more imaginative expansion of the earlier 'The Mystery of the Baghdad

Chest'. In fact, at one point the collection was to be called *The Mystery of the Spanish Chest and other stories.*

Of the ten 1960s titles only two are pure whodunits, the last examples of the genre that Christie was to write. *The Mirror Crack'd from Side to Side* (1962) and *A Caribbean Mystery* (1964), both Miss Marple novels, employ clever variations on a plot device that had appeared before: a character seeing something surprising, shocking or frightening over someone's shoulder. The other Marple novel of the decade was *At Bertram's Hotel* (1965), a nostalgic journey into the past for the elderly detective and, one suspects, her creator. Though all three Poirot novels of this decade are disappointing – the Christie magic is missing from the development of each – the fundamental plot ideas are as inventive as ever: in *The Clocks* (1963), a stranger's body found in a room full of incorrect clocks; in *Third Girl* (1966), a girl who thinks she 'may' have committed a murder; and in *Hallowe'en Party* (1969), a child is drowned while bobbing for apples. The best novels of this decade were, ironically, the two non-series titles, *The Pale Horse* (1961) and *Endless Night* (1967). Both of them were innovative, experimental and sinister – black magic murder to order in the former and a wholly original reworking of the Ackroyd trick in the latter – each showing an aspect of the Queen of Crime not heretofore seen.

Some old friends make welcome reappearances. Mrs Oliver has a solo run in *The Pale Horse*, which affords us a glimpse into the creative process of a mystery writer and, perhaps, into that of her creator; and appears with her old friend Poirot in both *Third Girl* and *Hallowe'en Party*. Tommy and Tuppence solve their penultimate case in *By the Pricking of my Thumbs* (1968). Age has not withered their spirit of adventure and the case they investigate, the disappearance of an elderly lady from a retirement home, is dark and sinister.

The elderly Christie is reflected in many of the books of this decade. Poirot's appearance in *The Clocks* is almost a cameo as he emulates an armchair detective and reflects on his magnum opus, a study of detective fiction; and in *Third Girl* he does unconvincing battle with the London of the Swinging Sixties. Miss Marple has aged since her previous appearance and agrees to a live-in companion in *The Mirror Crack'd from Side to Side.* Tommy and Tuppence are middle-aged grandparents and most of the characters in *By the Pricking of my Thumbs* are similarly elderly. And this book, as well as *Hallowe'en Party* and *At Bertram's Hotel,* is a journey into the past.

While *The Mousetrap* continued its inexorable success story with another new record in 1962 (the longest running play in London), Christie's only new play of this decade was another experiment. *Rule of Three* (1962) consists of three one-act plays, each totally different in style and content. Two years earlier saw a dramatisation of *Five Little Pigs* as *Go Back for Murder,* but both offerings received a cool critical reception.

In the cinema the four Margaret Rutherford Marple films were released – or should that be 'escaped'? – much to Christie's horror; only one, *Murder She Said,* was based on an authentic Marple novel, *4.50 from Paddington.* Of the other three, two were based on Poirot novels and one was a completely original script; and in all of them Miss Marple is unrecognisable, literally and metaphorically, as the elderly denizen of St Mary Mead. As a direct result, the 1964 Marple novel, *A Caribbean Mystery,* carried on its title page the reclamation 'Featuring the original character as created by Agatha Christie'. The following year, 1965, found *Ten Little Indians* transposed from an island off the coast of Devon to an Austrian ski resort (but filmed in Dublin!), but with the innovation of The Whodunit Break – a ticking clock-face reprised the suspects and murders for one minute to help the audience decide on the villain. *The Alphabet Murders* appeared in 1966, bearing almost no similarity to its inspiration, *The ABC Murders,* to the extent of including a cameo appearance from Miss Marple. (All five films came from the same production company.) A more faithful adaptation was the 1960 screen version of *Spider's Web*, from the play of the same name. Also in the world of cinema, Christie worked on an adaptation of the Dickens novel *Bleak House*, but although she produced a script ('I quite realise that a third or more of the present script will have to go') in May 1962 the film was never made. And Hercule Poirot debuted on US television in *The Disappearance of Mr. Davenheim* in 1962.

In 1965 Christie published *Star over Bethlehem*, a miscellany of Christmas poetry and short tales, and in October of that year she finished work on *An Autobiography*. This was a project she had worked at, on and off, for the previous fifteen years and although the book would not be published until after her death she enjoyed reviewing her life; it fell to her daughter, Rosalind, to edit the vast amount of material to produce the 1977 book. As we know from the recent release of recordings of the 'writing' of her *Autobiography*, Agatha Christie used a Dictaphone for many years. It is difficult to say with any certainty when this practice began, but in a radio interview as early as 1955 she said, 'I type my own drafts on an ancient faithful machine I've owned for years. And I find a Dictaphone useful for short stories or for re-casting an act of a play, but not for the more complicated business of working out a novel.' The implication is that she was practised in the use of the machine; and, of course, as far back as 1926, her most infamous title, *The Murder of Roger Ackroyd*, featured that piece of equipment as a plot device.

The photograph of Agatha Christie with the Dictaphone dates from the late 1950s. The resultant tapes, or more accurately Dictabelts, still exist for many of the titles from the succeeding decades. By that stage, no doubt, the elderly Christie found it physically easier to sit in her chair and 'speak' her novels into a machine and then correct a draft typed by her secretary. The less detailed notes for the last half-dozen novels can be seen as reflecting this procedure. The exhaustive plot experimentation and variations-on-a-

*Agatha Christie, photographed in Winterbrook House in the 1950s, using a Dictaphone.*

theme of the Notebooks of yesteryear are replaced by plot highlights which she considered sufficient for this method of writing. This procedure meant that the later novels were both more verbose in narration and less tight in construction than the earlier, more compactly written books; to echo her own words, the Dictaphone was not suitable 'for the complicated business' of constructing a detective novel.

In 1967 she co-operated with the first book to be written about her work, G.C. Ramsey's *Agatha Christie: Mistress of Mystery*. Although a slight book viewed from today's perspective, it was the first to impose order on the chaos of title changes, both transatlantic and domestic, and variations in short-story collections; thus it was as welcome to Christie's agent and publisher as it was to her fans. And it remains the only book about Christie which received her personal cooperation. In 1961 she received a doctorate from Exeter University, where today an archive of her papers is held. That was also the year in which Christie was declared by UNESCO to be the world's best-selling writer.

‿‿‿

## The Pale Horse
### 6 November 1961

————————◄○►————————

A list of names is found on the body of a murdered priest but what do they have in common? Is there such a thing as murder by suggestion? Are the elderly women in Much Deeping really practising black magic?

————————◄○►————————

*And I looked, and behold a Pale Horse,*
*And his name that sat on him was Death*

*Revelation 6:8*

Although written in 1960 and published the following year, *The Pale Horse* had an inspiration from Agatha Christie's youth. Mr P was a pharmacist who, almost half a century earlier, instructed her in the preparation and dispensing of drugs. One day he showed her a dark-coloured lump that he took from his pocket, explaining that it was curare which he carried around with him because it gave him a feeling of power. As she writes in *An Autobiography*: 'He struck me, in spite of his cherubic appearance, as a possibly dangerous man. His memory remained with me so long that it was still there waiting when I first conceived the idea of writing my book *The Pale Horse.*'

One of the strongest titles of the last fifteen years of her career, the book has a horribly plausible plot, a very unusual poison and a genuine feeling of evil pervading the usual whodunit element.

Notebook 58 has two pages of Notes on 'Voodoo' just before the notes for *The Pale Horse*. Phrases such as 'Blood Pact – the sacrifice of a pig – snake vertebrae mingled – the asson or sacred rattle – Legba, the God who removes the barrier – Abobo, a ritual exclamation' are all noted. The application of these researches can be seen in Chapter 6 of the novel.

Although the notes are scattered over five Notebooks, the basic plot was established early on, as were some of the characters. Notebook 38 contains a sketch of the opening pages and the coffee bar scene, with the important hair-pulling incident, appears in the novel exactly as it does here; although the woman is not found dead, but dies shortly after Father Gorman's ministrations. It seems that from the beginning thallium was to be the murder method.

The Thallium Mystery

Start somehow with a list of names e.g.
Sarah Montfort

Anthony West
Mrs. Evershed
Lilian Beckett –
Jaspar Handingly – All of them dead

A woman – hospital nurse – found dead – the place
     ransacked – she says list – all dead

They are all dead
Begins – coffee bar – the girls fight – one pulls out fistful of
     other one's hair
Police? Girl is good sport – says didn't really hurt

The formula – paid agents – women who go round – report
     on medicine bottles etc. – they do several houses in
     neighbourhood – report on the N.H. service

The mechanics of the aptly named 'death broker' as well as
some of his potential 'customers' are considered, although
Poirot was abandoned in favour of her second possibility:
'plain', i.e. a non-series novel:

Book
Thallium? Series of poisonings going back over years? Hair
     falling out only symptom in common
Poirot?
Plain?
A 'Death Broker' – you pay – the person concerned goes –
     by various natural causes
Idea like killing off jury (or Ten Little Niggers?)
No apparent connection – But there is one. What?

The idea of the Murder Syndicate arranged by (?) Osborne
– a strange dual personality – a respectable family – not a
bad lot – leaves home, wild, comes back the Prodigal Son
– but middle class respectability not enough for him – when
Father dies – well off – opens branches in 3 districts run by

his assistants – he is at other ones always – actually has a second life abroad?

It is not entirely clear if Dr Corrigan, mentioned in the following extract as a possible partner in crime, was to have been a relation of Ginger's, but Osborne was the villain of the piece from the start. And the outline below is accurately reflected in the published novel, although not all of the elements – Dr C is not 'in it' (he is a police surgeon) and Venables' name is not on the original list – were incorporated; and the names of the three 'witches' were to change:

Ideas
(1)  Ginger is Ginger Corrigan – Heiress to money?
     (a) Her would-be killer is in Fete party – man's wife
     (b) Doc. C.[orrigan] is in it – he and Osborne? Object
     – to set up big research unit abroad
(2)  Osborne – a double life character – father was
     respectable prosperous old fashioned pharmacist –
     other O. ran off as boy – went on stage – impersonator
Rough idea of how the racket is worked – The organisation?
     Double life – a chemist (shop)

A rich man – crippled – collects silver – his name will be 'on
     list' (false) – his niece or nephew will be framed.
Others – 1st Business man – office – or meet in park
         2nd weird sisters – ritual
         3rd employed person to make enquiries as to
     medicines etc. by victims – Consumer research it –
     replacing of some medicament by thallium

Head man Dr. C? Osbourn
False head adam's apple – Mr Vuillaumy [Venables] Rich
     eccentric

Next:
Samuel disbarred lawyer
3 W[eird] Sis[ters]
Thelma French – Sybil White (or Greek name) – Alison
Wilde – cook – village witch

Does Osborne come to Fete from Bournemouth – ~~accosts~~
 – comes to Mark – rang up Dr. Corrigan
or police? Saw the man – describes him – scene in chemist's
 shop at Bournemouth

One intriguing possibility was the inclusion of Miss Marple. The novel features a number of elderly women in a small village, as well as Mrs Dane Calthrop her old friend from *The Moving Finger*, so Miss Marple would have felt quite at home. Christie toyed with two ideas for involving her, both very feasible: as a neighbour of one of the victims or as a great-aunt to Mark Easterbrook:

The Pale Horse Extra notes

Near Miss Marple one of the 'Names' lives
 Is 'Mark' Miss M's great nephew (Raymond's son)
Three 'weird' sisters – living at the 'Pale Horse' formerly an
inn – inside is picture framed – formerly the Inn Sign at end
Mark (?) cleans it – the rider skeleton appears – Miss M
gives quotation from Revelations
 Thelma Grey is owner of Pale Horse – her family came
from Ireland – witchcraft – her gr[eat]-gr-gr-etc. aunt burnt
as a witch (probably all lies somebody says!). She talks
about witchcraft – and what it is

Finally, Notebook 6 has an unexpected jotting:

Pale Horse Play?

Expresso 2 girls – Andrew startled

That's all – nothing more exists. It is difficult to see how the novel could have transferred successfully to the stage. Perhaps the discussion on *Macbeth* and its Three Witches encouraged Christie to consider an adaptation?

Although thallium – the murder method in *The Pale Horse* – was used by her great con-temporary Ngaio Marsh in her 1947 novel *Final Curtain*, it was Christie's novel that gained notoriety in the UK in June 1972 when Graham Young was convicted of the murder of two workmates, and the attempted murder of two more, using the same poison. Both the novel and Agatha Christie were mentioned during his trial. Although Young denied having read *The Pale Horse*, an enterprising reporter contacted Christie to get her reaction. She explained that she had used it in the novel as it was unusual and interesting for a detective novelist, being tasteless and odourless as well as difficult to detect.

ᗡᗢᗢ

## *The Mirror Crack'd from Side to Side*
### 12 November 1962

─────────────◀◉▶─────────────

What was it that film actress Marina Gregg saw in her home, Gossington Hall in St Mary Mead, that caused her to 'freeze', just before a murder was committed there? Further attempts on Marina's life and three more deaths follow before Miss Marple can explain that look of doom.

─────────────◀◉▶─────────────

*Out flew the web and floated wide;*
*The mirror crack'd from side to side*
*'The curse has come upon me,' cried*
*The Lady of Shalott.*

Tennyson, *The Lady of Shalott*

*The Mirror Crack'd from Side to Side* is the last of the village murder mysteries. Christie began work on this in late 1961 but when the manuscript was submitted, in April 1962, there was a spate of concerned correspondence between her agent and publishers and at one stage it was doubtful if the book would be ready in time for the Christmas market. The early mention of German measles in the first draft was considered such a giveaway – although its complete omission was felt to be unfair – that a rewrite was called for. The reader at Collins successfully predicted not only the killer but the motive also, long before the first murder was even committed. And after its publication the problem rumbled on with the receipt of a letter from an angry American reader bitterly complaining about the motive and its lack of sensitivity to a tragedy in the life of the well-known actress Gene Tierney. Despite a reply from Edmund Cork to the effect that Agatha Christie knew nothing about this until long afterwards, the accusation still surfaces from time to time.

The first six pages of Notebook 39 contain an embarrassment of riches in the shape of plot ideas. The first page is confidently headed 'Miss M Book' and in the course of the following pages the plot devices of *The Clocks*, *A Caribbean Mystery* and *The Mirror Crack'd from Side to Side* are all sketched, along with echoes of 'The Case of the Caretaker' (where Dr Haydock encourages her to unravel a 'nice' murder) as well as a short idea – the girl and the nasty fall – that appears as a throwaway scene in Chapter 2 of *The Mirror Crack'd from Side to Side*:

> Dr Haydock – getting old – Miss M says can't knit – Dr H suggest unravel – you've always had an interest in murder to say nothing of more than your fair share of it. Proceeds to tell her a story.

> At the Development – a girl looking over a house has a nasty fall – has man with her pushed her

Dr H's story – Is it story of Clocks – typist – blind woman – dead man

Miss M with Jenny in West Indies – the frog faced Major – his gossip – glass eye – appears to be looking different direction from what he really is

Eventually she settles on the 'Development Murder' (as it is referred to throughout) and we find 71-year-old Agatha Christie still working at full creative stretch at an age when most people have retired:

Jessica Knight – M asks her to go to chemist? Then she gets up, slips her coat on and goes for walk. The Development – entering a strange country – scraps of talk – near accident? Man and girl – looking at cottage – her fall – Heather Badcock

Notebook 4 has the germ of the idea that is the main plot device of the book:

The Rubella idea – Reason for crime – child has been born defective owing to one natal infection – while the 'fan' has grim determination not to miss meeting her idol

And Notebook 8 develops this further with a rough sketch of the first few chapters:

Development Murder
Chapter I Miss Marple and Development – her walk – when old place was Protheroes – the Bantry's – young women who remind her of various people – then a Hilda Glazebrook – one of those tiresome gushing women. Patience Considine – Actress and Film star – Hilda's hero worship – bit about German measles – no ill effects – P's look – as though frozen

The contentious four words ('bit about German measles') appear very near the beginning of the notes, indicating Christie's intention of playing dangerously fair with the reader. In the event she rewrote this and other similar references, and avoided mentioning German measles until almost the end of the novel.

The bulk of the plotting is in Notebook 52, and once the setting of Gossington Hall and its new inhabitant was decided, and the 'rubella idea' established, the book was smoothly drafted:

> Miss M unravelling – Marina Gregg buys Bantrys old house – Mrs B in lodge
>
> Her husband Arthur Rossiter (?) quiet intelligent man – dark horse?
> Heather Beasly (?) in a 'development' house – Miss M – out walking – falls down – Heather picks her up – cup of tea – talk etc. about Marina Gregg? Story of H. going with measles etc. – Mr Beasley bank clerk? Insurance agent? House agent? School teacher?
>
> Encounter between M[arina] and H[eather] – husband there (Does Mrs B recount all this later to Miss M?)
>
> Some nonsense H said (first mention of G measles?) – Well M answered her – but there was a minute or two – and she said it quite absent-mindedly and as though she was thinking of something else – mechanically – said it so often before – but her eyes staring – over Heather's head – as though she saw something – something terrible – at what?
> Well – staircase
> Who was coming up

The idea of looking over the shoulder and seeing something amazing/frightening/puzzling features in a few Christie novels, and each example culminates in credible, and different explanation. The earliest example is in *The Mysterious Affair at Styles*, followed a few years later by another instance in *The Man in the Brown Suit*. Significant other examples are included in *Appointment with Death* and *Death Comes as the End*. Two years after *The Mirror Crack'd from Side to Side*, Miss Marple is presented with a similar puzzle when Major Palgrave sees something disturbing over her shoulder in *A Caribbean Mystery*. The answer to that riddle is her most daring and original solution and may, indeed, have been inspired by the reference to Nelson in the extract below.

A minor point about *The Mirror Crack'd from Side to Side* is the fact that Mrs Bantry relates all of the dramatic events of the reception back to Miss Marple. Why did Christie not arrange that Miss Marple, under some pretext, attend the party herself? This could have been easily set up and would have overcome the necessity to interpret Marina's actions as filtered through a third, and sometimes fourth, person. But perhaps that is the very reason that she did not: Miss Marple would have seen too much. As it is, the jogging of the arm and the dropping of the sleeping draught into the glass is glossed over, although in reality this would be difficult to stage-manage. This is also a rare example of the use of a fictitious poison.

For the most part the people Christie originally listed (or versions thereof) appear in the finished book:

Now People

Kathleen Leila Carlyn [Margot Bence] – adopted child from slum family – mother wrote letter – then her own [Marina's] child comes – she makes settlement on adopted children – girl and 2 boys –

Does Lara come to board with Cherry – (a pal her sister has picked up) or working somewhere as hairdresser or as a photographer (best?)

Ella Schwarz [Zeilinsky] – social secretary – in love with Jason

Heather's husband Arthur

Mary Bates –a widow – husband dead in a rather peculiar way (car accident?)

Carlton Burrowes – surprise guest – used to know Marina

Who were on stairs or coming up?

Ms Sage – just over his head – frozen stare – at what – or whom?

A. Picture on wall – subject? Death of Nelson!!
B. Carlton Burrowes – Alfred Klein – one a friend
C. The other brought by him
D. A photographer girl from Homes and Gardens
E. Ella Schwarz
F. Arthur Badcock
G. Mary Baine
H. Very elderly man

She recovers herself – usual charm to Heather – Dormil – uses it on her – H. puts it down (to talk) M. puts hers down – to stretch out both hands turning round – knocks H's drink – have mine – tomato juice instead

The 'Homes and Gardens' photographer, Margot Bence, carries echoes of the adopted children in *Ordeal by Innocence* from four years earlier. The widow Mary Bates (subsequently listed as Baine) does not figure in the story and Carlton Burrowes may be an early version of Ardwyck Fenn.

The biggest surprise is the inclusion in the above list of the 'Death of Nelson' (complete with double exclamation marks) as the subject of the all-important picture on the stairs. In the novel it is the Madonna and Child motif of the painting that causes both Marina to 'freeze' and Miss Marple's theory to be vindicated. Is it possible that at this stage in the planning Christie had not decided on the reason for the look of doom? Unlikely as it might appear, this would seem to be the case, as some of the other options for the 'frozen' stare are listed and eventually included in the novel.

And, finally, Miss Marple explains . . .

Miss M says – I've been very stupid – medical book – shuts it

The Meeting – Miss M wants to stand on stairs – the light – 'I understand better now'
   She took an overdose? Very easy to do – or perhaps someone gave it to her
   To Dermot – Very simple Doom has come upon me cried was Heather – doom came on her as a direct result of what she once did – many years ago – meaning no harm but lacking consideration – thinking only of what an action meant to her. She did because she went to an Entertainment to see and meet Marina Gregg at a time when she was suffering from German measles

In Christie novels last-minute revelations of hidden identities abound, but even the most devoted reader cannot accept that Arthur Badcock, portrayed and perceived as dull and insignificant, was once the husband of famous, glamorous Marina. In Chapter 8 iii he is described as looking like 'a piece of chewed string. Nice but wet.' True, Marina's first marriage, 'an early one which didn't count', is mentioned in Chapter 3, but to accept that he happens to live in the small village where she happens to buy a house, that neither of them mention it and that no one else is aware of it, is expecting too much of the reader's indulgence. For sheer unbelieveability this coincidence ranks with the revelation of Miranda's parentage in *Hallowe'en Party*, the identity of Louise Leidner's first husband in *Murder in Mesopotamia* and that of Stoddart-West's mother in *4.50 from Paddington*.

## *Rule of Three*
### *The Rats; Afternoon at the Seaside; The Patient*
### 20 December 1962

◄○►

Over forty years after her career began Christie was still experimenting when *Rule of Three* was first presented at the Duchess Theatre, London. Reviews were not good however and along with *Fiddlers Three*, which never had a West End run, it lowered the curtain on her golden age of theatre. Although rarely staged nowadays *Rule of Three* shows that, even after a lifetime of hoodwinking her audience, Agatha Christie still had the ability to surprise and entertain. Each play shows a different aspect of the Queen of Crime, aspects that are both unexpected and atypical. Of the three plays, *Afternoon at the Seaside* is the most unlikely play ever to have come from her pen; *The Rats* is not a whodunit but a claustrophobic will-they-get-away-with-it; while *The Patient* is the essence of Christie.

As early as 1955, in Notebook 3, Christie was including *Rule of Three* in a list of 'Projects'. The same list also considers what were to become *4.50 from Paddington* ('New Book Miss M?' below) and the next Westmacott novel, eventually titled *The Burden*. At that stage the three projected plays were to be adaptations of existing, and mutually contrasting, stories; both 'Accident' and 'The Rajah's Emerald' are from *The Listerdale Mystery* and 'S.O.S.' is included in *The Hound of Death*. It is worth noting that 'The Rajah's Emerald' has a thematic connection – the disappearance of jewels on a beach – with *Afternoon at the Seaside*; and both are light-hearted in tone. The grim poisoning short story 'Accident' had already been adapted in 1939 by Margery Vosper as *Tea for Three*, a short one-act play.

General Projects 1955

Angle of Attack   Mary Westmacott

The Unexpected Guest      Play 3 Acts

Three Plays (Rule of Three?)

1. Accident?
2. Rajah's Emerald?
3. S.O.S.?

New Book   Miss M?    P? –

By Notebook 24, two of the eventual titles, C and B below, were included in the following jotting, 'S.O.S.' (although with a question mark) still remaining as the third. Inexplicably, they are listed on the page in reverse alphabetical order; when presented *The Rats* is performed first, followed by *Afternoon at the Seaside*, and culminating with *The Patient*.

Rule of Three   3 1-Act plays for P.S. [Peter Saunders, her producer]

C. The Patient
B. Seaside Holiday – I do like to be beside the seaside
A. S.O.S.? [sic]
 The Locket
 Christmas Roses
 Green Paint Or Telephone Call –

Though the remaining references are elusive, the 'telephone call' in the second list is probably the seed of *The Rats*, where the phone-call sets the trap into which 'the rats' are lured; and 'Green Paint' may be a cryptic reference to the proposed innovation she had in mind for the end of *The Patient* (see below).

ᕔᕕᕗ

## The Rats

<>

Adulterous lovers Sandra and David each receive a phone call inviting them to the flat of a mutual acquaintance. When they try to leave they discover that they are locked in – and there is a dead body in the Kuwait Chest.

<>

*The Rats* is somewhat similar to the Poirot story 'The Mystery of the Baghdad Chest', and its later and more elaborate version, 'The Mystery of the Spanish Chest', in which a suspicious husband hides in the eponymous chest hoping to catch his wife and her lover *in flagrante*; in *The Rats*, when Sandra and David realise that they have been lured to the flat, they suspect a similar trap, but the play develops in a more macabre fashion. It does retain the clue of the little heap of sawdust beneath the chest which, in the story, gives Poirot 'furiously to think'. Notebook 24 contains almost five pages of notes:

The Rats

Flat belongs to the Torrances – rather bare – a Kuwait chest is centre – high up into roof – built in cupboards – a dark divan covered with curtains etc. – a long ply wood table – some modern chairs – one or two pieces of Persian pottery – a big Arab long nosed beak nosed coffee pot

Body in ~~cupboard~~ – Baghdad Chest – Oh! My God – It's Robert – Police will come – girl and man discover body of her husband – Alec arrives – a Mischa like person – says he got phone call

Although there have been gay characters in Christie before this (Mr Pye in *The Moving Finger*, Murgatroyd and Hinch-cliffe in *A Murder is Announced* and Horace Bindler in 'Greenshaw's Folly'), Alec in *The Rats* is the most unequivocal and stereotypical example and far more sinister than, for example, Christopher Wren in *The Mousetrap*. He is described in the script as 'the pansy type, very elegant, amusing, inclined to be spiteful' and his love for Sandra's former husband is openly discussed. The Mischa reference, above, is puzzling. It is unlikely to refer to the Russian actor Mischa Auer who played Prince Nikita Starloff – in effect, Anthony Marston – in the 1945 screen version of *And The There Were None*.

## Afternoon at the Seaside

A family afternoon on the beach culminates in the
capture of a jewel thief and some unexpected revelations
– and a resolve to go elsewhere for next year's holiday.

Reminiscent of a saucy English seaside postcard, *Afternoon at the Seaside* is Agatha Christie's most unlikely play. It is set entirely on a beach and involves, at one point, a female character changing into her swimsuit onstage. The plot, for Christie, is slight and the humour is at times forced but there is one surprise, representing a new variation on an old Christie theme. Ironically the notes are extensive, almost forty pages, albeit with a lot of repetition. There is much speculation about the naming both of the families (the aptly named Mr and Mrs Sour, described as 'whiners', become Mr and Mrs Crum) and the beach huts:

| Sea View | (Mon Repos) | Wee Nook |
|---|---|---|
| Mrs. Montressor | Mr Wills Mrs Wills | Genevieve Batat |

At the Seaside

| Iniskillen | Bide a Wee | Mon Repos |
|---|---|---|
| Mr Sour | Wilkinson | ~~Arlette~~ |
| Child | ~~Mr Robbins~~ | ~~Incognita~~ |
| Mrs Sour | ~~Mrs. Robbins~~ | Yvonne |
| (Whiners) | Wilkinson | |

But further into the notes there are flashes of the Queen of Crime in the unmasking, not of the villain, but of the policeman – or to be strictly accurate, the policewoman:

Read in paper – robbery at Aga Khan – emeralds/sapphires –

Beach
Mon Desir
Policewoman Alice Jones acting as vamp
Young man and his girl quarrel – another young man and
    they bring down deck chairs –

Her ability to spin variations on a theme has not deserted her, even in this short, untypical effort, and some ideas are reminiscent of the Christie of old. The 'switch of trousers' device has distinct echoes of 'The Rajah's Emerald' from *The Listerdale Mystery*:

Does detective arrive – search the huts? Find emeralds?
Or does old Grubb find it in bucket?
Or child kick pile of sand – Grubb picks out emeralds
God bless my soul

Reasonable possible ideas
Or switch of trousers – Percy gets in the wrong ones

Somers (weakly and gentlemanly – really cat burglar)
Or counterfeit money
Or put into wrong hut
Does Percy get hit with beach ball
Or blackmail

## *The Patient*

Mrs Wingfield is paralysed as a result of a fall from the
balcony of her home. Her doctor has found a way to
communicate with her and is about to do so in the
presence of her family. But someone doesn't want her
to tell the truth of that fateful afternoon.

It is a shame that so few Christie fans are familiar with *The
Patient*, as, in many ways, it is the essence of Christie: a closed
setting, a limited family circle of suspects, a crafty distribu-
tion of suspicion; and one of her most artfully concealed
clues. Unlike the other two plays in this trilogy, it is a pure
whodunit with a stunning curtain line. Yes, it is contrived (an
immobilised patient communicating via a once-for-Yes-twice-
for-No light switch) but so are many other detective plots,
including some of her own best titles. Notes for the play
appear in Notebooks 22 and 24:

The Patient

Nursing Home – Doctor and Nurse (Patient there?
Or wheeled in later)
    Is latter the one who has established communication –

The Patient -

Room in Nursing Home. Entry of doctor
& relations (?). Psychological - nothing organic
        Nurse - Her contact thro' patient -
Conscious - (Black nurse?)
        N - Says she thinks -
S.O.S. idea - Man (relation? police)
Notices that she thinks

        S.O.S. He asks her — one for
Yes - Twice for No -


        Do it

        Possible ending
A nurse introduced - really Police woman -
apparently guilty -

Possible scene.

Patient Sees, murderer -
        Sheds him.

N - Is a' Nurse who really was
relation & killed husband.

*A sketch and notes for* The Patient *from Notebook 64.*
*Note the reference to 'S.O.S.' the short story from* The Hound
of Death *that, like* The Patient, *also features an
unusual method of communication.*

Sales talk by Inspector – jewellery disappeared
   Mrs. X badly injured – paralysed – unable to
communicate – ingenious nurse pressure of fingers –
apparatus with red bulb – Patient wheeled in –

Patient wheeled in – nurse by her (Bond) or interne
Questions spelled out Murder
        Mirror
        Bathroom
Saw someone        Yes
Someone you knew        Yes
Is that person in the room now  Yes
Spell out the name   A – B
B –        Yes
Collapse reported by nurse? interne? –

Take off the mask – I know well enough who you are
Curtain falls – My God – you!

Alternative end – gloves – coated in phosphorescent paint
– hold up your hands – Lights out – Guilty Hands!

Even at this late stage in her theatrical career Christie was experimenting, as the last two notes above show. Incredibly, she wanted the curtain to fall, or the lights to black out, *before* the murderer was unmasked. This would have been the ultimate Christie twist, with the shock somewhat mitigated by a recording of her own voice asking the audience whom they thought the killer was.

Not surprisingly, however, the idea was not a winner. It was abandoned after a flurry of telegrams from the pre-London tryout in Aberdeen to the author, who was abroad. With a track record of glittering theatrical success, it does seem a very odd idea, akin to reading a Christie whodunit and finding the last chapter missing.

### The Clocks
### 7 November 1963

———————◄○►———————

A roomful of clocks showing the wrong time,
a blind woman, a dead man and a hysterical girl –
when Colin Lamb explains the story to his friend,
Hercule Poirot decides that the situation is so
bizarre that the explanation must be simple.
Developments prove otherwise.

———————◄○►———————

Published between two Miss Marple whodunits, *The Clocks*
was the first Poirot novel since *Cat among the Pigeons* in 1959.
Appearing in only three chapters, he acts, literally, as an
armchair detective, with Colin Lamb bringing him the
information to enable them both to arrive at a conclusion.

*The Clocks* is an uneasy mix of spy story and domestic
murder mystery with little in the way of clues to help the
reader distinguish between the two. There are, as usual,
clever ideas – the telephone call and the broken shoe, the
adoption of a ready-made plot, the conversion of secrets to
Braille – but the overall explanation is a disappointment. If
the spy angle had been dropped and the inheritance plot
elaborated the result would have been a tighter book. And,
as she has done in many previous titles, Christie introduces
an unsuspected, but in this case unnecessary, relationship in
the closing chapters.

A fascinating interlude with Poirot occurs in Chapter 14
when we read of his forthcoming study of detective fiction.
He mentions several milestones of the genre: *The Leavenworth
Case, The Adventures of Arsene Lupin, The Mystery of the Yellow
Room, The Adventures of Sherlock Holmes.* He goes on to discuss
a number of authors, some of whom, although fictional, are
identifiable: Cyril Quain with his attention to detail and

unbreakable alibis is Freeman Wills Crofts; Louisa O'Malley with her milieu of brownstone mansion in New York is Elizabeth Daly. Florence Elks is more difficult to identify but is perhaps Margaret Millar, a writer Christie admired, as she stated in a 1974 interview. A Canadian who set most of her novels in the USA, Millar has order, method and wit, although not the abundance of drink to which Poirot refers. Two other writers are mentioned but both are firmly fictional: Garry Gregson, who is an important element in the plot of *The Clocks*, and, of course, Ariadne Oliver.

The other area for speculation is the parentage of Colin Lamb. When they meet, Poirot asks after Colin's father and wonders why he is not using the family name. In G.C. Ramsey's *Mistress of Mystery* (1967) Christie is quoted as confirming that Colin is Superintendent Battle's son.

In Notebook 4, on a page dated 1961, an alphabetical listing of plot ideas includes the inspirations for *The Mirror Crack'd from Side to Side* and *A Caribbean Mystery*; on that list idea F is a brief outline of *The Clocks*. And a year later the tentative title appears on a listing of future books.

F. The Clock – as beginning – typist – dead body – blind old lady

1962
Notes for 3 books

Y. The Clocks (?)
Z. Carribean [sic] Mystery
X. Gypsy's Acre

But in fact the plot for *The Clocks* goes back a lot further than that. In late 1949 Agatha Christie devised a competition, in which competitors were asked to complete a short story, of which she had written the opening. It concerned a typist, Nancy, arriving at a house and letting herself in to the front room. There she finds a collection of clocks, a dead man and a blind woman. Twelve years later Christie herself resurrected the story and set about expanding it. The main difference between the two is that the clocks in the short story all show different, and wrong, times whereas the clocks of the novel all show the same, but equally wrong, time. Unsurprisingly the character names are also different, as is the street address; but the similarities are striking – the description of the clocks is identical and the 'Rosemary' clock is specifically mentioned; the telephone call making the appointment is a mystery and the blind woman, it transpires, is Nancy's mother. Ironically the explanation of the presence of the clocks is more convincing in the prize-winning solution than in the novel.

In its earlier incarnation the short story is called 'The Clock Stops'; this is also the title used in Notebook 8 where fifty pages of plotting is contained. A list of possible characters, most of whose names will change, and a possible motive, are the first considerations:

> Mildred Pebmarsh – fiftyish – blind – had been a librarian
> – now teaches Braille
> Alice Dale – young stenographer (Is her second name
> Rosemary) Does Alice, flying out of house, collide with Colin
> Dead Man
> Miss Curtis    Head of typing firm
> Colin Lamb – young man – journalist? Doctor? Investigator?
> On vacation

Christie sketches the motive scenario more than once. Elements of each sketch were used in the final version, which has much in common – an unexpected arrival from abroad endangering a criminal impersonation – with *Dead Man's Folly*:

> Money involved – something with money (gain)
> A middle aged woman inherits vast fortune from an uncle

in Canada? (Advertised?) S. America? (or written to Mrs. Bristow?) Actually real Mrs. Bristow is dead and Bristow has remarried (or not?). He decides that he and his wife will claim – was he small builder? Bankrupt – settled in her place. Anyway no one knows he has a first wife. But senior partner of firm of solicitors knows real Mrs. B. So he comes down to (No. 6? 19?) is received, drugged and killed. Taken across diagonal to No. 19 – 61?

Unsatisfactory person marries nice girl – goes abroad – actually she dies and he marries again – a woman who was sec[retary] to det. story writer – his wife poisoned but he won't marry her. Fortune left her – she plays invalid. Papers brought for her to sign – O.K. Later someone who knows her well comes – they prepare – plot hers – (from favourite employer) her name is Rosemary – uses old clock. Is girl's name Alice Rosemary called after his mother? Mother is dead – some mystery about her. A. is illegitimate

Further elaboration follows; the first possible explanation of the clocks is (thankfully) discarded and the second one adopted:

Point of various things

(1) Clocks – the time (Fast?) (Slow?) 3–25
Possibly – Rosemary faded carriage clock – press 3 – 2 – 5 contains a secret compartment – clocks works have been taken out (a reference to time of a murder – it took place on a Saturday night in Oct. (daylight saving!)

(2) Rosemary – the name of someone connected with Martindale – Alice or M. Pebmarsh

The whole is a plot – invented by Rosemary Western (a Mrs. Oliver) now dead and adapted for use as camouflage by her secretary who is – Martindale? Pebmarsh? Mrs. Bristow at No. 61 Pam or Geraldine

Fortune left to Mrs X (Argentine? Australia? S. Africa?). Actually she has died abroad and husband remarried almost at once. Only one person knows Mrs X by sight. It is this member of law firm who has come over. They plan murder – but not to let him be identified. Elaboration and clocks etc. is suggested by plot of an unpublished book. Mrs X or Miss Martindale was private secretary to a Creasey detective story writer.

The reference to 'a Creasey detective story writer' is unexpected. John Creasey was a hugely prolific writer – producing over 500 titles under a variety of pen names – of most types of crime novel, with the exception of detective stories. In Chapter 28 Poirot explains the original meaning of the clocks as they feature in the unpublished manuscript; it was a code to the combination to the safe, concealed behind a reproduction of the Mona Lisa, containing the jewels of the Russian royal family. He describes the plot as '*Un tas de bêtises*, the whole thing', in other words, nonsense.

The all-important story of Edna and her damaged shoe appears alongside the timetable for the fateful lunch-hour:

Edna in outer office with stiletto heel that has come off – describing where and how she bought buns and came back to office

Timing here to be consistent
1.30 – 2.30 Alice lunch interval
12.30 – 1.30 L[unch] interval for ?
Edna leaves office 12.30 o'clock – returns by
12.50 – no call comes through before 1.30
1.30 Miss M goes out
        or
Edna goes out 1.30 – back 1.50 – better
No call before 2.30
Miss M goes out 12.30 – 1.30

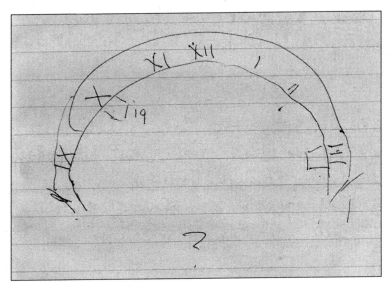

*A sketch from Notebook 8 during the plotting of* The Clocks.
*Christie was experimenting with a combination of the numerals from
a clock-face and a possible sketch of Wilbraham Crescent.*

Christie experimented throughout the notes with various neighbours, some of whom made it into the novel. Aspects of the following jottings – 'quiet gardening type', 'Cat lover woman', and the children – appear, but adapted and rearranged. Interestingly, the 'secretary to a bestseller writer' becomes a major plot feature; but the character chosen for this important role is not a resident of Wilbraham Crescent. Despite the alteration of house numbers between Notebook and novel, and the cryptic illustration in Chapter 6, these are not important elements. The use of a Crescent is a useful, though not entirely convincing, method of isolating the suspects:

Neighbours

No. 60 Man wife children – man sporty talkative, wife v. quiet

62 Couple of women – Pam and Geraldine – develop their characters

No. 18 Mainly cats?

No. 19 Middle aged man – a gardener – invalid wife? Got a blind spinster sister

Where is my murder and <u>why</u>

(1) Quiet gardener man – carries victim in sack
(2) One of the two women – Geraldine? – has been secretary to a bestseller writer (Mrs. O?!!) – has taken various details from one of her discarded plots
(3) Heart man with wife and children
(4) Miss Pebmarsh

Neighbours

16. Cat lover woman with draperies, accusative of one of the others (? which) because he killed my cat [Mrs Hemming at No. 20]

20. 2/3? awful children (later one of them says something) like B.B.'s children 10, 7, 3? Harassed fond mother children like Miss P [the Ramsays]

61. Mr. Bland – unimaginative man, sandy hair, freckled, commonplace – builder in small way near bankrupt – then wife comes into money. Thinking of living abroad – the wife would like it – I don't know myself – can't get any decent food abroad [no. 69]

62. 2 women? One former secretary to thriller writer or young man living with mother. He is weakly looking – she is really a man? Arty husband and wife – a son Thomas

~~69~~ 60. Middle-aged man – quiet gardening type – went with wheelbarrow sacks etc. [Mr McNaughton] Could have a flirty spinster sister

One of the problems with the book, though, is that there are too many neighbours and that they are not clearly enough delineated to fix them in the mind, while the lengthy interviews with them offer little in the way of information, either for the police or the reader.

Some ideas were not pursued, but some appeared at a later stage; the first has an element of the plot of the next Poirot novel, *Third Girl*, where a female character has two distinct 'lives' miles apart, the family of each unaware of the existence of the other:

Clocks

Miss Pebmarsh – forty? fifty? blind – who is she?

Idea – Really a Miss or Mrs X has a well authenticated life in small town Torquay or Wallingford; companion lives with her or perhaps she has a room as P[aying] G[uest] in people's house – goes away occasionally to stay with relations – 'Universal Aunt' sees her across London. Returns in due course – says she is a missionary – sister of a missionary. Came home with ill health – there <u>was</u> such a person – but lost track of.

And, as can be seen below, another early possibility was to combine the 'Greenshaw's Folly' idea with *The Clocks*; in the short story a secretary does indeed go to Greenshaw's Folly to begin work:

Typist sent from agency to G's Folly alone there – finds body – or blind woman who nearly steps on it. Clocks all an hour wrong Why? So that they will strike 12 instead of 1

Further ideas followed, some of which – the 'thriller' plot, the claimed husband, the postcards from abroad – found their way into the book:

Man next door does murder of blackmailer. Takes advantage of Miss P's blindness – kills man with dagger?

Or strangles? – carries him in through window – then rings up typewriting agency. Some reason for asking for that particular girl? Is her name Rosemary – clocks just a fancy touch (obvious really – contrived) mistake – one clock is at a quarter to nine

A 'thriller' plot – some secret process – man almost gets it – is killed – scrawls a few words – 61 – L

A woman whose lover is murdered
    "        "    daughter    "    A 14
    "        "    son        "    (revenge)

Idea put about is that a woman Mrs U meets Mr C at hotel – is to take him down in car. Later she calls for baggage – goes to Victoria . . . and travels with man like him (passport?) latter sends p.cs from abroad <u>or</u> his luggage is in hotel unclaimed. Mr C at Cresc. is killed . . . taken across to 19 – Mr Curry – later woman will turn up and claim him as husband. Mr C disappears

Vasall like – plans photographed during [lunch?] hour – 2 overcoats alike? – or bus or train. Miss Pebmarsh – (caraway seed? aniseed?) Found by agent – or agent writes it as dying

This last outline is very cryptic. 'Vasall' is a reference to the real-life spy John Vassall, a British civil servant who was arrested as a spy in September 1962 and subsequently convicted. This would have been a high-profile event during the genesis of *The Clocks*. The '2 overcoats' is probably a ploy used to effect a quick change of appearance in order to avoid detection; the bus/train possibility is probably another escape route plan. The caraway seed/aniseed reference is probably to the hoary old plot device of using either as a means of tracking a quarry, a variation of which is used in the denouement of *N or M?*

*The Mirror Crack'd from Side to Side*, published the previous year, and *A Caribbean Mystery* the following year, were the last 'pure' whodunits Christie was to write but *The Clocks*, despite its promising opening, remains an inexplicably disappointing offering.

## A Caribbean Mystery
### 16 November 1964

---

While holidaying in the West Indies, Miss Marple is
subjected to the endless reminiscences of Major Palgrave.
After his sudden death she regrets not paying more
attention when he talked about a murderer he knew.
Is it possible that the same killer is planning
another crime on St Honore?

---

In *A Caribbean Mystery* Christie used memories of a holiday in Barbados a few years earlier and despatched Miss Marple to solve her only foreign case, although before beginning *4.50 from Paddington* the idea had been briefly considered:

Miss Marple – somewhere on travels – or at seaside

The notes for *A Caribbean Mystery* are scattered over fourteen Notebooks, although many are no more than jottings of isolated ideas that Christie subsumed into *A Caribbean Mystery* when she came to write it in 1963. Notebook 4 shows early musings and in Notebook 48 we find speculation about two couples:

1961 Projects

Carribean [sic] – Miss M – after illness – Raymond and Wife – Daughter – or son? Bogus major Taylor – like a frog – he squints.

Idea A  Couples  Lucky and Greg  Evelyn and Rupert [Edward]
   Greg very rich American – Lucky wants to marry young chap – however pretends it is Rupert – has affair with him. Point is to be R. kills Greg or Evelyn kills G by mistake for R. Really it is young man kills Greg

Despite the presence of two couples with almost identical names in the novel, none of the various permutations and combinations considered here found their way into *A Caribbean Mystery*. In Notebook 35 she lists what were to become three novels, although the alphabetical sequence is odd. Perhaps this is the order in which she intended to write them, although they were actually published in the order below:

1962 Notes for 3 books
Y. The Clocks (?)
Z. Carribean [sic] Mystery
X. Gypsy's Acre [*Endless Night*]

Some of the ideas Christie jotted down in the various Notebooks – the frog-faced Major, someone telling long-winded stories about murder, the administration of hallucinogenic drugs and a husband who 'saves' his wife a few times only to 'fail' to save her at some later stage – do appear in the novel. She also reminds herself a few times about 'The Cretan Bull' from *The Labours of Hercules* and its use of hallucinogens:

Look up datura poisoning as administered by Indian wives to husbands – and re-read Cretan Bull

Book about Cretan Bull idea – insanity induced by doses of Belladonna

Play or Book – depending on root idea of Murder Made [sic] Easy or Cretan Bull – everything closing round <u>one</u> person gradually – engineered by someone else

A man's wife hangs herself – he cuts her down in time. Really man is preparing the way for her suicide . . . Does this tie in with what doctor or other officer remembers of another case – same man

Story about – woman hanged herself – husband cut her down in time – hushed up

One fact strikingly revealed by the Notebooks is how different a story *A Caribbean Mystery* could have been. In early drafts in Notebook 3 we see the germ of a bizarre idea, not pursued, which is elaborated in Notebook 18. Note also the early possibility of including Hercule Poirot. I can only speculate that Poirot was dropped in favour of Miss Marple as Christie, now as elderly as her creation, had spent a happy holiday in the Caribbean; and Poirot had already solved at least two seaside mysteries: *Evil under the Sun* and 'Triangle at Rhodes'.

(Happy idea) West Indian book – Miss M? Poirot
    Girl crippled by polio – has given up her young man
– goes out to where they were going on their honeymoon
– she has nurse with her – a rather doubtful character – girl
kills anyone who is happy

West Indies
    Miss Marple and possibly Jean Brent – Polio victim and a hospital nurse Doran Watson (Miss? Mrs.?)
    Could start with the girl – Jean – crippled – tells fiancé she must give him up – he protests – everyone applauds her – then given a trip because she wishes she could get away. Raymond must perhaps make an arrangement with Mrs.

Watson who is going with an old Mr. Van Dieman (rich) –
(to give him massage every day?) . . .

If a warped Jean who hates to hear other people's
happiness is the murderer – how does she bring it about.
Poison? Narcotic? Tranquillisers? Substitution of same Pep
pills – What drug

Combine Polio Jean – (or car accident) sacrifice with frog
faced Major (West Indies)

Three consecutive pages in Notebook 3 contain three important elements of *A Caribbean Mystery*:

Book about Cretan Bull idea – insanity induced by doses of
Belladonna.
2 pairs husband and wife – B and E apparently devoted
– actually B and G (Georgina) have had an affair for years
– Brian, G's husband doesn't know? Really it is a different
husband and wife – husband is a wife killer. Old 'frog'
Major knows – has seen him before – he is killed

And it is in Notebook 18 that we get the main source of
misdirection: the idea of the glass eye:

A different story by Major P – his glass eye rests on ? (1) ?
(2) but really on Jean and Nurse Boscombe

Interestingly, the original typescript at the end of Chapter 23
and after the 'Evil Eye . . . Eye . . . Eye' clue, includes an extra
sentence – *'Miss Marple gasped.'* This may have been considered too daring and does not appear in the published
version. And in Notebook 23 we get a rough sketch, literally,
of the all-important scene, with the Major looking over Miss
Marple's shoulder. Here Christie draws, probably for her own
clarification, the physical set-up as Miss Marple listens to the
Major's story and misinterprets his gaze:

After lunch Miss Marple talking to Maj –
verandah steps

          Miss M          Mollie Tim

Quartette      Maj.

Tim doing accounts with Mollie – Maj. talking – pulls out
snap look up and sees the man in the snap

          Left eye  R. eye

Notebook 58 is still considering very basic character setting
and a slightly different version of the story told by Major
Palgrave. Here, the CID man who investigated the crimes
tells the story directly to Miss Marple. At this stage in the
planning there is no mention of the hotel owners – just the
quartet. But there was to be a Christiean twist, not adopted
for the novel, even with this limited field of suspects.

Carribean [sic] Mystery

A quartet [of] friends
Mr and Mrs R. Rupert and Emily – English – friends of many
years standing – one pair app[ear] very devoted. One day –
wife confides they never speak to each other in private –
husband (to girl) says wonderful life together – which is lying?

The CID man is in County district in England – man's phone
broken down – he walks into town – (car at garage) for
doctor – they get back – wife is dead – heart? – man terribly
upset – it worries CID man – remembers man – has seen
him before – remembers – in France – and his wife had died
– same thing in Canada – then marries an American woman
– comes to Tobago – CID man found dead

But is it really the woman – The dog it was that died
          The wrong man or wrong woman dies – of heart trouble

so that you suspect the wrong pair – really Mrs Rupert is
the one with her fads and illnesses – she and chap are
having an affair

Finally, we can see the amount of thought that went into
the Major and his story, elements of which appear in three
Notebooks:

Problem of Major P

<u>Points</u>   Why did Major not recognise his murderer before?
     No new comers to the island – Edward, Greg, Van D
Jackson all known to him
     Answer by Miss M? – Major had <u>not</u> seen the man himself
– this was a story told him – he had only glanced at snap –
then kept it as a curiosity – he takes it out preparatory to
showing it to her looks at it – looks up, seeing suddenly <u>the
man in the photograph</u> – hastily stuffs it back again

Possibilities  (1)  Major had several murderer stories that he
                    had picked up in course of travel
               (2)  Could Miss M – (or Esther) have
                    misunderstood
               (3)  (Not supported!) Esther lied – why?

The murderer story is different – could be either a man or a
woman.
     Does Kelly tell Miss M – how Palgrave told him a story
– this indicates that it was a woman

Miss M with Jenny in West Indies
     The frog faced Major – his gossip – glass eye – appears to
be looking different direction from what he really is – 3
husband and wives applicable – Chuck and Patty (affair?)
– Greg and ~~Sarah~~ Evelyn

∽✕∾

## *At Bertram's Hotel*
### 15 November 1965

———————◄○►———————

Miss Marple's nephew treats her to a stay in Bertram's
Hotel, a relic of Edwardian opulence in London. While
enjoying its old-fashioned, and somewhat suspicious,
charm, she becomes involved in a disappearance,
robbery and murder.

———————◄○►———————

*At Bertram's Hotel* was the second Marple novel in as many
years and like its predecessor the title page included the
reminder 'Featuring Miss Marple The Original Character
as created by Agatha Christie'. This appeared as a result of
the recent incarnations of the character on screen in the
Margaret Rutherford travesties.

While the setting of this novel is typical Christie and
Marple, our expectations are confounded in the denouement when an even more breathtaking conspiracy than that
of *Murder on the Orient Express* is revealed. The notes for the
novel are evenly divided between three Notebooks. Notebook
27 has two dated pages, 'October 30th' and 'November 17th
[1964]', and the first page of Notebook 36 is dated 'October
'64'. Notebook 23 would seem to pre-date the notes in the
other two, as the following extract shows:

Bertram's Hotel

Description of it – Mayfair St. etc. – Edwardian comfort
– fires – porters . . . Tea and muffins – 'Only get muffins at
Bertrams'. Points about hotel – a nucleus of 'landed gentry'
– old style Miss Marple points out later – 'pockets' left over
really no-one like that left – No, 'Bertrams' hotel belongs to
two Americans – (never seen!). They cash in by deliberately

recreating the nucleus (at low prices) to give the right
atmosphere – then Americans and Australians etc. come at
large prices.

Meg Gresham [Bess Sedgwick] – her career – well born?
rich? Ran away with Irish groom. Then married Parker
Whitworth – enormous man – then Duke of Nottingham –
then Count Stanislaus Vronsky – Dirk Chester – film star –
or Op. singer

Amalgamate this with frog-faced old major Ronnie
Anstruther and Miss Marple – staying a week in London.
His talk about murder – same chap – saw him again –
different name – same kind of death – medical fellers
seemed satisfied – quite all right – only different name again
– Looks at someone coming

The general set-up is the same as the novel but the mention
of the 'frog-faced Major' (possibly a forerunner of Colonel
Luscombe, the guardian of Bess's daughter, Elvira) and his
talk about an earlier murder had appeared in 1964's *A Caribbean Mystery*, so these notes were probably written prior to
that. Despite this, much of the plot is accurately sketched;
but it is sketched at least three times in the course of the
notes, each adding little or nothing to the earlier, possibly an
indication that Christie's powers of weaving variations were
waning.

Ideas
Bertram's is a HQ – of a crime organization – mainly bank
robberies? Train robberies? No real violence – Money is
taken in respectable luggage to Bertram's. Certain people
take it there – rehearsed beforehand – they are usually
actors – character actors and they double for certain
people – Canon Penneyfather, General Lynde, Fergus
Mainwaring – country girl – Mr and Mrs Hamilton Clayton?
– Contessa Vivary – Ralph Winston

Resume of story
Bess Sedgwick – an outlaw rich loves dangerously – Resistance
– racing car falls for foreign criminal – handsome – attractive
Stan Lasky. She combines with him and they plan robberies
on a colossal scale – this has now been going on for (5 years?)
(longer?) HQ is Bertram's Hotel which changes hands – has a
lot of money spent on it and people of the gang are infiltrated
into it. Henry is its controlling brain and Bess is his partner –
the Americans are its titular owner – but really a façade for
Henry – there is a shuttle service – jewels or bank notes pass
through Bertram's in the hands of old fashioned 'clients',
elderly ladies – clerics – lawyers – Admirals and Colonels –
pass out next day – with rich American to Continent

While there is very little in any of the Notebooks about the
murder of Michael Gorman, the commissionaire at Bertram's
and an important figure from Bess Sedgwick's past, our old
friend the chambermaid gets yet another airing. Although
the setting of a hotel would seem to be idea, it was not to be.
Again:

Circumstances of murder?
Meg – breakfast tray by bed – Kidneys, mushrooms, bacon,
tea – chambermaid – evidence – as to conversation between
Meg and husband (Chester? Stanislaus?) Anything the matter?
She is opening letters. 'No, nothing' – This evidence clears
husband – also chambermaid collects tray – not waiter –

Bertrams   Points
Murder – woman in bed – chambermaid's evidence – took
her breakfast in bed – quite all right then (9 a.m.) body
not found until 12 – really killed – at 8.30. Man (in evening
dress) as waiter takes in breakfast tray – strangles her –
knifes her – shot? Then goes down and out. In it are
chambermaid and Richards

## *Third Girl*
### 14 November 1966

———————————◄○►———————————

When 'third girl' Norma Restarick approaches
Poirot with a story of 'a murder that she might have
committed', he is intrigued. When she disappears,
and a murder is committed at her apartment block
and his friend Mrs Oliver is coshed, Poirot enters the
unfamiliar world of Swinging Sixties London.

———————————◄○►———————————

Having made little more than a cameo appearance in his
previous case, *The Clocks*, Poirot tackles old problems in a new
setting in *Third Girl* and this time his involvement is more
active. Like some other novels from Christie's last decade,
*Third Girl* is verbose; there are many passages, and indeed
chapters, which could, and arguably should, have been
omitted: the detailed description of Long Basing (Chapter 4)
and much of Mrs Oliver's trudge around London (Chapter
9). The plot itself, despite its promising beginning, requires a
considerable suspension of disbelief, and the Swinging Sixties background is largely unconvincing. The impersonation
disclosed in the final explanation is difficult to accept, calling into question the entire basis of the novel. *Third Girl* is the
weakest book of the 1960s.

This uncertainty is mirrored in the notes. They are
scattered over six Notebooks and ninety pages but they are
repetitive, unlike the Christie of yesteryear. There are nevertheless ideas that she considered but ultimately rejected,
although, as will be seen, some of them were utilised, three
years later, in *Hallowe'en Party*.

When we meet Poirot in the opening chapter he has just
completed his magnum opus on detective fiction, a project
on which he had previously been working during *The Clocks*.

Mrs Oliver makes her second appearance of the decade having already featured, *sans* Poirot, in *The Pale Horse*. She would appear again in *Hallowe'en Party* and for the last time in *Elephants Can Remember*. It can be no coincidence that Mrs Oliver, and the now very elderly Miss Marple, both characters with which Dame Agatha had now much in common, appear in over half of the last dozen novels.

A major element of the plot of *Third Girl* concerns the drugging of Norma Restarick. This has echoes of *A Caribbean Mystery* when Molly Kendal was the victim of a similar plot; and, a quarter century earlier, the poisoning of Hugh Chandler in 'The Cretan Bull', the seventh Labour of Hercules, is undertaken for a similar sinister reason.

Mr Goby from *After the Funeral* makes a brief appearance. And is Chief Inspector Neele the same policeman, though not of the same rank, who investigated, alongside Miss Marple, the deaths at Yewtree Lodge in *A Pocket Full of Rye*? Is Dr Stillingfleet, moreover, the medical man who featured in 'The Dream'?

The intriguing opening scene is sketched over half a dozen times, with little variation, in four separate Notebooks. This premise would seem to have been the starting point of the novel and the one unalterable idea throughout the notes.

> Poirot breakfast – Girl – Louise – I may have committed a murder. 3 girls in a flat Louise and Veronica – Judy – (Claudia Norma Townsend). One of these three girls. What does she mean by 'she thinks she may have committed'

> Poirot at breakfast – girl calls 'She thinks she may have committed a murder.' 'Thinks' Doesn't she know? No clearness – no precision. 'I'm sorry – I shouldn't have told you – you're too old'

> Poirot at breakfast table – Norma (an unattractive Ophelia) says she may have committed a murder – then tells Poirot he is 'too old.'

Suggestions – Chap I – P. at breakfast

Poirot at the breakfast table – thinks she may have committed a murder. Disappointed by P – too old – recommended by Mrs. Oliver – makes excuse – goes. Poirot worried

And this, from Notebook 27, a page after the final notes *At Bertrams Hotel*, is probably the initial note for the 1966 'Christie for Christmas'.

Idea A          July – 1965

Poirot at his breakfast table (The Late Mrs. Dane). P. at breakfast – George[60] announces – a – pause – young lady. I do not see people at this hour. She says she thinks she may have committed a murder. 'Thinks? It is not a subject on which one should be in doubt.' Girl – unkempt – Poirot regards her with pain etc. G[eorge] and P discuss – neurotic?

Mrs Oliver's visits to Borodene Mansions in Chapters 3 and 7, and Poirot's to Long Basing in Chapters 4 and 5, are sketched thoroughly in Notebook 26:

Mrs Oliver visits Borodene Court – a flat – 3 girls
Claudia – confident, efficient good background
Frances – Arts Council or Art Gallery.
Norma
Milkman mentions to Mrs O. Lady pitched herself down from 7th floor. Mind disturbed – had only been in flat a month
Decoration of flat – all similar built-in furniture and wallpaper – one wall with huge Harlequin

---

60   George appears as both George and Georges in *Third Girl*. In the Notebook he appears without the 's'.

> Poirot at Long Basing – visits Restaricks – pretends to know
> Sir Rodney. On leaving has a snoop before he and Mary
> encounter the Peacock (David) also snoopy. Later Poirot
> gives lift to David

And the essence of the plot is captured in the following paragraph from Notebook 42:

> Frances in an art racket – David works with her – gallery 'in'
> it. She runs picture shows abroad – he forges pictures. She
> meets McNaughton, he and Restarick whose brother dies
> suddenly – he takes R's place – R's passport faked by her.
> She goes back to England – once there assumes part of
> Mary – blonde and wig – Mrs Restarick – visit Uncle Rodney
> – furniture in store – picture 'cleaned' – substitute painted
> by David of McNaughton. Katrina found by Mary – dailies
> – Mary up and down to London, Frances to Manchester
> – Liverpool – Birmingham etc. Frances gets Norma to
> Borodene Court – she seldom sees F – but thinks she is
> going mad because she <u>dreams</u> F is M

Most of the salient points of the plot are covered but the words 'assumes part of Mary' are easier to read than to imagine. They involve a character playing a continuing dual role. It is difficult for the reader to believe that, even in Norma's drug-induced twilight existence, the same person could have been accepted as her flatmate and her stepmother. Impersonation has frequently played an important part in Christie's fiction – Carlotta Adams in *Lord Edgware Dies*, Sir Charles Cartwright in *Three Act Tragedy*, Miss Gilchrist in *After the Funeral*, Romaine in 'The Witness for the Prosecution' – but in each of these cases the impersonation is a one-off episode and not a long-term arrangement. And in three of these instances the impersonator is a professional actor.

The sequence of events in Chapter 22 is outlined in Notebook 42:

Frances speaks to porter, goes up in lift – inserts key etc.
Hand rises slowly to throat – sees herself in glass – her look
of frozen terror. Then screams and runs out of flat – grips
someone – killed – she has just returned from Manchester?
Dead body – 2 hours dead. F. comes by train from
Bournemouth? – changes to Mary – meets David – where
are Claudia? Andrew? Mary?

And there are flashes of Christie's old ingenuity – the odd/
even numbers, the different/same room scenario – in this
extract from Notebook 49; elements of this note surfaced in
the book although the practicality of the idea is questionable.
The reference to 'Swan Court' is to the actual apartment
block in which Christie had a flat for much of her life:

An idea
Girl or (dupe of some kind) taken to flat – go up in lift –
one of kind you can't see or count floors. Room has very
noticeable wall paper – Versailles? Cherries? Birds? She
swears to this – believing it – describes it minutely. Actually
that room and wallpaper is somewhere else. Wallpaper is
put on same night – it is all prepared – cut etc. – pasted on
– would take a couple of hours not more – but it would
have to dry off and therefore would be described as a damp
room – 'had patches' of damp on it or a room with the
noticeable paper would be papered over with another
paper. The similarity of rooms in a block like Swan Court in,
say, opposite sides of building – odd and even numbers if
some flats furniture would be the same

Much of the detail explored in the following extract from
Notebook 50 was to change but some concepts – the drugging and scapegoating, the fake portrait and the subterfuge
with regard to flat numbers – remained:

Girl doped by other girls (Claudia? Frances?) ~~friends~~ hears a
shot – comes to find herself shooting out of window – other
girl supporting her and pistol really discharged by her –
Lance they get in and fix him up – bandages etc. He and
(Cl?) (Frances?) are 'in it' together against simple Norma.
Later she is again 'doped' a second brain storm – result – a
young artist is shot – girls give evidence for Norma – police
can't shake them but don't believe them.
(B)? The Picture by Levenheim A.R.A. is of her mother ~~Lady~~
~~Roche~~ in country house. Actually picture is copied by young
David McDonald – only face of (Mary?) is substituted –
then David is shot. Norma suspected and believes herself
she did it. Thought to be a sex crime.
C. <u>Or</u> is Arthur Wells – Mary's husband – painted into
picture
D. <u>Or</u> Arthur and Mary – Sir R – can't see A very well but
believes he is his nephew. A man with a stroke – is bribed to
impersonate Arthur at a specialist.
[E] Painting – a Lowenstein – (L is dead) worth £40,000 –
insured. Copy false – seen on one evening – party

Points of interest
Double flat – 71 7th floor (faces W), 64 6th floor (faces E)
Police called to which?

Finally, in the following extracts, all from Notebook 51, there
are glimpses of the Christie of yesteryear with the listing
of ideas and the consideration of possible combinations of
conspirators (throughout these sketches the David of the
book appears as Paul):

Norma – are her words connected with home –
stepmother? Her own mother – Sonia – old boy?
Or
3rd girl activities – is boy friend (Paul) a Mod – like a Van
Dyk [sic] – brocade waistcoat – long glossy hair – is he the

evil genius – is he in it with Claudia? with Frances?
Narcotics?

Does Norma get keen on him – she acts as a go between for
them? A girl – an addict – dies really because she is found to
be a police agent getting evidence – killed by Paul or
Claudia – (Frances) – they make Norma believe that she
brought her an over strength dose of purple [hearts] (some
new name) Technically she might be accused of murder –
they do this to get her finished and say they will protect her
– she really is fall guy if necessary – she thinks of getting
help from Poirot – they decide she is danger – they'll get rid
of her. What is Norma's job? Cosmetics Lucie Long
powders etc. N[orma] packs things

2nd idea
Paul is really police spy – he tangles with the girls
3rd idea
Paul is in it with Sonia
4th idea
Paul is in it with Mary Wells. Sir Rodney – rich – his nephew
and wife come to live – or his niece and her husband. Niece
dies – widower is married – 2nd wife sucks up to old man –
then Sonia arrives also sucks up to him – he alters his will
5th idea
Sonia and Sir Paul linked together – he is impersonating
real Sir R
6th idea
Mary Restarick – her beautiful blue eyes – tells Poirot how
she got Norma to leave home – better for her – because she
hates me. Shows Poirot a chemist's analysis – arsenic? Or
morphia. Norma says – I hate her – I hate her – does boy
friend ~~old boy dies~~ see her (he says) walking in sleep – puts
something in glass. He tells her – will of old Rodney forged
– by Norma?
7th
Poirot and Mary – her beauty – blue eyes – about Norma –

glad she went – I didn't know what to do – takes from
locked drawer an analyst's report – Arsenic? Or morphia? –
hated me because of her mother

Sadly Christie's former ingenuity is missing from these scenarios (note, for example, that Ideas 6 and 7 are very similar). Even if some of the ideas here – Paul/David as a police spy, Norma as a go-between – had been utilised, little difference would have been made to the fundamental situation.

### *Endless Night*
### 30 October 1967

Penniless Michael Rogers woos and marries Ellie,
an enormously wealthy American heiress. They build a
dream house in the country but their blissful existence is
ruined by a spate of unpleasant incidents. A fatal accident
follows and a monstrous plot is gradually revealed.

*Every Night and every Morn*
*Some to Misery are born*
*Every Morn and every Night*
*Some are born to Sweet Delight,*
*Some are born to Sweet Delight,*
*Some are born to Endless Night.*

Blake, *Auguries of Innocence*

The Collins reader, in a report dated 23 May 1967, found *Endless Night* 'prodigiously exciting to read. The atmosphere is doom-laden from the beginning and all the minor tricks and ornaments are contrived to heighten the effect.' Phrases such as 'dazzling sleight-of-hand', 'handled with great assurance' and 'Mrs. Christie has, as always, been very clever' are scattered through the report.

In an interview for *The Times* in the month following publication Christie admitted, 'it's rather different from anything I've done before – more serious, a tragedy really. In some families one child seems born to go wrong . . . Usually I spend three or four months on a book but I wrote *Endless Night* in six weeks. If you can write fairly quickly the result can often be more spontaneous. Being Mike wasn't difficult.' She began drafting in America in late 1966 when she accompanied Sir Max, who was on a lecture tour.

*Endless Night* is Agatha Christie's final triumph, her last great novel and the greatest achievement of her last quarter century. It is written by an elderly upper middle class woman in the voice of a young working class male; it recycles her most famous trick forty years after she originated it; it is totally unlike anything else she ever wrote; and finally, it is a return to the multiple death scenarios of *And Then There Were None* and *Death Comes as the End*. By the end of the novel all the main protagonists – Ellie, Greta, Mrs Lee, Santonix, Claudia Hardcastle – are dead; and Michael is behind bars, at best, for life.

The plot is an amalgam of at least four earlier plot ideas.

First, with a narrator as the villain of the piece, comparisons with *The Murder of Roger Ackroyd* are inevitable. It should be remembered that even before this, Agatha Christie had experimented with the narrator-murderer device in 1924 in *The Man in the Brown Suit*. The ploy came to fruition in 1926 with *The Murder of Roger Ackroyd*, a village murder mystery narrated by the local doctor, who is unmasked by Poirot as a blackmailer and a murderer. Forty years later she added another twist to it with *Endless Night*.

While *The Murder of Roger Ackroyd* is a whodunit, *Endless Night*, for much of its length, seems to be merely a novel with menacing undertones, and only at its conclusion is it revealed as a carefully plotted crime novel with a devastating climax. So while it is utterly unlike anything that Agatha Christie had written before, nobody expected her to repeat her dazzling Ackroyd trick of forty years earlier. But it should be remembered that Agatha Christie made a career out of doing what nobody expected.

Second, *Endless Night*'s plot set-up is identical to *Death on the Nile*. Two lovers collude to install a charming villain into the life of a wealthy heiress; the plan is to marry and subsequently kill her. The lovers fake a serious argument and are, to all appearances, at daggers drawn. Although the mechanics of the murder in each case are totally different, the similarities are too obvious to ignore and unlikely to be mere coincidence. In *Endless Night* there is also an unexpected development when Michael begins to harbour unanticipated feelings for the ill-fated Ellie.

Third, its greatest, and most obvious, similarity is to the Marple short story 'The Case of the Caretaker', first published in January 1942 and 'The Case of the Caretaker's Wife' (qv): a wealthy heiress marries the local ne'er-do-well and is murdered in exactly the same way as Ellie Rogers. *Endless Night* is a much expanded form of these stories, but presented in such a radically different way as to make it seem a new story.

Fourth, *The Mysterious Affair at Styles* also features a collusive couple who stage a very public argument, thereby convincing listeners, and readers, that they hate each other. They, like their counterparts in *Endless Night*, have doctored the victim's existing medication, allowing both of them to be absent at the time of the crime.

The earliest note below dates from 1961 and appears in a list of ideas that includes *A Caribbean Mystery*, *The Mirror Crack'd from Side to Side* and *The Clocks*:

Husband – wants to marry rich wife – get rid of her – employs someone to threaten her – grudge – he intercepts

sweets – etc. saves her life several times – her death in the
end comes through fear – running from a 'ghost' – she falls

Although there are strong hints in this jotting of *A Caribbean
Mystery* ('saves her life several times'), the idea of marrying a
rich wife and employing someone to threaten her is the basis
of *Endless Night*.

The following year it is listed with her proposed titles
for 1963 and 1964, after *The Mirror Crack'd from Side to Side*
had been delivered to Collins. There is no mention yet of the
eventual title and the references to it throughout the notes
are always as 'Gypsy's Acre', the scene of the legend that
seems, from the dedication, to have provided the germ of the
book. Nor is there any indication at this early stage of the
method of telling, one of the crucial features of the novel.
Note also that 'Gypsy's Acre' is listed as 'X', an indication,
perhaps, that she intended to work on this before the other
two, which are listed as Y and Z.

1962
Notes for 3 books
Y. The Clocks (?)
Z. Carribean [sic] Mystery
X. Gypsy's Acre

X Gypsy's Acre
Piece of land and road – tea at pub – story about accidents
there – husband plans to kill wife – faked motor accident?

Two years before publication we find a further elaboration,
much of which finds its way into the novel: the gypsy, the
story, the horse, the 'accident':

Oct 1st 1965
A. Gypsy's Acre
Place where accidents happen – etc. – A woman seen

(gypsy?) by husband – asks people – really has heard story already – but pretends it is the first time – a bit upset – a sceptical young fellow – but therefore more easily upset. Wife interested – not nervous – then one day, wife sees gypsy figure – and so on – working things up. Does gypsy figure catch bridle of horse – (stick pin in). Husband at accident – someone sees it from window – she is badly injured – shock – dies – really morphine

One definite omission from the novel is the reference to the husband as 'a sceptical young fellow', not a description that could ever apply to Michael Rogers; and he is not present at Ellie's 'accident'. Note also that at this stage there is still no mention of the husband as the architect of his wife's death, much less as the narrator of the story.

Notebook 28 adds an important plot device or, to be strictly accurate, borrows it from 'The Case of the Caretaker':

The Cyanide Murder – capsules – the tranquilliser.
Someone dies (W) – falls down stairs – thrombosis? –
heart? – an open window. Body found 2 or 3 hours after
death. Y – gives friend one of her capsules; Z – dead –
a link is apparent between Z and W – this leads everyone
astray

Originally this idea was to have been a different type of book but, as can be seen from below, the cyanide capsule was instead subsumed into *Endless Night*. The jotting also observes the important medical fact that the body must be either in the open air or not seen by a medical person until some time after death, in order for the potassium cyanide fumes to dissipate.

By October 1966 the novel was taking recognisable shape, but before she settled on Greta, however, Christie experimented with various other female characters:

1966 – Oct. – (in U.S.A.) Projects – Gypsy's Acre
Adventurer – Jason – good looking – Australian? American?
His meeting with old Mrs. Lee – the story – Accident Mile <u>or</u>
Claire Holloway – teaches at a Girl's School or College – her
old friend Anne – Marie – Claire – cousin – Jason – or an au
pair girl Sidonie – her brother or Hildegarde – point is
Hildegarde and J – are in it together – contrived accident.
H is a Valkyrie girl. Use Pot. Cyanide idea – capsule

The idea of a good-looking foreigner, Jason, is abandoned
for Michael Rogers, a ne'er-do-well from a working class background. And when Hildegarde becomes Greta – compared
to a Valkyrie a few times in the course of *Endless Night* – we
have arrived at the lethal pairing at the heart of the novel.

But some ideas were abandoned:

Gypsy's Acre – up for sale – auction – talk at pub where
auction is held. Auctioneer a stranger to neighbourhood –
hints round about – it goes for very little – auctioneer
puzzled. Old man tells him You'm foreigner here –
accidents – bad luck on it – Old Mrs. Lee

'Whoever you're acting for, you've done a bad turn to
him – no credit to him – he'll be dead within the year –
(They have been paid by someone wanting to get it
cheap)

Does auctioneer have accident getting home – young
man with pince-nez like Ed(ward) Bolan – clever – Hotel
built? Or flats – with room service or home for old people
–? Or old house used for that – Fleet House – girl at house
(Mothercub type) hospital nurse – finds old lady dead –
from the home

Eventually, we get to the final and vital idea that was to
set *Endless Night* apart from virtually everything else that
Agatha Christie wrote. Note that originally she intended
the narrator to be an architect intent on building a house,

but in the novel the role of Ellie's architect was given to the enigmatic Santonix instead:

> Idea? Told in first person – by an architect
> 'I first heard about Gypsy's Acre from old Simon Barlow'
>     etc. looks at it. The perfect house – meets girl
> What do you want
> I want thirty thousand pounds
> What for?
> To build a house

Without its unreliable narrator this would have been a different, and possibly indifferent, novel. Two sides of an eternal triangle conspiring to kill the third, is not new either to crime fiction in general, or even to Agatha Christie in particular. The originality lies in what ingenious variation the writer can weave into it. If *Endless Night* had been told in the third person much of its devastating impact would have been defused. But almost at the end of her career, when everyone assumed that Agatha Christie had played all the tricks she possibly could, she confounded everyone. Again.

Oddly, although the Collins report on *Endless Night* was enthusiastic – 'the difficult gimmick is fairly played', and 'the murder is pretty ingenious' – the fear was that the critics would maul it, presumably because it was such an atypical 'Christie for Christmas'. In the event the novel received some of the best reviews that Christie had enjoyed: 'one of the best things Mrs Christie has ever done' (*Sunday Times*); 'Christie at topmost peak' (*Evening Standard*); 'Wickedly ingenious murder mystery' (*Scotsman*); 'the most devastating [surprise] that this surpriseful author has ever brought off' (*Guardian*).

The dedication of *Endless Night* is 'To Nora Prichard from whom I first heard the legend of Gypsy's Acre'. Nora Prichard was Mathew Prichard's other grandmother, his father's mother. She lived in the real location of Gypsy's Acre

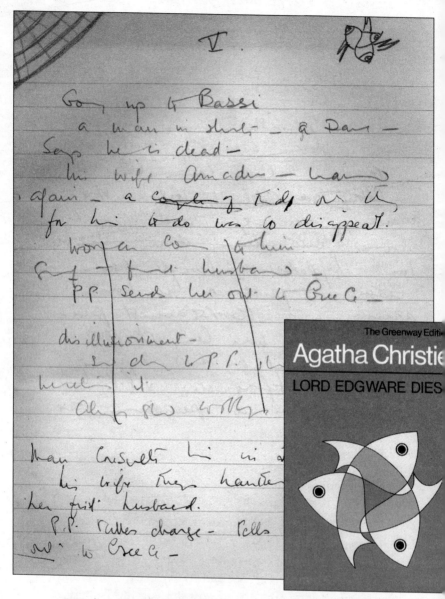

*This page from Notebook 66 is one of many examples in the Notebooks of Agatha doodling the three intertwined fishes, as sketched by Lois Hargreaves in 'The House of Lurking Death' (Partners in Crime). The symbol was subsequently used as the cover design on the Greenway Collected edition of Agatha's books, begun in the late 1960s and published throughout the 1970s.*

near Pentre-Meyrich in the Vale of Glamorgan in Wales, where many years earlier a nearby gypsy encampment was cleared and the head gypsy cursed the land. After numerous road accidents subsequently occurred in the vicinity, this possibly apocryphal tale gathered support.

## By the Pricking of my Thumbs
11 November 1968

On a visit to Tommy's Aunt Ada in Sunny Ridge Nursing Home, Tuppence meets Mrs Lancaster. Her subsequent disappearance intrigues Tuppence, who decides to investigate. This quest brings her to the village of Sutton Chancellor where the mystery is finally solved, but not before Tuppence's own life is in danger.

*By the pricking of my thumbs,*
*Something wicked this way comes.*

Shakespeare, *Macbeth*

Tommy and Tuppence Beresford are the only Christie characters to age between their first and last appearances. In their first adventure, *The Secret Adversary* (1922), they are 'bright young things', in 1941's *N or M?* they are worried parents and by the time of *By the Pricking of my Thumbs* they are middle-aged. The chronology of their lives and ages does not bear close scrutiny, however, and gets even more complicated and, in fact, inexplicable, by the time of their final adventure *Postern of Fate* in 1973.

The notes for *By the Pricking of my Thumbs* are more unfocused than usual. They repeat the same scene with only minor variations, suggesting a lack of plot clarity. And although the scenes in Sunny Ridge are intriguing, they are not enough to sustain an entire book. When Tuppence embarks on her investigation, the novel begins to flag and, unlike Christie's plotting in her prime, with a minimum of tweaking the final revelation could have been completely different with a totally different villain unmasked. Ironically, in Notebook 36 we find a note Christie wrote to herself: 'Rewriting of first half – not so verbose – 1st three or four chapters good – but afterwards too slow'.

Notes are contained in two Notebooks, 28 and 36, and extend to just over fifty pages. We have, in Notebook 36, a clearly dated starting point for the writing of this novel just over a year before it appeared in the bookshops. The early pages of this Notebook encapsulate the opening of the plot. The first and second sections of the novel, 'Sunny Ridge' and 'The House on the Canal', are then sketched between Notebooks 28 and 36:

Behind the Fireplace – Oct. 1967
Tommy and Tuppence go to visit disagreeable Aunt Ada –
she takes dislike to Tuppence who goes and sits in the
lounge – old lady in there sipping milk – says it's a very nice
place – are you coming to stay here?
It wasn't your poor child, was it?
No – I wondered – the same every day – behind the fireplace
– at ten minutes past eleven exactly.
Then she goes out with her milk – Aunt Ada dies in her
sleep four days later
Possible ideas for this
Is Mrs Nesbit the aunt or mother of a Philby or a Maclean
[i.e. the British spies] – some well-known public character
who defected to an enemy country. Were there papers?
Hidden behind grate? Child knew secrets of Priest's Hole.
Aunt Ada dies – funeral – call at the home – does Tuppence
see picture

Notebook 28 begins again with, broadly speaking, the same scene and set-up. And in it, we find the only Notebook reference to one of the most sinister and incomprehensible motifs in all of Christie: an elderly lady, a glass of milk and a story about a child's body behind the fireplace. This bizarre episode also surfaces in *The Pale Horse* (Chapter 4) and *Sleeping Murder* (Chapter 10). A possible explanation from within the plot of *By the Pricking of my Thumbs* is offered by the extract above; but it is not very convincing. The idea is repeated but not developed, and the suggested reasons are not utilised in the finished novel.

> Grandmother's Steps
> T and T – they visit nursing home for aged or slightly mental
> – Tommy's Aunt Amelia – (scatty? Tommy Pommy Johnnie?)
> Tuppence left in sitting room – old lady sipping milk
> 'Was it your poor child? It's not quite time yet – always the
> same time – twenty past ten – it's in there behind the grate,
> everyone knows but they don't talk about it. It wouldn't do'
> Shakes her head.
> 'I hope the milk is not poisoned today – sometimes it is – if
> so, I don't drink it, of course'
> Tuppence (on drive home) begins idly to think about it.
> 'I wonder what she had in her head – whose poor child? I'd
> like to know Tommy' [Chapters 2/3]
>
> The House – kindly witch – the jackdaw – heard through
> wall? They go in – jackdaw flies away – a dead one – the
> doll. Tuppence makes enquiries – goes to churchyard – vicar
> – elderly – a bossy woman doing flowers in church. Vicar
> introduces her to Tuppence – she invites Tuppence in to
> coffee. Tuppence goes to house agent in Market Basing
> [Chapters 7/8/9]

A month later more plot developments, as well as possible characters, are considered. Some of these – the painted boats and the superimposed name – were adopted, while it is possible that 'The House by the Canal' was under consideration as a title:

Nov 1st [1967]
The House by the Bridge or the Canal
Some points
The picture is of a small hump-backed bridge over a canal – across the bridge is a white horse on the canal bank – there is a line of pale green poplar trees – tied up to the bank, under the bridge are a couple of boats. An idea is that boats are an afterthought added some time after the picture was painted. Suppose a name was painted John Doe – murderer – over that the boats were painted. Someone either knew about this or someone did it

Ideas to pursue – or discard
1. Picture – boat superimposed – beneath it – 'Murder' [or] 'Maud'
'Come in to the garden, Maud' a clue
'The black bat, Night, hath flown' – who painted it?
2. Baby farmer idea (at Sunny Ridge? Before Old Ladies Home?) Child really was dead and buried in chimney of sitting room there
3. Could cocoa woman be the killer woman

Possible people involved?
The artist Sidney Boscowan
The friendly witch Mrs Perry
Big lumbering husband Mr Perry
Vicar Rev. Edmund Shipton
Active woman Mrs Bligh

Tommy features little in the book until Chapter 10 when he starts to track Tuppence. One of his first tasks is to find out more about the painting in Aunt Ada's room:

How does Tommy start his search?
Picture gallery – Bond St. – Boscowan – quite a demand for
them again. Mrs. Boscowan lives in country. Tommy goes
to see her – has Tuppence been there? Interested in her
husband's pictures. Tells her how this picture was given him
by aunt now dead – she was given [it] by an old lady, a Mrs.
Lancaster – no reaction. [Chapters 10 and 12]

Some of the ideas Christie noted in November 1967 were not
pursued at all; others were partially adopted. The first one
below was rejected possibly because of its similarity to a plot
device in *The Clocks*, five years earlier; the second has elements that were utilised – the pregnant actress and the name
Lancaster – but the surrounding ideas were discarded:

Does this <u>really</u> centre round a paperback – a thriller <u>read</u>
by old Mrs Lancaster? Does Tommy find that out? He reads
it in train, goes to Sunny Ridge, finds book was in library
– Mrs L. very fond of crime stories – comes home
triumphantly and debunks Tuppence

Country small lonely house – to it comes down beautiful
girl – actress – going to have child. Man marries her – but
he now wants to marry rich boss's daughter so wedding is
kept quiet (in local church) – under another name – he tells
girl baby is dead? Or he kills girl. Who is Mrs Lancaster?
Someone who lives near churchyard – sees body being
buried in old grave

Five further sketches of the murderous back-plot appear; but
as can be seen, each sketch is substantially the same, apart
from a brief consideration of a homicidal Sir Philip Starke:

Nov. 12 [1967]
Alternatives
X Mrs Lancaster – alias Lady Peele – of batty family – barren

– went queer. Husband loved children – she 'sacrificed' them. He gets his devoted secretary Nellie Blighe – sends her to ~~nursing~~ Old Ladies Home

Dec[ember]
Sir Philip Starke – loved children – his wife Eleanor – mental – (abortion) jealous of children – kills little girls. Nellie Bligh secretary – is also mental nurse.
Disappearance of child (Major Henley's) – Does Nellie and Philip bury one of them in churchyard – Lady S – in various homes. Friendly witch's husband was <u>Sexton.</u>

Was she Lady Peele – barren – had had abortion – was haunted by guilt – it was she, jealous, who killed any protégés of her husband. In asylum – released – then husband employs a faithful secretary to put her in old people's home – 'Miss Bates' the one who was doing the church – she adores Peele

Candidates for murder
Lady Sparke – neurotic – mental. Did she kill her children? She was released – Philip and Nellie Bligh hid her – took her to homes. Does an elderly woman go in also – does she die? Mrs. Cocoa?

Story gets about that Sir Philip's wife left him because he was the killer

Coming directly after the shocking and inventive *Endless Night*, *By the Pricking of my Thumbs* suffers, inevitably, by comparison. But although for the most part the book is a series of reminiscences with little solid fact, the opening chapters are certainly intriguing, conveying something of the old Christie magic, and the denouement is unsettling. The underlying themes of madness and child murder, combined with scenes set in graveyards and deserted houses, could well have justified, as suggested by the first-edition blurb, written by Christie herself, the title *By the Chilling of your Spine*.

### Hallowe'en Party
10 November 1969

A bobbing-for-apples game goes horribly
wrong at Rowena Drake's teenage party. One
of the guests, Mrs Oliver, approaches her friend
Hercule Poirot who subsequently visits Woodleigh
Common and, in the course of his investigation,
uncovers a long-forgotten crime as well as
the killer at the Hallowe'en party.

The notes for *Hallowe'en Party* provide the clearest example in the whole of the Notebooks of a definite starting and finishing date. The first page of notes in Notebook 16 is headed 'Jan. 1st 1969' and forty-five pages later we read:

July 7th Halloween Party completed

Chapter 1 to 21 inc. ending p. 280 to be sent or taken to H[ughes] M[assie]. 3 or 4 chapters to go to Mrs Jolly [her typist] on Dictaphone rolls 1 to 9. Continue corrections and revisions in them commencing P. 281 and send on to H. M.

Agatha Christie was now 78 and although six months for a full-length novel is impressive, it is a long way from the 1930s and 1940s when she finished two or three novels a year. It is entirely possible that the idea for this novel was hatched during a visit to America, where Hallowe'en was a bigger holiday, in late 1966, when she accompanied Sir Max Mallowan on a lecture tour. Although she toyed with the idea of an 11-plus, rather than a Hallowe'en, party for young teenagers, the basic plot device was set from the beginning. Yet again Mrs Oliver appears, as she does in four of the final dozen titles that Christie wrote. Also making a reappearance is the policeman Spence from *Mrs McGinty's Dead* and *Taken at the Flood*; and he was to appear again three years later in *Elephants Can Remember.*

Themes, ideas and plots from earlier titles abound. There are strong echoes throughout of *Dead Man's Folly*. In both we have a child murdered during a game, witnesses to an earlier murder presenting a danger to a hitherto safe killer and the creation of a thing of beauty as a grave – a folly in one novel and a garden in the other. As will be seen, a short story from 35 years earlier, 'How Does Your Garden Grow?' was also in her mind. *Dead Man's Folly, Mrs McGinty's Dead* and *The Labours of Hercules* are specifically mentioned in Chapter 4, 5 and 11 respectively; the inspiration for the radio-play *Butter in a Lordly Dish* is referred to in Chapter 11, Miss Bulstrode from *Cat among the Pigeons* is recalled in Chapter 10 and a brief allusion towards the end of Chapter 16 may have provided the basis for 1971's *Nemesis*. Mrs Drake's looking over the staircase (Chapter 10) has distinct similarities to Marina Gregg's in *The Mirror Crack'd from Side to Side*. And the opening line of Chapter 17 is almost identical to that in 'The Case of the Perfect Maid'.

Like many of the late titles, both the notes for *Hallowe'en Party* and the book itself are diffuse and unfocused. Alongside new ideas are some from earlier titles but the many meandering conversations do not coalesce into a coherent and ingenious detective novel. Compare the set-up with similar titles from earlier decades – *Dumb Witness, Taken at the Flood* and *Mrs McGinty's Dead* where Poirot arrives in a small town to investigate a suspicious death – and we can appreciate the decline in the quality of the books from *Endless Night* onwards. Apart from *Passenger to Frankfurt* all of the titles after 1967 are journeys into the past, each one weaker than the previous, although all are predicated on a compelling basic idea.

Apart from name changes, the following extracts outline the basic situation that sets the plot in motion, although it has to be asked why Miranda (Mifanwy in the notes) does not admit earlier that she, and not Joyce, was the original witness. And the later revelation of her parenthood beggars belief.

Jenny Butcher – Mrs. O's friend on Hellenic cruise – widow – husband was (leukaemia?) or polio victim – contracted it abroad – a scholar? Man of intellect – child Mifanwy eleven or twelve – did father die at Ephesus? Stroke?

Is it Mifanwy who saw murder? Her father's? or her father kill Jenny's lover? Or – her father – or mother – or mother's sister still alive and living in Woodlawn Common kills brother (or mental defective). Anyway Mifanwy saw a murder – tells her older friend Joyce. Joyce boasts about this at party as her adventure. Mifanwy was not at party – ill that day – cold?

Mrs Oliver is at Party – helping a friend – friend is:
Jean Buckley? Or Gwenda Roberts ?
Her family consists of: Daughter of 14 – Twin boys Henry and Thomas 12 – A husband – Doctor? G.P.

Bobbing for apples? Looking glass? (future husband) Snap Dragon – talk about origins of these rites – snapdragon – should be Christmas

The following, from Notebook 16, appears almost verbatim in Chapter 1. Here we see resonances of an earlier Christie as she tantalises the reader with hints of an earlier crime:

Joyce – 'Oo-er – I saw a murder once'

Grown up – 'Don't say silly things, Joyce'

Beatrice 'Did you <u>really</u> – really and truly?

Joan 'Of course she didn't – she's just making it up'

Joyce 'I <u>did</u> see a murder – I did – I did'

Ann 'Why didn't you go to the police about it, then'?

Joyce 'Because I didn't know it <u>was</u> a murder'

With the usual name changes – Mary Drake becomes Rowena and Sonia Karova is Olga Seminoff – she lists some characters:

Possible characters

Mary Drake – Giver of party (?)

Mother or step-mother of Joyce [Mrs Reynolds]

Alistair Drake – fair – good-looking – vague

Sonia Karova – Au pair girl came to Barrets Green four or five years earlier

The Drakes – old Miss or Mrs. Kellway an Aunt lived with them – dies suddenly – left a will hand written, leaving money to Sonia – former wills left money to Alistair

Girl ran away – never found – or – girl's body found – or au pair girl disappeared – went off with a young man

A school teacher – Miss Emlyn – her body found – seen with a man

The notes hint that much of the plot remained elusive:

A garden made out of a quarry by Mrs. Llewellyn Browne – rich eccentric elderly woman mad on gardens – sunk gardens – saw one in N. Ireland – spent a lot of money.

David McArdle – young, artistic landscape planner – rumoured to be an elderly woman's fancy – to make money out of them.

Also au pair girl Alenka – looked after old lady – she was keen on David – (refer to *Cornish Mystery* – she thinks husband is giving her arsenic)

Au pair girl – looked after old Mrs. Wilberforce – Aunt dies – her will found later – hidden in Chinese jar – (under carpet?) – money left to Olga – A supposedly written by her – but it was a forgery

Mary Drake – rich runs place – husband – Julian – polio victim? – weak – works on board of hospital – draws beautifully – forges – or – is Mr. Drake her second husband – first one was polio victim – did she kill him? In order to marry No. 2

But eventually on pages headed 'May 20th' and '31st' [1969] we find the following:

Idea – Sonia (Olga) (Katrina) was friends with John Leslie Ferrier – he had a conviction for forgery. Michael induces Leslie to forge will – offers him money – Leslie then killed (knifed by Michael) – Or – Hit and Run by car. Mary in with him her husband killed (hit and run) Soon after he inherits – man in car – car was pushed from somewhere 15 miles away, Michael at a meeting in London

Sequence –

A. Mrs. L.B. makes will or codicil – Michael hears about it (from Olga)
B. Gets Leslie to forge a codicil – pays him money – knifes him after a row between jealous girls.
C. Death of Mrs. L.B. (overdose)
D. Death of polio nephew – his wife adored him – Mrs. Mary had people playing bridge.
E. Mrs. L.B. had written draft codicil of my will. She had written it – or shown it to girl – then changed its position (work out details). Possibly in library.

Ideas and Points May 31st

A. Cleaning woman goes to Mrs. Oliver about seeing codicil
B. Poirot opens letter – Hungarian Herzoslovakian friend – has visited family – Olga Seminova – young man Olga was going to marry
C. Poirot and Michael Wright – in wood – he was with Miranda.
D. Miss Byways and hedges – Doctor dispensary – has cooked up prescription – little bottle of pills
E. Leonard or Leopold was near Michael and Miranda – sly – knows something – nasty little eavesdropper – is Leopold the next victim? Leopold – scientific bent – eavesdropper – possible juvenile blackmailer – or his sister Ann

This is, in fact, the plot she adopted, although why Mrs Llewellyn-Smythe should have written a codicil and then hidden it is never fully explained in the novel. And is it at all likely that 11-year-old Leopold should blackmail a double murderer?

The influence of the short story 'How Does Your Garden Grow?' can be seen in the extract below. Both feature an elderly lady ignoring her family to leave her fortune to a foreign companion and the subsequent scapegoating of that legatee. The 'shells' is a reference to the plot of the earlier story, where strychnine is concealed in an oyster and the shells later hidden in plain sight as a decoration in the garden:

What did Joyce see? Mary Drake comes out from back door – shells – sticks them by path

# The Sixth Decade 1970–1976

'Thank God for my good life, and all the love that has been given to me.'

*An Autobiography*

─────────◄○►─────────

**SOLUTIONS REVEALED**

*Curtain: Poirot's Last Case* • *Death on the Nile* • *Endless Night* •
*The Murder of Roger Ackroyd* • *Nemesis* • *Sad Cypress*

─────────◄○►─────────

In September 1970 Agatha Christie celebrated her eightieth birthday and, with a little selective arithmetic, it was also the year of her eightieth book. Extensive press coverage, both at home and abroad, greeted the publication on her birthday – 15 September – of *Passenger to Frankfurt*.

On the first day of the following year Agatha Christie became Dame Agatha, to the delight of her global audience. As she worked in Notebook 28 on that year's book, *Nemesis*, she wrote 'D.B.E.' (Dame Commander of the British Empire) at the top of the page. A book more impressive in its emotional power than in its plotting, *Nemesis* is, like its 1972 successor *Elephants Can Remember*, a journey into the past where 'old sins cast long shadows'. And the last novel she wrote, *Postern of Fate* (1973), is a similar nostalgic journey and the poorest book of her career (with the possible exception of the curiosity that is *Passenger to Frankfurt*). To counterbalance these disappointments, 1974 saw the publication of *Poirot's Early Cases*, a collection of short stories from the prime of the little Belgian and his creator, not previously published in the UK.

Coinciding with these reminders of the vintage Poirot, one of his most challenging cases, *Murder on the Orient Express*, was filmed faithfully and extravagantly by Sidney Lumet, working with an all-star cast. A massive critical and popular success worldwide, it became the most successful British film ever and created a huge upsurge of interest in the now frail Agatha Christie. Her last public appearance was at the Royal Premiere in London, where she insisted on remaining standing to meet the Queen. Her publishers knew that a new book would be unable to satisfy the appetite of the vastly increased Christie audience created by the success of the film. So Sir William Collins convinced Dame Agatha to release *Curtain: Poirot's Last Case*, one of her most ingenious constructions, written when she was at the height of her powers. Another global success followed its appearance in October 1975, heralded by a *New York Times* front-page obituary of Hercule Poirot.

On 12 January 1976, three months after her immortal creation, Dame Agatha Christie died at her Wallingford home. International media mourned the passing of, quite simply, 'the writer who has given more enjoyment to more people than anyone else' (*Daily Telegraph*); the perennial *Mousetrap* dimmed its lights and newspapers printed pages on 'the woman the world hardly knows'. She was buried at Cholsey, near her Oxfordshire home, and a memorial service was held in May at St Martin-in-the-Fields in London. *Sleeping Murder*, another novel from Christie's Golden Age, and the 'final novel in a series that has delighted the world' (to quote the blurb) was published in October and presented Miss Marple's last book-length investigation. Dame Agatha's *An Autobiography* followed in 1977 and *Miss Marple's Final Cases*, a collection of previously uncollected short stories, in 1979.

Apart from the unparalleled success of *Murder on the Orient Express*, the much-underrated screen version of *Endless Night* had appeared in 1972. Despite Dame Agatha's objection to a love scene at the close of the film, this adaptation remains a faithful treatment of the last great novel that Christie wrote. The previous year the last Christie play, *Fiddlers Five* (reduced to *Fiddlers Three* in a subsequent version in 1972), was staged, but its lack of critical and popular success ruled out a West End production. In 1973 Collins published *Akhnaton*, her historical play, written in 1937 but never performed; and her poetry collection, called simply *Poems*, was also issued in 1973.

The final six years of Agatha Christie's life saw some of her greatest successes – her Damehood, the universal successes, in two separate spheres, of *Murder on the Orient Express* and *Curtain* – but also the publication of some of her weakest titles. But by then it didn't matter. Such was the esteem and affection in which she was held by her worldwide audience that *anything* written by Agatha Christie was avidly bought by a multitude of her fans, many of whom had had a lifelong relationship with her.

❧

## Passenger to Frankfurt
### 15 September 1970

―◄○►―

Diverted by fog to Frankfurt Airport,
Sir Stafford Nye agrees to the fantastic suggestion
of a fellow passenger. On his return to England he
realises that he has become involved in something
of international importance – but what? A further
assignation leaves him little wiser. What is Benvo?
And who is Siegfried?

―◄○►―

Published on her eightieth birthday, this was claimed to be Agatha Christie's eightieth book and, despite the dismay with which the manuscript was greeted by both her family and her publishers, it went straight into the best-seller lists and remained there for over six months. The publicity attendant on the 'coincidence' of her birthday and her latest production certainly helped, but *Passenger to Frankfurt* remains the most extraordinary book she ever wrote. Described, wisely, on the title page as 'An Extravaganza' – the description went some way towards mitigating the disappointment felt by both publishers and devotees – and showing little evidence of the ingenuity with which her name is still associated, this tale of international terrorism and engineered anarchy is difficult to write about honestly. Most devotees, myself included, consider it an aberration and, but for the fact that it is an 'Agatha Christie', would never have read it the first time, let alone re-read it over the forty years since its first appearance. Like other weaker novels from the same era, it begins with a compelling, if somewhat implausible, situation, but it degenerates into total unbelievability long before the end. Only in the closing pages of Chapter 23, with the unmasking of a completely unexpected, albeit incredible, villainess is there a very faint trace of the Christie magic.

The idea of stage-managed anarchy brought about by promoting student protest and civil unrest is not new in the Christie output. It reaches back as far as the mysterious Mr Brown in *The Secret Adversary* and also makes an appearance, 30 years later, in *They Came to Baghdad*. While both these examples demand some suspension of disbelief on the part of the reader, *Passenger to Frankfurt* demands a higher and longer suspension. The other echo from earlier works, and one that can be appreciated only now, after the publication of the alternate version of 'The Capture of Cerberus', is the subterfuge about a fake/real Hitler character and the method of concealment. This element of the plot is identical in both the short story and the novel, written thirty years apart.

The other surprise about this novel, apart from the unlike-liness of the plot, is the fact that throughout her life Christie evinced little interest in politics. And yet the entire thrust of the novel is political, with politicians and diplomats meeting regularly and, it must be said, implausibly in attempts to maintain political stability. Such scenes are dotted through-out the book; although, despite these meetings and endless conversations, nothing happens. Most of the conversations, whether private or political, meander aimlessly and uncon-vincingly and swathes of the book could be removed without making any notable difference.

The character of Matilda Cleckheaton is, in many ways, a Marple doppelganger – elderly, observant, worldly-wise and devious. But her stratagem for dealing with 'Big Charlotte' is in the highest degree unlikely and unconvincing.

*Passenger to Frankfurt* was written in the year of publication and Notebook 24 has three dates – '1970', 'February 1970' and '16th February 1970' – on pages 12, 14 and 17 respec-tively. Christie realised that the year of her eightieth birthday would inevitably involve publicity and that the 1970 'Christie for Christmas' would have to be finished earlier than usual for a September publication. Some selective arithmetic had to be done to arrive at the significant figure of 80 titles. Only by counting the American collections – *The Regatta Mystery* (1939), *Three Blind Mice* (1950), *The Under Dog* (1951) and *Double Sin* (1961) – all of which contained stories not then published in Britain, as well as the Mary Westmacott titles, could this all-important figure be arrived at.

In an interview conducted shortly after the publication of the book Christie denied that any of the characters were based on real-life politicians but that her inspiration for writing the book was her reading of the daily newspapers. She cited especially reports of rebellious youth and the fact that youth can be more easily influenced than older people. She was at pains to emphasise that, personally, she was 'not in the least interested in politics' and that the novel was apolitical in the sense that anarchy could originate from either the Right or the Left. Much of this is echoed in the Introduction to the novel where she also discusses her ideas and where and how she got them. 'If one idea in particular seems attractive, and you feel you could do something with it, then you toss it around, play tricks with it, work it up, tone it down, and gradually get it into shape.' It is a sad irony that, of all her novels, *Passenger to Frankfurt* is one where the ingenious ideas that proliferated in other novels are notable only by their absence.

The opening gambit of the airport swap is one that, nowadays, would be practically impossible; in the less terrorist-conscious days of the late 1960s, when the book was plotted, it was just about feasible. But this feasibility does not extend to believability: is it remotely likely that anyone would agree to hand over their passport to a total stranger and then take a drink with the assurance of that stranger that the drug that it contained was harmless? This ploy is considered in six Notebooks with the earliest, in the first extract below, dating back to around 1963. As usual, details of names and airport locations were to change, but the basic situation remains the same:

Possibilities of Airport story (A)
After opening in central European airport (Frankfurt)
(Venice) – diversion of plane – substitution of girl for
Sir D

Starts at European airport – woman, tall, sees a medium man wearing a distinctive cloak and hood. Asks him to help her – Sir Robert Old – she takes his place – he takes knock-out drops. Later woman contacts him in London. Thriller

D. Book
Starting at airport – substituting – Robin West –
international thinker type

B. Missing passenger

B. Passenger to Frankfort [sic]
Missing passenger – airport – Renata – Sir Neil Sanderson

B. Passenger to Frankfurt
Sir Rufus Hammersley – his cloak – med[ium] height –
sharp jutting feminine chin.

In Notebook 23 the first sketch above – 'Possibilities of Airport story' – continues at 'A' below. But the scenario considered after the postcard and 'near escape' idea goes in a completely different direction from the one adopted in the novel. The 'Girl murdered' idea is rather similar to that of Luke Fitzwilliam's reading of the death of Miss Pinkerton following their meeting on the train in *Murder is Easy*. These notes appear on a page directly preceding the plotting of 1964's *A Caribbean Mystery* and this timeline is confirmed by the date of the proposed postcard, November 1963.

A. Advertisement?
Postcard? Frankfort 7-11-63 Could meet you at Waterloo
Bridge Friday 14th 6 p.m.
B. Sir D. is called upon by a rather sinister gentleman –
questioned about incident at Frankfort – D. is alert – non-
committal. Shortly after, a 'near escape' – gas? car steering
trouble? electric fault? Then a visit from the 'other side'
apparently friends of girl
Or
Girl murdered – her picture in paper – he is sure it is the girl
at the airport – it starts him investigating – he goes to the
inquest.

Notebook 28A contains the plot-line that Christie actually adopted and the following short paragraph, listed as Idea B, neatly encapsulates it. Although the calculation about the age of the supposed son would seem to place the writing of this note in 1969, Idea C on the following page is part of the plot of *Endless Night* (1967) and is followed a few pages later by extensive notes for *By the Pricking of my Thumbs* (1968). Unusually, here also is the exact title, spelling apart, of the projected book:

Passenger to Frankfort [sic]
Missing passenger – airport – Renata – Sir Neil Sanderson
London Neil at War Office or M.14. His obstinacy aroused
– puts advertisement in. Frankfort Airport Nov. 20th Please
communicate – passenger to London etc. Answer –
Hungerford Bridge 7.30pm
What is it all about? She passes him ticket for concert
Festival Hall. Hitler idea – concealed in a lunatic asylum –
one of many who think they are Napoleon or Hitler or
Mussolini. One of them was smuggled out – H. took his
place – Hitler – H. Bormann – branded him on sole of foot
– a swastika – the son born 1945 now 24 – in Argentine?
U.S.A.? Rudi Schornhorn – the young Siegfried

The following extract from Notebook 49 dates from the mid 1960s. Idea A on the same list became *Third Girl* and Ideas C and D never went further than the four-line sketches on the page of this Notebook. This outline tallies closely with the finished novel although there is no mention of the ticket and passport swap.

B. Passenger to Frankfurt
Sir Rufus Hammersley – His cloak – med[ium] height –
sharp jutting feminine chin. Fog in airport – flight diverted
– the young woman – not noticeable – thinks he has seen
her before – likeness – she will be killed – because of the fog
– diverted elsewhere – Miss Karminsky – passenger – he is
found in passage by loos – no money or papers
He gets money sent him – then asked to go to Intelligence.

He has a sixth sense and a feeling of partisanship. His
things searched. Advertisement – wants to see you again –
Hungerford Bridge – Nov. 26th Ticket at concert. What is it
all about

Probably because this novel did not involve clues and suspects
and alibis, the usual components of a Christie detective novel,
there is little in the way of notes or ideas that were considered
and discarded. In fact, it is fair to say that there is little in the
way of plot at all in *Passenger to Frankfurt*. Apart from speculation about rearranging some sections, the notes for the novel
are mostly of the names of people and their countries and
the interminable meetings that fill the book. The following
early notes show uncertainty about the arrangement of some
passages in the opening chapters. The seemingly odd reference 'Lifeboat' is to the name of the periodical used to
conceal the safe return of Sir Stafford's passport.

Chapter 3
Car incident p. 51 – or keep it as original – or keep it on p. 46
Last page rearranged – Start at breakfast – Interview at
ministry. After ministry interview into Mrs. Worrit – clothes
cleaned – man – panda?
Rings Matilda – arranges to go down next week. Dinner
with Eric – on way home car business – Lifeboat – passport
– advertisement idea

A passage of considerable interest is the one concerning
the antecedents of Siegfried, 'the young hero, the golden
superman' of Chapter 6. Chapter 17 of *Passenger to Frankfurt*
contains distinct echoes of the 'new' version of 'The Capture
of Cerberus' (qv). Remarkably, after a 30-year gap, the central idea of the short story is recycled in the novel: the asylum
with its many incarnations of the famous and infamous. In
each case there is confusion about the 'fake' and the 'real'
Hitler (Hertzlein in the short story) and the eventual release

of the 'real' one. A major difference in the short story is that the newly released character has become a force for good and not evil, as in the novel.

> Are you suggesting he is Hitler?
> No, but he believes he is.
> Statistics – Borman hid him there – he married a girl – child was born – swastika branded on
> child's foot – Renata has birth certificate [Chapter 17]

Some characters from earlier titles reappear. Mr Robinson, first mentioned in Chapter 3, and Colonel Pikeaway in Chapter 4, both appeared in both *Cat among the Pigeons* and Colonel Pikeaway also appeared in *At Bertram's Hotel*; these two shadowy figures would make a further reappearance in *Postern of Fate*. Matilda Cleckheaton's nurse, Amy Leatheran, on the other hand, is unlikely to be the same Amy Leatheran who narrated *Murder in Mesopotamia*; she is described in Chapter 20 of *Passenger to Frankfurt* as a 'tactful young woman'. Other interesting passages include a discussion, in Chapter 6, of *The Prisoner of Zenda*, to be discussed again by Tommy and Tuppence in *Postern of Fate*; an inadvertent naming of two Christie plays in a paragraph of Chapter 11; and a distinct reference, in Chapter 22, to the basis of the 1948 radio play *Butter in a Lordly Dish*. More personally, Lady Matilda's discussion of medicines in Chapter 15 is an echo of Christie's own description, in *An Autobiography*, of her work in the dispensary in Torquay.

Overall, the decline that began with *Third Girl* reached its nadir with *Passenger to Frankfurt*; the superb *Endless Night* beams out like a shining light among the last half-dozen novels. But there can be little doubt that the only reason that *Passenger to Frankfurt* was published was that it had the magic name 'Agatha Christie' on the title page.

∽✢∾

## *Nemesis*
## 18 October 1971

────────◄○►────────

At the posthumous request of Mr Rafiel, from
*A Caribbean Mystery*, Miss Marple joins a coach tour of
'Famous Houses and Gardens'. She must use her natural
flair for justice to right a wrong. But she is mystified
by a lack of clues – until one of her fellow
travellers is murdered.

────────◄○►────────

Like its predecessors, *By the Pricking of my Thumbs* and
*Hallowe'en Party*, and its successors, *Elephants Can Remember*
and *Postern of Fate*, *Nemesis* is concerned with a mystery from
the past. Retrospective justice is what Miss Marple is asked,
by the deceased Mr Rafiel, to provide. And, similar to the
letter received by Poirot at the outset of *Dumb Witness*, the
posthumous correspondence from Mr Rafiel is very short on
detail.

In one way *Nemesis* is the most surprising novel that
Christie wrote in her declining years. As with most of the
novels from her last decade *Nemesis* is rambling and repetitive,
and it is disappointing as a detective novel. The coach tour,
which promises much as a traditional Christie setting, is
almost a red herring. And unlike the classic settings of *Murder
on the Orient Express*, *Death in the Clouds* and *Death on the Nile*,
where a mode of transport isolates a group of suspects, the
vital characters in *Nemesis*, the three sisters, are all to be
found outside the coach.

Yet, though it is not a great detective novel – clues to its
solution are remarkable only by their absence – considered
solely as a novel it is a revelation. Its theme is 'Love – one of
the most frightening words there is in the world', according to
Elizabeth Temple at the close of Chapter 6. The mainspring

of the plot is the smothering, corrosive love of Clotilde Bradbury-Scott for the girl Verity. As a counterbalance to this claustrophobic situation there is the love of Verity for Michael Rafiel; but this love is also destined for tragedy. The doomed worship of Verity by Clotilde is the root cause of three deaths – the object of that love and the brutal killing of two innocent onlookers. This hitherto unexplored theme has powerful emotional impact, especially in the closing explanation which, unusually for Miss Marple, takes over fifteen pages.

Like the novel itself, the notes for *Nemesis* are not very detailed. The bulk of them concern the crime in the past and its possible variations. The idea of the three sisters and the tomb disguised as a greenhouse seems to have been settled in the early stages of planning. This has distinct echoes of a similar plot device in *Hallowe'en Party*, where a sunken garden fills a similar role; and, earlier again, *Dead Man's Folly*, which features a folly as a grave. The notes for *Nemesis* are in four Notebooks and, as can be seen from the first extract below, work on it began just a year before publication. Note the incorrect name 'Raferty' instead of Rafiel:

Oct. 1970
Chapter I
Miss Marple at home reading Times – glances at Marriages – then Deaths. A name she knows – can't quite remember. Later in garden remembers Carribean [sic] – Raferty, the dying millionaire.
Chapter II Letter from lawyer in London.

The Three Sisters – invitations to Miss Marple – Mr. Rafiel – old manor house – a body concealed there
Clothilde
Lavender
Alicia
What kind of a house? What garden

A Greenhouse – wreathed over with polygnum – fell down
or collapsed in war

This list of characters from Notebook 6 reflects, with the
exception of the Denbys and Miss Moneypenny, that of the
completed novel.

People on Tour
Mrs. Risely-Porter (Aunt Ann) Elderly dictatorial a snob
And niece Joanna Cartwright (27)
Emlyn Price (Welsh and revolutionary)
Miss Barrow and Miss Cooke (spinster friends)
Miss Moneypenny (Cats) [possibly Miss Bentham or
Lumley]
Mr and Mrs. Butler Americans middle-aged
Colonel and Mrs. Walker (Flowers? Horticulture)
Mr Caspar (Foreign) about 50
Elizabeth Peters [Temple] Retired headmistress
Schoolgirl and brother – Liz and Robert Denby
Professor Wanstead

A section of Notebook concerning the murder of Elizabeth
Temple appears almost word for word in Chapter 11, 'Accident'. Details differ – the school is Fallowfield, not Grove
House Park, and it is Joanna Crawford and not Mr Caspar
who provides most of the details of the rock fall – but in
essence this extract is an accurate précis:

Death of Elizabeth Peters, late headmistress of Grove
House Park Girls' School – or is she in hospital? Does Miss
M go and see her?
Does Emlyn Price come and tell Miss Marple of accident?
She goes to local hotel to see other travellers – group talk
and chat. Either Miss Cooke or Robert Denby describe what
they saw – 4 or 5 boys climbing up – throwing stones –
pushing a rock – local boys. Mr Caspar later says that was

not what happened – it was a woman. Tells Miss Marple –
he was a botanist and had wandered by himself. Professor
Wanstead speaks to Miss Marple – mentions Mr. Rafiel –
suggests Miss Marple should go and visit her. He stresses
Rafiel told him about her

It must be said however that as a murder method, rolling a
rock down a hillside in the hope of hitting a moving target
is, at best, imprecise; thirty-five years earlier, on the banks
of the Nile, Andrew Pennington discovered this when his
murder attempt on Linnet Doyle failed, literally, to achieve
its target. And for the middle-aged murderess in *Nemesis* it is
also incredibly unlikely, if not impossible.

The essence of the plot appears in Notebook 28 and, apart
from a few details – Gwenda and Philip are forerunners of
Verity and Michael – is reproduced in the book. It would
seem to have been written early in the plotting as it appears
directly ahead of a page dated 'Jan. '71'; and it is written
straight off with no deletions or changes. The ruse of the
'pinched' car and the obliterated body has familiar echoes
from *The Body in the Library*, 30 years earlier.

Elizabeth Peters 60 retired headmistress
A girl in her school – one of the 3 sisters had taken her up, trip
abroad art galleries. Girl had finally come to live with her – girl
was murdered by 19 or 20 years old young man – picked her
up in car (evidence that he did). Body found 20 miles away
– face disfigured – identified by Miss C – says a mole by elbow
or above knee – a small silver cross or some other trinket –
pregnant – 6 weeks only. A scarf (Persian? or Italian?) Red hair
– auburn or black hair – Girl used to take local bus to nearby
Town – meet Philip there – C[lothilde] finds out Gwenda and
Philip – baby coming – going to marry. Strangles her – hides
body in garden – plans another girl whom she knows – drugs
her – drives her in car she has pinched 20 miles away in quarry
– obliterates features – moles – jealous

Midway through Notebook 28 we find a touching note. In the 1971 New Year Honours list Agatha Christie became Dame Agatha, a fact that she noted as she resumed work on *Nemesis*. On a more practical note, this means that she was less than halfway through the novel at the beginning of the year, with the submission date three months away. And she was 80 years of age.

> D.B.E. [Dame of the British Empire]
> Nemesis – Jan 1971
> Recap – death of Mr. Rafiel in Times – Miss Marple
> Point reached – Elizabeth Peters retired headmistress –
> accident as climbing – stones and rocks rolling down
> hillside – concussion – hospital
> Professor Wansted and Miss Marple

As she tidied the manuscript Christie listed the characters again, this time with a few additions. The final proofs were corrected by Dame Agatha while she recovered from a broken hip in June/July 1971, at which stage she also wrote the jacket blurb.

> Notes on 'Nemesis' March 18th '71
> Elizabeth Temple School Fallowfield
> Justin (?) Rafiel
> Michael Rafiel – Verity Hunt
> Miss Barrow – Miss Cooke – or Miss Caspar
> The Old Manor – Jocelyn St. Mary
> Clothilde Bradbury Scott – Lavinia – Anthea
> Archdeacon Bradshaw Bradley Scott?
> Emlyn Price
> Joanna Crawford Mrs Riseley-Porter
> Professor Wanstead
> Broadribb and Schuster (Solicitors)

She also gives a proposed list of chapters, with some notes to herself:

This list is not exactly reflected in the novel, but the suggested title of the opening chapter here is surely better than that eventually decided upon. 'Overture' is not thematically inked with any other chapter, while 'Births Marriages and Deaths' is both accurate and intriguing.

∿

## Fiddlers Three
### 3 August 1972

⟨○⟩

It is very important that businessman Jonathan Panhacker should live until Wednesday 18th as he has made a financial arrangement with his son, Henry, to inherit £100,000 on that date. When he unexpectedly dies, the Fiddlers Three conspire to make sure he is still 'alive' for a few more days.

⟨○⟩

This is the last play written by Agatha Christie and the only one not to receive a West End run. After a glorious and record-breaking playwriting career, this last work was a sad curtain call. Her previous dramatic offering, *Rule of Three*, was not particularly well received and it was ten years before she again felt tempted to try a script. *Fiddlers Three* is a two-act comedy thriller but, unfortunately, it has not enough of either to be a successful blend and falls between two uneasy extremes. It has a complicated history. In its first incarnation, *Fiddlers Five*, it premiered on 7 June 1971; the following year on 3 August a revamped version was presented as *Fiddlers Three*. In the intervening year Christie amalgamated some characters to reduce the number of Fiddlers.

The set-up is relatively straightforward. If Jonathan Panhacker lives until Wednesday 18th his financial arrangement with his son, Henry, to inherit £100,000 on that date will come to pass. In his turn, Henry has promised to invest the money in a business scheme with Sam Fletcher and Sam Bogosian. When Jonathan suddenly drops dead, Henry, Sam and his secretary, Sally, the Fiddlers Three of the title, scheme to keep him 'alive' until the 18th. This involves a double impersonation, a dubious death certificate and a revelation about an earlier murder. Complications arise in Act II when various people who knew Jonathan arrive at their hideaway hotel demanding to see him.

In common with the later books, the play contains good ideas but her earlier genius for exploiting them has deserted her; if she had written this play twenty years earlier a more compelling plot would have emerged. There is an unlikely impersonation and some unconvincing business with pill bottles before the play culminates in the unmasking of an improbable murderer. It cannot be coincidence that many of her later plays – *Spider's Web, The Unexpected Guest, Verdict, The Rats* and *Fiddlers Three* – feature this type of a will-they-get-away-with-it situation; although she frequently manages to reveal a murderer also.

Unsurprisingly, her producer Peter Saunders was not anxious to present it in the West End, fearful that it would receive a critical mauling. As it was, the local press was hardly kinder and phrases such as 'entertaining, amusing but undemanding play', 'lightest vein – bordering on farce' and 'the plot is predictable, witless and shallow' peppered what reviews there were.

As early as October 1958, the first seeds were sown in Notebook 15, although it would be over a dozen years before she began to cultivate them seriously. Obviously, even this late in her career, she was revisiting her faithful Notebooks to find exploitable ideas:

Oct. 1958

Projects

A Play – light-hearted (a Spider's Web type) Where? – girl's school?

Or Cheating Death parties? Pretending a death? or smuggling away a natural death – devoted fluffy secretary? – a silly type deliberately chosen? Boardroom – K. doubles as wife and corpse – wig etc. – Grand muddle –

The 'girl's school' idea surfaced the following year as *Cat among the Pigeons* and the 'Cheating Death parties' was briefly pursued in Notebook 39 below. 'Smuggling away a natural death' was the one that provided the basis of *Fiddlers Three*.

Notebook 4 contains most of the plotting, but, as often with the later book titles, the notes themselves are vague and unfocussed although the list of characters is accurate. A minor mystery about this play is the naming of the two main characters; Panhacker and Bogosian are two of the most unusual names in the entire Christie output.

Scene – an office
Mr Willis Stanley a bit off – story
His friend Mr. Bogosian
Nellie (M) devoted rather talkative and scatty

The Penthouse owner – Very rich man lives in W. Indies
His son ~~or nephew~~? Make over all his English assets
Going to finance – only a fortnight to go

Then goes up after lunch – or is lift out of order – so he
comes in here – sits in other room – found dead

M. says it will be her husband or brother – Go out to buy
    me an onion [to induce tears]
Jeremy ~~Brooker~~ Brown

That's all right – he's got to be alive – Geraldine – Go on
upstairs with things

Gina
Sally Lee
Sam Fletcher
Jan Bogosian
Henry Panhacker
Solomon Panhacker
An Air Hostess
Detective Inspector Wylie
Mr. Moss

Various titles were considered and *This Mortal Coil* appears
on an early script:

This Mortal Coil
Operation Deadline
Sixpence Off
Deadline
Fiddle de Death

In Notebook 39, under the mysterious heading 'M and J
Play',[61] we find two attempts at a 'death duties' play. The first
sketch has echoes of 'Jane in Search of a Job', originally

---

61  In his book *Curtain Up: Agatha Christie – A Life in Theatre* Julius
    Green speculates that this is a reference to Margaret Lockwood –
    star of *Spider's Web* – and her daughter Julia.

published in August 1924 and collected ten years later in *The Listerdale Mystery*:

> Death duties – girl is dead – great fortune is coming to her
> – idea is she has to appear alive for one more week. Man
> advertises for young lady – 5ft 7in, fair – hair slight build,
> blue eyes etc. First scene interesting girls whittled down
> – one is chosen to impersonate girl – J

The second is nearer to the eventual plot, but this was not developed until Notebook 4 where it becomes recognisably *Fiddlers Three*:

> Death Duties – a natural death body has to be hidden for a
>     week – impersonation by M or J – undertaker helps.
>     Office – M and her two employers
> Mr Leonard – big, bouncy, common
> Mr Arkwright – melancholy – dreary
> They are in a jam – what to do
> Sally!

### Elephants Can Remember
6 November 1972

---

At a literary dinner, Mrs Oliver is asked to investigate
the double death years earlier of Sir Alistair and
Lady Ravenscroft. Did he kill her and then himself
or was it the other way round? Hercule Poirot
journeys into the past to arrive at the truth.

---

The adage 'Old sins have long shadows' runs like a motif through *Elephants Can Remember*, the last Poirot novel that

Agatha Christie wrote. At its heart is a plot involving typical Christie ploys – mistaken identity, impersonation and misconstrued deaths – culminating in a last chapter reminiscent of the closing scene in *Five Little Pigs* with a group of people gathering at the scene of an earlier tragedy in order to learn the poignant truth. If it had been written twenty years earlier there can be little doubt that the plot would have been developed in a more ingenious fashion. As it is, the book is a series of conversations, with little action; and like its successor, *Postern of Fate*, the chronology of the earlier crimes will not bear close examination.

Old friends make reappearances: Mrs Oliver plays a large part and Superintendent Spence reminisces in Chapter 5 about *Mrs McGinty's Dead*, *Hallowe'en Party* and *Five Little Pigs*, all stories where Poirot investigates past crimes, the first two also in the company of Mrs Oliver. In Chapter 10 Miss Lemon, Poirot's secretary, appears briefly. Mr Goby, described in Chapter 16 as 'a purveyor of information', first appeared in *The Mystery of the Blue Train*, and also conducted enquiries on behalf of Poirot in *After the Funeral* and *Third Girl*.

There can be little doubt that it is Agatha Christie herself rather than Ariadne Oliver who muses throughout the first chapter on the difficulties of eating with false teeth, the horror of giving speeches, the difficulties of dinner-party companions and the unwarranted effusiveness of fans. And the passage in the same chapter in which Albertina remonstrates with Mrs Oliver about her diffidence is echoed in *An Autobiography* when Christie describes how the wife of the British ambassador to Vienna had encouraged her to abandon her natural shyness and declare to reporters, 'It is wonderful what I have done. I am the best detective story writer in the world. Yes, I am proud of the fact . . . I am very clever indeed.'

There are fewer than twenty pages of notes, scattered over four Notebooks. Notebook 5 contains six pages of notes but only the first few lines are relevant to the finished novel. In strong legible writing at the top of the first page of Notebook 5 we read:

Elephants Remember – Jan. 1972

Despite its incongruity in a crime novel it would seem that the title, or a slight variant of it, was settled from the beginning. The elephant motif recurs throughout the book – often in defiance of logic – with an early reference in the first chapter to Mrs Burton-Cox's teeth.

In the following extract Mrs Gorringe is the forerunner of Mrs Burton-Cox and, although their discussion about hereditary violence is not used, the last idea, a godchild and her fiancé, is. Details from this extract – Mrs Oliver's birthday and the 'bull in the field' memory – tally exactly with Chapter 1.

Mrs. Oliver – Poirot

Does a problem come to P? or Mrs. O? Lunch for literary women – Mrs. Oliver – Mrs. Gorringe

Mrs G. 'Do you think that if a child had grown up she might have been a murderer- murderess?'

Boys pull fly's legs off but they don't do it when they grow up – just boyish fun. Are you very interested in these things?

Not really – it's just because of one particular thing – a god child I've got – she's got a boyfriend – she wants to marry him. (Interruption – Speeches) They go and sit and look at the Serpentine.

All so long ago – everyone would have forgotten. People don't forget things that happen when they were children

– Mrs. O remembers cows a bull in a field – a birthday and
something to do with an éclair. It's like elephants –
elephants never forget

After a brief detour to consider an alternative and to remind
herself to re-read an early Poirot short story with a very
similar plot, Christie outlines the opening of *Elephants Can
Remember* in Notebook 6, almost exactly as it appears in the
published novel:

Idea A
Husband and wife – she says her husband is poisoning her
– (wants to believe it) attracted to a young man who
pretends he is in love with her – actually is also courting
niece tells wife he is pretending this to deceive husband.
Really, he and niece are in on it. Re-read 'Cornish Mystery.'

Idea B
Mrs. O goes to literary lunch – bossy female buttonholes
her. I believe Celia Ravenscroft is your god-daughter? My
son wants to marry her. Can you tell me if her mother killed
her father or was it [her] father killed [her] mother.
Celebrated case – you must remember – both bodies on
cliff – both shot.

Mrs. O goes to Poirot or does she get Celia to come and
see her. Modern – violent – intellectual girl – says definitely
of course mother shot him – gives reason – story of what lay
behind it. Mrs. O gets interested. Talks to Poirot

A few pages later we find a variety of ideas, some of which
found their way into the finished book. These notes are
somewhat confused and confusing – references to the wife/
sister are not always clear – but the underlying plot of two
sisters, one husband and lifelong jealousy ending in murder
and impersonation eventually emerged. There is an echo of

the Christie of old in the listing of alternatives, although most of them are variations on a theme.

### Further ideas

Is it actually Col. R has shot himself – wife is <u>not</u> his wife – a sister in law – elder sister of wife – has been in nursing home or mental Home for killing children – unfit to plead

Or Col. R's sister or his first wife – a tragedy in India – she is paroled from mental home. Dressed in wife's clothes and wig. Wife pretends to be sister – identifies body.

Sisters one is mental – kills children – unfit to plead – in Broadmoor
or
Colonel's sister – devoted to him – jealous of his wife. Paroled – comes to house – kills brother – wife shoots her – dresses her in wig and clothes – stages it all – identifies wife's body –
or
India Col. has wife/sister? – mental kills child – Ayah accused – poisons herself. But was it the ayah? Could it have been sister in law or the mother? [Chapter 7]

Story about Mrs. Ravenscroft sister in India – nervous breakdown – killed a child – hushed up taken back to England – nursing home.
Story – Wife and mother killed child
Story – Sister of Col – or Mrs. R – said to be accident. Goes now to England in private mental home – released – lives with a qualified mental nurse – nurse dies – sister in law marries.

There is a reference to twins – an idea dotted throughout the Notebooks – which is adopted, although not exactly as Christie here speculated. And the second reference below, from Notebook 6, is a plot very similar to the Marple short story 'The Case of the Perfect Maid'; apart from the idea of twins, it has little to do with *Elephants Can Remember*.

> Twin idea – 2 girls born same day – one girl tells her they are identical – nobody knows them apart

> Lalage and Lorna identical twins – born same day but really not identical – look quite different – come from Australia or New Zealand. Lalage plays part of both sisters – 3rd person in house is Stephanie (really Lorna). Play part of maid or one time au pair girl – foreign accent etc. actually looks like her Aunt (mother's sister Francesca)

One of the ideas appears in Chapter 6 as a red herring:

> Colonel R – is doing reminiscences of his days in India – girl secretary comes – takes dictation from him and does typing. Suggestion that there was something between them

Despite showing a glimpse in the final chapter of the Christie of yesteryear, *Elephants Can Remember* remains a disappointment. Like the books published on either side of it, there are too many rambling conversations that give the reader little solid information but merely repeat what we have already been told. The central idea has possibilities and there is certainly material for a long short story. It could have been a disappointing swan song for Poirot but the Queen of Crime had reserved a dazzling final performance, *Curtain: Poirot's Last Case*, for the little Belgian.

## *Akhnaton*
### Published 14 May 1973

◄○►

Spanning a period of sixteen years, the play concerns
the attempts of the young King Akhnaton to introduce
a new religion to Egypt. His failure spells tragedy for
himself, his queen and, ultimately, Egypt.

◄○►

Called by Christie's husband, Sir Max Mallowan, 'the most
beautiful play' she ever wrote, *Akhnaton* is based on the real-
life Pharoah Akhnaton of Egypt in 1375 BC. Although written
in 1937 it was not published until 1973, with a blurb written
by Agatha Christie herself. Shortly after its completion Christie sent it to the actor (later Sir) John Gielgud. His reply,
which she kept, expressed his admiration for the play while
declining to become involved in a production. In fact *Akhnaton* was never professionally produced, but it was seen in the
Westcliff Agatha Christie Theatre Festival in 2001; the one-
off presentation used a minimum of setting and props and
was, in essence, an elaborate reading.

    Although by no means a typical Agatha Christie play, it
does contain Christie-like elements – there is a death by
poisoning, masterminded by an unsuspected villain using an
innocent party.

    There are forty pages of notes for this play, including
extensive background material. The very first page begins
with a cast list (in the published version Mutnezmet, Nefertiti's sister, has become Nezzemut), and this is followed by a
sketch of the opening scene:

Queen Tyi
Horemheb
Eye

Nefertiti

Mutnezmet

Tutankhamun

The father of Tyi

The mother of Tyi

The High Priest of Amon

The High Priest of Re

A Priest of Ptah

Act I Scene I

Amenhotep the Magnificent is near to death – the king of Mitanni sends the image of Ishtar of Niniveh to Egypt (second time such a procedure happened) in hopes that the Goddess might exorcise the evil spirits which were causing the King's infirmity. The Goddess passes through.

Horemheb talks with the father and mother of Tyi talk together. The High Priest of Ammon talks to Horemheb – on evils of foreign marriage – Queen Tyi appears with her son. –

The early pages of Notebook 61 show seven scenes for Act I, four for Act II and two for Act III. A redrafting ten pages later brings it closer to the published version, which has three scenes each for the first two Acts and four for the third with an Epilogue. The notes show this Epilogue as the last scene of the play.

In between the drafts there are notes on

Indulgences – A verdict of acquittal sold by Scribes – pardoned names inserted in the blanks.

Heart scarab – 'O my heart rise not up against me as a witness'

Gold collars as gifts –

The book *From Fetish to God* by Budge is also mentioned on the very first page and there are page references to it

throughout the notes. This research is similar to that undertaken by Christie for *Death Comes as the End* from books
loaned to her by Stephen Glanville, the dedicatee:

> Visit by Tyi in 12th year of A's reign – description of clothes
> P.155
> Tribute? – A scene showing it being brought' P.151
> Description of Palace for scene P.138

One of the earliest quotations, presumably from this book, is
reproduced with minor variations to form almost the closing
lines of the play. The last traces of Akhnaton are erased, soon
to be replaced by 'the divine Amon, King of Gods':

> How bountiful are the possessions of him who knows the
> gifts of that God (Amon). Wise is he who knows him.
> Favoured is he who serves him, there is protection for him
> who follows him.

### Postern of Fate
### 29 October 1973

While shelving books in her new home Tuppence
Beresford finds a hidden message concerning the
mysterious death of a previous inhabitant. With the help
of Tommy she investigates a mystery from the distant past,
unaware that new danger is very much in the present.

> *Four great gates has the city of Damascus . . .*
> *Postern of Fate, the Desert Gate, Disaster's Cavern,*
> *Fort of Fear . . .*
>
> Flecker, *Gates of Damascus*

*Postern of Fate* was the last book Agatha Christie wrote and the initial notes are clearly dated November 1972, almost exactly a year before publication. It is arguable that her agent and publisher should never have asked for another book after *Elephants Can Remember.* Although H.R.F. Keating reviewed *Postern of Fate* charitably in *The Times* with the ambiguous phrase 'She stills skims like a bird', there is no doubt that it is the weakest book Christie ever wrote. The most interesting passages are those where we get a glimpse of the private Agatha Christie. Old Isaac's reminiscences in Book II, Chapter 2 ('Introduction to Mathilde, Truelove and KK') echo Christie's own memories of her childhood as described in Part I of *An Autobiography.* Many of the books mentioned by Tommy and Tuppence in the early chapters of the book – *The Cuckoo Clock, Four Winds Farm, The Prisoner of Zenda, Under the Red Robe* – are still to be found on the shelves of Greenway House, her Devon home. The description of The Laurels bears more than a passing resemblance to Ashfield, her beloved childhood home, even down to the monkey puzzle tree in the garden; and the first UK edition has on the jacket a photo of Bingo, Christie's own family dog and the inspiration for the novel's Hannibal. And when Tuppence complains about the effects of old age or the vagaries of workmen ('They came, they showed efficiency, they made optimistic remarks, they went away to fetch something. They never came back'), we can be certain that this is the elderly Christie speaking.

Interesting though these insights are – and they were to be superseded within a few years by publication of *An Autobiography* – they do not make a detective novel and there can be no argument that *Postern of Fate* is even a pale imitation of the form at which, for half a century, she excelled. The novel's intriguing opening premise, the coded message in the book, clearly shows that advancing age did not prevent Christie having ideas; what was missing was the ability to develop them as she would have even a decade earlier. All of the final half-dozen novels, from *By the Pricking of my Thumbs* onwards, begin with a fascinating idea – the disappearance of an elderly lady from her retirement home, the drowning of a child while bobbing for apples, the supposed double suicide of an elderly couple – but none of them is explored with anything approaching the ingenuity of Christie's yesteryear. As recently as two years earlier, *Nemesis* begins with a situation very similar to that of *Postern of Fate*: a message from the dead that demands an investigation. But the decline in those two years is all too evident and dramatic.

Not surprisingly this decline is mirrored in the two Notebooks, 3 and 7, which contain the plotting notes. There are fewer than twenty-five pages of notes and they vary between scattered jottings and complete paragraphs. Many of the notes are reminders to amend sections already written and there is none of the plethora of ideas normally associated with the Notebooks. Note that the page numbers below do not refer to the published version but, in all probability, to the proofs.

> Continue next from P.120
> March 9th [1973]
> P.135 Letter or money in leather wallet
> P.56 Name of village or market town? Must be mentioned in first chapter?
> P.75 about M.R. Car accident? Change to illness

The book was completed by May 1973 and the editor at Collins wrote diplomatically in mid-June to say that he 'enjoyed your latest novel very much', remarking especially on the splendid character of Hannibal the dog and the wise comments on old age. He also mooted the idea of changing the title, despite the presence of the quotation, to *Postern of Death*, a suggestion that obviously was not well received. Further correspondence and phone calls were needed to rectify 'certain discrepancies' – whether references to the war refer to the First or Second World War, exactly who killed Isaac, and the splitting of some long chapters into shorter ones. With all of this clarification it is surprising that no one spotted the impossible chronology of the Beresfords' children. In *N or M?* Deborah, their daughter, is involved in war work; in Book III Chapter 16 of *Postern of Fate*, set thirty years later, she is described as 'nearly 40'.

Some old friends reappear – the mysterious Colonel Pikeaway and Mr Robinson – and there are numerous references to the Beresfords' earlier cases. They reminisce about *The Secret Adversary* in 1922, their exploits as *Partners in Crime* in 1929 and their war-time spy adventure in *N or M?*. Oddly, although they remind each other frequently about these, neither of them mentions their most recent adventure *By the Pricking of my Thumbs*, a mere five years earlier. The murder method in *Postern of Fate*, foxglove leaves as poison, has echoes of the early short story 'The Herb of Death' from *The Thirteen Problems*. And note the reference, in Book II, Chapter 2, to the idea of taking pot-shots at departing visitors; this was the unsociable habit both of Richard Warwick, the victim in *The Unexpected Guest*, and Christie's brother Monty when he settled in Devon on his return from Africa.

For even the most devoted reader of Christie *Postern of Fate* is a challenge. Despite its intriguing premise – 'Mary Jordan did not die naturally. It was one of us. I think I know which' – the book never explores this enigma in any organised way. The investigation, such as it is, consists mainly of pointless and long-winded conversations, endless reminiscences and far too many inconsequential characters. What little plot there is would have benefited from the excision of at least a hundred pages, but it is doubtful if even this ruthless exercise would make any overall difference. Yet the book went into the best-seller charts within weeks of publication – and stayed there. But there can be no doubt that at this stage fans automatically bought each new title just because it *was* the new 'Christie for Christmas'.

The opening of the book is almost exactly as sketched below:

Notes for Nov. 1972 and Plans
Opening suggestion for a book
Tuppence says 'What a load of books we have.' Starts
looking at books – takes some out – looks at them – laughs
– finds a letter in book shoved behind shelf. Seems to
indicate a murder

This is followed by speculation about the title, with 'Doom's Caravan' and 'Death's Caravan' leading the field and heading the following page; and by the quotation that actually appears in the book:

Book T[ommy] and T[uppence] Title?
Doom's Caravan?
Swallow's Nest
Postern of Fate?

Doom's Caravan

Pass not beneath, O Caravan, or pass not singing
Have you not heard
That silence where the birds are dead yet
Something pipeth like a bird?
Pass not beneath, O Caravan, Doom's Caravan
Death's Caravan

In the early pages of Notebook 3 Christie considers various ideas, some of which were discarded – a homicidal spinster aunt, a woman doctor – and some adopted – the census entries, hidden papers, Regent's Park. At this stage Mary is still a German spy.

Points

Death – accidental? – of Alexander. Horseradish picked by
mistake was foxglove leaves
Digitalin – Death from Heart –
Who picked them? Who cooked them (a) Cook (b) Girl
helping (c) Woman doctor? Goes round garden with one of
the children. Aunt or perhaps mother of illegitimate child
– who grown up as her nephew – in army or navy. Mary
Robinson (governess) German girl, very beautiful, is German
spy – takes plans to London – Regent's Park – Queen Mary's
garden. Tommy by reason of some of his contacts (in N or
M) – Census entries – who was in the house those 2 (?) dates
Spinster Aunt – she poisons German Mary R
Simon a school friend staying there – Recognises M.R.
– pointed out to him as a woman by an Army god father or
an older friend – or a foreign officer an [Australian] who
in 1921 or thereabouts has a cottage a place like Dittisham
[a village near Agatha Christie's Devon home] – (Reason –
papers might be hidden there)

A list of characters from Notebook 7 includes a Miss Price-
Ridley, who is surely a relative of Mrs Price Ridley, Miss
Marple's neighbour in St Mary Mead; a character bearing
this name does make a brief appearance in *Postern of Fate.*
This is the sort of irritating mistake that an editor should
have spotted.

Points Doom's Caravan
People
Dorothy called Dodo – Miss Little – big woman –
nicknamed The Parish Pump
Griffin – old – full of memories
Miss Price Ridley
Mrs Lupton – supports herself on 2 sticks – remembers the
Parkinsons, [the] Somers – also Chattertons
Place called Hallquay [Book I, Chapter 5]

And, inexplicably, in the middle of Book III, Chapter 7, after a discussion of their adventures in *The Secret Adversary* and *N or M?*, we find Tommy and Tuppence having the following conversation. The version below, from Notebook 7, is reproduced almost exactly in the novel:

> Swallow's Nest said Tuppence 'That's what the house was once called.'
> 'Why shouldn't we call it that again'
> 'Good idea', said Tuppence
> Birds flew from the roof over their heads
> Swallows flying south, said Tommy. 'Won't they ever come back?'
> 'Yes they'll come back next winter through the Postern of fate', said Lionel

This is followed by brief mention of Isaac's death, the most casual murder in the entire Christie canon. The sang-froid with which his murder is greeted is rivalled only by the casual attitude to, and implausibility of, the shooting of Tuppence.

> Isaacs Death
> Inquest – after inquest – Isaac's household – a niece or wife – Nellie – a lodger who has not been there very long – 2 lodgers perhaps. Mention by Nellie of Cambridge or an envelope on which Cambridge has been written – Boat Race that day – a bet made [Book III, Chapters 9 & 10]

In Notebook 28 Christie considers some scenarios for the opening chapter, eventually settling on C below. The reference to Harrison Homes is to the real-life charity, providing accommodation for the independent-minded elderly, with which she was closely involved:

*An extract from Notebook 7 and the plotting for* Postern of Fate.
*Note the legibility of the handwriting.*

Large numbers of books – Tuppence is going to sort them
out – take some to hospital? Or Harrison Homes – some
old lady knows something
A. Is there something in a book – 2 pages stuck together
B. or is there some letters or print which spell out words –
a message
C. Such a sentence as 'Mary Robinson did not die naturally.
It was one of us – I think I know which one.'

This is followed by a careful working out of the code found
by Tuppence in her copy of R.L. Stevenson's *The Black Arrow*.
The extract starts out accurately, although judicious editing
has been done to avoid writing it out in its entirety. Eventually, isolated words only are used and sense and logic are lost,
a sentiment echoed by Tommy when Tuppence shows him

her discovery. Note, however, the change of the name from Robinson here to Jordan in the published version; and the incorrect spelling of 'naturally' as 'naturaly' in the code even though it appears correctly in the body of the note. Very little of this working out appears in the published novel.

> The Black Arrow R. L. Stevenson
> Matcham could not restrain a little cry and even Dick started with surprise and dropped the windac from his fingers but to the fellows on the lawn this shaft was an expected signal. They were all afoot together tightening loosening sword and dagger in the sheaths. Ellis held up his hand, the white of his eyes shone – let . . . . . . . the men of the Black Arrow had all disappeared and the cauldron and the ruined house burning alone to testify . . . . Not in time to warn these one from (from) upper quarters I have these I and striking I will / Duckworth and Simon red with / Is the arrow hurry ellis whistle / Space their house and dead
> MARY/ROBINSON/DID/NOT/DIE/NATURALY/IT/
> WAS/ONE/OF//US/I/THINK/I/KNOW/WHICH/
> ONE

It is touching to imagine the 83-year-old Queen of Crime carefully copying and underlining her code; and to remember that it was the last ingenious idea she was to devise.

## *Curtain: Poirot's Last Case*
### 22 September 1975

———————◄○►———————

A frail Poirot summons Hastings to Styles, the scene
of their first investigation and now a guest house.
Poirot explains that a fellow-guest is a murderer.
Convinced that another killing is imminent he asks
Hastings to help prevent it. But who is the killer
and, more importantly, who is the victim?

———————◄○►———————

'Do you know, Poirot, I almost wish sometimes that you
would commit a murder.'

'Mon cher!'

'Yes, I'd like to see how you set about it.'

'My dear chap, if I committed a murder you would not
have the slightest chance of seeing – how I set about it! You
would not even be aware, probably, that a murder had
been committed.'

'Murder in the Mews'

'I shouldn't wonder if you ended up by detecting your
own death,' said Japp, laughing heartily. 'That's an idea,
that is. Ought to be put in a book.'

'It will be Hastings who will have to do that,' said Poirot,
twinkling at me.

*The ABC Murders, Chapter 3*

These telling and prophetic exchanges, both between Poirot
and Inspector Japp, may have sowed the seeds of a shocking
idea in Christie's fertile brain. *The ABC Murders*, begun in
1934 and 'Murder in the Mews', completed in early 1936,
both pre-date *Curtain*. But, as will be seen, she had been
considering such a plot for some years.

*Curtain: Poirot's Last Case* is the most dazzling example of literary legerdemain in the entire Christie output. It is not only a nostalgic swan song, but also a virtuoso demonstration of plotting ingenuity culminating in the ultimate shock ending from a writer whose career was built on her ability both to deceive and delight her readers. It plays with our emotional reaction to the decline, and eventual demise, of one of the world's great detective creations, and it also recalls the heady days of the first case that Poirot and Hastings shared, also in the unhappy setting of the ill-fated country house Styles.

The return to Styles was inspired; it encompasses the idea of a life come full circle, as Poirot revisits the scene both of his momentous reacquaintance with Hastings, and of his first great success in his adopted homeland. Like Poirot himself, Styles has deteriorated from its glory days and, instead of having a family gathered under its roof, is now host to a group of strangers; and one of them (at least) has, as in yesteryear, murder in mind. And the claustrophobic atmosphere of the novel is accentuated by having only two short scenes – those depicting Mrs Franklin's inquest and funeral and a visit to Boyd Carrington's house – set elsewhere. The novel also toys with the vexed question of natural versus legal justice and this is not the first time that a classic Christie has explored this theme. *And Then There Were None* and *Murder on the Orient Express* are both based on this difficult concept; and *Ordeal by Innocence*, *Five Little Pigs*, *Mrs McGinty's Dead* and 'The Witness for the Prosecution' further explore this theme.

But as usual with Christie, and certainly the Christie of the 1930s and 40s, almost everything is subservient to plot; throughout her career, the theme of justice – natural versus legal, justice in retrospect, posthumous free pardons – is merely the starting point for an ingenious exercise in ratiocination. Two of her greatest titles – *And Then There Were None* and *Murder on the Orient Express* – are predicated on this theme but in each case the moral dilemma is secondary to the machinations of a brilliant plot. Discussion of justice is perfunctory in each title; plot mechanics override any philosophical consideration.

When was *Curtain* written? There are no dated pages among the notes for *Curtain*, but there are two likely parameters. *Sad Cypress*, mentioned in Chapter 3 ('the case of Evelyn [Elinor] Carlisle'), was published in March 1940 with a US serialisation beginning in November 1939. The address on the manuscript of *Curtain* is 'Greenway House', which Christie left in October 1942 on its requisition by the US navy.

But from the evidence of the Notebooks it would seem that it was written earlier, rather than later. The clearest evidence for this is in Notebook 62, whose early pages contain the notes for the stories that make up *The Labours of Hercules*, beginning with 'The Horses of Diomedes' (page 3) and 'The Apples of the Hesperides' (page 5) published in *The Strand* in June and September 1940 respectively. The first page also contains a short list of 'Books read and liked' and the latest publication date involved is 1940. Sandwiched between this list and notes for 'The Horses of Diomedes' is a page headed unequivocally 'Corrections Curtain'; page 4 continues with the corrections and the final revisions appear below the half-page of notes for 'The Apples of the Hesperides'. Combined with the reference on the first page of the novel to 'a second and a more desperate war', this would seem to place the writing of this novel in the early days of the Second World War.

For the reader, the main difficulty with *Curtain* is one of fitting the case into the Poirot casebook, containing as it does inevitable chronological inconsistencies for a book written thirty-five years before its 1975 publication. It is impossible to state with any certainty when the book is set. Although he has been married for over fifty years, Hastings has a 21-year-old daughter. Poirot has declined dramatically since his previous appearance three years earlier in *Elephants Can Remember*; and even the most generous estimate must place his age at around 120. In Chapter 3 there are references to cases that were all written, and published, during the late 1930s or early 1940s: 'Triangle at Rhodes', *The ABC Murders, Death on the Nile, Sad Cypress* (whose main character oddly, is referred to as Evelyn, instead of Elinor, Carlisle). Countess Vera Rosakoff (*The Big Four,* 'The Capture of Cerberus', 'The Double Clue') is also mentioned in the same chapter and the bloodstained butcher, also from *The Big Four,* is mentioned in passing in Chapter 5. There is an enevitable mention in Chapter 15 of the original Styles case as happening '20 years ago and more' a reference vague enough to have little chronological significance.

The question that has to be asked, but unfortunately cannot be answered, is: Did Christie write *Curtain* intending it to appear long after many 'future' cases of Poirot had been published, or did she write it *as if* she was writing it after many such cases had been published? Are references to 'long ago' (Chapter 7) *actually* to long ago or to the 'long ago' Christie imagined would have elapsed by the time the book was published? There is no indication on any of the the original typescripts of any major deletions or updating, putting paid to the theory that the resurrected manuscript received major surgery to remove obvious chronological anomalies. One of the surviving typescripts contains minor corrections, and these correspond to the list of corrections in Notebook 62, dating from the early 1940s, possibly 1940 itself.

But if you accept that the book was written many years prior to publication and treat it as a 'lost' case, then these problems disappear and it is possible to enjoy this masterwork of plotting for what it is – the ultimate Christie conjuring trick. Technically it is a master class in plotting a detective story. Arguably there is no murder, although there are three deaths: Colonel Luttrell attempts to murder his wife, while

Mrs Franklin attempts to murder her husband; Hastings proposes to murder Allerton and is responsible for the unintentional murder (i.e. manslaughter) of Mrs Franklin; and Poirot's 'execution' of Norton is followed by his own suicide.

Hastings' intended murder of Allerton is foiled by Poirot, who realises what he means to do. Mrs Franklin, thanks to an innocent action by Hastings, is hoist with her own petard. Colonel Luttrell's shooting of his wife is a failure because, as Poirot puts it, 'he wanted to miss.' And Poirot, in effect, executes Norton. In this regard, it should be remembered that Poirot was not above taking the law into his own hands and had done so, to a greater or lesser degree, throughout his career. In *The Murder of Roger Ackroyd, Peril at End House, Dumb Witness, Death on the Nile, Appointment with Death* and *The Hollow*, he 'facilitated' (at least) the suicide of the culprit. And in *Murder on the Orient Express* and 'The Chocolate Box' he allowed the killers to evade (legal) justice.

References to *Curtain* are scattered over nine Notebooks. Notebooks 30, 44 and 61 each have a one-page reference, while another half a dozen have a few pages each. The bulk of the plotting is in Notebooks 62 and 65 (ten pages each) and Notebook 60 with over forty pages. It is difficult to be sure if this was because Christie mulled it over for a long time, jotting down a note whenever she got an idea, or because the plotting of it presented a challenge to even her creativity. I would incline towards the latter theory, as many of the jottings are a reiteration of the same situation with minor changes of name, character, profession or other detail. This would seem to indicate that the basic idea (Styles as a guest house and Poirot as an invalid inhabitant) remains the same and that, as she intended this to be Poirot's swan song (and the notes confirm this), she wanted it to be stunning; as indeed it is.

In *Curtain* Agatha Christie played her last great trick on her public. Throughout her career she fooled readers into believing the innocent guilty and, more importantly, the guilty innocent. Her first novel made the most obvious parties the guilty ones; a few years later she made the narrator the murderer. Throughout the 1930s and 1940s she rang the changes on the least likely character – the investigating policeman, the child, the likeable hero, the supposed victim; she had everyone guilty and everyone victim. She even repeated the Ackroyd trick, unrecognisably, in her last decade. So by the time of *Curtain* her only remaining, least likely character was the one she chose – Poirot, her little Belgian hero. And in so doing, her title was also the only possible one: *Curtain.*

The idea of a 'last case' for Poirot was one that Christie toyed with intermittently while plotting earlier titles. The following references are scattered through seven Notebooks and all refer to such a case, often with the name *Curtain* included:

Curtain
Poirot investigates story of death believed caused by ricin

B. Poirot's Last Case
Styles – turned into convalescent home or Super Hotel

A. Poirot's Last Case
History repeats itself – Styles now a guest house

Double murder – that is to say: A poisons B [and] B stabs A
but really owing to plan by C (perhaps P's last case?)

Curtain
Letter received by Hastings on boat. His daughter with him
– Rose? Pat? At Styles

The Unsolved Murder – Poirot's Last Case?

~~The~~ Curtain
H[astings] comes to Styles – has heard about P[oirot]

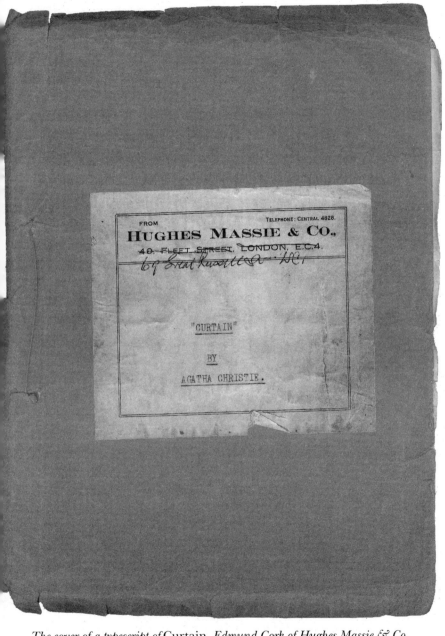

FROM
TELEPHONE: CENTRAL 4828.

## HUGHES MASSIE & CO.,
40, FLEET STREET, LONDON, E.C.4.

"CURTAIN"

BY

AGATHA CHRISTIE.

*The cover of a typescript of* Curtain. *Edmund Cork of Hughes Massie & Co. was Christie's agent from* The Murder of Roger Ackroyd *onwards.*

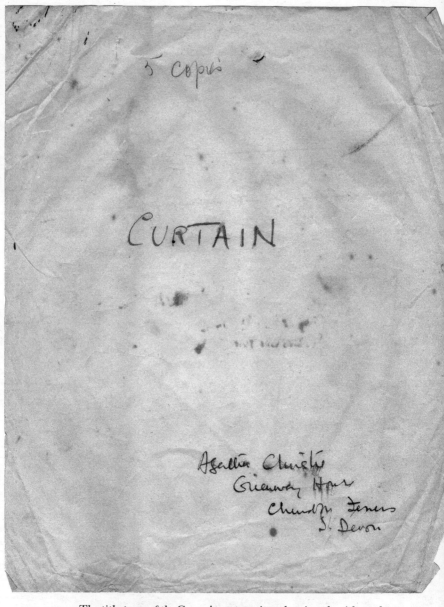

*The title page of the **Curtain** typescript, showing the title and name-and-address in Christie's own handwriting.*

Short Stories
Scene of one – Road up to Bassae? (Hercule's last case)

That last, very short and cryptic example from Notebook 60 refers to the Temple of Bassae in Greece, one of the places that Christie visited on her honeymoon. Both *An Autobiography* and Max Mallowan's *Memoirs* mention it, mainly because it involved a ten-hour mule ride. At first glance it seems that she was considering it as a possible setting for *Curtain* but it is far more likely that it is the last of *The Labours of Hercules*, with its varied international settings, that she had in mind, although in the end the idea came to nothing.

Possible characters are considered in six Notebooks, with Hastings and/or his daughter appearing in many of the lists:

The people
Sherman is the man who likes power – attractive
personality. Victim is Caroline

Curtain Characters
Judith – H's daughter
Mrs Merrit – tiresome invalid
Her husband – tropical researcher medicine
Girl – B.Sc. has done work for him – very devoted
Or
Judith
Miss Clarendon – nurse companion – fine woman –
experienced – mentions a 'case' of murder – 'I once had to
give evidence in a murder case'
Sir C. Squire – fine English type – wants to fight – H.
terrifically taken by him –

2nd set of people?
Betty Rice (old friend of Landor) – A difficult life – her
husband takes drugs
Dr. Amberly – clever man tropical medicine

Mrs Amberly tiresome invalid but with charm
Sir Roger Clymer – old school tie – fine fellow – has known
Mrs A[mberly] as girl
Miss Clarendon – a nurse companion
A girl, Betty, and her friend come down together – she is an
archaeologist or B.Sc. or something in love with Dr. Amberly
Or
Judith H's daughter
Superior and unpleasant young man? (Mrs A's son by
former marriage?)

At Styles
Dr Amory – keen man of forty-five – wants to go to Africa,
study tropical medicine
His wife, Kitty – invalid imaginaire – a blight but attractive
Governess Bella Chapstowe
Nurse companion Miss Oldroyd
Martin Wright – cave man – naturalist

People
John Franklin
Adela Franklin
Langton
Nurse Barrett
? Mrs. L[angton] (Emilia?)
Roger Boyd
Old Colonel Luxmoore
Mrs Luxmoore

People there
The Darwins – Fred – patient, quiet – his wife querulous
He wants to go off to Africa – his wife won't let him
Betty Rousdon – a girl staying there – very keen on his work
Wife's companion – Miss Collard – principal false clue
John Selby – cave man – fond of birds – a naturalist –
becomes great friends with Joan Hastings

Girl and mother (latter impossible)
Young man who wants to marry her
Has Selby a wife?

Col. Westmacott and wife – (like Luards?) some secondary
resentment between them
Langdon – lame man – keen on birds – (has alibi <u>genuine</u>
for some previous case)
P[oirot] – invalid – thinks Egypt etc. not George another
valet – (not really helpless)
Triangle drama
(Hastings daughter?) sec. to scientific man – nagging invalid
wife who won't let him go to S. America

Some characters seem to have been decided early on and,
apart from name changes (e.g. Langdon/Langton), remained
constant until the finished novel. They include a doctor
interested in tropical medicine and his invalid wife, under
various names (the Amberleys/Merrits/Darwins/Amorys/
Franklins); a young professional woman (Betty Rousdon/'a
Girl'/Judith) in love with him and his work; a nurse companion (Miss Collard/Oldroyd/Clarendon/Nurse Barrett); an
'old school tie' (Roger Boyd/Sir C. Squire/Sir Roger Clymer);
a naturalist (Sherman/Martin Wright/Selby); and the owners
of Styles (the Westmacotts/Luxmoores). These remain, in
one form or another, through most of the notes. The young
professional woman was not always Hastings' daughter,
Judith; this amendment was introduced possibly in order to
give Hastings the necessary motive for murder.

Note the one-time proposal to use the name Westmacott
for the owners of Styles. Although it is now well known that
Mary Westmacott is a pseudonym for Agatha Christie, at the
time these notes were written it was a carefully preserved
secret. The reference to the Luards above is to an infamous
murder case in 1908.

Eventually, in Notebook 60, we get the listing that is nearest to the novel. At this point, as in some of the earlier listings, there was to be a Mrs Langton. However, Langton as a 'loner' makes more sense, psychologically as well as practically.

People
Judith Hastings
John Franklin
Barbara Franklin
Nurse Campbell [Craven]
Sir Boyd Carrington
Major ~~Neville~~ Nugent [Allerton] (seducer) really after Nurse
Col and Mrs Luttrell own the place
Miss Cole – handsome woman of 35
Langtons [Norton]

Chapter 2 of the novel lists the cases on which Poirot bases his assertion that a death will take place at Styles and some of the scenarios below, from Notebooks 60 and 65, tally closely with that chapter though details have been selected and amalgamated:

The Cases
On a yacht – a row – man pitched another overboard – a quarrel – wife had had nervous breakdown
Girl killed an overbearing aunt – nagged at her – young man in offing – forbidden to see or write to him
Husband – elderly invalid – young wife – gave him arsenic – confessed
Sister-in-law – walked into police station and admitted she'd killed her brother's wife. Old mother (of wife) lived with them bedridden [elements of the Litchfield Case]

Curtain The Cases
Man who drinks – young wife – man she is fond of – she kills husband – arsenic? [the Etherington Case] (Langton's her cousin – or friend?)

Man in village – his wife and a lodger – he shoots them both
– or her and the kid (It comes out L[angton] lived in that
village) [elements of the Riggs Case]
Old lady – the daughter or granddaughter – elder polishes
off old lady to give young sister a chance [elements of the
Litchfield Case]

The only scenario not to appear is the first one. In many ways
these recapitulations are reminiscent of a similar set-up in
*Mrs McGinty's Dead*, where four earlier and notorious murder
cases affect the lives of the inhabitants of Broadhinny.

The following extract, from Notebook 61, appears as Idea
F in a list that includes the germs of *Sad Cypress* ('illegitimate
daughter – district nurse') and 'Dead Man's Mirror' ('The
Second Gong – Miss Lingard efficient secretary') and is
immediately followed by detailed notes for *Appointment with
Death*, published in 1938. As this jotting was probably written
around late 1936 ('Dead Man's Mirror' was first published in
March 1937) this would put the early plotting of *Curtain* years
ahead of its (supposed) writing. The theory that Christie
wrote *Curtain* and *Sleeping Murder* in case she was killed in
the Blitz begins to look questionable, as the 1940 Blitz was
an unimagined horror four years earlier. Nor can it have
been a book held in reserve in case of a 'dry' creative season;
*Curtain* could only be published at the end of Poirot's (and
Christie's) career. Ironically, despite the fact that this is a very
precise and concise summation of *Curtain*, this Notebook
contains no further reference to it.

The Unsolved Mystery    Poirot's Last Case?
P very decayed – H and Bella [Hastings' wife, whom he met
in *The Murder on the Links*] come home. P shows H
newspaper cuttings – all referring to deaths – about 7 – <u>4</u>
people have been hanged or surprise that no evidence. At
all 7 deaths <u>one person</u> has been present – the name is cut
out. P says that person X is present in house. There will be

another murder. There is – a man is killed – that man is really X himself – executed

And this extract, from Notebook 62, mentions another important point – the absence of George and his replacement with another 'valet':

> Hastings arriving at the station for Styles – Poirot – black hair but crippled – Georges away – the other man – a big one – quite dumb
> After dinner (various people noted) P in his room gives H cases to read – X

Notebook 65 recaps this with some added detail – Poirot and Egypt, the sadism angle – but the note about warning the victim is puzzling. As he says in Chapter 3, Poirot knows from his experiences in *Death on the Nile* and 'Triangle at Rhodes' how fruitless such warnings are. And warning the victim in this case is impossible as he does not know who that victim is to be. So why is the 'Warn the victim?' question answered with 'I have done that'?

> ~~The~~ Curtain
> H comes to Styles – has heard about P from Egypt – has arthritis – Georges is back with him – Master much worse since he went to Egypt.
> I am here because a crime is going to be committed. You are going to prevent it
> No – I can't do that
> Warn the victim?
> I have done that
> It is certain to happen because the person who has made up his mind will not relent
> Listen –
> The story of 5 crimes – H stupefied – no motive in ordinary sense? No – spoilt – sadistic

The first 'murder', that of Mrs Luttrell by her husband, is considered in Notebook 60. The finished novel follows these notes accurately, even down to the quotation from *Julius Caesar*:

> Col L shoots Mrs L – rifle not shot gun as he thinks – prepared by 'brother' batman story – then good shot – quick etc. Accident. He is terribly upset that night – cares for her – remembers her as 'girl in a blue dress' [Chapter 9]

> P goes down – finds Colonel and Langton – former has been shooting rabbits – Langton flattering him. Talk of accident – he talks of shot beater etc. BC [Boyd Carrington] comes along – tells story of batman – goes off. Langton says he'll never be bullied or henpecked – Langton quotes 'Not in our Stars, dear Brutus but in ourselves.' Col. shoots at rabbit – shoots Mrs – bending over flowers. Franklin and Nurse attend to her. ~~Colonel~~ latter comes later to Colonel – says it's all right, Colonel all broken up – talks of her and old days – where he met her [Chapter 9]

> H[astings] has conversation with Nurse. She asks about Styles – was in murder case once. Talks about Mrs Franklin. Boyd Carrington comes up 'Good looking girl' – come and see house. H goes with him – the house – his uncle – a very rich man – has everything – lonely. About Col L – fine shot [Chapter 7 iii]

There are three sketches of Hastings' proposed murder and two of his unintentional 'murder', all from Notebook 60.

> H decides (goaded by Langton) to kill 'seducer' of Judith – J. very secretive – plants Boyd as decoy – really when with Franklin. Boyd a boaster – fond of travel – carrying on with pretty hospital nurse. P. drugs H so that he wakes up next morning and has not killed B – his relief

Hastings plans a murder. Gets tablets from Poirot's room or from Boyd's own room – P drugs him

Conversation between BC, Langton, Judith and H. BC – his magnetic personality – goes off. Langton tries to persuade Judith she wouldn't have the courage etc. He comes to reassure Hastings she wouldn't really do anything. Then tries to warn him – is it wise to let her see so much of Atherton – married etc. He looks through glasses – shows his bird – then snatches them away – changes subject – he can see the figures. Goes in very unhappy – very worried. Personal problem ousts all others. Judith comes out of his room – H upset – speaks to her – she flares out – nasty mind – spends a night of increasing anxiety – the following day Langton tells him – rather unlovely story (quote him) – Atherton and a girl – she committed suicide. He goes to Judith – real row – H. is miserable. Hangs about – I could kill the fellow – Langton says not really – one hasn't the guts when it comes to it. H goes upstairs to see P (with L) – passes A's room – he is talking to someone – (nurse) that's fine, my dear – you run up to town – I go so and so – send a wire you can't get back – will go to other D – etc. Finds L – pulling him away. I'll go to her – No, you'll make things worse. L goads him – one feels responsible. H makes up his mind – it's his duty to save her. Gets drug – waits up – P makes him drugged chocolate. He sleeps. Next morning – his relief – tells P – P reassures him – you can't lead other people's lives for them – points out just how he would have been found out [Chapters 11 and 12]

More points
It is <u>Hastings</u> who kills Mrs F. He changes glasses or cups so that she gets it, not husband

Everyone asked up afterwards. She is lying on divan – coffee – makes it herself. Crossword – everyone there – at

least ~~Nurse~~ F. J. BC. Coles and H. Col and Mrs L L. Miss
Cole. The stars – they go out to look – H puzzling over
crossword. BC comes back – picks up Mrs [Franklin] in his
arms – carries her out laughing and protesting. H's eyes fill
remembering Bella. J comes in – he disguises his feeling by
pretending to look in bookcase – swings it round – muddle
about 'Death.' J gives him correct word – he replaces book.
Goes out with her – they come back – take their places. J by
request brings medicine – F goes off to work. Dead the next
day [Chapter 13]

There is an irony in the fact that having 'saved' Hastings
from an intentional murder, Poirot is unable to save him
from committing an accidental murder. And, arguably, the
explanation of Mrs Franklin's death is as big a surprise to the
reader as the explanation in Poirot's letter at the end of
the book.

There are also a few versions of the death of Langton/
Norton, all of them in Notebook 60, but none of them
include a shooting:

Langton tells H he has an idea about murder. P stops him
'Dangerous' – he goes to P's room that evening. Chocolate
put in trintium. He dies at once. H woken by striking
against his door – looks out – Sees L – go into own room
– limp, dressing gown etc. Next day – found dead – key of
his room in own pocket – locked. P says gave him trintium
tablets 1/10 – by mistake in 1/100 box. P says <u>his</u> fault – H
knows better – says to P same method – always a mistake
– P agrees

P has had door key stolen – had new one made – (old
room!) (a mention of P coming <u>after</u> Langton) P has
trintium tablets for high blood pressure – takes them –
induces tolerance. Shares chocolate with L – L dies. P
wheels him to room – returns and plays part of L in dressing

gown – hair – his own is wig – fake moustache – deliberately for Hastings. Goes in and locks door

Mrs Langton – Emilia – realises truth – tells Hastings so – kills herself – cuts throat. Langton arrested – P's machination – limp – razor blade dropped – blood on it etc. fingerprint – L and Hast. <u>only</u> – L put in invalid chair and pushed to room

Emilia realises L is insane. First writes letter saying she is afraid of him, then ~~cuts her~~ shows herself in his dressing gown and limping, hides razor (wiped) with blood on it – then cuts her throat. P's point is to lie – say L left him at 12.10. Or guillotine idea – L to put his head down – steel shutter

P sends for L – confronts him with story. L admits it all, shows himself in his true colours –Emilia hears it all. P gives him narcotic – goes to Emilia's room. She has killed herself with razor. P takes L along, lets him hold razor – blood on it, on him. Then leaves room waking up H – shows himself in L's dressing gown hiding razor in pot. H finds it

It is difficult to think of any advantage this blood-soaked method might have, over the shooting eventually settled on. Especially as the bullet wound has the added symbolic resonance of the Mark of Cain; this was also a significant clue in *And Then There Were None*, making one wonder which came first. The 'guillotine' idea is one of the most bizarre in the entire Christie opus.[62]

The notes for *Curtain*, in both quality and quanity, show a professional working at the height of her considerable powers. The manipulation of plot variations, the exploration

---

62   Coincidentally or otherwise, this is a plot feature of Carter Dickson's *The Magic Lantern Murders* (1936).

of character possibilities, the evocation of earlier crimes, all culminating in an elegiac letter from the dead, combine to display the unique gifts of the Queen of Crime.

### *Sleeping Murder*
### 11 October 1976

Gwenda Reed's new house evokes disturbing memories and her attendance at a performance of *The Duchess of Malfi* confirms her suspicions that, as a child, she witnessed a murder there. Miss Marple's advice to 'let sleeping murder lie' is ignored and a murderer prepares to kill again.

Although published ten months after Christie's death, *Sleeping Murder* was written during the Second World War and, like *Curtain*, placed in safekeeping to appear only after its author's death. Or so, until an examination of the Notebooks, we thought . . .

Notes for *Sleeping Murder* appear in Notebooks 17, 19, 33, 44, 63 and 66, an indication of its convoluted genesis. It underwent two changes (at least) of title and its history is linked with *Taken at the Flood*, which in turn is linked with *They Do It with Mirrors*. The Notebooks also show that at various times it was to involve a motif from the Mr Quin story 'The Dead Harlequin' of a person looking down at a dead body on the floor; it could have been a Poirot title and, even more amazingly, a Tommy and Tuppence novel. And despite the assertion that it was written during the Blitz, the Notebooks reveal a very different timescale for its creation.

The first page of Notebook 19 is headed:

Cover Her Face
The Late Mrs. Dane
They Do It with Mirrors

As we shall see, *Cover Her Face* was the one-time title for *Sleeping Murder*. The promising title 'The Late Mrs. Dane' was not pursued although it appears in the early sketches for *Sad Cypress* and *The ABC Murders*.

*Sleeping Murder* was originally called *Murder in Retrospect*, the title on one of the surviving typescripts and the title of Chapter 5 of the novel. Then the American publishers of *Five Little Pigs* used this title in 1942, so the stored typescript was renamed *Cover Her Face*. All was well until P.D. James used |the latter title in 1964 for her first detective novel. Agatha Christie herself, in a 1972 letter to her agent, suggested *She Died Young*. Eventually Miss Marple final case was published as *Sleeping Murder*. But, as can be seen in the following extract, the title *Cover Her Face* appears in the Notebooks in connection with what is recognisably *Sleeping Murder*:

Cover her Face
     The House – recognition – door – Staircase etc. Poirot and girl at Duchess of M – her story

Cover her Face
     . . . in the train – then the house – feeling of knowing it – the wall paper in this room – (inside closet) – ~~the door~~ but it was the door that really shook her

The complex history of this novel is best exemplified by a brief quotation from Notebook 63:

Helen – Start with the house and the girl and Tuppence (?) or friend – Raymond West and wife – the things happening one by one – then the theatre – Malfi – a T and T story? A Miss M story? An HP story?

> Helen Rendall – suicide – hanged herself – her husband
> sold the house and went abroad.
> Now who killed her? – Her brother – eminent surgeon
> – Doctor? – Husband? shell-shocked – girl's husband? H is
> P's second wife – young, flighty – a lover – Fergus –
> chauffeur or lover

The only real certainty in all of this plotting is a girl buying a house that contains memories from her earlier life, and we can see from the above extract that Christie was undecided about even the detective, mentioning Miss Marple, Poirot and Tommy and Tuppence. Presumably, depending on the detective she chose, a different book, and possibly a different plot, would have followed. This vacillation about the detective also raises questions about the book being written specifically as Miss Marple's last case; if it was created as her final investigation Miss Marple would have been a given from the start.

Notebook 17 has a clear outline of the first four chapters. The heroine's name, later to change to Gwenda, is here Gilda, although her husband's remains the same:

> Gilda – young married woman arriving Plymouth or
> Southampton – feels ill – stays night then hires car – drives
> slowly through Southern England. Feeling of coming home
> – evening – down into the valley – board up – visit to house
> agent – (former owners?). She buys it – writes letter
> to husband (or takes it furnished? unfurnished?)
> Incidents – the path – the door – the wallpaper – sends
> telegram to London – to Giles aunt Miss M? – or to Giles
> cousin Miss M is <u>her</u> aunt – or to the Crests – theatre –
> some young people – etc. – Cover her face – she rushes out
> and home. Joan asks her – Miss M. comes up with hot
> water bottles and hot coffee and sugar. The next morning
> . . . Gilda tells her all about it – Helen etc.

Notebook 66 begins as Notebook 17 but then diverges briefly to a different idea before returning to the *Duchess of Malfi* theme. Also included in this jotting is the notion of a father in a mental hospital for a murder he may or may not have committed, an idea which appears in *Sleeping Murder*:

> Cover her Face
>     Start with girl and friend (f[emale]) find house [in] Sidmouth – queer things etc.
>     Husband comes (or is coming) – A's fear – consults local doctor – really crook? He advises her to leave neighbourhood – later window box falls on her – 'the house hates me') – play – Duchess of Malfi etc. – etc. – Helen. Is her father in loony bin because he thinks he killed his young wife

Notebook 44 confuses the issue further with mention of a soldier and Poirot:

> Theatre party
>     Duchess of Malfi – Cover her Face – girl screams – taken out – won't go home with fiancé – young soldier – goes with Poirot. A man looking down at someone dead – the man with the hand – not only that – familiar house – seen it all before

And Notebook 33 shows the potential Harlequin connection:

> Continuation of Harlequin and Helen?
>     Girl (Anne) comes down stairs and sees girl dead and man/woman bending over her – (grey hands) Helen

Eventually, with the plot well in hand and Miss Marple firmly installed as the detective, Christie is able to follow her alphabetical plan:

A. Love letter in bureau to Musgrave? [mentioned in Chapter 17 iii by Erskine]
B. Newspaper adv. seen by the ex-servant [Chapter 12]
C. Servant 1? 2? heard that H. afraid of someone [Chapter 14]
D. 3 servants – 1. Nurse flighty – out that night . . . . (She is C [above])
   2. Cook – Mrs. F's servant – very young at time
   3. Lily – very young at time – say housemaid – clothes wrong – saw something out of window? [Chapter 14]
E. Fane in office – gentle, repressed – never married – possessive mother [Chapter 13]
F. Miss M and mother – learns about Jackson's boy – also about man on way out – Major M [Chapter 16]
G. Jackson [Affleck] – left under a cloud – (in Fane's office?) made good – member of an accounting firm – 2nd murder – Lily? Nurse? [Chapter 21 and 22]
H. Major and Mrs. Musgrave [Erskine] – Gwenda talks to him – lovely girl – yes, I fell in love with her – my wife – young children – suppose I did the right thing – came down to Dilmouth because I wanted to see where she lived once [Chapter 17]
I. Miss M says – body can always be put where you want it – in garden – following on J. [Chapter 23]
J. Dr. Kennedy with G. Gil and Miss M – the 3 men – which? Then subsequent lives – Miss M. asks how a man would feel – lonely – want to talk [Chapter 23 is the nearest match]

In a somewhat lacklustre book the alibi for the Lily Kimble murder shines out as a prime example of Christie ingenuity. As with all the best Christie ploys it is simplicity itself and appears in the book much as outlined in Notebook 17:

Circumstances of Lily's killing
    Writes (against husband's advice) to Dr. K – He when he comes to see G[iles] and G[wenda] finds Marple – brings her letter – says he has asked her to come on Tuesday by 4.30 train changing at Dillmouth Junction. G and G get there at 4.30. Actually he tells her to come by 2.30 train – two letters – just the same – except for time

Overall, however, *Sleeping Murder* is not in the same class as other titles written in the early 1940s: *One, Two, Buckle my Shoe*, *Evil under the Sun* or *The Body in the Library*. And, from the evidence the Notebooks, we now have a possible reason in.

Notebook 14 contains the first reference to a date in conjunction with this book, September 1947:

Plans Sept. 1947

Dying Harlequin
Cover her face (Helen)
~~Crooked House (The Alt~~[eration]~~s)~~ Done

And it is this reference that completely contradicts all the theories we have received about the date of the book's creation. There is no other novel that could possibly fit the description of 'Cover her face (Helen)' so it is definitely a reference to the book that we know as *Sleeping Murder*. But if it was only in the planning stages (and a very early stage to judge by the brevity of the note) in September 1947 the writing of it is placed much later than heretofore presumed.

This complication is underlined on the following page when we read a date over a year later again, with still only the barest outline of the plot:

Plans Nov. 1948

<u>Cover her Face</u>

The girl (or young wife) has memories – come back –
point it – 'Helen' is dead at foot of stairs – 'Grey fingers'.
Advertisement for Helen Gilliat (name found in a book) –
answered by Dr. Gilliat – a plastic surgeon – it was his
sister?

Although a plastic surgeon does not appear in *Sleeping Murder*, the reference to 'Grey fingers' here and 'the man with the hand' above, is reflected in the final confrontation in the book, when their disturbing significance becomes apparent. Clearly there was still a lot of planning to complete. So we can move the writing of it nearer to 1950, i.e. almost ten years later than the supposed 1940 date.

There are yet further indications that this book was written several years after the war. In the following extract from Notebook 19 ('girl at theatre – stumbles out' clearly identifies *Sleeping Murder*) we find a reference to 'in the war years', a phrase which would surely be written only long after the war had ended:

Jimmy Peterson comes from U.S.A. to look up Val (who was
over there in the war years). Girl at theatre – stumbles out
– young man follows her

Two final points support the theory that *Sleeping Murder* was not written during the war. First, why write, in the early 1940s, a 'final' case for Miss Marple when at that point her only full-length case had been *The Murder at the Vicarage*, published in 1930, and *The Body in the Library* would not appear until 1942? And second, in Chapter 24 i of *Sleeping Murder* Inspector Primer mentions the 'poison pen trouble down near Lymstock', a direct reference to *The Moving Finger*, published in 1943.

Overall, *Sleeping Murder* is a disappointing climax to Miss Marple's career. While a perfectly adequate detective story it is not in the same class as *Curtain: Poirot's Last Case*; or, indeed, *A Murder is Announced*, the real apex of Miss Marple's career. The possibility that it was written much later than previously suspected would go a long way towards explaining why.

# POSTSCRIPT

## Unused Ideas

'Unless I get a rough sketch of my idea down, it will go'
*Mrs McGinty's Dead*, Chapter 24

'I'm never at a loss for a plot'
*Cards on the Table*, Chapter 4

---◄○►---

### SOLUTIONS REVEALED

'The Affair at the Victory Ball' • 'The Case of the Perfect
Maid' • *Death in the Clouds* • *Death on the Nile* • *Endless Night*
• *Five Little Pigs* • *4.50 from Paddington* • 'The Jewel Robbery
at the Grand Metropolitan' • 'The Listerdale Mystery'
• *The Mirror Crack'd from Side to Side* • 'Miss Marple Tells
a Story' • *A Murder is Announced* • *The Mysterious Affair at
Styles* • *One, Two, Buckle my Shoe* • *Peril at End House* •
*A Pocket Full of Rye* • 'The Sign in the Sky' • *The Sittaford
Mystery* • *Sparkling Cyanide* • 'Strange Jest' • *Tape-Measure
Murder*' • 'The Third-Floor Flat' • *Three Act Tragedy* •
'The Tuesday Night Club' • 'The Unbreakable Alibi'
• 'The Witness for the Prosecution'

---◄○►---

There is a story, possibly apocryphal, that detective novelist
Nicholas Blake (in real life the Poet Laureate Cecil Day
Lewis) offered to buy some plot ideas from Christie but

she replied that she intended using them all herself. The Notebooks are littered with such ideas, varying in length from two words to several paragraphs. Some examples went no further than the page on which they appeared while others provided the basis of much-elaborated, and often much-disguised, plots. And some – the chamber-maid, the twins – appeared more than once in the Notebooks and some – 'poor little rich girl' and 'offered post abroad' – more than once in published stories.

I have arranged these ideas into broad categories although by their very nature these are somewhat arbitrary. The first examples are brief notes.

> Twins – point is not identical – Twins identical – one killed in railway smash?

> Identical twins – claimant assumes identity of sister (killed in railway smash) rich widow

These are just two of the ten versions of the 'twins' idea that litter the Notebooks. A railway smash and a false identity are minor features of *Murder in Mesopotamia*. Twin sisters also feature in *Elephants Can Remember* and twins are the light-hearted solution to Tommy and Tuppence's *Partners in Crime* cases.

––––– • ◆ • –––––

> Mirrors
>     Man or woman – she gets post or chums up with another woman – they come to hotel together.
>     Background of one is all right – cathedral town etc. Have been in A.R.P. together – they give alibi to man

The heading 'Mirrors' confirms what a confusing history *They Do it with Mirrors* had. The only tenuous connection to that novel is the idea of giving an alibi.

––––– • ◆ • –––––

*Despite its heading, this page from Notebook 19 has no connection
with 'Mirrors' Unused idea. It is the page open on Christie's lap
in this 1946 photograph.*

Nitro benzene – point is – it sinks to bottom of glass – woman takes sip from it – then gives it to husband

Camphor in capsule

Murder by lipstick – lip burnt first – cigarette given wrong end first

Strychnine or drug absorbed through skin

Influenza depression virus – Stolen? Cabinet Minister?

Lanolin poison? Strychnine? The poison that makes everything yellow (applied to dress – very misleading as another girl had yellow dress (1931)

Lanoline rubbed into skin

Despite regular use of poison as a murder method, these are just a few of the extra ideas Christie considered. Poison absorbed through the skin made an appearance in *Death Comes as the End* and a poison which 'sinks' is a feature of *The Mysterious Affair at Styles*. 'Murder by lipstick' is particularly imaginative.

———— •◆• ————

Chambermaid in hotel accomplice of man – evidence always accepted and clinches case

Chambermaid story – a hotel – Torquay? Riviera? Spain? Majorca? English better

The chambermaid idea, of which the above are just two examples, appears ten times in the Notebooks. Evidently the idea of a dishonest chambermaid was one that held possibilities for Christie as she utilised it in both 'The Jewel

Robbery at the Grand Metropolitan' and 'Miss Marple Tells a Story'. The second jotting is vague enough to fit anything.

———•◆•———

> Legless man – sometimes tall – sometimes short

A 'legless man' – who could completely alter his appearance – is another idea with ten appearances in the Notebooks, although nothing was ever made of it. Christie's fellow detective novelist John Dickson Carr used this device definitively in his 1938 novel *The Crooked Hinge.*

———•◆•———

> Stabbed through eye with hat pin

This untypically gruesome idea appears in four Notebooks, its attraction probably the difficulty of identifying the means of death.

———•◆•———

> Isotope idea – Carbon 14 – hypodermic injection (for typhoid?) normal procedure. He (?) is going abroad – appointment with local doctor – his place is taken by impostor who gives so-called typhoid injection.

Inspired by a visit to a laboratory during a US visit in the 1960s, this idea – the impersonation of a doctor in order to poison a patient – has strong echoes of *One, Two, Buckle my Shoe.*

———•◆•———

> Committee crime – Mr Llewellyn – tiresome woman – makes speech – drinks glass of water
>
> Glass of water – Dr Haydock . . . Suicide because of anonymous letter? At Harton Parva – the vicar's sister –

vinegary woman – the school teacher – at village shop
vicar's sister gets groceries – lays down letters – girl slips
one in

These jottings both appear in the same Notebook, the first in a list of projected Miss Marple short stories, and it seems very much Miss Marple's territory. The seeds of *The Moving Finger* can be seen in the 'suicide because of anonymous letters' idea and the method of inserting a letter in an otherwise innocent bundle appears in Chapter 13 of that novel.

———•◆•———

Disappearance of actress – strange behaviour of head
gardener

This wonderfully enigmatic combination of ideas appears in Notebook 65 alongside the notes for *And Then There Were None*, although it dates from much earlier in Christie's career. The suspicious head gardener, again Miss Marple territory, does make a brief appearance in 'Ingots of Gold'.

———•◆•———

A blonde millionaire's daughter kidnaps herself so as to get
away to marry young man

This surfaces three times in the Notebooks, each time specifying a blonde perpetrator. It sounds relatively non-criminal and may have been intended as a light-hearted story, not unlike the Tommy and Tuppence adventure, 'A Pot of Tea'.

———•◆•———

Tom, Dick or Harry come to Bridge – point – none of them
existed!

Tempting though it is to believe that this is a reference to *Cards on the Table*, it appears in a list headed 'Ideas 1940', four years after that title.

———•◆•———

Infra Red photograph

This unusual idea may have been inspired by her interest in photography during her archaeological work with Sir Max Mallowan. Somewhat surprisingly, it appears in a list of possible Miss Marple stories.

———•◆•———

Dangerous drugs stolen from car – doctor very upset – excitement in village

Dangerous drugs stolen from doctor's car – X goes touring in car – follows a doctor in strange town – or Doctor himself is criminal – later marries dead patient's wife or daughter

Despite an appearance in five Notebooks, this idea never appears as a plot device in its own right, although it is one of those considered in *Hickory Dickory Dock* as a means of obtaining poison. Our old friend the doctor (statistically the most homicidal profession in Christie) resurfaces here and although the idea was jotted down in the late 1930s, the second note may be the inspiration for Dr Quimper in *4.50 from Paddington.*

———•◆•———

A false Hercule P. – he is in some hotel lunching re-growing one of his moustaches which have been burnt – wild out of the way spot

The 'wild out of the way spot' may be the snowbound Swiss mountain-top of 'The Erymanthian Boar', but the moustache regrowing was never explored despite its appearance in two other Notebooks.

———————————◇———————————

All of the following appear separately from the plotting of the story in which they ultimately appeared and are perfect examples of Christie's imaginative cultivation of even the smallest seed of an idea into a fully formed bloom; and, with customary inventiveness, she often used an idea more than once.

> ✳ Poor little rich girl – house on hill – luxury gadgets etc.
>   – original owner

From a list, dating from the late 1930s, of possible Miss Marple stories, this is surrounded by notes for *N or M?* and *Curtain*. The idea is incorporated into 'The Case of the Care-taker/Caretaker's Wife' and, much expanded, into the 1967 novel *Endless Night*.

> ✳ Hargreaves case – young man and girl – she suspected
>   – swears to him she is innocent – he warns her – her
>   innocence is proven – she then admits she is guilty

Obvious strong echoes here of one of her greatest short story (and subsequent stage) successes, 'The Witness for the Pros-ecution', this appears immediately after a page dated June 1944 where she is sketching ideas for a 'play on moral issue involving husband and wife'.

> ✳ Witness in murder case – quite unimportant – offered
>   post abroad – hears indirectly it is a fake offer – or
>   servant – cook?

From a list of 'Ideas A–U' dating from the early 1940s, this device had already been used in the 1924 Mr Quin story 'The Sign in the Sky', and briefly in Chapter 6 of *Why Didn't They Ask Evans?*. And in the early stages of *The Big Four* this ploy is used on Poirot himself.

⁎ Invisible ink – written (will?) Or print a different
document

'Motive vs. Opportunity' and 'The Case of the Missing Will' both feature this idea. But as those two stories had originally appeared in the 1920s this jotting, from the late 1930s, cannot be their starting point. It appears on a long list a few pages before the initial notes for *The Labours of Hercules*.

⁎ Not identical twins – one sister pretends to be 2 – totally
different looking woman – (invalid) pretends to be maid
– really 2 of them

The idea of non-identical twins appears again and again in the Notebooks and this variation, the basis of 'The Case of the Perfect Maid', appears four times, twice in one Notebook.

⁎ Spoof butler

This brief note is difficult to date but may have been under consideration for one of Tommy and Tuppence's *Partners in Crime* adventures, although the rest of Notebook 65, where it appears, is taken up with *And Then There Where None*. The short story 'The Listerdale Mystery', published in December 1925, concerns a 'spoof butler' but it seems more likely that this jotting became the basis of *Three Act Tragedy*.

⁎ Or Japp – unhappy with D.P.P. A case – yes – not
happy – asks Poirot will he check up on it. Young
man – bitter – difficult

Appearing just ahead of a page dated September 1947, this eventually became *Mrs McGinty's Dead*, but not with Japp (long retired) but Superintendent Spence from *Taken at the Flood*. The bitter young man is the already convicted James Bentley.

> ✳ Short Marple Stories A. Poison Pen – big hearty girl is it

One of a long list of similar cryptic ideas, this is sandwiched between the plotting of *Sparkling Cyanide* and *N or M?*. It is obviously the germ of *The Moving Finger*, although a 'big hearty girl' is not 'it' at the end of that novel.

> ✳ . . . with teeth projecting, discoloured or white and even (better for short story)

The teeth of the victim are one of the first anomalies noticed by Miss Marple when she views *The Body in the Library*.

> ✳ Stamp idea – man realises fortune – puts it on old letter – a Trinidad stamp on a Fiji letter

The 'stamp idea' appears at least eight times, with minor variations, in the Notebooks. It is used in the Marple story 'Strange Jest' and is also a plot feature of *Spider's Web*.

> ✳ See a pin and pick it up all the day you'll have good luck (dressmaker has been already – comes again – woman is dead)

This is the basis of 'Village Murder'/'Tape-Measure Murder' and a ploy of Poirot's in 'The Under Dog'. The idea of a murderer returning and 'discovering' the body also featured in *The Sittaford Mystery*.

> ✳ Old lady in train – tells girl (or man) she is going to

> Scotland Yard – a murderer at work – she knows next
> victim will be the vicar – Girl takes job in village etc.

This jotting – although without the vicar or job-taking – from a list dated January 1935 – is the basis for *Murder Is Easy*. The novel itself is one of the few for which there are no notes.

———————————◄○►———————————

There are numerous references to nursery rhymes scattered through the Notebooks, although some defeated even Christie's fertile imagination and went no further then brief jottings. In Notebook 31 we find the following list:

1948 Short story for Nash's [Magazine]

A. Hickory Dickory Dock
Complex about the word Dock – a terror story – danger –
   girl in job – finds out something – (the people who
   wanted to pull the hall down) starts in hotel – rich
   people – crooks

B. Little Boy Blue
Where are you going to my pretty maid?
C. This is the way the gentlemen ride
Little Brown Jug – (My wife likes coffee and I like tea she
   says she's very fond of me)
D. Ding Dong Dell
E. Pussy Cat, Pussy Cat where have you been?
F. Town Mouse Country Mouse
G. Lucy Locket

This list for a series of nursery-rhyme themed short stories was not pursued: perhaps *Nash's* simply changed their minds. No Christie short stories appeared in *Nash's* later than 1933, after the final six Parker Pyne stories. The only rhymes to appear at all, and in very different guises at that, were the first two. 'Hickory Dickory Dock', as it appears above, seems to have little, if any, connection with the rhyme or, indeed, with the Poirot novel which appeared eight years later. The last six words ('starts in hotel – rich people – crooks') seem to foreshadow *At Bertram's Hotel.*

'Little Boy Blue' eventually appeared, although in much altered form and very briefly, in *Taken at the Flood* where, Adela, the mystic of the Cloade family, receives the message 'Little Boy Blue'. Remembering the last line of the rhyme – 'under the haycock fast asleep' she interprets this as a sign that Robert Underhay is still alive.

Despite the fact that 'Ding Dong Dell' appears in Notebook 18 and again in Notebook 35 with the added note (see below), it was never used. And, apart from a brief reference to 'Pussy-cat, Pussy-cat, where have you been' in the final page of *An Autobiography*, none of the rest appear either.

Three further references to nursery rhymes are scattered through the Notebooks:

One, two, 3 – 4 –5 Catching fishes all alive

Ding Dong Dell – Pussy's in the Well – ? An old maid murdered

Old King Cole?

Although at first glance it seems that none of these were ever used, a closer look at the last one reveals that its last line provided the title for Christie's final play, *Fiddlers Three*, whose complicated genesis is discussed in 'The Sixth Decade'.

––––––––––––––⊸◦⊶––––––––––––––

These more elaborate ideas have strong connections with published titles.

## MURDER-DISCOVERED-AFTERWARDS

Mirrors or some other book
Murder discovered afterwards – 5 years or 2 years like
Crippen? Statements taken – all quite definite – no result.
(Poirot goes over it or Miss M) talk to people – or poison
case because poison is so difficult to trace (exhumation)
Possibility of husband being accused – liked a young
woman (secretary?)
Resented by his family – particularly eldest son – She is
~~marries him~~ going to marry him afterwards – son won't
speak to her – real rift (actually son and girl are in it
together)

This jotting immediately follows notes for *The Mousetrap* and *They Do It with Mirrors*, so it is reasonable to assume that it comes from the late 1940s or early 1950s. The phrase 'Statements taken' contains echoes of *Five Little Pigs*, the husband and secretary idea foreshadows *Ordeal by Innocence* and the proposed solution is somewhat similar to that of *They Do It with Mirrors*. The staged 'rift' has appeared before – *The Mysterious Affair at Styles, Death on the Nile*, and would again in *Endless Night*. But while individual elements appear in various titles, this combination of ideas does not appear in a finished work. The reference to *Mirrors* at the beginning is further evidence of the complicated genesis of that novel.

———•———

## THE VICTORY BALL

Victory Ball idea
Six people going to dance or dance in house
Murderer is Harlequin? Or Pierrot?
Possible people?

~~Janey facial surgeon (murdered?)~~
Columbine – sister S. American
Pierette – girl who might have married Monteith
Pulchinella – Mrs Carslake
Harlequin – brother S. American
Pierrot – Lord Monteith – in love with Lola [possibly Columbine]
Pulchinello – brother of Monteith (heir)

This was, presumably, to be a more elaborate variation on the very first Poirot short story, 'The Affair at the Victory Ball', published in *The Sketch* on 7 July 1923 and collected in *Poirot's Early Cases*. In this story the solution turns on the murderer assuming at different times the costumes of both Harlequin and Pierrot. And, of course, the Harlequin theme provided Christie with another series character, *The Mysterious Mr Quin*. There are also brief notes dated 'June 1944' in Notebook 31, for a play, or possibly a ballet, based around the Harlequin figures. 'A Masque from Italy', one of the poems in *The Road of Dreams*, her 1924 poetry collection, is based on the same characters. Inspiration for all of these came from the china figures in the drawing room of her childhood home, Ashfield, and they can now be seen in the restored drawing room of Greenway House. Oddly, the plastic surgeon idea recurs here in somewhat unexpected surroundings.

———◆·———

## THE 'PRIME MINISTER' AND COMPANION

Man like Asquith or Burdett Coutts [both British MPs]
– very ambitious – Junior clerk in firm – marries rich woman
– head or daughter in firm – older than he is – she dies very
conveniently for him. He becomes a big noise with the
unreserved power she has left him.

Now – Did he really do away with her? Evidence of weird servant or companion acquits him absolutely but girl in question knows something. Say, e.g. like Gladys in 13 Problems she really committed crime quite unwittingly following his orders – later blackmails him. Or servant girl helped him – afterwards talking with friend – confidential friend etc. helps her in 2nd murder

Some of the ideas explored here did surface in a few later titles. Notebook 35, where these notes appear, also contains the notes for *One, Two, Buckle my Shoe* and there are distinct echoes of Alistair Blunt from that novel in the biographical sketch. The connivance, albeit unwitting, of a servant girl is an element of both the short story 'The Tuesday Night Club', the first of *The Thirteen Problems,* and the novel *A Pocket Full of Rye.* The variation of a friend helping the servant to commit a second murder is however a fresh, and distinctly original, development.

———◆———

## THE FORTUNE TELLER

Fortune teller found dead    Japp and Poirot
Greta Moscheim found by some bright young people – one of them's a friend of Greta
Michael O'Halloran – P. says saved him from a murder charge – Ah, now a little matter of a defaulting bookmaker.
People – cocktail party
Jane Brown
John Colley B.B.C. young man
Lady Monica Trent
Greta Moscheim – last person to see her alive
Mrs. Edgerton – a letter (found in flat?) from her young man in East Africa (but she hadn't heard from him for 4 months). Greta was helping her – so psychic – husband –

(suspicious) was reading her – Mrs Edgerton – says woman with a deep melancholy voice – deep contralto voice

Death of Zenobia
P. visits Japp have found Michael O'Halloran – they go along – flat – divisional surgeon and inspect the body

Fortune teller woman – Mrs De Lucia. She is very successful because in partnership with young man (or girl) who tips her off. If young man – he pretends to disapprove violently – she also blackmails. Young man is in love with Sue – sister to someone in a matrimonial tangle. De Lucia is really his wife so he has to get rid of her. Stages quite a drama over someone's fortune – something about letters? The post? Brought in from door – puts her death after 6.30 pm or whatever it is. So p[artner?] comes to flats – kills De L – goes on up to Sue – they go out to cinema. Comes back – no key – he goes up in lift – discovers body etc.

The murder of a fortune teller appears in four Notebooks but these are the two most detailed versions. As can be seen, it was to be a variation, or an elaboration, of the short story 'The Third Floor Flat', first published in January 1929. The second outline appears sandwiched between pages extending 'The Market Basing Mystery' into 'Murder in the Mews', so this idea seems to date from the early 1930s, further confirmed by the presence of Japp.

It may well be that Christie was toying with the elaboration of early short stories and this was her version of 'The Third Floor Flat'. If so, it is indeed an elaboration, as the only plot devices common to both are the use of the service lift and the 'finding' of the body. A fortune-teller appears in 'The Blue Geranium' from *The Thirteen Problems* although with entirely different surrounding material.

———————————◄○►———————————

Apart from short, single ideas there are more elaborate examples that, despite development beyond a few sentences, still did not always result in a story. Many of these ideas seem very promising and fragments of some of these ideas were used, perhaps slightly adapted, in published works. This was one of the advantages that Christie saw in the chaos of her Notebooks when she wrote in *An Autobiography*, 'What it's all about I can't remember now; but it often stimulates me, if not to write that identical plot, at least to write something else.'

## THE CLUEDO CASE

Book idea
George speaks to Poirot – his sister in law – she 'obliges' – giving evidence – but offered a very good post in Eire [Ireland] – can she take it? (or something [in] France).
Or perhaps she is a 'Nannie' who now does a lot of 'cooking' in the house.
What evidence? Murder case but her evidence is quite unimportant
She saw Professor Plum in the library – with the candlestick.
Shall the people be
~~General~~ Col. Mustard
Mrs. White – Housekeeper? ~~Or Col. M's sister~~
Miss Scarlet – young woman of doubtful morals – engaged to son? or secretary to Plum
Mrs. Peacock – Colonel's sister
Reverend Green – Former owner – in neighbourhood
Professor Plum – Old friend of Mustard
Result of conversation
'Nannie' or 'Daily Help' dies after cup of tea?
Now – what did she see or know that she didn't know she knew
A Point of Time
The siren goes on a Monday at a certain time. She says it

always 'gives her a turn.' The point is siren went off at 11.30 and she has just said Professor Plum down stairs at 11.25 (really 11.35). Electric clock has been stopped and put on again

What a wonderful idea – the ultimate deviser of detective puzzles whose name is forever associated with the country-house murder mystery adapting the classic country-house murder mystery board game; and what a shame that it was never fully developed. This sketch appears in Notebook 12 between detailed notes for 1954's *Spider's Web* and the Marple short story 'Sanctuary', so the mid 1950s seems to be the most likely date of composition. This also tallies with the 1949 release date of Cluedo.

In many ways this sketch reads like an elaborate version of the 1924 Mr Quin short story 'The Sign in the Sky' in which a housemaid mentions seeing a 'sign' – the Hand of God, in reality the smoke from a passing train – at the time her mistress, Vivien Barnaby, is shot. Although during the investigation the time of the shot is taken from the clocks in the house, in reality the time of the train is accurate and the clocks have been altered by the murderer. Not realising the importance of her evidence, the maid is subsequently offered, and accepts, a lucrative position in distant Canada. The variation in the unused idea above is a siren and an electric clock, but it is essentially the same plot. Unreliable clocks or watches are plot features of *The Murder at the Vicarage*, *Murder on the Orient Express* and *Evil under the Sun*.

The 'Nannie dying' idea featured in *Crooked House*; and the 'post abroad' ploy appears in 'the witness in murder case' idea above. A character knowing something (dangerous to the killer) without realising its significance was a regular feature of Christie plots. Sir Bartholomew Strange in *Three Act Tragedy*, Miss Sainsbury Seale in *One, Two, Buckle my Shoe*, Agnes Woddell in *The Moving Finger*, Heather Badcock in *The Mirror Crack'd from Side to Side* all die without knowing why.

And the unfortunate Mrs De Rushbridger, also in *Three Act Tragedy*, dies because she knows nothing.

———— •◆• ————

## THE PLASTIC SURGEON

Old man is crook – played market etc. Or surgeon – plastic
Wife was hospital nurse – ill – heart – had to give up her job
– nursed old man – married him –
happy in a quiet way – had had love affair with young
medical student.
Morgan and Eiluned – son and wife – strong feelings
~~Selina   dau~~ Kathleen – daughter – (Nurse Vernon?)
They have to live together in 'Crooked House' because of
War difficulties.
Old man holds purse strings – two children – Serena and
Edward
Tutor? Young man – wounded in War – a cripple – Miles
Dr. Kirkpatrick – Suggestion is that Gertrude killed him – or
Miles
Money is left to her
Possibly Dr. Kirkpatrick is her old boyfriend – he intends to
marry Kathleen
Triangle
Country House Rich man dead in (1) office (2) study in
suburban house
Crooked Mile (Dr. plastic surgeon – crook)
Old man like gnome – young hospital wife nurse

Crooked House
Crippled soldier with scarred face – old man is treating him
for war wounds – but <u>not</u> war wounds – really a murderer
Combine with Helen idea – man convinced he is a
murderer. Doctor persuades him and says he will remake
his face

Crooked Man
Old gnome like man – plastic surgeon – (struck off for
unprofessional conduct – did surgery for crooks) – young
dumb house wife – boisterous son – hard intellectual wife
– grandchildren?
Intelligent boy? girl?
Fantastic persons in the house – young crippled tutor – in
love with wife

Although all of these extracts contain definite elements (and the title) of *Crooked House* – a young tutor, an old gnome-like man holding the purse-strings and a young wife – and all come from Notebook 14, they are included here because they also feature the Plastic Surgeon idea. With three attempts over a dozen pages it would seem that this idea was one that appealed to, but ultimately defeated, Christie. And there are foreshadowings of at least two other novels. The 'rich man dead in office' from the first extract explicitly presages *A Pocket Full of Rye*; and both 'Combine with Helen idea' and 'man convinced he is a murderer' have strong echoes of *Sleeping Murder*.

———— •◆• ————

## THE LOCUM DOCTOR

Next Detective novel
Villain is doctor (locum) – Lies about time of death. But he
is the one to suspect murder – not satisfied with cause of
death – therefore he is free of suspicion and can add poison
to a 'sample' he has taken – and which can only have been
prepared by
wife
foreign girl in house
etc.
Actually that preparation was harmless – poison was

administered by doctor himself in something else – <u>before</u>
– or later (capsule?). Motive – will marry daughter – plain –
devoted. 2 person crime – he and daughter?

Book – Dr. Scofield – called in after discovery of body –
gives time of death incorrectly. Dr. S (who is locum)
suspects what real doctor (busy careless chap) has not
– chronic poisoning by member of household. Takes sample
of food (or vomit) – sends for analysis – sure enough there
is poison – he gives a warning to household – that night the
old man dies – Poison? Bashed? Appearance of robbery –
doctor fixes time of death at such a time (wrong).
Police surgeon arriving later can only give wide latitude
of time

The first of these notes appears in Notebook 53 alongside notes for the 1954 radio play *Personal Call* and the novels *They Do It with Mirrors*, *After the Funeral* and *Destination Unknown*, all published 1952–4. So it is reasonable to assume that the sketch dates from the early to mid 1950s. And some of the ideas do feature in 1957's *4.50 from Paddington*. Dr Quimper, hoping to marry the devoted daughter (and heiress), adds poison to the curry sample, having doctored the drinks jug earlier. But it has to be asked why the villainous doctor of the first extract should draw attention to a murder instead of certifying it a 'natural' death.

The 'foreign girl in house' scapegoat appears in 'How Does Your Garden Grow?', and *Hallowe'en Party*. Oddly, the second sketch directly precedes the main plotting for *4.50 from Paddington*, although there is less connection between the two.

———•◆•———

## THE 'HANDED TO' IDEA

Interesting idea that many murderers are loose. Experiment by saying to people 'Getting away with murder' etc.
Dropped teacup just as it is being handed to someone. Inference – the hander has dropped it (wife or husband recently conveniently dead) – really the 'handed to.'
Experimenter shortly after has near escapes – being gunned for. Result – investigation – more near escapes – actually investigations also apply to 'recipient' this not seen till by surprise at end

This outline seems to date from the early 1950s, as it appears during the plotting 1952's *They Do It with Mirrors*. Here Christie experimented with yet another variation on misdirecting the reader. In many of her poisoning dramas – *Three Act Tragedy, The Mirror Crack'd from Side to Side, Five Little Pigs* – the 'hander', not surprisingly, was the killer, but the 'handed to' is a new twist.

———— •◆• ————

## THE BRITISH MUSEUM

British Museum Story
S.S., Keeper of Babylonian Dept., has been stealing objects and replacing them with electrotypes in parchment unheard of in B.M. laboratories. Sir James Dale, director, gets wind of this but decides to hush the matter up.
Dobson who has been passed over for director is suspected as he has been very bitter – he went to see Sir James last thing with a dagger he wanted to buy for the Museum – wound is like one made by such a dagger.
Slightly batty old gentleman (Olin?) gives show away by handling some stuff of his and saying it didn't feel right

The idea of a short story set around the British Museum appears in three other Notebooks but this, from Notebook 30, is the most elaborate version. The setting had an obvious appeal for Christie because of her connection, via Max Mallowan, with the Museum. The idea of 'electrotypes' surfaced in *Murder in Mesopotamia*.

———◆———

## THE BOMBED BUILDING

Man trapped under bombed building – Nurse at AT crawls in and rescues him. He says do you want to be rich? She thinks funny idea.
Now!
He presses something into her hand – paper? Formula?
Afterwards man visits her – asks – she senses danger – the paper? Hides it.

This dates from early in the Second World War, appearing on a list between the ideas for *The Moving Finger* and *Towards Zero*. It sounds more spy story than detective story with its overtones of secret formulas, and the Nurse may well be a prototype for Victoria Jones in *They Came to Baghdad* and Hilary Craven in *Destination Unknown*. The 'bombed building' idea is the starting point for *Taken at the Flood*.

————◄○►————

Foreign settings, reflecting Christies's lifelong love of travel, also featured. The first example is particularly intriguing.

## THE HELLENIC CRUISE

There are two lengthy sketches in the Notebooks of a murder plot during a Hellenic cruise, possibly inspired by Christie's own cruise to Greece in the late summer of 1958. Chronologically this makes sense: the first extract below is sandwiched between the pages of notes for 1959's *Cat among the Pigeons*; the second extract, from Notebook 15, appears alongside notes for 1961's *The Pale Horse*.

> Book with Hellenic cruise setting
> A murderer
> Possible scene of actual murder Ephesus or could be electrocuted during lecture on deck
> People
> Lecturers – little man with beard his wife calls him Daddee – a professor
> Young schoolmaster type of man – uncouth and rather dirty – superior in manner
> Miss Courtland – a Barbara type – two schoolmistresses travelling together – one has had a nervous breakdown
> Mrs. Oliver??
> The 2 spinsters idea could be combined with this. The 'friend' schoolmistress came on deliberately – have planned to kill someone going on cruise – camouflaging it by going with a friend, really sending money to friend anonymously to pay expenses. Alibis helped by the two of them being places – but M[iss Courtland or, possibly, Murderer?] makes friend believe that she occasionally has short lapses of memory – appear to be very devoted.
> Motive?

Although a possible plot involving two female friends is a recurring motif in the Notebooks, the sketch here is different; here one friend is the dupe, rather than the partner-in-crime, of the other. The reference to 'Barbara' is probably to Barbara Parker, Max Mallowan's long-time assistant and, after the death of Dame Agatha, his wife for the last year of his life. The idea of convincing someone that they suffer from memory loss had earlier appeared in 'The Cretan Bull', the seventh Labour of Hercules, and in *A Caribbean Mystery*. It would seem from the ambiguous phrase 'appear to be devoted' that the friend with the nervous breakdown in her background is set to be the dupe of Miss Courtland, the putative murderer. And the reference to electrocution 'during lecture on deck', not a very obvious murder method, would suggest that Christie had something definite in mind, although what it was remains a mystery.

The second outline, while retaining essentially the same characters, adds some new scenarios to the first:

Hellenic cruise – murder – where? Ephesus? During lecture in the evening on deck?
By whom committed – and why
A Miss Marple?
Wife decides to kill husband? Or she and her lover? Say she has had lovers – one, a foreigner? an American? Dismisses him abruptly because she knows he will react – actually he is framed by her and another lover whom she pretends she hardly knows? Possibly Cornish Mystery type of story?
Academic background – woman like J.P.? or like M.C.
Anyway 2 people in it – and a fall guy!
Or a Macbeth type of story – ambitious woman – urges on husband – husband turns out to have a taste for murder.
Perhaps murder is done when someone is sleeping on deck
– or Murder is Easy idea – monomaniac who believes everyone who opposes him dies – this is really suggested to him by woman who hates him.
One of lecturers little man with beard – his wife calls him Dadee – encounters young schoolmistress – rather dirty – Miss Cortland (a Barbara type! Good Company).
Mrs Oliver ?!!
Two Schoolmistresses travelling together (one has had nervous breakdown). One of them is murderer – she sent money anonymously to ill friend to enable her to come too

> – impresses on friend that she has 'black outs' short lapses
> if memory so that friend and she have alibis together

If Christie had adapted plot devices from either *Murder is Easy* or 'The Cornish Mystery', we can be sure that she would have rendered them unrecognisable, as she did with *Death on the Nile/Endless Night* and *Dead Man's Folly/Hallowe'en Party*.

Elements from each extract can be found elsewhere: the stage-managed dismissal has echoes of *Death on the Nile* and 'two people and a fall guy' is similar to 'Triangle at Rhodes'. And there are some compelling new variations: the husband who, after initial reluctance, 'turns out to have a taste for murder' and the anonymous gift of money to set up an alibi. The references to 'J.P.' and 'M.C.' have proved elusive but may simply refer to two of Christie's fellow passengers on the cruise.

Miss Marple, a few years before her only foreign case, *A Caribbean Mystery*, makes a brief appearance. Interestingly, Mrs Oliver was intended to appear, whichever scenario was chosen. Ariadne Oliver, Agatha Christie's alter ego, is a prolific detective novelist with a foreign detective, the Finnish Sven Hjerson, one of whose cases is *The Body in the Library*. Doubtless she would, like her creator, have been using the trip as a background for her next masterwork.

———— •◆• ————

## THE GIRL-IN-THE-BAHAMAS

These examples, all from different Notebooks, show Christie experimenting with an intriguing idea before eventually deciding to send Miss Marple, who is not mentioned here, to essentially the same place, St Honore, and have her solve Major Palgrave's murder in *A Caribbean Mystery*:

> Girl gets job – sent out to Bahamas – plane brought back.
> She goes back to flat – another girl there acting as her

West Indies Book
Begins girl secretary – told by Company to go to Barbados
(Tobago) on business – meet certain executives there –
passage paid etc. Goes off from London Airport – Shannon
etc. – then back again following evening – her flat occupied
by someone else – she and boy friend decide to investigate

How about girl gets job – a flat is given her – after a month
she is sent to Barbados – return of plane she goes to flat –
finds dead body or finds she is supposed to have died
– young man she telephones him – they discuss it – what is
the point? Person to die first – a lawyer – head of solicitor's
firm? New member of a country solicitors? A Q.C.?

The common denominator of the West Indies was the *idée
fixe* of these jottings, probably inspired by a family holiday
there in the early 1960s.

◄○►

There are also notes for unrealised plays.

## THE MOUSETRAP II

Mousetrap II?
A reunion dinner – the survivors of revolution? war (Airman
and passengers lost in desert)
Man gate crashes – a lawyer? elderly? Mannered? Felix
Aylmer[63] type or a [Sir Ralph] Richardson.[64]
A murder – here – one of group is a murderer – one of
group is a victim. Doesn't know victim

---

63  Felix Aylmer played Sir Rowland Delahaye in the first production
of *Spider's Web* (1954)
64  Ralph Richardson played Sir Wilfrid Robarts, in a 1983 TV remake
of *Witness for the Prosecution*.

End of Scene – I'm the prospective victim amn't I? (Really murderer)

Possibility of house in street Soho hired for party – waiters hired for joke! One man is waiter – brings drink to guest – later enters as guest – with moustache.

Death at the Dinner – man drinks – dies – a doctor present says this glass must be kept. It is then he puts poison in it – real drink was poisoned earlier – before dinner

(A mixture of 3 Act Tragedy (Sir Charles) and Sparkling Cyanide?) Is wrong person killed?

The biggest mystery about this sketch is the reason for calling it 'Mousetrap II', as it has nothing in common with that famous play. Perhaps it was so called in the hope of another stage success that might rival the record-breaking title? It is also difficult to date this extract as most of the contents of Notebook 4, from which these notes are excerpted, remain unpublished. Much of it is taken up with notes for the relatively unknown play *Fiddlers Five* (later *Fiddlers Three*), first staged in 1971, so it seems reasonable to assume this extract dates from the late 1960s. Strength is also lent to this argument by the fact that *The Mousetrap* was, by then, a record-breaker.

As Christie herself states, there are strong similarities with *Three Act Tragedy* – the subterfuge with glasses, the cryptic note 'Doesn't know victim', the guest disguised as a waiter/butler – and *Sparkling Cyanide* – the unexpected death at the dinner table and a similar waiter/guest ploy, a ruse also adopted by the killer in *Death in the Clouds*. The oddly specific reason outlined for the reunion – survivors of a revolution – has echoes of the revolution in Ramat that culminated in murder at Meadowbank School in *Cat among the Pigeons*. And the prospective victim as murderer was a favourite throughout Christie's career: *Peril at End House, One, Two, Buckle my Shoe, A Murder is Announced, The Mirror Crack'd from Side to Side*. Despite these echoes of earlier novels, this late in her career Christie was still coming up with original ideas: the trick with the glass did not feature in any of her earlier poisonings.

———•—•———

## THE REUNION DINNER

Reunion Dinner 3 Act Play
Collinaris Restaurant
Waiter – old man like a tortoise
Waiter – young Italian type (conversation between them about this dinner)
Victor Durel – business type (approves menu etc. – wines)
Valentine Band (Clydesdale? Harborough?) – rich furs and so on
Major Allsop – sharp practice type company partner
Isadore Cowan – old Jew
Janet Spence – Middle aged, forthright (missionary? UNESCO?!)
Captain Harley ex pilot – now rich
Lowther – Company lawyer
Canon Semple (not a Canon – an actor pretending)

The Dinner
Before it begins Durel makes speech – object of dinner
The plane came down – our miraculous preservation – ~~two~~ three of our number left us – to the memory of our missing friends – Joan Arlington – Gervase Cape – Richard Dymchurch. Canon says grace – For what we are about to receive may the Lord
Conversation?
The old man waits about watching – pours wine

Possibilities
1. Wine – a truth drug?
2. Wine – poison for somebody

3. Canon is shown to be not a canon – but CID? Or oil
surveyor
4. Victor Durel points out – item out paper tonight – two
skeletons have been found on an oil survey –
Joan A[rlington]? R[ichard Dymchurch]? G[ervase Cape]?
5. Isadore asks Harley about circumstances – dismissed for
error of judgement – but very well off?
Suggests: was it an error of judgement? Or were you paid
to put down jet there

These very detailed notes from Notebook 52 may be connected to the previous entry, from Notebook 4, although the
two Notebooks seem to date from different years. The idea of
survivors of an air crash is common to both and there are
indications that, in each scenario, poison is the murder
method. The full names (even of the missing characters) and
backgrounds included would seem to indicate that considerable thought went into this unused idea. This Notebook also
contains the notes for *The Mirror Crack'd from Side to Side* and
*The Clocks*, both published in the early 1960s, and is directly
ahead of the notes for the screen adaptation of Dickens's
*Bleak House*, on which Christie worked in 1962. Puzzlingly,
therefore, it would seem that this more detailed sketch
preceded the first sketch, discussed above. UNESCO had
recently designated Christie the most translated writer, apart
from the Bible, so the exclamation mark after their name
may be a private joke.

This is untypical Christie territory – survivors of a plane
crash, someone paid to 'put a jet down', skeletons found
during an oil survey – although a truth drug features in
*A Pocket Full of Rye*. During the 1950s she published two
'foreign travel' titles – *They Came to Baghdad* and *Destination
Unknown* – and the latter does contain much air travel as
well as a crashed plane. But while the background to the
plot outlined above may contain adventurous concepts, the
murder plot is Christie on home ground: a poisoning during

dinner at a restaurant ('Yellow Iris', *Sparkling Cyanide*); a clergyman who is not a clergyman (*Murder in Mesopotamia*); a middle-aged missionary (*Murder on the Orient Express*); a detective in disguise (*The Mousetrap, And Then There Were None*). The description of the elderly waiter as 'like a tortoise' has distinct echoes of Lawrence Wargrave from Chapter 13 of *And Then There Were None*; this possibility is further strengthened when we read the 'old man waits about watching'. And is it pure coincidence that there are ten characters listed – eight guests and two servants?

––––––––––––––––◄○►––––––––––––––––

And, finally a very special and surprising Unused Idea . . .

## THE EXPERIMENT

The following brief notes all appear in lists of ideas for both short stories and novels. The first is Idea E on an 'A to J' list dated January 1935, which includes the original ideas for 'Problem at Sea', *Sad Cypress* and *They Do It with Mirrors*.

> The Experiment    Mortimer – How does murder affect the character?

This heads a short list that includes *A Pocket Full of Rye* and *They Do It with Mirrors*, indicating a late 1940s date:

> Mortimer – his plans – first killing and so on – his character gradually changes

This next jotting appears a few pages ahead of the notes for *Curtain* and a page of corrections for *The Body in the Library*, indicating almost a decade earlier:

> Man (or woman) who experiments in murder (goes queer)

And the final jotting appears alongside notes for *The Moving Finger* and *Sparkling Cyanide*:

> Mortimer – experimental murder

Although all four were written during her most productive and inventive period, it was not until the final year of her creative life that Christie elaborated on this plot. Perhaps she had been doing what she wrote of in *An Autobiography*, 'looking vaguely through a pile of old notebooks and [finding] something scribbled down'; or perhaps the inspiration resurfaced from somewhere in her subconscious. The idea, as evidenced by its four Notebook appearances, was obviously one that attracted her and one that she had never tackled in any way in her published work; yet, at the time of the early notes, it would have been almost impossible for her to have attempted it with Collins Crime Club waiting for her annual 'whodunit'. It was not until the twilight of her career that she (and they) felt comfortable publishing titles like *The Pale Horse*, a murder-to-order thriller with supernatural overtones, and *Endless Night*, a psychological suspense story with a dark secret. And this idea would have fitted into the same category.

In Notebook 7 Christie began developing the idea. Here Mortimer has disappeared, to be replaced first by Jeremy and later by Edmund:

> Jeremy – discusses with friends – murders
> What difference would it make to one's character if one had killed someone?
> Depends what the motive had been – Hatred? Revenge? Gain? Jealousy?
> No – No motive – for no reason just an interesting experiment. The object of the crime – oneself – would one be the same person – or would one be different. To find out one would have to commit homicide – observing all the

time oneself – one's feelings, keeping notes.
Needed a victim – carefully selected but definitely not
anyone that one wished dead in any way. 'I have killed
– now am I the same person I was? Or am I different – do
I feel – fear? regret? pleasure? (surely not!)
People to imagine and [in]vent
The victim
Various suggestions. A woman who has cancer or a heart
condition. It can suggest itself as a mercy killing.
The killer
Man? Woman? Possibly woman get excited, she too decides
to try the experiment also. Man (Jeremy) does not realise
what she is doing
Afterwards J finds he is excited, nervous – doctor or nurse is
suspicious. J begins to lay clues of who the culprit may be
and some reason why. J begins to feel he might do another
murder – Lay the clues

Edmund (Harmsworth) Murdock debates with friends –
Murder – How would it feel to be a [killer?]
Girl or woman – tells about shoplifting or stealing – or
falsifying accounts.
Edmund and Lancelot go away debating
Points to be safe – victim – man or woman
Who should be obliterated – ('unfit to live') (no motive no
advantage to be gained) (Someone must gain and profit)
Feelings of operation must be closely studied – will X's
character alter (no one must share knowledge)

Astonishingly, these notes, from November 1973, are for the
novel to appear in 1974 following the disappointing *Postern of
Fate*. As can be seen, this outline is far superior, both in concept and approach; even the notes read better than those for
*Postern of Fate*, the last book Christie wrote. Here, at the age
of 83, Christie was experimenting with a novel totally unlike
anything she had written before. Sounding somewhat similar

Book?

Edmund (Harmsworth) - Murdock

Debates with friends - Murder
        How would it feel to be a —?
Girl or woman — tells about shoplifting or
Stealing — or falsifying accounts —

    Edmund + Lancelot go away debating.

Points To be safe — Victim — Man or woman
who should be obliterated — ("unfit to live")
(no motive — no advantage to be gained
(Someone must gain and profit—)

    Feelings of operator must be closely
Studied — Will X's character alter)
(no one must share Knowledge)

Someone at original Conversation might be
(although not suspected) be actually involved —
possibly even (guilty) Final Surprise?
                or has planned the
whole thing —

*From Notebook 7 this is one of the last pages Agatha Christie wrote when*
*she was too frail to develop this fascinating sketch into one Final*
*Unused Idea Christie for Christmas.*

to Meyer Levin's *Compulsion* (1956), a work of 'faction' based on the infamous 1924 Leopold and Loeb true-life murder case, where two US college students murdered a small boy solely as an experiment – this would have been a radical departure. It seems remarkable that after the previous half-dozen weak novels Christie should be even planning something like this. Whether she had the ability, at this stage, to carry off such a demanding concept is debatable but these notes confirm, once again, that it was her powers of development, and not her powers of imagination, that were waning.

And lest there be any lingering doubt, the devious hand of the Queen of Crime is very evident in the last phrase, with its final – absolutely final – Christie twist:

Someone at original conversation might be (although not suspected) actually involved – possibly even (guilty) final surprise? Or has planned the whole thing

# APPENDIX 1

# *Agatha Christie Chronology*

Dates of publication refer to the UK editions

**1921**
*The Mysterious Affair at Styles*

**1922**
*The Secret Adversary*

**1923**
*The Murder on the Links*

**1924**
*The Man in the Brown Suit*
*Poirot Investigates*:
  The Adventure of 'The
    Western Star'
  The Tragedy at Marsdon
    Manor
  The Adventure of the Cheap
    Flat
  The Mystery of Hunter's
    Lodge
  The Million Dollar Bond
    Robbery
  The Adventure of the
    Egyptian Tomb
  The Jewel Robbery at the
    Grand Metropolitan

  The Kidnapped Prime
    Minister
  The Disappearance of
    Mr Davenheim
  The Adventure of the
    Italian Nobleman
  The Case of the Missing Will
*The Road of Dreams* (poetry)

**1925**
*The Secret of Chimneys*

**1926**
*The Murder of Roger Ackroyd*

**1927**
*The Big Four*

**1928**
*The Mystery of the Blue Train*

**1929**
*The Seven Dials Mystery*
*Partners in Crime*:
  A Fairy in the Flat/A Pot of
    Tea

The Affair of the Pink Pearl
The Adventure of the Sinister
   Stranger
Finessing the King/The
   Gentleman Dressed in
   Newspaper
The Case of the Missing
   Lady
Blindman's Buff
The Man in the Mist
The Crackler
The Sunningdale Mystery
The House of Lurking Death
The Unbreakable Alibi
The Clergyman's Daughter/
   The Red House
The Ambassador's Boots
The Man Who Was No. 16

**1930**

*The Mysterious Mr Quin:*
   The Coming of Mr Quin
   The Shadow on the Glass
   At the 'Bells and Motley'
   The Sign in the Sky
   The Soul of the Croupier
   The Man from the Sea
   The Voice in the Dark
   The Face of Helen
   The Dead Harlequin
   The Bird with the Broken
      Wing
   The World's End
   Harlequin's Lane
*The Murder at the Vicarage*
*Black Coffee* (stage play)
*Behind the Screen* (radio serial,
   co-authored)
*Giant's Bread* (as Mary
   Westmacott)

**1931**

*The Sittaford Mystery*
*Chimneys* (stage play)
*The Floating Admiral* (co-
   authored)
*The Scoop* (radio serial,
   co-authored)

**1932**

*Peril at End House*
*The Thirteen Problems:*
   The Tuesday Night Club
   The Idol House of Astarte
   Ingots of Gold
   The Blood-Stained Pavement
   Motive vs. Opportunity
   The Thumb Mark of St Peter
   The Blue Geranium
   The Companion
   The Four Suspects
   A Christmas Tragedy
   The Herb of Death
   The Affair at the Bungalow
   Death by Drowning

**1933**

*Lord Edgware Dies*
*The Hound of Death:*
   The Hound of Death
   The Red Signal
   The Fourth Man
   The Gypsy
   The Lamp
   Wireless
   The Witness for the
      Prosecution
   The Mystery of the Blue Jar
   The Strange Case of Sir
      Arthur Carmichael
   The Call of Wings

The Last Séance
S.O.S.

*Unfinished Portrait* (as Mary
Westmacott)

**1934**

*Murder on the Orient Express*
*The Listerdale Mystery*:
  The Listerdale Mystery
  Philomel Cottage
  The Girl in the Train
  Sing a Song of Sixpence
  The Manhood of Edward
    Robinson
  Accident
  Jane in Search of a Job
  A Fruitful Sunday
  Mr Eastwood's Adventure
  The Golden Ball
  The Rajah's Emerald
  Swan Song
*Why Didn't They Ask Evans?*
*Parker Pyne Investigates*:
  The Case of the Middle-aged
    Wife
  The Case of the Discontented
    Soldier
  The Case of the Distressed
    Lady
  The Case of the Discontented
    Husband
  The Case of the City Clerk
  The Case of the Rich
    Woman
  Have You Got Everything You
    Want?
  The Gate of Baghdad
  The House at Shiraz
  The Pearl of Price
  Death on the Nile
  The Oracle at Delphi

**1935**

*Three Act Tragedy*
*Death in the Clouds*

**1936**

*The ABC Murders*
*Murder in Mesopotamia*
*Cards on the Table*

**1937**

*Dumb Witness*
*Death on the Nile*
*Murder in the Mews*:
  Murder in the Mews
  The Incredible Theft
  Dead Man's Mirror
  Triangle at Rhodes
*Wasp's Nest* (TV play)
*Yellow Iris* (radio play)

**1938**

*Appointment with Death*
*Hercule Poirot's Christmas*

**1939**

*Murder is Easy*
*Ten Little Niggers/And Then There*
  *Were None*

**1940**

*Sad Cypress*
*One, Two, Buckle My Shoe*

**1941**

*Evil under the Sun*
*N or M?*

**1942**
*The Body in the Library*

**1943**
*Five Little Pigs*
*The Moving Finger*
*And Then There Were None* (stage
　play)

**1944**
*Towards Zero*
*Absent in the Spring* (as Mary
　Westmacott)

**1945**
*Death Comes as the End*
*Sparkling Cyanide*
*Appointment with Death* (stage
　play)

**1946**
*The Hollow*
*Murder on the Nile/Hidden
　Horizon* (stage play)
*Come, Tell Me How You Live*
　(memoir)

**1947**
*The Labours of Hercules*:
　Foreword
　The Nemean Lion
　The Lernean Hydra
　The Arcadian Deer
　The Erymanthian Boar
　The Augean Stables
　The Stymphalean Birds
　The Cretan Bull
　The Horses of Diomedes
　The Girdle of Hyppolita

　The Flock of Geryon
　The Apples of Hesperides
　The Capture of Cerberus
*Three Blind Mice* (radio play)

**1948**
*Taken at the Flood*
*Butter in a Lordly Dish* (radio
　play)
*The Rose and the Yew Tree* (as
　Mary Westmacott)

**1949**
*Crooked House*

**1950**
*A Murder is Announced*

**1951**
*They Came to Baghdad*
*The Hollow* (stage play)

**1952**
*Mrs McGinty's Dead*
*They Do It with Mirrors*
*The Mousetrap* (stage play)
*A Daughter's a Daughter*
　　(as Mary Westmacott)

**1953**
*After the Funeral*
*A Pocket Full of Rye*
*Witness for the Prosecution* (stage
　play)

**1954**
*Destination Unknown*
*Spider's Web* (stage play)
*Personal Call* (radio play)

**1955**
*Hickory Dickory Dock*

**1956**
*Dead Man's Folly*
*A Daughter's a Daughter* (stage play)
*Towards Zero* (stage play)
*The Burden* (as Mary Westmacott)

**1957**
*4.50 from Paddington*

**1958**
*Ordeal by Innocence*
*Verdict* (stage play)
*The Unexpected Guest* (stage play)

**1959**
*Cat among the Pigeons*

**1960**
*The Adventure of the Christmas Pudding:*
  The Adventure of the Christmas Pudding
  The Mystery of the Spanish Chest
  The Under Dog
  Four and Twenty Blackbirds
  The Dream
  Greenshaw's Folly
*Go Back for Murder* (stage play)

**1961**
*The Pale Horse*

**1962**
*The Mirror Crack'd from Side to Side*
*Rule of Three* (3 one-act plays):
  Afternoon at the Seaside
  The Rats
  The Patient

**1963**
*The Clocks*

**1964**
*A Caribbean Mystery*

**1965**
*At Bertram's Hotel*
*Star over Bethlehem* (poetry and stories):
  Star over Bethlehem
  The Naughty Donkey
  The Water Bus
  In the Cool of the Evening
  Promotion in the Highest
  The Island

**1966**
*Third Girl*

**1967**
*Endless Night*

**1968**
*By the Pricking of my Thumbs*

**1969**
*Hallowe'en Party*

**1970**
*Passenger to Frankfurt*

**1971**
*Nemesis*

**1972**
*Elephants Can Remember*
*Fiddlers Five/Fiddlers Three* (stage
   play)

**1973**
*Postern of Fate*
*Poems* (poetry)
*Akhnaton* (stage play)

**1974**
*Poirot's Early Cases*:
  The Affair at the Victory
    Ball
  The Adventure of the
    Clapham Cook
  The Cornish Mystery
  The Adventure of Johnnie
    Waverly
  The Double Clue
  The King of Clubs
  The Lemesurier Inheritance
  The Lost Mine
  The Plymouth Express
  The Chocolate Box
  The Submarine Plans
  The Third Floor Flat
  Double Sin
  The Market Basing Mystery
  Wasp's Nest
  The Veiled Lady
  Problem at Sea
  How Does Your Garden
    Grow?

**1975**
*Curtain: Poirot's Last Case*

**1976**
*Sleeping Murder*

**1977**
*An Autobiography* (memoir)

**1979**
*Miss Marple's Final Cases*:
  Sanctuary
  Strange Jest
  Tape-Measure Murder
  The Case of the Caretaker
  The Case of the Perfect
    Maid
  Miss Marple Tells a Story
  The Dressmaker's Doll
  In a Glass Darkly

**1982**
(in *The Agatha Christie Hour*):
  Magnolia Blossom

**1991**
*Problem at Pollensa Bay*:
  Problem at Pollensa
    Bay
  The Second Gong
  Yellow Iris
  The Harlequin Tea Set
  The Regatta Mystery
  The Love Detectives
  Next to a Dog
  (Magnolia Blossom)

**1997**
*While the Light Lasts*:
  The House of Dreams
  The Actress
  The Edge
  Christmas Adventure

The Lonely God
Manx Gold
Within a Wall
The Mystery of the Baghdad
    Chest
While the Light Lasts

**2008**
(in *Hercule Poirot: The Complete
    Short Stories*):
Poirot and the Regatta
    Mystery

**2009**
(in *Agatha Christie's Secret
    Notebooks*):
The Capture of Cerberus
The Incident of the Dog's Ball

**2011**
(in *Agatha Christie's Murder in
    the Making*):
The Man Who Knew

The Case of the Caretaker's
    Wife

**2012**
*The Grand Tour*
(in *Ask a Policemen*):
    Detective Writers in England

**2014**
*Hercule Poirot and the Greenshore
    Folly*

**2015**
*Little Grey Cells: The Quotable
    Poirot*

**2018**
(In *Bodies from the Library*):
    The Wife of the Kenite

**2019**
*Murder, She Said: The Quotable
    Miss Marple*

# APPENDIX 2

## Alphabetical List of Agatha Christie Titles

*4.50 from Paddington* **1957**
*ABC Murders, The* **1936**
*Absent in the Spring* (as Mary Westmacott) **1944**
*Adventure of the Christmas Pudding, The* (Short stories) **1960**
*After the Funeral* **1953**
*Agatha Christie Hour, The* (short stories) **1982**
*Akhnaton* (stage play) **1973**
*And Then There Were None* (stage play) **1943**
*Appointment with Death* **1938**
*Appointment with Death* (stage play) **1945**
*At Bertram's Hotel* **1965**
*Autobiography, An* (memoir) **1977**
*Behind the Screen* (radio serial, co-authored) **1930**
*Big Four, The* **1927**
*Black Coffee* (stage play) **1930**
*Body in the Library, The* **1942**
*Burden, The* (as Mary Westmacott) **1956**

*Butter in a Lordly Dish* (radio play) **1948**
*By the Pricking of my Thumbs* **1968**
*Cards on the Table* **1936**
*Caribbean Mystery, A* **1964**
*Cat among the Pigeons* **1959**
*Chimneys* (stage play) **1931**
*Clocks, The* **1963**
*Come, Tell Me How You Live* (memoir) **1946**
*Crooked House* **1949**
*Curtain: Poirot's Last Case* **1975**
*Daughter's a Daughter, A* (stage play) **1956**
*Daughter's a Daughter, A* (as Mary Westmacott) **1952**
*Dead Man's Folly* **1956**
*Death Comes as the End* **1945**
*Death in the Clouds* **1935**
*Death on the Nile* **1937**
*Destination Unknown* **1954**
*Dumb Witness* **1937**
*Elephants Can Remember* **1972**
*Endless Night* **1967**
*Evil Under the Sun* **1941**

*Rule of Three* (3 one-act plays) **1962**

*Sad Cypress* **1940**

*Scoop, The* (radio serial, co-authored) **1931**

*Secret Adversary, The* **1922**

*Secret of Chimneys, The* **1925**

*Seven Dials Mystery, The* **1929**

*Sittaford Mystery, The* **1931**

*Sleeping Murder* **1976**

*Sparkling Cyanide* **1945**

*Spider's Web* (stage play) **1954**

*Star over Bethlehem* (poetry and stories) **1965**

*Taken at the Flood* **1948**

*Ten Little Niggers/And Then There Were None* **1939**

*They Came to Baghdad* **1951**

*They Do It with Mirrors* **1952**

*Third Girl* **1966**

*Thirteen Problems, The* (short stories) **1932**

*Three Act Tragedy* **1935**

*Three Blind Mice* (radio play) **1947**

*Towards Zero* **1944**

*Towards Zero* (stage play) **1956**

*Unexpected Guest, The* (stage play) **1958**

*Unfinished Portrait* (as Mary Westmacott) **1934**

*Verdict* (stage play) **1958**

*Wasp's Nest* (TV play) **1937**

*While the Light Lasts* (short stories) **1997**

*Why Didn't They Ask Evans?* **1934**

*Witness for the Prosecution* (stage play) **1953**

*Yellow Iris* (radio play) **1937**

# Index of Titles

# Acknowledgements

This book has benefited greatly from the encouragement and assistance of many people whose names do not appear on the title page.

First and foremost, my thanks go to Mathew Prichard and his wife Lucy. The very existence of this book is due to Mathew's generosity. He unhesitatingly agreed to my writing about the Notebooks and granted me complete and unfettered access to all of his grandmother's papers. And he and Lucy also extended me limitless hospitality on many occasions.

David Brawn, HarperCollins, for his faith in the project and Steve Gove for his eagle-eyed editing. My brother Brendan read an early draft and his positive words gave much encouragement; and with his wife, Virginia, he provided me with a home-from-home (but with superior technical back up!). And Joseph and Francis for proof-reading.

My friend and fellow Christie devotee, Tony Medawar, made many helpful suggestions as well as sharing his research with me.

And for various reasons Jane Alger, Eurion Brown, Robyn Brown, Pete Coleman, Patricia and Noel Donnelly, Julius Green, David Headley, Katie Lusty, John Perry, Karl Pike, John Ryan, Michael Sands, John Timon, Andy Trott, Elaine Wiltshire and Nigel Wollen.

Of the many books written about Agatha Christie, the following have been most helpful:

Barnard, Robert, *A Talent to Deceive* (1980)

Campbell, Mark, *The Pocket Essentials Guide to Agatha Christie* (2006)

Morgan, Janet, *Agatha Christie* (1984)

Green, Julius, *Curtain Up: Agatha Christie – A Life in Theatre* (2015)

Osborne, Charles, *The Life and Crimes of Agatha Christie* (1982)

Sanders, Dennis and Lovallo, Len, *The Agatha Christie Companion* (1984)

Sova, Dawn B., *Agatha Christie A to Z* (1996)

Thompson, Laura, *Agatha Christie, An English Mystery* (2007)

Toye, Randall, *The Agatha Christie Who's Who* (1980)